T0393679

John Williams: Music for Films, Television and the Concert Stage

Contemporary Composers

General editors
Massimiliano Locanto
Massimiliano Sala

Volume 1

Publications of the Centro Studi Opera Omnia Luigi Boccherini
Pubblicazioni del Centro Studi Opera Omnia Luigi Boccherini
Publications du Centro Studi Opera Omnia Luigi Boccherini
Veröffentlichungen des Centro Studi Opera Omnia Luigi Boccherini
Publicaciones del Centro Studi Opera Omnia Luigi Boccherini
Lucca

John Williams
Music for Films, Television and the Concert Stage

edited by
Emilio Audissino

⚜

BREPOLS
TURNHOUT
MMXVIII

D/2018/0095/89

ISBN 978-2-503-58034-0

Printed in Italy

Contents

Introduction: John Williams, Composer

A new series of musicological books — 'Contemporary Composers' — is inaugurated with a volume on John Williams. That might seem an odd choice, perhaps an audacious one, and in the past the fact of opening a musicological series with a *film* composer — or better, a *Hollywood* film composer — would have probably been looked upon as something utterly outrageous. Nowadays, the presence of film music in the legitimate venues of so-called 'classical' music is substantial and diffused, and cannot be ignored, whether one likes it or not[1]. Pieces from the film-music repertoire are being played not only in themed concerts — some 'Friday Night at the Movies' concert by the Chicago Symphony Orchestra, to name one instance — but alongside venerable pieces from the 'proper' concert repertoire too. Moreover, entire films are now presented with an orchestra playing the film's original score live. In these presentations the famous and beloved scores have a large part in attracting the audience to the shows, and the film screenings acquire a component of live performance that makes them closer to opera[2]. In the near future, people will perhaps say, «Tonight let's go see Shore's *The Lord of the Rings*» as they used to say, «Tonight let's go see Verdi's *Rigoletto*». In the present day, film music has indeed replaced opera and tone poems as the outlet for programmatic symphonic/orchestral music targeted at popular audiences. Moreover, the short forms typical of the concert arrangements of film scores seem to be more akin to the accelerated pace of the age we live in and the limited spare time we have. Typically presented in the form of modular suites, three/five-minute overtures or, in the longest cases, ten/fifteen-minute medleys or "Excerpts from...", film-music concert pieces present a shortened, 'shrunk' if you like, form in which techniques and processes of the symphonic repertoire are applied in a condensed mode. If some effect would take five minutes to build and deliver in a symphony, in a film-music piece it might be given only thirty seconds[3]. These short

1. The phenomenon is examined in Lehman 2018.

2. The phenomenon that I call 'multimedia film' (Audissino 2014a), which is also known as 'Film Concerts Live', after one of the most successful organizations that today distribute such shows, Film Concerts Live!, a joint venture between the talent management agencies IMG Artists and Gorfaine/Schwartz. See <http://filmconcertslive.com>, accessed February 2018.

3. For example, the «condensed leitmotiv» (Brown 1994, pp. 97-118).

forms were not invented by film music but have a longer history of their own[4]; yet, the growing interest for compressed structures could be traced back to the diffusion of recorded music in the early twentieth century, which made the records audience as large as, if not larger than, the audience of live concerts. Seventy-eight rpm discs could allocate only three/four minutes per side, which prompted not only song writers but composers as well to take into account this time limit to fashion their pieces accordingly. Duke Ellington, famously, composed some of his 'serious' pieces precisely within these new formal limits[5]. The concise language and condensed techniques of film music have found in these short forms the ideal vehicle for the concert presentation of this repertoire. But why this long digression? Because the vastly heightened presence of film music in today's concert programmes and its increased acceptance — compared to three decades ago — are largely the results of John Williams's work.

Building Bridges

As I have claimed elsewhere[6], the importance of Williams does not lie so much in the quality and dramaturgical effectiveness of his music — which at this point is largely undisputed. The importance of Williams lies in how he has managed to build bridges. He acted as the linking figure between the film-music style of the classical Hollywood cinema and the New Hollywood — the reason I have called him a 'neoclassical' composer[7]. Today, he is virtually the only surviving practitioner of old-fashioned symphonic scoring in the orchestral-pop landscape of Hollywood music[8]. He has bridged the gap between the world of 'art' concert music and that of 'commercial' film music with his fourteen seasons as Music Director and Principal Conductor of the Boston Pops Orchestra; his Boston Pops conductorship was seminal to the legitimization of film music as a proper repertoire for concert programmes and also for the popularization of 'multimedia presentations' of film music — Williams has also been a pioneer of live conducting to film[9]. More importantly, he has enormously contributed to the bridging of the gap between the realm of 'absolute' music and that of 'applied' music. Surely other past and present composers have worked in both — Erich Wolfgang Korngold and Ennio Morricone, to name just two. Yet, probably no other have been so equally successful in both and have expressed such equal satisfaction

4. On the past equivalents of today's formats used to adapt film scores for concert presentations, see Audissino 2014a, pp. 35-42.

5. For example, Ellington's «"Diminuendo in Blue" and "Crescendo in Blue", companion pieces that filled both sides of a 78». (Gioia 2011, p. 171).

6. Audissino 2014b, p. 203.

7. *Ibidem*, pp. xxiv-xxvi, 84-85.

8. Audissino 2017.

9. Audissino 2013.

for both. Korngold, eventually disillusioned with the film business, used to admit that «a film composer's immortality lasts from the recording stage to the dubbing room»[10]; Morricone has stated: «I did not approach film music by vocation: I thought I would be one of the many composers who earn little money but write what they want. [...] Of course I would like to make up for the time I lost, but I definitely do not think it is possible: I am the film composer and nobody sees me as another kind of composer, even if I always make some attempts[11] [...] I regret not doing in my life what I would have liked»[12], and he refused for a long time to conduct film music in concerts[13]. This sense of disappointment, perhaps guilt, and almost of shame, that could too frequently be found in classical-trained composers who applied their talent to cinema was the result of long-standing prejudices against film music, prejudices that were vehemently inflated and disseminated by Hanns Eisler and T. W. Adorno in their 1947 book about (against?) film music[14]. The general idea was that those who entered the film-music field were lesser composers who would not be able to have a 'proper' career in art music and had to compromise and resign to accept jobs in a debasing and merely commercial arena; or opportunistic and venal composers who sold out in order to 'make a quick buck'.

These prejudices have seemingly never been taken into serious consideration by Williams, and have never prevented him from applying his compositional skills to whatever genre/area of music he encountered, 'unashamedly': «I consider movie music as a legitimate art form like a symphony or an opera»[15], he confessed. On a previous occasion he said: «You and I both know if Richard Wagner were alive today, he'd own his own movie studio. He'd produce his own films. [...] Mozart would be writing film scores. He'd be Sondheim to the ninth power»[16]. And he once noted that «only one half of one percent of the music written in the 19th century is anything we ever hear today; surely there must be at least that percentage of good music written for films»[17]. He has never shown any sign of frustration about his film career, never accepting, for example, the provocations of his friend and colleague André Previn who has reiteratedly urged him to retire from Hollywood and focus on concert music[18] — Previn, formerly a film composer who quit his Hollywood career to concentrate on concert music, famously confessed that «No matter where I went to conduct, my reputation seemed tarnished by Hollywood glitter. To have written a Broadway show is okay, even admirable; having played a lot of jazz is okay, but

10. Korngold in Thomas 1991, p. 79.
11. Morricone in Miceli 1982, pp. 309-310 (translated from Italian).
12. Morricone in *ibidem*, p. 321 (translated from Italian).
13. Morricone in *ibidem*, p. 313 (translated from Italian).
14. Adorno – Eisler 2007.
15. Williams in Ponick 2004, no p.
16. Williams in Vernier 1988, no p.
17. Williams in Dyer 1980a, no p.
18. Stearns 2017.

less admirable. But somehow, having worked in Hollywood is like being a well-known whore»[19]. Williams has always seemed to be quite happy with his multifaceted profile, balancing his conducting career, film-composing career, and concert-composing career in a rather unprecedented way and with surprisingly constant and consistent results in all fields. One might object that his serene content can be a pose, the feigned public persona of a shrewd businessman who knows that it is not advisable to bite the hand that feeds you — perhaps he secretly holds a grudge for not being the next Elliott Carter. All speculations are legitimate, but confronted with the question, Williams replied, «I think of myself as a film composer, [...] I'm not a frustrated concert composer»[20]. One might downplay his achievements by noting that his multi-success eclectic career might have been the lucky fruit of the changing of times, of him happening to be in the right place at the right time with the right collaborators — Has Williams helped *Star Wars* through his music or has *Star Wars* helped Williams through its visibility? He is the first one to admit — in his trademark modesty — that: «there's an element of chance in that, an element of luck, the moment of reception in the marketplace, if I can put it that way, so many factors that are almost sociological and beyond the competence of someone like me to analyze for you. [...] I've been very fortunate to be associated with some films that have found their way into that place and that the music can go successfully along with it and support it»[21]. Speculations aside, Williams is an artist who has managed to make his undeniable talent fruitful in every musical arena he has entered and has always applied himself to his best to any musical commission regardless of its genre/destination. The Associate Conductor of the Boston Pops at the time of Williams's tenure, Harry Ellis Dickson, noted that: «I love his great seriousness. [...] I've learned a good deal from him. He taught me to value music that I would have looked down upon. He once said that a tune by Jerome Kern can be as beautiful in its way as a song by Schubert. And he is right»[22]. And the following assessment is from his first concert as Boston Pops newly appointed conductor:

> At his first concert with the Pops in New York, the orchestra players were greatly impressed with the seriousness and sensitivity Williams brought to a violin concerto he performed with assistant concertmaster Emanuel Borok. But what seems most impressive is that his scrupulous care for details and stylistic purity seems to have universal application. He approaches classical and popular music alike with the same respect, adventurousness and love[23].

19. Previn in THOMAS 1997, p. 42.
20. Williams in MOSS 2002.
21. Williams in MANGAN 2002.
22. Dickson in PFEIFER 1993, no p.
23. PFEIFER 1980.

Introduction

Biographical Notes

Born in Flushing, Queens (NY) in 1932, John Towner Williams came to be exposed to music from a very early age. His father, John Francis, was a percussionist who worked both in the CBS Radio Orchestra, in the 'Raymond Scott Quintette' — famous for his swing-jazz descriptive music, like *Powerhouse* (1937) — and later as a session musician in Hollywood studios. Through his father's work, John Jr. had the opportunity to get in touch with a variety of musical genres and an array of instrumentalists. He himself 'flirted' with the trombone, the trumpet, the clarinet, the cello, the bassoon, eventually deciding to 'get engaged' to the piano and pursue a career as a classical recitalist. When his family relocated to Los Angeles in 1948, he became a pupil of Robert Van Eps, a pianist who also worked as an orchestrator in the film business, and later studied composition and counterpoint with Mario Castelnuovo Tedesco and at the UCLA. Having already demonstrated his skills as an arranger for the school's band when he attended the North Hollywood High School, he later applied those skills and further honed them during his stint in the Airforce, where he was assigned to the military band as a conductor and arranger. After the discharge, in 1955, he was admitted to the Juilliard School in New York City, in the class of Madame Rosina Lhévinne, with Van Cliburn as one of his classmates. While studying there as a classical pianist, he also played gigs as a jazz pianist in the city's clubs, and developed an increasing interest in composition. In 1956 he moved to Los Angeles and landed a job as a pianist in the Columbia Pictures orchestra. He also worked in the recording industry, arranging and conducting the band for artists such as Mahalia Jackson and Vic Damone, while also 'cutting sides' with his own jazz band, under the name of Johnny Williams, or John Towner. As a pianist in Hollywood, he worked under some of film music's biggest names, past and present: Alfred Newman, Dimitri Tiomkin, Henry Mancini, Jerry Goldsmith, Elmer Bernstein… From the piano bench, he soon climbed the music-department ladder up to the composer's position, having passed through the richly formative experience of arranging and orchestrating. In the second half of the 1960s he was already working as a full-time composer in television shows and film comedies, also conducting the recording sessions. At the end of the decade, in 1968, he received the first of his currently fifty-one Oscar nominations, for his arrangements for *Valley of the Dolls* (Mark Robson, 1967). In the 1970s he was typecast as the 'disaster movie' composer of choice, penning the scores to *The Poseidon Adventure* (Ronald Neame, 1972), *Earthquake* (Mark Robson, 1974), and *The Towering Inferno* (John Guillermin, 1974). A young director and long-time admirer of Williams's work hired him for his first feature film, *Sugarland Express* (1974): that director was Steven Spielberg, and that was the first of twenty-eight collaborations (not counting the TV shows and the short films), making the Spielberg/Williams duo the most successful, enduring, and solid director/composer partnership in film history, probably surpassing the Fellini/Rota. In mid-1970s Williams had already become one of the most respected composers in Hollywood, having won his second Oscar for *Jaws* (Steven Spielberg, 1975), with an outstanding score that was essential to shape the film's drama and tension and already showed — with its references to Herrmann and Korngold — important signs of the 'neoclassical' restoration that Williams would soon accomplish. Williams's 'Hollywood neoclassicism' came completely to the fore with *Star Wars* (George Lucas, 1977), with which he brought back the rich symphonic late-romantic sound that was typical of the 1930s/1940s Hollywood cinema and had been declared dead and buried in the 1960s/1970s. With *Star Wars* Williams became a film-music superstar: «[Williams's work on *Star Wars*] gave vast audiences a type of film music which, from the 1950s onwards, seemed hopelessly compromised if not completely lost, and this created a veneration for Williams that has no precedent»[24]. Williams has since been particularly sought after for adventure, fantasy, and space films — from *Superman* (Richard Donner, 1978), to the *Indiana Jones* saga (Steven Spielberg 1981-ongoing), to the first three *Harry Potter* films (Chris Columbus/Alfonso Cuarón, 2001-2004). This high-budget projects have often overshadowed Williams's versatility and his other compositional sensibilities: from the schizophrenic approach (half tonal, half aleatoric *bruitism*) to the schizophrenia thriller *Images* (Robert Altman, 1972), the darkly sensual scores to De Palma's *The Fury* (1979) or *Dracula* (John Badham, 1979), the gently restrained and chamber music-like works for *Stanley and Iris* (Martin Ritt, 1990) and *The Book Thief* (Brian Percival, 2013), the sensitive poignancy of *Schindler's List* (Steven Spielberg, 1994), the jazzy scores to *Catch Me if You Can* (Steven Spielberg, 2002) and *The Terminal* (Steven Spielberg, 2004), the ethnic experimentations of *Memoirs of a Geisha* (Rob Marshall, 2005) and *Munich* (Steven Spielberg, 2005), to the minimalist touch of *The Post* (Steven Spielberg, 2017). Besides this busy film career, Williams also held for fourteen seasons the position of Music Director and Principal Conductor of the Boston Pops Orchestra — 'America's Orchestra', one the most televised and recorded ensemble of light symphonic music — and continues to this day to appear with the ensemble as their Laureate Conductor. He has also nurtured a parallel prolific composing career in concert music, began in the 1960s with *Essay for Strings* (1965) and the *Flute Concerto* (1969), steadily sustained, and still ongoing — at the time of writing this, a new piece, *Highwood's Ghost*, is in preparation to be premiered at the Tanglewood Music Festival in the summer of 2018. Williams has also served as America's quasi-official composer, regularly summoned to provide music for such landmark national events as the 1984 Olympic Games in Los Angeles, the rededication of the Statue of Liberty in 1986, the centennial Olympics in Atlanta in 1996, the 2002 Winter Olympics in Salt Lake City, the inauguration of President Barack Obama's first term in 2009.

24. Miceli 2009, p. 49 (translated from Italian).

In all these endeavours, Williams has always shown a very well-balanced tension between an idealism for artistic excellence and a practical realism. In a 1989 interview he declared that he is constantly reaching for the best possible result:

> The pursuit of excellence is what life ought to be about. It's trying to get closer to God, to imitate the perfect state. The odyssey to find perfection should define humanity. This thought comes into my consciousness when I'm working. If I forge my music better, if I shape it better, if I make it better, I am happier than if I hadn't tried. [...] I'm never frustrated by music. What can be frustrating is not being able to solve problems in a given piece. You have to address yourself to your own inadequacies. [...] The ideal always seems to elude me. I always want to do better[25].

At the same time, he has always shown a solid realism for the limitations and constraints one has to constantly face. Well-trained in the film-scoring business, Williams often compares his job to that of a journalist, always tied to strict deadlines: «I live with deadlines everyday. [...] I need to do a certain amount every day; if I don't, the next day I have twice as much, so I can't really go back and fuss and obsess»[26]. Williams has also always acknowledged the limitations and competition that film may impose on music:

> In many ways writing for film is very restricted. If you have two minutes and 31 seconds to do something, you can't have more if you think you need it. Then you find yourself acoustically in competition with wagon wheels, gunshots, space ships sweeping back and forth, and you thank God for the soundtrack LP where the public can get the other 80 percent of the music they never heard in the film. And the problems continue right down to the level of the neighborhood theater, where the reproduction equipment is in bad shape. It is soul-destroying, if you think about it. But you can also think of it as sympathetically human; like everything worth doing, it is full of difficulties[27].

In old Hollywood, the motto of Warner Bros. mogul Jack Warner was: «I don't want it good. I want it Tuesday». The accepted and well-managed tension between quality and constraints, ideals and practicalities, art and commerce, «good» and «Tuesday», has allowed Williams to be successful across six decades of career.

All these traits and multifaceted achievements make Williams a truly *contemporary* composer, an example for those who wish to break the barriers from one artistic genre to another, to get rid for good of the old distinction between 'high brow' and 'low brow'

---

[25]. Williams in CHRISTY 1989.

[26]. Williams in BOOTH 2004, no p.

[27]. Williams in DYER 1980B, no p.

music, and to accept the practicalities that any working composer has to deal with. With the flourishing of jazz and its refined developments that could legitimately compete with 'art music' in terms of sophistication and innovation, with the 'Third Stream', with the various progressive rock and jazz movements, one of the teachings of the past twentieth century is that these barriers are already imploding, and perhaps the quicker this implosion is completed the better it is, because this way we can move on without the impediment of old 'romantic prejudices'[28] that sometimes still haunt the art of music. These prejudices have targeted Williams with particular vehemence. Besides more or less overt accusations of conservatism (his music helps manipulate viewers into regressive socio-political positions), bad musical taste (it sounds too loud and too American), musical amateurism (in particular when the Hollywood composer dared to guest-conduct such 'art-music' institutions as the Los Angeles Philharmonic), using ghost writers (the inveterate misunderstanding about the use of orchestrators[29]), and outmoded musical language (romanticism all over again), the most frequent charge is that of plagiarism[30]. Williams is typically said to have based his success on poaching from the style of past composers, when not even on stealing melodies and ideas — «*Star Wars* sounds like Holst meets Korngold; *E. T.* is Hanson's *Symphony No. 2*, *Home Alone* is Tchaikovsky's *The Nutcracker*...». It is worth here clearing the air about the alleged 'plagiarism', so that we can address Williams's music in the following pages without preconceptions[31]. The accusation of plagiarism has recently been debunked by James Orosz, who rather calls Williams a «paraphraser»:

> All music is intertextual; virtually any piece includes moments that remind us of another musical work. [...] [I]f one piece is explicitly based on another, we can say, following Gérard Genette, that the two have a hypertextual relationship — that a hypotext has served as a model for a newly composed hypertext. [...] Williams is remarkably canny in how he adapts music from another source [...] He likely does paraphrase, but he certainly does not plagiarize. [...] Even when Williams paraphrases music from other sources, this can hardly be considered a flaw of his working method. [...] The fact that so many accuse Williams of having an aesthetically dubious method of composition is presumably a consequence of his fame. Globally, he is perhaps the most well-known living composer of orchestral music [...] and it follows that the biggest name makes for the biggest target. Yet Williams's creative process places him not only in the company of other film composers but also in that of countless composers of concert music who use pre-existing material as their starting point for crafting a new piece[32].

---

[28]. Audissino 2014a.

[29]. To clear that misunderstanding, see Audissino 2014b, pp. 136-138, but also Ian Sapiro's chapter in this volume.

[30]. I have already discussed and objected to these accusations in Audissino 2014b, pp. 134-144.

[31]. In his chapter in this volume, Mervyn Cooke also discusses this issue.

[32]. Orosz 2015, pp. 1, 318-319.

I have myself addressed this issue in these terms:

> Igor Stravinsky reportedly said that «lesser artist borrow; great artists steal». Borrowing here means a superficial and opportunistic act — I don't have something and I need to borrow it from someone else. Stealing means to take possession of it, it is a more assimilative and personal act. If one appropriates someone else's music, that music becomes part of the composer and is likely to be transformed, personalised by the new owner — if I borrow something I don't have the authority to personalise it, which I have if I steal it and become the new owner. The criticism of those who blame Williams for plagiarising other composers is based on a misunderstanding: Williams does not secretly borrow but "patently steal"[33].

Williams has always had no problems in acknowledging the influences of other composers on his music: «There are stylistic similarities which were really done on purpose and there are a couple of chords [in *Star Wars*] which I call "The Planet" chords which are not quite the same but very similar to Holst's [*The*] *Planets*, [...] I did it intentionally as a kind of statement as saying this is a homage to Holst»[34]. He has also clarified that — given film music's need to immediately convey specific atmospheres, periods, and milieus — the act of citing music is not different from that of a set designer who introduces references to specific styles in the set decorations to create specific ambiances:

> A lot of these references are deliberate. They're an attempt to evoke a response in the audience where we want to elicit a certain kind of reaction. Another thing is that, whenever one is involved in writing incidental music — where you have specific backgrounds, specific periods, certain kinds of characters and so on — the work is bound to be derivative in a certain sense. The degree to which you can experiment, as you can in a concert work, is very limited. You're fulfilling more of a role of a designer, in the same way that a set designer would do a design for a period opera[35].

Moreover, in our post-modern times — or even post post-modern — the quotation, elaboration, transformation, combination, re-enactment of past styles and artefacts is at the very basis of the current aesthetics, something by now widely accepted[36]. So, one could also say that Williams the «paraphraser» is perfectly in line with the combinatory aesthetic of contemporary art. Why keep forcing a (idealized) Romantic aesthetic of uncompromising originality on our different period of time?

[33]. AUDISSINO 2017, p. 230.

[34]. Williams quoted in GRACE 1983, no p.

[35]. TERRY 1981, p. 21.

[36]. On 'originality', see MERA 2017.

John Williams Studies

The academic literature on Williams has seen an increase in the last few years — with journal articles, book chapters, Master's dissertations and Ph.D. theses — after a period of almost complete neglect. Yet, the academic publications are still surprisingly few if compared to Williams's importance in the musical landscape of the late-twentieth/early twenty-first century[37]. I beg to differ with Janet K. Halfyard who claims that this is simply due to the fact that Williams is still alive and so «this is perhaps less surprising given musicology's preference for looking at a complete opus, meaning that most of the work on individual composers tends to be done after they have died»[38]. At the time of writing this, both Howard Shore (fourteen-year younger than Williams) and Stephen Sondheim (almost same class as Williams) are still alive, and yet they have already been honoured with a musicological book devoted to *The Lord of the Rings* scores (Adams 2010) and an *Oxford Handbook of Sondheim Studies* (Gordon 2015) — and Halfyard herself has authored a monograph on Danny Elfman's *Batman* (Halfyard 2004), with Elfman being still around and twenty-one-year younger than Williams. And if we consider the substantial literature on Ennio Morricone, particularly in the Italian language[39], I cannot but still be surprised (pace Halfyard) that before 2014 there was not a single monograph in English on Williams. I am not convinced by this 'posthumous scholarship' argument and I think that, even if Williams is still working, studies of circumscribed periods, stylistic areas, and single scores can and should be done. It is high-time to set in motion the 'John Williams Studies'. The recent announcement that Williams has bequeathed all his archives (scores, manuscripts, sketches...) to the Juilliard School of Music opens up unprecedented possibilities for scholars to study his work in philological and analytical ways that have been so far precluded by the inaccessibility of the materials[40].

When I was contacted by the Centro Studi Opera Omnia Lugi Boccherini (Lucca) to be commissioned a book on Williams to inaugurate their new series on contemporary composers, I found the request and timing particularly auspicious. Their idea was to treat Williams as a composer, not only as a *film* composer, and this was a much welcome act of barrier-breaking and bridge-building. I would like to express, in particular, my appreciation to Massimiliano Sala and Roberto Illiano, for their trust and support. And, as always, many thanks to Jamie Richardson. I have had the honour of assembling and

[37]. There are only three academic books on Williams: one in German that focuses on his collaboration with Steven Spielberg (Moormann 2010), one in French that provides an introduction mostly focussed on his film works (Tylski 2011), one in English that offers an historical and stylistic survey of his film music (Audissino 2014b). On the neglect of the musical academe, see also Emile Wennekes's chapter in this volume.

[38]. Halfyard 2015, p. 231.

[39]. For example, Miceli 1994.

[40]. <https://www.juilliard.edu/news/131971/academy-award-winning-composer-and-conductor-john-williams-bequeath-concert-and-film>, accessed March 2018.

coordinating an international team of scholars who enthusiastically collaborated to address the many facets of Williams's career and highlight the fine-grain thematic, harmonic, and timbral details and the dramaturgical acumen that make his music (for whatever medium or rostrum) unmistakable. This is not a biography of the composer — to the disappointment of the fan community, I guess — and hence bibliographical information and trivia are not to be found here. While my previous Williams monograph (Audissino 2014b) was a work of historiography and film-music stylistics penned by a film historian/ film musicologist and presenting only a limited selection of musical analysis, the present volume mostly accommodates contributions from music theorists and musicologists and possesses a predominantly musicological imprint, making the whole balance decidedly tipped towards Music Studies rather than Film Studies. Though, in all those cases in which Williams's *film* music was under investigation, proper attention has been devoted to the interaction of music with the other cinematic components, and the decision-making behind the compositional choices has been linked to the formal/narrative requirements of the film at hand. All the scholars featured here have both keen ears for the music and keen eyes for the film — thus reinforcing another bridge, the one between Film Studies and Music Studies which, although already built, is always a bit shaky and in need of acts of consolidation and restructuring.

This Volume's Contents

Part One, 'John Williams and the Musical Landscapes: Film, Television, Jazz, and Concert Halls', provides a series of studies of Williams's work in different musical realms. Mervyn Cooke's chapter surveys Williams's work in cinema by concentrating on the manifold influences that have shaped his musical language and the variety of idioms that he employs — traversing the full gamut from diatonicism to atonality — and closes with a discussion that reframes the criterion of 'originality'. Paula Musegades points her attention to Williams's work in television, first tracing his formative experience in the last days of the studio system, and then examining his approach to television scoring — with particular attention to *Checkmate* and *Alcoa Premiere* — to show that the 'Hollywood neoclassicism' that would fully emerge in his most famous film works can already be found in these early scores. Ryan Jones brings us in the territories of jazz and popular music, studying Williams's handling of these idioms specifically with regard to the 'jazzy' score to *Catch Me if You Can*, which is studied with the help of insightful contributions from saxophonist Dan Higgins and the analysis of a 2003 Boston Pops concert in which Williams conducted a three-piece suite from the film score. Emile Wennekes offer us a discussion of Williams's output for the concert hall, his *absolute musik*, opening the survey with considerations about why Williams's name is missing in some important 'Who's Who' of contemporary concert music, and then demonstrating the deft balance between art and craftsmanship. Sebastian Stoppe closes this first part with a presentation of the status of Williams's film music in the concert programmes with selected examples, starting with a discussion of the post-Williams years at the Boston Pops Orchestra, then moving to the New York Philharmonic, and then to Leipzig's Gewandhaus Orchestra.

Part Two, 'The Williams Touch: Style and Musical Dramaturgy' zooms in on the linguistical, formal, timbral, and dramaturgical traits that characterize Williams's writing. One of Williams's trademark is his memorable musical themes, and Mark Richards concentrates on how Williams manipulates these themes for dramaturgical purposes through variations, also discussing the various types of variations employed and proposing a style-based periodization of Williams's film production. Frank Lehman tackles Williams's *magnum opus*, the *Star Wars* saga, and thoroughly compiles a commentated catalogue of all the themes and motifs appeared so far, introduced by a discussion of the concept of leitmotiv as used in Williams's music and of the criteria behind the compilation of the catalogue. Benefiting from conversations with the orchestrators Conrad Pope and Paul S. Henning, Ian Sapiro looks into another fundamental trait of the 'John Williams sound', the orchestral colour and voicing, and does so by examining the role of the orchestrators (thus dismantling the suspect that the Williams Sound is not Williams's merit) and by illustrating how the different instrumental groups of the orchestra are typically utilized. Nicholas Kmet further elaborates and exemplifies the importance of orchestration in Williams's music by exploring how the use of the orchestra changed across the *Star Wars* films, showing how the 'prequel trilogy' presents a different sound than the 'classic trilogy'. Joakim Tillman casts light on the connection between Williams's writing strategies and the narrative demands of the films, studying his film-music dramaturgical prowess applied to the depiction of villains, from Darth Vader to the clumsy burglars in *Home Alone*. Jamie Lynn Webster remains within a dramaturgical focus and on the connections between compositional choices and narrative needs, and explores how Williams's style has changed in his *Harry Potter* trilogy to adapt to the sensibilities of the different directors, and also offers an in-depth analysis of some key sequences, like Aunt Marge's balloon-like inflation.

Part Three, 'Case Studies', (as clarified by the title itself) is a selection of essays that point their attention to single works. Laura Anderson's study of *Angela's Ashes* investigates the musical depiction of national identity and, specifically, how Williams has managed to infuse a 'lilt' of Irishness to the film without opting for musical solutions that may sound too 'Oirish', as happened with his score to *Far and Away*. Chloé Huvet focusses on *E. T.: The Extra-Terrestrial* and studies how Williams's score cooperates with the overall sound design to tell a story that is more bitter-sweet and less 'happy-ending-ish' than most Spielberg critics think. David Ireland examines the Spielberg/Williams collaboration in historical dramas, with a particular focus on *Munich* and its sparse use of music that departs from the most familiar big romantic sound that people associate with the composer, showing that the unscored quasi-documentary moments are contrasted by moments of meaningful musico/visual incongruence. Irena Paulus tackles an often neglected output of the Spielberg/Williams production, *War of the Worlds*, whose score is strongly divergent from Williams's typical style and instead features harsh dissonance and atonal episodes, to the point that Paulus, in the provocation that opens the chapter, wonders whether this score can be seen as a sign of Williams's desire to embrace atonality. Tom Schneller takes us in the area of concert music and offers us an examination of one of Williams's most personal concert work, the *Violin Concerto*, whose writing was prompted by the sudden death of the composer's wife; after a biographical background on the events that led to the composition, Schneller traces the struggle between loss and acceptance within the musical form of the piece. Stefan Swanson concentrates on another less popular Spielberg/Williams production, *A. I.*, demonstrating how the score strongly supports a not-so-positive interpretation of the controversial ending, too often charged with sentimentalism; on the contrary, we are deceived into thinking that we are watching a happy ending, while it is not happy at all.

Finally, Part Four offers some perspectives on Williams's music from the performers' viewpoint. The first contribution is an interview with Boston Pops Principal Conductor and Music Director Keith Lockhart. Frank Lehman and I have met with Maestro Lockhart and asked him about the challenges and demands that Williams's music requires from the orchestra and the conductor, how Williams intervenes on the concert versions of his film repertoire, and the technicalities and difficulties that the live accompaniment of entire films entails in the topical and expanding phenomenon of 'Film Concerts Live'. In the second contribution, Maurizio Caschetto met with world-renowned piano recitalist Simone Pedroni to discuss the performer's rendition of Williams's music and specifically his piano repertoire, with a focus on the piano-solo suite *Conversations*, but also on what it is that makes this composer's music appealing and rewarding to musicians.

Envoy

A volume on John Williams is a very appropriate opener for the new series 'Contemporary Composers', not only because of Williams's vast impact on contemporary music but also because this choice is a strong statement about the need to completely supersede the old barriers that used to separate concert music (*absolute musik*) from film music (the worst type of *gebrauchsmusik*, according to Adorno and others). All *good* music *is* good music, regardless of its genre and finality, something that Williams's work has evidenced. And John Williams should not be considered a *film* composer, but a *composer*, one of the most influential of our time.

Emilio Audissino
University of Southampton

Bibliography

Adams 2010

Adams, Doug. *The Music of «The Lord of the Rings» Films: A Comprehensive Account of Howard Shore's Scores*, Van Nuys (CA), Alfred Music, 2010.

Adorno – Eisler 2007

Adorno, Theodor Ludwig Wiesengrund – Eisler, Hanns. *Composing for the Films*, (1947), London-New York, Continuum, 2007 (Continuum Impacts).

Audissino 2013

Audissino, Emilio. 'Archival Research and the Study of the Concert Presentations of Film Music. The Case of John Williams and the Boston Pops Orchestra', in: *The Journal of Film Music*, vi/2 (2013), pp. 147-173.

Audissino 2014a

Id. 'Overruling a Romantic Prejudice. Forms and Formats of Film Music in Concert Programs', in: *Film in Concert, Film Scores and Their Relation to Classical Concert Music*, edited by Sebastian Stoppe, Glücksstadt, VWH Verlag, 2014, pp. 25-43 (AV-Medien).

Audissino 2014b

Id. *John Williams's Film Music: «Jaws», «Star Wars», «Raiders of the Lost Ark», and the Return of the Classical Hollywood Music Style*, Madison (WI), University of Wisconsin Press, 2014 (Wisconsin Film Studies).

Audissino 2017

Id. 'John Williams and Contemporary Film Music', in: *Contemporary Film Music: Investigating Cinema Narratives and Composition*, edited by Lindsay Coleman and Joakim Tillman, Basingstoke, Palgrave MacMillan, 2017 (SpringerLink: Bücher), pp. 221-236.

Booth 2004

Booth, William. 'Shark Attack?! John Williams Liked the Sound of That', in: *The Washington Post*, 5 December 2004.

Brown 1994

Brown, Royal S. *Overtones and Undertones: Reading Film Music*, Berkeley (CA), University of California Press, 1994 (Music).

Christy 1989

Christy, Marian. 'John Williams' Pursuit of Excellence', in: *The Boston Globe*, 4 July 1989.

Dyer 1980a

Dyer, Richard. 'John Williams Bows In', in: *The Boston Globe*, 11 January 1980.

Dyer 1980b

Id. 'Q&A with John Williams. Pops' Conductor Talks about His New Beat', in: *The Boston Globe*, 27 April 1980.

GIOIA 2011
GIOIA, Ted. *The History of Jazz*, Oxford-New York, Oxford University Press, [2]2011.

GORDON 2015
GORDON, Robert. *The Oxford Handbook of Sondheim Studies*, Oxford-New York, Oxford University Press, 2015 (Oxford Handbooks).

GRACE 1983
GRACE, Bob. 'John Williams: Scoring Big in the Movies', in: *The Houston Chronicle*, 13 November 1983.

HALFYARD 2004
HALFYARD, Janet K. *Danny Elfman's «Batman»: A Film Score Guide*, Lanham (MD), Scarecrow Press, 2004 (Scarecrow Film Guides, 2).

HALFYARD 2015
EAD. '*John Williams's Film Music: «Jaws», «Star Wars», «Raiders of the Lost Ark», and the Return of the Classical Hollywood Music Style* by Emilio Audissino (review)', in: *Music, Sound, and the Moving Image*, IX/2 (2016), pp. 231-236.

LEHMAN 2018
LEHMAN, Frank. 'Film-as-Concert Music and the Formal Implications of "Cinematic Listening"', in: *Music Analysis*, XXXVII/1 (March 2018), pp. 7-46.

MANGAN 2002
MANGAN, Timothy. 'The Movies' Music Man', in: *The Orange County Register*, 7 July 2002.

MERA 2017
MERA, Miguel. 'Screen Music and the Question of Originality', in *The Routledge Companion to Screen Music and Sound*, edited by Miguel Mera, Ronald Sadoff and Ben Winters, New York, Routledge, 2017 (Routledge Companions), pp. 38-49.

MICELI 1982
MICELI, Sergio. *La musica nel film: arte e artigianato*, Fiesole, Discanto Edizioni, 1982 (Contrappunti, 13).

MICELI 1994
ID. *Morricone, la musica, il cinema*, Milan, Ricordi, 1994 (Le Sfere, 23).

MICELI 2009
ID. *Musica per film: storia, estetica, analisi, tipologie*, Lucca, LIM; Milan, Ricordi, 2009 (Le Sfere, 49).

MOORMANN 2010
MOORMANN, Peter. *Spielberg-Variationen: Die Filmmusik von John Williams*, Baden-Baden, Nomos, 2010 (Schriftenreihe Filmstudien, 57).

MOSS 2002
MOSS, Stephen. 'The Force Is with Him', in: *The Guardian*, 4 February 2002.

Orosz 2015
Orosz, James. 'John Williams: Paraphraser or Plagiarizer?', in: *Journal of Musicological Research*, xxxiv (2015), pp. 299-319.

Pfeifer 1980
Pfeifer, Ellen. 'Williams: «I Never Intended to Conduct in Public»', in: *Boston Herald American*, 28 April 1980.

Pfeifer 1993
Ead. 'Passing the Baton', in: *Boston Sunday Herald*, 9 May 1993.

Ponick 2004
Ponick, T. L. 'Movie Music Raised to Its Rightful Place by Composer', in: *The Washington Times*, 3 December 2004.

Stearns 2017
Stearns, David Patrick. 'André Previn Says He Keeps Telling John Williams, «John, Stop It with the *Star Wars*»', in: *The Philadelphia Inquirer*, 12 October 2017, <http://www.philly.com/philly/entertainment/arts/andre-previn-says-he-keeps-telling-john-williams-john-stop-it-with-the-star-wars-20171012.html>, accessed February 2018.

Terry 1981
Terry, Kenneth. 'John Williams Encounters the Pops', in: *Downbeat*, March 1981, pp. 20-22.

Thomas 1991
Thomas, Tony. *Film Score: The Art and Craft of Movie Music*, Burbank (CA), Riverwood Press, 1991.

Thomas 1997
Id. *Music for the Movies*, second expanded and updated edition, Beverly Hills, Silman-James, 1997.

Tylski 2011
John Williams: Un Alchimiste musical à Hollywood, edited by Alexandre Tylski, Paris, L'Harmattan, 2011 (Univers musical).

Vernier 1988
Vernier, David. 'Magnificent Modern Maestro', in: *Digital Audio*, March 1988.

John Williams and the Musical Landscapes: Film, Television, Jazz, and Concert Halls

A New Symphonism for a New Hollywood: The Musical Language of John Williams's Film Scores

Mervyn Cooke
(University of Nottingham)

The renaissance of symphonic film scoring trailblazed by John Williams since the 1970s has earned him an indelible place in histories of film music — not perhaps as a pioneering innovator, but as a superb consolidator of a wide range of stylistic elements in his efforts to maintain venerable traditions of film composing while at the same time modernizing them to ensure they are both accessible and meaningful to a younger generation of movie-goers. This chapter provides an overview of the various influences on, and characteristics of, Williams's mainstream orchestral idiom as it came to dominate blockbusters of the so-called New Hollywood school — principally those directed by George Lucas and Steven Spielberg — and beyond. It also examines how music which clearly delights in paying both explicit and implicit acts of homage to often readily identifiable compositional exemplars can circumvent potential charges of a lack of originality, and also provide a coherent listening experience. Both these considerations are inextricably tied up with the manner in which narrative-driven film music articulates a story's dramatic thrust, while at the same time achieving a structural (though, it might be argued, by no means essential) autonomy which has ensured the success of so much of Williams's music in the concert hall and in the medium of soundtrack recordings. As will be shown, a crucial — and often overlooked — model for this manner of film scoring is ballet, rather than the more usually cited operatic paradigm.

Helen Mitchell's concise account of the fall and rise of the 'symphonic' film score charts the story from the very earliest use of the adjective in this context (1915), through the high period of prolific orchestral film scoring in the Golden Age of the Hollywood studio system (*c*1930-1950), then the various dips in the fortunes of such scores in the following decades, and finally to the work of Williams and others in the New Hollywood era[1]. Mitchell adopts the simplest definition of 'symphonic', i.e. «scored for the instruments of the symphony orchestra», without intending to connote any specific style[2]. It might be

1. Mitchell 2009.
2. *Ibidem*, p. 175, fn. 1.

noted, however, that (especially in Europe) 'symphonic' also suggests that a musical work «is extended and thoroughly developed», both features of much of Williams's film output[3]. Emilio Audissino defines Williams's style more precisely as «symphonic neoclassicism», referring not to the neoclassical aesthetics of some early twentieth-century composers but instead signalling a revival of the 'classical' style of Golden Age filmmaking and film scoring[4]. Audissino sees the peak of this neoclassical trend as occurring between *Jaws* (Steven Spielger, 1975) and *Return of the Jedi* (Richard Marquand, 1983), and its musical characteristics were to persist well beyond that period. As this essay hopes to show, in an unusual inversion of the more orthodox trajectory of a composer's stylistic development, Williams's career began with a diversity of modern and vernacular influences and then, post-*Jaws* and *Star Wars* (George Lucas, 1977), increasingly espoused more conservative stylistic ingredients which were closely modelled on late-romantic and early twentieth-century orchestral music as filtered through the influence of Hollywood composers of the Golden Age.

Williams's best known scores from the years before the New Hollywood watershed were those for the all-star disaster genre in which he nearly became typecast: *The Poseidon Adventure* (Ronald Neame, 1972), *Earthquake* (Mark Robson, 1974) and *The Towering Inferno* (John Guillermin, 1974), along with the mountaineering thriller *The Eiger Sanction* (Clint Eastwood, 1975). The scores for all these films lack the 'big theme' mentality of the later Spielberg and Lucas blockbusters, and instead of the often lush neoromantic quality of Williams's later music there is generally a more widespread use of dissonant, athematic and fragmentary cues which (since the innovative work of film composers such as Leonard Rosenman and Jerry Fielding in the 1950s and 1960s) have seemed ideally suited to scenes of violent action, suspense and horror. There is generally less music than in the almost wall-to-wall scoring of some of the later films, and occasionally the listener is reminded of Williams's contemporaneous concert music: for example, intensely elegiac string writing similar to that in the *Violin Concerto* (1974), and somewhat reminiscent of Berg, captures the sombre, desolate mood as survivors precariously leave a shattered building in *Earthquake*.

Although, collectively, Spielberg's *Jaws* and Lucas's *Star Wars* have long been considered the obvious turning point towards a more traditional approach to orchestral scoring, Spielberg's *Close Encounters of the Third Kind* (1977) is also significant on account of its deliberate strategy of keeping two different layers of musical idiom concurrently in play. Williams felt the movie on the one hand required a 'romantic' level, utilizing readily recognizable tonal elements; on the other, it also demanded a 'non-tonal' level, for which he used the terms «chaos», «disassociated» and «abstract»[5]. This duality was to remain broadly in evidence throughout Williams's career, and returned particularly

---

3. Larue n.d.

4. Audissino 2014, p. 84. On the filmic definition of 'classical', see *ibidem*, p. xxv.

5. Williams 2001, video.

strongly in Spielberg's *A. I. Artificial Intelligence* (2001), but the romantic impulse in the meantime had became increasingly crystallized and foregrounded in his other work for Spielberg and Lucas.

Modernist Hollywood

Williams once listed amongst his favourite music the work of Bernard Herrmann, Jerry Goldsmith and Peter Maxwell Davies[6]. The last, who wrote little film music, might seem an unlikely choice; but, as we have already seen, Williams's early film composing demonstrated a proclivity for sometimes unsettling modernist cues, and this was to remain in evidence in his later output when a plot required it[7]. The fondness for Herrmann and Goldsmith is more revealing, given that before the neoromantic watershed of *Star Wars* Williams's style reflected his admiration for their originality and resourcefulness in harnessing sometimes idiosyncratic musical inspirations to powerful dramatic ends.

Williams cited the music to Alfred Hitchcock's *Vertigo* (1958) and Brian De Palma's *Obsession* (1976) as his favourite Herrmann scores[8]. Not surprisingly, the chance to compose his own score for Hitchcock (*Family Plot*) in 1976, the year before *Star Wars*, elicited some Herrmann-like touches, alongside overtly French influences and a tongue-in-cheek heavenly chorus (the latter a suggestion of the director's) — the two last geared towards capturing what Hitchcock had described as the 'impressionism' of the film's *séance* scenes[9]. This assignment was quickly followed by the opportunity to score De Palma's *The Fury* (1978), which includes some of Williams's most Herrmann-influenced music in a fitting tribute to the composer who would have been the director's first choice had he not died in 1975[10]. The Herrmann influence may also be heard in *The Eiger Sanction* and *Jaws*: see, for example, the latter's cue "The Underwater Siege"[11], with its mesmeric multiple harp glissandi and pulsating string ostinati. Herrmann, who was notable for his innovative music for sci-fi films, influenced Williams's contributions to this genre, too. *Close Encounters* is a case in point, with some cues again reliant on ostinati and also inhabiting the low tessitura for which Herrmann had a particular fondness. In *Star Wars* ("The Death Star / The Stormtroopers"), Williams seemingly quotes the ominous three-note "madness" motif for cellos and basses which occurs in several of Herrmann's scores, most famously that to Hitchcock's *Psycho* (1960) — an apparently

---

6. Darby – Du Bois 1990, p. 524.

7. See the chapter on *War of the Worlds* in this volume.

8. Darby – Du Bois 1990, p. 524. Both these films have similar and darkly fantastic plots involving female doppelgängers.

9. Williams 2005.

10. Audissino 2014, pp. 223-224.

11. All titles given in roman type and inverted commas are track titles from the relevant soundtrack album. The album details are given at the end of this chapter.

direct borrowing which Williams later said had not been intentional[12]. Other Williams scores paying homage to Herrmann's distinctively brooding style include *The Witches of Eastwick* (George Miller, 1987) and *Minority Report* (Steven Spielberg, 2002), Williams commenting of the latter's noir-ish ambience that Herrmann — whom he described as his «old mentor and friend» — was «the grandparent of the score»[13].

The most obvious fingerprint of Goldsmith's scoring techniques to have left its mark on Williams is a proclivity for low, dissonant piano lines and pounding percussion rhythms as economical means for promoting a sense of threat. Passages of this kind occur in Williams's early contributions to the disaster genre, as well as in *Star Wars* and *The Empire Strikes Back* (Irvin Kershner, 1980): representative examples from the sci-fi franchise are heard at *c.* 40 seconds into the cue "Landspeeder Search / Attack of the Sand People" in *Star Wars*, and *c.* four minutes into the cue "The Battle of Hoth" in *The Empire Strikes Back*. It also seems likely that Goldsmith's penchant for Stravinskyan rhetoric, especially when redolent of the rhythmic dynamism and crushing dissonances of *The Rite of Spring*, was at least in part responsible for similar tendencies in Williams's idiom (for more on which, see below). These Goldsmith-related features were to remain prominent in Williams's later music for modern-set action sequences — in contrast to the neoromanticism of his quasi-Golden Age musical swashbuckling — and a particularly good example is the score to Spielberg's *Jurassic Park* (1993). Although the experimentation distinguishing Goldsmith's avant-garde score to *Planet of the Apes* (Franklin J. Schaffner, 1968) is occasionally echoed in Williams's work, Goldsmith (following the example of Williams) also attempted to romanticize the sci-fi genre in his initial response to Ridley Scott's *Alien* (1979); the result was not deemed terrifying enough by the director, and had to be replaced by what the composer dismissively described as «a bunch of effects» assembled in haste, lamenting that «just writing fear all the time» was tedious[14]. Nevertheless, *Star Trek: The Motion Picture* (Robert Wise, released in the same year) did allow him the opportunity to follow Williams's neoromantic lead in the genre.

Musical Americana, whether the direct referencing of popular and/or vernacular idioms or the continuation of the tradition of nationalist orchestral scoring introduced to film music by the work of Aaron Copland, Hugo Friedhofer and others, is another area of Williams's film music which is kept mostly discrete from the neoromantic Golden Age techniques described below. Williams's concert fanfares, such as the Olympic Centennial piece *Summon the Heroes* (1996) — with its glowing brass writing and noble diatonic trumpet solos accompanied by sustained strings — strongly recall Copland's example, and Williams's film scores also tap Copland-like soundscapes for both the excitement of urban settings (see, for example, the brash main-title cue of *The Towering Inferno*) or the

---

12. Bond 2003, p. 10.
13. Quoted in Audissino 2014, p. 218.
14. Bond 2004, p. 13.

more dignified restraint of music associated with US presidents[15]. The Prologue to Oliver Stone's *JFK* (1991), for example, features multiple side drums and diatonic solo trumpet, and a cadential progression switching from the chord of the flattened seventh to the major dominant — a stock device in the scoring of westerns. (The noble trumpet timbre had already acquired an ironically darker hue in the more disturbing context of *Born on the Fourth of July* (1989), also directed by Stone.) A notable characteristic of this 'presidential' idiom, which is still ubiquitous in scores to contemporary US movies and TV series set in the White House, is the apparently direct equation of overtly military elements (drums and trumpets) with a domestic political setting; such musical gestures would seem out of place in films set in equivalent European political circles. More broadly, Copland's influence on Williams is heard in limpid diatonic writing (ultimately derived from the example of Stravinsky's neoclassicism) and a certain melodic angularity not dissimilar from a characteristic trait of Prokofiev's (see below): the track "Out to Sea" from *Jaws*, for instance, neatly brings together musical ingredients reminiscent of Copland, Friedhofer, neoclassical Stravinsky and Prokofiev, the music's essential diatonicism being its most obvious means of coherence. Given the importance of ballet music to film scoring, it is worth remembering that Copland's influence on film composers came as much from his seminal ballet scores and concert works, some with distinctively American subject-matter (*Billy the Kid*, *Rodeo*, *Lincoln Portrait*), as it did from his own film scores.

Williams's fondness for composing thrilling march themes as his boldest and most optimistic musical statements is a reminder that this was the most popular genre in XIX-century America, peaking with the work of John Philip Sousa and remaining deeply embedded in modern US culture, whether associated with the military, sporting fixtures, or its continuing influence on jazz, pop music and film music. As Williams commented: «One of the most significant aspects of the march is the nostalgia involved... I think that the Sousa march and the swingy march — the kind of marches the Bill Finegan and Glenn Miller bands played — go to some place in the American soul and are part of what defines us as a nation»[16]. The influence of popular band music on his military-style march for *Midway* (Jack Smight, 1976) was also discussed by Williams[17]. Amongst the most famous Williams marches are those he composed and subsequently judiciously recycled for action films which spawned lucrative franchises, principally *Star Wars*, Spielberg's *Raiders of the Lost Ark* (the first Indiana Jones movie, 1981) and *Superman* (Richard Donner, 1978). Audissino has pinpointed the specific musical characteristics which make these thrilling melodies sound so heroic[18]. Examples are to be found in films as diverse in nature as Spielberg's *1941* (1979) and *Jurassic Park* ("Journey to the Island"). The former is coloured

15. For further on the 'presidential' dimension of Williams's scoring, see Lehman 2015.
16. Quoted in Audissino 2014, p. 157.
17. Williams 2003.
18. Audissino 2014, pp. 154-156.

by a comedically nationalist slant, so it comes as no surprise to find Williams writing a parody of cowboy music for a P40 fighter pilot. March rhythms underpin many of the most celebrated themes composed for westerns in the 1950s and 1960s, a genre to which Williams himself contributed in his scores for Mark Rydell's *The Reivers* (1969) and *The Cowboys* (1972), the latter starring John Wayne. In these projects, the music balances vernacular styles (cowboy and hillbilly tunes, rustic instrumentation, hints of the blues) with fairly formulaic orchestral scoring reminiscent of Copland's cowboy-themed ballets — a huge influence on film scoring in the 1950s — and the scores to westerns by Elmer Bernstein and others. It was Williams's music for these two Rydell films that first inspired Spielberg to hire Williams, for *The Sugarland Express* (1974), a movie also replete with vernacular styles. Spielberg, an avid enthusiast for what he termed «pure symphonic film music»[19], had imagined Williams to be a veteran composer because of the traditional nature of his scoring, which had made him keen to learn more about «this modern relic from a lost era of film symphonies»[20].

Particularly striking is Williams's canny tapping of the traditional western's musical characteristics in other genres: both the *Star Wars* "Main Title" march and Indiana Jones's "Raiders March" energize their propulsive melodies by means of snappily syncopated rhythmic underpinning which recalls the prototypical example of this trick in the film-music literature: Bernstein's main-title music for *The Magnificent Seven* (John Sturges, 1960). This is significant because both *Star Wars* and *Raiders of the Lost Ark* perpetuate the pioneering spirit of adventure and exploration with which the western has always been associated: here we have, respectively, music for space cowboys (whose adventures are sometimes set in western-looking desertscapes) and an archaeologist jauntily wearing a cowboy's fedora. In this way Williams satisfyingly reinvented the strong vein of nationalistic post-Copland film scoring and its indelible association with particular genres.

Classical Hollywood

Lucas was at one stage considering adding «a country-and-western influence» to the music for *Star Wars*, alongside the 'classical' music he intended to commission from Williams[21]. This would have intensified the quasi-western feel of the movie, but it was the 'classical' dimension of Williams's celebrated orchestral score which did most to change both his own stylistic direction and the nature of the other blockbusters which followed. Lucas knew from the outset exactly what he wanted — «an old fashioned, romantic movie score» — and alighted on Williams because he knew him to be «very good with large orchestras»; Williams later warmly commended the director's bold decision to match his

[19]. Quoted in *ibidem*, pp. 108-109.

[20]. McBride 1997, p. 222.

[21]. Rinzler 2007, p. 115.

futuristic settings with essentially anachronistic music that charted «fairly familiar emotional ground» rather than relying on «futuristic cliché» or electronics[22]. After all, as the opening title card of each film in the franchise tells us, these stories are set in a future which is «a long time ago». In an interview conducted in 1997 to mark the twentieth anniversary of the first film in the series, Williams expanded on this view, commenting that the franchise «reached across cultural bounds and beyond language into some kind of mythic, shared remembered past — from the deep past of our collective unconscious, if you like». This attribute seemingly required music

> [...] that would put us in touch with very familiar and remembered emotions, which for me as a musician translated into the use of a 19th century operatic idiom, if you like, Wagner and this sort of thing. These sorts of influences would put us in touch with remembered theatrical experiences as well — all western experiences to be sure. We were talking about cross-cultural mythology a moment ago; the music at least I think is firmly rooted in western cultural sensibilities[23].

Contrary to popular belief, the excerpts from classical music included on the film's temp track were not intended to end up, Kubrick-like, in the final cut[24]. As noted elsewhere, however, they did result in some infamous near-plagiarisms on the composer's part, most obviously from Holst's *The Planets* and Stravinsky's *The Rite of Spring*. The opening of the main-title march has often been compared to the similarly uplifting theme Erich Wolfgang Korngold penned as his main-title music for *Kings Row* (Sam Wood, 1942), and another influence was Miklós Rózsa's music for *Ivanhoe* (Richard Thorpe, 1952), which was used for the main-title sequence on the temp track[25]. Other sources mention the use of Alex North's music for *Cleopatra* (Joseph L. Mankiewicz, 1963), extracts from Herrmann's scores for Hitchcock, and Bruckner's Ninth Symphony[26]. Yet the principal model Lucas had in mind was legendary Golden Age composer Max Steiner, famous (indeed, infamous) for his literal-minded and often slavish attention to catching the action — or 'mickey-mousing', as it is more disparagingly known. Spielberg, who had suggested to Lucas that Williams was his best bet to score the film, nicknamed the composer 'Max' for his adept use of this technique[27]. A particularly graphic Williams example occurs in *Family Plot* when Blanche is

---

22. *Ibidem.*

23. Byrd 1997, rpt. in Cooke 2010, p. 236.

24. Rinzler 2007, p. 266. The film's editor, Richard Chew, here somewhat implausibly suggests that one of the recordings Lucas used was «Dvořák's *The Planets* [*sic*]».

25. *Ibidem*, p. 273.

26. See, for example, Jeff Smith's research on Lucas cited at <http://originaltrilogy.com/topic/Star-Wars-The-Temp-Track/id/12014>, accessed January 2018. On the Bruckner, see Rinzler 2007, p. 273. The influence of Bruckner's Seventh Symphony on Williams's love music in *Superman* has been proposed in Winters 2012, p. 121.

27. See Rinzler 2007, p. 293, and Audissino 2014, p. 207.

drugged in the villains' basement garage, and explicit tributes to Steiner have been identified in the later scores for *Raiders of the Lost Ark*, *1941*, and *Home Alone 2: Lost in New York* (Chris Columbus, 1992)[28].

Yet Korngold's more opulent musical spirit remains the prime inspiration behind Williams's post-*Jaws* blockbuster scores. Among the direct correspondences between the two composers which commentators have noted are a resemblance between the main-title theme in *Superman* and Korngold's theme for Emily in *Devotion* (Curtis Bernhardt, 1946), as well as his main-title theme from *Kings Row*[29]. Not coincidentally, Korngold's music was enjoying something of a renaissance in the 1970s, thanks to the appearance of several LPs devoted to his flamboyant scores for Warner Bros. pictures from the 1930s and 1940s, beginning with the first instalment of RCA's series *The Classic Film Score* in 1972; this disc included the main-title music from *Kings Row*, as a result of which the record company was besieged with requests that they issue the entire score. In his liner notes to the eventual release of the complete *Kings Row* music in 1979, George Korngold put his finger on what had made his father's film music so successful, commenting that its «dramatic construction through the use of motifs is highly intricate in its detail while remaining easily accessible to the listener. Nothing bears this out more than the fact that the music heard here becomes (or remains) absolute music even when divorced from the picture»[30]. These remarks might be applied to Williams's film scores with equal aptness, as could the following description of Korngold's style by William Darby and Jack Du Bois:

> [It] can best be described as late romantic and eclectic. His orchestrations are lush, with an expected emphasis on strings (often divisi) and with a prominent role for harps, an instrumental combination which was to become a cliché in Hollywood music. His great facility and fluency of technique are accompanied by a strong lyric (sentimental) gift in melodic writing. Korngold follows in the footsteps of Richard Strauss by employing the whole arsenal of late romantic compositional techniques with consummate mastery[31].

Rightly pointing out that «Strauss provides the immediate source for Korngold's style», they then proceed to criticize the older composer's «notorious fluency», which

> [...] lies partly in slipping from one key to another without a true modulation, employing orchestrations as a plush substitute for content, offering a busyness of movement for long stretches in lieu of genuine thematic momentum. All of these Straussian attributes, normally viewed as defects in the classical music arena, constitute the modus operandi of such studio composers as Korngold, Steiner, and [Franz] Waxman[32].

---

28. Audissino 2014, pp. 167, 179, 209, 225.
29. Winters 2007, p. 41.
30. Korngold 1991.
31. Darby – Du Bois 1990, p. 160.
32. *Ibidem*.

But in one vitally important respect, Strauss's (and subsequently Korngold's) idiom was the ideal prototype for these Golden Age composers, and was to remain so for Williams: its skilful fusion (whether in the genres of opera or symphonic poem) of vivid narrative commentary, characterization and atmosphere with musical structures that can stand firmly on their own two feet when divorced from stage or screen.

Although it is tempting to regard Straussian elements in Williams's neoromantic music as having been filtered entirely through their Korngold incarnation, elements directly redolent of Strauss himself are to be found in many Williams scores. Some are obvious timbral and textural tendencies, such as a fondness for heroic and noble horn writing, and the general Alpine aura in the soundscapes of the early TV movie *Heidi* (Delbert Mann, 1968), while others are more precise. For example, one specific harmonic detail in Williams's music directly recalls Strauss: a shift from a major triad to the major triad a tone higher, while retaining the root of the first triad as a pedal point to create a last-inversion dominant-seventh chord — a device most memorably used by Strauss at the transcendental moment of his symphonic poem *Death and Transfiguration*. Examples of this harmonic fingerprint are to be found in Williams's scores to *Jaws* (end credits), *Superman* (main title), *The Empire Strikes Back* and *Return of the Jedi* (Yoda's theme), and *Jurassic Park* (the heroic trumpet theme in "Welcome to Jurassic Park"). Furthermore, Audissino highlights a quotation from Strauss's opera *Der Rosenkavalier* in *A. I. Artificial Intelligence*, where it serves as a gesture of homage to Stanley Kubrick — who might have directed the film and used this music in it, had he lived to do so[33].

Given that Korngold was particularly associated with Warner Bros.' swashbuckling adventures starring Errol Flynn, and that these films were influential on directors such as Lucas and Spielberg in both dramatic and musical parameters, it is not surprising that the carefully choreographed action sequences in the New Hollywood blockbusters often pay conscious homage to their Golden Age forebears. Williams recalled that his music for the exciting chase in *Jaws* during which the *Orca* pursues a barrel attached to the shark «becomes very Korngoldian […] you expect to see Errol Flynn at the helm of this thing»[34]. The tongue-in-cheek quality of the atmosphere here (which «gave us a laugh», recalled Williams) became a vital part of the Indiana Jones concept, which Williams described musically as «camp fun» in its allusions to old-style scoring practices — and these were appropriate enough, given that Indy's action adventures are set in the 1930s and Steiner was a self-confessed influence on these scores[35]. The impact of the combined Korngold-Strauss model on Williams's handling of action sequences can most readily be felt when comparing scenes involving sword fights or similar. Korngold's exuberant scoring for the sword fights in, for example, *Captain Blood* (Michael Curtiz, 1935), *The Adventures of Robin Hood* (Michael Curtiz and William Keighley, 1938) and *The Sea Hawk* (Michael Curtiz,

[33]. Audissino 2014, pp. 217-218.

[34]. Burlingame 2012.

[35]. Audissino 2014, pp. 152-153.

1940) is recalled in the sword fights of Spielberg's *Hook* (1991), which features a setting directly analogous to those of the pirates and privateers in *Captain Blood* and *The Sea Hawk*, *Indiana Jones and the Kingdom of the Crystal Skull* (Steven Spielberg, 2008), and even in the de rigueur light-sabre clashes of the *Star Wars* franchise. The basic approach is that of the Straussian symphonic poem, in which localized physical action can be caught via sporadic mickey-mousing, without sacrificing the structural autonomy of the cue as a whole — and cues of this kind can be substantial in length, often involving scant dialogue. (A lack of dialogue might be considered a godsend to composers writing in this manner, but the exaggerated sound effects in modern action sequences often drown out the carefully crafted music.) A good comparison is that between the climactic sword fight in *Robin Hood* and the vehicle-borne sword fight in *Crystal Skull* — a score in which one of the cues, as Audissino points out, was given the title "Swashbuckler" in its concert version[36].

The impact of Wagner on Williams's thematic techniques has often been identified, even though Strauss's subsequent development of Wagnerian leitmotivic procedures seems a more stylistically relevant model. Fancifully, perhaps, the music for the *Star Wars* franchise has even been viewed as Williams's *Ring* cycle[37]. As we saw above, Williams himself singled out Wagner when discussing his creative response to Lucas's idea that the *Star Wars* score should inhabit territory that was «emotionally familiar»[38]. He also recalled the specific initiative to imbue the *Star Wars* music with a leitmotivic construction:

> I didn't want to hear a piece of Dvořák here, a piece of Tchaikovsky there [...]. What I wanted to hear was something to do with Ben Kenobi more developed here, something to do with his death over there. What we needed were themes of our own, which one could put through all the permutations of a dramatic situation. This was my discussion and my dialogue with George — that I felt we needed our own themes, which could be made into a solid dramaturgical glue from start to finish[39].

Williams's leitmotives and their transformations range from the utterly simply to the ultra-sophisticated. As few as three notes can serve memorable narrative ends: consider, for example, the three-note motif for Voldemort in the *Harry Potter* franchise, which in its concise usefulness recalls the economy of Steiner's equally terse three-note motif for the title character in *King Kong* (Merian C. Cooper and Ernest B. Schoedsack, 1933). Like Korngold, in whose score for *Anthony Adverse* (Mervyn LeRoy, 1936) no fewer than 18 different themes have been identified and labelled[40], a Williams score can be a rich tapestry

---

36. *Ibidem*, p. 285 fn. 29.

37. BYRD 1997, rpt. in COOKE 2010, p. 237. On leitmotifs in *Star Wars*, see Frank Lehman's chapter in this volume.

38. *Ibidem*, p. 236.

39. Quoted in RINZLER 2007, pp. 292-293.

40. DARBY – DU BOIS 1990, pp. 161-162.

of multiple thematic developments, all closely tied in to narrative details; in composing scores for sequels, however, he can be highly selective in redeploying thematic material already familiar from the earlier film(s), as shown by the marked reluctance to trot out the "Raiders March" in *Indiana Jones and the Last Crusade* (1989)[41].

Specific Wagnerian touches in Williams's film scores include an alleged similarity between the "Tarnhelm" motif from the *Ring* (which juxtaposes two unrelated minor triads) and the "Imperial March" from *The Empire Strikes Back*[42], with its extra-musical associations of what Scott Murphy terms «antagonism, with offshoots of the eerie and sinister»[43]. Kathryn Kalinak, too, sees Williams's ambiguity between major and minor harmonizations here as suggestive of how Darth Vader's character is «both so threatening and so recuperable»[44]. (In fact, both the soundworld and melodic profile of Williams's theme seem much closer to Tchaikovsky's *Swan Lake*: see below.) A comparably mysterious harmonic ambiguity characterizes the music associated with the Ark in *Raiders of the Lost Ark*. Not surprisingly, given the common subject matter, "The Keeper of the Grail" in *Last Crusade* has something of the aura of *Parsifal*, an influence also audible in the music associated with the Force in *Star Wars*.

Oddly, it might be felt — given the cue's strong Wagnerian resonance — Spielberg heard an «English» musical atmosphere at work in "The Keeper of the Grail", describing this as an «English pastoral idiom in major modes with very positive intervals»[45]. True, Wagner (especially *Parsifal*) was a major influence on Elgar, most notably in the latter's *The Dream of Gerontius*, and perhaps Spielberg was unwittingly responding to this connection. "Hymn to the Fallen" in *Saving Private Ryan* (Steven Spielberg, 1998) also has something of the Elgarian *nobilmente* idiom about it, here flanked by the side drum and distant fanfares of the US presidential style, and also recalls Elgar's music in specific harmonic details. Williams recalled chatting to Hitchcock about Elgar while working on *Family Plot*[46], and Elgar's *La Capricieuse* was used as source music in Spielberg's *Schindler's List* (1993) — a film with a nondiegetic score echoing (alongside other influences) the intensity and lyricism of the British string-orchestra tradition. Williams's creative responses to English music are one obvious way in which his scoring can sound quite distinct from Hollywood precedents.

---

41. Spielberg commented in his note to the original soundtrack recording of *Indiana Jones and the Last Crusade*: «We felt [these] movies had grown up to the point that we didn't have to lean on your thrill button every time something heroic occurs as we had done in the previous two motion pictures». See also Audissino 2014, p. 126.

42. On the comparison of the "Imperial March" and the "Tarnhelm" motif, see Joakim Tillman's chapter in this volume.

43. Murphy 2014, pp. 482, 487. The substantial and wide-ranging volume on film music in which this essay appears contains remarkably little discussion of Williams's output.

44. Kalinak 1992, p. 31.

45. Spielberg, liner note to original soundtrack album of *Indiana Jones and the Last Crusade*.

46. Williams 2005.

Its influence first surfaces in the British TV movie *Jane Eyre* (Delbert Mann, 1970), where he composed «something that sounds like Yorkshire in the eighteen-sixties»[47]. Audissino additionally notes the echoes of music by Vaughan Williams and Delius on this score[48]. Some of the muscular orchestral counterpoint in *Jaws* ("Sea Attack Number One" and "Preparing the Cage") is redolent of Walton, a composer whose spirit more obviously conditioned the coronation-like "Throne Room" music in *Star Wars*, derived as it is from the idiom of ceremonial marches composed by both Walton and Elgar. There is a reference to a melody from the most celebrated of the latter's *Pomp and Circumstance* marches in Williams's comment that the music for the medal-presentation ceremony in this scene «is a kind of land of hope and glory bit [...] almost like coronation music, really, which the scene seemed to want»[49]. This style, also heard at the conclusion of the main titles, is particularly redolent of Walton's coronation march *Orb and Sceptre*[50]. The Elgar-Walton idiom recurs in "Lando's Palace", which is (heroically, if briefly) recapitulated at the mid-point of "The Clash of the Lightsabers" in *The Empire Strikes Back*. The score by Williams which is most thoroughly coloured by English influences is *War Horse* (2011), of which Spielberg noted that the music had been shaped not only by his film «but also by many of the picturesque settings of the poet William Wordsworth, whose vivid descriptions of the British landscape inspired much of what you are going to hear»[51]. This is particularly evident in the track "Dartmoor 1912", where a folklike modality and rhapsodic style strongly reminiscent of Vaughan Williams blossom into the inevitable Hollywood-style big melodic sweep, with an anachronistic hint of Copland's rodeo idiom for the horsemanship. In "Learning the Call" the quasi-folk modality, pentatonic flourishes and non-functional parallel triads remind us that — for all its 'English' sound — this manner of composing demonstrates Vaughan Williams's own absorption of the innovations of Debussy and Ravel.

Ballet

Experiencing the elegant choreography and neatly synchronized music of swashbucklers past and present might well suggest ballet as a more obvious progenitor of the musico-dramatic approach taken in these movies than the much-touted operatic origins of film music. After all, ballet is an art form which combines expressive movement, dynamic rhythms, deft characterization and colourful contrasts par excellence, and Sergei

47. Quoted in Audissino 2014, p. 206.

48. *Ibidem*, p. 90.

49. Rinzler 2007, p. 430.

50. On the pervasive influence of the Elgar-Walton march idiom on the scoring of British war films, see Cooke 2018. The influence of the action sequences in the British war film *The Dam Busters* (1955) on the portrayal of the attack on the Death Star in *Star Wars* has often been noted, not least because the British cinematographer Gilbert Taylor worked on both films.

51. Spielberg, liner note to original soundtrack album of *War Horse*.

Eisenstein pointed out that ballet had achieved a compelling conjunction of music and physical spectacle long before films traversed similar artistic territory[52]. When viewing *Star Wars* for the first time, Williams found himself «reacting to its atmospheres and energies and rhythms», all parameters which resonate with the ballet composer's remit[53]. While Korngold famously stated that film music was opera without the singing, an action sequence from *Robin Hood* has plausibly been likened to ballet by Audissino, who points out that (as in many ballet scores) the music — while «highly functional» — does not necessarily follow the action in slavish detail[54]. Ballet has in fact been a crucial, but under-appreciated, influence on film scoring throughout movie history. In Hollywood, balletic influences have been noted in the scores of Dimitri Tiomkin (who was married to a choreographer involved in the production of MGM's musicals, many of which involve interpolated ballet set-pieces) and Alex North (who was married to a dancer). North directly likened the writing of film cues to writing dances[55]. Cartoon music, too, has always been strongly influenced by ballet — a connection reaching its apotheosis in the explicitly balletic sequences of Disney's *Fantasia* (1940) — and the deft balancing of detailed mickey-mousing with an ongoing musical flow in cartoon shorts suggests parallels with Williams's post-Steiner action-catching in his more tongue-in-cheek adventure scores[56]. The cartoon connection was made by Williams himself when discussing the need in *Jurassic Park* to undertake «a massive job of symphonic cartooning»: «You have to match the rhythmic gyrations of the dinosaurs and create these kind of funny ballets»[57]. Kubrick, in a discussion of *A Clockwork Orange* (1971) during which he likened his protagonist's outlook on violence as «some great action ballet», commented more generally that «in cinematic terms, I should say that movement and music must inevitably be related to dance» and gave the specific example of his infamous use of Johann Strauss's "Blue Danube" waltz to accompany the spaceship docking sequence in *2001: A Space Odyssey* (1968)[58]. Similarly, Williams noted of the asteroid field in *The Empire Strikes Back*: «It has a musical piece that was like a ballet of flying spaceships and asteroids colliding»[59]. Earlier, one of the cues in *Jaws 2* (Jeannot Szwarc, 1978) had been entitled "Ballet for Divers".

Both Tiomkin and North had family backgrounds in Russia, and Russian ballet composers were a potent influence on both their own work and Williams's film scores. Tchaikovsky's music had of course been liberally plundered in the compilation scores of

52. Eisenstein 1948, p. 131.
53. Byrd 1997, rpt. in Cooke 2010, p. 235.
54. Audissino 2014, p. 17.
55. Cooke 2008, pp. 119-121.
56. The influence of ballet music on cartoon scoring was proposed in Dahl 1949.
57. Quoted in Audissino 2014, p. 131.
58. Quoted in LoBrutto 1998, pp. 338-339.
59. Byrd 1997, rpt. in Cooke 2010, p. 241.

the silent-film era, with his *Romeo and Juliet* fantasy overture and *Swan Lake* remaining firm favourites in the tracking of early sound films. It may, perhaps, have been the use of *Swan Lake* in Universal's groundbreaking *Dracula* (Tod Browning, 1931) that inspired the apparent allusion to this ballet's music in Williams's score to a much later *Dracula* (John Badham, 1979), notably in the end titles[60]. Echoes of Tchaikovsky's ballets in Williams's other film scores include the dark harmonic progression of the "Imperial March" in *The Empire Strikes Back* — strongly reminiscent of *Swan Lake* but here merged with the aura of Wagnerian symbolism mentioned earlier — and the ebullient descending scales and rapid sequential harmonic progressions of "The Adventures of Mutt" in *Crystal Skull*, as well as the similar scales, warmly expressive moments and bubbling flute solo in the "Finale" of the same film. Similar harmonic sequences recur in *Hook*, while Tchaikovsky's *Sleeping Beauty* is aptly quoted in a scene of cryogenic preservation in *A.I. Artificial Intelligence*. The vigorous brass turns in the original *Star Wars* score (for example, in "Shootout in the Cell Bay"), sound like a nightmarish distortion of the "Arab Dance" from *The Nutcracker*, a score more explicitly referenced as part of the Christmas atmosphere of the music to *Home Alone* (Chris Columbus, 1990) and *Home Alone 2*, where the Sugar Plum Fairy's celeste is showcased in the main-title sequences. In both of these films, too, the music for the family's desperate rush through the airport to catch their flight strongly recalls the Cossack *trepak* dance in the same ballet.

Rimsky-Korsakov, whose music exerted a strong influence on Golden Age Hollywood scoring, was not known as a ballet composer; but his pupil Stravinsky composed a succession of brilliant ballet scores which progressed from Rimskyan pastiche in *The Firebird* to the folk-based modernism of *Petrushka*, *The Rite of Spring* and *Les Noces*, followed by the neoclassicism of *Pulcinella* and its successors. Williams's most notorious nod to *The Rite* came in the music for the Dune Sea of Tattooine in *Star Wars*, which aped the eerie opening of Part II in Stravinsky's ballet; the 'flip side' of the LP had featured on the temp track because Lucas felt «nobody ever uses that side of the record»[61]. Williams's score is also reminiscent of Rimsky and early Stravinsky — especially *Firebird* — in its music for Princess Leia, which includes a noble diatonic horn solo above hazy strings and a thematic recapitulation stiffened by a horn countermelody à la Tchaikovsky. The same soundworld characterizes Leia's encounter with Han Solo ("Han Solo and the Princess") in *The Empire Strikes Back*, where gently chromatic harmonies above a pedal point resemble a feature of much late-romantic Russian music. This technique acquires a Khachaturian-like aura when the same theme returns by way of a tutti climax towards the end of "The Clash of the Lightsabers". In the same score, the allusion to *The Rite* is immediately followed by dancelike music for Jawa Sandcrawler, one of numerous self-contained and

60. As suggested by Emilio Audissino in a private communication.

61. Rinzler 2007, 273.

orchestrationally memorable passages in Williams's film music which seemingly support North's assertion that composing film cues is analogous to writing dance numbers. As Goldsmith was (more) prone to do, Williams occasionally resorts to pounding, repetitive string dissonances reminiscent of the "Augurs of Spring" in *The Rite*, for example at the mid-point of "The Tractor Beam / Chasm Crossfire" in *Star Wars*, and in several cues for *War of the Worlds* (2005), a film in which the invading tripods were likened by Spielberg to «scary ballet dancers»[62]. Audissino has also identified the influence of early Stravinsky in Williams's music for the flight to Neverland in *Hook*[63], while the thrilling march for the parade of the slave children in *Indiana Jones and the Temple of Doom* (Steven Spielberg, 1984) overlays the pseudo-archaic primitivism of the old Hollywood Romano-Biblical epics (brass flourishes in parallel fourths and fifths) with distinctly Rimskyan touches (glittering orchestration featuring exotic, swirling scales).

Williams's film scores are replete with echoes of the music of two of the greatest twentieth-century Russian ballet composers, Shostakovich and Prokofiev, both of whom (significantly) were also resourceful film composers whose output for theatre, cinema and concert hall shared common traits. Reviewing Prokofiev's *Romeo and Juliet* in 1949, for example, Iris Morley wrote: «One of the new things about this ballet is that the technique of the cinema is used to give a heightened sense of action; again and again the musical themes are broken and re-woven like the change in a camera's focus»[64]. Shostakovich's eclectic early ballets are less of an influence on Williams than his symphonies, hard-driving elements from which — especially reminiscences of the dynamic dance-of-death scherzo of the Tenth Symphony — are heard in in the "Forest Battle" of *Return of the Jedi*, "T Rex Rescue" in *Jurassic Park*, "Sea Attack Number One" from *Jaws*, and in much of Williams's battle music (for example, "The Battle of Hoth" in *The Empire Strikes Back*). Shostakovich's militaristic side-drum mannerisms occur in numerous contexts, including "Escape from Venice" and "Belly of the Steel Beast" in *Last Crusade*. It should be noted, however, that several earlier US composers had seen their symphonic styles unfairly likened to those of Russian composers, most notably in the case of George Antheil — who resented the comparison, but might have been amused by one critic's conclusion that «even if Antheil isn't exactly the American Shostakovich, I would see no real harm if the Russians suddenly began calling Shostakovich the Russian Antheil»[65]. Another generic hallmark of Russian influences, suggestive of the work of both Shostakovich and Prokofiev, is the sardonic, brittle march style — very different from Williams's robustly nationalistic march themes — encountered in "March of the Villains" in *Superman* and during the opening cue of *Last Crusade*.

62. Spielberg 2005.
63. Audissino 2014, p. 214.
64. Morley 1949, p. 31.
65. Bancolli 1949.

Antheil's Fifth Symphony (1948) was strongly influenced by Prokofiev's recently composed Fifth Symphony, notably in some of its jaunty melodic profiles and distinctively chugging repeated-chord accompaniments from the horn section. Both of these stylistic fingerprints are also widely encountered in Williams's film music. The Prokofiev influence on Williams's melodic and harmonic style often involves angular themes that leap upwards or downwards to alight on the sharpened fourth of the prevailing harmony, and the distinctive cadential ploy of following a sharply dissonant chord with a ringing consonance. Much of his orchestration (superbly realized by Herb Spencer from the composer's detailed instructions) suggests an intimate familiarity with the colourful instrumentation of Prokofiev's ballets *Romeo and Juliet* and *Cinderella*, and this connection is particularly striking when listening to André Previn's fine recordings of these scores with the London Symphony Orchestra, made (in 1973 and 1983 respectively) during the same era in which this ensemble recorded the first trilogy of *Star Wars* soundtracks. Another clear parallel with Prokofiev is the choral-orchestral music (heavily based on ostinati) for "Duel of the Fates" in the first film in the *Star Wars* prequel trilogy, *The Phantom Menace* (George Lucas, 1999), which recurs in the film's end credits and recalls Prokofiev's music for Eisenstein's *Alexander Nevsky* (1938). And the more buoyantly balletic Prokofiev soundworld accompanies Tom Cruise as he frantically pursues his own escaping eyes in *Minority Report*. The chugging repeated-chord accompaniment style is evident in the "Promenade" from *Jaws* and "The Asteroid Field" in *The Empire Strikes Back*, where some of the melodic material also carries Prokofiev's stylistic fingerprints. All the foregoing characteristics come together in "Parade of the Ewoks" from *Return of the Jedi*, the nearest Williams comes to a pastiche of Prokofiev's style — deliciously eccentric scoring for recorders notwithstanding — and in this instance seemingly modelled on the sardonic march from Prokofiev's opera *The Love for Three Oranges*, which the Russian composer himself wittily quoted at a dramatically apt moment in *Cinderella*. Similar conjunctions of Prokofiev's stylistic hallmarks are to be found in the dialogue-free shots of pleasure seekers on the idyllic beach in *Jaws 2* ("The Menu"), the music here making the playful nature of the scene balletic in effect, and "The Snake Pit" from *Crystal Skull*[66].

The dance of the title characters in *The Witches of Eastwick*, which includes some Prokofiev-like melodic angularity, is but one example of an association between the influence of Russian ballet music and the supernatural, while in other contexts (e.g. *Hook*, *Home Alone*, *E. T. the Extra-Terrestrial* [1982]) these resonances suggest the wonder of childhood. Both associations are potently combined in Williams's scores for the Harry Potter franchise, the first two films of which were directed by his *Home Alone* collaborator Chris Columbus[67]. Williams observed that his music for Harry Potter was more theatrical in nature than his other film work, and Audissino has drawn attention to the renewed influence of Tchaikovsky, Rimsky-Korsakov and early Stravinsky on the

[66]. On the Prokofiev influence in the score to *Jaws 2*, see Audissino 2014, p. 117.

[67]. On the Williams scores to the *Harry Potter* films, see Jamie Lynn Webster's chapter in this volume.

scores for the first two films[68]. The first movie in the series, *Harry Potter and the Sorcerer's Stone*[69], features a Williams score profoundly influenced by the soundworld of Prokofiev's ballets. Memorably described by Richard Dyer as «an agreeably lopsided and slippery waltz»[70], the well-known "Hedwig's Theme" from the "Prologue" demonstrates both the Russian composer's melodic angularity and dissonant-cadence harmonic strategy, while its juxtaposition of unrelated minor triads also taps the Wagnerian and *Swan Lake* resonances of Darth Vader's music[71]. In addition, the use of the celeste returns us to the soundworld of *The Nutcracker*, the instrument in this score functioning in time-honoured fashion as a timbre both innocent and eerily disquieting; the Tchaikovsky connection again briefly surfaces as Christmas is celebrated, as it did in the first two *Home Alone* films. The thematic material from the opening of *Sorcerer's Stone* acquires a more obviously balletic stamp in the later cues "Visit to the Zoo" and "Mr Longbottom Flies", while the parodic wrong-note harmonization in the horn ensemble's rendering of "Hogwarts Forever!" includes particularly clear examples of Prokofiev's dissonant-consonant cadential mannerism.

Conclusion: «A Solid Dramaturgical Glue from Start to Finish»

Playing the game of 'Spot the Influence' is great fun, especially when dealing with an idiom as eclectic as Williams's and, indeed, a genre of music which has always invited — and often strongly encouraged — the direct assimilation of tried and tested formulae from yesteryear. The game continues to be played on several websites, one of which is a blog devoted to the influence of Prokofiev on Williams and Russian influences on other US film composers such as James Horner[72]. But the game does, of course, raise two important questions. How, if at all, does Williams's music cohere? And, given the fairly obvious nature of many of the influences discussed here, what makes his music distinctive to the point when any aficionado can immediately spot a Williams score? In this connection it is worth noting that one fan-blog has been devoted exclusively to the relatively few cues in Williams's film scores which do *not* sound like Williams[73].

---

68. Audissino 2014, p. 226.

69. The film is known as *Harry Potter and the Philosopher's Stone* in the United Kingdom, after the original title of the book by J. K. Rowling on which it is based.

70. From an article in the *Boston Globe* quoted in Clemmensen 2001.

71. Williams once commented that the music for *Star Wars* was associated with the «fairy-tale aspect» of the story: see Rinzler 2007, p. 292.

72. See, for example, <http://www.classicalmpr.org/story/2015/10/20/star-wars-john-williams-influences>, and <http://tvtropes.org/pmwiki/pmwiki.php/SuspiciouslySimilarSong/Film>; the Williams/Prokofiev blog is at <http://www.jwfan.com/forums/index.php?/topic/19614-prokofiev-scores-that-influenced-film-music>, all three sites accessed January 2018.

73. <http://www.jwfan.com/forums/index.php?/topic/12936-john-williams-cues-that-dont-sound-like-john-williams>, accessed January 2018.

While the 'big theme' mentality of some of the post-*Jaws* blockbusters is for many moviegoers the most immediately comprehensible feature of the composer's style, there are of course a myriad of subtler ways in which his music makes its dramatic impact. In charting the quasi-Golden Age leitmotivic procedures of his most celebrated scores, as many commentators at all levels (from student essay to scholarly publication) are prone to do, the resourcefulness of the harmonic language is often neglected. Williams's harmonic vocabulary, to coin a phrase used by Spielberg of the composer's art more generally, is truly chameleon-like[74]. It ranges from the purest diatonicism to terrifying atonality according to dramatic context, with a huge range of tonal explorations in the rich territory between those two poles — and it is exactly the same fruitful post-tonal region that creates such memorable harmonic tension in the work of the twentieth-century composers whose music is occasionally echoed in the process, and who are products of what has aptly been termed «romantic modernism»[75]. By placing his own personal stamp on inherited harmonic languages, Williams succeeds in making his music sound both traditional and modern at the same time, and also achieves a perhaps surprising degree of stylistic cohesion in the process. To cite one specific example, Williams drew attention to his fondness for last-inversion seventh chords, in part a holdover from his early interest in jazz[76]. Harmony of this type is also ubiquitous in the music of Prokofiev, Sibelius and Walton, echoes of all of whose work abound in Williams's; yet when listening to such chords presented in the brashly optimistic spirit of the "Raiders March", or at around four minutes into the track "The Battle of Hoth" from *The Empire Strikes Back* (where they are another clear reminder of the coronation-march idiom), the overall effect seems unique to Williams. Such chords can also be related to a clichéd dissonance construction used melodramatically in old Hollywood scores, a trick which Williams deliberately emulated (as part of the «camp fun») to characterize the Nazis in *Last Crusade*: «the orchestra hits these 1940s dramatic chords, you know, seventh degree of the scale on the bottom, which is a kind of an old signal of some evil, militaristic doer»[77]. Furthermore, the luminous harmonies suggestive of Strauss's *Death and Transfiguration* discussed earlier are also last-inversion sevenths. Taken together, all these instances show Williams applying a well-worn harmonic formula — keeping a basic triad recognizable while creating tension or expectancy by adding a dissonant bass note — in ways that perfectly suit both the immediate dramatic needs of the story at hand and overall stylistic consistency.

---

74. In his liner note to the original soundtrack album of *Jaws*, Spielberg writes: «John is an artist of numerous styles. He is chameleon-like and vulnerable to the impulses of the film he is about to score».

75. FRANKLIN 2011, p. 32.

76. As an example of the interest generated amongst Williams's fans even by an awareness (or otherwise) of this specific harmonic detail, see <http://www.jwfan.com/forums/index.php?/topic/22832-indiana-jones-seventh-on-the-bottom>, accessed January 2018.

77. Quoted in AUDISSINO 2014, p. 153.

In addition to a fondness for last-inversion seventh chords, jazz influences sometimes help keep Williams's film scores relevant to the modern age. Such influences are also to be heard in Williams's concert music, for example the *Cello Concerto* (1994) and *Heartwood* (2002), where the influence is not the spiky restlessness of typical swing-era dance music but the rich «impressionistic harmonies» (Williams's own description) so typical of the sophisticated composing of Duke Ellington, Billy Strayhorn, Claude Thornhill and Gil Evans[78]. Then there are the big-band pastiche numbers in the film scores, such as "Swing, Swing, Swing" in *1941* (a direct response to Louis Prima's "Sing, Sing, Sing") or — everybody's favourite — the idiosyncratically scored Benny Goodman tribute which makes the performances of the cantina band in *Star Wars* so delicious[79]. The latter's updating of a traditional jazz style through a modernist perspective may be compared to the treatment of rococo style in "Jabba's Baroque Recital" from *Return of the Jedi*: in both cases the stylistic allusions are clear enough, but the eccentric treatment of them prevents the music from sounding either like pure pastiche or inappropriately dated. More subtly, this is also true of the homages to Henry Mancini and cool jazz in Spielberg's *Catch Me if You Can* (2002) — which are appropriate to the era in which the film is set, and where more up-to-date minimalist techniques are added to the stylistic mix. References to jazz, minimalism and klezmer characterize the same director's *The Terminal* (2004), while minimalism also surfaces in the journey to the submerged post-apocalyptic Manhattan in *A. I. Artificial Intelligence*, resonating with the style's historical association with New York City.

Owing to its eclectic nature, Williams's film music has sometimes been subjected to allegations of incoherence. In the harsh assessment of Norman Lebrecht, for example, these «patchwork soundtracks that borrow from the classics» merely succeed in «plastering movies with bits of what we know»[80]. In his detailed review of the score to *Sorcerer's Stone*, Christian Clemmensen laments the sense of *déja-vu* attendant on its indebtedness to musical gestures thoroughly familiar from the various *Star Wars* films and the fact that while «about half of the score [is] extremely tightly woven into the thematic tapestry [...] the rest of it was surprisingly anonymous». On his own admission, however, this is an «awkwardly nebulous complaint», and he concludes: «even if you buy into the argument that parts of this score exhibit Williams on auto-pilot, the music that comes from the composer even at those times is superior to most of what comes from the rest of the industry»[81]. In this context it should be noted that the old-fashioned notion that film scoring needs some

---

78. In his liner notes to the album *Yo-Yo Ma Plays the Music of John Williams*, which includes these two works, Williams recalls that one of the things that always fascinated him was the way Thornhill and Evans utilized the horn in a jazz context. As noted earlier, this instrument is particularly prominent in Williams's film scores.

79. On the genesis of the cantina band music, see Byrd 1997, rpt. in Cooke 2010, p. 242.

80. Audissino 2014, pp. 138, 140.

81. Clemmensen 2001.

kind of alchemical organic cogency in order to succeed should have been laid to rest long ago, and is these days viewed with increasing scepticism. The classically minded elitism which has inspired often fruitless searches for 'unity' in orchestral film scores has frequently overlooked the special needs of narrative film scoring, and thanks to the persuasive arguments of recent scholarship we can now view traditional scoring methods in more valid critical perspectives. Ben Winters, for example, has argued that what used to be universally regarded as nondiegetic scoring isn't really nondiegetic at all: «By recognizing the importance of the musical score to the scene's identity, and to both our and the characters' experience of the narrative, we acknowledge this music to be deeply implicated in the world it inhabits rather than the separated phenomenon that the proponents of a metaphysical, non-diegetic narrating voice might have us believe»[82]. Elsewhere Winters has reminded us that film music strongly driven by narrative requirements gains its «structural continuity» from closely following and commenting on the action[83]. When asked about the «architectural unity» of his scores to the first *Star Wars* trilogy, Williams (with characteristic modesty) replied that it was merely a «happy accident»: «the functional aspect and the craft aspect of doing the job of these three films has to be credited with producing a lot of this unity in the musical content the listeners perceive»[84].

Miguel Mera has revisited the entire question of originality in film scoring, or the specious need for it, and finds «there is danger in devaluing screen music's symbiotic relationship with sound and visuals at the expense of a false notion of intrinsic originality within musical material itself»[85]. He goes further by claiming that originality is in any case impossible to define «because of an inherent paradox between acknowledgement of the past and differentiation from it»[86], a comment which seems particularly telling for a richly allusive idiom such as Williams's. «I'm not thinking about stylistic purity»[87], the composer himself once said; and, indeed, in order to fulfil the role of musical chameleon required of any prolific film composer such a goal would be nigh on impossible, even if it were felt to be desirable. At the same time, Williams rejected the concept of pastiche, arguing that what he does is more challenging: «A pastiche is not that difficult. What is not easy is taking it a stage further and doing the real thing, with some sincerity»[88].

We live in an era when it is possible to become a successful film composer without the kind of technical (as opposed to technological) expertise which used to be a requirement for writing worthwhile music. Williams is a supremely gifted and traditionally

---

82. Winters 2017, p. 541.
83. Winters 2007, p. 33.
84. Byrd 1997, rpt. in Cooke 2010, p. 237.
85. Mera 2017, p. 38.
86. *Ibidem*, p. 48.
87. Quoted in Audissino 2014, p. 205.
88. Quoted in *ibidem*, p. 182. For further on the problematic nature of the concept of pastiche in this context, chiefly on account of its association with postmodernism, see *ibidem*, p. 267, fn. 1.

minded composer possessed of a technical brilliance that is encountered with increasing rarity in modern film scoring. If writing pastiche does not seem difficult to a composer as skilled as Williams, less capable composers — and this applies as much to those fixated on fragmented textures and atonality as it does to those with a limited grasp of tonal harmonies — can certainly find it daunting, if not impossible. One of the most infamously outspoken complaints against the alleged mediocrity of modern film scoring came from Elmer Bernstein, who said towards the close of the last century: «the tide running against good music is so strong that none of us who care are surprised or outraged any more when we hear dumb music accompanying a film»[89]. As we have seen, even in his mixed review Clemmensen concluded that when on «auto-pilot» Williams's music is undeniably «superior to most of what comes from the rest of the industry».

Perhaps to make sense of the stature of Williams's symphonic film scoring we need to return to the original meaning of 'symphony': a sounding together, or a symbiosis of harmonious elements. Unashamedly drawing attention to Williams's technical prowess, Sergio Miceli summarizes his achievement as one of «synthesis rather than innovation», and finds that the allusions to other composers in his own music are «numerous but very blurred and well integrated [...] nobody has ever weighed and mixed the ingredients so carefully»[90]. One might add that nobody has ever succeeded so well in capturing specific narrative needs in film scoring with such seeming effortless but technically virtuosic resourcefulness, making a virtue of sometimes graphic musical narration as «a solid dramaturgical glue». Christopher Palmer (who knew the working methods of Hollywood composers better than anyone) described Williams in 1990 as a «professional craftsman [...] a musician of taste and style, an artist [who] transforms and recreates what he borrows, repays his debts with interest»[91]. And only someone possessed of such formidable traditional composing skills could have produced such a huge corpus of internationally loved and respected orchestral music which — as Spielberg once put it — is «all at once familiar and original»[92].

Bibliography

Audissino 2014

Audissino, Emilio. *John Williams's Film Music: «Jaws», «Star Wars», «Raiders of the Lost Ark», and the Return of the Classical Hollywood Music Style*, Madison (WI), University of Wisconsin Press, 2014 (Wisconsin Film Studies).

Bancolli 1949

Bancolli, Louis. Review of George Antheil's music, *New York World Telegram*, 5 January 1949.

89. Quoted in Mitchell 2009, p. 189.
90. Quoted in Audissino 2014, p. 120.
91. Palmer 1990, p. 66.
92. Spielberg, liner note to original soundtrack album of *Indiana Jones and the Kingdom of the Crystal Skull*.

Bond 2003
Bond, Jeff. 'God Almighty! FMS Finally Talks to John Williams', in: *Film Score Monthly*, viii/1 (January 2003), pp. 10-13.

Bond 2004
Id. 'The Gold Standard', in: *Film Score Monthly*, ix/7 (August 2004), pp. 12-18.

Burlingame 2012
Burlingame, Jon. 'John Williams Talks *Jaws*', <http://www.filmmusicsociety.org/news_events/features/2012/081412.html?isArchive=081412>, 2012, accessed January 2018.

Byrd 1997
Byrd, Craig L. 'The *Star Wars* interview: John Williams', in: *Film Score Monthly*, ii/1 (1997), pp. 18-21; reprinted in Cooke 2010, pp. 233-244.

Clemmensen 2001
Clemmensen, Christian. Review of the soundtrack to *Harry Potter and the Sorcerer's Stone*, <http://www.filmtracks.com/titles/harry_potter.html>, 2001, accessed January 2018.

Cooke 2008
Cooke, Mervyn. *A History of Film Music*, Cambridge, Cambridge University Press, 2008.

Cooke 2010
The Hollywood Film Music Reader, edited by Mervyn Cooke, Oxford, Oxford University Press, 2010.

Cooke 2018
Cooke, Mervyn. 'A Bridge Too Far? Music in the British War Film, 1945-1980', in: *Music, Memory, Trauma and Nostalgia in European Cinema after the Second World War*, edited by Ewelina Boczkowska and Michael Baumgartner, New York, Routledge, forthcoming 2018.

Dahl 1949
Dahl, Ingold. 'Notes on Cartoon Music', in: *Film Music Notes*, viii/5 (May-June 1949), pp. 3-13; repr. in Cooke 2010, pp. 93-99.

Darby – Du Bois 1990
Darby, William – Du Bois, Jack. *American Film Music: Major Composers, Techniques, Trends, 1915-1990*, Jefferson (NC), McFarland, 1990.

Eisenstein 1948
Eisenstein, Sergei. *The Film Sense*, translated and edited by Jay Leda, (1943), new edition, London, Faber and Faber, 1948.

Franklin 2011
Franklin, Peter. *Seeing Through Music: Gender and Modernism in Classic Hollywood Film Scores*, Oxford-New York, Oxford University Press, 2011 (Seeing through Music).

KALINAK 1992
KALINAK, Kathryn. *Settling the Score: Music and the Classical Hollywood Film*, Madison (WI), University of Wisconsin Press, 1992 (Wisconsin Studies in Film).

KORNGOLD 1991
KORNGOLD, George. Liner notes to recording of Erich Wolfgang Korngold, *Kings Row*, Varèse Sarabande VCD47203, 1979; CD reissue 1991.

LARUE 2017
LARUE, Jan *et al.* 'Symphony', in: *Grove Music Online*, <http://www.oxfordmusiconline.com>, accessed January 2018.

LEHMAN 2015
LEHMAN, Frank. 'Scoring The President: Myth and Politics in John Williams's *JFK* and *Nixon*' in: *Journal of the Society for American Music*, IX/4 (2015), pp. 409-444.

LOBRUTTO 1998
LOBRUTTO, Vincent. *Stanley Kubrick: A Biography*, London, Faber and Faber, 1998.

MCBRIDE 1997
MCBRIDE, Joseph. *Steven Spielberg: A Biography*, London, Faber and Faber, 1997.

MERA 2017
MERA, Miguel. 'Screen Music and the Question of Originality', in *The Routledge Companion to Screen Music and Sound*, edited by Miguel Mera, Ronald Sadoff and Ben Winters, New York, Routledge, 2017 (Routledge Companions), pp. 38-49.

MITCHELL 2009
MITCHELL, Helen. 'Against All Odds: The Decline and Resurgence of the Symphonic Film Score in Hollywood', in: *The Journal of Film Music*, II/2-4 (2009), pp. 175-200.

MORLEY 1949
MORLEY, Iris. '*Cinderella* and *Romeo and Juliet*', in: *Tempo*, Prokofieff Number, n.s./11, (Spring 1949), pp. 30-32.

MURPHY 2014
MURPHY, Scott. 'Transformational Theory and the Analysis of Film Music', in: *The Oxford Handbook of Film Music Studies*, edited by David Neumeyer, Oxford-New York, Oxford University Press, 2014 (Oxford Handbooks), pp. 471-499.

PALMER 1990
PALMER, Christopher. *The Composer in Hollywood*, London-New York, Marion Boyars, 1990.

RINZLER 2007
RINZLER, Jonathan W. *The Making of «Star Wars»: The Definitive Story behind the Original Film*, London, Ebury Press, 2007.

Spielberg 2005
Spielberg, Steven. Interview for DVD bonus feature, *War of the Worlds* (dir. Steven Spielberg), Paramount/Dreamworks/Amblin VFC82029, 2005.

Williams 2001
Williams, John. Interview for DVD bonus feature, *Close Encounters of the Third Kind* (dir. Steven Spielberg), Columbia TriStar VFC06143, 2001.

Williams 2003
Id. Interview for DVD bonus feature, *Midway* (dir. Jack Smight), Universal VFC50425, 2003.

Williams 2005
Id. Interview for DVD bonus feature, *Family Plot* (dir. Alfred Hitchcock), Universal VFC27651, 2005.

Winters 2007
Winters, Ben. *Erich Wolfgang Korngold's «The Adventures of Robin Hood»: A Film Score Guide*, Lanham (MD), Scarecrow Press, 2007 (Scarecrow film score guides, 6).

Winters 2012
Id. '*Superman* as Mythic Narrative: Music, Romanticism, and the "Oneiric Climate"', in: *The Music of Fantasy Cinema*, edited by Janet K. Halfyard, Sheffield, Equinox, 2012 (Genre, Music and Sound), pp. 111-131.

Winters 2017
Id. 'Idolizing the Synchronized Score: Studying Indiana Jones Hypertexts', in: *The Routledge Companion to Screen Music and Sound*, edited by Miguel Mera, Ronald Sadoff and Ben Winters, New York, Routledge, 2017 (Routledge Companions), pp. 531-542.

Discography

• Korngold, Erich Wolfgang. *Kings Row: Original Motion Picture Score*, Varèse Sarabande VCD47203, 1979; CD reissue 1991.

• Williams, John. *Harry Potter and the Philosopher's [Sorcerer's] Stone: Music from and Inspired by the Motion Picture*, Warner Sunset/Nonesuch/Atlantic 7567930865, 2CD set, 2001.

• Id. *Indiana Jones and the Kingdom of the Crystal Skull: Original Motion Picture Soundtrack*, Concord Records 8807230856, 2008.

• Id. *Indiana Jones and the Last Crusade: Original Motion Picture Soundtrack*, Warner Bros. 7599258832, 1989.

• Id. *Jaws: Music from the Original Motion Picture Soundtrack*, MCA MCLD 19281, 1975.

• Id. *Jaws 2: The Original Motion Picture Soundtrack*, MCA 3045, 1978.

• Id. *Jurassic Park: Music From the Original Motion Picture Soundtrack*, MCA MCD 10859, 1993.

• Id. *Star Wars Trilogy*, 6CD box set of three 2CD sets of the original soundtracks of *Star Wars Episode IV: A New Hope*, S2K 92950; *Star Wars Episode V: The Empire Strikes Back*, S2K 92951; and *Star Wars Episode VI: Return of the Jedi*, S2K 92952; Sony Classical, 2004.

• Id. *Star Wars Episode I: The Phantom Menace. Original Motion Picture Soundtrack*, Sony Classical SK61816, 1999.

• Id. *Superman the Movie (Original Soundtrack)*, Warner Bros. Records 2BSK 3257, 1978.

• Id. *War Horse: Original Motion Picture Soundtrack*, Sony Classical 88697975282, 2011.

• Id. *Yo-Yo Ma Plays the Music of John Williams*, Sony Classical SK89670, 2002.

John Williams: Television Composer

Paula Musegades
(Brandeis University, Waltham, MA)

Majestic, haunting, swashbuckling, and atmospheric; these are just a few words often used to describe composer John Williams's film music. Interestingly, though perhaps not surprisingly, one finds similar labels in reviews of Williams's predecessors in the field. Lawrence MacDonald describes Erich Korngold's theme for *Kings Row* (Sam Wood, 1942) as a «majestic and noble melody that immediately grabs the viewer's attention»[1], while William Brogdon highlights «the hauntingly-presented ballad» in Dimitri Tiomkin's *High Noon* (Fred Zinnemann, 1952)[2]. Jon Burlingame notes Alfred Newman's «swashbuckling sounds [in] *The Prisoner of Zenda*» [John Cromwell, and Woodbridge Strong Van Dyke, 1937] while Mildred Martin applauds «the effectiveness of pantomime accompanied by an atmospheric score» in Max Steiner's *The Informer* (John Ford, 1935)[3]. Such associations between Williams's music and 'classic-era' film composers abound, with the clearest connection made by Emilio Audissino, who labels John Williams as a *neoclassical* film composer. He demonstrates how Williams blends the 'classical' musical approaches of Hollywood in the 1930s and 1940s, including late-Romantic dialect, rich orchestration, close adherence between musical gestures and visual actions ('Mickey-Mousing'), and a continuous stream of music, with more modern idioms. This, Audissino notes, simultaneously revives and updates the once dominant Hollywood sound[4].

While Audissino focuses primarily on Williams's film music, he also makes a compelling statement about the composer's early career in the television industry. He explains that it was a «good training ground for film composers», before adding further, «in this formative period, dividing his time between playing piano in studio orchestras

---

1. MacDonald 2013, p. 80.
2. Brogdon 1952.
3. Burlingame 1997, Martin 1935.
4. While traditional use of the term *neoclassic* in music refers to composers returning to the ideals of classicism and the classical period of music, Audissino adopts a different angle and refers to the 1930s and 1940s as the classical period of film composition in Hollywood. For a full discussion of Williams's neoclassical style, see Audissino 2014, pp. 122-127.

and composing in the Revue Studio music department, Williams had the opportunity of mixing with, and learning the tricks of the trade from some of the masters of Hollywood music»[5]. Spending nearly a decade in the field of television, Williams developed his skill in compositional versatility. From detective programs (*M-Squad* [1957-1960]) to anthologies (*Kraft Suspense Theater* [1963-1965]), and Westerns (*Tales of Wells Fargo* [1957-1962]) to children's science fiction (*Lost in Space* [1965-1968]), Williams learned to write for numerous genres, adhere to a small budget, and compose within restricted time frames, all necessary skills for success in the highly competitive entertainment industry. By studying the music of these television works, one finds early evidence of Williams's signature sound, including a blending of the late-Romantic style with modern twentieth-century dissonances and popular-music idioms.

This chapter looks specifically at Williams's compositional approach for two formative assignments during his television career, the detective series *Checkmate* (1961-1963), and the anthology show *Alcoa Premiere* (1961-1963). Building upon Audissino's position on Williams as a neoclassical film composer, I argue that even during the initial stages of his career, Williams practised his neoclassical style. While perhaps not as developed as his later scores for such blockbuster hits as *Jaws* (Steven Spielberg, 1975), *Star Wars: Episode IV – A New Hope* (George Lucas, 1977), and *Raiders of the Lost Ark* (Steven Spielberg, 1981), his blending of the classic Hollywood sound with modern twentieth-century music nevertheless helps mark these television scores as distinctly 'Williams'.

WILLIAMS'S FORMATIVE YEARS

Music maintained a consistent presence throughout Williams's young life, from childhood piano lessons, to studying at The Julliard School, to playing piano in jazz clubs. Eventually deciding to pursue a career in composition, he took this musical training with him to Hollywood. Despite Williams's initial plan, however, the majority of his early positions were not as a composer, but as a piano studio musician, with some of his first film credits including *Sweet Smell of Success* (Alexander Mackendrick, music by Elmer Bernstein 1957), *Funny Face* (Stanley Donen, music by Adolph Deutsch, 1957), and *South Pacific* (Joshua Logan, music by Richard Rogers and adapted by Alfred Newman, 1958). Perhaps one of his most important collaborations at this time, however, did not occur in film, but rather in television.

Playing piano on the influential jazz score for *Peter Gunn* (1958-1961), Williams was deeply immersed in composer Henry Mancini's compositional approach and the show's signature hard bop sound. Mancini was one of the first composers to employ a non-

5. *Ibidem*, pp. 60, 88-89.

diegetic jazz score for a television series, and he further challenged industry norm by creating individual scores for each episode. Instead of relying largely on standard library cues, which was common practice for television shows of the 1950s, Mancini treated every score as a new project and composed specific cues for each of the 114 episodes[6]. Like many composers in the field, however, he also reused musical ideas, namely the walking bassline of the opening action sequence and the driving *Peter Gunn* theme with its dramatic brass falls[7]. Through his consistent use of similar musical techniques with minor adjustments in orchestration, tempo, and rhythmic or melodic line, Mancini created cohesion for the series as a whole. This helped establish its edgy, private-eye style, while still catering to the specific demands of each episode. Williams, closely involved with the show's music, soon adopted and modified Mancini's approach for his own work on *Checkmate*.

In addition to Mancini's influence on his compositional style, Williams's position as a studio musician allowed him to meet many other players in the field. In fact, he credits much of his early film score training to his colleagues. As he explained

> The instrumentalists at that time, as now, were outstanding world-class players [...] My advantage was that I'd been playing with them for three or four or five years, as a colleague in the orchestra. I would go over to a horn player and say, «Have I got this too high?» or «Is this trill a little awkward? Would you rather play it here or there?». Just from one friend to another, without any particular professional pressure. And they'd all say, «no, put it here, put it there, do this»[8].

When one considers Williams's early Hollywood experience working with both the 'old guard' (Alfred Newman, Adolph Deutsch, and Dimitri Tiomkin) and the new (Elmer Bernstein, Henry Mancini, and Jerry Goldsmith), combined with first-hand feedback from the studio musicians, his many layers of training come to the foreground, with each experience contributing to his distinct musical voice.

---

[6]. This practice of using canned music was largely a result of the ongoing battles between the American Federation of Musicians (AFM) president, James Caesar Petrillo, and the union members. Throughout the 1950s, AFM taxed television producers 5% of their show's overall budget if they wished to hire musicians from the AFM, and this was *before* the studios even paid the musicians' wages. Producers were unwilling to accept such fees, so they began recording their music outside of the country. Furthermore, they relied primarily on library collections, which allowed them to reuse music in multiple episodes. As Jon Burlingame notes, «by 1955 four-fifths of all film and TV shows were being scored with so-called 'canned music' recorded overseas», which left many musicians in the AFM out of work (Burlingame 1997, p. 5). After extensive negotiations and restructuring within the union, however, they struck a deal with the studios who agreed to employ AFM members and create new scores for their programmes once again. This was an incredibly complex, lengthy, and heated process, and for a detailed look at the history, see Burlingame – Asner 1997.

[7]. Additionally, he often returned to similar compositional approaches during reoccurring events in various episodes. As Caps describes, «hard rock/jazz during a tough fight scene; then a rich ballad if, say, a swanky downtown woman came into the club...». Caps 2012, pp. 46-47.

[8]. Lunden 2009.

Upon first listening to Williams's early compositions, the more 'classical Hollywood' techniques — continuous underscoring, careful sync points, and colourful timbres — come quickly to the foreground. Interestingly, much of Hollywood at the time had moved away from this traditional sound. As Audissino explains, film scores of the 1960s relied more heavily on the 'closed musical number': «[i]nstead of a continuous stream of music based on interwoven leitmotifs, the score was structured through a series of isolated set pieces closed in themselves»[9]. Due to the typical format of television programs, with multiple commercial breaks throughout each episode, one typically finds closer musical connections between television music and the set pieces of 1960s film music than the continuous film scores of the 1930s and 1940s; it was difficult to achieve a continuous stream of music in this advertiser-sponsored medium. Furthermore, when one takes into consideration the minimal resources, small ensemble of studio musicians, and extremely limited time frames allowed for composing each score, it is not surprising that the expectation for television music did not include multi-scene continuity. Nevertheless, one finds that Williams often composed cues in his television music that were lengthier than the standard, and he included them not only in moments of intense action, but also under dialogue or character reflection. This, in turn, helped convey further information to the viewer about the narrative — a valuable asset when most television episodes had to depict an entire story arc in sixty minutes or less. Beginning with *Checkmate*, Williams's first assignment as the composer of the main theme and each episodes' score, one can clearly decipher these characteristics. While employing Hollywood's 'classic' film scoring techniques, Williams did so in a modern jazz-inspired style, providing an early indication of his neoclassical sound.

Checkmate

Falling largely under what Mareike Jenner calls a «Rational — Scientific — Genius detective drama», Eric Ambler's *Checkmate* (1961-1963) traces a team of three cool, detached detectives working in crime prevention[10]. The series was one of many private eye/detective programs that surged during this time[11]. With such predecessors as *M-squad* (1957-1960), *Richard Diamond, Private Detective* (1957-1960), *Peter Gunn* (1958-1961), and *Johnny Staccato* (1959-1960), *Checkmate* had plenty of approaches from which to draw.

[9]. Audissino 2014, p. 60.

[10]. The 'Rational - Scientific - Genius' style is in opposition to the 'Police Procedural' approach, which traces a team of police working together within the boundaries of the law on a solving a committed crime, as well as the 'Irrational - Subjective' approach, which relies upon gut instinct and challenges typical legal investigative practices. Jenner 2016, pp. 2, 15.

[11]. Rodman 2010, pp. 243-256.

While much of these detective shows employed chiaroscuro lighting, voiceovers, a femme fatale-like character, and frequent use of jazz, *Checkmate* steps slightly away from the crime noir aesthetic. It avoids the voiceover technique and rarely incorporates a femme fatale. Even the lead protagonists stand apart from their hard-boiled contemporaries; the three detectives, Don Corey (Anthony George), Jed Sills (Doug McClure), and Dr. Carl Hyatt (Sebastian Cabot) are clean-cut, articulate, and well educated. In fact, Jon Burlingame describes the series as «atmospheric and often intriguing [...] the class of the genre at that time»[12]. Likely picking up on this aesthetic shift, Williams too abandoned the strict crime-jazz sound so closely associated with other tougher and more violent series. Instead, he composed a jazz-inspired score that, while certainly categorized under television's crime-jazz umbrella, seems to push boundary classification by also incorporating more traditional film-scoring aesthetics, including motivic repetition, underscoring dialogue, and through-composed, atmospheric cues.

Furthermore, when scoring *Checkmate*, Williams largely avoided the closed-cue practice of his contemporaries, and he opted instead for the continuous underscoring of his film composer predecessors. He used subtler cues to slowly build up suspense throughout a scene — or several scenes — before erupting into forceful, assertive music for the action-packed sequences that inevitably follow in such a genre. He would create close correlations between the music and the plot, be it through enhancing an underlying narrative theme, suggesting a character's state of mind, or including direct sync points to accompany physical action. Finally, one hears early examples of Williams's approach to leitmotivic writing[13]. He often breaks longer melodies into smaller phrases or motives, which he weaves throughout an episode creating unity within the score. This technique helps invest the viewer further in the narrative, if only subconsciously, by incorporating brief glimmers of familiarity throughout the episode; the viewer can recognize those previously-heard musical motifs. With an investigation of select scenes from Williams's work on *Checkmate*, one hears his distinct compositional approaches come to the foreground; he stands apart from many contemporaries by daring to apply the film-scoring techniques of his predecessors in the lighter more 'trivial' form of television entertainment.

Looking closely at Williams's music for the episode "The Dark Divide" (Season 1, Episode 9), for example, one finds a compelling score that comments on the narrative both thematically and emotionally[14]. Featuring guest star Barbara Rush as Margaret Russell,

---

[12]. Burlingame 1996, p. 38.

[13]. Though the term leitmotif originates with Richard Wagner's compositions, this chapter employs Hollywood's adoption of the technique. In this situation, the term concerns connections between a musical motive and a specific character, idea, or emotion. The theme recurs throughout the film, and helps reinforce a clear narrative structure.

[14]. "The Dark Divide", *Checkmate*, Episode 9, directed by Don Weis, written by Robert Bloomfield and James Gunn, CBS, 19 November 1960.

"The Dark Divide" follows Checkmate Inc. as the three detectives investigate threatening phone calls that Margaret's aunt Edith (Irene Tedrow) receives about her niece's safety. The threats come from the beautiful Nikki Garnett, and through careful sleuthing, handwriting analysis, and hypnosis, Checkmate Inc. discovers the true identity of Nikki's character: she is the result of Margaret's «dissociative reaction». Nikki is Margaret's second personality, who wishes — in a confused state of logic — to kill her other half. Luckily, Don, Jed, and Carl solve the case and ultimately save Margaret from herself.

One of the most compelling components of the score for "The Dark Divide" concerns a leitmotif associated with both Margaret and Nikki. The leitmotif first sounds at the beginning of the episode immediately following Nikki's on-screen threat to aunt Edith; speaking in a phone booth with low-key lighting that casts dark shadows around her face, Nikki threatens Margaret's life. As she hangs up the phone and walks confidently towards her car, the theme begins in the high register of the soprano saxophone, and its descending leaps alternating with the chromatic passing tones dominate the A-minor theme (1:14)[15]. This blending of jazz instrumentation, syncopated rhythms, and chromatic harmony, helps the viewer recognize the show's detective genre due to the common association of jazz with crime[16].

In addition to reinforcing this linkage, the Nikki leitmotif holds greater significance as well. Not only associated with the dangerous side of Margaret's split personality — Nikki —, a variation of the theme is also used to convey her 'other' personality — Margaret. In this case, the Nikki leitmotiv sounds in broken phrases or variations in the flute, harpsichord, or piano. By abandoning the soprano saxophone for other instrumentation, and offering variations on the Nikki leitmotif, Williams contrasts Margaret's 'good' to Nikki's 'evil' personality. This offers subtle musical cues that guide the viewer who, like the detectives, strives to solve the case as the episode unfolds; the victim and criminal are the same person[17].

A complex tactic for a weekly television show, Williams's use of the leitmotiv in this episode has a film-scoring rather than a television-scoring quality. For example, it looks back to such films as *The Wizard of Oz* (Victor Fleming, 1939), in which composer Herbert Stothart scored the detestable character, Miss Gluch, with a menacing theme at the beginning of the film. This theme returns in variation accompanying the Wicked

15. "The Dark Divide", *Checkmate. The Complete Series*, NBC Universal Television, Timeless Media Group. DVD video, 2010.

16. For further discussion of jazz music in film noir and the detective genre, see BUTLER 2016, pp. 175-186.

17. Roughly ten years later, we see Williams take a more drastic approach to composing multiple personalities in his work for *Images* (Robert Altman, 1972). Focusing on the life of children's book author Cathryn (Susannah York), *Images* reveals the woman's schizophrenic double life. Williams reinforces the plot through an equally divided score by juxtaposing a melodic, piano-based theme with sudden bursts of atonal music during her psychotic episodes.

Witch of the West — played by the same actress. Both the Wicked Witch and Miss Gluch represent the film's antagonist when Dorothy is in Oz and in Kansas, respectively. At the same time, Williams's leitmotivic practice also anticipates his later film scores. Perhaps the strongest example comes from the *Star Wars* saga, specifically the "Darth Vader's Theme", which is introduced in full force to accompany the arch-villain's appearance in *The Empire Strikes Back* (Irvin Kershner, 1980). Williams uses this connection carefully in the prequel trilogy to foreshadow that the young Anakin Skywalker will become the dark lord, Darth Vader. In *The Phantom Menace* (George Lucas, 1999), one hears a brief suggestion of Darth Vader's theme when Obi-Wan Kenobi and Yoda discuss Anakin's future on Naboo. In *Attack of the Clones* (George Lucas, 2002), Williams alludes to "Darth Vader's Theme" when Yoda senses Anakin's attack of the Tusken raiders; this theme comes more strongly to the foreground later in the film when Anakin confesses his evil actions to Padmé. In *Revenge of the Sith* (George Lucas, 2005), the leitmotif occurs frequently, culminating in the accompaniment of Anakin's complete and definitive transformation into Darth Vader. This careful use of leitmotivs is clearly an effective and enduring compositional method for Williams, and is one that began as early as 1960.

While it is easy to recognize Williams's continued use of leitmotivs throughout his career, a consistent jazz-inspired style may not seem quite as evident. Upon closer investigation of his oeuvre, however, one finds evidence not only of brief nods to his early jazz background in the form of syncopated melodies and traditional jazz instrumentation, but also distinct jazzy cues within a vast array of films[18]. In Sydney Pollack's *Sabrina* (1995), for example, the score maintains a clear connection to the jazz genre. During the film's opening sequence, lounge-style jazz accompanies the introduction of the wealthy Larrabee brothers as they host an extravagant party at their home. Sounding diegetically, the music simultaneously sets the general atmosphere for the evening's soiree while associating the smooth refinement of easy-listening jazz with the younger brother, David (Greg Kinnear) (1:50-5:22)[19]. As this is a remake of Billy Wilder's 1954 film of the same name, Williams's use of easy-listening jazz, so prominent in the 1950s-60s, was a tasteful nod to the original *Sabrina*.

Creating a slightly different atmosphere in Spielberg's 2002 picture, *Catch Me if You Can*, Williams dominates the score with light, carefree jazz, filled with vibraphone, quick woodwind runs, and solo saxophone. This cool jazz style perfectly evokes the narrative's atmosphere; set in the 1960s, the film stars the suave Frank Abagnale Jr. (Leonardo DiCaprio), who successfully cons millions of dollars by impersonating an array of different professionals. Though unquestionably a crime narrative, Williams's spirited,

[18]. Traditional jazz instrumentation is often a combination of saxophone, trumpet, trombone, piano, bass, and drums. The number of instruments in each section depends on the desired sound (jazz combo vs. large ensemble).

[19]. *Sabrina*, DVD, Paramount Pictures, 1995.

finger-snapping score helps support the film's entertaining and breezy tone. Canvassing a wide range of films and genres, from Clint Eastwood's *The Eiger Sanction* (1975) to Steven Spielberg's *The Terminal* (2004), and the "Knight Bus" sequence in Alfonso Cuaron's *Harry Potter and the Prisoner of Azkaban* (2004), to the opening scenes in Spielberg's *The Adventures of Tintin* (2011), Williams's later film career reveals clear connections to the 'Johnny Williams' jazz practised in his works of the late-1950s and 1960s.

One also finds that Williams, both then and now, often divides his melodic lines into smaller fragments, which he then weaves throughout the episode or film. In nearly every score for the *Checkmate* series, for example, Williams breaks the show's main title theme into smaller motifs, and he intertwines these brief segments within the episode's cues[20]. Such recurrence of similar thematic ideas scored in different variations unifies the overall show. While this technique is not unique to Williams, his use of the strategy throughout *Checkmate* is particularly effective due to its connection to the jazz genre. Written in 12/8, the cue opens with an ostinato eighth note line in the electric guitar followed quickly by tightly syncopated hits in the French horn. Trumpets dominate the melody with chromatic glissandos in their upper register, before the trombones drive the cue to a conclusion playing sforzando triplet quarter notes. By intertwining this title music throughout *Checkmate*'s episodes, Williams helps further reinforce the relationship between jazz and the detective/crime genre.

A particularly effective use of this technique occurs in "The Cyanide Touch" (Season 1 Episode 3)[21]. The narrative focuses on college student Roddy Stevenson, whose car gets stolen one evening at a party. Racing away from the scene of the crime, the thieves run down Roddy's best friend, an innocent bystander, and kill him instantly. Roddy seeks revenge on Larry Forbes (Henry Jones), the man who hired the two car jackers, and attempts to get a confession from the man through the threat of death by cyanide. Driven by vengeance, Roddy stops at nothing in the name of justice for his friend.

Sonically depicting Roddy's fixation, Williams's initial variation on the opening *Checkmate* theme quickly associates the cue with both the murder and Roddy's discovery of the criminals (1:20)[22]. The music then leads directly into the opening credits as the original theme plays in its entirety. Taking full advantage of the established connection in the viewers' minds between the *Checkmate* theme and Roddy's need for revenge, Williams

[20]. In Williams's later film projects, one finds a similar buildup to the main theme. Slightly different from *Checkmate*, however, which relies upon motives from the opening title sequence, Williams initially avoids sharing the main theme in its entirety. Instead he works backwards, and offers brief selections of the melody as the narrative unfolds. These smaller motives eventually build up to the full theme, which then blossoms during a climactic portion of the film. Audissino calls this approach the «gradual disclosure of the main theme», noting *E. T.: The Extra-Terrestrial* (1982) as the most noteworthy instance. Audissino 2014, p. 126.

[21]. "The Cyanide Touch", *Checkmate*, Episode 3, directed by Don Weis, written by Stirling Silliphant. CBS, 1 October 1960.

[22]. "The Cyanide Touch", *Checkmate. The Complete Series*, *op. cit.* (see note 15).

floods the episode primarily with variations on the main theme; of the 16 separate cues, 13 of them include some reference to the melody. Two of the cues, one beginning at 7:17 and the other at 36:39, use long stretches of the theme largely untouched aside from changes in instrumentation and dynamics. The first occurrence sounds at a much quieter volume, with the main melody — originally scored for bright trumpets — now playing softly in the French horns. Despite this quieter volume, however, the consistent eighth note line in the electric guitar maintains its brisk pace in 12/8 time. This helps convey the scene's quiet intensity as Corey attends a police interrogation of the guilty car jackers; the longer presentation of the theme coincides with a movement toward justice as the police chief books the two men on charges of first degree man slaughter.

Brief variations of the theme permeate much of the next 30 minutes as Roddy, unsatisfied with the conviction of the two thieves, meticulously plans his revenge on Forbes. These short motives eventually culminate in one of the episode's most climactic moments: when Roddy successfully captures his victim, and drives him recklessly to meet his fate. Like many key moments in the episode, the car race takes place in the dark of night. Only passing streetlights illuminate the two men's faces, and this chiaroscuro enhances the scene's tension by leaving much of the sequence in shadow. Signaling Roddy's feeling of triumph, the *Checkmate* theme sounds in full force with the trumpets confidently playing the main melodic line once again. As the viewer has only heard pieces of the theme for the past 30 minutes, its full presentation complements Roddy's own feeling of success as his plans fall into place.

Williams's work on *Checkmate* played an important role in shaping his compositional style. While he adhered to a standard scoring approach by scoring both character emotions and the show's general atmosphere, he did so with jazz-inspired rhythms, harmonies, and instrumentation. This blending of styles gives us an early glimpse of Williams's now-familiar characteristic sound, which would come even further to the foreground in his next major project, *Alcoa Premiere* (1961-1963).

Alcoa Premiere

Williams's experience working for the small screen, and more specifically anthology television, had a large impact on his compositional versatility due to the sheer nature of anthology shows. As anthology programming involves a new storyline and cast of characters for each episode, Williams did not have the option to rework previous material as he did for *Checkmate*. Instead, he had to compose new music every week. *Alcoa Premiere* was a series hosted by Fred Astaire that often focused on dramatic and/or controversial subjects, and Williams scored each of the 28 one-hour episodes for seasons one and two. Reflecting on his experience in the medium, Williams recalled, «The shows I was assigned to were the hardest shows, the hour shows, which meant I had to write about 20-25 minutes of music a week, score it, and record it. It was a tremendous learning opportunity for me»[23]. Demanding new music appropriate to the wide range of topics explored from week to week, *Alcoa Premiere*'s quick turnaround strengthened Williams's ability to connect music and narrative at a highly efficient pace.

One of the ways Williams made these music-narrative connections was through sync points, which is when a physical action on screen aligns with a musical gesture. This was an approach frequently employed by Williams's predecessors in the business, especially Max Steiner, and one sees a particularly 'Steineresque' approach in the episode "Mr. Lucifer" (Season 2, Episode 5)[24]. Described in 1962 as a «satirical, tongue-in-script»[25] by daily newspaper *The Knickerbocker News*, the episode traces a modern-day Lucifer, played by Fred Astaire, and his secretary Elizabeth Montgomery, as the pair attempt to corrupt a seemingly perfect couple. Taking on the role of the comic composer with ease[26], Williams frequently scores the action through close mickey-mousing, which contributes to the narrative's absurdity by aurally punctuating both the physical and verbal humour[27].

Consider the episode's introduction as Fred Astaire presents the evening's story. The screen opens to a silhouette of the classic 'devil' image so clearly ingrained in the minds of the public; his horns, spiked tail, trident, and cape, make the character's persona unmistakable. He stands menacingly, wielding his trident from one hand to another, while Williams indicates the satirical horror of the scene through close mickey-mousing. A brash descending fourth in the low brass followed by a frantic upward glissando in the flutes and piccolo directly aligns with each of the devil's forceful gestures. With one final ascent in the flutes, the devil throws his cape over his shoulder and stands defiantly on-screen in silhouette. With such exaggerated movements accompanied by those clichéd sounds of 'danger' in the low brass and upper woodwinds, the viewer immediately recognizes the tone of the coming episode, which «pokes a bit of fun at our moral values… [for] a thoroughly entertaining hour»[28]. Furthermore, by primarily employing leaps of fourths, fifths, and sixths, while avoiding the true 'Devil's chord', the tritone, Williams further conveys the scene's lighter character, despite its potentially weighty topic.

---

23. Quoted in Audissino 2014, p. 88.

24. "Mr. Lucifer", *Alcoa Premiere*, Season 2 Episode 5, directed by Alan Crosland Jr., written by Alfred Bester, *ABC*, 1 November 1962, DVD, Film Collectors Society of America.

25. *The Knickerbocker News* 1962.

26. For additional examples of Williams's early role as a comic composer, see *Bachelor Flat* (Frank Tashlin, 1962); *John Goldfarb, Please Come Home!* (J. Lee Thompson, 1965); *How to Steal a Million* (William Wyler, 1966); *A Guide for the Married Man* (Gene Kelly, 1967).

27. The technique of Mickey-Mousing began in the field of animation before branching out to other film genres. It is a term that describes direct synchronization of movement and music, and it was often used during 1930s and 1940s.

28. *The Knickerbocker News* 1962.

An entirely different situation from the physical comedy of "Mr. Lucifer", "The Potentate" (Season 2 Episode 12) tells a darkly dramatic narrative concerning conspiracy and corruption within a small Soviet country. Adapting a narrative technique often employed in the detective genre, the episode depicts the conflicted emotions of the protagonist, comrade minister Tamarov, through voiceover. Throughout most of the narrative, Tamarov suspects his close comrade Andreas of treason, and grows increasingly paranoid as he considers possible repercussions for maintaining a friendship with the man.

Unlike Williams's aforementioned score for "Mr. Lucifer", in "The Potentate" he focuses on underscoring Tamarov's moments of deep introspection and shifting emotional state. Throughout the episode, Williams incorporates a two-part leitmotiv. Part one, the main theme for "The Potentate", offers a rather chromatic line. It spans a minor seventh, with the melody comprised largely of seconds, major and minor thirds, and perfect fourths. Part two, much less melodic, consists of wide intervallic leaps that often follow a steady pulse with clear timbral contrasts between the extreme high register of the woodwinds and upper strings and the low register of the horn, cello, and bass. As the narrative unfolds, Tamarov grows increasingly paranoid about his relationship with Andreas, and Williams conveys this loss of emotional composure through a shift in thematic presentation.

From the beginning of the episode, Williams makes it clear that the story is not a happy one. Unlike the humour instilled in "Mr. Lucifer", "The Potentate" opens with a solo French horn playing part one of the melody, which the strings promptly echo as the camera pans to the United Nations building in New York City. The shot fades into a meeting room where Tamarov is holding a press conference and we hear him thinking to himself: «tell a few jokes» and «don't be so stiff»[29]. In fact, Tamarov expresses his changing emotions in voiceover throughout most of the episode, a voiceover that Williams enhances with the music. During this opening scene, for example, the accompanying cue maintains its chromaticism in a slow, stately tempo, with occasional sforzando punctuation in the low brass, suggesting a hint of Tamarov's nerves hidden under his composed and relaxed confidence (0:50-1:30). Following the meeting's conclusion, however, Tamarov's friend, Andreas, seeks a private conversation regarding Tamarov's potential rise within the government. Uncomfortable with such treasonous talk, the comrade minister admonishes his friend, and his emotions change suddenly from cool confidence to astonishment and anger. Williams conveys this emotional shift by pitting high strings in minor thirds against the low brass, while moving part one of the melody down a third.

In other scenes, Williams employs slow ascending and descending lines, most often in the high strings and low basses respectively, helping reveal the complicated emotions of each sequence. Through a slowly ascending string line, for example, Williams suggests the minister's mounting tensions as he strives for a semblance of normalcy at home (10:07-

[29]. "The Potentate", *Alcoa Premiere*, Season 2 Episode 12, directed by John Brahm, written by William Fennerton and David Karp, *ABC*, 20 December 1962, DVD, Film Collectors Society of America.

10:49). Even more telling is the one-on-one conversation between Tamarov and Raknitch (Simon Scott), the latter once a protégé of Tamarov's. Seeking information from his younger friend, Tamarov listens closely to Raknitch's veiled statements about government politics, and reads closely into each insinuation. Though one may interpret Raknitch's comments as either positive or negative, Tamarov's anxiety and paranoia builds; he believes everyone knows of his connection to Andreas's potentially treasonous plot, and the slow ascent high in the violins puts the viewer similarly on edge.

In opposition to the musical ascent, Williams also relies on a downward melodic line conveying a feeling of despair or panic. As Tamarov sinks lower into his state of paranoia, this downward momentum reveals his darkening mood while foreshadowing a feeling of inevitability. One hears this when Tamarov enters a busy conference room following his conversation with Raknitch; the government will hold a ceremony later that day, and he wants to ensure that his position on the podium, number six in rank, has not changed. The slow downward movement in the score foreshadows his coming discovery; not only is his name absent from the sixth position, but it does not appear in the seventh, eighth, or ninth position either. In fact, Tamarov does not see his name at all. This entire sequence lasts about two minutes in length (25:30-27:10). Within the cue, Williams suggests the inevitable through a slow stepwise descent as Tamarov gradually discovers his missing placement on the podium (25:30) and accepts his fate (26:10). Meanwhile, smaller motivic descents with faster rhythmic movement play simultaneously, conveying Tamarov's alarm; though he may appear calm on the outside, panic rushes through his body, which the viewer fully comprehends thanks to Williams's cue. Tamarov has reached his breaking point.

From the playful comedy of "Mr. Lucifer" to the heavy drama of "The Potentate", Williams demonstrated early on his adaptability to compose for a wide array of genres and narratives. Despite this flexibility, however, fans most often celebrate Williams's work for its powerful and memorable themes in such films as *Jaws* (Steven Spielberg, 1975), *Superman* (Richard Donner, 1978), or *Jurassic Park* (Steven Spielberg, 1993). When stepping back and considering Williams's entire body of work, however, one might argue that one of his most remarkable compositional characteristics is his vast versatility. Williams has built on the adaptability he developed in television and tackled nearly every film genre, from comedies (*How To Steal a Million*, William Wyler, 1966) to epic disasters (*The Poseidon Adventure*, Ronald Neame, 1972), and romance (*Stanley & Iris*, Martin Ritt, 1990) to crime (*Sleepers*, Barry Levinson, 1996).

Conclusions

John Williams composed music for over thirty different television shows during the 1950s and 1960s alone, and there is a wealth of information yet to be uncovered. I hope this study of Williams's music for *Checkmate* and *Alcoa Premiere* provides a foundation for future research, and opens up further avenues to examine his compositional style. Ultimately, by investigating Williams's early works, one not only discovers the developing relationship between music and television in the 1950s-60s, but also better understands how Williams combined the stylistic influences of his colleagues, both past and present, with his multi-faceted musical training, and developed a distinct yet versatile compositional style that remains a part of his sound today.

BIBLIOGRAPHY

AUDISSINO 2014
AUDISSINO, Emilio. *John Williams's Film Music: «Jaws», «Star Wars», «Raiders of the Lost Ark», and the Return of the Classical Hollywood Music Style*, Madison (WI), University of Wisconsin Press, 2014 (Wisconsin Film Studies).

BROGDON 1952
BROGDON, William. 'Review: High Noon', in: *Variety*, 29 April 1952.

BURLINGAME 1996
BURLINGAME, Jon. *TV's Biggest Hits: The Story of Television Themes from «Dragnet» to «Friends»*, New York, Schirmer Books, 1996.

BURLINGAME 1997
ID. 'L.A. Music's First Family', in: *Variety*, 15 July 1997, <http://variety.com/1997/music/markets-festivals/l-a-music-s-first-family-1116677018>, accessed February 2018.

BURLINGAME – ASNER 1997
ID. – ASNER, Edward. *For the Record: The Struggle and Ultimate Political Rise of American Recording Musicians within Their Labor Movement*, Hollywood, RMA Recording Musicians Association, 1997.

BUTLER 2016
BUTLER, David. 'Film Noir and Music', in: *The Cambridge Companion to Film Music*, edited by Mervyn Cooke and Fiona Ford, Cambridge, Cambridge University Press, 2016 (Cambridge Companions to Music), pp. 175-186.

CAPS 2012
CAPS, John. *Henry Mancini: Reinventing Film Music*, Urbana, University of Illinois Press, 2012.

JENNER 2016
JENNER, Mareike. *American TV Detective Dramas: Serial Investigations*, New York, Palgrave Macmillan, 2016 (Crime Files Series).

LUNDEN 2009
LUNDEN, Jeff. 'John Williams' Inevitable Themes', in: *NPR.org*, 28 April 2009, <http://www.npr.org/sections/deceptivecadence/2012/11/10/164615420/john-williams-inevitable-themes>, accessed February 2018.

MacDonald 2013
MacDonald, Laurence E. *The Invisible Art of Film Music: A Comprehensive History*, Lanham (MD), Scarecrow Press, 2013.

Martin 1935
Martin, Mildred. 'Camera Angles Art of Screen Acting Enhanced and Advanced by Elisabeth Bergner and Victor Mclaglen', in: *The Philadelphia Inquirer*, 9 June 1935.

Rodman 2010
Rodman, Ronald Wayne. *Tuning in: American Narrative Television Music*, Oxford-New York, Oxford University Press, 2010 (The Oxford Music/Media Series).

The Knickerbocker News 1962
'A Devil of a Time', in: *The Knickerbocker News*, 1 November 1962.

"Catch as Catch Can": Jazz, John Williams, & Popular Music Allusion

Ryan Patrick Jones
(University of Wisconsin-Eau Claire, WI)

We have John's score — almost an hour of amazing music in the idiom of progressive jazz that was very popular in the 50s and 60s. I think Charlie Parker would be very proud of him[1].
Steven Spielberg on John Williams's score to *Catch Me if You Can*

In 1993, after nearly fifteen seasons as music director, renowned film composer John Williams stepped down from the Boston Pops podium. According to his successor, Keith Lockhart, Williams offered some telling advice to the young conductor: «He said, "I wouldn't spend a lot of effort trying to make your mark on the organization", Lockhart recalled. "It's older than both of us put together and will be here after we're gone. Just be a good steward and naturally it will begin to reflect your choices"»[2]. Stressing the familiar, long-time personal connection to his specific Boston audience, Williams's comments here hint at a chief ingredient of his own characteristic popular appeal to broader audiences the world over — an endearing, almost deferential authenticity. Whether from the stage or in any one of myriad media interviews he has granted over the years, Williams strikes the same gentle tone in an understated voice seemingly untouched by his staggering successes nor their paradigmatic impact. Indeed, owing in large part to his continued prolific film projects following his initial departure from the Pops, Williams's longstanding return to its podium each season is among the institution's most anticipated, promoted, and lucrative traditions.

So it was in the 2003 Boston Pops season, during one of these very returns as laureate conductor, that Williams opted to program live excerpts from his twentieth collaboration with Steven Spielberg, a 1960s period piece entitled *Catch Me if You Can* (Steven Spielberg, 2002). The performance featured his original studio alto saxophone soloist Dan Higgins alongside a separate, complementary set with celebrated vocalist Nancy Wilson[3].

1. Spielberg in Bouzereau 2003.
2. Lockhart quoted in Feinberg 2015.
3. This twentieth collaboration count is Williams's estimate. Williams in Bouzereau 2003.

Following after years of Williams's laureate programming more closely tied to recycling excerpts from *Star Wars* (George Lucas, 1977), *Superman* (Richard Donner, 1978), and *E. T.: The Extra-Terrestrial* (Steven Spielberg, 1982) to the *Indiana Jones* series, *Schindler's List* (Steven Spielberg, 1993), and even more recent selections from the *Harry Potter* juggernaut, the decidedly popular stylistic bent of the *Catch Me* score — framed by an unmistakable choice to showcase a popular singer from the same decade as the film's narrative setting — signaled a clear break with typical Pops selections, in favour of more exploratory stylistic presentations. With Williams's further investment to document this programme as part of the venerable PBS *Evening at Pops* series, this concert's widespread commitment to more experimental pop-inspired music was not only atypical, but writ large.

In fact little of Williams's cinematic output bespeaks his formative work in popular music settings, for the lush, late-nineteenth-century European style typifying his most well-known film scores inherently eschews commercial music. Even in those rarer instances where his writing does reference popular strains, Williams tends to recast them sufficiently enough as to mask their original source akin to the process by which he effected the familiar, yet suitably alien, 'swing' of his *Star Wars* "Cantina Band". Such successful pop flirtations, often placed as they are within otherwise symphonic soundtracks, beg larger questions. For instance, what would result if Williams were intentionally to fashion an entire film score after a popular medium? Could such an effort maintain an exclusive basis in pop? Which popular style would Williams prefer and why? How would this choice, as opposed to some other, affect the score's outcome? Just how faithful to this stylistic choice could his score remain? Might these efforts generate a hybrid style — one either distinct from, or grounded in, Williams's foregoing compositional voice? How might the introduction of popular music elements influence the composer's more traditional approaches to writing? How would performers respond to this hybrid style and what might that response imply?

Before his score for *Catch Me if You Can*, precious few of Williams's full cinematic efforts suggest a pop aesthetic. According to the composer, «Some of the music has a kind of sixties swagger to it and has a jazz saxophone that you would hear in that period. Actually, for me personally, it's kind of like a perfect regression because I would write some jazz music in the fifties and sixties when I [was] very young. *Catch Me if You Can* has been a good opportunity for me to revisit some part of myself that's been lying, slumbering dormant for a few decades now». As he adds, «*Catch Me if You Can* is certainly a deviation stylistically from the films that Steven has been doing through the years»[4]. In this sense, the extent to which the score for *Catch Me* represents a corresponding stylistic departure from Williams's milieu offers a unique opportunity to investigate further interrelated questions concerning the artistic consequences of the specific popular source model at hand (motivation and execution), its success (reception and legacy), and its efficacy in

4. Williams in *ibidem*.

advancing film narrative. Will music themes continue to operate leitmotivically — in Williams's oft-preferred Wagnerian mode — within this new pop-minded context, or in a less complicated network of variations? How might each of these aspects be affected when a composer with Williams's particular stylistic inclinations and long-running successful formulae encounters the popular music idiom?

Surveying his early compositional explorations of popular music, this discussion will frame analysis of Williams's later approach to invoking jazz sound and style against his customary compositional direction. While certain elements appropriated from jazz such as instrumentation and rhythmic interest clearly inform the *Catch Me* score, this study will further examine those ways in which this hybrid work is also indebted to the classical or art music tradition — most notably in its preference for notated improvisatory gesture over true improvisation. And yet, according to performer testimony, the work's principal challenges nevertheless seem to lie in the blended demands it makes of both classical and jazz technique. Just as its hybridized veneer may, for a time, conceal the work's broader allegiance to the concert music world, Williams's claims to revisit the pop writing of his earliest output within this soundtrack prove illusory. More revealing is Williams's live concert contextualization of his score at the Boston Pops, situating it among similarly qualified stylistic presentations such as self-described 'song stylist' Nancy Wilson[5]. While *Catch Me if You Can* references jazz with varying degrees of persuasion, what Williams achieves amounts to more of a clever, albeit multifaceted allusion to the popular music idiom — one that approaches an homage just shy of engaging the tradition directly. The resulting stylistic species has instead unearthed new sonic territory for cinematic and concert music alike.

From Jazz Clubs & Early Television to Cantina Bands: Williams's Formative Training Ground in Popular Music

Following military service during the early 1950s that included orchestrating and conducting duties, Williams returned to his native New York. As he would later discover, his inadvertent training directing Air Force bands had provided a seminal preparation for his later career scoring Hollywood productions, supplying repeated opportunity for long-term, close study and adaptation of various popular music styles. Reflecting upon these formative experiences, Williams recollected:

> I went in [to the US Air Force band] as a pianist and a brass doubler. […] [I] discovered that I could be useful in writing arrangements for our dance band. […] I could perhaps advance the harmonizations, add some tricks. […]

5. Wilson 2003.

> We did radio, we did endless dance sessions, officers club shows. [...] Certainly the best way to learn instrumentation is to live and play with and study other people as they study their instruments. [...] I had a tremendous education in the Air Force. [...] And I think, in my mind, [I] reference it still[6].

While attending the Julliard School — but before his supplemental training in composition at the University of California, Los Angeles — Williams also played in jazz clubs, no doubt further refining his popular music sensibilities within the burgeoning 1950s New York City hardbop scene.

Back in California by mid-decade, Williams soon found work as a studio pianist. Within a few years, he was contributing prolifically to early television music — first as a studio musician, and then, increasingly, as a composer in his own right. See TABLE 1.

TABLE 1: CROSS SECTION OF MUSIC FOR EARLY TELEVISION BY JOHN WILLIAMS (1958-1970)[7]

SERIES TITLE	TOTAL EPISODES	YEAR(S)
**Alcoa Theatre*	1	1958
**Markham*	1	1959
*Johnny Staccato****	3	1959
*Mr. Lucky****	29	1959-1960
**Goodyear Theatre*	1	1960
**Checkmate*	70	1960-1962
**One Step Beyond*	1	1961
**Alcoa Premiere*	58	1961-1963
**Wide County*	28	1962-1963
**Kraft Mystery Theatre*	2	1962-1963
**Kraft Suspense Theatre*	39	1963-1965
**Bob Hope Presents the Chrysler Theatre*	10	1963-1967
Lost in Space*	126	1965-1968
**The Tammy Grimes Show*	6	1966
**The Time Tunnel*	29	1966-1967
**Land of the Giants*	50	1968-1970

* Williams as composer of television main theme
** Williams as composer of incidental or 'stock' music for respective program
*** Williams credited as, simply, 'musician' or uncredited as a studio pianist

6. Williams quoted in LANG 2016.
7. 'John Williams', Internet Movie Database, <http://www.imdb.com/name/nm0002354/?ref_=fn_al_nm_1>, accessed February 2018.

After supplying orchestration and piano playing on the film adaptations of *Carousel* (Henry King, 1956) and *South Pacific* (Joshua Logan, 1958) respectively, Williams turned predominantly to the new television medium[8]. Now often credited as 'Johnny' Williams, the twenty-six-year-old's first television composition, the short-lived *Alcoa Theatre* (1958), was quickly followed by an impressive run of successful series during the 1960s – including the more favourably received fifty-eight-episode revival, *Alcoa Premiere* (1961). For most of these programs, Williams wrote the main theme alone; for others he gained occasional experience as a composer of incidental or 'stock' music and, eventually, even a limited engagement as an arranger for Bob Hope. (Other television programs for which the composer wrote limited episodic music, but not the main theme, included *M Squad*, during 1958 and 1959; *Wagon Train*, 1958-1964; *Gilligan's Island*, 1964-1965; and even *The Carol Burnett Show*, 1968.) Williams's most enduring work from this period aligns with his two most popular associations, *Checkmate* (1960) and *Lost in Space* (1965), together totalling nearly 200 episodes. The latter series, perhaps prophetically, also offered Williams his first chance to pen incidental music for a prominent science-fiction production, much of which anticipated many of the signature musical tropes he would later expand upon to establish the sound world of another wildly popular science-fiction franchise emergent within the coming decade, *Star Wars* (George Lucas, 1977).

A survey of these early television themes lays bare a number of common threads. Most channel a generic brand of big band instrumentation, arrangement, and rhythmic style typical of the more commercial efforts of the period. Almost all make use of lively melody and brassy writing in high registers punctuated by dramatic articulations and wide-ranging dynamic levels. Reliance upon jazz idioms is unmistakable. The scope and vision of Williams's *Checkmate* theme, for example, evinces a related big-band model and temperament, enough that this variety of Williams's writing even resembles the contemporaneous output of a mainstream band leader like Stan Kenton[9].

Sparingly one sees hints of components that will ultimately come to govern Williams's mature style, one free from popular markers — say, in his sweeping theatrical theme for the revamped *Alcoa Premiere* or, more directly, in his agitated scoring for *Kraft Suspense Theatre* (1963). (See Ex. 1, p. 46.)

---

[8]. It is worth noting that Williams also orchestrated the 1959 hit *Gidget* (Paul Wendkos) while providing uncredited piano playing on the classic *Some Like It Hot* (Billy Wilder) in the same year.

[9]. Stan Kenton's landmark *New Concepts of Artistry in Rhythm* (1952) album capitalized upon years of leading popular swing and progressive big bands in the 1930s and 1940s to cement his place among the most commercially successful jazz-inspired figures through the 1970s. Curiously, a 1965 collaboration between Williams and Kenton's longtime drummer, Shelly Manne, also produced a series of Gershwin arrangements for the album *Manne – That's Gershwin!* (Capitol Records). During the late 1940s, Kenton coined the term 'progressive jazz' as part of his promotional campaign. For further context on the origins and impact of this particular stylistic label, see Jones 2008.

Ex. 1: opening excerpt of Williams's *Kraft Suspense Theatre* theme (© 1963) with analysis from *Kraft Suspense Theatre*, ear transcription from the television soundtrack. Used in compliance with U.S. Copyright Act, Section 107[10].

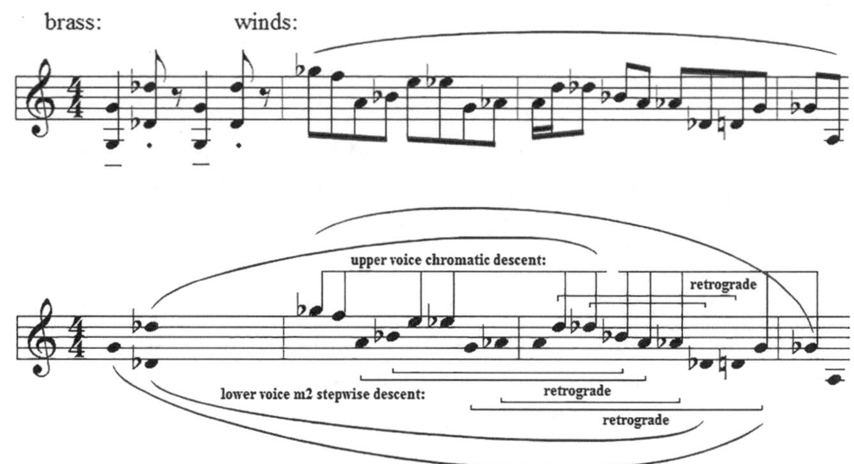

An abiding consistency pervades much of Williams's style and this fleeting passage offers an illustrative, if concentrated, case study of the unity and organicism that — even early in his output — inform his writing. As the diagram aligned below Ex. 1 chronicles, a dense network of interrelated patterns shape and quickly reinforce Williams's compositional choices, underpinning his melodic profile with a certain signature inevitability; one no less effective for its atonal hue. Note the careful balances in pitch class presentation (most prominently, G and D♭; to a lesser extent, B♭ and A) repeatedly underscored through multiple layers of structural emphasis. After an opening stress on the G-D♭ tritone dramatically declares the passage's governing intervallic parameters, the responding wind compound melody proceeds to reinforce and frame the centrality of these two pitches from concomitant angles. As the upper voice begins a chromatic octave descent from G♭ — interrupted at the structural D♭ only to resume its course at B♭ — the lower voice initiates a series of minor second retrogrades (sequenced first from A and B♭), eventually further used to re-emphasize D♭ once more just before the passage reaches its conclusion passing through G to G♭[11]. Less inspired by straight ahead jazz, Williams's opening tritone motive begets and dictates his entire melodic profile.

Even in the contour of his diatonic, jazzier score for *Lost in Space* — composed two years later — Williams maintains elements of this stylistic homogeneity, echoing the disjointed mood of its considerably more chromatic televised forerunner. (See Ex. 2, p. 47.)

10. 'John Williams Kraft Suspense Theatre Theme First Version', <https://www.youtube.com/watch?v=o3zHGN4yWtA>, accessed February 2018.

11. By skipping the intervening pitches C and B at this point in his chromatic descent, Williams inherently stresses these two remaining structural pitches (D♭ and B♭) — already highlighted within the passage by other means — that much more.

Ex. 2: opening melody to Williams's main theme for *Lost in Space* (© 1965 BMI), published by EMI Hastings Catalog Inc., ear transcription from the television soundtrack. Used in compliance with U.S. Copyright Act, Section 107.

Aptly suited to its roving program, the writing here seems intentionally directionless, even discombobulated by design. Albeit within the confines of G minor, an active, expansive intervallic profile all but pushes beyond the disjunct melody's expectable diatonic emphases on the tonic and dominant to suggest disorientation through abrupt shifts in register, metric displacement, and moderately open-ended phrasing[12].

It should be little wonder that nearly forty years later, as Williams prepared to revisit the 1960s and, naturally, his own contributions within it, traces of this particular brand of intervallic counterbalance and symmetry would re-emerge — namely, in the solo alto saxophone writing of his *Catch Me* score. Compare the compound melodic contour previewed in Ex. 3 here (ahead of the work's forthcoming expanded score discussion) with that outlined in Ex. 1 above:

Ex. 3: excerpted saxophone line from "Recollections", *Catch Me if You Can* (© 2002 BMI), published by Songs of SKG, ear transcription by C. A. Norling from the film's soundtrack. Used in compliance with U.S. Copyright Act, Section 107.

Such a correlation suggests that while adapting popular idioms for fusion with his personal style in a period piece such as *Catch Me if You Can* — a rare endeavour for the composer — Williams may favour turning at least partially to the same modernist models he had relied upon to bolster his own compositional textures during the very era targeted for tribute.

[12]. On Williams's work in television, see Paula Musegades's chapter in this volume.

Close stylistic parallels such as this also reflect a broader, fundamental dichotomy in Williams's scoring practices. Within this stratification, one may group a number of Williams's film scores under what might best be termed his primary composition mode. This approach — accounting for many projects the general listener would immediately associate with Williams — supplies the composer's mature film scores with his familiar, bold return to a neo-romantic, often expressly programmatic soundscape taking its cue from the early Korngold-Steiner studio era. Functionally, this style usually undergirds a complex network of leitmotives often orchestrated for a full symphony, sometimes operating across multiple unified film sequels (see *Jaws* [Steven Spielberg, 1975], *Star Wars*, *Superman*, *Indiana Jones*, and *Harry Potter*, among others). Works in this compositional mode also tend to be grounded in a functionally diatonic language, though definitive aberrations — chiefly modal inflections — routinely embellish this relative tonal clarity for emphasis and dramatic effect. In the case of the first *Star Wars* film, Williams discussed how this archaic choice of style came about as a function of balanced presentation and thematic development: «George [Lucas] [...] wanted a dichotomy to his visuals, an almost nineteenth-century romantic, symphonic score against these unseen sights. [...] This established the stylistic direction I went to in *Star Wars*, which is first, tonal, and second, orchestral. [...] For formal reasons, I felt that the film wanted thematic unity. I believed we needed melodic themes of our own which I could sort of bend around and put through all the permutations»[13]. As observed elsewhere, in this mode Williams patterns his writing after forerunning operatic paradigms exemplified by Richard Wagner. «A theme that appears in film two that wasn't in film one was probably a very close intervallic, which is to say note-by-note-by-note, relative to a theme that we'd had», as Williams explains: «We would have the Princess Leia theme as a the romantic theme in the first film, but then we'd have Yoda's music, which was unexpectedly romantic, if you like, in the second film, but not such a distant relative, musically speaking, intervallically [and] melodically speaking, to Princess Leia's music. [...] They're different, but they also marry up very well and you can interplay them in a contrapuntal way, and it will be part of a texture that is familial»[14]. This level of detailed melodic correspondence and adjustment lies at the core of Williams's primary compositional mode — a methodology he perfected over decades and for which he remains the leading exponent in Hollywood.

But there is also an alternative, secondary mode of composition Williams wields with nearly as much frequency — one that inherently retains his personal dramatic voice, but seems reserved for less overtly programmatic narratives. These scores devote their creative resources to establishing a particular overarching mood — or series of moods — connected to far fewer themes typically more austere and, quite often, distinctly modern in sound and nature. Here long-range leitmotivic relationships are exchanged for a less elaborate,

13. Williams 1993, p. 55.

14. Williams quoted in Byrd 1997.

general schema of theme and variations. In addition to some of his early work for television (briefly alluded to above), projects crafted along these lines include such film scores as *Close Encounters of the Third Kind* (Steven Spielberg, 1977), *Born on the Fourth of July* (Oliver Stone, 1989), *Jurassic Park* (Steven Spielberg, 1993), *Amistad* (Steven Spielberg, 1997), *Seven Years in Tibet* (Jean-Jacques Annaud, 1997), and *Angela's Ashes* (Alan Parker, 1999). Though not all of these scores are nearly as chromatically driven as the profiles of those sources featured in Exs. 1 and 3 would suggest, their collective language nevertheless deviates in prominent ways from typical film scores, inclining less regularly toward upholding traditional forms of tonality and making use of avant-garde elements. These deviations interrupt tonal contexts with expressive purpose, either through a carefully extended tonality, or, more rarely, by plunging headlong into decidedly atonal extremes, however briefly. While not hard-and-fast, these generalizations separating the leitmotivic approach from the less complex variation of themes are useful distinctions in confronting Williams's *modus operandi.* As subsequent analysis will demonstrate, the score for *Catch Me if You Can* is not only firmly entrenched in the latter compositional mode, but in some ways, expands it.

Interlaced with additional uncredited roles as the conductor of various projects, Williams's run of contiguous television work ended around 1970, after which — following intermittent, suitably transitional experience with the television-movie genre — he increasingly devoted more attention to scores for film proper in earnest[15]. A prominent film noir collaboration during this time with Robert Altman and Elliot Gould, *The Long Goodbye* (1973), even resulted in a crooning 'Johnny T. Williams' fifties jazz-influenced pop song by the same name with lyrics by Johnny Mercer (cleverly reinterpreted and rearranged in different styles throughout the film's diegetic music), complete with piano comping, a solo trumpet chorus, and ensuing call and response with famed vocalist Jack Sheldon. A lighter pop tune, "Make Me Rainbows" with lyrics by Alan and Marilyn Bergman, for the earlier Dick Van Dyke romantic comedy vehicle *Fitzwilly* (1967) offers a glimpse into the younger Williams's facility with the conventional jazz harmony of the period. (See Ex. 4 p. 50.) Though his ballad plots a relatively basic jazz chord progression, the sophistication and nuance of Williams's voicings within testify to a clear stylistic proficiency. Interestingly, thirty-five years later as laureate conductor of the Boston Pops, Williams would pair this tune with his more recent excerpts from *Catch Me if You Can.* (See Ill. 1, p. 66.)

Arguably Williams's most well recognized reference to the popular idiom — the so-called 'Cantina Band Song' (officially titled "Mad About Me") — is well documented in

[15]. Williams returned to mainstream television composition during the 1980s, most notably writing the main themes for *NBC News* (entitled "The Mission") and the Spielberg vehicle *Amazing Stories*, both premiering in 1985. Other prominent television work includes the *Olympic Fanfare and Theme* (1984) for television coverage of the games that persists today.

Ex. 4: transcription of the opening of Williams's "Make Me Rainbows", from *Fitzwilly* (© 1967 BMI), published by Primary Wave Tunes, printed as a vocal score by Unart Music Corporation (1967-1973). Used in compliance with U.S. Copyright Act, Section 107.

the exhaustive literature surrounding the *Star Wars* franchise[16]. In a recent edited volume of essays on science fiction film music, Seth Mulliken offers the following overview of its origins within a broader discussion of diegetic music: «Director George Lucas's original concept for the music of the cantina band was to "imagine several creatures in a future century finding some 1930s Benny Goodman swing band music in a time capsule or under a rock someplace… how they might attempt to interpret it"»[17].

In dutifully realizing his director's original vision, Williams set out to craft a swing-era, reed-inspired number with an appropriately alien twist. «We hired nine musicians, mostly jazz», he recalled, «they included one trumpet, two saxophones, one saxophone who doubled on clarinet, a Fender Rhodes piano, a Caribbean steel drum, assorted percussion, a drum, and an Arp synthesizer for the bass. I scored it so they sounded a little bit strange, almost familiar but not quite. We filtered them so that it clips the bottom end

16. MULLIKEN 2010, p. 91.

17. *Ibidem*.

of the sound. We attenuated the bottom end a little bit and reverbed them so that it slightly thins them out»[18]. In addition to its instrumentation, "Mad About Me" bears many stylistic trappings associated with Goodman's swing era: wah-wah trumpet, alternating clarinet lead and break work, pitch bends, and arranged contrasts between solo and soli writing. Its form, what Williams has termed a «five-part rondo», opens with a repeated three-part (ABC) section in which each part totals 16 measures conventionally grouped into four separate, four-bar phrases — for a recurring forty-eight-measure unit[19]. Though far from abnormal, this formal reluctance to conform with the era's ubiquitous preference for 32-bar song form (AABA) does offset those expectations more conventionally prompted by the tune's traditional sound and style. Similarly, Williams's harmonic setting benefits from a corresponding scrutiny. A series of somewhat atypical melodic inflections complement the otherwise ordinary circular progression (ii-V-I) closing his first A section. After sustaining a patently textbook diatonic vocabulary, the brief, subtle chromaticism of this cadential moment — namely the consecutive raised fifths colouring the supertonic and dominant chords — appears just peculiar enough to suggest a corrupting outside, if not actively 'alien', affect at work. (See Ex. 5.)

Ex. 5: Williams's "Mad About Me", ("Cantina Band #1", *Star Wars*, ©1977 BMI, published by Bantha Music/ Warner-Tamerlane) harmonic progression approaching first cadence, measures 13-16, ear transcription from the film's soundtrack. Used in compliance with U.S. Copyright Act, Section 107.

Perhaps these traits constitute part of Williams's choice to score his extraterrestrial nonet «so they sounded a little bit strange, almost familiar but not quite»[20]. But, intergalactic cabaret cards aside, even here, one sees a further hint of the composer's earlier practice within his secondary mode of composition. These inflections are more accurately artefacts from a finely honed chromatic past — fleeting but characteristic musical turns of phrase consistent with the same harmonic language Williams will not only resurrect, but greatly extend as part of an homage even less concerned with presenting genuine jazz than even Mos Eisley management.

[18]. Williams quoted in Kendall 1993, p. 48.

[19]. Williams quoted in Mulliken 2010, p. 91.

[20]. Williams quoted in Kendall 1993, p. 48. Elsewhere, Williams supplemented the account of his compositional process for "Mad About Me": «I went to the piano and began writing the silliest little series of old-time swing band licks, kind of a little off and a little wrong and not quite matching [...] a little out of tune and a little behind there, a little ahead there: it had all the foibles of a not-very-good human performance». Williams quoted in Byrd 1997, online.

Williams followed the cantina sequences with a similar venture for *Star Wars: Return of Jedi* (Richard Marquand, 1983), the vaguely disco "Lapi Nek", presented by Jabba the Hutt's house band with lyrics by Williams's son, Joseph[21]. Even the recent seventh instalment, *Star Wars: The Force Awakens* (J. J. Abrams, 2015), revisited this tradition with a corresponding cantina group, updating the featured pop style to reggae ("Jabba Flow"). In this instance Williams delegated the recasting of this music scene to *Hamilton* composer-performer Lin-Manuel Miranda and director J. J. Abrams. As Abrams revealed:

> I saw *Hamilton* [...] and at intermission, Lin-Manuel Miranda [...] says «Hey, if you need music for the cantina, I'll write it...». Basically we have a scene that's sort of our version of the cantina scene that John Williams, master composer, said, «J. J. Baby, I'd rather not write the music for that scene, because I'd rather write the [orchestral] score...». So, I end up emailing Lin Miranda [...] and now in the movie, in this one sequence, is music that Lin-Manuel Miranda and I wrote in *Star Wars*[22].

In an interesting parallel, reggae's origins in the 1970s are about as far removed from 2015 — roughly forty years — as had the original cantina band been from its 1930s swing source material in 1977.

CATCH ME IF YOU CAN: WILLIAMS'S POPULAR-CLASSICAL HYBRID

As far and away his most protracted dalliance with the popular music idiom, Williams's writing for *Catch Me if You Can* exemplifies his broader theme and variations mode of composition, and in many ways maps out a model approach for this method. While this score, alongside a candid integration of identifiably popular elements, fashions a subtle lyricism of recurring musical themes designed to recall central narrative themes across the film, they are more limited in number and variability than the comparable litany of themes comprising the dramatic escapades of more character-driven films under Williams's primary leitmotivic mode — especially those assuming serial proportions (*Star Wars*, *Indiana Jones*, *Potter*). «In all of those years», Williams observes, «we never really did a piece like this. *Catch Me if You Can*, it's really a sort of bon-bon, if you like. It's light, it's amusing and entertaining — oddly enough about a serious subject... Most of the music is playful and whimsical»[23]. *Catch Me* stands further apart for its marked effort at homage through popular music culture from the period in question. It deliberately

[21]. This selection was later replaced with the widely panned "Jedi Rocks" — an uneven rhythm and blues number overdubbed as part of the film's digitally remastered special edition released by Lucas in the late 1990s.

[22]. Abrams in FALLON 2015.

[23]. Williams in BOUZEREAU 2003.

abdicates Williams's lush nineteenth-century sound world, embracing instead a more modern-inspired popular style that loosely references jazz idioms in a daring attempt to strike a new tone. As the composer acknowledged, this score «presented some interesting musical changes and, slightly, challenges too from the other films»[24]. What is critically new about his approach to scoring this period piece is Williams's only partial embrace of the popular model. Styles that had previously coloured and more directly penetrated his earlier oeuvre — big band, pop song, and even the nascent modernist gestures informing the language of *Kraft Suspense Theatre* — are rejected in any wholesale form for a new, hybridized orchestral style that trifles with the popular.

The main title for *Catch Me* presents Williams's most conventional nods to jazz. Besides introducing the score's ubiquitous solo alto saxophone, the movement features walking bass lines, conventional pop voicing and harmony, Harmon mutes, and even percussive finger-snapping supplied by ensemble members. Unlike his strained "Cantina Band", this arrangement never quite reaches any critical swinging mass, preferring instead to hint at rhythmic interest by way of hemiola, sleights of hand in grouping and meter, and irregular accent à la Dave Brubeck — tried and true, if antiseptic, art music devices to compensate for authentic swing impulses.

Not insignificantly, selections comprising the full soundtrack alternate between Williams's writing and period-specific pop tunes designed to capture the flavour of the era. See Table 2.

Table 2: Popular Song Selections from *Catch Me if You Can* Soundtrack (Listed in Order of Album Presentation)

Recording	Performing Artist(s)	Year Issued
"Come Fly with Me"	Frank Sinatra	1958
"The Girl from Ipanema"	Stan Getz, João Gilberto, Astrud Gilberto, Antônio Carlos Jobim	1964
"Embraceable You"	Judy Garland	1940
"The Christmas Song"	Nat King Cole	1961
"The Look of Love"	Dusty Springfield	1967

While their story-telling application within Spielberg's period narrative is commonplace, these songs further provide an important context as they intermingle with Williams's score. «We also use period top forties hit tunes. But in this case», qualifies the director, «I really went for melody and mood as opposed to relevance with lyrics»[25]. Their regular, collective interruption of Williams's music unavoidably conditions its presentation — effectively

[24]. Williams in *ibidem*.

[25]. Spielberg in *ibidem*.

circumscribing the composer's own stylistic aims with definition and corroborating his intentions to channel specifically pop-minded material. And though the film's commitment to a pop dimension may be clear, its link to jazz is less apparent. As these musics work in tandem to triangulate the 1960s, the listener ultimately comes to regard Williams's edgier contributions as part of the decade's so-called 'progressive' jazz idiom.

Technical Matters: Interpretive Considerations Negotiating Classical & Jazz Technique

At the core of Williams's hybridization lie fundamental questions concerning the motivation, process, and assessment of a product intertwining opposed traditions. More pressing still are the choices confronting its interpreters. Soloist Dan Higgins (b. 1955), a Los Angeles studio musician who recorded saxophone for the original *Catch Me* film soundtrack, began his relationship with the Spielberg-Williams duo providing «very minimal roles» involving «just maybe a light colour» nearly a decade earlier[26]. His first collaboration supplied music for only a brief moment in *Schindler's List*. «Right at the beginning of the movie, where Schindler walks into a bar and there's an accordion and an alto sax and a drummer or a piano, or something — small little band in a night club», Higgins recounted. «I played the part, and [Williams] says, "Dan, that's just lovely. Could it sound more antique?" He never uses regular words, so I just backed off the microphone because I'm kind of a modern player and obviously this was a 1938 alto player. So I just changed my tone a little bit»[27].

Higgins would bring a telling versatility — informed by an indispensably apposite training background — to the *Catch Me* sessions. «I started out as a classical clarinet player», he remembered. «I transferred to the University of North Texas saxophone department. [...] At the time, it was four years of classical study and you played in the jazz band and you took improv, but you never took a jazz lesson, which I think is the key to my control of the instrument — that I studied classical». Comparing his own readiness to other players, Higgins asserted: «I see these kids come out to Los Angeles [...] and they [are] not good textural players. They're good improvisers, but [...] that's my ace in the hole — that I went to a school that had both. I didn't want to play the classical saxophone [...] and then, when I got to be better at it, I really embraced it. And that became a really great asset to have as... it's still the foundation of the instrument and feels good to know how to play it»[28]. Despite formal training as a classicist, Higgins considers himself a commercial jazz player. «I look back to the cassette of all the solos I transcribed. Cannonball [Adderley],

26. Higgins 2017.
27. *Ibidem*.
28. *Ibidem*.

Charlie Parker, Dave Sanborn, John Coltrane, and Tom Scott were my heavy hitters [...] not really any classical players. [...] I always gravitated to all of the odd classical pieces that had more modern harmony»[29].

For certain aspects — vibrato, intonation, and time — Williams's score undoubtedly demands classical technique. «A straight classical player will sound bad on this piece, and a straight jazz player will sound bad», Higgins assesses. Expounding upon the implications of this claim, he elaborates: «So, where do you draw the line? I'm in between, so it's a good fit for me. But when I've heard classical players — it just dies. And then I hear a jazz player try to play *Catch Me if You Can*, and he's out of tune and the vibrato is not legit. So I think you need to have your foot equally in both camps to pursue the piece and that may not be true of other saxophone literature where you can just be a classical player»[30]. Drawing a clearer distinction between the classical and jazz approach in more specific technical terms, Higgins focussed on his use of vibrato throughout the piece. As he notes, «The vibrato is a legit vibrato and it's not of the French style. It's just tighter, less amplitude, so it's not as corny. The jazz player vibrato is uncontrolled and it just comes and goes as however he sees fit. So, it's ragged and I didn't do any of that. Not one bar — because it never calls for it. I treated it like a classical thing, with a jazz tone, maybe. [...] I would play the vibrato like a classical player and it just worked»[31].

The absolutist position Higgins assumes to broker this crossbreeding speaks to the composer's skill and awareness in expressing his stylistic intentions. «I think [Williams] just interpreted [the score] in a classical sense», Higgins opined. «The notes are hip, and there's some jazz elements in there, but you just play it and play it nicely. And that's what you're going for». Over time, as aspiring players contacted the saxophonist to consult him over performance choices for *Catch Me*, his stance became amplified. «Somebody called me», Higgins shared, «and said, "Oh I've got to play this and John's going to be there and I got some ideas to bend the note and I'm going to do this", and I go, "Oh, good luck! I just played what was written and it seemed to work out". He wanted to improve on something. Just play it, you know?»[32].

Other performance dimensions of *Catch Me* draw similarly, if less profoundly, upon a certain jazz fluency. As Higgins acknowledged, «I certainly took liberties with [Williams's] articulations to make the thing swing a bit more because it might just be a broad slur or something. I think I could add that to it»[33]. The score's favoured timbres — solo alto

29. *Ibidem*.

30. *Ibidem*.

31. *Ibidem*.

32. *Ibidem*.

33. *Ibidem*. For the record, Higgins prefers a Vandoren Java reed, strength 3 (jazz brand) for its thinner and slightly more responsive tip. He has played his 1957 Selmer Mark VI alto saxophone — which he notes was designed specifically for the classical players of its day — since acquiring it in the 1970s.

saxophone and vibraphone — as well as its running collection of active rhythmic gesture both pervade the soundtrack and initiate references to jazz. But Williams's turn to jazz wavers, undeveloped and lacking in one key ingredient. «It was all written out», Higgins reports. «Every note. John doesn't leave much to chance. That isn't his style»[34]. Instead, Williams would cite other models to help his performers achieve the sound he was after: «Sometimes he would use jazz references [including Cannonball Adderley] with me. It was Red Norvo he wanted [vibraphonist] Alan [Estes] to [emulate] — who was a very soft, smooth player and not a hard-driving mallet player. [...] Some people can't hear the vibes and they think you're improvising. And I go, "Well, if I am, then the vibe player knows exactly what I'm going to do, because he's in there doing it!"»[35]. Williams's music for *Catch Me*, though appearing to present an improvised voice, merely simulates a deferential facsimile.

By even the most liberal definitions, almost all styles of jazz swing and all improvise. *Catch Me if You Can* exhibits neither of these components by any true benchmark. While the place for swinging has varied over jazz's century-long history, improvisation has remained at the centre of its expression and expectation, differentiating the genre from other popular music such rhythm and blues, rock, or country that locate improvised forums closer to their peripheries. While some moments of his score are strategically designed to approximate a stylized brand of swing, no part of the film's score is improvised, or designates sections for improvisation — even within formal cadenzas. Rather, Williams's writing — combined with Higgins's background and performance choices — effects an 'improvisatory' style. Though the composer's adoption of popular music idioms draws largely upon the later 1950s and 1960s jazz stylistic trends of his young adulthood, Williams's particular species of approach within this paradigm might more usefully be described not as straight ahead jazz, but perhaps best — however less satisfyingly — by the looser term, 'jazzy'. As Williams asserts, «I didn't want to write a jazz piece, only something to suggest the period»[36].

---

34. *Ibidem*. «The advantage of traditional notation», Williams observes with regard to composing *Catch Me*, «is that there can be more tightly constructed counterpoint than when people improvise. If the players were improvising, the bass player wouldn't really know what the saxophonist was going to do until it happened, but through traditional notation the piece sounds improvised, even though it has carefully controlled counterpoint». Williams quoted in Colburn 2004, p. 16.

35. Higgins 2017. According to Williams, «The tracer effect, in which the vibraphone duplicates every note of the saxophone solo, gives it a special glow. This is another aspect of the music that would be impossible if it were improvised». Williams quoted in Colburn 2004, p. 16.

36. Williams quoted in Colburn 2004, p. 16. Of course, this special brand of jazz-inspired orchestral writing is not without precedent. Models for this form of appropriation pervade the art music world, if not film scores, of the early half of the twentieth century, during which composers flirted with the new popular style to varying degrees. Among others, George Gershwin, Aaron Copland, Maurice Ravel, Darius Milhaud, and Igor Stravinsky each experimented with the instrumentation and distinctive rhythmic profile of jazz (including the American popular music traditions such as blues and ragtime that nurtured it) as a means to foster new sound and compositional direction — without coopting its central, definitive improvisational

"Catch as Catch Can": Jazz, John Williams, & Popular Music Allusion

Despite his intimations toward a jazz aesthetic — however equipped by his formative work in popular settings — Williams's 2002 *Catch Me* score emerged classically conceived with popular leanings. The call for a soloist who can tackle both traditions — to effect the actual work of shared stylistic spirit that Williams has captured here — is both warranted and inescapable. «Listen», Higgins confesses, «I'd rather listen to a classical player play it, than a jazz player. It's got to lean over there because it's excruciating to hear it [without a classical sensibility]. That's just no fun. But the classical player can be tight. [He or she] can be rather undynamic and not [have] enough fire on the articulation to really sell things. But that's fine»[37]. Higgins's internal counterpoint, in and of itself, testifies to the special challenge Williams's work extends and the original sound world it inhabits — no matter how much it may or may not dabble in a purely popular vein.

Catch Me if You Can Case Study: "Recollections (The Father's Theme)"

Outside its protracted treatment and sustained solo focus on the saxophone, the factor that sets Williams's "Recollections" (and much of the *Catch Me* score) most apart from his foregoing pop-inspired writing remains its extended tonal intricacies. Its relatively sudden shifts in both pitch centre and pitch collection closely track with much of the work's variation procedures and trajectory. Though hardly atonal, this extended harmonic language forsakes straightforward functionally diatonic progressions in favour of a local chromaticism that regularly promotes shifting tonal loyalties. In concert with those specific choices in instrumentation and rhythmic interest enumerated above, these fluctuations — along with their phrasing — are also primarily responsible for generating the piece's loose improvisatory melodic character.

Thematic material tied to this movement — chiefly its soft, lyrical 'father's' melody — once introduced, recurs broadly throughout the film score in an almost textbook 'reminiscence theme' capacity whenever a reflective or melancholy mood is justified. «There are a couple of scenes where [the main character is] linked musically with his father», Williams describes, «where he's alone, where he's tired of the chase»[38]. (See Ex. 6, p. 58.)

---

mode. For example, in his 1926 *Concerto for piano and orchestra*, Aaron Copland — who later clarified that its «short cadenza sounds like an improvised break, but is not» — wrote out each note of his cadenza «probably because», as the composer admitted, «I was not good at improvisation myself». Copland – Perlis 1984, p. 131. Owing to his painstaking study of jazz inflection and character, Copland's solo retains a distinctly improvisatory, if not outright improvised, feel.

[37]. Higgins 2017.

[38]. Williams in Bouzereau 2003.

Ex. 6: opening of Williams's "Father's Theme", from "Recollections", measures 5-8, from *Catch Me if You Can* (© 2002 BMI), published by Songs of SKG, ear transcription by C. A. Norling. Used in compliance with U.S. Copyright Act, Section 107[39].

Appropriately, in these brief reappearances — more specifically employed either to call to mind or directly accompany one of the protagonist's many on-screen returns to unresolved family issues — the theme itself remains stubbornly unaltered but for shrewd, related adjustments in timbre. Moreover, even these changes in voice are kept, analogously, to the originating saxophone's own *orchestral* family, often going only so far as to pass the theme not just to any woodwind, but, elegantly, to another reed instrument such as the oboe. Such is the mastery, too often overlooked, of Williams's craftsman precision in orchestrating the subtlest of narrative undercurrents in his films. In these ways, "Recollections" serves as the film's tonal and narrative nexus.

Conspicuously, the introductory phrase of "Recollections" opens on a harmonically indecisive octatonic pitch collection (A-B♭-C-D♭-E♭) stressing its highest opening pitch, D♭, through restatement. (See Ex. 7.)

Ex. 7: introduction to Williams's "Recollections" from *Catch Me if You Can* (© 2002 BMI), published by Songs of SKG, ear transcription from the film's soundtrack. Used in compliance with U.S. Copyright Act, Section 107.

While a forgiving pitch survey of this introduction might advocate for B♭ minor — reading the voice-leading of A natural to B♭ across measures 1 and 2 (and across the octave displacement of measure 3) as the move of a leading-tone resolving to its tonic — Williams's initial, angular choices here clearly resist harmonic transparency. But greater clarity quickly arrives within only a few more measures as the father's theme substitutes D♮ for D♭ to usher in a stronger B♭ pitch centre, if not outright B♭ major. (An intervening anacrusis run up a D phrygian scale leading directly into this main theme further prefigures this impending two-flat area.) However, even here, Williams's melody — like its introduction's emphasis on

[39]. I would like to extend my sincerest thanks to saxophonist Cody A. Norling for his detailed transcription of Dan Higgins's saxophone solo from the "Recollections" movement as released on the original commercial soundtrack recording of *Catch Me if You Can*. All figures featuring excerpts from "Recollections" derive from this transcription. Unless otherwise noted, all other transcriptions are the work of the author.

D♭ — concentrates on D and evades strong cadential movement to B♭. Note the interrupted leading tone-tonic resolution of A-B♭ through the truncated phrase elided and interpolated across measures 8 and 10. (See Ex. 8.)

Ex. 8: conclusion of Williams's "Father's Theme", from "Recollections (The Father's Theme)", measures 4-12, from *Catch Me if You Can* (© 2002 BMI), published by Songs of SKG, ear transcription from the film's soundtrack. Used in compliance with U.S. Copyright Act, Section 107.

In fact, with this early melodic transition to a B♭ centre, Williams's score inaugurates an important tension between D and D♭ pitch classes that will fuel his movement's central interest. This opposition will prove at issue throughout the movement's extensive intervallically manipulated variations, ultimately affirming D♮ at its conclusion.

Whatever his harmonic persuasions, Williams loses no time launching into chromatic obfuscation. Beginning with measure 13, he initiates a series of local variations on the father's theme undermining any enduring harmonic stability. Immediate sequencing introduces alternations between A♭-D♭ and A-D that begin to point the way to his D♮ outcome. (See Ex. 9.)

Ex. 9: chromatic variations on Williams's "Father's Theme", from "Recollections", measures 13-27, from *Catch Me if You Can* (© 2002 BMI), published by Songs of SKG, ear transcription from the film's soundtrack. Used in compliance with U.S. Copyright Act, Section 107.

Stemming from the restarted phrase begun and then extended in the second half of the original theme (see Ex. 8, p. 59, measures 9 and 10), the overarching phrase structure of these variations expands upon this idea, repeating the definitive opening octave of each phrase at different transposition levels (moving through A to A♭, C, and finally D to D♭) to elaborate chromatically and rhythmically on the material at hand. Phrase endings also transition from cadences on D to D♭ throughout the passage. Notice again the now familiar gesture of interrupting a leading tone (C♯) resolution across measures 23 and 24, elided this time into the opening pitch D of the following phrase. A rubato section at measure 28 initiates a second set of variations which themselves reconceive frequented intervals from earlier variations as a part of an ongoing process of embellishment and reference. For instance, compare the first phrase of measure 30 (from earlier Ex. 3) — itself loosely retrograded in the next phrase — to the contour of the opening phrase from the first set of variations in measure 13 of Ex. 9 immediately above. These are but the initial procedures by which Williams establishes tonal centres, alters (or modulates) them, and wends thematic interrelationships through his atmospheric assembly — decidedly unrestricted by a leitmotivic framework.

By comparison, consider a corresponding procedure from Williams's more conventional primary compositional mode. The following examples depart momentarily from "Recollections" to illustrate Williams's execution of a prototypical diatonic modulation — in this case, within a scene from *Star Wars: The Empire Strikes Back* (Irvin Kershner, 1980). This example demonstrates his approach to relaying specific narrative events through the reinterpreted harmonic transposition of established character leitmotives and their melodic permutation. Once Luke Skywalker fails to lift his X-wing fighter out of the Dagobah swamp, Williams sets the scene's central music process in motion. As Luke's music subsides along with his submerging ship, a timely pep talk from Yoda on the ways of the force ushers in his own leitmotiv. (See Ex. 10.)

Ex. 10: Williams's opening to Yoda's leitmotiv (in E lydian) from *The Empire Strikes Back* (© 1980 BMI), published by Bantha Music/Warner-Tamerlane, ear transcription from the film's soundtrack. Used in compliance with U.S. Copyright Act, Section 107.

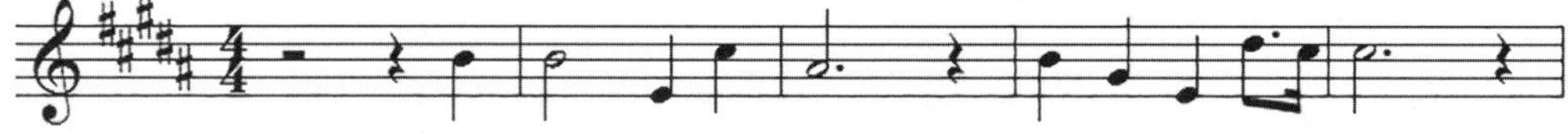

Cast in Williams's favoured lydian mode, Yoda's theme is marked by an opening falling perfect fifth, followed by another descent of a minor third transposed a step above to land on the raised fourth scale degree and emphasize the mode's definitive tritone. His monologue concluded, Yoda demonstrates by example, raising the ship out of the swamp himself in an inspired display. In preparation for this feat, Williams twice restarts Yoda's distinctive falling fifth in the scene's present mode of C lydian — first misstated in earnest by the French horn before the phrase elides into the oboe for correction. After a brief pause, the horn attempts the opening for a final time only to be interrupted as the two instruments gracefully join in duet precisely at the moment — a repeated, displaced C — where Williams effects a common-tone modulation to E lydian. Newly christened as a lowered submediant, the former tonic pitch now descends naturally to the dominant of the new mode commencing a more successful start to Yoda's theme, finally permitted to continue unobstructed. (See Ex. 11.)

Ex. 11: prototypical Williams common-tone modulation on Yoda's leitmotiv, "Yoda and the Force" from *The Empire Strikes Back* (© 1980 BMI), published by Bantha Music/Warner Tamerlane, ear transcription from the film's soundtrack. Used in compliance with U.S. Copyright Act, Section 107.

As the ship soars over the swamp, the music swells to a sudden, powerful climax built upon the very transformative interval by which Williams inaugurated Yoda's modulation. This same descending minor second (C-B), stated ever louder in the brass, repeats before expanding to a rising augmented second (C-D♯) enharmonically recalling Yoda's definitive minor third. A further ascent by a final perfect fifth (E-B) brilliantly reverses Yoda's opening interval just after as the X-wing fighter reaches its apex overhead and descends along with the music's register to touch down at the shoreline beside Luke. (See Ex. 12.)

Ex. 12: climactic intervallic variations on Yoda's modulation at X-wing apex, "Yoda and the Force" from *The Empire Strikes Back* (© 1980 BMI), published by Bantha Music/Warner-Tamerlane, ear transcription from the film's soundtrack. Used in compliance with U.S. Copyright Act, Section 107.

Inside a fairly short sequence, Williams wields a concentrated application of musical adjustment to unveil Yoda's abilities with striking dramatic effect. The pacing of this impressive, almost organic note-for-note harmonic orchestration of screen events is a hallmark of Williams's primary mode of film composition — directly programmatic, and devoted entirely to expressions of narrative precision and tonal clarity. "Recollections" is anything but. Governing the *Catch Me* score, his secondary mode manipulates wide-ranging moods with similarly less fixed harmonic and melodic statement. As Williams discusses: «For [Frank William Abagnale, Jr.]'s character [in *Catch Me if You Can*] — [though] he does go through all of these different permutations and disguises and so on — his music is really uniform. Whenever he's conceiving of a new scam, a new trick, this magical little music [...] invades his character and we go off with him on another escapade. And that little musical trigger is always the same»[40]. Gone is the investment in or usefulness of leitmotivic mimicry. The point here is to establish mood for contemplative reflection and variation through a prism of prevailing chromaticism.

As Williams's "Recollections" develops, his variations become more intertwined, revisiting earlier forms of embellishment and passing in and out of interrelated pitch centres lunging ever closer to D. The excerpt reproduced in Ex. 13 — from the piece's halfway point — reintroduces the distinctive opening dotted rhythm of the father's theme, now put through its own passing variations briefly implying D major. (See Ex. 13.)

Ex. 13: return of the "Father's Theme", from "Recollections", measures 45-53, from *Catch Me if You Can* (© 2002 BMI), published by Songs of SKG, ear transcription from the film's soundtrack. Used in compliance with U.S. Copyright Act, Section 107.

Further registral and agogic emphases on D are connected by a D locrian descending run at measure 48 immediately before a cadenza returns rather adamantly to B♭ major with a clear descending diatonic sequence accenting each successive triad of the key (I-vii°-vi-V-IV-iii-ii) in measures 54 and 55. Another locrian descent segues into a chromatic kaleidoscope of trills that conclude with a beleaguered leading-tone resolution to B♭ in measure 57. (See Ex. 14.)

Ex. 14: cadenza from "Recollections", measures 54-58, from *Catch Me if You Can* (© 2002 BMI), published by Songs of SKG, ear transcription from the film's soundtrack. Used in compliance with U.S. Copyright Act, Section 107.

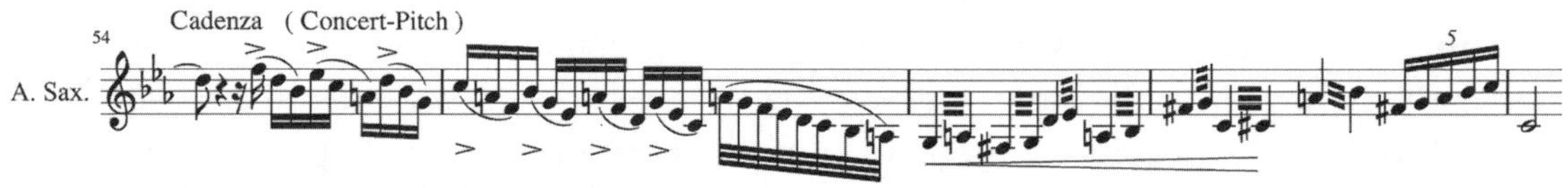

[40]. Williams in Bouzereau 2003.

At measure 59, the father's theme returns for the third and last time, now in the dominant pitch centre of D, making a final bid for the impending long-range resolution forecasted for the work's conclusion. (The leading tone G♯ is spelled enharmonically here as A♭.) Notice the customary chromatic variations on the original set of variations (again, deriving from measure 13 of Ex. 9 above) that follow the father's statement at measure 61. (See Ex. 15.)

Ex. 15: final statement of the "Father's Theme", from "Recollections", measures 59-63, from *Catch Me if You Can* (© 2002 BMI), published by Songs of SKG, ear transcription from the film's soundtrack. Used in compliance with U.S. Copyright Act, Section 107.

As his conclusion looms, Williams's texture suddenly shifts to stress briefly another non-committal octatonic collection (E-F-G-A♭), not unlike the scale referenced at the movement's cryptic introduction. Though sounding haphazard, the almost symmetrical, balanced pattern of these displaced octaves recalls the compound melodic retrograde contours of his main theme for *Kraft Suspense Theatre* (Ex. 1) four decades earlier. (See Ex. 16.)

Ex. 16: return of octatonicism anticipating conclusion of "Recollections", measures 68-70 with analysis, from *Catch Me if You Can* (© 2002 BMI), published by Songs of SKG, ear transcription from the film's soundtrack. Used in compliance with U.S. Copyright Act, Section 107.

It is also worth noting that this octatonic fragment (E-F-G-A♭), though referencing a separate collection, begins precisely where the earlier collection (A-B♭-C-D♭-E♭) would have resumed — with the pitch E. Moreover, the octatonic scale from which this collection is derived (based on A♭) deviates from the introductory octatonic collection (based on A) by only one other pitch, F♮ (versus F♯). Intensely interconnected pitch relationships such as these populate this movement as agents of compositional correspondence through which Williams mediates unity across its opening and closing.

The final moments of "Recollections" maintain the movement's overarching elements of rhythmic variation and chromatic camouflage while heralding its conclusive move to the prophesied D pitch centre. Note the final disruptions of the leading tone (C♯), including a clever emphasis on a premature tonic resolution displaced in an extreme low register just before the final pitch. (See Ex. 17.)

Ex. 17: "Recollections" conclusion, from *Catch Me if You Can* (© 2002 BMI), published by Songs of SKG, ear transcription from the film's soundtrack. Used in compliance with U.S. Copyright Act, Section 107.

Two basic observations may be drawn from this case study. First, over and above the more superficial elements of timbre and rhythm, it becomes increasingly clear that virtually no part of this piece is grounded in a popular music idiom. «There's not really a bluesy element or something you could do something with», offers Dan Higgins. «It's definitely chromatic, but it's not like jazz players going to a plus 11 as a way of getting above the harmony. […] It moves through different keys»[41]. Whatever popular models may have inspired the composer's concept for this project (what Williams described as «a kind of sixties swagger»), his resultant work veers sharply into a post-tonal art music context[42]. And while the contour of Williams's melody may approximate a jazz line to the uninitiated, his angularity ultimately owes more to Jacques Ibert than to Gershwin (never mind Charlie Parker). As Higgins appraises, «It's not rooted in the things that you could do a takedown to or want to play over»[43].

Second, if Williams's shift from D♭ to D♮ — in essence, a move from Bb minor to its parallel key, B♭ major — is common enough, his means of effecting it are less customary, especially in the arena of film music. Both his long-range voice leading and running variation technique are more closely bound up with art music practices tightly conceived from a complex chromaticism. In this case, the simple melodic abandonment of D♭ for D is achieved markedly differently from more traditional diatonic modulatory procedures that Williams employs adeptly elsewhere. Put simply, there is, fittingly, more of Abagnale's own troubled father than Darth Vader in the music of *Catch Me if You Can*.

41. Higgins 2017.
42. Williams in Bouzereau 2003.
43. Higgins 2017.

The Live *Catch Me* Experience: Programming Pop Concerts with the Boston Pops & Beyond

As part of his return for the 2003 Boston Pops season, Williams hosted Dan Higgins along with renowned singer Nancy Wilson for an instalment of the popular PBS program *Evening at Pops*. Keeping to the conventional Pops concert division of programs into three sections, or 'thirds', planned repertoire from each part of this concert highlighted mid-century music from a different perspective.

After the first third of this program presented film score selections surrounding this period — Laurence Olivier's *Richard III* (1955), Delbert Mann's *Jane Eyre* (1970), featuring George C. Scott and one of Williams's early film soundtracks, and outlier Orson Welles's *Citizen Kane* (1941) with music by Bernard Herrmann — Williams delighted his audience by walking through the logistics of film scoring itself. The second third opened with live demonstrations of real-time improvised accompaniment (sans orchestra) hailing from the silent era, followed by Williams conducting one of his own scored scenes from *Indiana Jones: The Last Crusade* (Steven Spielberg, 1989) screened above the orchestra. Higgins closed this third with excerpts from *Catch Me if You Can*, while the third third was devoted entirely to celebrated singer Nancy Wilson, an artist who Williams introduced to the stage as «the possessor of truly one of the best voices of her generation»[44]. Lastly, the program was capped off by at least one planned encore depending on time (in the case of Williams's visit, typically a selection from *E. T.: The Extra-Terrestrial*), and finally the Pops's eternal closer, Sousa's *Stars and Stripes Forever*. (See Ill. 1, p. 66).

Speaking to the differences in performing *Catch Me* in a live concert setting, Higgins conceded, «It's a little out of my area. [...] I think it's because it's a one-timer and you don't get that kind of edge as a studio player because you're punching in or fixing anything that's wrong. You have to gear up your mind and go straight ahead». Clarifying, he continued: «It's always thrilling because you just get to play. [In the studio] we rarely play it more than one time. But the little trio — bass, vibe, and I — will get together beforehand. [John] doesn't have time in those Pops rehearsals to get too detailed. And the orchestra is so good now you can do it with one rehearsal. [...] That's what's different: finally you get to play music without going tedious take after take, or with technical problems, or a noise, or something»[45]. A few scored differences do emerge between Higgins's live performance with the Boston Pops and his original soundtrack studio recording. Apart from orchestral cuts likely made for time, and a few embellished notes from Higgins, roughly three moments stand out where new passages were clearly added — written, not improvised — to the studio version of the score. The first briefly sets the saxophone line in loose call-and-response against the orchestra's

[44]. Williams 2003.

[45]. Higgins 2017.

* = Change/addition | Week 4, 2003 | FINAL NO. 2, 05/27/03

THE BOSTON POPS ORCHESTRA
KEITH LOCKHART, Conductor

Tuesday evening, May 27, 2003, at 8:00 [TV PREP]

JOHN WILLIAMS conducting

*4 Prelude to *Richard III* **[with cut!]** — Walton

14 Suite from *Jane Eyre* — Williams
At Lowood – To Thornfield – The Return

3 "The Inquirer," from *Citizen Kane* — Herrmann

SUBTOTAL TIME: 21

INTERMISSION

4 The Silent Era [no orch]
John Williams and Bob Winter, piano

12 Circus Train Chase, from *Indiana Jones and the Last Crusade* **[with discussion and demo]** — Williams

13 Escapades, for Alto Saxophone and Orchestra (from the film *Catch Me If You Can*) — Williams
DAN HIGGINS, saxophone
J. William Hudgins, vibraphone
Lawrence Wolfe, bass

3 Buckle Down Winsocki [new] — Martin/Blane-Williams/Nestico

SUBTOTAL TIME: 32

INTERMISSION

PRESENTING NANCY WILSON
with Llew Matthews, piano, John B. Williams, bass, and Roy McCurdy, drums

3 All of Me — Simmons/Marks-Matthews
5 Imagination — Burke/Van Heusen-Mishkin
3 It Don't Mean a Thing (If It Ain't Got That Swing) — Ellington-Nestico
3 Make Me Rainbows **[no orch, John Williams, piano]** — Williams/Bergman/Bergman
4 Embraceable You — Gershwin/Gershwin-Matthews
3 When October Goes — Manilow/Mercer-Matthews

SUBTOTAL TIME: 21
TOTAL TIME BEFORE ENCORES: 74
4 **ENCORE:** Flying Theme from *E.T.* — Williams
4 **ENCORE:** The Stars and Stripes Forever — Sousa
TOTAL TIME: 82

The Boston Pops Orchestra may be heard on
RCA Victor, Sony Classical and Philips Records.

ILL. 1: Production programme for 27 May 2003, *Evening at Pops* dress rehearsal presenting selections from *Catch Me if You Can* and Nancy Wilson. (Reproduced by permission of the Boston Symphony Orchestra.)

statement of the main "Father's Theme" during the "Recollections" inner movement. Two new duets highlighting the saxophone and vibraphone in further virtuosic flare are then added to open and close the final movement. No doubt these alterations represent the revisions included in Williams's print edition for the stand-alone collection of these set pieces — eventually entitled *Escapades for Alto Saxophone and Orchestra* — fashioned after the original score soon after the film's release.

As to preparation, «I practiced a lot harder for the live [performance] because it's such a physical piece for me», Higgins admitted. «I have to get up to where that's comfortable and I can have the endurance to play it. [...] The saxophone can sit around and play on jobs, but I'm not really practicing it. [...] So when I know I have a concert coming up I go to about a six-week run-up. A lot of that is not so much for the piece of music, it's for the stamina [...] to get up to recital quality»[46].

The concert's climax on the artistry of Nancy Wilson neatly complements many of the same factors informing the background and choices that led Williams to conceive *Catch Me if You Can*. Showcasing such standards as "All of Me", "It Don't Mean a Thing (If It Ain't Got That Swing)", and "Embraceable You", and referencing mainstream jazz and pop figures alike from Duke Ellington and George Gershwin to Johnny Mercer, Sammy Nestico, and Barry Manilow, Wilson's selections seem to strike an intentional stylistic balance. «If you've got to put me in a category», she observes, «basically I'm a song stylist. I like the term song stylist because it allows me the freedom to sing anything I like, anything I think will please my audience. It's about freedom. It's not about being in a category necessarily»[47].

The programming of Wilson's set invites the same conflation in style only just raised by Williams's blending of classical and pop idioms on the other side of intermission. «When I started professionally at fifteen», Wilson recalls, «I was singing what was the 'pop' of the day, and it was not considered jazz. When I starting signing, all the critics [responded], "Oh, jazz? Oh, you're kidding. No!" I was too commercial, I was too pop, and I liked it that way». Her comments about classification match Higgins's attempts to interpret Williams while straddling disparate stylistic expectation in his own performance. In negotiating distinctions between jazz and pop, Wilson further admits a similar indifference to improvisation, stressing her role as story teller. «I know that my roots are in R&B. I love jazz, but I don't scat», she acknowledges. «I don't think of myself in the traditional classic mode of an Ella Fitzgerald or a Billie Holiday. But I do read a lyric. It's about the lyrics. I want a story. I want to have a beginning and an end. I really want to talk»[48].

For the centrepiece of Wilson's set, Williams renewed his earlier pop tune, "Make Me Rainbows", (see Ex. 4, p. 50), featuring his own improvised piano accompaniment

---

46. *Ibidem*. As of this writing, a recording of Higgins's *Evening at Pops* performance may still be viewed at <https://www.youtube.com/watch?v=LlYRNBXygUc>, accessed February 2018.

47. Wilson 2003.

48. *Ibidem*.

skills in a rare, prominent display. «This is from 1967», Williams commented from the stage, «with a wonderful lyric by Alan and Marilyn Bergman. And there's a line in it, "Make me a room where I'll bloom out of season", which I thought was a lovely aspiration»[49]. As Wilson remembered, «When I first heard the song many years ago, I had never really realized until just recently that it *was* John's». Reaffirming her investment in text, Wilson welcomed the opportunity her duo with Williams afforded her «to be able to just do it directly and just to sing it in a different manner totally than I recorded it, and get the essence of what the song is about — it's really a beautiful lyric»[50]. Williams's savvy decision to exhibit an intimate performance of Wilson's own contradictions fashioned the best possible backdrop for his cherished Boston audience to receive a live concert presentation of his latest film work's inherent risks.

Since its May 2003 premiere at Boston Symphony Hall, programming of Williams's *Escapades for Alto Saxophone and Orchestra* has grown steadily, helped along in no small part by an edition published not long afterwards in association with the Hal Leonard Company[51]. «We've been back. We've done Tanglewood a couple of times», records Higgins, who also went on to record the final version of the edited work in September of 2016 — including a newly added cadenza for double bass — with Williams and the Recording Arts Orchestra of Los Angeles at Royce Hall (University of California, Los Angeles)[52]. In fact, counting additional engagements with the Los Angeles Philharmonic, the New York Philharmonic, and the Chicago Symphony, Higgins has personally performed the score live under Williams's direction on at least ten different occasions, averaging approximately one concert per year since 2003. As the *Escapades* arrangement has entered the classical saxophone repertoire over the last several years, a spate of recent performances across early 2017 alone starring such saxophone luminaries as Branford Marsalis, Timothy McAllister, and Christopher Creviston suggests no end to the allure of Williams's contribution to this literature[53].

***

Analytic intrigue notwithstanding, *Catch Me if You Can* has clearly proven popular in its own right. In his veiled effort to crossover with the popular idiom, Williams may well

49. Williams 2003.

50. Wilson 2003.

51. Other notable incarnations of the original score include a musical and a grade five arrangement for concert band.

52. Higgins 2017. One Tanglewood performance on 1 July 2011 replaced Nancy Wilson's set with another by James Taylor.

53. Marsalis performed with Orchestra Iowa on 10 and 11 March 2017, and McAllister soloed with the Knoxville Symphony Orchestra on 18 and 19 May 2017. Creviston was in recital with a piano arrangement at the University of Iowa on 28 March 2017. As a testament to this work's continued relevance, in January 2018 Williams's *Escapades* arrangement garnered him his twenty-fourth Grammy award.

have prospected some truly new stylistic strain — an appealing duality new generations of players and audiences have continued to discover and embrace, now far removed from the simple novelty of the composer's cachet. «The best thing about it», Higgins proposes, «is that it takes my area of work and brings it to the concert stage». Williams's manner of recasting the past in the present holds a compelling sway over nostalgic perspective on popular music history and significance. «To have him in our little world is great», Higgins remarks. «It makes [the studio musicians] feel that what they're doing has a lot of credibility because they're not in an orchestra and they've chosen this more commercial thing and they may be playing some fairly simple, mundane music day in and day out. And now they get this piece, this jewel»[54]. As he explains:

> It's a business, but John makes it not a business. He makes it a music happening wherever he goes with it and we just light up because we're just traveling at this other rate. I imagine in the fifties and sixties, every job was with all the great composers [like Jerry] Goldsmith. [...] Everything that I hear is juicy. Dated but juicy. And John always does some of that music. [...] Everybody gets melodies. There's heat. There's structure. There's harmony. It's just wonderful. [...] It's just one of those things where we're kind of keepers of the past, in a way, for the moment[55].

Though far closer to evoking the classical saxophone legacy of the last century than the commercial, the appeal of those innovative challenges forging Williams's unique sound world at this intersection of stylistic traditions continues to captivate performers and prove instructive for scholars on a variety of worthwhile, enduring fronts.

Bibliography

Bouzereau 2003

Bouzereau, Laurent. 'Scoring *Catch Me if You Can*'. Disc 2. *Catch Me if You Can*, directed by Steven Spielberg, DreamWorks Home Entertainment 90332 DVD, 2003.

Byrd 1997

Byrd, Craig L. 'Interview with John Williams', in: *Film Score Monthly*, ii/1 (January/February 1997), pp. 18-21, <http://www.filmscoremonthly.com/backissues/viewissue.cfm?issueID=10>, accessed January 2018.

Colburn 2004

Colburn, Major Michael J. 'John Williams Returns to Bands Where He Began 50 Years Ago', in: *The Instrumentalist*, lviii/11 (2004), pp. 12-17.

54. Higgins 2017.

55. *Ibidem*.

COPLAND – PERLIS 1984
COPLAND, Aaron – PERLIS, Vivian. *Copland: 1900 Through 1942*, New York, St. Martin's Press, 1984.

FALLON 2015
FALLON, Jimmy. Interview with J. J. Abrams, in: *The Late Night Show Starring Jimmy Fallon* (30 November 2015), <https://www.youtube.com/watch?v=-Z09yMczy2k>, accessed January 2018.

FEINBERG 2015
FEINBERG, Judy. 'At 20 years, Keith Lockhart keeps the Boston Pops on top', in: *The Patriot Ledger*, 2 May 2015.

HIGGINS 2017
HIGGINS, Dan. Personal interview with author, 31 May 2017.

JONES 2008
JONES, Ryan. '"Free Swing" and the Emergent Neophonic: Forging Progressive Jazz with Stan Kenton in the 1947 Dance Hall', in: *Jazz Research Journal*, II/1 (2008), pp. 29-54.

KENDALL 1993
KENDALL, Lukas. Liner notes, in: *«Star Wars» Trilogy: The Original Soundtrack Anthology*, 20th Century Fox CDs 07822-11012-2, 1993.

LANG 2016
LANG, Larry H. 'Interview with John Williams', 7 June 2016. Colonel Larry H. Lang, commander and conductor of The U.S. Air Force Band, <https://www.youtube.com/watch?v=HFXCfXkJSmA>, accessed January 2018.

MULLIKEN 2010
MULLIKEN, Seth. 'Ambient Reverberations: Diegetic Music, Science Fiction, and Otherness', in: *Sounds of the Future: Essays on Music in Science Fiction Film*, edited by Mathew J. Bartkowiak, Jefferson (NC) McFarland & Company, 2010, pp. 88-99.

WILLIAMS 1993
WILLIAMS, John. 'John Williams on *Star Wars* (Spring 1977)', liner notes, in: *Star Wars Trilogy: The Original Soundtrack Anthology*, 20th Century Fox CDs 07822-11012-2, 1993.

WILLIAMS 2003
ID. *Evening at Pops* (2003), in: *Evening at Pops*, WGBH/Boston Symphony Orchestra, episode #2705 2003, WGBH Media Archives, Boston MA, U.S.A.

WILSON 2003
WILSON, Nancy. *Evening at Pops* (2003), in: *Evening at Pops*, WGBH/Boston Symphony Orchestra, episode #2705 2003, WGBH Media Archives, Boston MA, U.S.A.

NO SHARKS, NO STARS, JUST IDIOMATIC SCORING AND SOUNDING ENGAGEMENT: JOHN WILLIAMS AS A 'CLASSICAL' COMPOSER[1]

Emile Wennekes
(UTRECHT UNIVERSITY)

IT WAS ONE OF THOSE BALMY AFTERNOONS in the Berkshires. Scene of the action: the impressive, open-air Koussevitzky Music Shed at Tanglewood, Lennox, Massachusetts. The date: the 4th of August, 2002. My parents-in-law, dressed-up to the nines, had invited us for a concert that would musically celebrate the 70th birthday of John Williams. That afternoon, Artist-in-Residence and birthday boy Williams conducted the Boston Symphony Orchestra in a programme of his own scores[2]. For me — a European musicologist — it was the first live encounter with Williams's concert-hall music. Soloist was the famous cellist Yo-Yo Ma. One of the pieces performed was *Concerto for Cello and Orchestra*, a commission by the B.S.O. which Ma had premiered eight years earlier to celebrate the opening of the other venue at Tanglewood, the rectangular Ozawa Hall. «Whatever virtues the concerto may have», Williams wrote, «can never surpass for me the experience of knowing and working with Yo-Yo Ma. Happily, and with complete justice, the world loves and reveres this man as I do and working with him is always a joyous journey to be treasured»[3]. Slightly to my surprise, this closing part of Williams's commentary on the concerto was not printed in the Tanglewood programme book of that year. Much more to my surprise, however, was that my father-in-law did not see any virtues at all in the performed piece. The music had not taken him on a «joyous journey», but instead on a grievous grade down from the classics. Himself an avowed admirer of

---

1. In admirable remembrance of Skip and Don Wilson.

2. The All-Williams programme opened with *Sound the Bells!*, after which *Concerto for Cello and Orchestra* was performed. After the intermission, "Immigration and Building" (from *American Journey*), *Heartwood*, "Rosewood" and "Pickin" (from *Three Pieces for Solo Cello*) followed. The finale was "Adventures on Earth" (from *E. T.: The Extra-Terrestrial*).

3. Quoted in the liner notes of the album *Yo-Yo Ma Plays the Music of John Williams*, Sony Classical 88697561452. See 2002 programme book, p. 31.

Williams's film music and married to a committed B.S.O. Overseer, he fully dismissed the composition as the sounding equivalent of the emperor's new clothes. During the intermission, an engaged discussion followed, centred around the question whether this music was humbug or high point. He bluntly criticized the non-critical audience as snobs, with no ear for real 'classical' music. It left me puzzled as to how to explain that, on the one hand, a composer was highly acclaimed for his quintessential film scores, while on the other hand, the scores that this same person created for the concert stage were unflinchingly condemned.

This cherished family anecdote is in many ways exemplary for the ambiguous reception of John Williams's music. One regularly encounters comments with a comparable tenor, for example as straightforwardly stated online, on 23 September 2001 by a certain Mr. Jose M. Martinez: Williams «does a fine work with film musical scores. But he is not a classical composer»[4]. Not just 'ordinary', albeit well-educated listeners, such as my late father-in-law, but also music scholars and critics struggle with this binary[5]. Others completely neglect one side or the other of William's double persona as a composer — when not even refusing to recognize both sides. This rejective approach is in line with an observation Emilio Audissino previously made: that John Williams has only «received little attention from essayists and critics, and sometimes a kind of ill-concealed animosity from scholars»[6].

The composer's absence in the literature is deafening. In Joseph Horowitz's *Classical Music in America: A History of its Rise and Fall* (2005), Williams is completely missing, both as film composer and as composer for the concert-hall. This, despite Horowitz's referring to «eclectics for whom neither Europe nor the concert-hall represent the measure of all things musical»[7]. Williams is equally absent in the 2017 reprint of Wilfrid Mellers's *Music in a New Found Land: Themes and Developments in the History of American Music* (originally from 1964). These may be older, perhaps dated publications, yet even in Richard Taruskin's monumental book series *The Oxford History of Western Music* (2005), Williams is nowhere to be found. Taruskin's five massive volumes define no less than musicology's present take on 'Western music'. They mark, yet they also mask. In them, Western music still «means what it has always meant in general academic histories: it means what is usually called 'art music' or 'classical music'»[8]. Film music is obviously still alien to said domain. But where the disregard of his film scores within the ambience of 'classical' (that is: elite)

4. <https://www.amazon.com/John-Williams-Treesong-Concerto-Schindlers/product-reviews/B00005M05E>. Accessed March 218.

5. For example, on the negative reception that Williams's *Concerto for Violin and Orchestra* received in first instance, see Tom Schneller's chapter in this volume.

6. Audissino 2014, p. 4.

7. Horowitz 2005, p. 539.

8. Taruskin 2005, vol. 1, p. xxii.

music may to a certain extent be defendable, even understandable — despite the significant mark these scores have put on the sound of the twentieth century —, the fact that he is not even mentioned in a footnote among the Lucullian amount of Western composers reviewed, is arresting. Leonard Bernstein and George Gershwin — to name just two composers who also had careers in multiple musical domains — did have the honour to be included by the above-mentioned publications, despite the fact that their contribution to the classical repertoire is quantitatively far less significant. The many prestigious awards and commissions Williams has received from illustrious classical institutions and individuals appear to be of absolutely no relevance when these are confronted with the agencies of a scholarly canon.

One of the conclusions a reader could therefore draw from these publications is that John Williams is not considered to belong to the classical music canon; that he is perhaps not 'good enough' for the canon. Perhaps his music is not even considered to be a proponent of 'art music'. However, according to Lawrence Kramer, «What makes a score 'classical' is the particular relationship between the way it is written and the way it is treated»[9]. To loosely adopt this remark: John Williams, as a composer of concert-hall music which is widely performed by classically profiled orchestras, ensembles and individual musicians, necessarily deserves to be treated just like any other 'classical' composer.

This chapter addresses this 'John Williams, the classical composer'. His 'classical' oeuvre[10] consists of works scored for symphony orchestra, chamber ensemble, and brass band. The compositions represent a great variety of musical genres, styles, lengths, and strengths. Fanfares and celebratory works for brass bands, as well as concerti for solo instruments and orchestral repertoire are most prominent. Some are programmatic in inspiration while others can be interpreted as being more 'absolute'. Celebrations and birthdays prompted several new additions to this oeuvre, whereas a handful of works was composed to celebrate sports events (for example, those for various Olympic Games).

In Williams's concert-hall oeuvre, he proves himself to be an artist who is indissolubly connected with the craftsman, or as the French so neatly term it: he blends *l'artiste et l'artisan*. The interwoven nature between these can be demonstrated by a tremendous richness of musical ideas which are cast in highly idiomatic scores for various instruments, all presented within tightly knit musical structures. One not even need look at the larger orchestral compositions to realize the richness. The synthesis of the artist and the artisan can just as effectively be demonstrated by a delicate short piece such as *Air and Simple Gifts* (2009), which I will discuss later in the chapter. Here, an eloquent representation of an old Shaker melody is both richly and colourfully featured in each individual instrument.

---

9. Kramer 2007, p. 81.

10. In this chapter, I refer to Williams's non-filmic scores either as 'classical' or as concert-hall compositions. I deem the term 'concert works', often used in the literature, confusing due to the fact that a large part of his 'classical' output exists of concertos for a solo-instrument with orchestral accompaniment.

When comparing the different personae of John Williams as a film-music composer and as a concert-hall composer, one might conclude that the musical material may not always differ that much; form and format however do — and style even more so. Williams the film composer and Williams the concert composer are two peas in a pod, yet they do differ at specific, crucial points. In his film scores, Williams expresses first and foremost the feelings and the ideas of the director; in his concert-hall music, we hear more of his personal engagement. Overt references and subtle homages to the jazz musicians he has admired since his youth (among them: Claude Thornhill, Billy Strayhorn and Duke Ellington) are thematically referenced. Williams's explicit political, social, and environmental involvement is even more salient. Those are manifested in celebratory pieces for famed (Democratic!) politicians, while in his various references to trees and wildlife, Williams expresses a rural nostalgia paired with Biblical inspiration. Even more conspicuous are the explicit references to the Civil Rights movement or the oppression of Native and Afro-Americans in the course of America's history. These references form noticeable topics in his concert-hall oeuvre, carved as they are in the titles of pieces and movements, as well as through the incorporation of texts by most notable authors, including U.S. Poet Laureate and Pulitzer Prize winner Rita Dove (b. 1952).

When John Williams uses referential titles for his compositions, it does not mean that these associations are to be interpreted as programmatic in a traditional sense, for example when the listener is enticed to follow a musical translation of some narrative, line by line. No; Williams opts for a more overarching idea via this direct denoting of trees, images, or situations. The connotation at large is essentially 'abstract'. Or, as he himself formulated it in his comments on *TreeSong* (2000), a composition inspired by a metasequoia tree in Boston's Public Garden: «The piece doesn't aspire to 'describe' the tree per se, but it does attempt, in my mind at least, to connect, to the degree possible, the great beauty and dignity of this magnificent conifer»[11].

Williams's concert repertoire is basically instrumental. Relevant to orchestration, there are similarities between Williams the film composer and his concert-hall doppelgänger. In both repertoires, we regularly encounter bombastic brass parts in open fifths, whipped-up percussion marches and optimistic sound, heroic melodies in lavish modal structures where major chords rule over minor harmonies. Yet, there are differences as well — in terms of idiom, structure, as well as harmonic language. Many of the orchestral compositions are multi-movement pieces that allude to classical forms, genres or tempo indications (such 'Cadenza', 'Scherzo', 'Rondo', 'Molto Allegro'). Movements of later works tend to be titled with more poetic license or association (take: 'The Tree Sings' or 'The Family Argument'). Williams often composes the movements back to back — *attacca* — without clear distinction or pauses between the subsequent parts, overall affording the music a through-composed touch.

---

[11]. Liner notes from the album *TreeSong – Violin Concerto – Three Pieces from Schindler's List.*

No Sharks, No Stars, Just Idiomatic Scoring and Sounding Engagement

In most of his orchestral pieces, Williams displays a consistent musical discourse, a gravitation towards diatonic or modal essentials spiced on occasion with more dissonant modernities. Since his *Concerto for Violin and Orchestra* (1974-76), the composer has landed on what he considers a personal style. Tom Schneller, in his analysis featured in this book, qualifies this personal style as a «synthesis of modernism and neoromantic expression»[12]. One can easily detect influences from Stravinsky, Ravel, Barber, Berg, Bernstein, Bartók, Copland, Elgar, Holst, Tchaikovsky, Richard Strauss, Richard Wagner and not to forget: John Philip Sousa — *bien étonnés de se trouver ensemble.*

Having mentioned this fraternity, one may idly qualify John Williams as a straight-limbed traditionalist, as a nostalgist. But it is just too lazy to refer to Williams as a *gazza ladra*, a thieving magpie, as Norman Lebrecht did[13]. More willingly, one could argue that Williams simply pays his respectful dues to Western music tradition, especially that of the late nineteenth century up and until the mid-twentieth, including jazz. In this sense, the following lines from *America, the Dream goes on* can perhaps be read as metaphorical of the composer's personal position towards music history:

> [...] the voices are changing,
> The song's the same as it sings from sea to sea,
> [...] as long as the music is strong and clear[14].

Strong in generating impressions with the ultimate twelve tones to choose from, Williams's music is clear in voice and fabric. Having said that, there are also substantial concert pieces which express a significantly freer, atonal sound world — a drifting away from anything diatonic to cling to, as a result of the triadic distortions, pan-tonality, ample use of octatonic scales, *et cetera*. Yet, harmonic language is just one of the components that characterize a style of a composer; preferred instrumental combinations is another. In this specific respect, Williams also distinctively digested Western tradition.

Orchestral Scores[15]

«The symphony orchestra [...] is one of the greatest inventions of our artistic culture», John Williams once stated, «Fabulous sounds it can produce and a great range of emotional

12. See Tom Schneller's article in this volume.

13. Lebrecht 2002. A rebuttal of Lebrecht's claims is in Audissino 2014, pp. 138-140.

14. Lyrics by Alan and Marilyn Bergman.

15. Unless otherwise stated, the observations in this chapter are primarily based on aural analyses by the author of recordings available online and on CDs, on widespread programme notes, as well as on Williams's web site <http://www.johnwilliams.org/compositions>. Additional information has been acquired via discussions on the <http://www.jwfan.com website>. (Both websites accessed March 2018.) Unfortunately, (orchestral) scores are not always available. Not all premiere dates could be traced in detail for this occasion.

capabilities»[16]. It can be argued that Williams realizes an even more variegated range of emotions and a more versatile spectrum of sounds and timbres in his 'classical' compositions than in an average film score by his hand. In the diversity of styles, scoring, tonal idioms, as well in the choice of specific genres, his concert-hall music offers much eclectic variation, so much so that generalizations can hardly do it justice. Consequently, the following section discusses Williams's classical works *grosso modo* per instrumental combination. The compositions which are reviewed here are specific, original compositions. Arrangements of (parts of) Williams's film scores, frequently found in live concert programmes, as well on audiovisual media and online formats, will be left unconsidered. For reasons of coherence and space, the stage musical *Thomas and the King* (1975; lyrics James Harbert)[17] will not be reviewed. Most fanfares for brass band are only mentioned in the passing.

Focussing on instrumentation, Williams's concert-hall music can roughly be divided into works scored for symphony orchestra (with or without instrumental soloists), compositions scored for diverse types of wind and string orchestras, and various chamber musical combinations. Vocal compositions (or those with vocal additions) are exceptions to the rule. Numerically, pieces scored for large orchestra stand out. Williams's symphonic scores commonly employ a conventional large, but not extra-large orchestra, with added piano and sometimes organ. The percussion section is multi-coloured. It offers various melodic possibilities in diverse registers, a rich spectrum of timbres, as well as a wealth of hit, strike, and bang possibilities (the way a sound is produced is part of the instrument's identity). In Williams's scores, a large percussion section contains chimes, gran cassa, snare drum, bells, piatti, ratchet, sizzle and suspended cymbals, triangle, tambourine, marimba, xylophone, vibes and celeste (often doubled with the piano). The wind section generally consists of three flutes (of which the third doubles as piccolo), three oboes (the third doubling on cor anglais), two to three clarinets (third doubling on A clarinet and/or bass clarinet), and two to three bassoons (third as contra bassoon). The brass section profiles four horns in F, three trumpets in C or B flat, two to three trombones with bass trombone, and often tuba. Timpani, harp and strings (first and second violins, violas, celli and double basses) complete the orchestra in many of Williams's scores[18].

This instrumentation was, however, not fully crystallized in the mid-sixties when Williams presented some experimental works. His first concert-hall composition was a 'semi-symphonic' score in big-band style (including rhythm section): *Prelude and Fugue* (1965)[19]. The piece was written for the progressive Los Angeles Neophonic Orchestra

16. Quoted in Audissino 2014, p. 127.

17. See <http://www.guidetomusicaltheatre.com/shows_t/thomasandtheking.htm>, accessed February 2018.

18. For more on the orchestral colours in Williams's music, see Ian Sapiro's chapter in this volume.

19. Premiered 29 March 1965, by the Los Angeles Neophonic Orchestra, conducted by Stan Kenton.

lead by jazz pianist Stan Kenton[20]. In just under ten minutes, the work offers a Third Stream[21], *film noir* atmosphere. Later that same year, Williams's expressive *Essay for Strings* was presented[22]. *Essay for Strings* is stretched out over some eleven minutes and is written in one movement. The composition is poignantly 'contemporary' in texture — more modern than most of Williams's later works, not neo-romantic in gesture this time, but rather expressionist. The main theme is written in a loosely configured serial idiom. After a nocturnal introduction, the expressive twelve-tone theme demands centre stage, performed in unison. The theme gradually gathers more and more rhythmical pulse and evolves into a groovy pizzicato episode. This groove persists in a lightly canonical whirlwind affecting the whole string orchestra, one section at a time until the unison motive dominates the entire ensemble once more. Finally, a short figure brings the work to a halt with an exclamation mark.

After *Essay for Strings*, André Previn also conducted the premiere of Williams's ("First") *Symphony* from 1966[23]. The *Symphony* was only performed twice (in Houston in 1968 and during a performance at the Royal Festival Hall, London, 1972). After these concerts, Williams withdrew the piece. All the references to the unreleased score are now meticulously deleted. In the opening *Allegro*, two basic melodies figure within a simple metric structure. The subsequent *Andante Sostenuto* is once again moderately jazz-inspired, embracing a flute solo that has the flavour of the later Eric Dolphy[24]. The concluding *Maestoso: Allegro Risoluto* relapses to the first movement, now using the melodic material for fugal variation and a waltz parody. Famous film composer Bernard Herrmann seems to have been instrumental in writing the *Symphony*. An anecdote describes how Herrmann called Williams after he had attended a performance and delivered a telling review by phone: «There was a nice tune in the second movement. Why ya covered (that) with all that stuff, with all that excessive orchestration!»[25]. A revision of the *Symphony* was scheduled for a performance in 1987, again by the Houston Symphony Orchestra (this time with an altered second movement and a rewritten finale). When push came to shove, however, this part of the programme was cancelled in favour of some of his film-music concert arrangements.

After John Williams had taken over the baton of the Boston Pops in 1980, he composed a series of short, occasional pieces especially for this orchestra. His predecessor Arthur Fiedler had already requested Williams to write a compact march to commemorate his 50th anniversary as conductor of the Pops, yet only posthumously, when Williams

20. Sparke 2010, pp. 194-201.

21. The fusion of jazz and classical music is qualified as 'Third Stream' by Gunther Schuller.

22. Premiered 6 December 1965, by the Houston Symphony Orchestra, conducted by André Previn.

23. Premiered 21 October 1968, by the Houston Symphony Orchestra, conducted by André Previn.

24. See Valverde Amador 2013, p. 36.

25. Smith 1991, p. 259.

himself had taken the helm, was he able to complete the piece for his predecessor, which came to be known as *Pops on the March* (1981)[26]. The five-minute tribute is centred around a four-part rhythmic cell which reflects the rhythm of Arthur Fiedler's name. From melodic onsets in the brass section, the cell leads to the woodwinds until the orchestra presents the theme in full. Via breaks and a second theme, as well as quotes from Sousa's *The Stars Stripes Forever*, the piece comes to a facetious finale. It is one of those pieces in which the artisan in Williams joyously and convincingly shakes hands with the imaginative artist, however very short the piece may be.

Esplanade Overture (1982)[27] is another short, less than five-minute introduction to a fictitious comedy for which the listeners themselves have to make up the narrative. The overture is a lavish and varied melodic scherzo with an ongoing drive, and abundantly orchestrated. It is «a colorful and bouncy work designed to show off the sections of the orchestra while celebrating the pleasures of music-making and music-listening on the Esplanade»[28], according to the original liner notes[29]. The *Overture* reworks parts of the score to *Monsignor* (Frank Perry), from the same year, in particular the cue «Reunion in Italy».

A Hymn to New England (1987)[30] originated as an underscore for the short film *New England Time Capsule* which functioned as an introduction to all the feature-length presentations in the Mugar Omni Theater at Boston's Museum of Science. Since Williams was fully immersed in completing new film scores, this time — exceptionally — he only composed the melodies. Boston Pops percussionist Patric 'Pat' Hollenbeck (b. 1955) orchestrated the music and arranged it to underscore the museum's IMAX movie. Condensed to a three-minute concert version, it features noble trumpets, hymn-like string tunes, all leading to a majestic, fully orchestrated final C-major chord, even augmented with an organ.

Besides his tribute march for Fiedler, Williams honoured two other conductors: Leonard Bernstein and Seiji Ozawa[31]. The short *For New York* (also known as *To Lenny! To Lenny!*) (1988)[32] was composed for Bernstein for the occasion of his 70th birthday and entails, among others, variations on themes from Bernstein's *Westside Story*. When principal B.S.O. conductor Seiji Ozawa celebrated his 25th anniversary with the orchestra, Williams marked this jubilee with the salute *For Seiji!* (1999, also known as *Tributes!*[33]) in the form of a dazzling, demanding concert for orchestra of about ten minutes. The composer himself

26. Premiered 28 April 1981, by the Boston Pops, conducted by John Williams.

27. Premiered 3 March 1983, by the Boston Pops, conducted by John Williams.

28. This remark refers to the Charles River Esplanade, the landmark park of Boston which houses a large open-air concert venue, the Hatch (Memorial) Shell, as well as the Arthur Fiedler Memorial Monument.

29. Quoted at <http://hmongbuy.net/video/qs92ZUIPkZw>, accessed March 2018.

30. Premiered 5 May 1987, by the Boston Pops, conducted by John Williams.

31. On the occasion of Andris Nelsons's appointment as the new Music Director of the B.S.O., Williams honoured him with the brass fanfare *A Toast!* (2014).

32. Premiered Summer 1988, at Tanglewood.

33. Premiered 22 April 1999, by the B.S.O., conducted by Seiji Ozawa.

qualified the piece as «a collection of musical thoughts and jottings that form a kind of Festschrift for orchestra»[34]. Based on the interval of a major second and «a five-note melodic idée fixe», it displays the richness of the orchestra in up-tempo while featuring miniatures for the soloists within the orchestra. To jointly celebrate the birthdays of Ozawa, Yo-Yo Ma and Itzhak Perlman, Williams composed the droll *Variations on Happy Birthday* (1995)[35], which includes a hilariously derailment through false notes, as well as the tune laboriously presented elsewhere by timpani and chimes.

A few years ahead of the festivities to commemorate the discovery of the Americas by Columbus in 1492, Williams had already composed his *Celebrate Discovery!* (1990)[36]. The piece makes use of all the appropriate clichés for such a celebratory occasion, yet it catches the audience occasionally off-guard. The just-under-four-minute homage commences with one of Williams's signature fanfare statements. Shortly after, however, he kicks the listener off balance by moving to a different harmonic atmosphere which engulfs the main theme with a prominent horn presence. A moment of introspection follows in which violins and cellos echo each other before the piece transports the listener back to the festive atmosphere introduced earlier.

More substantial is a composition for the occasion of the 2000 Millennium festivities, *American Journey* (1999)[37]. This is an orchestral suite of twenty-five minutes, with two narrators that quote famous poets and politicians. It is a revision of *The Unfinished Journey* that accompanied the eponymous multimedia presentation for the Millennium celebration, commissioned by then U.S. President Bill Clinton and directed by Steven Spielberg. We hear a voice-over by Clinton, with further collaboration by Poets Laureate Rita Dove, Maya Angelou and Robert Pinsky. Text writer Tim Willcocks further incorporated quotes by Abraham Lincoln and Martin Luther King. The composition moors at six thematic jetties; each alludes to a decisive historical event, together summarizing the twentieth century from an American perspective. "Immigration and Building" incorporates quotes from the epic adventure film *Far and Away* (Ron Howard, 1992). In its opening movement, the orchestra metaphorically reflects on the birth of the nation, with references to the erection of the Empire State Building and the construction of interstate highways. "The Country at War" features lyrical strings that meditate on the Second World War. "Popular Entertainment" is a scherzo summary of the world of entertainment, whereas "Arts and Sports" offers a whimsical escape, alluding to characters including baseball legends Joe DiMaggio and Mark McGwire. "Civil Rights and the Women's Movement" pays tribute to those who sacrificed their lives for said campaigns. This movement features a theme that recalls the combative, optimistic melody of "Dry Your Tears, Afrika" from the film *Amistad*

34. <https://www.pacificsymphony.org/tickets/ACF/the_music/tributes_for_seiji>, accessed March 2018.

35. Premiered 23 May 1995, by the B.S.O., conducted by John Williams.

36. Premiered 4 July 1990, by the Boston Pops Esplanade Orchestra, conducted by John Williams.

37. Premiered 31 December 1999.

(Steven Spielberg, 1997). The same mood is continued in "Flight and Technology", which functions as a heartening epilogue.

Parts of Williams's concert-hall repertoire exist in multiple orchestrations, one example being *Sound the Bells!*[38]. In 1993, Williams composed this piece which was inspired by Japanese temple bells and intended to be performed on a Boston Pops tour of Japan. Chimes, tubular bells, glockenspiel and other, comparable bell-sounding percussion instruments are displayed in the musical shop window, predominantly accompanied by brass. The work was offered as a wedding gift to the Japanese Crown Prince Naruhito and Masako Owada, and the success of it prompted Williams to subsequently arrange it for full orchestra.

On New Year's Day, 1995, Seiji Ozawa conducted a concert in Tokyo with his Saito Kinen Orchestra, also featuring violinist Isaac Stern and Yo-Yo Ma. The concert marked the 40th anniversary of the end of the Second World War. For the occasion, Williams had composed a short, five-minute orchestral piece with choral supplements, entitled *Satellite Celebration* (1994). The cantata with Japanese text was broadcasted throughout Japan. Williams reworked the piece without the chorus, renaming it *Song for World Peace* in 2002, and subsequently expanded the solos in the version premiered in 2012. This latter mainly profiles woodwinds and strings which sound out a contemplative desire for peace, including more elaborate solos for violin and cello.

For diverse sporting events, Williams composed occasional short works involving brass fanfares and marching drums; in these, the strings typically express their lyrical register, such as in *Olympic Fanfare and Theme* (1984)[39], or in the arresting, melodic modulations and folklore-colours displayed in *Olympic Spirit* (1988, the tune used for the NBC Seoul Games broadcasts) — *Indiana Jones* and *Jurassic Park* never seem too far away in the sound of many of these occasional pieces. *Summon the Heroes* (1995)[40], composed for the Centennial Olympic Games in Atlanta, 1996, may not directly recall an ancient Greek sports event, the opening fanfare rather runs the gauntlet of a medieval knight tournament in Hollywood splendour with a bit of *Jurassic Park* thrown in. The bombastic *Call of the Champions* (2001) was composed for the Salt Lake City Winter Olympic Games of 2002. Williams himself conducted the Utah Symphony and the Mormon Tabernacle Choir during the opening ceremony of the Games, with the massive choir vocalizing and performing the Olympic motto *citius, altius, fortius*[41]. If there is a partial oeuvre of Williams's orchestral, non-filmic work that does recall his soundtrack scores, then it is in celebratory pieces like these which reach out to a noticeably broader audience[42].

---

38. Premiered 10 June 1993, by the Boston Pops, conducted by John Williams.

39. Premiered 28 July 1984.

40. Officially premiered 19 July 1996, by the Atlanta Symphony Orchestra, conducted by John Williams.

41. Premiered 8 February 2002.

42. Other celebratory fanfares comparable in style and gesture are: *Fanfare for a Festive Occasion* (1980), *Jubilee 350 Fanfare, Liberty Fanfare* (1986), *Celebration Fanfare* (1986), *Winter Games Fanfare* (1988), *Fanfare*

No Sharks, No Stars, Just Idiomatic Scoring and Sounding Engagement

The opening of the Walt Disney Concert-hall in Los Angeles prompted Williams to compose the fifteen-minute composition *Soundings* (2003)[43], It is scored for an extensive orchestra with, for example, four flutes, six horns, even an additional synthesizer. Although through-composed as in a single movement, the piece addresses five different sounding phenomena. Each were allotted its own musical moment, enabling the orchestra to show off the acoustic specifics of the new hall: "The Hall Awakens", "The Hall Glistens", "The Hall Responds", "The Hall Sings", and "The Hall Rejoices".

The most recent addition to Williams's catalogue of occasional short pieces for orchestra is *Just Down the Street... On the Left* (2015)[44], written for the 75th anniversary of the Tanglewood Music Center. This four-and-a-half minute work kicks off yet again with a fierce brass fanfare while in a continuous drive all the colours of the orchestra are proffered their moment of glory, with twinkling glockenspiel passages, brass and chimes smashes, and repetitive pulsing strings.

Vocal Compositions with Orchestra

John Williams only composed a handful of vocal concert-hall pieces. While *American Journey* addresses patriotism, the previous cantata *America, The Dream Goes On* (1982), for vocal solo (tenor), chorus and orchestra, already celebrated this topic *a fortiori*. The short (some four and a half minutes), yet massively orchestrated piece is a galvanizing anthem in which American mythology, history and patriotism are concentrated into one heroic score. A prominent snare drumbeat immerses Ravel's *Boléro* into a military march, while the brass section builds a massive, pugnacious wall of sound — as if we witnessed the heroic entrance of the Romans in a Miklós Rózsa-scored film. In an ongoing crescendo, the lyrics are moved from vocal soloist to a large choir. The lyrics stem from the famed, Academy Award winning songwriting couple Alan and Marilyn Bergman (b. 1925 and 1929, respectively)[45]. An excerpt of the lyrics will suffice to illustrate the tone: «And the words that we read on the courthouse walls / And the words that make us free / And the more we remember the way we began / The closer we get to the best we can be. / Was there ever a time we forgot it's worth / All the struggles and the scars / If we leave to the children a sky full of hope / And a flag that's filled with stars. / America, America,

for Ten-Years Old (1988), *Fanfare for Michael Dukakis* (1988), *Fanfare for Prince Philip (Aloft... To the Royal Masthead)* (1992), *Fanfare for Fenway* (2012), *Fanfare "For the President's Own"* (2013).

43. Premiered 23 October 2003, by the Los Angeles Philharmonic Orchestra, conducted by John Williams.

44. Premiered 5 July 2015 by the Tanglewood Student Orchestra, conducted by Stefan Ashbury.

45. The Bergmans wrote texts for film, stage and television shows, and collaborated with an impressive number of artists of diverse stylistic plumage, among these Quincy Jones, Frank Sinatra, Michael Jackson, Barbara Streisand and Céline Dion.

and the dream goes on!». For some, the over the top patriotic flavour and its formulaic fabric make this cantata disputed within Williams's repertoire. Critical listeners have even deemed it 'corny', yet the piece is convincing in its sincerity, in Williams's heartfelt love for his country, moulded into an ear-worm melody. Five years later, Williams once again incorporated lyrics by the Bergman couple in *We're looking good!* (1987)[46], composed for the Special Olympics that year and available in two versions, for military band as well as for full orchestra. The vocal version was premiered with the inclusion of some 550 Olympic athletes from sixty-three countries singing the lyrics. The orchestral version had been premiered by the Boston Pops some two months before[47].

Seven for Luck (1997) is of a total different magnitude[48]. It is a song cycle for mezzo-soprano and full orchestra[49] setting to music seven poems by Rita Dove. In an interview, Dove reminisced on how the work was jointly created: «(W)e started by talking about what each of us imagined a cycle was meant to do, how the genre of the song cycle is very similar to that of the poem cycle, and we educated each other on the way those two things worked. I would begin writing a poem I imagined being sung and would send him fragments, a line here or there; or he'd call and say, "I hear flute, and a woman's voice" and actually hum a few bars! Then I'd write words to fit that melody, and eventually we were completing each other's sentences — whether melodic lines or actual lines of poetry. So that's one example of a strict collaboration»[50]. The cycle is approximately eighteen minutes and narrates the various stages of a woman's life, addressing such topics as going out, courting, love, pregnancy, adultery, and the like. The poems have been put to music with an African-American rhythmical flavour. The songs have perfect syllabic settings, explore the entire register of the voice and are delicately balanced between faster and slower passages. The specific poems are: "Song", "Chocolate", "Adolescence", "Black on a Saturday Night", "Serenade", "Expecting", "Starting Over". An excerpt from "Black on a Saturday Night" may illustrate their invocative atmosphere: «the wages of living are sin / and the wages of sin are love / and the wages of love are pain / and the wages of pain are philosophy / which leads definitely to an attitude / and an attitude will get you / nowhere fast so you might as well / keep dancing dancing till / tomorrow gives up with a shout, / 'cause there is only / Saturday night, and we are in it / black as black can, / black as black does, / not a concept / nor a percentage / but a natural law».

---

46. Premiered 5 May 1987, by the Boston Pops, conducted by John Williams.

47. Orchestral version premiered 5 May 1987, by the Boston Pops, conducted by John Williams.

48. Complete cycle premiered 25 July, 1998 by Cynthia Haymond (soprano) and the B.S.O., conducted by John Williams. The songs were originally composed for Kathleen Battle, but she never sang them.

49. An arrangement for soprano and piano is also available.

50. Gzemski 2016.

SOLO CONCERTS FOR STRING INSTRUMENTS

The 'opus meter' currently indicates some sixteen concertos for various solo instruments with orchestral accompaniment of diverse scoring. Williams concerti tend to be relatively short, generally somewhere around twenty minutes in length, and are, without exception, remarkably contemporary additions to the repertoires of the featured instruments. In the details, they often recall canonical pieces in displaying the wealth of possibilities the instruments have to offer, albeit not in a pastiche-like demeanour but more like a *connoisseur* who knows all the ins and outs of the solo instruments under consideration and how these were creatively treated by the grand masters of the past.

Pivotal is the (first) *Concert for Violin and Orchestra* (1974-1976; revised 1998)[51]. In his meticulous analysis for this volume, Schneller qualifies the concerto as Williams's «most intensely personal work» and as no less than «an American counterpart to Alban Berg's violin concerto»[52]. In some thirty minutes, the violin concerto is clearly a neoclassical composition, including a solo-cadenza, one which furthers proven forms and structures, but in a contemporary idiom. There are three overarching movements: "Moderato" / "Slowly" / "Broadly, Quickly". Clear, lyrical melodies alternate with contrasting subjects, all presented in a colourful orchestral palette which embraces atonal and chromatic elements.

Some twenty-five years later, Williams published a second violin concerto: *TreeSong* (2000)[53], a piece dedicated to Gil Shaham. The opening movement refers to the Chinese botanist Dr. Shiu-Ying Hu (1910-2012), author of the more-than-nine-hundred-page encyclopedia *Food Plants of China* (2005). Williams was introduced to her while she worked at Harvard in the late nineties. Hu was the one who had brought seeds of the prehistoric Chinese dawn redwood tree to the U.S., and North-American metasequoias — Williams's favourite tree — are descendants from those very same seeds. The concerto is written in Williams's characteristic modernistic, strongly chromatic musical language and embedded in a delicate, nonetheless rich orchestration. The slow opening movement is entitled "Doctor Hu and the Metasequoia". Reticently orchestrated with strings, piano, marimba, harp and celeste, the accompanying instruments provide a continuously reiterated, 'dreamily' framework for the soloist. The solo violin then kisses the melody glissandi to life via a four note motive in a misty meadow soundscape. The orchestra regains its full power in the central movement, "Trunks, Branches and Leaves". This is the quicker one of the three and contains the solo cadenza. After a series of climaxes with competitive brass parts and gentle horn accompaniment, the concerto gradually returns to the opening mood in the closing movement, "The Tree Sings".

---

51. Premiered by Mark Peskanov (violin) and the Saint Louis Symphony Orchestra, conducted by Leonard Slatkin.

52. See Tom Schneller's article in this volume.

53. Premiered July 2000, by Gil Shaham (violin) and the B.S.O., conducted by John Williams.

The most recent addition to Williams's violin concerti is the intimate, seven-minute miniature concerto *Markings*, for solo violin, strings and harp (2017), composed at the request of the famous German violinist Anne-Sophie Mutter[54]. After a melancholic, minor-mode mood in the opening theme which incorporates an open-string passage, a light wink to Alban Berg's concerto, this new concerto leads to a brief but fiery, syncopated middle section, with virtuoso violin figurines. The soloist subsequently surges forward to an unaccompanied cadenza which gradually returns to the pensive atmosphere of the outset before culminating in a daring, sustained, high-register tone.

Williams also embraced other members of the violin family. *Concerto for Viola and Orchestra* (2009)[55] is a three-part composition dedicated to violist Cathy Basrak. The piece opens with a lyrical viola melody in a subdued mood. The second movement, entitled "Family Argument", puts the viola and the timpani centre stage while they commence a competitive duet. In the end, the viola is revealed to be the winner. The final movement features the cadenza, accompanied by harp.

Concert for Cello and Orchestra (1993-1994)[56] is a four-movement piece ("Theme and Cadenza" / "Blues" / "Scherzo" / "Song"), of which each movement melts *attacca* into the next episode, forging an overarching form which makes it sound like a one-part composition. After being repeated four times, the short blasts by brass and timpani are followed by the soloist immediately taking centre stage and launching full speed in low to high registers, interrupted once more by the repeated short brass blast. The orchestra accompanies in repetitive short figurines, while the solo cello gradually glides into a virtuoso cadenza, displaying double stops in pleasing consonants as well as thrilling dissonants, moving faster and higher to its apex, sustained until the piece has reached its slower second part. While piano and percussion paint a subtle, clustered décor, the cello now settles into bluesy scales and blue notes[57], performed in pizzicati and portamenti. The following triple time "Scherzo" is again velocity driven, cruising toward an orchestral climax which briefly works as a contemporary counterpart to Paul Dukas's *L'Apprenti sourcier*, but just like in the old days, the broom-like cello will not acquiesce. In the closing statement, flutes and horns introduce the cello's lyrical song, distantly accompanied by the harp.

The cello concerto was composed for Yo-Yo Ma, just like the following work, *Heartwood: Lyrical Sketches for Cello and Orchestra* (2001)[58], a one-movement piece of around fifteen minutes. The composition is inspired by the book *Heartwood: Meditations*

---

54. Premiered 16 July 2017, by Anne-Sophie Mutter (violin) and members of the Boston Symphony, conducted by Andris Nelsons.

55. Premiered 26 May 2009 by Cathy Basrak (viola) and the Boston Pops, conducted by John Williams.

56. Premiered July 1994, by Yo-Yo Ma (cello) and the B.S.O., conducted by John Williams.

57. Williams himself refers to the ghosts of Ellington and Strayhorn which appear to «waft around the atmosphere». Liner notes of the album *Yo-Yo Ma Plays the Music of John Williams*.

58. Premiered August 2002 by Yo-Yo Ma and the B.S.O. conducted by John Williams.

on Southern Oaks (1998) with black-and-white photographs of trees by William Guion. The photographer combined these portraits with thirteenth century Islamic poetry. In *Heartwood*, Williams combined an artist's impression of nature with his personal recollections of historic jazz of the 1930s and 40s. On the one hand, «the deep vertical sonorities set out in the piece, particularly by the brass», evoke images of great trees, he explained. On the other, the composer refers to the Claude Thornhill Orchestra: «I heard in this music [...] the rich impressionistic harmonies favoured by Thornhill which he usually presented in a reflective and moody setting. In what was then essentially a dance orchestra, he featured the French horn, making his music seem unusual and even eccentric at the time»[59].

Elegy for cello and orchestra (2002)[60] is a re-arrangement of the *Elegy* Williams had previously scored for cello and piano (1997, See: chamber music section below).

The harp as a solo instrument was featured in *On Willows and Birches* (2009), for harp and orchestra[61]. This two-movement composition of around fifteen-minute length displays woodwinds, percussion, celesta and strings without the double bass section as accompanying partners to the virtuoso harp in the first part, entitled "On Willows". The second part, "On Birches", calls for additional oboes, bassoons, horns, extra harp and double basses. The percussion section is also altered in the final movement. The "Birches" movement contrasts the first with the cadenza most notably through its syncopated rhythmical pulse and pronounced metrical changes. The title of the piece has a double source of inspiration. The Biblical Psalm 137 («By the waters of Babylon...») includes the ornate line «we hanged our trees upon the willows», whereas the second movement refers to Robert Frost's early poem "Birches"[62]: «One could do worse than be a swinger of birches».

Surprisingly, given his background as a pianist, the piano is only modestly present in Williams's concert catalogue, merely represented by the *Scherzo for Piano and Orchestra* (2014), a nine-and-a-half-minute, straight-forward pulsing piece. From a repetitious beat reminiscent of Stravinsky's *Sacre*, the piece moves on to more open, tranquil spots where the piano gets a good hammering through some dexterous key smashing. Bartókian interruptions and dialogues between soloist and orchestra follow in fast-running scales, up to the homophone trembling that finalizes the rousing Scherzo. American-Chinese pianist Lang Lang premiered the piece with the China Philharmonic Orchestra conducted by Li Jian[63] during the Music for Summer Air Festival in Beijing[64].

---

59. Liner notes of the album *Yo-Yo Ma Plays the Music of John Williams.*

60. Orchestral version premiered 24 February 2002, by Yo-Yo Ma (cello) and the Los Angeles Philharmonic Orchestra, conducted by John Williams.

61. Premiered in Boston, 23 September 2009 by Ann Hobson Pilot (harp) and the B.S.O. conducted by John Williams.

62. Referred to by Williams as «On Birches», <http://www.jw-collection.de/classical/harp.htm>, accessed March 2018.

63. Premiered in Beijing, 1 July 2014.

64. The catalogue of pieces for solo and orchestra is to be augmented in summer 2018 with a new piece for cello, harp and orchestra, written for Leonard Bernstein's centennial celebrations at the Tanglewood

Solo Concerts for Wind Instruments

Concerto for Flute (1969) is one of Williams's most avant-garde pieces and received its premiere only in 1981. Its modernist flavour is reminiscent of Webern's *Klangfarben*, exotically spiced with the sound world Tōru Takemitsu created in his *November Steps*, which featured the Japanese wooden flute, shakuhachi, and the short necked lute, the biwa (1967). Williams's fourteen-minute concerto flows in one continuous stream, divided into four components of different tempi. The orchestra is thinned out for this occasion to encompass only strings, harps, celeste, piano and percussion. The flute's timbre is inspired by the shakuhachi and showcases contemporary performing techniques like lip bends, a non-vibrato playing style, overblowing, slapping and an ample use of harmonics. Its mystic, modernist opening profiles fast arpeggi in an almost improvisational flow that leads to a cadenza in the second part. The finale is written in a brisk 6/4 beat.

The *Concerto for Oboe and Orchestra* (2011)[65] was written for Keisuke Wakao of the B.S.O. It has a tripartite structure in which the slower movement (a pentatonically oriented "Pastorale") is placed in-between two faster ones, the opening "Prelude" and the bedazzling rondo finale entitled "Commedia" with its witty, deceptive conclusion. The oboe part features, first and foremost, the instrument's purity of sound, eloquently and elegantly exhibited with at times rather complex, chromatic passages. In order to fully be able to flaunt the soloist, the orchestra is reduced here to only strings (not even the harp is included).

The *Concerto for Clarinet and Orchestra* (1991)[66] is also conceived in three movements (of which the first presents a cadenza): "Maestoso", "Calmo" and "Con Brio". In the opening movement, the clarinet tickles staccato figurines like jumping jacks until the more lyrical side of the instrument takes over. The similar harlequin-like cadenza is followed by a tranquil central section which exhibits an enjoyable, timeless modernist voice. In just a few steps, the clarinet melody moves from high up to deep down. The finale speeds off in virtuoso motives against a backlash of repetitive winds and pizzicato walking strings.

In many respects, the aforementioned *Concerto for Oboe and Orchestra* deviates from Williams's other concerto for a reed instrument, the concerto for bassoon and full orchestra titled *The Five Sacred Trees* (1995)[67]. The five *attacca* propelling movements indeed refer once

Festival and called *Highwood's Ghost*, after the alleged ectoplasmic inhabitant of Highwood Manor, in Lenox, Massachusetts.

65. Premiered in Boston, 25 May 2011, by Keisuke Wakao (oboe) and the Boston Pops, conducted by John Williams.

66. Premiered in Los Angeles, 13 April 1991 by Michele Zukovsky (clarinet) and the Riverside County Philharmonic, conducted by John Williams.

67. Premiered in New York, 15 April 1995 by Judith LeClair (bassoon) and the New York Philharmonic, conducted by Kurt Masur.

more to trees, yet this time spiritually contextualized within ancient Celtic mythology. An extended solo of the featured instrument opens a movement called "Eó Mugna", which means the great oak. In the subsequent movement, "Tortan", a tree, according to Williams, associated with witchcraft, the bassoon is jointly highlighted with the violin. "Eó Rossa", the third movement, refers to the yew tree and features a solo for harp, flirting around the bassoon. The short transitory part "Craeb Uisnig" leads to the closing "Dathi", a gloomy and reflective movement. The concerto was written for the celebration of the New York Philharmonic's 150th anniversary.

The *Concerto for Horn and Orchestra*[68] exceeds most other concertos in length; it clocks some thirty five minutes. The score comes adorned with an image of a medieval woodcut of a hunter blowing an animal horn. The titles of the individual movements also unveil literary sources of inspiration. Quoted are an oratory hymn by Frederick W. Faber, a Welsh ballad, a line from poet Emily Dickinson, a varied children's nursery rhyme and the like. The impressive piece opens with the movement "Angelus: Far Far Away, like Bells, at Evening Pealing" which indeed figuratively commences with meditative chimes. Luring horn motives gradually speed up and finally the orchestra returns to its pensive opening mood. The second movement, "Battle of the Trees: Swift Oak… Stout Guardian of the Door" features the horn in break neck speed in infuriatingly complicated passages and impelling tempo. The interconnected movements "Pastorale: There Came a Day at Summer's Full" and «The Hunt: The Hart Loves the High Wood» open with a grieving oboe melody, while the horn tries to establish dialogues with highlighted instruments within the orchestra. It slides into the subsequent movement in which Schoenbergian shades are transformed into something similar to a swinging machine, gradually acquiring a mechanical pulse. The closing part is not an up-tempo finale, but a subdued "Nocturne: The Crimson Day Withdraws". It feels like an extensively stretched *lamento*. In the concerto, the horn is required to play extremely high and extremely low notes; pitches have to be altered by hand et cetera, all of which involving very difficult techniques.

The *Concerto for Trumpet and Orchestra* (1996)[69] is a three-movement composition for soloist and large orchestra that takes again about twenty minutes. Like other Williams's concerti, it is a sample sheet of playing techniques and styles: lyrical in the first two, more virtuoso parts and belligerent in the third. It features cadenzas in the opening and closing movements, whereas the orchestral trumpet section is repeatedly called on for flamboyant assistance. Not only do we hear typical Williams brass fanfares, in the finale of the first movement, but the soloist is heavily backed-up by his orchestral *confrères* as well.

---

68. Premiered 29 November 2003, by Dale Clevenger (horn) and the Chicago Symphony Orchestra, conducted by John Williams.

69. Premiered October 1996 by Michael Sachs (trumpet) and the Cleveland Orchestra conducted by Christoph von Dohnány.

The *Concerto for Tuba and Orchestra* (1985)[70] is equally an interconnected, three-part composition. The cinematic-sounding opening bars show minimal motives in the string section. The tuba then jovially, yet adeptly interferes. Jointly descending triplets lead to a virtuoso cadenza. The second movement introduces the *alter ego* of the tuba, now offering a mysterious and mellow tune. The finale is a triumphant "Rondo", slightly 'à la Turk'[71]. Although starring the tuba, the concerto also features the flute, English horn, the horn quartet and a trio of trumpets, all instruments that Williams qualifies as «his pets in the orchestra»[72]. In Williams's film scores, the tuba was previously highlighted with a big solo in the Dick van Dyke film *Fitzwilly* (Delbert Mann, 1967), as well as in *Star Wars vi: Return of the Jedi* (Richard Marquand, 1983), when Jabba the Hutt was so comically characterized by a tuba solo.

Compositions for Wind Ensemble

Although fanfares for brass band are not featured in this overview, some brief attention for works for wind ensemble is apt and appropriate. Around the mid-twentieth century, the modern wind ensemble emancipated itself from the military band into a class of its own. Williams's atonal *Sinfonietta for Wind Ensemble* with percussion (1968) can be qualified as his own contribution to this liberation. The genre name *sinfonietta* refers to a symphonic gesture on a smaller scale. This one is a brief, seventeen-minute composition in three movements. The piece commences with a "Molto Allegro", profiling two contrapuntally competing themes: one ascending, the second more fugally conceived. The "Lento Assai" middle movement merges influences from Claude Thornhill and the Second Viennese School idiom. The concluding "Allegro Molto" profiles distinctive jazz flavoured chords, walking bass passages and is, in its contemporary-style writing, once again an exemplary exponent of Williams's contribution to Third Stream repertoire from the sixties[73]. The *Sinfonietta* was initially recorded for Deutsche Gramophone by the Eastman Wind Ensemble conducted by Donald Hunsberger (b. 1935). This eventually led to a commission for a composition to celebrate the 50th anniversary of the famous Eastman School of Music: *A Nostalgic Jazz Journey* (1971). This work recalls the Big Dance Band era of the 1940s and 1950s, according to Hunsberger: «While using contemporary improvisational techniques in various sections, the whole work is an exciting view of a wonderful period in America's popular culture»[74].

---

70. Premiered in Boston, 8 May 1985 by Chester Schmitz (tuba) and the Boston Pops, conducted by John Williams.

71. My association here is always a wound down version of Dave Brubeck's *Blue Rondo à la Turk*. «Round, round, round a melody / Round, round, round a harmony…».

72. Programme book New York Philharmonic Orchestra, May 2016, p. 36.

73. Akkerman 2004.

74. Cipolla – Hunsberger 1994, p. 305.

CHAMBER MUSIC[75]

Williams's first chamber music compositions date even further back than his first credits as a film composer (*Daddy-O*, 1958), a never-premiered 1951 *Piano Sonata* and an unfinished *Wind Quintet* of about the same date. Apart from these (rejected) youth works, a gap of half a century unfolded before Williams returned to the more intimate chamber concert stage. Over a timespan of almost two decades, he has since composed a substantial oeuvre of various instrumental combinations which especially stands out in its more liberal attitude towards tonality.

Elegy for Cello and Piano (1997)[76] was composed for a funeral service in Los Angeles, as a gift for a befriended violinist who tragically lost her children. It is part of a suite of small pieces which Williams and a handful of colleagues had written especially for this sad occasion. For his contribution, Williams reverted to a cello motive he had previously used in *Seven Years in Tibet* (Jean-Jacques Annaud, 1997). He expanded the melody to a six-and-a-half-minute, introspective, yet lyrical tone poem in one ongoing motion. Some fifteen years later, Williams's re-scored the piece for orchestra and cello (see above).

Three Pieces for Solo Cello (2001)[77] has an anthropological stance to it, being a tribute to African-American culture. «I thought that the cello might be especially well-suited to express the vernacular manner of musical speech and rhythmic inflection that characterize this most important 'root-source' of American music», Williams wrote in the liner notes[78]. The bluesy opening piece "Rosewood" is inspired by the steel-fronted guitar played by the workers «as they tried to ease the pain of their long hours in the field»[79]. The middle piece "Pickin'" refers to the techniques of cotton picking and banjo-picking. "The Long Road North" was inspired by the poem of the same name by Rita Dove and embraces a lullaby-like lyricism of a mother comforting her child.

Williams's involvement with native American culture is another time part and parcel of *Conversations* (2012-2013) for piano[80]. The piece consists of four movements[81] which feature imagined encounters between (jazz) musicians and slaves. In a musical hide and seek, jazz pianist Phineas Newborn Jr. catches up with former slave Elizabeth Freeman,

---

75. Left out of this overview is also the piano duet *Silent film* (2003). That piece was written to accompany silent film footage, therefore occupying a middle ground between Williams's film and concert music.

76. Performed by John Williams (piano) and John Walz (cello).

77. Premiered 4 August 2002, by Yo-Yo Ma (cello).

78. Liner notes from the album *Yo-Yo Ma Plays the Music of John Williams*. The movement, with its thriving guitar part, also recalls the score for the film *Rosewood* (John Singleton, 1997).

79. *Ibidem*.

80. Gloria Cheng premiered movements 1 and 2 at Tanglewood, 10 August 2012, and movements 3 and 4 in Los Angeles, 12 November 2013.

81. 1: "Phineas and Mumbett"; 2: "Claude and Monk"; 3: "Chet and Miles"; 4: "Strays, Duke… and Blind Tom". See also the interview with pianist Simone Pedroni in this volume for further remarks.

also known as Mumbett (movement 1). In the second movement, Claude Thornhill winks at Claude Debussy in his encounter with Thelonious Monk. Chet Baker and Miles Davis are up next, while Billy Strayhorn and Duke Ellington finally meet another former slave, Blind Tom, while they cheer the genesis of stride piano technique.

In *Duo Concertante* (2007)[82], a thirteen-minute piece in three movements, Williams flirts with the late-Romantic idiom. The opening "Maestoso" offers a splendid tension between extendedly stretched, dramatic chords by the eight strings that are used as their building blocks, before setting off to a race through tonal scales. In the subsequent "Cadenza-Adagio" — occasionally reminiscent of *Schindler's List* (Steven Spielberg, 1994) — each of the instruments have their own «mini-soliloquies»[83] in an interactive dialogue. These subsequently flow out into a lyrical conversation between the two string instruments over passages full of trills, leading, *attacca*, to an arousing "Allegro" finale. The opening movement is revisited once more in a final cadence, added as an afterthought.

Air and Simple Gifts (2009) for clarinet, piano, violin and cello is probably the most famous chamber music piece by John Williams. It was first performed[84] in Washington D. C. during the first inauguration of Barack Obama as the 44th President of the United States, on 20 January 2009, an event witnessed live by millions of people as well as broadcast worldwide. The piece is not so much an original composition as an arrangement, a personal take on the 1848 Shaker song *Simple Gifts*, composed by Joseph Brackett, in turn made famous through Copland's incorporation in his *Appalachian Spring* (1944). The song's reference to American pioneers of the nineteenth century is at the same time appropriate for the U.S. Presidential ceremony and rhymes with Williams's own personal and continued involvement with America's history. In less than four and a half minutes, Williams offers a brief trilogy. The modal conceived "Air" is introduced by violin, cello and piano. This in turns leads to the presentation of the "Simple Gifts" melody and its subsequent variations, initially by the clarinet and interspersed by recollections of the "Air". Via an excursion that explores diverse tonal highways and byways, the chain of cadences finishes in a 'Presidential' D major.

A second composition which features clarinet and string instruments is *Quartet La Jolla*[85] for violin, cello, clarinet and harp (2011)[86]. It is a five-movement composition of about

---

82. Premiered 17 August 2007, by Victor Romanul (violin) and Michael Zaretsky (viola).

83. Liner notes of the album *Duos for Violin and Viola* by Victor Romanul and Michael Zaretsky. Artona CP31-304.

84. The performance was not live but mimicked. The unpredictable weather conditions in January would most likely have negatively influenced the tuning of the costly instruments used. The piano's hammers were decoupled from the keys, the bows of the string instruments were soaped, both in order to stifle their sound.

85. La Jolla refers to the SummerFest(ival) of the La Jolla Music Society (CA).

86. Premiered 20 August 2011, by John Bruce Yeh (clarinet), Deborah Hoffman (Metropolitan Opera Orchestra), Cho-Liang Lin (violin), Joshua Roman (cello).

thirty minutes duration. It is centred around the harp which displays an impressionistic disposition. After the vivid "Introduction", a lyrical "Aubade" follows. A rapid "Scherzo" leads to a second lyrical movement, now entitled "Cantando". The piece features a lovely clarinet song which pairs its bluesy feeling with snippets of Copland and Bartók, all the while accompanied by the pizzicato playing cello. In the closing movement, the violinist leads the rest of the musicians into a dazzling "Finale".

A Young Person's Guide to the Cello (2011)[87] is a witty, six-and-a-half-minute solo piece. It nods to Benjamin Britten's educational composition *The Young Person's Guide to the Orchestra: Variations and Fugue on a Theme of Purcell* (1946) which presents the technical possibilities, colours and individual instruments of a large symphony orchestra. Williams's miniature pendant comparably shows «everything that a cello can do»[88], as cellist Lynn Harrell described it in an interview. Open strings, flageolets in octaves to broken triads, pizzicati, tremoli, double stops, semi Bach quotations, et cetera — they can all be consumed via this comical composition.

Rounds for classical guitar (2012)[89] is far more 'serious' in conception, but it equally offers a *tour d'horizon* of instrumental possibilities on a par with the cello piece. The approximately seven-minute piece was composed for the Spanish guitarist Pablo Sáinz Villegas. It is an attractive, highly idiomatic guitar composition which makes ample use of legato and apoyando techniques, tremoli, flageolets, sequences and reminiscences of Phrgyian modes. This composition is written in a free atonal style that may remember of the guitar pieces by his former teacher, Mario Castelnuovo-Tedesco. In that sense, with *Rounds*, John Williams has come full circle.

By Means of a Coda

The ambiguity between John Williams the film composer and John Williams the 'classical' composer has already been addressed. Even Seiji Ozawa, Artistic Director and Conductor in Residence of the B.S.O. once honestly confessed: «Many people — I was one of them — misjudged [Williams] as a composer… But I found out when I studied his pieces. His knowledge and background and training, how he does his music [demonstrates] a very high standard and deep musicianship»[90].

87. Premiered at the Daniel Pearl World Music Day, 30 October 2011, by Lynn Harrell.

88. <http://www.opuscello.com/lynn-harrell>, accessed February 2018.

89. Premiered at the Parkening International Guitar Competition (Malibu [CA]) 2 June 2012 by Pablo Sáinz Villegas (guitar).

90. Quoted in Audissino 2014, p. 191.

A profound study of Williams's 'classical' compositions remains a desideratum. This chapter is one[91] of the initial attempts to systematically survey his oeuvre through sketching some thematic characteristics and signalling some red threads. It is an attempt to chart the individual pieces through, admittedly, somewhat impressionistic descriptions in a compositional 'railway schedule', to guide the interested listener (or performer, or programmer) through Williams's repertoire. Further research is required since scores have been so far largely unavailable, were withdrawn by the composer, or are yet to be published[92]. More in-depth theoretical work (comparable to Tom Schneller's diverse exemplary analyses, the insightful studies by Frank Lehman, the dissertation by Greg Akkerman, among others[93]) are needed, as well as more qualitative analyses. Having lived with this oeuvre for a few months — or should I say «having been on a joyous journey with Williams's music» — by now, I completely agree with Ozawa's conclusion about Williams's very high and deep musicianship. If you will, it represents the perfect blend of the artist and the artisan. Williams's 'classical' repertoire is not simply a by-product of his silver screen successes, but an oeuvre which eloquently caters to diverse audiences and orchestral combinations. Should the metaphorical emperor indeed be dressed in new clothes, then these are of no less than excellent quality and fabric, and are, as well, tightly tailored.

John Williams is an all-round, quintessential American composer. He does not discriminate between genres or mediated formats. The qualification 'American' does, however, not come without complications which cannot be further elaborated in this context. «The semiotics of national music [or for that matter: a national composer] is not determined solely by differences from a perceived 'universal' language, still less a "mainstream of compositional evolution" running through Austrian and German composers, from Bach to Schoenberg, but by internal developments and dialogue within traditions»[94], as Matthew Riley and Anthony D. Smith argued in their book *Nation and Classical Music: From Handel to Copland*. Said tradition, however, should not be interpreted as solely musical (in the case of Williams: a European, late-romantic heritage, fused with jazz and popular influences), but one which participates in a constant, lively conversation with its cultural roots; one which is also — and in principle — open to critical, historical awareness. And this all is typically Williams, in the idiomatic scoring and sounding engagement of his 'classical' music oeuvre.

---

91. Others are Valverde Amador 2013 and Barton 2013, pp. 102-111.

92. At the time of writing this, it has been announced that Williams will donate his whole archives (film and concert scores, sketches, manuscripts…) to the Juilliard School of Music in New York. <https://www.juilliard.edu/news/131971/academy-award-winning-composer-and-conductor-john-williams-bequeath-concert-and-film>, accessed March 2018.

93. Akkerman 2004, Lehman 2015, Schneller 2013.

94. Riley – Smith 2016, p. 15.

Bibliography

Akkerman 2004

Akkerman, Greg. *An Original Composition in a Postmodern Confluent Style for Orchestra and An Analysis of Escapades for Alto Saxophone and Orchestra by John Williams*, Ph.D. Diss., Greeley (CO), University of Northern Colorado, 2004.

Audissino 2014

Audissino, Emilio. *John Williams's Film Music: «Jaws», «Star Wars», «Raiders of the Lost Ark», and the Return of the Classical Hollywood Music Style*, Madison (WI), University of Wisconsin Press, 2014 (Wisconsin Film Studies).

Barton 2013

Barton, Ton. *A Musical Biography of John Williams*, electronic print, Mall Publications, 2013, pp. 102-111.

Cipolla – Hunsberger 1994

The Wind Ensemble and Its Repertoire: Essays on the Fortieth Anniversary of the Eastman Wind Ensembles, edited by Frank J. Cipolla and Donald Hunsberger, Rochester (NY), University of Rochester Press, 1994 (Donald Hunsberger Wind Library).

Gzemski 2016

Gzemski, Sarah. 'An Interview with Rita Dove', in: *Blog for the University of Arizona Poetry Center*, 26 October 2016, <https://poetry.arizona.edu/blog/interview-rita-dove>, accessed February 2018.

Horowitz 2005

Horowitz, Joseph. *Classical Music in America: A History of Its Rise and Fall*, New York, London, W.W. Norton & Company, 2005.

Kramer 2007

Kramer, Lawrence. *Why Classical Music Still Matters*, Berkeley (CA), University of California Press, 2007

Lebrecht 2002

Lebrecht, Norman. 'John Williams – The Magpie Maestro', in: *La Scena Musicale*, 20 November 2002, <www.scena.org/columns/lebrecht/021120-NL-williams.html>, accessed March 2018.

Lehman 2015

Lehman, Frank. 'Scoring the President: Myth and Politics in John Williams's *JFK* and *Nixon*', in: *Journal of the Society of American Music*, ix/4 (2015), pp. 409-444.

Mellers 2017 (1964)

Mellers, Wilfrid. *Music in a New Found Land: Themes and Developments in the History of American Music*, (1964), New York, Routledge, 2017.

Riley – Smith 2016

Riley, Matthew – Smith, Anthony D. *Nation and Classical Music: From Handel to Copland*, Woodbridge, Boydell Press, 2016 (Music in Society and Culture).

Schneller 2013
Schneller, Tom. 'Modal Interchange and Semantic Resonance in Themes by John Williams', in: *Journal of Film Music*, vi/1 (2013), pp. 49-74.

Smith 1991
Smith, Steven C. *A Heart at Fire's Center: The Life and Music of Bernard Herrmann*, Berkeley (CA), University of California Press, 1991.

Sparke 2010
Sparke, Michael. *Stan Kenton: This is an Orchestra!*, Denton (TX), University of North Texas Press, 2010 (North Texas Lives of Musicians Series, 5: Book Collections on Project MUSE).

Taruskin 2005
Taruskin, Richard. *The Oxford History of Western Music*, 6 volls., Oxford-New York, Oxford University Press, 2005.

Valverde Amador 2013
Valverde Amador, Andrés. *John Williams: vida y obra*, Seville, Editorial Berenice, 2013 (Cine).

John Williams's Film Music in the Concert Halls

Sebastian Stoppe
(Leipzig University Library)

Introduction

Film music has its roots in late-romantic concert music. A number of composers of so-called 'serious music' also composed for the film, such as Igor Stravinsky, Dmitri Shostakovich or Sergey Prokofiev. And some Golden Age film composers such as Erich Wolfgang Korngold and Miklós Rózsa came from the concert-music realm and, once they started their association with Hollywood, continued to pen works for the concert stage too[1]. Film music had to struggle for a long time against the prejudice that saw it as music not to be taken seriously; it was regarded as a «neglected art»[2]. Leigh Stevens expressed the opinion that «the problems of promoting the use of film music in the concert hall are manifold, but the most serious deterrent to its use in such surroundings is the theory held by many composers that motion picture music [...] ha[s] [not] anything specific to say»[3]. Nevertheless, film-music concerts have experienced a blossoming in the recent years. There is a large variety, from programmes that only perform film music in concert halls without any additional element to large-scale events in multi-purpose halls where film music is accompanied by film clips or provides the live accompaniment to entire films. This chapter examines the role of John Williams's film scores in this context. Are there any special features of Williams's film music that make it particularly suitable to the concert hall? How does the performance practice of his film music differ in comparison to classical concerts? Are there any pieces that are played more frequently than others, and if so, why?

Within the framework of this chapter, systematic consideration can only be made to a rudimentary extent. For this reason, I look at the post-Williams era of the Boston Pops

[1]. See Neher 2012, p. 669.

[2]. The quote refers to the title of Prendergast 1977. See also Sullivan 2008, pp. 32-33.

[3]. Stevens 2006, p. 339.

Orchestra, from 1994 onwards[4] and the development of the New York Philharmonic's film-music concerts. In addition, I examine the film-music concerts of the Gewandhaus Orchestra Leipzig, which took place in the 2000s under the direction of John Mauceri and in which Williams's music was prominently represented[5]. My investigation ends with a look at some more recent concerts that show that film music is becoming more and more accepted in the concert programmes.

CAN FILM MUSIC EXIST WITHOUT FILM?

Film is a peculiar art form as it combines a number of pre-existing art forms such as visual arts, photography, drama, acting, literature and music into a *Gesamtkunstwerk*, a sort of total work of art. From this point of view, one could argue that film music has a meaning only in relation to the corresponding film, and that it can exist only if it stays in constant contact with its film. On the other hand, film music is an element that is quite easily separable from the completed film. Unlike production design, cinematography, or acting, it does exist separately both as a sound recording and (in many cases) in musical notation as a score. Typically, the film composer is also the first of all the creative collaborators who is able to watch the almost finished film[6]. Seen in this light, the roughly finished film serves as an inspiration for the composer and a film score does not differ much from programme music in the first place. Thus, the film narrative can be considered the music's programme. (John Williams typically starts his work by watching a rough cut of the film[7].) The extra-musical idea is not only the point of origin, not only the seed from which the music emerges, but its presence constitutes a constant frame of reference[8]. Zofia Lissa argues that «in the film, the picture explains the illustrative musical structures; in the autonomous programme music, this explanation is carried out individually and subjectively by each listener on the basis of the respective sound structure»[9]. Wolfgang Thiel reminds us that «as a rule, there is no soundtrack listener in the true sense of the word, but rather the film

[4]. AUDISSINO 2013 already provides a detailed analysis of the period in which Williams was music director.

[5]. The Gewandhaus Orchestra concerts are available in the Gewandhaus Archive as programme booklets as well as audio recordings. I would like to thank the Gewandhaus zu Leipzig and especially Claudius Böhm and Thomas Händel, who gave me access to the archive.

[6]. Although it may happen that some film scores are made before or during the shooting, the composer usually works with a rough cut of the film and not with a script. In this way he already has an idea of what the finished film is going to look like.

[7]. A prominent exception is *Hook* (Steven Spielberg, 1991). Originally conceived as a musical, Williams worked on his score in an early production phase, with the script as a reference.

[8]. See STOPPE 2014, p. 13.

[9]. LISSA 1965, p. 117. Own translation.

viewer who receives the multi-layered art form "sound film"»[10]. And Kristjan Järvi argues, that «anybody in the concert hall who visit a concert doesn't listen to pure music, absolute music like we have been educated to listen, but they actually see a concert and they listen by looking, you know, not only hearing»[11].

Seen in this light, film scores tell a film through musical means[12]. «If the composer has an adequate musical vocabulary, tells the story with taste and care and follows the rules common to both music and drama, the result will be music, good music, and it will be played in concert halls»[13]. Essentially, one could go as far as saying that even music composed directly for the concert hall is designed to tell a story: «What are tone poems or even Mahler symphonies? They are stories»[14].

WILLIAMS'S FILM MUSIC IN THE CONCERT HALL

With regard to his film scores, Williams has always distinguished between the music actually used in the film and the album presentations. This is evident, for example, in the fact that his soundtrack albums often contain music in different chronological order than in the film or that individual cues are newly arranged into longer cues. During the recording sessions, Williams sometimes even records individual cues specifically arranged for the upcoming album[15]. This way of working shows that Williams does not regard film music as inseparable from the film; the music (at least portions of it) can have a separate existence[16].

Williams had his breakthrough as a film composer in the early 1970s[17], and with *Jaws* (Steven Spielberg, 1975) and *Star Wars* (George Lucas, 1977) Williams became a household name in Hollywood. And *Star Wars* was the first score in the Williams

---

10. THIEL 1981, p. 16. Own translation.

11. JÄRVI 2014, p. 134.

12. Of course, there are exceptions like many scores by Hans Zimmer, for example, who is described as «acting more as a music producer, talent scout, and sound designer than as a composer stricto sensu» (AUDISSINO 2017, p. 223). Some Zimmer scores were performed live as a symphonic suite, like *Gladiator* (Ridley Scott, 2000), although «his music had to be substantially adapted for the live symphony orchestra» (*ibidem*, p. 223). However, even 'ambient music' that does not follow traditional compositional techniques should not be automatically disqualify from concert performance.

13. STEVENS 2006, p. 339.

14. JÄRVI 2014, p. 135. See also WINTERS 2014, pp. 134-146.

15. Both practices are particularly evident in the soundtrack album for *Star Wars Episode 1: The Phantom Menace* (George Lucas, 1999) or *E. T.: The Extra-Terrestrial*, for example.

16. These kind of adaptations are not unusual. For example, Ennio Morricone arranged a number of his film scores for a separate performance, and Howard Shore adapted his score for the *Lord of the Rings* trilogy into a six-movement symphony, which is intended for a stand-alone performance.

17. See AUDISSINO 2014, p. 104. In 1971 Williams received his first Academy Award for his adaptation of the music of *Fiddler on the Roof*.

canon to be successfully and widely performed in concert as stand-alone music. «On 20 November 1977 Zubin Mehta conducted a thirty-minute-long-suite with the Los Angeles Philharmonic in front of 17,500 people in a sold-out concert at the Hollywood Bowl in Los Angeles. This was the first one of the many "Star Wars concerts" to follow»[18]. «[...] Between 1978 and 1979 there were around 400 performances of the "Star Wars Symphonic Suite" — Williams's concert arrangement distributed by Warner Bros. Music»[19]. However, Williams did not appear as a concert conductor until after these achievements, considering himself «mostly a recording-stage conductor»[20]. It is likely that it was the popularity of the *Star Wars* suite performances that led to Williams's appointment as Arthur Fiedler's successor at the Boston Pops Orchestra[21]. When he became conductor-in-residence and music director of orchestra in 1980 (a post he held until the end of 1993), Williams had a privileged rostrum on which he could premiere some concert arrangements from his own film scores, and this circumstance certainly promoted an increase in the number of film-music concert arrangements. Williams's appointment was the first time a Hollywood film composer was appointed music director of an important musical institution like the Boston Pops Orchestra[22]. Emilio Audissino argues that Williams's conductorship with the Boston Pops Orchestra has been instrumental in helping the film-music repertoire gain a better reputation. The Boston Pops Orchestra had already performed film music under Williams's predecessor, Arthur Fiedler, «though Fiedler would select film music akin to the pop-song repertoire»[23]. On the contrary, Williams saw film music to be on a par with classical music: «If Fiedler considered film music akin to pop music, Williams thought that the film-music repertoire could provide pieces akin to concert music»[24]. He brought in philological accuracy in the performance of the film-music repertoire — either contemporary or from the past — by employing the original orchestrations and «if the original was not available, Williams commissioned an arrangement based on the authentic orchestration, reconstructed from surviving orchestral parts and from the film's original music track»[25]. In his inaugural Boston concert on 29 April 1980, Williams premiered two concert pieces from the *Star Wars* sequel *The Empire Strikes Back* (Irvin Kershner, 1980), even before the film itself was released[26].

---

[18]. *Ibidem*, p. 81. Mehta also recorded the suite for an album on the Decca label together with an excerpt from the music for *Close Encounters of the Third Kind*.

[19]. Audissino 2013, p. 153.

[20]. Audissino 2014, p. 185.

[21]. See *ibidem*, p. 82.

[22]. See Audissino 2013, p. 151.

[23]. *Ibidem*, p. 149. Often performed as last part of the programme, it included «show tunes from Broadway musicals — which would increasingly replace the traditional excerpts from operas and operettas-jazz, marches, [...] orchestral versions of popular songs, and, eventually, film music» (*ibidem*).

[24]. *Ibidem*, p. 153.

[25]. *Ibidem*, p. 154.

[26]. See *ibidem*, p. 156.

The Post-Williams Era in Boston

In 1993, Keith Lockhart succeeded to Williams as music director of Boston Pops, while Williams assumed the role of 'Laureate Conductor'. At this point it is worth examining to what extent the Boston Pops continue to programme Williams's film music. To this end, I have analysed the programmes of both the Boston Symphony and the Boston Pops from 1994 to 2017[27]. The main question of this research is which pieces by Williams (here limited to the film-music repertoire) have been performed.

Table 1: Overview of the Film Music Works by John Williams Performed by the Boston Pops Orchestra since 1994

March from *1941*
Swing, Swing, Swing from *1941*
The Battle of Hollywood from *1941*
For Always from *A. I. Artifical Intelligence* (arr. Karam)
The Duel from *The Adventures of Tintin*
The Sea Battle from *The Adventures of Tintin*
Dry Your Tears, Afrika from *Amistad*
The Lanes of Limerick from *Angela's Ashes* (for solo harp)
Theme from *Angela's Ashes* (arr. for cello quartet Dejardin)
Two Concert Pieces from *Angela's Ashes*
Suite (A Child's Tale) from *The BFG*
[Suite from] *The Book Thief*
Escapades from *Catch Me If You Can*
Excerpts from *Close Encounters of the Third Kind* (Hal Leonard Signature Edition)
Excerpts from *Close Encounters of the Third Kind* (Pops version)
Overture from *The Cowboys*
End Title from *Dracula*
Night Journeys from *Dracula*
Adventures On Earth from *E. T.: The Extra-Terrestrial* [= Excerpts from *E. T.*]
Finale from *E. T.: The Extra-Terrestrial*
Flying Theme from *E. T.: The Extra-Terrestrial* [= Title Song from *E. T.*]
Stargazers from *E. T.: The Extra-Terrestrial*
E. T.: The Extra-Terrestrial: The Movie [complete movie, live to projection]
Three Million Light Years from Home from *E. T.: The Extra-Terrestrial*
Cadillac of the Skies from *Empire of the Sun*
Exsultate Justi from *Empire of the Sun*
Jim's New Life from *Empire of the Sun*
Excerpts from *Far and Away* (Pops version)
Suite from *Far and Away* (Hal Leonard Signature Edition)
Suite from *Far and Away* (Manuscript version)

[27]. The Boston Symphony Orchestra has made its programmes available in a digital archive at <http://archives.bso.org>, accessed February 2018 However, Boston Pops concerts are not yet fully accessible: according to the website there are currently about 1000 concerts available.

Theme from *Far and Away*
Film Music Montage I [excerpts from *Star Wars*, *Raiders of the Lost Ark*, *Jaws*, *Superman*, and *E. T.: The Extra-Terrestrial*]
Film Music Montage II [excerpts from *Jurassic Park*, *Home Alone*, *Star Wars Episode II – Attack of the Clones*, Hook, *Close Encounters of the Third Kind*, and *Harry Potter and the Sorcerer's Stone*]
The Chamber of Secrets from *Harry Potter and the Chamber of Secrets* (Manuscript version)
Fawkes the Phoenix from *Harry Potter and the Chamber of Secrets* (Hal Leonard Signature Edition)
Fawkes the Phoenix from *Harry Potter and the Chamber of Secrets* (Manuscript version)
Aunt Marge's Waltz from *Harry Potter and the Prisoner of Azkaban*
Bridge to the Past from *Harry Potter and the Prisoner of Azkaban* (Tanglewood on Parade 2004 arrangement)
Suite from *Harry Potter and the Prisoner of Azkaban*
Witches, Wands and Wizards from *Harry Potter and the Prisoner of Azkaban* (Tanglewood on Parade 2004 arrangement)
Harry Potter's Wondrous World from *Harry Potter and the Sorcerer's Stone*
Hedwig's Theme from *Harry Potter and the Sorcerer's Stone*
Nimbus 2000 from *Harry Potter and the Sorcerer's Stone*
Suite from *Harry Potter and the Sorcerer's Stone*
Grand Suite from *Harry Potter*
Main Title from *Heidi*
Merry Christmas, Merry Christmas from *Home Alone 2* (arr. Bricusse)
Holiday Flight from *Home Alone*
Somewhere in My Memory from *Home Alone*
Home Alone: The Movie [complete movie, live to projection]
Three Selections from *Home Alone* (with chorus, arr. Bricusse)
The Flight to Neverland from *Hook*
Three Pieces from *Hook*
A Whirl Through Academe from *Indiana Jones and the Kingdom of the Crystal Skull*
Irina's Theme from *Indiana Jones and the Kingdom of the Crystal Skull*
Swashbuckler (The Adventures of Mutt) from *Indiana Jones and the Kingdom of the Crystal Skull*
The Crystal Spell from *Indiana Jones and the Kingdom of the Crystal Skull*
Opening Sequence from *Indiana Jones and the Last Crusade*
Scherzo for Motorcycle and Orchestra from *Indiana Jones and the Last Crusade*
Parade of the Slave Children from *Indiana Jones and the Temple of Doom*
Suite from *JFK*
Suite from *Jane Eyre*
Man Against Beast from *Jaws*
Out to Sea / Shark Cage Fugue from *Jaws*
Excerpts from *Jaws* (Pops version)
Jaws: The Movie [complete movie, live to projection]
Theme from *Jaws*
Theme from *Jurassic Park*
With Malice Toward None from *Lincoln*
Theme from *Meet the Press*
Brush on Silk from *Memoirs of a Geisha*
Confluence from *Memoirs of a Geisha*
Sayuri's Theme from *Memoirs of a Geisha*
Suite from *Memoirs of a Geisha*
Three Selections from *Memoirs of a Geisha*
A New Beginning from *Minority Report*

The Mission Theme (Theme for *N. B. C. Nightly News*)
Monsters, Beauties, and Heroes [medley including *Jaws* and *Superman*]
[Theme from] *The Patriot* (long version)
Raiders of the Lost Ark: The Movie [complete movie, live to projection]
Marion's Theme from *Raiders of the Lost Ark*
Opening from *Raiders of the Lost Ark*
Excerpts from *Raiders of the Lost Ark* (Pops version)
Raiders March from *Raiders of the Lost Ark*
Suite from *The Rivers*
Piano Solo from *Sabrina*
Hymn to the Fallen from *Saving Private Ryan*
Hymn to the Fallen from *Saving Private Ryan* (arr. for brass ensemble Bocook)
Immolation from *Schindler's List*
Remembrances from *Schindler's List*
Theme from *Schindler's List*
Three Pieces from *Schindler's List* [= Theme, Jewish Town, Remembrances]
Hell's Kitchen [from *Sleepers*]
Reunion and Finale from *Sleepers*
Star Trek through the Years (arr: - Calvin)
Anakin's Theme from *Star Wars Episode I – The Phantom Menace*
Duel of the Fates from *Star Wars Episode I – The Phantom Menace*
The Flag Parade from *Star Wars Episode I – The Phantom Menace*
Battle of the Heroes from *Star Wars Episode III – Revenge of the Sith*
Cantina Band from *Star Wars Episode IV – A New Hope* (full orch. version)
Main Title from *Star Wars Episode IV – A New Hope*
Princess Leia's Theme from *Star Wars Episode IV – A New Hope*
The Asteroid Field from *Star Wars Episode IV – A New Hope*
Throne Room & End Title from *Star Wars Episode IV – A New Hope*
The Imperial March from *Star Wars Episode V – The Empire Strikes Back*
Yoda's Theme from *Star Wars Episode V – The Empire Strikes Back*
Luke and Leia from *Star Wars Episode VI – Return of the Jedi*
Star Wars Trilogy: Film Montage
Excerpts from *Star Wars* Trilogy (Pops version)
Grand Suite from *Star Wars*
March of the Resistance from *Star Wars: The Force Awakens*
Rey's Theme from *Star Wars: The Force Awakens*
Scherzo for X-Wings from *Star Wars: The Force Awakens*
The Jedi Steps and Finale from *Star Wars: The Force Awakens*
Love Theme from *Superman*
March from *Superman*
Pops Excerpts from *Superman* (Pops version)
Viktor's Tale from *The Terminal*
Main Title from *Towering Inferno*
A Tribute To George Lucas and Steven Spielberg [medley including *Jaws*, *Star Wars*, *Raiders of the Lost Ark*, and *E. T.: The Extra-Terrestrial*]
Dartmoor, 1912 from *War Horse*
Escape from the City from *War of the Worlds*
Devil's Dance from *The Witches of Eastwick*

A review of the programme booklets shows that Williams's film music is still regularly featured; the list above comprises around 120 different titles. Even though Williams has regularly conducted concerts as the 'Laureate Conductor' after 1994, Keith Lockhart has also included Williams's pieces in his programmes, and the Boston Symphony Orchestra under Seiji Ozawa has also performed some pieces from *Schindler's List* (Steven Spielberg, 1993), for example. The chart below shows the number of performances in which one or more of Williams's music pieces has been featured (taking into account performances by both the Boston Pops and the Boston Symphony Orchestra).

Number of Film Music Concerts
by the Boston Pops and Boston Symphony Orchestra since 1994

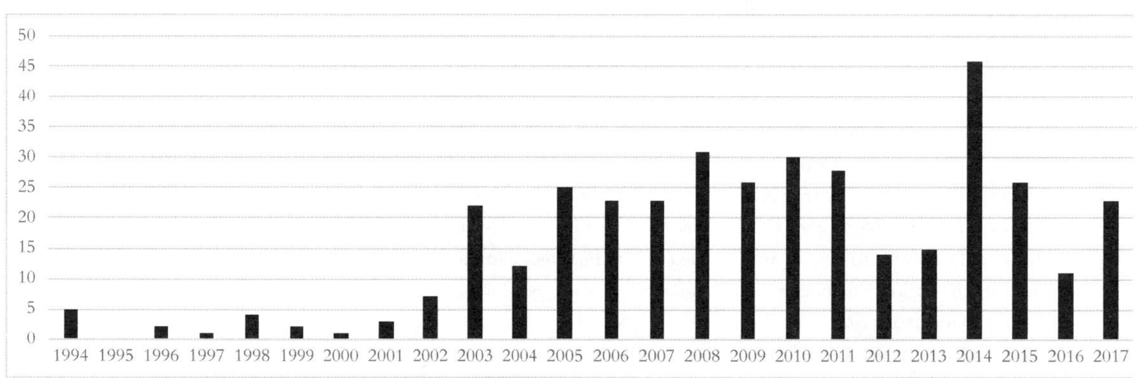

It is noticeable that a veritable boom in the number of performances began in the early 2000s and the trend continues to this day. Williams's policy to treat film music as serious music and, accordingly, to include it into the concert programmes has had a long-term influence.

Another topical phenomenon of the present time is to perform entire film scores (by Williams and other composers) as a live accompaniment to the films they were written for (this is commonly referred to as 'live to projection'). Williams also had an influential role in this 'film concert' phenomenon[28]: in 2002, for the 20th anniversary of *E. T.: The Extra-Terrestrial* (Steven Spielberg, 1982), he conducted the entire score with a live orchestra at the premiere of the restored version of the film[29]. From the Williams canon, Keith Lockhart conducted live to projection the score to *Home Alone* (Chris Columbus, 1990) on 26 and 27 December 2014, *Raiders of the Lost Ark* (Steven Spielberg, 1981) on 26 August 2016, and *E. T.: The Extra-Terrestrial* on 12 and 13 May 2017, and continued these 'film concerts' with *Jaws* on 25 and 26 May 2017. However, the question might be whether this live-to-

[28]. For an example, see <http://filmconcertslive.com>, accessed February 2018.

[29]. See Audissino 2014, p. 192. A making-of documentary of this unique concert with the Recording Arts Orchestra of Los Angeles can be found on the *E. T.: The Extra-Terrestrial* DVD edition from 2002.

film performance can still be interpreted as a film-music concert, since the 'concertante' character of the music is lost[30]. These cases can be compared to ballet music as part of a scenic performance *vis-à-vis* as a ballet suite arranged for a stand-alone performance.

When looking at the archive material, it is also noticeable that Williams has maintained his habit of performing newly composed film music with the Boston Pops during the post-1994 era. The concerts at Symphony Hall on 1 and 2 June 2012, for example, included "Dartmoor 1912" from *War Horse* (Steven Spielberg, 2011) and "The Duel" from *The Adventures of Tintin* (Steven Spielberg, 2011). In the following 2013 concert, he performed "Three Pieces" from *Lincoln* (Steven Spielberg, 2012); in 2016 Williams arranged his film music for *Star Wars: The Force Awakens* (J. J. Abrams, 2015) into a five-movement suite and performed it at the Tanglewood Music Festival on 13 August 2016. On 19 August 2017, Williams combined forces with Boston Symphony Orchestra's music director Andris Nelsons, who not only conducted the first half of the programme but also contributed a trumpet solo — being an accomplished trumpet player as well — for the piece "With Malice Toward None" from *Lincoln*.

Table 2: Programme of "John Williams's Film Night", Tanglewood, Boston Pops Orchestra, Andris Nelsons/John Williams, 19 August 2017

Korngold, Erich Wolfgang	March from *The Adventures of Robin Hood*
Herrmann, Bernhard	Scene d'Amour from *Vertigo*
North, Alex	Forest Meeting/Love Theme and March from *Spartacus*
Williams, John	The Duel from *The Adventures of Tintin*
Williams, John	End Titles from *Dracula*
Williams, John	Adventures on Earth from *E. T.: The Extra-Terrestrial*
- Intermission -	
Williams, John	The Adventures of Mutt from *Indiana Jones and the Kingdom of the Crystal Skull*
Williams, John	Excerpts from *Close Encounters of the Third Kind*
Williams, John	Parade of the Slave Children from *Indiana Jones and the Temple of Doom*
Williams, John	Suite from *Far and Away*
Williams, John	With Malice Toward None from *Lincoln*
Williams, John	The Chamber of Secrets from *Harry Potter and the Chamber of Secrets*
Williams, John	Fawkes the Phoenix from *Harry Potter and the Chamber of Secrets*
Williams, John	Harry's Wondrous World from *Harry Potter and the Sorcerer's Stone*
Williams, John	March from *1941* (Encore)
Williams, John	Theme from *Schindler's List* (Encore)
Williams, John	The Imperial March from *The Empire Strikes Back* (Encore)

[30]. The term 'concertante' refers to the performance of film music as a concert piece without the film being shown synchronously. However, there are also film-music concerts in which still images, film excerpts or visual animations are projected onto a screen to accompany the concert suites. I also consider the latter to be a concert performance.

Nelsons commented about film music:

> The genre makes the music sometimes to follow certain rules. [...] It is all the same with ballet music by great composers like Tchaikovsky. You can hear when it is a symphony or a ballet music. The ballet music you can hear is written for dancing, and, obviously, it sounds different than a symphony but it is still genius. And I think the same in this case for Korngold. Of course, I have conducted a few of his pieces for symphony [orchestra], then, of course, listened to his film music. The quality of writing is the same. It is really great and I don't divide there for if it's Korngold classical or it's Korngold Hollywood. It's the same composer in a different genre[31].

This was the first time ever that the Principal Conductor of the Boston Symphony Orchestra conducted a Boston Pops film-music concert, a sign that film music is now an accepted part of the regular concert repertoire[32].

Williams in New York

The first mention of a Williams film score in a New York Philharmonic programme was on 9 December 1987 in a 'Young People's Concert' conducted by Leonard Slatkin[33]. Slatkin selected a wide range of different marches from Beethoven's "Turkish March" to the "Wedding March" by Mendelssohn, Tchaikovsky's "Nutcracker March", Siegfried's "Funeral March" from Richard Wagner's *Götterdämmerung*, to Williams's "Imperial March" from *The Empire Strikes Back*[34]. In the programme booklet itself there is no sign of the need to justify the presence of a film-music piece amongst the other pieces.

Table 3: Programme of «Young People's Concert», New York Philharmonic, Leonard Slatkin, 9 December 1987

Beethoven	Turkish March from *The Ruins of Athens*
Mendelssohn	Wedding March from *A Midsummer Night's Dream*
Gounod	*Funeral March of a Marionette*
Berlioz	March to the Scaffold from *Symphonique Fantastique*
Tchaikovsky	March from *The Nutcracker*

31. BSO music director Andris Nelsons interviewed by Ron Della Chiesa for the WCRB 99.5 broadcast of the concert.

32. The BSO recently announced that the «John Williams's Film Night» will once again be conducted by Andris Nelsons and John Williams at the 2018 Tanglewood Music Festival.

33. The New York Philharmonic Orchestra Archive is digitally available at <http://archives.nyphil.org>, accessed February 2018, and contains more than 13,000 printed programmes among other things.

34. In the internal programme listing the piece is mistakenly called «The Imperial March (Darth Vadar's [*sic*] Theme)».

Wagner	Siegfried's Funeral March from *Götterdämmerung*
Prokofiev	March from *The Love for Three Oranges*
Williams	Imperial March from *The Empire Strikes Back*

Nevertheless, it would take nearly 20 years before Williams's film music is performed again by the New York Philharmonic. On 10 February 2004, Williams himself made his debut as a guest conductor with a programme consisting exclusively of his own works. Particular prominence had the "*Harry Potter* Suite", the "Tribute to the Film Composer" and "Escapades" from *Catch Me if You Can* (Steven Spielberg, 2002). The "Tribute to the Film Composer" is a medley showcasing Hollywood's most famous film themes, which Williams presented on the occasion of the 74th Academy Awards ceremony in 2002, where he was musical director[35].

Table 4: Programme of «The Art of the Score», New York Philharmonic, John Williams, 10 February 2004

Williams, John	Olympic Fanfare and Theme
Williams, John	Selections from *Close Encounters of the Third Kind*
Williams, John	Suite from *JFK*
Williams, John	Suite from the *Harry Potter* films (Hedwig's Theme, Fawkes the Phoenix, Nimbus 2000, Harry's Wondrous World)
arr. Williams, John	Tribute to the Film Composer
Williams, John	Selections from *Far and Away* (County Galway, June 1892; The Fighting Donnellys, Joseph and Shannon, Blowin' Off Steam [The Fight], Finale)
Williams, John	Escapades from *Catch Me if You Can*
Williams, John	Theme from *Schindler's List*
Williams, John	Adventures on Earth from *E. T.: The Extra-Terrestrial*
Williams, John	For New York (Encore)
Williams, John	Main Title from *Star Wars* (Encore)
Williams, John	The Mission (NBC News Theme) (Encore)

[35]. This work consists of a medley including "As Time Goes By" from *Casablanca* (Michael Curtiz, 1942); "Theme" from *Nuovo Cinema Paradiso* (Giuseppe Tornatore, 1988); "Overture" from *Citizen Kane* (Orson Welles, 1941); "Theme" from *E. T.: The Extra-Terrestrial*; "Theme" from *Exodus* (Otto Premiger, 1960); "Love Theme" from *The Godfather* (Francis Ford Coppola, 1972); "Theme" from *Rocky* (John G. Avildsen, 1976); "Main Title" from *Out of Africa* (Sydney Pollack, 1985); "Theme" from *Jaws*; "Theme" from *The Magnificent Seven* (John Sturges, 1960); "My Heart Will Go On" from *Titanic* (James Cameron, 1997); "Theme" from *The Natural* (Barry Levinson, 1984); "Theme" from *Patton* (Franklin J. Schaffner, 1970); "Theme" from *The Pink Panther* (Blake Edwards, 1963); "The Murder" from *Psycho* (Alfred Hitchcock, 1960); "The River Kwai March" from *The Bridge on the River Kwai* (David Lean, 1957); "Theme" from *The Sea Hawk* (Michael Curtiz, 1940); "Lara's Theme" from *Doctor Zhivago* (David Lean, 1965); "Love Theme" from *Spellbound* (Alfred Hitchcock, 1945); "Main Title" from *Star Wars*; "Tara's Theme" from *Gone With the Wind* (Victor Fleming, 1939); "20th Century Fox Fanfare" and "Warner Bros. Fanfare". With an average performance time of 4.30 minutes, many pieces are only quoted briefly.

On 12 April 2005, the New York Philharmonic performed another film-music concert under the direction of Leonard Slatkin, with Itzhak Perlman as a soloist.

Table 5: Programme of «An Evening of American Cinematic Musical Magic», New York Philharmonic, Leonard Slatkin, 12 April 2005

Newman, Alfred	20th Century Fox Fanfare
Rózsa, Miklós	Overture to *El Cid*
North, Alex	Love Theme from *Spartacus*
Chaplin, Charles	Smile from *Modern Times* (arr. John Williams)
Newman, Alfred	Cathy's Theme from *Wuthering Heights* (arr. John Williams)
Steiner, Max	Theme from *Now, Voyager* (arr. John Williams)
Korngold, Erich Wolfgang	Marian and Robin's Love Theme from *The Adventures of Robin Hood* (arr. John Williams)
Bernstein, Leonard	*On the Waterfront* Symphonic Suite from the Film
Bernstein, Elmer	Theme from *The Magnificent Seven*
Kamen, Michael	Scherzo (Marking Homework) from An American Symphony *(Mr. Holland's Opus)*
Raksin, David	Theme from *Laura*
Goldsmith, Jerry	Main Title from *Patton*
Barry, John	Main Theme from *Out of Africa*
Williams, John	Theme from *Far and Away*
Williams, John	Theme from *Schindler's List*
Gardel, Carlos	Tango (Por una cabeza) from *Scent of a Woman* (arr. John Williams)
Morricone, Ennio and Andrea	Theme from *Cinema Paradiso*
Shore, Howard	Symphonic Suite from *The Fellowship of the Ring*
Williams, John	The Imperial March from *The Empire Strikes Back* (Encore)

The first half of the programme was dedicated to the Golden Age composers, including three pieces arranged by Williams for violin and orchestra — Charlie Chaplin's "Smile" from *Modern Times* (Charlie Chaplin, 1935), Max Steiner's "Theme" from *Now, Voyager* (Irving Rapper, 1942) and Erich Wolfgang Korngold's "Love Theme" from *The Adventures of Robin Hood* (Michael Curtiz, William Keighley, 1938). In the second half there was a section dedicated to the film composers who died in 2004 — Elmer Bernstein, Jerry Goldsmith and David Raksin — and the concert ended with a selection of contemporary film scores, including a symphonic suite from Howard Shore's *The Lord of the Rings: The Fellowship of the Ring* (Peter Jackson, 2001). In this last section, Williams was prominently featured with pieces from *Far and Away* (Ron Howard, 1992), *Schindler's List*, Williams's own arrangement of Carlos Gardel's tango "Por una cabeza" and "The Imperial March".

In the two years that followed, Williams was once again an integral part of the New York concert schedule, this time as a guest conductor himself. On 24 and 26 April 2006, two concerts with identical programmes were held, with Steven Spielberg and Martin Scorsese as hosts.

Table 6: Programme of «Lights! Camera! Music»,
New York Philharmonic, John Williams, 24 and 26 April 2006

Herrmann, Bernard	Death Hunt from *On Dangerous Ground*
Herrmann, Bernard	The Inquirer from *Citizen Kane*
Herrmann, Bernard	Ballad of Springfield Mountain from *The Devil and Daniel Webster*
Herrmann, Bernard	Gallop: The Whip from *Currier and Ives Suite*
Herrmann, Bernard	Scène d'amour from *Vertigo*
Herrmann, Bernard	Music from *Psycho* (Prelude, The Murder)
Herrmann, Bernard	Two Selections from *Taxi Driver* (Night Piece for Orchestra, Prelude/Night Prowl – Blues)
Herrmann, Bernard	Prelude from *North by Northwest*
Williams, John	Theme from *Jaws*
Williams, John	Excerpts from *Close Encounters of the Third Kind*
Williams, John	Out to Sea/Shark Cage Fugue from *Jaws*
Williams, John	Excerpt from *Indiana Jones and the Last Crusade*
Williams, John	Theme from *Schindler's List*
Williams, John	Finale from *E. T.: The Extra-Terrestrial*
Williams, John	Prayer for Peace from *Munich* (Encore)
Williams, John	Main Title from *Star Wars* (Encore)
Williams, John	The Mission (NBC News Theme) (Encore)
Williams, John	For New York (Encore)

Williams dedicated the first half of the concert to his colleague Bernard Herrmann, with a sweeping selection from his film-music works. In the second half, the focus was on the ongoing cooperation between Williams and Spielberg. Williams performed his own compositions for *Jaws*, *Close Encounters of the Third Kind* (Steven Spielberg, 1977), *Indiana Jones and the Last Crusade* (Steven Spielberg, 1989), *Schindler's List* and *E. T.: The Extra-Terrestrial*. As encores, excerpts from *Munich* (Steven Spielberg, 2005), the "Mission Theme" for the NBC News and the "Main Title" from *Star Wars* were performed. A similarly presentation of Williams's film music can be found in the programme of the three concerts from 14 to 16 September 2007; here Williams performed "Sayuri's Theme" from *Memoirs of a Geisha* (Rob Marshall, 2005).

Table 7: Programme of Unnamed Concert,
New York Philharmonic, John Williams, 14-16 September 2007

Williams, John	Sound The Bells!
Williams, John	Flight to Neverland from *Hook*
Williams, John	Suite from *Jane Eyre* (Lowood, To Thornfield, Reunion)
Williams, John	Suite from the *Harry Potter* films (Hedwig's Theme, Aunt Marge's Waltz, Harry's Wondrous World)
Bock, Jerry	Selections from *Fiddler on the Roof* (adapt. John Williams)
Whiting	Hooray for Hollywood from *Hollywood Hotel* (arr. John Williams)

Lane/Lerner	You're All the World to Me from *Royal Wedding*
DePaul/Mercer	Bless Your Beautiful Hide from *Seven Brides for Seven Brothers*
Previn/Comden/Green	I Like Myself from *It's Always Fair Weather*
Fain/Freed	The Worry Song from *Anchors Aweigh*
Brown/Freed	Singin' in the Rain from *Singin' in the Rain*
Williams, John	Sayuri's Theme from *Memoirs of a Geisha*
Williams, John	A Tribute to George Lucas and Steven Spielberg
Williams, John	Theme from *Sugarland Express* (Encore)
Williams, John	The Olympic Spirit (Encore)
Williams, John	The Mission (NBC News Theme) (Encore)

Since then, Williams has been a regularly performed composer in the repertoire of the New York Philharmonic. In particular, his music from *Schindler's List* is frequently featured, for example, in a concert on 2 December 2009, where it was the only film-music piece to be included in the programme alongside works by Liszt, Bruch and Tchaikovsky.

Williams himself appeared again as a guest conductor on 25 October 2011 with Gil Shaham as a soloist. In this concert Williams once again chose, in addition to his own compositions, to perform pieces by Golden Age composers as well as the aforementioned "Tribute to the Film Composer". Shaham played the violin solo in Williams's arrangement of "Por una cabeza", in "Excerpts" from *Fiddler on the Roof* (Norman Jewison, 1971), and in "Three Pieces" from *Schindler's List*.

Table 8: Programme of «John Williams: A Night At The Movies», New York Philharmonic, John Williams, 25 October 2011

Whiting	Hooray for Hollywood from *Hollywood Hotel*
Korngold, Erich Wolfgang	March from *The Adventures of Robin Hood*
Herrmann, Bernard	Scène d'amour from *Vertigo*
North, Alex	Forest Meeting / Love Theme and March from *Spartacus*
Williams, John	Selections from *Close Encounters of the Third Kind*
	Adventures on Earth from *E. T.: The Extra-Terrestrial*
arr. Williams, John	Tribute to the Film Composer
Gardel, Carlos	Tango (Por una cabeza) from *Scent of a Woman* (arr. John Williams)
Williams, John	Three Pieces from *Schindler's List* (Remembrances, Krakow Ghetto Winter '41, Theme)
Bock, Jerry	Excerpts from *Fiddler on the Roof* (adapt. John Williams)
Williams, John	Main Title from *Star Wars*
Williams, John	Theme from *Sabrina* (Encore)
Williams, John	Yoda's Theme from *Star Wars* (Encore)
Williams, John	The Raider's March from *Raiders of the Lost Ark* (Encore)
Williams, John	Imperial March from *Star Wars* (Encore)

Conductor David Newman performed an all-Williams programme on 24 May 2016, where he gave the New York premiere of "Rey's Theme" from *Star Wars: The Force Awakens*.

Table 9: Programme of «A John Williams Celebration», New York Philharmonic, David Newman, 24 May 2016

Williams, John	For New York
Williams, John	Excerpts from *Close Encounters of the Third Kind*
Williams, John	Selections from *Jane Eyre* (Lowood, To Thornfield)
Williams, John	Sayuri's Theme from *Memoirs of a Geisha*
Williams, John	Harry's Wondrous World from *Harry Potter and the Sorcerer's Stone*
Williams, John	The Barrel Chase from *Jaws*
Williams, John	*Born on the Fourth of July*
Williams, John	Motorcycle Chase from *Indiana Jones and the Last Crusade*
Williams, John	Theme from *Schindler's List*
Williams, John	Rey's Theme from *Star Wars: The Force Awakens*
Williams, John	Throne Room and Finale from *Star Wars*
Williams, John	Flying Theme from *E. T.: The Extra-Terrestrial* (Encore)

Newman also conducted entire Williams film scores live to film: on 12 and 13 May 2017 *E. T.: The Extra-Terrestrial*, and in September and October 2017 all the film scores for the *Star Wars* classic trilogy plus *The Force Awakens*. Like Boston Pops, the New York Philharmonic has markedly increased the presence of film music since the beginning of the 2000s.

John Williams in Concert Halls Worldwide

Like Williams, conductor John Mauceri is a pioneer and an advocate of the concert presentation of film music, and he already led numerous film music concerts with the Hollywood Bowl Orchestra in the 1990s[36]. In the 2000s, Mauceri was a regular guest conductor with the Leipzig Gewandhaus Orchestra and played a major role in the distribution of concertante film-music performances worldwide. Like Williams, Mauceri emphasizes the value of film-music: «movie music is not a genre of music. [...] What differentiates it from other music is its frequent requirement to fit within a specific and pre-existing amount to time to do whatever it needs to do. Great music written for the cinema is great music»[37]. As an example, he cites Howard Shore's *The Lord of the Rings* Symphony, which was performed more than 100 times in the first two and a half years after its release[38]. However, he admits that «most music written for the cinema, like all those forgotten symphonies, string quartets, operas and ballets, is not [great music]»[39].

[36]. See Audissino 2014, p. 194. Mauceri was also a regular guest conductor with the Boston Pops Orchestra in the 1980s.

[37]. Mauceri 2006, p. 60.

[38]. See *ibidem*, p. 59. Mauceri also had a significant role in preparing Shore's source materials for the symphonic performance.

[39]. *Ibidem*, p. 60.

All of Mauceri's concerts with the Gewandhaus Orchestra had an overarching theme that was personally chosen by Mauceri:

> When I was first invited to conduct Leipzig's Gewandhaus Orchestra [...] I was asked to bring music from Hollywood composed by those Germans who had fled the Nazi era and who brought their European-trained genius to a new medium: sound film. Although my first program was exclusively music written for Hollywood films, I soon began programming concerts that *included* film music, but were based around some idea, like Love and Death, Time and Space, Two Worlds, Big and Little Heroes[40].

Like Williams, Mauceri also regards film music as a legitimate repertoire, not only for film-music concerts but also included in concert-music programmes. It is no surprise that all but one of Mauceri's concerts with the Gewandhaus Orchestra also included Williams pieces.

TABLE 10: PROGRAMME OF «MUSIC FROM HOLLYWOOD», GEWANDHAUS ORCHESTRA, JOHN MAUCERI, 14 AND 15 JANUARY 2000

Waxman, Franz	*Sunset Boulevard* - A Sonata for Orchestra (arr. John Mauceri)
Waxman, Franz	Suite from *A Place in the Sun*
Gershwin, George	An American in Paris
Korngold, Erich Wolfgang	Symphonic Suite from *The Adventures of Robin Hood*
Rózsa, Miklós	The Prince and the Princess from *The Thief of Bagdad*
Williams, John	Dinosaur Theme from *Jurassic Park**
Williams, John	Final Scene from *Schindler's List***
Newman, Alfred	20th Century Fox Fanfare
Williams, John	Throne Room and End Title from *Star Wars*
Williams, John	Flying Theme from *E. T.* (Encore)

*. Despite the alternate title, this is actually Theme from *Jurassic Park*.
**. Despite the alternate title, this is actually Theme from *Schindler's List*.

As can be seen, Williams is featured rather prominently and shares the programme with film composers from the Golden Age and with George Gershwin's *An American in Paris* — not a film score but an outstanding example of programme music. For the second concert on 20 and 21 December 2001, Mauceri focused on «Love and Jazz» and the only Williams piece was "Cantina Band" from *Star Wars*[41]. For the third concert, the programme's theme was «American Journeys» and Williams was again on the list.

---

40. *Ibidem*, p. 60. Emphasis in original.

41. This is a little bit surprising because Williams has been no stranger to jazzy scores, albeit his latest entry in this genre, *Catch Me if You Can*, had yet to be composed at that time However, Mauceri could have included "Swing, Swing, Swing" from *1941* (Steven Spielberg, 1979).

Table 11: Programme of «American Journeys»,
Gewandhaus Orchestra, John Mauceri, 10 and 11 January 2003

Weill, Kurt	The Seven Deadly Sins - Ballet chanté
Williams, John	Liberty Fanfare
	Oh, Shenandoah! (arr. Carmen Dragon)
Newman, Alfred	Selznick International Pictures Fanfare
Steiner, Max	Suite from *Gone with the Wind*
Morricone, Ennio	Theme from *The Untouchables* (arr. Henry Mancini)
Barry, John	Music from *Dances with Wolves*
Bernstein, Elmer	Music from *The Magnificent Seven*
Williams, John	Suite from the *Harry Potter* movies*

*. There is no further indication in the archives which particular film or suite is meant. Unfortunately, there is no archived recording of this concert, so therefore it is not possible to determine which piece has actually been played at this time.

Carrying on with his inclusive policy, Mauceri not only performed film pieces by Steiner, Morricone, Barry and Bernstein but also included non-film music entries such as the American traditional song "Oh Shenandoah", Williams's "Liberty Fanfare"[42] and Kurt Weill's ballet music "The Seven Deadly Sins"[43]. The presence of Williams's "*Harry Potter* Suite" in an America-themed programme might seem unmotivated — being *Harry Potter* quintessentially British — but the film version is American (produced by Warner Bros.).

The presence of Williams was stronger in the fourth and fifth Mauceri concerts from late 2003 and early 2005.

Table 12: Programme of «Myths and Wonder»,
Gewandhaus Orchestra, John Mauceri, 19 and 20 December 2003

Wagner, Richard	Ride of the Valkyries from The Valkyrie
Holst, Gustav	Jupiter, the Bringer of Jollity from The Planets
Dukas, Paul	L'apprenti sorcier
Williams, John	Music from *Harry Potter and the Chamber of Secrets* (Fawkes the Phoenix, Dobby the House Elf, The Chamber of Secrets)
Shore, Howard	Music from *The Lord of the Rings*
Williams, John	Theme from *Jurassic Park*
Williams, John	Music from *Close Encounters of the Third Kind**
Rózsa, Miklós	Music from *Ben Hur* (Overture, Parade of the Charioteers, Love Theme, Miracle and Finale)

[42]. Williams composed this piece in 1986 on the occasion of the 100th anniversary of the Statue of Liberty.

[43]. Weill's piece was composed and premiered in 1933 in Paris, France. The ballet tells the story of the singer/dancer Anna (the roles are performed separately on stage) who encounters the seven deadly sins on her journey through seven American cities.

Williams, John	Music from *Harry Potter and the Sorcerer's Stone*** (Encore)
Williams, John	Music from *Raiders of the Lost Ark**** (Encore)

*. This is actually Excerpts from *Close Encounters of the Third Kind*, published by Hal Leonard.
**. This is actually Hedwig's Theme from *Harry Potter and the Sorcerer's Stone*.
***. This is actually Raiders March from *Raiders of the Lost Ark*.

Mauceri's theme for the first of these concerts was «Myths and Wonder». Mauceri coupled Wagner with Shore (*The Lord of the Rings*) as well as with Holst and Dukas, adding an extensive selection from the Williams repertoire. Here, Mauceri seemed to be stressing some narrative similarities between Dukas's *L'apprenti sorcier* and *Harry Potter* — who is himself a 'sorcerer's apprentice'. Holst was paired with "Excerpts" from *Close Encounters of the Third Kind*, while the Williams set was completed with music from *Jurassic Park* (Steven Spielberg, 1993), *Raiders of the Lost Ark*, and more music from the first three *Harry Potter* films. For the concert called «Big and Little Heroes» Mauceri selected "Somewhere In My Memory" from *Home Alone*, together with "Something Wicked This Way Comes" from *Harry Potter and the Prisoner of Azkaban* (Alfonso Cuarón, 2004) and "Exsultate Justi" from *Empire of the Sun* (Steven Spielberg, 1987), thus forming a «triptych» — as Mauceri himself called it during the concert — for children's choir[44].

Table 13: Programme of «Big and Little Heroes»,
Gewandhaus Orchestra, John Mauceri, 28 and 29 January 2005

Korngold, Erich Wolfgang	Fanfare from *King's Row*
Wagner, Richard	Siegfried-Idyll WWV 103
Wagner, Richard	Siegfried's Death and Funeral Music from Götterdämmerung
Korngold, Erich Wolfgang	Robin and his Merry Men from the Symphonic Suite of *The Adventures of Robin Hood*
Williams, John	Bugler's Dream/Olympic Fanfare
Elfman, Danny	Music from *Edward Scissorhands*
Shore, Howard	Finale from *The Lord of the Rings: The Fellowship of the Ring*
Rózsa, Miklós	Love Theme from *El Cid*
Williams, John	Somewhere in my Memory (from *Home Alone*)
Williams, John	Something Wicked This Way Comes from *Harry Potter and the Prisoner of Azkaban [= Double Trouble]*
Williams, John	Exsultate Justi from *Empire of the Sun*
Arnold, David	Music from *Tomorrow Never Dies*

44. On the archive recording, Mauceri explicitly thanks John Williams for the opportunity to perform these pieces and emphasizes that this is a European premiere. It can therefore be assumed that Mauceri, in the same way as Williams frequently did, used a manuscript version and not the published Hal Leonard score for performance. In his Leipzig concerts, Mauceri did this in any case with Howard Shore's *Lord of the Rings* Symphony, from which he performed excerpts in advance.

Again, he combined these film-music pieces with pieces by Richard Wagner and Williams's concert miniature "Olympic Fanfare and Theme"[45]. Mauceri's last concert with the Gewandhaus Orchestra in 2008 only featured "Excerpts" from *Close Encounters of the Third Kind* — surprisingly, as in a programme titled «Time and Space» one would have expected more Williams 'space' music. Mauceri's pro-film music policy seems to have had little influence on the orchestra, though: after the era of Mauceri's guest conductorship, Williams's and other film music have virtually not appeared again in the programmes of the Gewandhaus Orchestra[46]. Yet, in the following years other important 'classical music' institutions would show important changes of attitude towards the film-music repertoire.

In 2014, the Los Angeles Philharmonic scheduled a one-off John Williams Gala Concert at the Walt Disney Hall under the direction of music director Gustavo Dudamel[47]. Dudamel prepared a selection from both Williams's film-music and concert-music repertoires: "Soundings", "Three Pieces from *Schindler's List*", "Cadenza and Variations from *Fiddler on the Roof*" (with Itzhak Perlman as the soloist)[48], "Escapades from *Catch Me if You Can*", "The Duel" from *The Adventures of Tintin*, "Dry Your Tears, Afrika" from *Amistad* (Steven Spielberg, 1997), and "Throne Room and Finale" from *Star Wars*. Williams — who attended the entire concert — was invited onstage to conduct the encore, "The Imperial March" from *The Empire Strikes Back*. In 2015, at the Waldbühne arena, the Berlin Philharmonic Orchestra held a concert called «Lights, Camera, Action» under the baton of Sir Simon Rattle. The programme featured rarely performed pieces from *Mutiny on the Bounty* (Lewis Milestone, 1962) by Bronislau Kaper, *The Big Country*

---

45. Composed in 1984 for the Los Angeles Summer Olympics.

46. However, the Gewandhaus Orchestra had a one off film-music concert in 2009 as part of its season finale. Here, Williams was featured with his concert arrangements of "Flight to Neverland" from *Hook* and suites from *Harry Potter and the Sorcerer's Stone*, *Star Wars: Episode 1 – The Phantom Menace*, and *E. T.: The Extra-Terrestrial*. It is interesting to note that the suite from *Star Wars: Episode 1 – The Phantom Menace* is rarely performed in its entirety, compared to the material from the other *Star Wars* films. However, the Gewandhaus Orchestra's performance omitted the chorus part in the final piece of the suite, "Duel of the Fates". In 2018, BSO music director Andris Nelsons took over the post of *Gewandhauskapellmeister* — which is equivalent to music director — in addition to his Boston commitment. This might lead to a policy change. For the 2018-2019 season, a dedicated Pops concert featuring film music is already scheduled with the Gewandhaus Orchestra and guest conductor Keith Lockhart.

47. In fact, Dudamel is a well-known admirer of Williams's film music and was invited to conduct the end title cues of *Star Wars: The Force Awakens* during the scoring sessions. Dudamel is credited for his conducting duties in the end credits of the film as well as in the album credits. In 2009, Dudamel — appointed the new music director of the Los Angeles Philharmonic — had already invited Williams as guest conductor for a three-part series of film music concerts entitled «Music from the City of Angels». See Audissino 2014, p. 196.

48. Despite the alternate title, this is actually "Excerpts of *Fiddler on the Roof*" as published by Hal Leonard.

(William Wyler, 1958) by Jerome Moross, or Scott Bradley's theme from the *Tom and Jerry* animated shorts, but also showcased some of the repertoire's staples like Korngold's suite from *The Adventures of Robin Hood* or Rózsa's selections from *Ben Hur* (William Wyler, 1959). Notably, the programme also included Edvard Grieg's *Piano Concerto in A* with Lang Lang as a soloist, showing that Rattle — like Mauceri — had no particular reservations in combining film music with the traditional concert repertoire. Williams's music was presented at the very end of the programme: *Raiders of the Lost Ark*, *E. T.: The Extra-Terrestrial*, and *Star Wars* to bring the concert to a rousing end. Talking at the audience, Rattle emphasized that «no film music concert would be complete without John Williams», continuing that «my children said to me that if we did not play *Raiders of the Lost Ark*, they would not attend. However, it's superb music!»[49]. On 3 and 6 September 2015 Simone Pedroni conducted Milan's Giuseppe Verdi Symphony Orchestra and Chorus in the first all-*Star Wars* programme featured in a regular 'classical' concert season. In July 2016 the concert was reprised, with the addition of new music from *The Force Awakens*. More recently, Keith Lockhart conducted a BBC Proms Concert on 20 July 2017 in celebration of Williams's 85th anniversary.

CONCLUSION

During his time with the Boston Pops Orchestra Williams has been a major player in making film music a legitimate choice for concert presentations. Williams has been a pioneer and an example for conductors all over the world wishing to include film music in their concert programmes and thus supersede the prejudice that sees it as a minor art form. As Sullivan commented, «No one has been more successful over a longer span than Williams in bridging Hollywood and Carnegie Hall»[50]. The Boston Pops Orchestra and the New York Philharmonic in particular, but also other orchestras, have recorded a marked increase in film-music concerts to the last years. And Williams's music is an almost constant presence in both the film-music programmes and in those programmes that combine concert music with film music[51]. Williams has the ability to take a film's story

49. Own translation. Rattle made his speech in German.

50. SULLIVAN 2008, p. 32.

51. As regards the performance of film music in concert, the biggest difference between film music and 'regular' concert music is availability. While concert music is available in practically all cases through music publishers either for sale or rent, this is rarely the case with film music. Usually, the copyright of the film score is transferred to the production company or to the film studio, both for the sound recording and the score itself, and the majority of companies show little interest in the publication of a performable score. At times, copies remain with the composer or other persons involved in the production process, which then are sometimes transferred as an estate to university libraries or private collections (see POOL – WRIGHT 2011, p. 103). In these cases many scores consists only of conductor's scores, a condensed version of the score

and re-narrate it through musical means, which is not different from what happens with tone poems or other types of applied music that are sometimes held in higher esteem than film music.

Bibliography

Audissino 2013

Audissino, Emilio. 'Archival Research and the Study of the Concert Presentations of Film Music: The Case of John Williams and the Boston Pops', in: *Journal of Film Music*, vi/2 (2013), pp. 147-163.

Audissino 2014

Id. *John Williams's Film Music: «Jaws», «Star Wars», «Raiders of the Lost Ark», and the Return of the Classical Hollywood Music Style*, Madison (WI), University of Wisconsin Press, 2014 (Wisconsin Film Studies).

Audissino 2017

Id. 'John Williams and Contemporary Film Music', in: *Contemporary Film Music: Investigating Cinema Narratives and Composition*, edited by Lindsay Coleman and Joakim Tillman, Basingstoke, Palgrave Macmillan, 2017, pp. 221-236.

Järvi 2014

Järvi, Kristjan. '«A Soundtrack to Our Lives…»', in: *Film in Concert: Film Scores and Their Relation to Classical Concert Music*, edited by Sebastian Stoppe, Glückstadt, Verlag Werner Hülsbusch, 2014 (AV-Medien), pp. 131-144.

Lissa 1965

Lissa, Zofia. *Ästhetik der Filmmusik*, Berlin, Henschelverlag, 1965.

Mauceri 2006

Mauceri, John. 'Did You Hear That? The Challenge of Programming Concerts Lies in How We Really Listen', in: *Symphony*, (November/December 2006), pp. 55-63.

Neher 2012

Neher, Erick. 'Movie Music at the Philharmonic', in: *The Hudson Review*, lxiv/4 (2012), pp. 668-674.

Pool – Wright 2011

Pool, Jeannie G. – Wright, Howard Stephen. *A Research Guide to Film and Television Music in the United States*, Lanham (MA), Scarecrow Press, 2011.

with the less important parts omitted (see *ibidem*, p. 97), so that the full scores have to be reconstructed, re-orchestrated, and parts extracted and copied for performances. This is especially the case with many Golden Age music. John Williams is one of the few film composers whose work is widely available from a music publisher for both sale and rental. The 'Hal Leonard Signature Edition' offers a series of concert arrangements from his film scores, arranged by Williams himself. In addition, the Juilliard School announced in 2018 that it has received a bequest from Williams of his complete library of film music scores as well as his composing sketches.

Prendergast 1977

Prendergast, Roy M. *Film Music: A Neglected Art: A Critical Study of Music in Films*, New York, Norton, 1977.

Stevens 2006

Stevens, Leigh. 'Music in the Films: The Promotion of Film Music in the Concert Hall', in: *The Journal of Film Music*, 1/4 (2006), pp. 339-340.

Stoppe 2014

Stoppe, Sebastian. 'Film Composing between Art and Business', in: *Film in Concert: Film Scores and Their Relation to Classical Concert Music*, edited by Sebastian Stoppe, Glückstadt, Verlag Werner Hülsbusch, 2014 (AV-Medien), pp. 11-23.

Sullivan 2008

Sullivan, Jack. 'Is Movie Music the New Classical?', in: *Symphony*, (November/December 2008), pp. 30-35.

Thiel 1981

Thiel, Wolfgang. *Filmmusik in Geschichte und Gegenwart*, Berlin, Henschelverlag, 1981.

Winters 2014

Winters, Ben. *Music, Performance, and the Realities of Film: Shared Concert Experiences in Screen Fiction*, Hoboken, Taylor and Francis, 2014 (Routledge Research in Music, 9).

The Williams Touch:
Style and Musical Dramaturgy

The Use of Variation in John Williams's Film Music Themes

Mark Richards
(Florida State Univeristy, Tallahassee, FL)

Williams is perhaps best known for his film music themes, most of which are based on eight-bar models that divide into discernible halves of 4+4 bars, each half usually containing two short ideas of two bars each[1]. Though this type of thematic structuring has been the norm for the majority of Hollywood film history[2], Williams's themes include variation more frequently than is typical for Hollywood films. More specifically, many of his themes for films from the mid 1970s through the early 1990s rework the initial idea such that it is not merely repeated or contrasted with, but varied.

From one point of view, variation within a film theme serves very practical purposes. The similarity of varied and initial ideas facilitates the recognition of such themes should they move beyond their first idea, which they usually do. This is an important consequence in film, where an audience's attention is divided among the narrative, images, dialogue, sound effects, and music. At the same time, since a varied idea involves both similarity to *and* difference from the initial idea, it provides a built-in sense of balance between coherence and variety, an especially effective technique for the richly leitmotivic scores Williams often writes, in which a small handful of themes typically permeates the film.

Yet from another point of view, themes with varied ideas can be interpreted as describing key narrative elements in a musical manner. Specifically, Williams's main themes from the mid 70s to the early 90s not only tend to paint a vivid picture of their narrative association through their melody, harmony, rhythm, and instrumentation, but themes with particular associations are also linked even more deeply to their narrative meanings

---

1. These eight-bar theme types frequently appear as sections of larger thematic structures such as those based on models of sixteen-bar periods, AB or ABA binary forms, and the like. However, in order for themes to group together in a consistent manner and to limit the scope of the present study, when such larger structures were encountered, only the theme type of its opening section, based on an eight-bar model, was included for analysis.

2. See my article, Richards 2016, Ex. 41.

by way of their thematic structure. In order to more fully appreciate the central role that variation plays in Williams's film music, an understanding of how these themes are constructed is necessary. I therefore divide this chapter into four parts: Part I lays out the theoretical framework for thematic structures. Part II describes the ways in which Williams varies a theme's initial idea and how it impacts the theme's expression. Part III illustrates the theme types that result from these varied ideas and how they help to communicate their narrative association. And Part IV explores tendencies of these themes with regard to time period and narrative association across Williams's entire career. The goal is to begin to construct a picture of how themes in Williams's film music operate musically to convey specific aspects of the film's narrative.

Part I: Theme Categories, Classes, and Types

If a film music theme is defined as a distinctive passage of music with a narrative association in the film[3], then all themes may be said to fall into one of three broad categories: *grammatical themes*, *motto themes*, and *discursive themes*[4]. Grammatical themes are generally based on eight-bar models and divide into beginning-end halves such as the antecedent and consequent of the traditional period form. By contrast, motto themes are shorter than grammatical ones, and although they may be looped into an ostinato, like Williams's main theme for *Jaws* (Steven Spielberg, 1975), structurally they achieve only a beginning portion and never venture into a second half that would become an answering end portion. Finally, discursive themes are relatively long themes that either lack the grouping into halves of grammatical themes or contain more than two such groupings, like Williams's main theme for *Catch Me if You Can* (Steven Spielberg, 2002). The result is a sizable theme that does not signal where it will end and thus gives a run-on impression by continually spinning its material out. Most of Williams's themes fall into the grammatical category, hence they will be the focus of this chapter.

Grammatical themes are further divided into four large classes that are defined by the relationship of the theme's second half to its first, as shown in Table 1: *sentence*, *clause*, *period*, and *composite*.

---

3. On a theme constituting a distinctive musical idea, see Cook 1992, p. 9, who remarks that the term 'theme' (in Western music generally) «refers to some readily recognizable musical element which serves a certain formal function by virtue of occurring at structural points». See also Bribitzer-Stull 2015, p. 34, who comments that, in order for it to be recognizable, «a theme must employ (and retain) a variety of identifiable musical parameters. These may include, but are not limited to: contour, rhythmic content, pitch content, length, orchestration, texture, register, tempo, harmonic progression, harmonic function, and contrapuntal framework».

4. This breakdown of themes into three large categories and the taxonomy of theme classes and types given below are discussed in detail in Richards 2016.

Table 1: Second Halves of Grammatical Themes

	1st Half	2nd Half	Formal Term for 2nd Half
Sentence	x ————————>	Acceleration	Continuation
Clause	x ————————>	Variation	Divergence
Period	x ————————>	Return	Antecedent
Composite	x ————————>	Contrast	Departure

In sentences, the second half begins with an acceleration in relation to the first half in terms of phrase structure, harmony, or surface rhythm. In clauses, the second half begins with a variation of the preceding idea in the first half. In periods, the second half begins as a return to the opening of the first half. And in composites, the second half begins with material that contrasts with the first half but does not accelerate. Each type of second half is described with a formal term, as shown in the figure.

Variation may occur between the two halves as in the clause, but it may also arise between the two ideas of a single half, particularly the first, which may be structured in one of three ways, as shown in Table 2.

Table 2: First Halves of Grammatical Themes

	1st Half	
	Idea 1	Idea 2
Presentation	A	A
Antecedent	A	B
Development	A	A2

Within a first half, the second idea may repeat the first idea to form a *presentation*, contrast with it to form an *antecedent*, or vary it to form a *development*. What I call the *basic form* of each theme class is that which is generally the most common in the film repertoire. The sentence and clause usually begin with a presentation, whereas the period and composite usually begin with an antecedent[5]. The *developing form* of a theme, which begins with a development, is therefore less common than the basic form. Themes may also adopt a first half that is the opposite of its typical layout (i.e., repetition instead of contrast or contrast instead of repetition). These are what I call the *hybrid form* of each theme. With four theme classes and three possible forms within each class, there are a total

[5]. Occasionally, a presentation will include a number of basic ideas other than two, usually one or three. When it contains only one, I term the structure a *monofold sentence* whereas when it contains three, I term it a *trifold sentence*. For more detail on these structures, see Richards 2011, pp. 190-196.

of twelve grammatical theme types, all of which are shown schematically in Table 3, the 'x' ending many themes indicating a variable position in which any material may occur[6].

Table 3: Twelve Types of Grammatical Theme as Determined by the Relationship of the Second Half to the First, and the Second Idea to the First

2nd Half Compared to 1st Half				
	BASIC FORM	DEVELOPING FORM	HYBRID FORM	
Acceleration	**Sentence** *Presentation* A A$^{(r)}$ *Continuation* Accel	**Developing Sentence** *Development* A A2 *Continuation* Accel	**Periodic Sentence** *Antecedent* A B *Continuation* Accel	SENTENCE
Variation	**Clause** *Presentation* A A$^{(r)}$ *Divergence* A2 x	**Developing Clause** *Development* A A2 *Divergence* A3 x	**Periodic Clause** *Antecedent* A B *Divergence* B2 x	CLAUSE
	HYBRID FORM	DEVELOPING FORM	BASIC FORM	
Return	**Sentential Period** *Presentation* A A' *Consequent* A x	**Developing Period** *Development* A A2 *Consequent* A$^{(r)}$ x	**Period** *Antecedent* A B *Consequent* A$^{(r)}$ x	PERIOD
Contrast	**Sentential Composite** *Presentation* A A$^{(r)}$ *Departure* B x	**Developing Composite** *Development* A A2 *Departure* B x	**Composite** *Antecedent* A B *Departure* C x	COMPOSITE
	Similar	Varied	Different	
		2nd Idea Compared to 1st Idea		

[6]. For the analysis of Williams's themes, Zacharopoulos 2017 adopts the period and several subtypes of the sentence according to the number of identical or varied ideas the theme states successively. Hence these categories do not distinguish between an idea's repetition and its variation, which, as I illustrate below, is a crucial distinction both for the patterns of associations that Williams's themes take on and for the division of his film scores into style periods. Zacharopoulos's categories, however, cannot simply be mapped onto those presented here since they rely on fundamentally different concepts. As I discuss below, the developing period and clause are two forms that are central to Williams's film themes but remain inaccessible within his categories. His period category for instance, includes not only my developing period, but the basic and sentential forms as well. Likewise, depending on the number of basic or varied ideas involved, clauses are categorized as trifold sentences such as the main theme from *Presumed Innocent* (Alan J. Pakula, 1990), as unfolding sentences such as the Irish theme from *Far and Away* (Ron Howard, 1992), or even sentences with dissolving third statements (Princess Leia's theme from *Star Wars* [George Lucas, 1977]). I therefore prefer the methodology outlined in the present chapter, which allows themes with variation to be separated from other types.

Part ii: Techniques of Variation in Williams's Film Themes

With the above theme types in place, we may now examine more precisely how Williams incorporates variation into the structure of his film themes. Most of his grammatical themes that employ variation do so through the manipulation of the first idea, called the *basic idea*. The resulting *developing idea* includes both similarity to and difference from the basic idea and may appear at any point after the initial basic idea[7]. Regardless of where the developing idea occurs, however, Williams employs four main techniques to refashion the basic idea into a developing one, as shown visually in Table 4. While these techniques tend to occur singly in any developing idea, they occasionally occur successively in the same idea[8].

Table 4: Means of Varying the Basic Idea To Create a Developing Idea

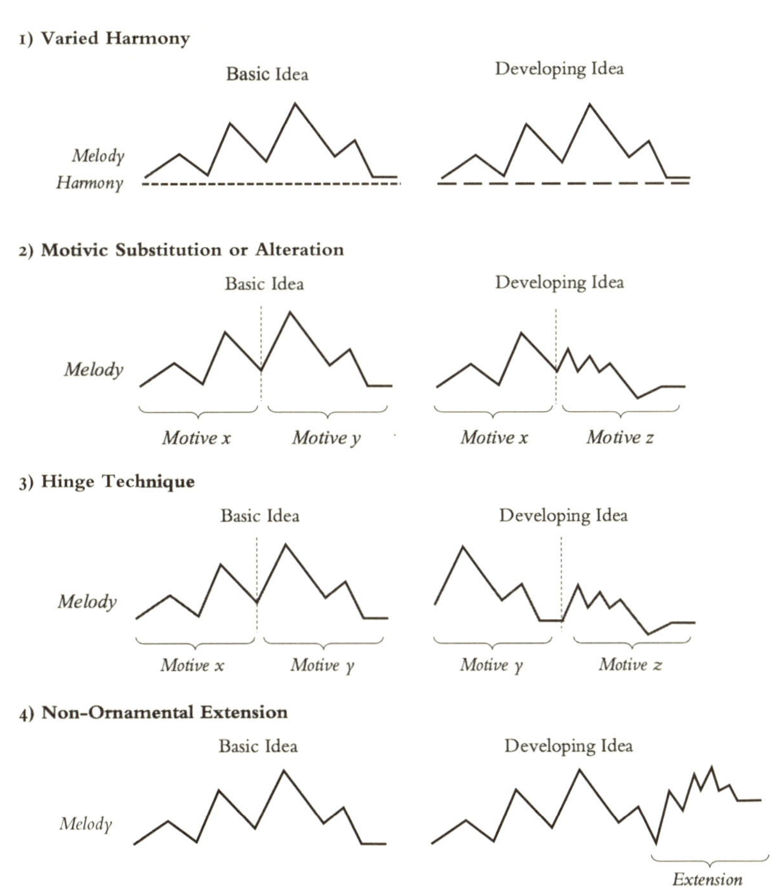

7. The term 'basic idea' is from Caplin 1998 whereas 'developing idea' is from Richards 2016.

8. See, for instance, "Parade of the Ewoks" in Ex. 5 and the "Force Theme" in Ex. 7.

Varied Harmony (Rhythm and Contour Essentially Intact)

A common device is to essentially retain the rhythm and contour of the entire basic idea but to vary its harmony, perhaps with smaller ornamental changes to the melody that do not drastically affect its structure. A good example occurs with the "Remembering Childhood" theme from *Hook* (Steven Spielberg, 1991), given in Ex. 1[9].

Ex. 1: variation in the "Remembering Childhood Theme" from *Hook* (© 1991 BMI), published by EMI Intertrax Music Inc, reduced from *The Flight to Neverland*, printed by Hal Leonard. Used in compliance with the U.S. Copyright Act, Section 107.

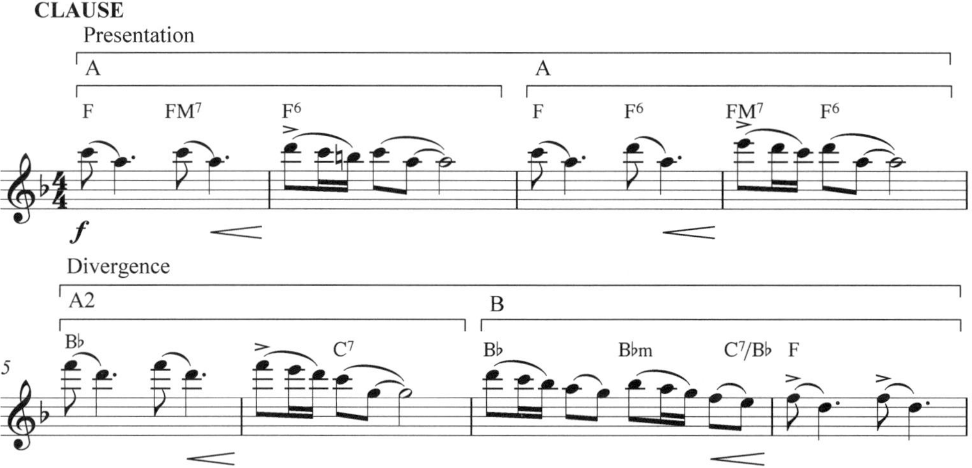

The opening basic idea begins with a repeated interval of a falling third from scale degree $\hat{5}$ to $\hat{3}$ of the major scale, a figure that appropriately evokes the world of a child through its appearance at the start of many traditional children's songs such as "Ring Around the Rosy", "This Old Man", "Rain, Rain, Go Away", and even the taunting "Nyah Nyah" song. These falling-third figures are set in a Lombard rhythm (i.e., reversed dotted rhythm) and flow into a turn figure set in a long-short-short rhythm that returns to the falling third with a closely-related syncopated figure. The second idea restates the first

[9]. Musical examples in this chapter are reductions of the original orchestral textures. Those with relatively simple textures are transcribed with two staves while those with very active or complex textures are instead notated in the manner of a lead sheet with a single staff of melody and chord symbols so as to maintain focus on the melodic ideas. Moreover, some examples are re-notated in a metre that clarifies the length of the basic idea as two perceived bars of music. See CAPLIN 1998, p. 35, which states that «what a listener perceives as "one full measure" of music does not necessarily correspond to the notated bar lines of the score. We thus need to distinguish between a *real*, experiential measure and a *notated* measure. The former, which may or may not correspond to the latter, is the only valid measure for an analysis of form based on our musical experience». The re-notated examples include the main themes from *Hook*, *Star Wars*, and *Close Encounters of the Third Kind*.

almost exactly as the rhythm and contour are preserved, forming a presentation. A few of its notes are raised up a step, and the harmonic extensions of the supporting F major chord are slightly shifted to accommodate the change in melody. But these alterations are minor and essentially leave the basic idea intact. With the third idea, the rhythms of the Lombard, long-short-short, and final syncopation are all preserved exactly as in the first idea, and the contour is the same except for the new downward inflection ending the long-short-short figure. The harmony, however, now breaks away from the unwavering F major support of the presentation, moving to a B♭ major chord and even changing to a C^7 within the same idea. The fact that two chords now accompany the idea rather than one produces an acceleration in the harmonic rhythm, a device that is typically associated with sentence continuations, which drive the theme toward its end. Consequently, although this third idea is clearly related to the preceding ideas, its harmonic alterations introduce fundamentally different material, breaking the pattern of repetition with the first two ideas and signalling that the theme is entering its second portion. In other words, what is stated here is not another basic idea, but a developing idea based on variation.

Motivic Substitution or Alteration

Another common technique for producing developing ideas in Williams's themes is the substitution or alteration of a portion of the basic idea, almost always after the head of the idea. The fanfare theme from *Superman: The Movie* (Richard Donner, 1978), given in Ex. 2 (p. 126), illustrates this concept.

Here, the basic idea comprises two distinct motives, labelled x and y. Both motives are composed only of scale degrees $\hat{1}$ and $\hat{5}$ of the major scale, and elaborate the intervals of the perfect fifth (C-G) and perfect octave (C-C, the highest and lowest notes)[10]. This emphasis on relatively large and very consonant intervals conveys a feeling of strength and heroism, and the on-beat march rhythm along with the militaristic triplet give the sense of a powerful force, both of which aptly describe the Superman character[11]. In the second idea, motive x is retained exactly while motive y is replaced with a new motive, z, which is given a fuller texture, louder dynamic, and a dotted rhythm that almost seems to speak the character's name[12]. Moreover, this new motive closes like a half cadence, on dominant harmony — quite a change from the constant tonic harmony that underpinned

[10]. MATESSINO *ET AL.* 2007 notes that the theme's emphasis on $\hat{1}$and the $\hat{5}$ above it (tonic and dominant) is an element that was preserved from two Superman themes in other media, both of which rise through the full major triad from tonic to dominant: one by Sammy Timberg for animated shorts in the 1940s and another attributed to Leon Klatzkin for the 1950s television series.

[11]. For more detail on this interpretation, see my blog post on the theme, RICHARDS 2013C.

[12]. As the film's director, Richard Donner, recalls, «the day we went into a recording studio, and we ran the opening credits, [and] as "Superman" came on the screen, I swear to God, if you listen carefully, it literally, the music, speaks the word». See THAU 2001.

Ex. 2: variation in the "Superman Fanfare" from *Superman: The Movie* (© 1978 BMI), published by Warner-Barham Music LLC, reduced from "Superman March", printed by Hal Leonard. Used in compliance with the U.S. Copyright Act, Section 107.

the opening basic idea. The second idea's combination of both similarity to and difference from the basic idea renders it a developing idea. This in turn renders the theme's first half a development within a developing period.

Hinge Technique

The two above variation techniques for developing ideas are the most widespread in Williams's film themes, but there are two others that appear occasionally. The first involves a restating of the basic idea's last motive as the first motive of the next idea, or what I call *hinge* technique[13]. The main-title theme from *Star Wars*, shown in Ex. 3, provides a fine instance of the technique.

---

[13]. I introduce this term in Richards 2016, paras. 49-51, using as examples the *Star Wars* main-title theme and "Gabriel's Oboe" from Ennio Morricone's score for *The Mission* (Roland Joffé, 1987).

Ex. 3: variation in the "Main Title" theme from *Star Wars* (© 1977 BMI), published by Bantha Music/ Warner-Tamerlane Publishing Corp., reduced from *Star Wars: Suite for Orchestra*, printed by Hal Leonard. Used in compliance with the U.S. Copyright Act, Section 107.

DEVELOPING PERIOD
Development
A1 A2
x y y y2
Consequent
A1 A2

Once again, the basic idea breaks down into two motives, x and y. And like the *Superman* fanfare, the two motives depict the strength, power, and heroism of the film's main character, Luke, through the emphasis on the perfect fifth (B♭-F) and octave (B♭-B♭, the highest and lowest notes), the on-beat articulation of most notes, and the triplet figure[14]. But with the second idea, motive y is relocated in the unit, appearing at the beginning rather than the end. Although motive x is completely omitted here, the restatement of motive y immediately after its initial appearance creates a clear connection between the first and second ideas. With the following y2 motive, however, the contour of motive y is altered, leaping down instead of up, the final note is omitted, and the harmony sounds an appropriately swashbuckling 'cowboy cadence' to complete the theme's first half[15]. With the hinge technique, then, it is the juxtaposition of motive y with itself that creates the clear similarity to the basic idea while the repositioning of the motive and omission

14. For more on motivic manipulation in the entire rounded binary structure of this theme, see my blog post, Richards 2013b.

15. Lehman 2013, para. 4.12, Schneller 2013, pp. 55-56, and Morrell 2013-2015, vol. 1, ch. 3, p. 13, likewise note the cowboy cadence in this theme. However, while film-music scholars regularly suggest that the cadence or modal triadic writing in general derives from Aaron Copland's Americana-styled music, Lehman 2013, fn. 47, cautions against such a link, raising as possibilities influences from Thomson or Ives, or original thought in the case of Moross and his landmark score for *The Big Country* (William Wyler, 1958).

of motive x involves enough difference to distinguish it from the basic idea and instead produce a developing idea[16].

Non-Ornamental Extension

The final means by which a developing idea may be formed in Williams's themes is by a non-ornamental extension added onto an essentially intact basic idea. Consider the main theme to *SpaceCamp* (Harry Winer, 1986), shown in Ex. 4.

Ex. 4: variation in the main theme from *SpaceCamp* (© 1986 BMI), published by ABC Circle Music/ Marjer Publishing Company, ear transcription from the film's soundtrack. Used in compliance with the U.S. Copyright Act, Section 107.

DEVELOPING SENTENCE
Development
A
A2
B♭
Continuation
Fragmentation
Dm
E♭

This theme is associated with the sense of awe the adolescent characters share for the wonders of outer space, and the structure of its basic idea expresses a musical version of this sentiment. The basic idea encompasses a gradual stepwise motion up the major scale from degree $\hat{1}$ to $\hat{3}$ (B♭-C-D). Note, however, that there is a slight pause on the second note through the tie, then the initial ascent from $\hat{1}$ to $\hat{2}$ is repeated in a faster rhythm before leaping up to scale degree $\hat{5}$. This chain of events suggests being captivated by something positive, beautiful perhaps, and repeatedly striving to attain it. After the first 'reach' up to $\hat{5}$, the following $\hat{3}$ suggests modest progress from the initial earthbound tonic. The following idea replicates this trajectory with the exception of a larger leap upward, to $\hat{7}$ rather than $\hat{5}$, before falling back to the same scale degree $\hat{3}$. The larger

[16]. As I demonstrate in RICHARDS 2015, "Across the Stars", the main theme to *Star Wars, Episode II: Attack of the Clones* (George Lucas, 2002), possesses not only the same thematic structure as the original film's main theme for Luke, but also very similar motivic material. As a result, the later theme can be heard as a darkened, pessimistic version of the original, establishing an appropriate musical opposition between the tragic fate of Anakin and Padme's love and the heroic fate of Luke.

leap seems to imply a more outstretched reach for the source of captivation, while the return to $\hat{3}$ now becomes a stepping stone to greater heights. Upon arriving at $\hat{3}$, the idea is extended up several steps, now reaching scale degree $\hat{7}$ in the more 'attainable' manner of stepwise motion. The extension not only continues the stepwise ascent begun with the basic idea, but also possesses its own hesitant pause, now on $\sharp\hat{4}$, a chromatic note borrowed from the Lydian mode that in film has, among other things, come to signify wonder and amazement[17]. The stepwise ascent continues into the theme's final notes, where it reaches a euphoric tonic degree at the very top of the scale, but now over the IV chord instead of the tonic. Although this tonic degree is in one sense stable since it is the tonic, its accompanying change of harmony renders it the fifth of the chord, which sits high atop the chordal root (understood as a perfect fifth below it). The emotional implication is both one of satisfaction at having achieved a desired goal (such as reaching outer space), and yet having one's sense of wonder suddenly expanded upon reaching that goal (as though experiencing the sheer vastness of space once arriving there). With its seamless integration into the material of the basic idea and the material that follows, it would be difficult to dismiss this extension as merely ornamentation of a repeated basic idea. Instead, the extension adds substantial difference to the material, producing a developing idea within another small-scale development and, with the fragmentation that follows it, a developing sentence overall.

Part iii: Theme Types with Developing Ideas in Williams

As we have seen, a developing idea can define different theme types depending on its position in the theme. Of the twelve types of grammatical themes, six include at least one developing idea: the basic, developing, and hybrid forms of the clause (which contain variation by definition) and the developing form of the other three theme classes (sentence, period, and composite). Of these six possible forms, Williams displays a distinct preference for only two: the developing period and the clause, shown schematically in Table 5. As before, each 'x' below is a variable representing any material.

---

[17]. As noted by Lehman 2012, pp. 31-32, and Schneller 2013, pp. 68-71. On p. 69, Schneller indicates that the *SpaceCamp* theme in particular intensifies these associations by twice transposing the Lydian I–II$\sharp$ progression up a step, reproducing it on a larger scale. On the Lydian mode in general, Karlin – Wright 2004, pp. 227-233, similarly points out that it «has been used many times to evoke a sense of other-worldliness», which certainly applies to this film, as does the observation in Lehman 2012, p. 14, fn. 2, that the Lydian aspects of this score, among several others, create an «empyrean» effect. Hence, in addition to the otherworldly association of the mode in film, I would add that this quality is generally a positive one.

TABLE 5: DEVELOPING PERIOD AND CLAUSE

Developing Period				
	Development		Consequent	
	A	A2	A	x
Clause				
	Presentation		Divergence	
	A	A	A2	x

Of the six theme types with a developing idea, these are the only two to include both a repetition *and* a variation of the basic idea, ensuring both unity and variety within the theme's structure.

Developing Period

While the developing period was seen earlier with the themes from *Superman* and *Star Wars*, Ex. 5 gives another instance in "Parade of the Ewoks" from *Return of the Jedi* (Richard Marquand, 1983) that is worked out quite differently.

Ex. 5: developing period, "Parade of the Ewoks" from *Return of the Jedi* (© 1983 BMI), published by Bantha Music/Warner-Tamerlane Publishing Corp., reduced from *Music from the Star Wars Saga*, printed by Hal Leonard. Used in compliance with the U.S. Copyright Act, Section 107.

Here, the basic idea begins with a three-note motive on a dotted rhythm that, together with the 4/4 time, on-beat articulations, accompanying staccato chords, and soft dynamic, suggests the inconspicuous military might of the Ewoks. At the same time, the accompaniment's inclusion of the note E in the B♭ major chords expresses the Lydian mode, which here evokes a positive, otherworldly quality[18]. The melody includes D♭ as well, which clashes with the accompaniment's D♮. But since these D♭s are in such a high register, their clashing impact is minimized, the result being more playful than fearful — an affect that captures a central aspect of the creatures' role in the film. The second idea begins just as the first did, then continues its rhythms with altered intervals, and replaces the rhythm of its last bar with a longer note that signals the end of the first half. Clearly, this second idea is a developing one, rendering the first half a development. The second half opens with the same basic idea as the first, forming a consequent, but alters the last few notes so as to end more conclusively, on the tonic note. This developing period is therefore composed of four ideas that are either identical or variations of one another. Given the playfulness of the theme, its construction from a single idea and its variations, along with the crystal clear symmetry between the two halves, indicates a kind of simplicity, one that evokes something of a child-like innocence, which is yet another aspect of the Ewoks that this theme manages to express[19].

Clause

As noted earlier, the other very common theme type in Williams that incorporates developing ideas is the clause. Like the developing period, this theme type has already appeared above, in the theme from *Hook*, but a more extensive treatment of the form is heard in the main theme from *Close Encounters of the Third Kind* (Steven Spielberg, 1977), shown in Ex. 6 (p. 132).

Although this theme is, in a sense, associated with Devils Tower (the location where humans finally meet the aliens face-to-face), its appearances in the film rather identify it as a theme of awe-filled discovery at gradually learning more about the significance of the Tower[20]. With this in mind, consider the theme's opening three notes, the first of which is set to a BM^7 chord in the accompaniment that clearly establishes B as the tonic. In motive x, with the G♯ in the melody moving to A♯ as scale degrees $\hat{6}$ and $\hat{7}$ in B major, we would expect the

[18]. It is notable that the Lydian mode is also a central aspect of another of Williams's prominent *Star Wars* themes: that for Yoda who, like the Ewoks, is a small alien creature who assists the Rebels in their cause.

[19]. Reinforcing this interpretation is Williams's orchestration of the theme, which includes a toy piano when it first appears in the film and when it returns in the end credits.

[20]. Just as the significance of the tower is slowly disclosed in the film, so is its theme, at first appearing only in fragments and only reaching its full form with the end credits, after the aliens have been fully revealed and as the full splendour of their mothership is revealed. Audissino 2014 calls this technique in Williams's scores «gradual disclosure of the main theme» (p. 126), citing examples in *E. T.*, *Jaws*, and later in the book, in *Raiders of the Lost Ark* (p. 178).

Ex. 6: clause, "Devils Tower Theme" from *Close Encounters of the Third Kind* (© 1977 BMI), published by EMI Gold Horizon Music Corp., reduced from *Excerpts from Close Encounters of the Third Kind*, printed by Hal Leonard. Used in compliance with the U.S. Copyright Act, Section 107.

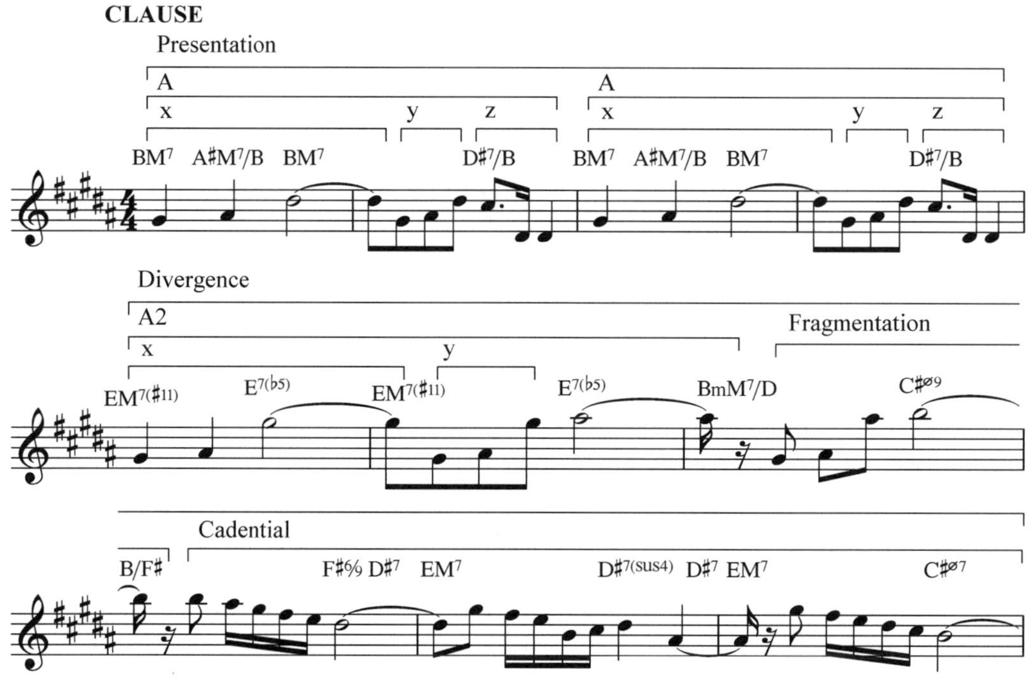

following note to be the tonic, B. But instead, the melody leaps up to D♯ ($\hat{3}$), another note in the B major chord. This act of reaching to a note beyond the nearest goal suggests an exuberance that cannot be contained simply by rising stepwise up the scale to B. Yet at the same time, it also deprives the figure of its expected goal tone and thus evades resolution. The entire basic idea is then repeated to form a presentation, extending this evasiveness across the clause's entire first half. Along with the theme's major-mode setting, one can well interpret the first half as reflecting the main characters' emotions in the film's moments of discovery; namely, being immersed in a trance-like state brought on by an overwhelming feeling of awe.

A developing idea then begins the second half, motive x now reaching more energetically to G♯, and motive y stretching even further to A♯, a resolution to B now palpably imminent, especially with motive z now being omitted. Indeed, B does follow in the next iteration of the reaching figure, but it is harmonized with a C♯ half-diminished chord, then a cadential 6/4 chord, both of which render the B a dissonance that does not attain the comfort of a stable, consonant chord tone. Nevertheless, the cascading contours that follow in the melody imply a gleeful celebration, as though revelling in one's awe and the discoveries it brings. This expression is emphasized at the theme's end, where, although ending on B, the harmonic support is once again the half-diminished seventh on C♯, even here avoiding resolution on a tonic B major chord.

Developing Clause

The remaining theme types discussed in this section appear far less frequently than the developing period and clause. I include them here because they are represented by at least one example from a well known film. The first of these is the developing clause, given schematically in Table 6.

Table 6: Developing Clause

Developing Clause				
	Development		Divergence	
	A	A2	A3	x

With this theme type, it may seem that three successive similar ideas ought to be grouped together within the same portion of a theme. But in developing clauses, the third idea brings about greater change than does the second idea, hence pointing in a new direction that signals the onset of the second half. One instance is the "Force Theme" from *Star Wars*, shown in Ex. 7.

Ex. 7: developing clause, the "Force Theme" from *Star Wars* (© 1977 BMI), published by Bantha Music/ Warner-Tamerlane Publishing Corp., reduced from *Star Wars: Suite for Orchestra*, printed by Hal Leonard. Used in compliance with the U.S. Copyright Act, Section 107.

While this theme throughout the entire saga does indeed accompany scenes in which a character uses or discusses the Force, its association is more specifically with the Jedi, taken individually or as a group. And although the theme appears in a variety of contexts involving one or more Jedi or those with Force powers, its main purpose seems to be to depict their various struggles[21]. The theme's basic idea encapsulates the beginning of such a struggle in its melodic structure. After a pickup on $\hat{5}$, the idea begins with a slow rise through scale degrees $\hat{1}$, $\hat{2}$, and $\hat{3}$ of the minor scale (with $\hat{2}$ being slightly ornamented with the $\hat{3}$ and $\hat{4}$ of the triplet figure) before returning to its opening note on the low $\hat{5}$. This initial shape, of a slow stepwise rise then a quick leaping fall, suggests encountering a setback in attempting to achieve a difficult goal, even while making gradual progress. This general depiction of a struggle continues to play out over the rest of the theme. With the following developing idea, notice that the first five notes retrace the entire basic idea (omitting the ornamental $\hat{3}$-$\hat{4}$ figure), though now altered, being compressed into a smaller space. This compression leaves room to expand on the idea's material with a triplet figure that rises to $\hat{5}$, the highest note yet, before falling a step to $\hat{4}$. Once again, forward progress has been tempered by a setback. Notice, however, that the harmony of this scale degree $\hat{4}$ is the major IV, a chord that would be minor within the minor scale that is implied in the theme and thus is a sign of hope within a negative environment[22].

The next developing idea begins like the second, with the same compressed version of the basic idea's outline. But now, the previous idea is itself reworked as the large leap from $\hat{3}$ down to $\hat{5}$ (A♭-C) is omitted and its triplet material instead appears in a dotted rhythm. This dotted motive extends the rising motion up to a climactic tonic, which, as the highest note in the theme and in its harmonization with the major VI chord, is another positive sign within the negative minor mode. The final contrasting idea not only differs from the previous ideas in its rhythm, but in its contour as well, as it closes the theme by outlining a fall from $\hat{5}$ to $\hat{1}$ rather than a rise. Overall then, the expression of struggle depicted individually in the theme's first three ideas (i.e., increasingly greater heights yielding more quickly to a final descent) is reproduced across the theme as a whole, more powerfully imparting the protracted and arduous nature of the Jedi struggle[23].

---

[21]. No doubt, it is this sense of struggle with its incorporation of both positive and negative affects that grants the theme such versatility in the *Star Wars* saga and thus distinguishes it from the other themes in the original film. Indeed, as Adams 1999, p. 23, points out, this theme is «the only heroic *A New Hope* theme in which Williams employs large downward intervallic leaps (although it still begins with a characteristically rising perfect fourth). The other major heroic character themes all reach out with a sense of yearning and impetuousness».

[22]. Murphy 2014, p. 488, notes that two-chord progressions in film music of a minor tonic to its major subdominant (as here with i-iv), or a major tonic to its minor dominant — which he labels 'm5M' and 'M7m', respectively — tend to be associated with experiences of wonderment, optimism, success, or transcendence. Clearly, the most pertinent of these associations in the "Force Theme" are the central two: optimism and success, or perhaps more fittingly in this case, optimism for success.

[23]. I also discuss this struggle-infused contour of the "Force Theme" in Richards 2013a.

Varied Period Forms

So far, this study has focused on developing ideas as the main source of variation in Williams's film music themes. The potential for varying ideas, however, also extends to basic ideas that return in period forms. Even when a basic idea returns in a period, that returning basic idea can be varied without destroying the sense of return it expresses. In particular, when the head of the third idea is more similar to that of the initial idea than is the second, a sense of return is activated and overrules the variation component as a determinant of the theme type[24]. I refer to such theme types as *varied periods*, which, in the present corpus, are found to occur only in the basic form of the period. In other words, the varied period is a special case of the basic period, which is why I do not list it as a separate theme type in the comprehensive table of grammatical themes in Table 3.

"Rey's Theme" from *Star Wars – The Force Awakens* (J. J. Abrams, 2015), given in Ex. 8, is a prominent instance of the varied period in its basic form. More than simply being a musical label for the film's main character, "Rey's Theme" depicts the character's traits in this film in an unusually subtle manner — specifically, the latency of her powers with the Force[25].

Ex. 8: varied period, "Rey's Theme" from *The Force Awakens* (© 2015 BMI), published by Utapau Music, reduced from *Star Wars, The Force Awakens: Suite for Orchestra*, printed by Hal Leonard. Used in compliance with the U.S. Copyright Act, Section 107.

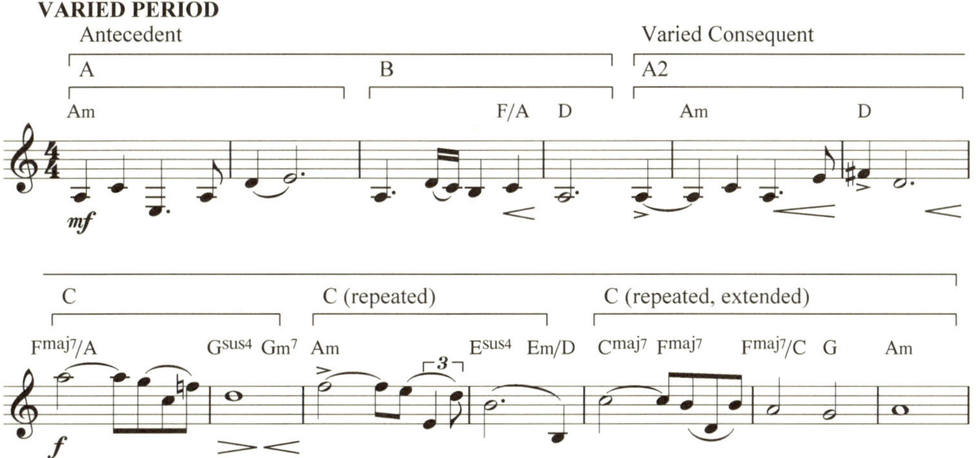

The theme is in 4/4 time and most of the notes in its basic idea are set to on-beat rhythms, the others being in a slow dotted rhythm. The idea thus makes a veiled

24. As described in Richards 2016, para. [21].

25. For more on how this theme depicts Rey's other character traits, see Richards 2017.

implication of a march, which hints at a strength that Rey possesses but has not yet fully expressed. This interpretation is further supported by the accompaniment, which injects the militaristic long-short-short, or 'gallop', rhythms throughout that are heard on their own in the theme's introductory portion (not shown).

The contrasting idea that follows continues with a different melodic profile of on-beat rhythms and a slow dotted rhythm (now slightly decorated with sixteenth notes). More importantly, the harmony turns conspicuously from the minor tonic chord to the major subdominant, IV. As we have seen, this progression at the end of a second idea is a prominent facet of the "Force Theme" and thus here it suggests that Rey's hidden powers are linked to the Force[26].

The developing idea that follows begins with a syncopation, then plays out much like the basic idea as it starts on the same tonic harmony, exactly repeats its rhythm, restates its opening two notes, and retraces its contour up until the final note. Yet the harmony retains the Force-theme-like i-IV motion that characterized the contrasting idea, perhaps suggesting that, as Rey reappears throughout this film's narrative (or returns, as a period's basic idea does), though she will not be completely transformed, she will undergo noticeable changes on account of her interactions with the Force. The use of a varied period allows the theme to capture these relatively subtle changes while explicitly associating them with their source in the narrative.

Part IV: Stylistic Trends in Williams's Themes with Variation

The above analyses have shown that Williams's treatment of variation-based themes can be interpreted individually, as musical manifestations of character traits or narrative ideas in the film. But it is also valuable to view these themes from two broader perspectives: their style period, and a more general categorization of their association. I examine each of these in order below.

Dividing Williams's film scores into style periods has, as far as I am aware, not yet been suggested in published scholarship. Useful indications are provided, however, by changes in Williams's thematic structures over the course of his career thus far. In order to obtain data in a reasonably objective manner, I set out with the intention of selecting the main theme from each film he has scored. Exceptions arose in several cases. In a handful of scores from the 1960s and early 70s, Williams was given thematic material on which to base the score. These include films with a popular song written by another composer and musicals, for which Williams was again given material by other composers. Hence, I did not include themes from these films. From the late 1970s onward, Williams began to

[26]. Williams further emphasizes this relationship in the end credits, where the ideas of Rey's theme appear in alternation with those of the "Force Theme" over the same i-IV progression.

write for sequels to films he had scored. While most sequels are generally furnished with the same main theme as the original film, Williams typically writes new themes as well, and thus, in order to obtain more data for the study, I selected from sequels the secondary theme that seemed the most prominent, some of which can actually overshadow the main theme, as "The Imperial March" does in *The Empire Strikes Back* (Irvin Kershner, 1980). Finally, for *Not with My Wife, You Don't!* (Norman Panama, 1966), I selected two themes that were equally prominent, befitting the narrative about two men vying with equal fervour for the affections of the same woman.

The resulting data set of Williams themes is shown in Appendix 1. Table 7 distils this information, highlighting notable trends with the shaded areas[27].

Table 7: Notable Trends in Frequencies for Grammatical Theme Types across Williams's career

Year	# Main Themes in Year	Theme Type			Theme Category		
		% Sentence (Basic)	% Clause (Basic)	% Developing Period	% Grammatical	% Discursive	% Motto
1958	1	100	0	0	100	0	0
1960	1	100	0	0	100	0	0
1961	1	0	0	0	100	0	0
1962	1	0	0	0	0	100	0
1965	2	50	0	0	100	0	0
1966	6	33	17	17	83	0	17
1967	3	0	0	0	100	0	0
1969	2	50	0	0	100	0	0
1970	2	50	0	0	100	0	0
1972	5	20	20	0	100	0	0
1973	4	25	25	0	100	0	0
1974	4	0	25	75	100	0	0
1975	2	0	50	0	50	0	50
1976	3	0	0	0	100	0	0
1977	3	0	33	33	67	0	33
1978	3	0	0	33	100	0	0
1979	2	0	50	0	100	0	0
1980	1	0	100	0	100	0	0
1981	2	0	0	0	100	0	0
1982	2	0	0	0	100	0	0

27. Note that 2017 includes *The Last Jedi* (Rian Johnson) but not *The Post* (Steven Spielberg) since the latter's release postdates this writing.

1983	1	0	0	100	100	0	0
1984	2	0	0	100	100	0	0
1986	1	0	0	0	100	0	0
1987	3	0	0	33	100	0	0
1988	1	0	100	0	100	0	0
1989	3	0	0	33	100	0	0
1990	3	33	33	0	100	0	0
1991	2	50	50	0	100	0	0
1992	2	0	0	50	100	0	0
1993	2	0	50	0	50	50	0
1995	2	0	50	0	50	0	50
1996	1	0	0	0	100	0	0
1997	4	0	0	0	75	0	25
1998	2	0	0	0	100	0	0
1999	2	50	0	0	50	50	0
2000	1	0	0	100	100	0	0
2001	2	0	0	50	100	0	0
2002	4	0	0	25	50	25	25
2004	2	50	0	0	100	0	0
2005	4	0	0	0	50	0	50
2008	1	0	0	0	100	0	0
2011	2	0	0	0	50	0	50
2012	1	0	0	0	100	0	0
2013	1	0	100	0	100	0	0
2015	1	0	0	0	100	0	0
2016	1	0	0	0	100	0	0
2017	1	0	0	100	100	0	0

Notice that, up to 1973, basic sentences had usually comprised a substantial portion of the selected themes but that with 1974, sentences disappear for over a decade and only appear sporadically thereafter. Instead, clauses and developing periods become consistent in his output — the two theme types I mentioned above as the most common to include developing ideas. Further evidence stems from Williams himself, who describes the untimely death of his wife, Barbara Ruick, in March of 1974 as a «pivotal moment» in his life and career: «after that point, in my writing, in my approach to music, in everything I was doing, I felt clear about what it is I was trying to do and how I could do it with whatever small gift I may have been given»[28]. Although all of this suggests 1974 as a major

[28]. See Williams 2014.

turning point in Williams's film music, I would suggest that his new efforts did not come to full fruition until he scored *Jaws* in 1975. It is with this score that Williams's main themes begin to be exceedingly tailored to their particular association, fusing a wealth of musical techniques that as a whole conjure up a very specific mental image. Also consider that the number of films he scores per year drops in 1975 from four or five in 1972-1974 to only two, and in the years following, the number almost always falls into a range of one to three. For all the above reasons, I understand *Jaws* as a stylistic watershed in Williams's career.

TABLE 7 shows another change that becomes apparent in 1993. At this point, grammatical themes, which hold a near monopoly in this corpus up to that year, now regularly yield to discursive and motto themes. 1993 was the year Williams officially retired from his position as conductor of the Boston Pops Orchestra «to devote more time to serious musical compositions», a decision he announced in December 1991, shortly before his sixtieth birthday[29]. One will also notice an increase in his scoring of more serious, drama films and a shift away from the action and fantasy genres for which he became known. But perhaps more pertinent are the changes that took place in filmmaking more generally from about 1990 onward due to the increased reliance on digital technology. With regard to Williams specifically, Emilio Audissino observes that the composer's scores for the second *Star Wars* trilogy (which began in 1999) were less melodic and more modular than those for the first trilogy, and speculates that this was the result of two influences: 1) a sound mix that, in contemporary films generally, has become «too thick to allow space for the same melodic flow and leitmotivic network as in the first trilogy», and 2) last-minute film edits that have become easy with the aid of computer editing but can interfere with longer melodic lines in the score[30]. In both cases, short motto themes or patchwork-like discursive themes are typically more adaptable than grammatical ones, of which Williams tends to state the entire first half when they appear[31]. And indeed motto and discursive themes become more regular in Williams's film scores starting from about 1993, which therefore seems another stylistic turning point in Williams's film scores.

Finally, there is some evidence to regard 2008 as the beginning of a fourth period. With that year's lone score, that for *Indiana Jones and the Kingdom of the Crystal Skull* (Steven Spielberg), there is a return to grammatical themes as the prevalent category of theme in the corpus from there to the present, the motto theme of *The Adventures of Tintin* (Steven Spielberg, 2011) being the sole exception. The large-scale trends in theme class across the style periods is most clearly evident when the percentage of each class per period can be compared, as in APPENDIX 2. I would also point out that, like 1975, Williams's productivity in film scoring drops, now to only one or two films per year. While this fourth period is defined by themes from only eight films, I nevertheless find the evidence compelling

[29]. CATALANO 1991.

[30]. AUDISSINO 2017, pp. 228-229.

[31]. As noted in ZACHAROPOULOS 2017, p. 248.

enough to justify such a division. With these turning points in place, we may divide Williams's film scores into four style periods, named simply by their chronology, as shown in TABLE 8[32].

TABLE 8: WILLIAMS'S FOUR STYLE PERIODS IN HIS FILM MUSIC

STYLE PERIOD	YEARS	FILMS (BEGINNING – END)
First	1958-1975	*Daddy-O* – *The Eiger Sanction*
Second	1975-1992	*Jaws* – *Home Alone 2*
Third	1993-2005	*Jurassic Park* – *Munich*
Fourth	2008-present	*Indiana Jones and the Kingdom of the Crystal Skull* –

Having identified style periods, it is now possible to track within each period the percentage of themes in the corpus that make use of substantial variation. APPENDIX 3 shows the number and percentage of each theme type Williams wrote across the four style periods. Of the twelve grammatical theme types, six employ developing ideas: the four developing forms of each theme class and the basic and hybrid clause. There are also varied periods, which are forms of the basic period. TABLE 9 shows the results of collecting all of the variation-based theme types together into a single category.

TABLE 9: FREQUENCIES OF VARIATION-BASED MAIN THEMES PER STYLE PERIOD

STYLE PERIOD	YEARS IN PERIOD	# MAIN THEMES IN STYLE PERIOD	% VARIATION-BASED THEMES
1st	1958-1975	32	38
2nd	1975-1992	36	53
3rd	1993-2005	26	31
4th	2008-present	8	50

In a separate study, I determined frequencies of theme types and categories across the corpus of scores nominated for the Academy Award for Best Original Score (or its equivalent)[33]. As shown in TABLE 10, the frequency of variation-based themes in each of Williams's style periods is always higher than in the corresponding period of the Oscar corpus (excluding Williams)[34].

32. Even so, there are cases in which Williams writes main themes that, in their structuring, harken back to those of his second period. Examples include the developing period that opens Hedwig's theme from *Harry Potter and the Sorcerer's Stone* (Chris Columbus, 2001), and Irina's theme from *Indiana Jones and the Kingdom of the Crystal Skull*, which opens with a developing clause.

33. See RICHARDS 2016.

34. The two corpuses compared here end with 2015 since that was the last year included in the earlier study.

Table 10: Comparison of Frequencies of Variation-Based Main Themes in Williams and in Oscar-Nominated Scores By Other Composers

Period	Williams Corpus	Oscar Corpus
1958-1975	38	24
1975-1992	53	46
1993-2005	31	21
2008-2015	50	6

Whereas a sizable proportion of themes in each period are variation-based, the frequency is substantially higher in the second and fourth periods, the former in large part due to an increase in the proportion of clauses and developing periods.

This relationship between variation and the second period, however, runs somewhat deeper. Of the 40 themes in the second period, 18 are variation-based. After viewing each film, I determined the main association of each theme in its film. In total, 14 of the 40 themes have an association that involves an element of what can broadly be referred to as fantasy. Such elements include the supernatural, imagined worlds, and sentient aliens and robots. Table 11 summarizes these findings, with variation-based themes highlighted by being shaded in the rightmost column.

Table 11: Associations and Theme Types of Main Themes in Williams's Second Period

Year	Film	Association of Main Theme or (for Sequels) Most Prominent Secondary Theme	Fantasy Element in Association?	Theme Type
1975	*Jaws*	Antagonist – Shark		Motto
1976	*Family Plot*	Antagonists – Shoebridge and accomplices		Period
1976	*The Missouri Breaks*	Love / Bonding – Tom and Jane		Sentential Period
1976	*Midway*	Protagonist – US military		Period
1977	*Black Sunday*	Antagonists – Dahlia and Michael		Motto
1977	*Star Wars*	Protagonist – Luke	x	Developing Period
1977	*Close Encounters of the Third Kind*	Location – Devils Tower	x	Clause
1978	*The Fury*	Supernatural powers – Psychic abilities	x	Developing Trifold Sentence
1978	*Jaws 2*	Protagonists – Adolescents sailing		Sentential Period
1978	*Superman: The Movie*	Protagonist – Superman	x	Developing Period
1979	*Dracula*	Antagonist – Dracula	x	Clause

1979	*1941*	Protatgonist – Air Force pilot Kelso		Period
1980	*The Empire Strikes Back*	Antagonist – Darth Vader	x	Clause
1981	*Raiders of the Lost Ark*	Protagonist – Indiana Jones		Sentential Period
1981	*Heartbeeps*	Love / Bonding – Aqua and Val	x	Developing Composite
1982	*E. T.: The-Extra-Terrestrial*	Love / Bonding – E. T. and Elliot	x	Developing Clause
1982	*Monsignor*	Protagonist – Father Flaherty		Composite
1983	*Return of the Jedi*	Secondary Characters – Ewoks	x	Developing Period
1984	*Indiana Jones and the Temple of Doom*	Treasure / Secondary Characters – Sacred Stones / Slave Children	x	Developing Period
1984	*The River*	Protagonists – Garvey family		Developing Period
1986	*SpaceCamp*	Emotion – Awe, breakthrough		Developing Sentence
1987	*The Witches of Eastwick*	Antagonist – Daryl	x	Period
1987	*Empire of the Sun*	Protagonist – Jamie / Jim		Developing Period
1987	*Superman IV: The Quest for Peace*	Antagonist – Nuclear Man	x	Period
1988	*The Accidental Tourist*	Protagonist – Macon		Clause
1989	*Indiana Jones and the Last Crusade*	Love / Bonding – Indiana and Henry Jones		Period
1989	*Born on the Fourth of July*	Protagonist – Ron		Period
1989	*Always*	Love / Bonding – Pete and Dorinda	x	Developing Period
1990	*Stanley and Iris*	Love / Bonding – Stanley and Iris		Sentence
1990	*Presumed Innocent*	Protagonist – Rusty		Clause
1990	*Home Alone*	Love / Bonding – Kevin and family		Period
1991	*Hook*	Emotion – Childhood wonder	x	Clause
1991	*JFK*	Emotion – Patriotic and moralistic hope		Sentence
1992	*Far and Away*	Love / Bonding – Shannon and Joseph		Developing Period
1992	*Home Alone 2: Lost in New York*	Emotion – Joy of Christmas		Period

Strikingly, 12 of these 14 fantasy-associated themes, or 86%, also have a variation-based structure[35]. Compare this with the non-fantasy themes in the list, of which only 6

[35]. The two exceptions are the main theme for *The Witches of Eastwick* (George Miller, 1987), which is associated with the devil in human form, and "Nuclear Man's Theme" from *Superman IV: The Quest*

of 21, or 29%, have a variation-based structure. In short, these figures suggest that, when Williams wrote a prominent fantasy-based theme during his second period, the theme's structure was almost always a variation-based type. This is not to say that variation-based themes are exclusive to fantasy associations, but rather that, between 1975 and 1992, fantasy associations are given a theme with variation on nearly every occasion.

Whether done consciously or not, I would suggest that this relationship has to do with a fundamental similarity between fantasy and variation-based themes. Both constitute what might be called imaginative developments of an established source. Fantasy is, after all, a kind of reshaping of the people, places, and principles that we understand as constituting the real world. Thus, the established source it develops is our perceived reality. In a similar way, variation-based themes reshape the rhythms, intervals, and harmonies of its own established source, the initial basic idea. Since this idea is generally distinctive enough to fulfil the function of a leitmotif by itself, it can be said to succinctly characterize the sound world or musical reality of the theme.

These themes therefore reimagine musical ideas in a way that parallels the way in which fantasy aspects of film narratives reimagine reality, infusing the themes with a subconscious connection to their association. But as we have seen in some of the analyses, variation-based themes from Williams's second period can also be understood as capturing many of the idiosyncrasies of each individual association whether it is the jaw-dropping awe of gradually discovering aliens in *Close Encounters* or the long and arduous struggles of the Jedi in *Star Wars*. Although many of Williams's second-period themes are celebrated in part because they occur in highly-exposed blockbuster films, without doubt it is the tight relationship between these themes and their association that have allowed many to progress beyond a memorability in the film in question and instead achieve an iconic status in the history of Hollywood music.

---

for Peace (Sidney J. Furie, 1987), which are set as basic periods. These fantasy associations differ from the others of this style period in that they contain significant comedic elements. In both cases, although the associated character is the antagonist, he is also something of a comic relief. Notably, there seems to be a connection in this style period between films that draw on the comedy genre and main themes with any sort of period structure, as 6 of 7 (or 86%) of such main themes are set as a theme type from that class. These comedy films include *Family Plot* (Alfred Hitchcock, 1976), *1941* (Steven Spielberg, 1979), *Heartbeeps* (Allan Arkush, 1981), *The Witches of Eastwick*, *Always* (Steven Spielberg, 1989), *Home Alone* (Chris Columbus, 1990), and *Home Alone 2: Lost in New York* (Chris Columbus, 1992). Of these, only *Heartbeeps* lacks a period form, being instead a developing composite. But I would point out that, although I selected the love theme from this film since it is the most prominent theme throughout, the theme that bookends the film in the main title and end credits (and may also be considered a main theme) begins with an eight-bar sentential period. Hence, one could argue that all of Williams's main themes for comedies during this era take on some sort of period structure.

Appendix 1

Analyses of 101 Main Themes or Most Prominent Secondary Themes by John Williams from Feature Films or Television Films

'Melodic Material in Cue' refers to sections distinguished by their motivic material or by material of a different function (especially introductory material such as an opening fanfare vs. the start of the theme proper).

'Melodic Statement in Section' refers to one of multiple statements of the same melodic material within a section.

List of films from Wikipedia: <https://en.wikipedia.org/wiki/List_of_compositions_by_John_Williams>, accessed February 2018.

Films excluded from this list:

Year	Film	Reason for Exclusion
1960	*Because They're Young*	Pop song by Duane Eddy in main title is the main theme
1963	*Diamond Head*	Pop song by Hugo Winterhalter in main title is the main theme
1963	*Gidget Goes to Rome*	Pop song by George David Weiss in main title is the main theme
1964	*The Killers*	Pop song by Henry Mancini is the main theme
1967	*Valley of the Dolls*	Pop song by André Previn in main title is the main theme
1969	*Goodbye, Mr. Chips*	Music arranged by Williams
1971	*Fiddler on the Roof*	Music arranged by Williams
1973	*Tom Sawyer*	Music arranged by Williams

#	Year	Film	Location of Theme	Melodic Material in Cue	Melodic Statement in Section	Theme Category	Theme Type
1	1958	*Daddy-O*	Main title	1st	1st	Grammatical	Sentence
2	1960	*I Passed for White*	Main title	1st	1st	Grammatical	Sentence
3	1961	*The Secret Ways*	Main title	2nd	1st	Grammatical	(Varied) period
4	1962	*Bachelor Flat*	Main title	1st	1st	Discursive	---
5	1965	*None but the Brave*	Main title	2nd	1st	Grammatical	Period
6	1965	*John Goldfarb, Please Come Home!*	Main title	1st	1st	Grammatical	Sentence
7	1966	*The Rare Breed*	1:20:58	---	---	Grammatical	Developing period
8	1966	*How to Steal a Million*	Main title	1st	1st	Grammatical	Sentence
9	1966	*The Plainsman*	Main title	2nd	2nd	Grammatical	Period
10	1966	*Not with My Wife You Don't*	27:49	---	---	Motto	---
11	1966	*Not with My Wife You Don't*	1:21:12	---	---	Grammatical	Clause
12	1966	*Penelope*	Main title	1st	1st	Grammatical	Sentence
13	1967	*A Guide for the Married Man*	Main title	1st	1st	Grammatical	Period
14	1967	*Fitzwilly*	Main title	1st	1st	Grammatical	Sentential period
15	1967	*Heidi*	End credits	2nd	1st	Grammatical	Sentential period

16	1969	*Daddy's Gone a Hunting*	Main title	1st	1st	Grammatical	Sentence
17	1969	*The Reivers*	Main title	3rd	1st	Grammatical	Period
18	1970	*Storia di una Donna (Story of a Woman)*	12:00	---	---	Grammatical	Sentence
19	1970	*Jane Eyre*	Main title	3rd	1st	Grammatical	Developing sentence
20	1972	*The Cowboys*	Main title	1st	2nd	Grammatical	Composite
21	1972	*The Screaming Woman*	End credits			Grammatical	Clause
22	1972	*Images*	Main title	1st	1st	Grammatical	Period
23	1972	*The Poseidon Adventure*	Main title	2nd	1st	Grammatical	Sentence
24	1972	*Pete 'n' Tillie*	Main title	1st	1st	Grammatical	(Varied) period
25	1973	*The Long Goodbye*	Main title	1st	1st	Grammatical	Developing sentence
26	1973	*The Man Who Loved Cat Dancing*	Main title	1st	1st	Grammatical	Sentence
27	1973	*The Paper Chase*	35:25:00	1st	1st	Grammatical	Monofold sentence
28	1973	*Cinderella Liberty*	1:13:35	1st	1st	Grammatical	Clause
29	1974	*Conrack*	Main title	1st	1st	Grammatical	Developing period
30	1974	*The Sugarland Express*	Main title	1st	1st	Grammatical	Developing period
31	1974	*Earthquake*	Main title	last	1st	Grammatical	Clause
32	1974	*The Towering Inferno*	Main title	1st	2nd	Grammatical	Developing period
33	1975	*The Eiger Sanction*	Main title	2nd	1st	Grammatical	Clause
34	1975	*Jaws*	Main title	---	---	Motto	---
35	1976	*Family Plot*	14:17	---	---	Grammatical	Period
36	1976	*The Missouri Breaks*	End credits	---	---	Grammatical	Sentential period
37	1976	*Midway*	End credits	---	---	Grammatical	Period
38	1977	*Black Sunday*	End credits	---	---	Motto	---
39	1977	*Star Wars*	Main title	1st	2nd	Grammatical	Developing period
40	1977	*Close Encounters of the Third Kind*	End credits	3rd	1st	Grammatical	Clause
41	1978	*The Fury*	Main title	1st	1st	Grammatical	Developing trifold sentence
42	1978	*Jaws 2*	End credits	2nd	1st	Grammatical	Sentential period
43	1978	*Superman: The Movie*	Main title	2nd	1st	Grammatical	Developing period
44	1979	*Dracula*	Main title	1st	1st	Grammatical	Clause
45	1979	*1941*	End credits	1st	1st	Grammatical	Period
46	1980	*The Empire Strikes Back*	End credits	4th	1st	Grammatical	Clause
47	1981	*Raiders of the Lost Ark*	End credits	1st	1st	Grammatical	Sentential period
48	1981	*Heartbeeps*	End credits	3rd	1st	Grammatical	Developing composite
49	1982	*E. T.: The Extra-Terrestrial*	End credits	4th	1st	Grammatical	Developing clause
50	1982	*Monsignor*	Main title	2nd	1st	Grammatical	Composite
51	1983	*Return of the Jedi*	End credits	4th	1st	Grammatical	Developing period
52	1984	*Indiana Jones and the Temple of Doom*	End credits	2nd	1st	Grammatical	Developing period
53	1984	*The River*	End credits	2nd	1st	Grammatical	Developing period

54	1986	*SpaceCamp*	End credits	1st	1st	Grammatical	Developing sentence
55	1987	*The Witches of Eastwick*	End credits	1st	1st	Grammatical	Period
56	1987	*Empire of the Sun*	1:07:15	---	---	Grammatical	Developing period
57	1987	*Superman IV: The Quest for Peace*	45:46	---	---	Grammatical	Period
58	1988	*The Accidental Tourist*	9:05	---	---	Grammatical	Clause
59	1989	*Indiana Jones and the Last Crusade*	End credits	2nd	1st	Grammatical	Period
60	1989	*Born on the Fourth of July*	End credits	1st	1st	Grammatical	Period
61	1989	*Always*	End credits	2nd	1st	Grammatical	Developing period
62	1990	*Stanley and Iris*	End credits	2nd	1st	Grammatical	Sentence
63	1990	*Presumed Innocent*	End credits	1st	1st	Grammatical	Clause
64	1990	*Home Alone*	End credits	5th	1st	Grammatical	Period
65	1991	*Hook*	End credits	1st	1st	Grammatical	Clause
66	1991	*JFK*	End credits	1st	1st	Grammatical	Sentence
67	1992	*Far and Away*	Main title	2nd	1st	Grammatical	Developing period
68	1992	*Home Alone 2: Lost in New York*	End credits	2nd	1st	Grammatical	Period
69	1993	*Jurassic Park*	20:23			Discursive	
70	1993	*Schindler's List*	End credits	1st	1st	Grammatical	Clause
71	1995	*Sabrina*	Main title	1st	1st	Grammatical	Clause
72	1995	*Nixon*	Disc 2 - 1:34:50	---	---	Motto	---
73	1996	*Sleepers*	Main title	1st	1st	Grammatical	Period
74	1997	*Rosewood*	End credits	2nd	1st	Grammatical	Period
75	1997	*The Lost World: Jurassic Park*	2:05:25	3rd	2nd	Grammatical	Composite
76	1997	*Seven Years in Tibet*	End Credits	1st	1st	Grammatical	Developing clause
77	1997	*Amistad*	Main Title	1st	1st	Motto	
78	1998	*Saving Private Ryan*	End Credits	3rd	1st	Grammatical	Composite
79	1998	*Stepmom*	1:28:34	---	---	Grammatical	Period
80	1999	*Star Wars, Episode I: The Phantom Menace*	End Credits	4th	3rd	Discursive	---
81	1999	*Angela's Ashes*	End Credits	1st	1st	Grammatical	Sentence
82	2000	*The Patriot*	End Credits	2nd	1st	Grammatical	Developing period
83	2001	*A. I.: Artificial Intelligence*	End Credits	1st	1st	Grammatical	Composite
84	2001	*Harry Potter and the Philosopher's Stone*	End Credits	3rd	1st	Grammatical	Developing period
85	2002	*Star Wars, Episode II: Attack of the Clones*	End Credits	4th	1st	Grammatical	Developing period
86	2002	*Minority Report*	End Credits	3rd	1st	Motto	---
87	2002	*Harry Potter and the Chamber of Secrets*	End Credits	3rd	1st	Grammatical	Composite
88	2002	*Catch Me if You Can*	Main Title	1st	1st	Discursive	---
89	2004	*Harry Potter and the Prisoner of Azkaban*	End Credits	3rd	1st	Grammatical	(Varied) period
90	2004	*The Terminal*	End Credits	1st	1st	Grammatical	Sentence
91	2005	*Star Wars, Episode III: Revenge of the Sith*	End Credits	5th	1st	Motto	---

92	2005	*War of the Worlds*	End Credits	2nd	1st	Motto	---
93	2005	*Memoirs of a Geisha*	End Credits	1st	1st	Grammatical	Developing clause
94	2005	*Munich*	End Credits	1st	1st	Grammatical	Composite
95	2008	*Indiana Jones and the Kingdom of the Crystal Skull*	5:45	---	---	Grammatical	Developing clause
96	2011	*The Adventures of Tintin: The Secret of the Unicorn*	Main Title	---	---	Motto	---
97	2011	*War Horse*	End Credits	---	---	Grammatical	Sentential composite
98	2012	*Lincoln*	1:47	---	---	Grammatical	Period
99	2013	*The Book Thief*	End Credits	3rd	1st	Grammatical	Clause
100	2015	*Star Wars, Episode VII: The Force Awakens*	End Credits	4th	2nd	Grammatical	(Varied) period
101	2016	*The BFG*	End Credits	1st	1st	Grammatical	Period
102	2017	*Star Wars, Episode VIII: The Last Jedi*	End Credits	4th	1st	Grammatical	Developing period

Appendix 2

Percentage of Each Theme Class per Style Period

Style Period	Grammatical	Discursive	Motto
1st	94	3	3
2nd	94	0	6
3rd	69	12	19
4th	87.5	0	12.5
Total	87	4	9

Appendix 3

Grammatical Theme Types per Style Period

Note: Types that had no instances in the corpus are not listed in the table.

Dev = Developing
Sent = Sentential
Mono = Monofold
Tri = Trifold
Var = Varied

TOTAL NUMBER

Style Period	Total Number of Themes per Style Period in Corpus	Sentence				Clause		Period				Composite		
		Mono	Dev Tri	Basic	Dev	Basic	Dev	Basic	Dev	Sent	Var	Basic	Dev	Sent
1st	32	1	0	9	2	4	0	5	4	2	2	1	0	0
2nd	36	0	1	2	1	7	1	9	8	3	0	1	1	0
3rd	26	0	0	2	0	2	2	3	3	0	1	5	0	0
4th	8	0	0	0	0	1	1	2	1	0	1	0	0	1
Total	102	1	1	13	3	14	4	19	16	5	4	7	1	1

PERCENTAGE

Style Period	Total Number of Themes per Style Period in Corpus	Sentence				Clause		Period				Composite		
		Mono	Dev Tri	Basic	Dev	Basic	Dev	Basic	Dev	Sent	Var	Basic	Dev	Sent
1st	32	3	0	28	6	13	0	16	13	6	6	3	0	0
2nd	36	0	3	6	3	19	3	25	22	8	0	3	3	0
3rd	26	0	0	8	0	8	8	12	12	0	4	19	0	0
4th	8	0	0	0	0	13	13	25	13	0	13	0	0	13
Total	102	1	1	13	3	14	4	19	16	5	4	7	1	1

BIBLIOGRAPHY

ADAMS 1999

ADAMS, Doug. 'Sounds of the Empire: Analyzing the Themes of the *Star Wars* Trilogy', in: *Film Score Monthly*, IV/5 (1999), pp. 22-25.

AUDISSINO 2014

AUDISSINO, Emilio. *John Williams's Film Music: «Jaws», «Star Wars», «Raiders of the Lost Ark», and the Return of the Classical Hollywood Music Style*, Madison (WI), University of Wisconsin Press, 2014 (Wisconsin Film Studies).

AUDISSINO 2017

ID. 'John Williams and Contemporary Film Music', in: *Contemporary Film Music: Investigating Cinema Narratives and Composition*, edited by Lindsay Coleman and Joakim Tillman, London, Palgrave Macmillan, 2017, pp. 221-236.

BRIBITZER-STULL 2015

BRIBITZER-STULL, Matthew. *Understanding the Leitmotif: From Wagner to Hollywood Film Music*, Cambridge, Cambridge University Press, 2015.

CAPLIN 1998

CAPLIN, William E. *Classical Form: A Theory of Formal Functions for the Instrumental Music of Haydn, Mozart, and Beethoven*, Oxford-New York, Oxford University Press, 1998.

CATALANO 1991

CATALANO, Peter. 'John Williams to Leave Boston Pops', in: *Los Angeles Times*, 21 December 1991.

COOK 1992

COOK, Nicholas. *A Guide to Musical Analysis*, New York, Norton, 1992.

KARLIN – WRIGHT 2004

KARLIN, Fred – WRIGHT, Rayburn. *On the Track: A Guide to Contemporary Film Scoring*, New York, Routledge, [2]2004.

LEHMAN 2012

LEHMAN, Frank. *Reading Tonality Through Film: Transformational Hermeneutics and the Music of Hollywood*, Ph.D. Diss., Cambridge (MA), Harvard University, 2012.

LEHMAN 2013

ID. 'Hollywood Cadences: Music and the Structure of Cinematic Expectation', in: *Music Theory Online*, XIX/4 (2013).

MATESSINO *ET AL.* 2007

MATESSINO, Mike – KENDALL, Lukas – ELDRIDGE, Jeff. *«Superman»: The Music (1978-1988)*, 8 CDs, liner notes, Hollywood (CA), Film Score Monthly, 2007.

Morrell 2013-2015
Morrell, Brian. *How Film and TV Music Communicate*, 3 vols., unpublished, 2013-2015, <http://www.brianmorrell.co.uk/filmbooks.html>, accessed February 2018.

Murphy 2014
Murphy, Scott. 'Transformational Theory and the Analysis of Film Music', in: *The Oxford Handbook of Film Music Studies*, edited by David Neumeyer, Oxford-New York, Oxford University Press, 2014, pp. 471-499.

Richards 2011
Richards, Mark. 'Viennese Classicism and the Sentential Idea', in: *Theory and Practice*, xxxvi (2011), pp. 179-224.

Richards 2013a
Id. 'John Williams Themes, Part 1 of 6: The Force Theme', blog post, 2 March 2013, in: *Film Music Notes*, <http://www.filmmusicnotes.com/john-williams-themes-part-1-the-force-theme/>, accessed February 2018.

Richards 2013b
Id. 'John Williams Themes, Part 2 of 6: *Star Wars*, Main Title', blog post, 9 March 2013, in: *Film Music Notes*, <http://www.filmmusicnotes.com/john-williams-themes-part-2-star-wars-main-title/>, accessed February 2018.

Richards 2013c
Id. 'John Williams' *Superman* Theme (*Superman March*)', blog post, 15 July 2013, in: *Film Music Notes*, <http://www.filmmusicnotes.com/john-williams-superman-theme-superman-march/>, accessed February 2018.

Richards 2015
Id. 'Celebrating *Star Wars* Themes, Part 5 of 6: Across the Stars', blog post, 7 December 2015, in: *Film Music Notes*, <http://www.filmmusicnotes.com/celebrating-star-wars-themes-part-5-of-6-across-the-stars/>, accessed February 2018.

Richards 2016
Id. 'Film Music Themes: Analysis and Corpus Study', in: *Music Theory Online*, xxii/1 (2016).

Richards 2017
Id. 'Themes and Their Musical Meaning in *Star Wars, Episode vii: The Force Awakens*', blog post, 7 December 2015, in: *Film Music Notes*, <http://www.filmmusicnotes.com/themes-and-their-musical-meaning-in-star-wars-episode-vii-the-force-awakens/>, accessed February 2018.

Schneller 2013
Schneller, Tom. 'Modal Interchange and Semantic Resonance in Themes by John Williams', in: *Journal of Film Music*, vi/1 (2013), pp. 49-74.

Thau 2001

Thau, Michael. 'Making Superman: Filming the Legend', in: *«Superman»: The Movie*, directed by Richard Donner (1978), DVD, Disc 1, Side B, Burbank (CA), Warner Home Video, 2001.

Williams 2014

Williams, John. *Behind the Score: The Art of the Film Composer*, interview by Tavis Smiley, Los Angeles County Museum of Art, 17 March 2014. The pertinent excerpt is available at <www.youtube.com/watch?v=bE9IWvLz6Dk>, accessed February 2018.

Zacharopoulos 2017

Zacharopoulos, Konstantinos. 'Musical Syntax in John Williams's Film Music Themes', in: *Contemporary Film Music: Investigating Cinema Narratives and Composition*, edited by Lindsay Coleman and Joakim Tillman, London, Palgrave Macmillan, 2017, pp. 237-262.

The Themes of *Star Wars*: Catalogue and Commentary

Frank Lehman
(Tufts Universiy, Medford, MA)

The musical universe of *Star Wars* is defined by its themes. Recurrent and memorable melodies have occupied a uniquely prominent place in the franchise's soundworld — a prominence reinforced by repetition in countless forms of auxiliary media, from commercials and concerts to radio programs, television shows, and games. Accordingly, thematic materials have received intense and consistent attention in both technical and critical discourses surrounding the series. In discussing his contributions to the franchise, composer John Williams has generally shown more interest in what he often terms «melodic identifications» than other aspects of the scoring process[1]. Commentators and scholars have followed Williams's example in identifying and interpreting these materials, sometimes at the expense of other noteworthy elements of the *Star Wars* scores, such as the structure of action set-pieces and source/diegetic cues[2]. Non-thematic areas of interest aside, the privileged spot themes occupy in the cultural imagination surrounding *Star Wars* is fully warranted. But as is often the case with an artistic touchstone of such inescapability, sheer familiarity has not always implied deep understanding, and many aspects of thematic structure and usage that could benefit from systematic analysis have been left unexamined in favour of more superficial or informal approaches.

The goal of this chapter is to provide a thorough catalogue of recurrent thematic materials in the *Star Wars* musical universe, including the Original Trilogy (Episodes 4-6), Prequel Trilogy (Episodes 1-3), and the current entries in the Sequel Trilogy (Episodes 7-8)[3]. My aim is not to overthrow conventional wisdom surrounding the thematic

[1]. The composer uses this phrase in many interviews, especially during and after the Prequel Trilogy. See, for example: Moss 2002, Reed 2009, and Handy 2015.

[2]. Among the academic work on these scores, notable contributions include Kalinak 1992, Buhler 2000, Paulus 2000, Lerner 2004, Audissino 2014, Richards 2015, Lehman 2017a and Lehman 2017b.

[3]. The films under discussion are, in chronological order: Episode 4, *A New Hope* (George Lucas, 1977); Episode 5, *The Empire Strikes Back* (Irvin Kershner, 1980); Episode 6, *Return of the Jedi* (Richard Marquand, 1983); Episode 1, *The Phantom Menace* (George Lucas, 1999); Episode 2, *Attack of the Clones* (George Lucas, 2002); Episode 3, *Revenge of the Sith* (George Lucas, 2005); Episode 7, *The Force Awakens*

constituents of the *Star Wars* saga, but rather to add clarity and rigour in areas where they are needed. Moreover, I do not plan to closely analyse the structure and development of each and every theme, measure by measure; this would be a valuable undertaking, but one for another essay. My hope is that this thematic catalogue, compiled in a systematic and exhaustive manner and with an eye for the complexities — and inconsistencies — of (leit) motivic scoring, will offer a useful and authoritative reference source for anyone studying these films in the future[4].

Compiling a thematic catalogue is not nearly so straightforward as one might assume given the instant recognizability of (some of) these thematic materials. A substantial portion of this essay is dedicated to exploring issues which arise when identifying recurrent musical thoughts in an evolving, decade-spanning musical text like *Star Wars*. These issues are not matters of secondary importance, but indeed central concerns for any scholarly approach to theme-rich film music, and for this reason they are presented before the catalogue itself, with a series of three sections that lay out the necessary conceptual groundwork for the rest of the project: thematic categories, labels and semantic flexibility, and patterns of usage.

Thematic Categories

Before undertaking any sort of sustained study of this musical corpus, it is necessary to specify the exact scope and definition of that which is being catalogued. This is not so easy. Already, I have used the somewhat vague placeholder 'thematic materials' instead of the more expected (and theoretically burdened) term *leitmotif*. The *Star Wars* films are swirling with recurring musical themes, phrases, and style-topics, and it is crucial to define our terms in a way that distinguishes genuine leitmotifs from the numerous incidental compositional ideas which do not fall into that more strictly delimited category. Achieving definitional clarity is complicated by the inconsistent application of the strictly *Wagnerian* conception of leitmotif, both in the composition and reception of the *Star Wars* scores[5]. Even in Richard Wagner's mature operas, where leitmotifs are deployed at their seemingly

(J. J. Abrams, 2015); and Episode 8, *The Last Jedi* (Rian Johnson, 2017). As more thematic material is added to the saga, updates will be made to the online version of this catalogue, available at <www.franklehman.com>, accessed January 2018, like all the websites mentioned in this article.

[4]. Up to this point, the most sustained cataloguing of thematic materials in this series has been undertaken in trade magazines such as *Film Score Monthly*, online sites such as *Wikipedia* and the *John Williams Fan Network*, and liner notes for soundtrack releases (see especially Kendall 1993 and Matessino 1997a-c).

[5]. Leitmotif-*ala*-Wagner has itself historically been both under- and/or over-defined, depending on context. Indeed, scholar of leitmotif Matthew Bribitzer-Stull, notes the existence of «decades of explanatory vagueness and complexity» — a complexity compounded by two hundred years worth of «competing kinds of thematic recall in dramatic music»; as a result, he dedicates an entire chapter of his monograph on the subject to defining leitmotif. See Bribitzer-Stull 2015, pp. 7-11 and *passim*.

most paradigmatic, there is striking variation in style and usage: the leitmotif technique means a quite different thing in *Das Rheingold* than it does in *Tristan* or *Götterdämmerung* or *Parsifal* — and, indeed a different thing to Wagner in his *own* writings as it does for his small army of acolytes and proselytizers like Hans von Wozlogen. So it is as well with *Star Wars*. Leitmotif principle means something vastly different in 1977's Episode 4: *A New Hope*, where now iconic themes were introduced for the first time, and in 2017's Episode 8: *The Last Jedi*, with forty years of musical memory and shifting scoring practices — plus six other entries in the franchise — informing Williams's ever-evolving approach.

In the interest of giving the clearest possible description of leitmotif, one whose underlying definitional assumptions are laid bare, I submit that in the *Star Wars* series, a leitmotif is a musical idea in possession of the following four characteristics[6]:

1) Distinctiveness: musical idea has a clear and unique melody, without being wholly derived from – or a subsidiary section within – another theme or motif.

2) Recurrence: musical idea is intentionally repeated more than two times across more than two discrete cues, and within in the final mix of the soundtrack.

3) Variation: musical idea's repetitions are not exact.

4) Intentionality: musical idea's repetitions are compositionally intentional, and do not require undue analytical detective-work to notice.

Together, the attributes of distinctiveness, recurrence, variation, and intentionality serve to separate out leitmotifs from many other types of musical material in the *Star Wars* series. Consider the most heavily used leitmotif in the entire series — what is usually referred to as the "Force Theme". Here we see a form of melodic identification in which these four attributes are in clear operation. The theme 1) is formally clear and memorable on a melodic basis, and stands on its own, despite bearing a family resemblance to a handful of other motifs; 2) it is heard across numerous different cues; 3) it is stated with obvious variations in texture, harmony, orchestration, and so on; and 4) it has variants that are manifestly the product of Williams's creative intention, not an accident or a hidden secret. All other musical materials which exhibit these four properties are included in Part One of the catalogue, which enumerates the franchise's 'true' leitmotifs.

The "Force Theme" possesses a few stronger attributes which makes it not only a leitmotif, but what may be termed a *Principal Motif*. These additional characteristics are:

---

[6]. Note that, unlike some theorists like Justin London (2000), I do not hold brevity to be a mandatory feature of a leitmotif. Many of the *Star Wars* leitmotifs are quite long-breathed, but have memorable melodic hooks which can detach from the larger thematic structures, standing in for longer themes and being more readily worked into non-diegetic musical prose. Brevity is thus a common aspect of how leitmotifs are treated in situ, but is neither an innate nor obligatory characteristic.

5) Abundance: musical idea occurs in more than one film, and with more than ten iterations overall.

6) Meaningfulness: musical idea attaches to an important subject or symbol, and accrues additional meaning through repetition in different contexts.

7) Development: musical idea is not only varied, but subjected to compositionally significant development and transformation across its iterations.

The presence of these stronger attributes means the difference between a recurring musical idea with a limited structural/symbolic role and one truly *integral* to the overall evolution of the *Star Wars* soundscape. Principal motifs are, as a result, much fewer in number than generic leitmotifs, amounting just under fifteen — the Main/Luke, Rebel Fanfare, Force, Leia, Darth Vader/Imperial March, Han & Leia, Yoda, Emperor, Young Anakin, Anakin & Padme, Rey, Kylo Ren, and Resistance leitmotifs. Of these, a little more than half appear in more than four of the movies. Appropriately, Episode 4 introduces the most new principal leitmotifs of all the films — four in total, namely Main/Luke, Force, Leia, and Rebel Fanfare motifs.

Of these principal leitmotifs, the "Force Theme" occupies a position of clear privilege in the series, as it is the most pervasively heard and well-developed musical idea in the franchise, and the only one to appear in genuinely *new* forms in every entry. The "Force Theme" also bears a deep semantic resonance, becoming associated with the Force, the Jedi Order, heroes like Obi Wan Kenobi, and the influence of destiny in general. (That is not to say it is semantically fixed — indeed, often the theme serves as a neutral or 'all-purpose' signifier, particularly in Episode 3 and 8.)

The criteria for these principal leitmotifs are quite stringent, and many other famous themes do not make cut. For instance, despite being the most prominent and memorable new musical idea in Episode 1, "Duel of the Fates" (and the three motivic subcomponents that define it) never undergoes any musical development in later films — Williams deigns only to give it a superficial orchestrational change in Episode 2, and its appearance at the climax of Episode 3 is tracked verbatim from Episode 1.

The determination of what is and is not a principal leitmotif has nothing to do with *potential* dramatic or compositional interest: many of Williams's most inventive themes are sparingly utilized, sometimes to the point of neglect. This is most glaring in the case of the exquisite "Luke and Leia" theme, which is abandoned after receiving only two airings during the diegetic runtime of *Return of the Jedi*, and eventually revived for a one final, poignant rendition at the end of *The Last Jedi*. Other themes which must be considered such missed opportunities include the leitmotifs for the droids, Lando, Anakin, Jar Jar, Qui Gon, and Shmi, and depending on its role in later entries in the Sequel Trilogy, "Jedi Steps"[7]. Whether the existence of this corpus of under-utilized materials amounts to a

---

7. Williams's aversion to thematic call-backs, such as evident in interviews concerning his scoring of *The Force Awakens* (Keegan 2016), seems earnest, and can have good dramatic justification; by avoiding the

deliberate creative choice rooted in Williams's dramatic instincts, or a regrettable absence of follow-through stemming from leitmotivic forgetfulness is difficult to say, though it is one contributor to the overall lack of systematicity in these scores compared (fairly or not) to Wagner's music dramas, and, to a lesser extent, Howard Shore's better-integrated but compositionally more pedestrian *Lord of the Rings* scores[8].

While Williams is plainly not possessed of the same radical organicist impulses of Wagner, many of the *Star Wars* themes do nevertheless bear structurally and symbolically important *family resemblances* with one another. These resemblances do not necessarily amount to a strong ancestor/descendent relationship — no single true leitmotif can be said to be fully derived from another — but rather include genetic similarities across various musical parameters. The "Imperial March", for instance directly spawns only a small handful truly derivative motifs – a short melodic figures in Episodes 3, 5, 6, and 8. However, when it comes to genetic affinities, the "Imperial March" has a much wider reach. Its melodic and harmonic ties with "Anakin's Theme" in Episode 1 are obvious (and made all but explicit in its concert arrangement). More subtle but no less potent similarities are clearly at work in Kylo Ren's two motifs and "Jedi Steps" in Episode 7[9].

Incidental Motifs

Williams utilizes a wide-variety of musical materials which recur in one form another, but which either a) occur only twice, b) are too indistinctive to seize the listener's attention to qualify as leitmotifs, or c) are not subjected to any sort of variation, even of a superficial variety. Part Two of the catalogue enumerates these incidental motifs, many of which have until now not been recognized in the musicological literature surrounding these films. In cases where the semantic content of an incidental motif is vague or underdetermined, a more neutral music-theoretic label, such as "Ominous Upper Neighbour Figure", is given, in contrast to the evocative titles borne by true leitmotifs. In other cases, the semantic target

---

Imperial March in Episode 7, for instance, Williams seems consciously attempting to avoid using that theme as a crutch, instead allowing the score to have its own thematic identity, with another Dark Side disciple, Kylo Ren, garnering materials that sound like unformed or poseur versions of their more well-established motivic ancestor.

8. There is an inverse situation: some materials (both leitmotivic and incidental) *do* return in unexpected, perhaps even unmotivated ways. The revival of a sentimental theme from Episode 1 during Finns confession scene in Episode 7 is an example of such a semantically arbitrary — if emotionally well fitting — recurrence.

9. I make two exceptions to the distinctiveness condition: "Luke and Leia" from Episode 6 and the "Conspiracy motif" from Episode 2. The former is a clever recomposition of Lukes theme, imbued with harmonic material of Leias leitmotif. The latter is manifestly a derived from the basic idea of that same films Love Theme ("Across the Stars"). In both cases, clear structural connections between these themes are never drawn out explicitly or exploited, and consistent differences of orchestration and articulation obscure the compositional derivation.

of incidental motifs seems to be clear — observe the host of musical particles which attach to the villainous First Order in Episode 7, or the almost sub-audible male chanting that accompanies Supreme Leader Snoke. Yet despite the symbolic clarity of these materials, their actual structural make-up is too vague, too melodically ill-defined to secure them a place in musical memory such as true leitmotifs must be capable of achieving. (Snoke's material does ascend to the level of leitmotif in Episode 8, thanks more to the louder mixing of the score than any newfound gain in melodic distinctiveness.)

The "Victory Fanfare" in Episode 6 is a prime example of an incidental motif. At the ending of the first act's Sail Barge Battle, and later the climactic Battle of Endor, Williams presents a pair of closely related celebratory fanfares. Both emphasize lydian harmony, both signify success for the protagonists, both are conveyed through brassy orchestration, and both conclude with a shared melodic and rhythmic figure, $\hat{1}$-$\hat{3}$-$\hat{5}$-$\sharp\hat{4}$-$\hat{2}$-$\hat{1}$. However, despite these similarities, there are simply too few recurrences to render the idea *motivic* in a constructive sense. And while it conveys clear semantic content, the fanfare does not *accumulate* it, performing essentially the same associative task upon both iterations.

An additional category of incidental motifs can also be described: musical ideas whose structural similarities may arguably be too slight to definitively attribute them to Williams's creative process. There is little evidence that Williams closely studies previous scores when writing a new entry into the *Star Wars* canon, and seems largely uninterested in drawing subtle interconnections between musical materials of minor or passing importance — in fact, he has confessed to not having seen most of them, as indicated in a recent interview[10]!

For example, there is a "Sentimental Descending Progression" figure which arises first in the "Victory Celebration" in the Episode 6 Special Edition (where it harmonizes a VI-v-III progression), and later "It's Working" in Episode 1 (where it harmonizes VI-VII-III) and "Across the Stars" in Episode 2 (once again VI-v-III). But this likeness, while compelling when noticed, is both inexact and quite possibly an accident — more probable the product of Williams approaching scenes of warmth and melodrama with similar Debussyian modal harmony than an attempt to unite disparate scenes with a truly obscure musical call-back.

Set-Piece Themes

Not all of Williams's creative energies are poured into musical themes and motifs. A substantial amount of the *Star Wars* soundscape is occupied with non-leitmotivic underscore, and in those special cases where music is allowed to breathe and come to the foreground, one can find some Williams's most original compositional ideas in any given entry into the series. Themes for these one-off set-pieces may be strikingly memorable, and can lend a

10. Desborough – Watts 2016.

single cue considerable unity and interest as so-called 'pure' or 'absolute' music. Examples of such cues include the Flag Parade (Episode 1), the Chase Through Coruscant (Episode 2), the Immolation Scene (Episode 3), the Asteroid Field Chase (Episode 5), and the Dark Side Beckons (Episode 6). Because of their highly constrained scope, it is impossible for these one-cue wonders to achieve the accumulation of meaning (or, often, variation) that is characteristic of leitmotifs. In a handful of cases, materials originally conceived of as set-piece themes can ascend to incidental-motivic status when they are resurrected in subsequent films: this is the case, for instance, with central syncopated idea from "Here They Come" from Episode 4, which was later recycled, with minimal alteration, for various battle sequences in Episode 6. And, upon its orchestrationally and harmonically varied resurgence in Episode 8, "Here They Come" finally qualifies as a true — if still only marginally developed — leitmotif.

Style-Topics and Non-Melodic Motifs

Musical themes and motifs may be categorized according to their formal structure. Using the typology of musical themes developed by Mark Richards[11], each entry in the catalogue is described as one of three structural archetypes: a *grammatical theme* (wherein a melody can be divided into a clear and balanced beginning and ending half); a *discursive theme* (which are lengthy and cannot be easily divided into a clear beginning or ending half); or a *motto theme* (which are brief and also cannot be broken into autonomous subsidiary functions)[12]. Among true leitmotifs, grammatical themes are the norm, while incidental motifs are more likely to based on mottos or discursive structures. In underscore, leitmotifs are frequently presented in only partial version, meaning that even the longest-breathed grammatical themes are often heard as mottos, their melodic hooks standing in for the fuller musical idea. At the same time, many leitmotifs, including the "Main Theme", "Imperial March", and "Yoda's Theme", have multiple sub-sections, like a contrasting A- and B- theme or bridge; these are treated as incidental motifs, as they tend to occur very rarely outside of concert arrangements. Other themes include distinct polyphonic sub-components, including "Duel of the Fates", "Battle of the Heroes", and "Rey's Theme".

Not all recurrent musical materials with semantic value in the *Star Wars* series are melodic in character; some may involve associative harmonies, timbres, or rhythms, while never exhibiting a single or consistent melodic hook. The series would not be the same without its sinister i → ♭vi progressions, its Ravelian brass lines moving in rapid parallel motion, its profusion of march rhythms, dissonant pedal-points, and so on. These non-

[11]. Richards 2016.

[12]. Grammatical themes can be further subcategorized into a number of forms. In Richards's typology, these include the *period*, *sentence*, *clause*, and *composite*. This taxonomic approach to theme structure in Williams's music is expanded substantially in Richards's own contribution to this volume.

melodic materials may be sorted into a broad category of *style topics*, with subcategories such as of leit-harmony, leit-timbre, leit-gestures and so on. Style topics form an essential component of the *Star Wars* sound, but necessarily lack the definition afforded by clear, hummable melody.

The clearest example of a non-leitmotivic style-topic is that of the low male voice. Deep, wordless vocals are strongly associated with the Dark Side, and characterize nearly every appearance of The Emperor's leitmotif since the character's big introduction in Episode 6. However, as a pure timbre, the male voice is also a detachable entity that is still capable of signifying, albeit with less lexical definition, matters pertaining to the negative side of the force — for example, the characters of Count Dooku in Episode 2 and Supreme Leader Snoke in Episode 7, or the ominous locale of the Coruscant Opera House in Episode 3.

Labels and Semantic Flexibility

In some cases, names for leitmotifs suggest themselves. We may take Williams at his word, for example, when he refers to "Yoda's Theme", first heard in *The Empire Strikes Back*, as a way of labelling the melody that attaches to the diminutive Jedi master. Other themes, however, are not so clear cut. The "Force Theme", for example, has occasioned some vigorous debates regarding proper name. Arguments have been put forth, especially online and especially by novitiate analysts, for referring to it as "Luke's Theme", "Obi Wan Kenobi's Theme", "Jedi Theme", and even "Main Theme". The multiplicity of labels for this particular melodic identification has several sources: the fact that in Episode 4, it does seem (loosely, inconsistently) associated with Kenobi; that in subsequent films, the prequels especially, it has a symbolically flexible character, finding its way into many dramatic situations where the single label "Force Theme" seems insufficient to articulate its semantic content; and that Williams, while often referring to the melody as the "Force Theme", never provided it with a named concert arrangement like other principal leitmotifs.

In general, the more often a musical idea is heard, the more chances it has to defy any labels that may be placed on it. No one will confuse the semantic target of the "Luke and Leia" theme in Episode 6, as it is heard only twice during that film's dramatic action, each time in connection with the brother/sister relationship between those two characters. Far less easy to assign a meaningful label, however, is something like the constellation of motifs and themes that incorporate a figure based on or alluding to the "Dies Irae"; despite not being truly an autonomous theme, it is nevertheless leitmotivic, heard with great frequency and in connection with a great many different targets (e.g. the death of Luke's aunt and uncle, Anakin's murderous confession, the slaughter of Ewoks, the extermination of the Jedi, introduction of Rey, and more).

Even symbolically unambiguous thematic materials can be used in a way that does not slavishly adhere to a single signified[13]. Yoda's theme, for instance, is heard late in Episode 5 when the character is not literally present. One could either justify this as an insinuation of the lessons Yoda has imparted to Luke, or pass it off as a free treatment of topically or expressively appropriate motivic material. Attempts to rationalize 'unruly' leitmotifs can easily veer into contrivance, as interpreters try to 'correct' ostensibly misbehaving themes by offering non-obvious justifications for their employment. At the same time, contrivance is not always unwarranted, and we should not downplay the extent to which drawing non-obvious connections is an inextricable part of the listening process, particularly given the explicitly mythical and allusive nature of these fantastic narratives.

Labelling recurrent thematic materials thus involves an interpretive balancing act. On one hand, a particle of musical meaning should be named with a degree of specificity that enables identification and reflects real patterns of deployment and association. At the same time, one must consider whether a strategic open-endedness is warranted, the sort of which admits atypical or aberrant uses and the semantically mutability inherent in any musical thought, leitmotivic or not. In this catalogue, I privilege names which Williams himself has lent to the themes, with a few garnering alternative labels when useful. I also indicate whether or not a recurring theme is ever deployed in a semantically flexible manner, or instead is locked into referring to a single, clear symbolic target. Once again, the "Force Theme" is the paradigmatic case of a semantically flexible leitmotif, while a motif such as "Jabba's Theme" or "Parade of the Ewoks" is quite constrained to the target literally suggested by its thematic label[14].

Further refinement of the way leitmotifs are interpreted in terms of semantic content is beyond the scope of this chapter, but one additional distinction is worth adumbrating: the difference between leitmotivic use and mention[15]. The use/mention distinction hails from the philosophy of language, where it describes how certain linguistic utterances carry meaning while others refer specifically back to the discourse itself or units therein. Put quite simply, it is the difference between a word and that same word placed within in quotation marks. Although obviously not words in a real linguistic sense, leitmotifs do carry semantic content and can be employed in either integral (direct, unmediated, immersive) or citational (e.g. indirect, mediated, self-conscious) ways, depending on context. The most clear-cut instance of this in the *Star Wars* films is the quasi-diegetic cue "Threepio's Bedtime Story"

---

[13]. The most famous example is the usage of "Princess Leias Theme" upon the death of Obi Wan Kenobi in Episode 4, which the composer claims was justified because of the sweeping romantic tenor of the leitmotif, rather than its specific lexical content (Adams 1999). Buhler notes this semantic flexibility is typical of themes associated with the Light Side of the Force in the OT, and contributes to the protean, mythical quality of those films storytelling apparatus.

[14]. "Parade of the Ewoks" does bear a few passing potentially accidental similarities in earlier music in ROTJ, in the original Sail Barge Battle cue and some of the Emperors Throne Room scenes.

[15]. See Lehman 2017a for more detail on this distinction with respect to *Star Wars*.

in Episode 6, which self-consciously quotes a number of previously integral leitmotifs in gently humorous way, though many other less overt examples of themes falling between the poles of pure use and pure mention may also be located with some effort[16].

Patterns of Usage

Mapping the *Star Wars* music universe requires knowing not only what a recurring theme is, but where and when it occurs. In order to limit the scope of this catalogue, and focus on the most definitive *Star Wars* texts, I have narrowed this study to materials originally written by John Williams as appear in the nine live-action films (Episodes 1-8 and *Rogue One*, designated by "R" in the catalogue), omitting uses in other media (television, video games, amusement parks, etc.) and materials composed or arranged by others, including Joel McNeely, Michael Giacchino, Kevin Kiner, Chris Huelsbeck, Gordy Haab, and John Powell.

This still leaves an enormous span of non-diegetic underscore to parse. With the exception of the "Main Theme" (both A- and B-sections), all leitmotifs appear for the first time within the non-diegetic score proper. While not relevant to the development of these materials during the dramatic action *per se*, Williams's End Credits cues typically showcase important themes from their respective movies, most artfully in the miniature suites devised for Episodes 5 and 7. The credits for all seven films begin with an invariant statement of the "Main/Luke Theme" in E-flat or D-flat major, followed by a blast of the "Rebel Fanfare", after which point new material is be presented. (Some interstitial and concluding passages is also recycled across films.) Four of the films — Episodes 3, 4, 5, 6 — end with triumphant orchestral *tuttis*, while three end softly, either with ominous presentiment of the "Imperial March" (Episodes 1, 2) or, in the case of Episode 7 and 8, a gentle celesta rendition of the "Main/Luke Theme" and "Rey's Theme" respectively.

With the exception of Episodes 4 and 5, thematic restatements featured in the End Credits are essentially identical to versions presented in autonomous concert suites and arrangements, with only minor altered transitions and abridgements. Of these, only two concert arrangements — "The Adventures of Jar Jar" and "Battle of the Heroes" — are basically identical to their underscore sources, though the former is a series of multiple spliced-together short cues from different parts of Episode 1, and the latter includes a short introduction and coda not present in the original set-piece from Episode 3. Typically, concert arrangements have a loose arc form, being structured around three or four rotations

---

[16]. Of all the franchises leitmotifs, "The Imperial March" / Vaders leitmotif) seems most susceptible to being mentioned, particularly in Episodes 1 and 2 where, when not subtly incorporated into young Anakins thematic material, tends towards overt and on-the-nose thematic deployment. The single straightforward usage of the theme in Episode 7 and 8 also acts in this self-quotational fashion.

of a given theme, presented with increasing orchestral density and volume. Many feature contrasting episodes between thematic statements ("Princess Leia's Theme", "Parade of the Ewoks") or even distinctive contrasting themes ("Across the Stars") or pseudo-developmental middle sections (the "Imperial March", "March of the Resistance"). Most idiosyncratic is Episode 8's "The Rebellion is Reborn", which serves as an arrangement for *two* motifs (Rose and Luke's Exile), which it presents and develops in alternation. Not every major theme earns a dedicated concert arrangement, particularly in the case of mottos and discursively structured melodies. However, two of the most important leitmotifs — the "Rebel Fanfare" and "Force Theme" — do feature as thematic *components* within other concert suites and set-pieces, most prominently in "Here They Come" for the former and "Throne Room and Finale" for the latter.

The thematic catalogue makes a note of each theme's first unambiguous airing in the chronologically earliest score — including retroactively tracked themes, as with a version of Jabba's creepy leitmotif, originally composed for Episode 6 but inserted into the Special Edition of Episode 4 in 1997. Often, these first annunciations are important in defining the theme's significatory and affective content, and in a few cases, they are offered in an already full and definitive form — most notably "Rey's Theme". More often, associative materials are initially presented in a tentative or embryonic fashion, particularly in the OT. For example, four of the most important themes in Episode 4 — the "Rebel Fanfare", "Imperial Motif", "Force Theme", and "Leia's Theme" — are all introduced in the first cue in an understated way: beneath dialogue or sound-effects, as an incomplete musical phrase, and/or without an obvious symbolic target. For this reason, it is also worth including information on the most definitive, foregrounded, and complete renditions of a given theme. This is, of course, something of a subjective determination, though in a few cases (e.g. the "Force Theme" during the famous Binary Sunset sequence), the theme's presentation is so iconic as to make the selection an obvious choice. In cases where no truly foregrounded iterations of a theme exist (e.g. "Jabba's Theme"), the most formally complete statement is listed instead.

Given the iconicity of so much of the franchise's themes, and the frequent comparisons with the thematic process of Wagner (for whom motivic saturation was a goal, particularly in his final operas), one might expect a substantial proportion of the soundtrack for these films to be devoted to leitmotifs — perhaps even a majority. However, the amount of time spent stating these materials is surprisingly low: at most 36% of the final soundtrack in Episode 5 and as low as 20.5% in Episode 2[17]. Given that most of these films are suffused

[17]. The percentages are as follows: Episode 1 (22%), 2 (20.5%), 3 (25.5%), 4 (24.5%), 5 (36%), 6 (29.5%), 7 (27%). In order to determine relative prevalence of leitmotifs, the author tracked thematic usage with a stopwatch while screening the most recent official digital release of each film (meaning the Special Editions are used for the three members of the Original Trilogy). Timings refer only to the dramatic action of each respective film, beginning right after the invariant Main Title and concluding the moment the End Credits

with non-diegetic music, approaching almost wall-to-wall scoring in places, this means that a largely unacknowledged portion of musical time is composed of athematic underscore. And while the number of motifs employed unsurprisingly grows with each new film as Williams's thematic library expands, this does not correlate with increasing motivic saturation. If anything, the tendency following Episode 5 is towards greater concision and restraint, with fewer cues in the Prequel Trilogy spun primarily out multiple leitmotifs in succession, and new themes that are comparatively constrained in terms of scope, usage, and development.

Emblematic of this shift between trilogies is the basis of climactic battle sequences on original action set-pieces (i.e. "Duel of the Fates", "Battle of the Heroes") that, while leitmotivic according to the criteria laid out in this essay, lack the breadth of development that characterizes the iconic themes of the OT. This tendency continues, with some modifications, in the ST. Episode 7, while citing many of the OT's motifs, adheres more to the PT's leaner approach to thematic scoring at a moment-to-moment level. A few exceptional portions of the soundtrack — notably the cue "Han and Leia" and everything from Rey and Kylo Ren's final duel to the Credits — end up contributing substantially and disproportionately to the overall percentage (27%) of leitmotivic scoring during Episode 7's runtime. The recent entry at the time of the authoring of this essay is Episode 8, which features by far the most cited leitmotifs (25!), though few beyond "The Force", "Rey", "Rose", "Resistance", and "Kylo Ren A" are substantially developed.

The relative abundance or paucity of motivic material in a given film should not be taken as a mark of its aesthetic coherence. Episode 5 possesses arguably the most compelling and tightly argued score, with its leitmotifs being well-integrated with spans of highly memorable athematic scoring, and each of the three new principal themes earning its own dramatic arc over the film's runtime[18]. However, the strengths of Episode 5's soundtrack, while undeniable, have as much to do with its being the most compelling and tightly constructed *film* as a whole as it does with Williams's thematic process. Compare with Episode 2, a critical low-point in the series according to many fans, which happens to have the lowest percentage of its soundtrack occupied by leitmotifs. Even so, the film has the clearest thematic through-line of any of the prequels by far, thanks to the thoughtfulness with which its central theme, "Across the Stars", is rolled out and developed. Furthermore,

---

appear. Timings reflect music as it occurs in context, not as written; thus artificially tracked, repeated and edited cues are included, while cut or rewritten are excluded. Only true leitmotifs were considered towards this total; the inclusion of incidental motifs contributes marginally (at most 10% in the case of Episode 2) to the percentages.

[18]. Extensive usage of a single them brings with it certain expressive potentialities, such as the ability to suggest inescapability — very much the case, and with good dramatic justification, with the "Imperial March" in Episode 5. At the same time, restraint also comes with its own dramatic powers: part of the significance of "Luke and Leia" in Episode 7 stems from its rarity, arising only twice, but both times at crucial moments. (See the "Glorification of Brünhilde" motif in Wagners *Ring*.)

Episode 2's score is also suffused with an unusually high number non-melodic motifs and timbres — most prominently and idiosyncratically its use of unpitched percussion. While incapable of grabbing the listener's attention in the same way as principal leitmotifs can, these non-melodic elements nevertheless imparts a distinctive colour to the soundtrack, a propulsive and exotic tint quite unlike the other entries in the series.

Conclusion

It is worthwhile to step back and consider what the purpose of compiling a thematic catalogue is. We must be careful to acknowledge the underlying agenda in ascribing this idea of leitmotivic organization, derived from musical practices of the nineteenth century, to a contemporary composition — albeit one of a profoundly retrospective and nostalgic character — such as the *Star Wars* musical universe. We can only rely on composer intent so far. Beyond occasionally invoking the leitmotif concept in interviews, Williams himself has never expressed much knowledge about or interest in Wagner's theoretical writings, nor indeed his operas either. To the extent that Williams's contribution to film music history may be called "Wagnerian", it is Wagnerian at several levels of remove — Wagner by-way-of a group of far more chronologically proximate and readily acknowledged cinematic models such as Steiner and Korngold.

The fidelity with which Williams hews to the originary Wagnerian conception of leitmotif (and mid-twentieth century cinematic appropriations thereof) may be invoked, depending on the commentator, as a means to several opposed ends:

1) Elevating Williams's scores as compositionally unified and legitimate according to the standards of art music. This is a typical attitude of fans and film music enthusiasts.

2) Denigrating his scores as imperfect or facile replications of those same art music standards. This is the typical attitude of classical music purists and detractors who focus on compositional originality and influence.

3) Critiquing his scores as a revival of an intrinsically defective or problematical musical practice. This is a rather less common attitude, as it requires a sceptical stance towards both Wagnerian music drama and Hollywood scoring practices; it is embodied, before the fact, in Adorno and Eisler's polemics on Wagner and Hollywood, and is gestured towards at in James Buhler's important essay on the scores of the original *Star Wars* trilogy[19].

---

[19]. See Adorno – Eisler 2007, Adorno 2005, and Buhler 2000. This attitude is related to, but not implicative of, a kind of meta-analytical critical stance towards habits of motivic analysis and hermeneutics, and the larger desire to draw connections between musical ideas in order to demonstrate musical value; such a view is expressed in, for example, Abbate – Parker 1989 and Abbate 1991. The feverish way in which fans strove to link Reys leitmotif in Episode 7 to scores of other themes shows exactly how irresistible this impulse remains, even when Williams himself in his description of the scores provides little grounds for such

Cataloguing motifs is therefore not a neutral task, and it is probably impossible to operate fully without one of the three above agendas as a motivating force. My own agenda falls somewhere between the first and third options: I maintain that the integrity of these scores resides at least in part in their ingenious motivic interconnectedness, though the extent of this interconnectedness is easily misunderstood and exaggerated, and owes to an impulse well-worth examining through a (self-)critical lens. And, given the increasing number of 'cinematic universes' with complex webs of motifs and musical identifications, this is an impulse scholars of film music should be acutely aware of as they compile such catalogues for other multimedia franchises.

Star Wars Catalogue, Part One: Leitmotifs

Ear transcriptions from: *Star Wars – Episode IV: A New Hope* [4] (© 1977 BMI, published by Bantha Music/Warner-Tamerlane); *Star Wars – Episode V: The Empire Strikes Back* [5] (© 1980 BMI, published by Bantha Music/Warner-Tamerlane); *Star Wars – Episode VI: Return of the Jedi* [6] (© 1983 BMI, published by Bantha Music/Warner-Tamerlane); *Star Wars – Episode I: The Phantom Menace* [1] (© 1999 BMI, published by Bantha Music/Warner-Tamerlane); *Star Wars – Episode II: Attack of the Clones* [2] (©2002 BMI, published by Bantha Music/Warner-Tamerlane); *Star Wars – Episode III: Revenge of the Sith* [3] (© 2005 BMI, published by Bantha Music/Warner-Tamerlane); *Star Wars – Episode VII: The Force Awakens* [7] (© 2015 BMI, published by Utapau Music); *Star Wars – Episode VIII: The Last Jedi* [8] (© 2017 BMI, published by Utapau Music). Used in compliance with the U.S. Copyright Act, Section 107.

Star Wars Catalogue, Part Two: Incidental Motifs

Ear transcriptions from: *Star Wars – Episode IV: A New Hope* [4] (© 1977 BMI, published by Bantha Music/Warner-Tamerlane); *Star Wars – Episode V: The Empire Strikes Back* [5] (© 1980 BMI, published by Bantha Music/Warner-Tamerlane); *Star Wars – Episode VI: Return of the Jedi* [6] (© 1983 BMI, published by Bantha Music/Warner-Tamerlane); *Star Wars – Episode I: The Phantom Menace* [1] (© 1999 BMI, published by Bantha Music/Warner-Tamerlane); *Star Wars – Episode II: Attack of the Clones* [2] (© 2002 BMI, published by Bantha Music/Warner-Tamerlane); *Star Wars – Episode III: Revenge of the Sith* [3] (© 2005 BMI, published by Bantha Music/Warner-Tamerlane); *Star Wars – Episode VII: The Force Awakens* [7] (© 2015 BMI, published by Utapau Music); *Star Wars – Episode VIII: The Last Jedi* [8] (© 2017 BMI, published by Utapau Music). Used in compliance with the U.S. Copyright Act, Section 107.

contrived explanations. See for example, an interview with the composer conducted by Byrd 1997, and a motivic summary by Lehman 2015.

Original Trilogy Themes

Theme Label	Melodic Basic Idea or Incipit	Initial / Iconic Statements	Principal Motif	Structure	Underscore / End Credits Uses	Semantic Flexibility
Main/Luke A	B♭ Fm7sus4 B♭	4 [0:00:28] 4 [1:27:23]	Y	Grammatical	1,2,3,4,5,6,7, 8, R 1,2,3,4,5,6,7, 8, R	Y
Rebel Fanfare	A F♯ A F♯ C C B C B A F♯	4 [0:02:06] 4 [1:05:25]	Y	Motto	3,4,5,6,7,8,R 1,2,3,4,5,6,7,8,R	Y
Force/Obi Wan/ All-Purpose	Gm (D) Gm C	4 [0:04:53] 4 [0:25:38]	Y	Grammatical	1,2,3,4,5,6,7,8,R 3,7	Y
Leia	E F♯m7♭5/E E	4 [0:05:07] 4 [0:21:40]	Y	Grammatical	3,4,5,6,7,8,R 3,4,8	Y

Imperial Troops		4 [0:06:40] 4 [0:15:09]	N	Motto	4,R —	N
Imperial Ships/ Death Star	 Am/C C♯m/C	4 [0:08:48] 4 [0:36:54]	N	Motto	4,6,8,R —	N
Jawas	 G⁷	4 [0:12:58] 4 [0:16:54]	N	Discursive	4 —	N
Jabba	 Gm D♭m	4 [0:52:44] 6 [0:14:43]	N	Discursive	1,4,6 —	N
Here They Come!		4 [1:34:34] 8 [2:02:14]	N	Motto	4,6,8 8	N

Throne Room	D♭ G♭/B♭ A♭7 G♭ G♭/F E♭m7 A♭7 Fm7 B♭m7 G♭	4 [1:59:24] 4 [1:59:24]	N	Grammatical	4,6 3,6	N
Darth Vader/ Imperial March	Gm E♭m/G♭ Gm E♭m/G♭ Gm E♭m/G♭ E♭m Cm7♭5 Gm	5 [0:01:55] 5 [0:19:37]	Y	Grammatical	1,2,3,5,6,7,8 1,2,5	Y
Han & Leia/Han	D♭ E♭m7♭5/D♭ E♭♭/D♭ A♭7 D♭	5 [0:03:32] 5 [0:50:51]	Y	Grammatical	5,6,7,8 5	Y
Droids	B♭ G♭m B♭	5 [0:06:44] 5 [0:44:24]	N	Grammatical	5 —	N
Yoda	C D/C C D/C	5 [0:49:43] 5 [1:12:11]	Y	Grammatical	1,2,3,5,6,8 5,8	Y

Boba Fett		5 [1:06:13] 5 [1:28:28]	N	Motto	5 —	Y
Lando/Cloud City	Ema7 F♯m7/E D/E Ema7 D7/E Ema7 F F/C	5 [1:21:31] 5 [1:47:18]	N	Grammatical	5 —	N
Emperor	Gm B♭m/F Gm C♯m -ma7	6 [0:38:17] 6 [1:55:22]	Y	Grammatical	1,2,3,6,8 —	Y
Ewok March	B♭sus♯4	6 [1:03:50] 6 [1:29:04]	N	Grammatical	6 6	N
Ewok Fanfare		6 [1:05:50] 6 [1:47:10]	N	Motto	6 6	N

Luke & Leia	C♭7/D♭ D♭ C♭7/D♭ D♭	6 [1:20:24] 6 [2:03:32]	N	Grammatical	6,8 6	N

Prequel Trilogy Themes

Theme Label	Melodic Basic Idea or Incipit	Initial / Iconic Statements	Principal Motif	Structure	Underscore / End Credits Uses	Semantic Flexibility
Droid March	Cm D7♭5/C Cm Fm/A♭ Cm/G Gm Fm Cm	1 [0:10:11] 1 [1:49:07]	N	Grammatical	1,2,3 —	N
Darth Maul	Fm/A♭ G♭m/B♭♭ Fm/A♭ D♭m/F♭ C♭m/E♭ Bm/D Fm/A♭	1 [0:27:43] 1 [0:51:22]	N	Motto	1 —	N
Jar Jar	C D♭ C	1 [0:28:55] 1 [0:33:22]	N	Grammatical	1 —	N

Young Anakin	 A B/A G♯7/A A F7/E E7♭5/B♭ B♭ Asus4	1 [0:32:41] 1 [1:35:12]	Y	Grammatical	1,2,3 1,2	N
Qui Gon	 Cm /E♭ /D /B /A♭	1 [1:11:08] 1 [1:16:50]	N	Grammatical	1 —	N
Shmi	 Dm (pandiatonic)	1 [1:15:00] 2 [1:23:17]	N	Discursive	1,2,3 —	Y
Duel of the Fates A (Theme)		1 [1:46:36] 1 [1:53:35]	N	Motto	1,2,3 1	Y
Duel of the Fates B (Fanfare)	 Em Esus4 Esus2 Em F♯sus2 Cm	1 [1:50:18] 1 [1:52:26]	N	Motto	1,2,3 1	Y

Duel of the Fates C (Ostinato)		1 [1:50:30] 1 [1:52:21]	N	Motto	1,2,3 1	Y
Death/Funeral	 G♯m G♯sus2 G♯madd6 G♯m C♯madd6/E G♯madd6 G♯m	1 [2:07:17] 3 [2:10:57]	N	Motto	1,3 —	N
Conspiracy	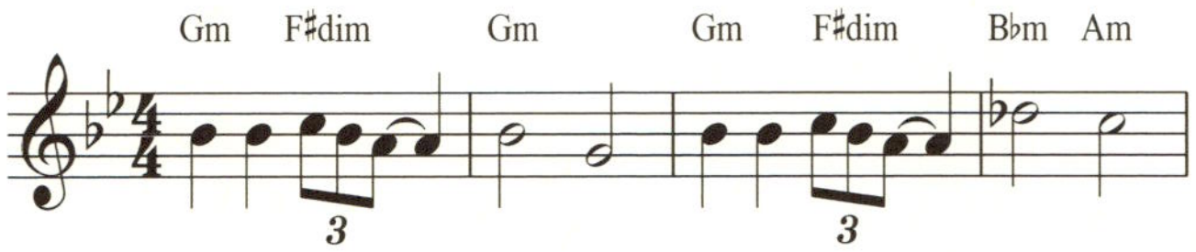 Gm F♯dim Gm Gm F♯dim B♭m Am	2 [0:04:21] 2 [1:16:29]	N	Motto	2 —	N
Gloomy Courtship	 E♭7♭5 C/A♭ D♭add6 Esus4/D E/D D C♯	2 [0:09:50] 2[0:55:02]	N	Grammatical	2,3 2	N
Across the Stars (Anakin & Padme)	 Dm Gm/D Dm Am/E B♭ Am F A/E	2 [0:29:06] 2 [1:44:05]	Y	Grammatical	2,3 2	N

Pastoral Courtship	$Dsus^4$	2 [0:47:46] 2 [0:50:00]	N	Discursive	2 —	N
Dies Irae	F♯m F♯º/C♮ F♯m F♯º/C♮ F♯m F♯º/C♮ F♯m F♯º/C♮	2 [1:24:02] 3 [1:21:24]	N	Motto	1,2,3,4,6,7 —	Y
General Grievous		3 [0:08:18] 3 [0:27:35]	N	Motto	3 —	N
Battle of the Heroes	Dm B♭/D Dm Am/D Em/D Dm	3 [1:47:53] 3 [1:56:50]	N	Motto	3,8 3	N

Sequel Trilogy Themes

Theme Label	Melodic Basic Idea or Incipit	Initial / Iconic Statements	Principal Motif	Structure	Underscore / End Credits Uses	Semantic Flexibility
Map	Dm G♯m Dm G♯m Dm G♯m	7 [0:02:40] 7 [0:52:41]	N	Motto	7 —	N
Kylo Ren A (Aggressive)	C♯m	7 [0:06:11] 7 [1:50:07]	Y	Motto	7,8 7	N
Kylo Ren B (Hesitant)	C♯m Am (F♯dim) C♯m Am (F♯dim)	7 [0:26:30] 7 [1:55:34]	N	Motto	7,8 7	N
Kylo Ren C (Menacing)		7 [1:30:31] 8 [0:02:15]	N	Motto	7,8 7	N

First Order	Dm E$^{7\flat5}$/D Dm Dm E$^{7\flat5}$/D Dm B♭/D Ddim/A	7 [0:09:32] 7 [1:29:29]	N	Motto	7 —	N
Rey A (Primary)	Am Asus$^{2/4}$ Am Am F/A D^7/F♯	7 [0:12:16] 7 [1:18:50]	Y	Grammatical	7,8 7,8	Y
Rey B (Chimes)	Am Asus$^{2/4}$ Am Asus$^{2/4}$ Am	7 [0:11:38] 8 [2:13:45]	N	Motto	7,8 7,8	N
Poe	A♭ B♭ Cm F	7 [0:21:53] 7 [1:16:23]	N	Motto	7,8 7	N
Pursuit/Finn	D^{7}sus^4 ———	7 [0:30:00] 7 [0:48:09]	N	Motto	7 7	Y

Snoke	 N.C. Appx. 15mb	7 [0:51:50] 8 [0:16:10]	N	Discursive	7,8 —	N
March of the Resistance A	 Am E Am Am	7 [1:15:27] 7 [1:21:02]	Y	Grammatical	7,8 7,8	N
March of the Resistance B	 Gm D/G Gm Gsus2/4	7 [0:58:27] 8 [0:41:40]	N	Motto	7,8 7,8	N
Tension		7 [1:43:03] 8 [0:27:20]	N	Motto	7,8 8	Y
Jedi Steps	 Gm E♭/G Gm Gsus2/4 Gm Gsus2	7 [2:05:10] 7 [2:05:30]	N	Grammatical	7,8 —	N

Luke in Exile	 Am F/A Am Asus^2 Asus^2 Asus^4 Am	8 [0:20:20] 8 [0:58:30]	N	Motto	8 8	Y
Desperation		8 [0:28:06] 8 [1:51:09]	N	Motto	8 8	Y
Rose	 D♭ E♭/D♭ D♭ E♭/D♭ D♭ E♭ F	8 [0:38:28] 8 [1:08:00]	Y	Grammatical	8 8	N

INCIDENTAL MOTIFS

MOTIF LABEL	MELODIC BASIC IDEA OR INCIPIT	CLEAR STATEMENT	USES
Main/Luke (Bridge)		4 [1:28:41]	4,5,6
Imperial Rhythm		4 [0:02:30]	4,5,6, R
Planetary Descent Figure		4 [0:07:21]	1,2,4
Scum and Villainy		4 [0:14:34]	4
Imperial Troops Ostinato		4 [0:55:04]	4

Imperial March Precursor		4 [1:13:27]	4, 6
Octatonic Battle Motif		4 [1:48:16]	4,6
Descending Tetrachords		4 [1:36:42]	4,6
Ominous Ostinato		5 [0:15:17]	5
Ominous Neighbor Figure		5 [1:04:45]	5
Ominous Upwards Arpeggio		5 [1:53:23]	5

Yoda (Bridge)		5 [0:56:10]	5
Imperial March (Bridge)		6 [0:02:40]	6
Lydian Fanfare		6 [0:35:31]	6
Revelatory Arpeggios		6 [0:43:15]	6
Cascading Trumpet Lines		6 [1:26:44]	6
Baroque Battle Motif		6 [1:34:10]	6, R

Ewok Casualties		6 [1:43:14]	6
Sentimental Modal Progression		6 [2:06:16]	1,6
Sith Whispers		1 [0:04:16]	1
Water World		1 [0:13:15]	1
Anakin Variant		1 [0:36:25]	1
Neutral Conversation Music		1 [0:41:37]	1,7

Jedi Business		1 [1:27:58]	2
Ominous Arpeggios		2 [0:41:06]	2
Shmi Death		2 [1:27:20]	2
Chromatic Interjection		2 [2:07:19]	2
Arena/Republic March		2 [1:48:25]	2, 3
Battle Drums		3 [0:01:43]	3

Happy Landing		3 [0:23:24]	3
Sith Mystery		3 [0:45:08]	3
Lament		3 [1:20:55]	3
Apocalyptic Minor Triads		3 [1:55:37]	3,7
Battle of the Heroes (Ostinato)		3 [1:51:40]	3
Battle of the Heroes (Bridge)		3 [1:51:39]	3

Expansive Positive Phrase		7 [0:16:29]	7
Chase Ostinato		7 [0:21:22]	7
Rey (Gallop)		7 [0:11:48]	7, 8
Rey (Variant)		7 [1:08:15]	7
Tragedy		7 [1:09:30]	7
Resistance Heroism		8 [0:08:00]	8

Catastrophe		8 [0:08:55]	8
Snoke's Chamber		8 [1:43:05]	8

Bibliography

Abbate 1991
Abbate, Carolyn. *Unsung Voices*, Princeton, Princeton University Press, 1991.

Abbate – Parker 1989
Abbate, Carolyn – Parker, Roger. 'Introduction: On Analyzing Opera', in: *Analyzing Opera: Verdi and Wagner*, Berkeley (CA), University of California Press, 1989 (California Studies in 19th-Century Music, 6).

Adams 1999
Adams, Doug. 'Sounds of the Empire: Analyzing the Themes of the *Star Wars* Trilogy', in: *Film Score Monthly*, (June 1999), pp. 22-25.

Adorno 2005
Adorno, Theodor Ludwig Wiesengrund. *In Search of Wagner*, (1963), translated by Robert Livingstone, London, Verso, 2005 (Verso Modern Classics).

Adorno – Eisler 2007
Id. – Eisler, Hanns. *Composing for the Films*, (1947), rpt. London, Continuum, 2007.

Audissino 2014
Audissino, Emilio. *John Williams's Film Music: «Jaws», «Star Wars», «Raiders of the Lost Ark», and the Return of the Classical Hollywood Music Style*, Madison (WI), University of Wisconsin Press, 2014 (Wisconsin Film Studies).

Bribitzer-Stull 2015
Bribitzer-Stull, Matthew. *Understanding the Leitmotif: From Wagner to Hollywood Film Music*, Cambridge, Cambridge University Press, 2015.

Buhler 2000
Buhler, James. '*Star Wars*, Music and Myth', in: *Music and Cinema*, edited by James Buhler, Caryl Flinn, and David Neumeyer, Hanover (NH), Wesleyan University Press, 2000, pp. 33-57.

Byrd 1997
Byrd, Craig. 'Interview with John Williams', in: *Film Score Monthly*, (January/February 1997), pp. 18-21.

Desborough – Watts 2016
Desborough, James – Watts, Halina. '*Star Wars* Composer Has Made a Very Surprising Confession about the Films He Helped Make Famous', in: *The Mirror*, 26 December 2016, <http://www.mirror.co.uk/tv/tv-news/star-wars-composer-made-very-9497097>, accessed January 2018.

Handy 2015
Handy, Bruce. 'John Williams Says His New Star Wars Score Will Include the Original Themes', in: *Variety*, 21 May 2015, <https://www.vanityfair.com/hollywood/2015/05/john-williams-star-wars-the-force-awakens>, accessed January 2018.

KALINAK 1992

KALINAK, Kathryn Marie. *Settling the Score: Music and the Classical Hollywood Film*, Madison (WI), University of Wisconsin Press, 1992 (Wisconsin Studies in Film).

KEEGAN 2016

KEEGAN, Rebecca. '*E. T.*, *Jaws*, *Star Wars* Composer John Williams Honored at American Film Institute', in: *Los Angeles Times*, 10 June 2016, <http://www.latimes.com/entertainment/movies/la-et-mn-john-williams-aft-lifetime-achievement-20160606-snap-story.html>, accessed January 2018.

KENDALL 1993

KENDALL, Lukas. '*Star Wars* Trilogy: The Original Soundtrack Anthology: An Analysis', Liner Notes to the CD, New York, Arista Records, 1993.

LEHMAN 2015

LEHMAN, Frank. '7 Things we Learned about *Star Wars: The Force Awakens* from Its Music', in: *Mashable*, 12 December 2015, <http://mashable.com/2015/12/31/star-wars-music-theory/#r_wIk_DbM8qm>, accessed January 2018.

LEHMAN 2017A

ID. 'Leitmotivic Use vs. Mention', in: *Musicology Now*, 10 January 2017, <http://musicologynow.ams-net.org/2017/01/quick-takes-on-rogue-one-leitmotivic.html>, accessed January 2018.

LEHMAN 2017B

ID. 'What The Sith Lord Said: Monologic Narration and Reflexivity Leitmotivic Scores', talk given at *Music and the Moving Image Conference*, NYU, May 2017.

LERNER 2004

LERNER, Neil. 'Nostalgia, Masculinist Discourse, and Authoritarianism in John Williams' Scores for *Star Wars* and *Close Encounters of the Third Kind*', in: *Off the Planet: Music, Sound and Science Fiction Cinema*, edited by Philip Hayward, Eastleigh, John Libbey Publishing, 2004 (Perfect Beat, 2004.6, 2/3), pp. 96-108.

LONDON 2000

LONDON, Justin. 'Leitmotifs and Musical Reference in the Classical Film Score', in: *Music and Cinema*, edited by James Buhler, Caryl Flinn, and David Neumeyer, Hanover (NH), Wesleyan University Press, 2000, pp. 85-95.

MATESSINO 1997A

MATESSINO, Michael. 'A New Hope for Film Music', Liner Notes for the CD *Star Wars Special Edition: A New Hope. The Original Motion Picture Soundtrack*, New York, BMG Entertainment, 1997.

MATESSINO 1997B

ID. 'John Williams Strikes Back', Liner Notes for the CD *The Empire Strikes Back Special Edition: The Original Motion Picture Soundtrack*, New York, BMG Entertainment, 1997.

MATESSINO 1997C

ID. 'Return of the Composer', Liner Notes for the CD *Return of the Jedi Special Edition: The Original Motion Picture Soundtrack*, New York, BMG Entertainment, 1997.

Moss 2002

Moss, Stephen. 'The Force is With Him', in: *The Guardian*, 3 February 2002, <https://www.theguardian.com/film/2002/feb/04/artsfeatures>, accessed January 2018.

Paulus 2000

Paulus, Irena. 'Williams versus Wagner, or an Attempt at Linking Musical Epics', in: *International Review of the Aesthetics and Sociology of Music*, xxxi/2 (2000), pp. 153-184.

Reed 2009

Reed, Josephine. Transcript from Radio Interview with John Williams, in: *Art Works*, National Endowment for the Arts, 2009, <https://www.arts.gov/file/2432>, accessed January 2018.

Richards 2015

Richards, Mark. 'Celebrating *Star Wars* Themes', Series on blog *Film Music Notes*, 8 November 2015, <http://www.filmmusicnotes.com/celebrating-star-wars-part-1-of-6-uses-of-the-force-theme>, accessed January 2018.

Richards 2016

Id. 'Film Music Themes: Analysis and Corpus Study', in: *Music Theory Online*, xxii/1 (2016), <http://www.mtosmt.org/issues/mto.16.22.1/mto.16.22.1.richards.html>, accessed January 2018.

Star Scores: Orchestration and the Sound of John Williams's Film Music

Ian Sapiro
(University of Leeds)

The film music of John Williams is often seen as synonymous with the sound of the symphony orchestra and, as Kathryn Kalinak notes, «contemporary literature on film music has credited John Williams, virtually single-handedly, with returning the classical film score to its position of pre-eminence»[1]. However, such broad generalizations overlook the nuance and development of Williams's use of instrumental resources and the role that orchestration plays in constructing the distinctive sound of his film music. Indeed, while to a large extent his scores remain strongly thematic in structure and for the most part the orchestra remains his ensemble of choice, the ways in which musical material is scored, and the balances and timbral combinations employed in his film music have been subjected to sometimes subtle and at other times not so subtle shifts and developments. This chapter draws on interviews I have carried out with two orchestrators who have worked on John Williams's film scores — Conrad Pope and Paul S. Henning — alongside evidence drawn from other interviews and studies to explore the processes by which Williams's scores have been and are orchestrated. Following this, aural analysis of excerpts from some of his scores — the musical products — will facilitate discussion of these processes in practice, thereby enabling a proper consideration of the role of orchestration in the sound of John Williams's film music.

Film-Score Orchestrators

Orchestrators are used by almost all major film composers in the process of taking ideas from their head to the scoring stage. John Williams is no different to his colleagues in this regard, and he is similarly not immune from criticism and questioning over this activity. Russell Lack, for example, queries the extent to which Williams's signature sound

[1]. Kalinak 1992, p. 188.

is a result of what he terms the use of «a variety of different orchestrators and arrangers»[2], a view perhaps reinforced by a quick survey of Williams's projects on the IMDB, which reveals twenty-six credited orchestrators. However, these listings lack suitable nuance, and overlook the fact that for the most part these professionals were brought in to work under a lead orchestrator with whom Williams had an established working relationship. It is clear from evidence drawn from interviews with those who have worked for the composer that aside from when pictures have required new versions of existing music — such as "Por una Cabeza", which is performed diegetically in *Schindler's List* (Steven Spielberg, 1993)[3] — arrangement has never played a part in his working practice[4]. There are, to date, only six people with more orchestration credits on John Williams scores than the composer himself (who has five), as shown in Table 1, below[5]. Williams maintained strong working relationships with four orchestrators — Herbert Spencer, John Neufeld, Conrad Pope and Eddie Karam — who orchestrated or led orchestration teams on his scores over a forty-four year period from *A Guide for the Married Man* in 1967 (Gene Kelly, orchestrated by Spencer) to *War Horse* in 2011 (Steven Spielberg, orchestrated by Karam). The orchestration of his more recent scores has been handled by JoAnn Kane Music Service (JKMS), under the direction of Mark Graham, but even this arrangement has deep roots. JKMS has handled the music preparation activities for Williams's scores for many years, and Graham worked as a music librarian on several Williams projects prior to taking on the role of 'head of music preparation'.

Table 1: Professionals with More Orchestration Credits for John Williams's Scores than the Composer Himself

Orchestrator	Orchestration Credits
John Neufeld	24
Herbert Spencer	22
Conrad Pope	20
Eddie Karam	11
Angela Morley	8
Alexander Courage	7
John Williams	5

2. Lack 2002, p. 329.

3. The arrangements in this picture were created by Angela Morley, John Neufeld and Williams himself.

4. I have discussed the differences between orchestrating and arranging in film-music elsewhere. See Sapiro 2016, p. 38 and 46 for definitions of orchestration and arrangement.

5. These figures have been collated using IMDB credit listings for John Williams's film projects. While it might well be the case that others have worked on more jobs than the number on which they were credited, the point made here about those personnel working under a small number of lead orchestrators is nonetheless still valid.

Speaking in 1978, Williams commented that Spencer had been his orchestrator of choice since they first worked together in the late 1960s[6], and while others worked alongside Spencer on some projects, Conrad Pope notes that it was not until *Indiana Jones and the Last Crusade* (Steven Spielberg, 1989) that Williams began to seek a new orchestrator to take over from his long-time colleague[7]. John Neufeld was one of three additional orchestrators on that project, and «through his personality and his abilities, sort of won the audition so to speak»[8]. Pope's first work for Williams was as a proof reader, checking over Neufeld's orchestrations for *Born on the Fourth of July* (Oliver Stone, 1989), and his initial orchestration for the composer was the end credit music for *Hook* (Steven Spielberg, 1991), just after Spencer had retired. Pope became a regular part of the orchestration team two years later on *Jurassic Park* (Steven Spielberg, 1993), having worked for and with Neufeld on James Horner's scores in the interim, and the two of them scored for Williams consistently up to *Harry Potter and the Sorcerer's Stone* (Chris Columbus) in 2001, by which time JKMS had begun music preparation work on Williams's scores. Pope's presence acts as something of a constant across the following decade, during which Neufeld gradually retired from the business (he has credits for just three pictures after *Harry Potter*), and Edward (Eddie) Karam became the last (to date) of Williams's regular orchestrators (starting with the first *Harry Potter* film).

In an interview about the seventh *Star Wars* film (*The Force Awakens*, J. J. Abrams, 2015) with Scott Yoho for "MakeMusic", creators of music-publishing software Finale, Mark Graham outlines the change in process since *War Horse* (2011), simply stating: «John Williams writes very detailed handwritten sketches. On the [*Star Wars*] prequels, these sketches went to orchestrators. The orchestrators would write pencil scores and we would copy parts into Finale. But for the past six or seven years, John has just sent the sketches directly to us. We put them straight into Finale»[9]. Graham's description of the difference in process is informative, but his mention of six or seven years appears to be a slight over-estimate given that Williams's 2011 scores were orchestrated by Pope and Karam rather than at JKMS[10]. Furthermore, his comments should not be read as suggesting that orchestrators are no longer involved in the realization of Williams's scores. Rather, these

[6]. Elley 1978.

[7]. Pope 2017.

[8]. *Ibidem*.

[9]. Mark Graham in Yoho 2017.

[10]. Audissino 2017, p. 225 suggests that Williams carried out his own orchestrations for both *Lincoln* (Steven Spielberg, 2012) and *The Book Thief* (Brian Percival, 2013), but Graham's comment indicates strongly that these scores were actually orchestrated through JKMS, albeit that it would not be unusual for the composer to have done some of this work himself. Audissino observes further that Williams orchestrated *The Force Awakens* himself, and while this may have been his intention he actually shares orchestration credits with Paul S. Henning and William Ross for this picture. The involvement of orchestrators may have been partly a result of the significant revisions required to the score as the film was made. See Burlingame 2015.

professionals now come under the umbrella of JKMS along with copyists, librarians and myriad other role-holders, and their work on the scores is managed by Graham rather than them answering directly to the composer. It is within this environment that Paul S. Henning has, to date, accrued three orchestration credits for Williams's scores including *The Force Awakens* (2015) and *The BFG* (Steven Spielberg, 2016)[11].

These changes of lead orchestrator(s) enable Williams's scores to be broken down into four broad time periods — 1967-1990 (Spencer); 1991-2004 (Neufeld/Pope); 2001-2011 (Pope/Karam); 2012-present (JKMS) — albeit that there is some overlap at the 'transition points' as shown in TABLE 2, below. While developments in scoring practice might be expected to result in some changes in the way that Williams's scores are orchestrated, partitioning the films in this way allows for some comparative analysis of the ways in which instruments are used over time.

TABLE 2: OUTLINE TIMELINE OF LEAD ORCHESTRATORS SHOWING WILLIAMS'S SCORES BREAKING DOWN INTO FOUR MAIN OVERLAPPING PERIODS

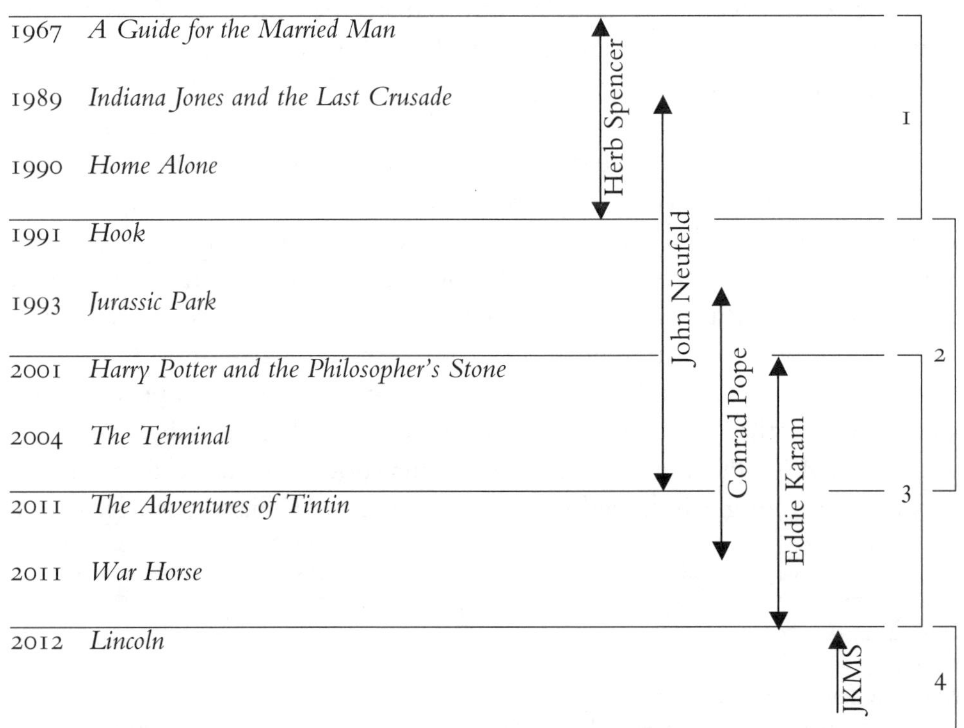

[11]. At the time of our interview HENNING 2017 stated that he had orchestrated on three John Williams scores, but could not reveal the identity of the third project.

Orchestration and Composition

While the intention of this chapter is to consider the role played by orchestration in defining the 'John Williams sound', this inevitably and necessarily requires some consideration of compositional practice. Film composer Trevor Jones «cannot see how you can conceive a piece of music without thinking of it in terms of audio colouration»[12], and others including Dario Marianelli and Heitor Pereira have expressed similar thoughts regarding the inseparability of timbral considerations from musical composition[13]. Unlike most of his colleagues, Williams does not use computers and digital audio workstations when he composes, working initially at the piano and creating hand-written sketches as he has done across his long career[14]. However, far from precluding consideration of instrumentation as the music is created, Williams observes that in his opinion «the colour counts as much as the tune, sometimes even more so» when scoring a film[15]. Indeed, having learned his craft in an era when composers had no option but to hear the orchestra in their head, he is arguably more capable of understanding the full sonic effect of his scores than many younger composers, and this comes across in his sketches. Pope asserts that when orchestrating for Williams, «it's not simply painting by numbers like so much of the MIDI stuff that you get, where somebody's basically written a piano composition and assigned a colour to particular notes. There's something a little bit more organic about John's writing for the orchestra, because it's definitely not a piano piece»[16].

In 1980, Williams outlined his basic working practice in a BBC documentary on the music of *Star Wars*, stating that «at the piano I'll sketch on a 10- or 8-line sketch pad, so on 6, 8 or 10 lines of sketch I can indicate very precisely what the orchestration ought to be»[17]. The programme shows Herbert Spencer seeking clarification on some markings on the composer's sketch, and it is readily apparent that the selection of instrumental line-up and the main orchestrational decisions were taken by Williams himself without any consultation with his orchestrator. This modus operandi has not changed across his career, Pope noting that in his experience «there was never really any discussion [about the instrumental line up]. Out of all the people I've worked for, John always had a very set idea of what he wanted and what he needed», and Henning confirming that even on his most recent scores «you don't have a lot of creative input on the way his music sounds in the final orchestration, because he's really done that for himself»[18]. In an interview for the *Boston Globe* in 1989, Pat Hollenbeck, who was one of those drafted in to work alongside

---

12. Jones 2007.
13. Sapiro 2016, p. 26.
14. Thomas 1991, p. 334; *TrailerAddict* 2013, 4:03-4:17.
15. *Gramophone* 2005.
16. Pope 2017.
17. John Williams speaking in Buckton 1980, 49:02-49:12.
18. Pope 2017; Henning 2017.

Spencer on *Indiana Jones and the Last Crusade* that year, described orchestrating for Williams as «taking his notes from the little green paper and putting them in the big yellow paper»[19]. However, given the number of film-music composers to whom such an epithet has been attached, and that the BBC documentary shows both Williams's sketch and score paper to be off-white, this is perhaps a slightly over-romanticized description of the process.

Despite all of this, however, there is some flexibility in the orchestration at times, Graham observing that they «sometimes have to deal with [...] the woodwinds, in terms of assigning particular instruments» when they work on Williams's music at JKMS[20]. Pope comments similarly that when he worked for Williams in the 1990s and 2000s there would sometimes be «latitude in the woodwind writing», though he continues, saying «and sometimes the brass and sometimes the strings even»[21], perhaps indicating that in recent years the composer has taken greater control over the sound of his scores than he used to exercise. Here, perhaps, there is also evidence of a change in knowledge base among those actually carrying out the scoring: while Pope suggests that «everything I needed to know was on the sketch, and by that I mean that I knew exactly how many woodwinds to put on things as soon as I saw what the chords were, how thick things were in the strings, what the brass voicings were, and what the general context was», Graham notes that «often I have to make a decision on instruments to cue in case he might want more sound in a particular place»[22]. While it is clear that the composer has always been able to change the orchestration of a cue, the implication is that Spencer, Neufeld, Pope and Karam would have understood the precise instrumentation that Williams wanted and would not have needed to provide additional cues to enable the sound to be changed on the scoring stage. Similarly, Pope feels that «earlier John Williams scores were fashioned in a particular way, and in recent years the woodwind tuttis have not been fashioned in that way»[23], which seems to be a reflection of the shift from experienced orchestrators to this work being done through JKMS. However, it is also important to consider broader changes in approaches to film scoring when evaluating this point. Since the widespread advent of samples and mock-ups there has been a marked decline in the use of the woodwind ensemble in film scores, with these instruments generally utilized to present solo lines if they are included at all in contemporary orchestral music. While Pope's observation may be accurate, it seems highly likely that changing trends in film scoring are at least partly responsible for differences in the way that these instruments are orchestrated in Williams's more contemporary works[24].

19. Pat Hollenbeck in Gonzalez 1989.

20. Graham in Yoho 2017.

21. Pope 2017.

22. *Ibidem*; Graham in Yoho 2017.

23. Pope 2017.

24. For more on industry-wide changes to the use of woodwind see Sapiro 2016. An increased focus on brass, percussion, strings and electronics at the expense of woodwind means that the contemporary film-music orchestra might even be interpreted as a pop band in which the rhythm section has been supplemented

Orchestrating from Williams's Compositional Sketches

> John really doesn't use an orchestrator per se any more. His sketches are so complete at this point. There are sixteen staves so they're not to the point where you could copy the parts off of them — it's still a condensed score — but almost all of the entire orchestration is within those sixteen lines. There are almost no creative decisions that you make other than some basic voicings that he might leave to chance in woodwinds and brass[25].

Henning's observation highlights the development of Williams's sketches over the course of his career to date, progressing from the 6, 8 or 10 lines of the late 1970s that the composer himself talked about, to something approaching double that number on his latest projects. Karlin and Wright discuss compositional sketches in *On the Track*, identifying composers producing anything from 2 to 14 staves of music, though Williams is not on their list, and sixteen lines would exceed anything that is included[26]. Richard Davies notes that in addition to detailing all of the melodic, harmonic and structural elements of a cue (as required to meet Union regulations), Williams's sketches «even designate individual instruments»[27], and Pope suggests that they are best thought of using the German term «particell»[28], since the material is much more akin to a short score than to what might be thought of either traditionally or contemporarily as a film-music sketch. The strings are presented over five staves with all divisis and splits marked in the music, and Williams's particells include textual information concerning doublings across the ensemble. This cross-cueing saves him time when writing, since he only needs to notate a musical line once but still provides the orchestrators with all of the information needed to construct the individual instrumental parts, albeit that they have to trace each instrument across the score carefully. Additionally, and very unusually, Williams sketches at absolute concert pitch, meaning that as well as being 'in C', every instrument including those that transpose by whole octaves is written at the pitch at which it sounds; piccolos, contrabassoons and double basses are therefore presented on several ledger lines and must be carefully transcribed by the staff at JKMS[29].

Further evidence of Williams's keen awareness of instrumental timbre can be found in textual markings on the sketches. Henning observes that the phrase 'colour of' is often included to help the orchestrators and performers understand how a line relates to others

with 'horns' and strings. This, perhaps inevitably, can result in what Audissino 2017, p. 222 calls «a simplified orchestral sound resembling [...] rock/techno/pop music arranged for orchestra».

25. Henning 2017.

26. Karlin – Wright 2004, pp. 323-324.

27. Davies 2010, p. 109.

28. Pope 2017.

29. Henning 2017.

within the ensemble, «so if the clarinets are doubling the violins he'll say "colour strings" for the clarinet, so the clarinet knows that it's not a solo and that it's actually meant to just outline something else»[30]. Such attention to orchestrational detail again highlights the importance to Williams of instrumentation and timbral balance, and why it is a key if subtle component of his musical voice.

The 'John Williams Sound'

Before exploring some scores aurally to identify the key markers of the 'John Williams Sound', it is necessary to consider additional factors that may influence the way in which music is orchestrated. Firstly, and perhaps most obviously, Williams often draws on orchestrational practices that are commonly found in and beyond music for films, such as the employment of codified instrumental timbres. It is unsurprising, for example, that the main themes for the *Star Wars*, *Indiana Jones* and *Superman* films feature brass instruments, since that is a typical musical marker for heroism, and in each of these cases the main theme represents the hero of the plot (Luke and the title characters respectively). Notwithstanding this, and without meaning to dismiss consideration of other musical elements, nuanced exploration of *how* this music is scored for brass can help to identify why the sonic representation of these characters and the use of established (perhaps even clichéd) sounds is distinctively Williamsian.

As already discussed, scoring conventions have developed quite significantly over the course of Williams's career, not least as a result of the widespread implementation of digital technologies in both film scoring and film making, and the resulting impacts on the instrumental sound of film scores since the turn of the twenty-first century. This has led to a dissociation between 'orchestral' and 'symphonic' scores[31], and may have impacted on the way in which orchestration is utilized in Williams's music. Similarly, Williams has moved away from the 'traditional' symphony orchestra on some of his more recent scores: for example *Catch Me if You Can* (Steven Spielberg, 2002) is based around a small jazz ensemble and is written within that genre, *The Adventures of Tintin* (Steven Spielberg, 2011) makes substantial use of saxophones and converts part of the orchestra into a quasi-big-band ensemble, and *The Book Thief* (2013) is scored without 'heavy brass', instead favouring the harp, piano and synthesizer. The rest of this chapter considers key elements of Williams's orchestration and their contribution to the characteristic sound of his music, with examples drawn from a range of scores to support these observations.

---

30. *Ibidem*.

31. Audissino 2017, p. 231, n. 4.

Synthesizers

Perhaps the most surprising element of a typical Williams orchestration is the inclusion of synthesizers. These instruments are more commonly associated with contemporary composers whose approach relates more closely to that of Hans Zimmer than to Williams, but there is actually a long history of synthesized sound in Williams's scores. Audissino notes the inclusion of synths in three scores — *Heartbeeps* (Allan Arkush, 1981), *SpaceCamp* (Harry Winer, 1986) and *Presumed Innocent* (Alan J. Pakula, 1990)[32] — and Pope recalls that synthesizers were also used in *Always* (Steven Spielberg, 1989)[33]. Of particular note here is that while the synth sounds are quite obvious in *Heartbeeps* and *Presumed Innocent*, in *Space Camp* and *Always* they are used within the context of symphonic orchestral scores as part of the ensemble. Pope recalls that Williams would meet with his synth players prior to the first recording session, «and sort of audition sounds. In his sketch he would indicate things like "synth voice", and we weren't quite sure what that synth voice would be until we heard it (laughs) [...]. He knew it had to have a synth sound and he had an idea in his head but it wasn't a concrete idea until a couple of days before the first recording session»[34]. Synthesizers remain part of Williams's typical ensemble, creating a fusion of electronic and acoustic elements in his scores. However, whereas in most contemporary film scores this sort of combination is achieved by 'sweetening' the acoustic recording through the addition of the mock-up[35], Williams considers the electronic sound as part of the live ensemble, «usually doubling other things in the strings or a woodwind part or keyboards or percussion»[36].

Celeste

Williams's subtle inclusion of synthesizers is epitomized through his frequent use of celeste. Pope identifies this timbre as something that the composer may actually be known for, but as Henning observes, «he doesn't actually use a real celeste and hasn't done for some time»[37]. Henning's experience is mirrored by that of Pope, who believes that Williams «never, in my experience in the years I worked for him, actually used a real celeste»[38]. Rather, he prefers a sound created by pianist Randy Kerber, with whom Williams has worked for many years, particularly since the real instrument can be quite

---

32. *Ibidem*, pp. 226-227.
33. Pope 2017.
34. *Ibidem*.
35. Sapiro 2016, p. 94.
36. Henning 2017.
37. *Ibidem*.
38. Pope 2017.

temperamental in the way it reacts to the room and the atmospheric conditions in which it is being played. The opening of "Hedwig's Theme" from *Harry Potter and the Sorcerer's Stone* (2001) is probably one of Williams's best-known celeste solos, and consideration of this passage on the film's soundtrack album offers a good opportunity to evaluate the nuance of the timbre[39]. In contrast to "The Dance of the Sugar Plum Fairy" from Tchaikovsky's *Nutcracker*, recorded using a real celeste by Williams and the Boston Pops Orchestra in 1984[40], Kerber's artificial sound is arguably warmer than that of the actual instrument. There is fractionally less directness in the attack, a characteristic that helps the sound to blend effectively with the harp, piano and tuned percussion instruments that are also mainstays of many Williams scores, and it sounds «almost like a vibraphone»[41], which is a subtle but significant difference from the more glockenspiel-like tone of the real celeste.

Percussion

That Williams should be so concerned with the sound of the celeste is no surprise given the fastidiousness with which he deals with the percussion section. Henning observes that the composer will «track down what every percussion instrument is doing»[42] across a score, and Pope agrees that Williams is «very specific about percussion»[43]. Tuned percussion — notably glockenspiel, marimba, vibraphone and xylophone — is a key part of Williams's orchestral colour and, as noted above, it is often employed in tandem with harps and keyboard instruments to create textural changes in a cue. The marimba also features in Williams's less-orchestral scores such as *Catch Me if You Can*, *The Adventures of Tintin* and *Memoires of a Geisha* (Rob Marshall, 2005), about which Pope recalls:

> On *Geisha* one of the things that John said was to be sure that the marimba parts are good (laughs). So I orchestrated the marimba parts and I took them to Alan Estes — he's [...] the main marimba and mallet guy for John — and I remember Alan looked at them and he first said "these are impossible", which is very typical when working with John's stuff. I said "do I have to write it for two people?", and he started playing and he said "no this isn't so bad, but this is imposs..., no and this isn't impossible either". And he said, "well actually it's all doable" (laughs); this is very typical with John[44].

39. WILLIAMS, John. *Harry Potter and the Sorcerer's Stone, Original Motion Picture Soundtrack*, Atlantic Records, 2001 [MP3], track 19, 0:00-0:34.

40. ID. *Prokofiev: Peter & The Wolf; Tchaikovsky: Nutcracker Suite*, John Williams, Boston Pops Orchestra, Universal International Music, 1984 [MP3], track 4, 0:08-0:37.

41. POPE 2017.

42. HENNING 2017.

43. POPE 2017.

44. *Ibidem*.

As this anecdote indicates, Williams's knowledge of the capabilities of each instrument (and, of course, his regular players) enables him to utilize them very effectively in his scores. Indeed, Pope suggests that one of the key strategies that can be learned from Williams's approach to orchestration «is try to make the score as musical as possible with as few percussion effects as possible. When you hear the percussion it should be in support of a musical arrival and a musical moment»[45], and this philosophy is evident across his output. For example, while snare drum and cymbals characterize many of his march themes from *1941* (Steven Spielberg, 1979) to *Indiana Jones and the Kingdom of the Crystal Skull* (Steven Spielberg, 2008)[46], such scoring is not used indiscriminately for cues of this type. The march from *Superman* (Richard Donner, 1978) and those in some of Williams's more recent scores including "The March of the Resistance" from *The Force Awakens* and the giants' march, "Fleshlumpeater", in *The BFG* all avoid this military reference, reserving this instrumentation for climactic points and instead often making use of timpani to support the bottom of the texture and push the music forward.

Piano and Harp

There are some Williams scores, notably *The Book Thief*, in which the piano is showcased as a solo instrument, but more routinely it is used to add colour and movement to the music alongside tuned percussion and harp. It can sometimes be difficult to hear the piano within the mix because of how closely integrated it is into the score, doubling other instruments to alter the resulting sound with a subtle injection of extra attack, brightness or depth, but its distinctive tone also rises out of the ensemble on occasions, such as parts of "The Secret of the Scrolls" from *The Adventures of Tintin*. The piano and harp play key roles in filling the centre of the orchestral texture in this cue, the steady repeated piano notes at the outset generating a sense of instrumental momentum, and both instruments playing scalic and arpeggiated passages that thicken the harmony as the music progresses[47].

This sort of harp writing is typical of Williams, who also employs the instrument to double melodic lines and chordal harmonies, notably those played by the strings. Glissandi — probably the most clichéd harp technique — are reserved for moments where the sound supports and enhances the music, reflecting Pope's observation, above, regarding Williams's use of percussion. Just about all of these uses can be heard in the music for *Seven Years in Tibet* (Jean-Jacques Annaud, 1997), notably during the closing credits, which

45. *Ibidem*.

46. And presumably beyond, given that a fifth *Indiana Jones* movie has been announced for release in 2020.

47. Williams, John. *The Adventures of Tintin, Music from the Motion Picture*, John Williams, Sony Music, 2011 [MP3], track 3, 0:00-2:02.

utilizes multiple harps to increase the timbral possibilities available to the composer[48]. Similarly, Williams's effective utilization of glissandi can be found in "Hedwig's Theme" when it is heard at the opening of *Harry Potter and the Prisoner of Azkaban* (Alfonso Cuarón, 2004). Harp glissandi are placed alongside the running scalic figures played by the violins and synthesized celeste while another harp doubles the pizzicato cellos in an eight-bar passage that ably demonstrates the ways in which Williams uses the instrument to enhance the sound of the ensemble[49]. The first harp brings a sense of flow and smoothness to the forefront of the texture while the second adds brightness and an element of subtle sustain — a longer decay on the sound — to the bass line that underpins the phrase.

Strings

As discussed earlier, the strings are effectively fully orchestrated in Williams's sketches and can, to a large extent, simply be copied out into the full score. However, just as with the rest of the orchestra, this does not preclude the use of orchestrational knowledge to enhance the impact of the composer's instrumentation. Pope suggests that adding some of the violas or cellos at pitch with the violins can improve the overall balance or weight of a line, a technique that he used on a number of Williams's scores and which is derived from a practice employed by Eugene Ormandy when he was conductor of the Philadelphia Orchestra. He explains:

> There's a raptor attack in *Lost World* and it was all violins and they went up to a high four-line G♯ or something above the staff, sort of crawling up because they're being chased by raptors. And I thought «this is perfect for a little more body. Let's put the violas on it too», because the violas can actually play higher than they generally do in Hollywood. [...] Very typically for me we'd sometimes double some cellos and the violins. The mid-register's one of the most problematic areas in the orchestra to be heard and sometimes with strings you need to achieve more body. [...] I remember once on one of the last ones I did with John, I guess it was *Crystal Skull*, I got to one of these areas and he had been very specific about the voicing of something. I thought, «oh no, this is the area where generally I'd add the violas» [...] and when they recorded it, it wasn't good enough and John came back and he said «add the violas»[50].

---

[48]. Id. *Seven Years in Tibet, Original Recording Remastered*, John Williams, Yo-Yo Ma, Sony Classical, [1997] 2005 [MP3], track 14.

[49]. Id. *Harry Potter and the Prisoner of Azkaban, Music from and Inspired by the Motion Picture*, Atlantic Records, 2004 [MP3], track 1, 0:41-0:49.

[50]. Pope 2017. Pope seems to be referencing the music heard in Williams, John. *The Lost World: Jurassic Park, Original Motion Picture Soundtrack*, MCA, 1997, <https://www.youtube.com/watch?v=we9rHcFXsIo&list=PLA368E634C4663E59&index=9>, accessed February 2018, track 9 — high swirling strings are clearly audible at around 2:20.

It is, of course, impossible to identify the application of this technique without access to sketches and scores, since a well-balanced string line on a soundtrack recording could just as easily be the result of what Williams indicated on the sketch. Nonetheless, the instance Pope mentions during recording for *Indiana Jones and the Kingdom of the Crystal Skull* demonstrates that Williams was aware of and happy about the addition of violas or cellos to appropriate violin lines, and while he did not indicate it on the sketch in this case he added this doubling at the session to correct the balance of the cue.

Brass

Brass instruments are fundamental to many of Williams's most iconic themes, and as already noted, in several cases this links to the use of established musical codes for heroism and bravery. However, it is the way that the brass is orchestrated that gives these themes Williams's distinctive sound. In several scores including those in the *Star Wars* and *Indiana Jones* series he features the trumpet section playing a theme in unison, giving the music a bravura that would be missing from a solo line, and Williams is also unafraid of using a wide pitch range without changing between instruments in the brass section. During the "Bike Chase" sequence in *E. T.: The Extra-Terrestrial* (Steven Spielberg, 1982) Williams takes the horns up to a D_5 (a written top A), and the trumpets and trombones up as far as $A\flat_5$ and $A\flat_4$ respectively, meaning that he can present unbroken melodic lines in each instrument and thereby retain timbral coherence within phrases[51]. Similarly, when the "Raider's March" returns in the closing credit music for *Kingdom of the Crystal Skull*, the trombones not only play the complete melody, but continue with the countermelody when the trumpets begin the next iteration of the theme. In both phrases Williams takes the trombones up to $B\flat_4$ rather than passing the line to the horns or low trumpets. By contrast, the main theme from Alan Silvestri's score for *Back to the Future* (Robert Zemekis, 1985) moves between instruments as the register changes[52]. The first phrase (D_4–$B\flat_4$) is played by horns in octaves (0:28), moving to trumpets and trombones in octaves (0:33) as the register increases in the second phrase ($A\flat_4$–$E\flat_5$), and when the melody repeats a perfect fourth higher this instrumentation is retained (0:39 and 0:44). While the orchestration of the melody is doubtless energizing and dramatic, the moment when the trumpets complete the four-phrase melody in their upper register (up to $B\flat_5$) is somewhat pre-empted by them doing the same thing in the middle of the passage, and it lacks some impact as a result. Arguably a more Williamsian orchestration would have been to use horns in unison to

[51]. Williams, John. *E.T. The Extra Terrestrial, Original Soundtrack: 20th Anniversary Remaster*, John Williams, Universal-Island Records, [1982] 2002 [MP3], track 20. The "Bike Chase" is 4:20-7:58 within this track.

[52]. Silvestri, Alan. *Back to the Future, Music from the Motion Picture Soundtrack*, The Outatime Orchestra, Universal Music Catalogue, 1985 [MP3], track 3.

present the whole melody across the first two phrases, followed by unison trumpets and unison trombones one octave apart when the theme repeats a perfect fourth higher[53].

Woodwind

The use of woodwinds in film scoring was discussed earlier in this chapter alongside Pope's observation that woodwind tuttis sound different in recent Williams scores relative to older pictures. "One Small Face" from *The Book Thief* is a good example of a contemporary Williams score that features the woodwind choir, the track opening with a slow piano introduction before the melody is presented by the woodwind in octaves over an oscillating and sustained accompaniment in strings and harp[54]. The balance between the upper and lower octaves is quite noticeable in the mix (0:40), with a clear division in the orchestration between flutes and oboes on the upper line and the cor Anglais, clarinets and horn on the lower line. The third phrase of the melody (0:55) introduces a third octave of music as the woodwind ascend — still grouped as before — leaving the horn in a lower register, before the horn re-joins the lower woodwind to complete the melody and the track (1:03). The scoring places the cor Anglais in a relatively powerful register and it cuts through the rest of the woodwind with reasonable presence as a result, while the upper line is quite flute-heavy and seems a little detached texturally from the rest of the instrumentation. Given Williams's usual working methods it is unclear precisely who took the decision to balance the passage in this way. Based on the testimony from Pope and Henning, it seems likely that the composer did not provide detailed information about the woodwind allocations on the sketch, instead writing the melody on the woodwind staves and marking it as 8va without specifically telling the orchestrator — or the JKMS staff in this case — how to spread the material across the instrumental parts within the woodwind section.

An example of a similar passage can again be found in "Hedwig's Theme", which dates from twelve years previously[55]. As with the cue from *The Book Thief*, a woodwind-section melody enters after an initial passage on a keyboard instrument — in this case the (fake) celeste — and it is accompanied by moving material in strings, harp and, on this occasion, celeste (0:45). Based on the audible timbres and the register of the theme, the melody is presented on alto flue, cor Anglais and bassoon, supported by vibraphone and harp, with all of these instruments playing in unison. The avoidance of octaves and

[53]. The opening of the track, which features the main motif twice, is scored with the first iteration on horns and the second on trumpets, giving it more of a 'Williams sound' than the melody that follows it.

[54]. WILLIAMS, John. *The Book Thief, Original Motion Picture Soundtrack*, Sony Music Classical, 2013 [MP3], track 1.

[55]. ID. *Harry Potter and the Sorcerer's Stone, Original Motion Picture Soundtrack*, Atlantic Records, 2001 [MP3], track 19.

placement of both the alto flute and cor Anglais in strong tessituras helps the flute and double-reed timbres to blend, creating a strong and focused sound that retains some brightness despite the low register. The inclusion of harp brings additional brightness and attack, while the vibraphone provides body and resonance to the overall timbre of the melody line. The finale of *Kingdom of the Crystal Skull* is similarly constructed though combines different timbres, opening with low flute and clarinet in unison supported by the celeste (which is barely audible, occasionally coming to the fore as the pitch rises)[56]. When the melody repeats (0:26) the orchestration is enlarged through the addition of an oboe in unison with the other woodwinds and a horn playing one octave below, the former providing additional penetration and the latter greater depth of tone as the music builds towards a fuller statement of the theme led by the violins (0:46).

The timbral focus found in the cues from *Harry Potter* and *Indiana Jones* is somewhat diffused in *The Book Thief*, though the presence of a woodwind chorale of any sort is unusual in a contemporary film, and can perhaps be seen as an orchestrational fingerprint of a Williams score despite changes in the nuance within the section over time. Indeed, recalling his work with John Neufeld on Williams's scores in the early 1990s, Pope identifies a conscious change in approach to woodwind instrumentation in particular:

> [...] flutes can be very bright in the upper register but because of the physics of the flute — that it's blown across a mouthpiece — the attack doesn't have a lot of point on it [...] so what Neufeld would do was add E♭ piccolo oboe with the flutes whenever it was getting too high [for the regular oboe ...]. The E♭ piccolo clarinet [...] has that cheeky quality to its tone colour, whereas the A♭ clarinet has a very smooth tone, which I think is why John Neufeld used that with John [Williams] on some of the stuff in *Hook*. I don't know if you know how discordant *Hook* sounds, but in fact you are listening to a lot of exotica that you probably are not aware of. But it seemed after that that Williams basically said «let's not do that any more, since these instruments are not that readily available»[57].

It seems very unlikely that any orchestrator who has started in the business in the digital era would ever have scored for the E♭ piccolo oboe or the A♭ clarinet. Indeed, neither instrument is included in the orchestration textbooks by Samuel Adler and Alfred Blatter[58], and as older practitioners such as Neufeld have retired there have been fewer orchestrators with knowledge of these instruments' existence, let alone how they might be employed to enhance a score. Pope also observes that the orchestrational relationship between woodwind and brass instruments in Williams's scores has changed over time,

---

56. Id. *Indiana Jones and the Kingdom of the Crystal Skull, Soundtrack*, John Williams, Concord, 2008 [MP3], track 19.

57. Pope 2017.

58. Adler 2002, pp. 193-217; Blatter 1997, pp. 98-116.

commenting that «on *Force Awakens* there are doublings that I would not do and I don't think John Neufeld would do»[59]. While in some respects this might be a result of changes in scoring styles in the digital era, Pope's comment also relates to the idea of woodwind being used to amplify the brass by bringing out the «upper partials» of the sound[60]. This technique can be heard in various Neufeld orchestrations including "The Ultimate War" from *Hook*, "Dennis Steals the Embryos" from *Jurassic Park* and "The Sith Spacecraft and the Droid Battle" from *The Phantom Menace* (George Lucas, 1999)[61], and the "Scherzo for X-Wings" from the seventh instalment of the *Star Wars* saga provides a useful point of contrast. While the cue features Williams's typical brass writing with trumpets in unison often playing in their most dynamic register, the role of the woodwind in supporting some of the brass seems somewhat diminished. While there are occasional flourishes, the 'upper partials' are not as apparent as they are in the cue from the earlier *Star Wars* film (or the other examples given above), and the sound is less musically 'brilliant' than that of its predecessors.

Conclusions

John Williams's orchestrational style, as with other aspects of his compositional aesthetic, can be traced back through Korngold to composers such as Wagner, Mahler and Richard Strauss. Indeed, the eight unison horns at the opening of Mahler's Third Symphony, the violas doubling the violins at pitch at the start of the second movement of his First Symphony, and the woodwind tutti supported by triangle in this same passage, all connect orchestrationally and sonically to Williams's symphonic film scores. Thematicism probably remains the most widely recognized trait of Williams's musical style, but this should not trivialize the role of other musical characteristics[62]. From initial considerations of instrumentation at the point of composition through detailed indications on his sketches and changes at recording sessions, Williams's idiomatic writing and his ear for balance are critical elements in his compositional and orchestrational processes. His scoring strategy is clearly modified by the specific demands of the projects on which he works, but the consistent application of orchestrational techniques such as those highlighted in this chapter

59. Pope 2017.

60. *Ibidem*.

61. Williams, John. *Hook, Original Motion Picture Soundtrack*, Epic Soundtrax, 1991 [MP3], track 16; Id. *Jurassic Park, Original Motion Picture Soundtrack*, Universal-Island Records Ltd, 1993 [MP3], track 9; Id. *Star Wars: Episode 1 – The Phantom Menace, Original Motion Picture Soundtrack*, John Williams, London Symphony Orchestra, Sony, 1999 [MP3], track 5.

62. This situation is not helped by the actual film scores being unavailable for study, and publications like Hal Leonard's series "John Williams Signature Edition" consisting of isolated or amalgamated film cues that have usually been reorchestrated for concert performance.

set Williams's film scores apart from those by other composers, emphasizing the key role of orchestration in the 'John Williams sound'.

Bibliography

Adler 2002

Adler, Samuel. *The Study of Orchestration*, London, W.W. Norton and Company, ^{3}2002.

Audissino 2017

Audissino, Emilio. 'John Williams and Contemporary Film Music', in: *Contemporary Film Music: Investigating Cinema Narratives and Composition* edited by Lindsay Coleman and Joakim Tillman, Basingstoke, Palgrave Macmillan, 2017, pp. 221-236.

Blatter 1997

Blatter, Alfred. *Instrumentation and Orchestration*, New York, Schirmer Books, ^{2}1997.

Buckton 1980

Buckton, David. *Star Wars: Music by John Williams*, BBC, 18 May 1980, <https://www.youtube.com/watch?v=N3V3QZZa2qw>, accessed March 2018.

Burlingame 2015

Burlingame, Jon. 'Film Score Icons Williams, Morricone and Horner Loom Large in Oscar Race', in: *Variety*, 9 December 2015, <http://variety.com/2015/music/awards/oscar-icons-williams-morricone-and-horner-loom-large-in-scorerace-1201657637>, accessed March 2018.

Davies 2010

Davies, Richard. *Complete Guide to Film Scoring: The Art and Business of Writing Music for Movies and TV*, Boston, Berklee Press, ^{2}2010.

Elley 1978

Elley, Derek. 'The Film Composer: 3 – John Williams', in: *Films and Filming*, xxiv/10-11 (1978), pp. 20-24 and 30-33, <http://www.jw-collection.de/misc/interview/elley.htm>, accessed March 2018.

Gonzalez 1989

Gonzalez, Fernando, 'Orchestrating Indiana Jones (1989)', in: *The Boston Globe*, 18 June 1989, p. 91, <http://www.jwfan.com/?page_id=4522>, accessed March 2018.

Gramophone 2005

'John Williams Interview: «It's not Hard Work that Makes Success; It's Sustained Hard Work that Makes Success»', (2005), in: *Gramophone*, <https://www.gramophone.co.uk/feature/john-williams-interview-its-not-hard-work-that-makes-success-its-sustained-hard-work-that>, accessed March 2018.

Henning 2017

Henning, Paul S. Unpublished interview with the author, August 2017.

Jones 2007
Jones, Trevor. Unpublished interview with the author, October 2007.

Kalinak 1992
Kalinak, Kathryn. *Settling the Score: Music and the Classical Hollywood Film*, Madison (WI), University of Wisconsin Press, 1992 (Wisconsin Studies in Film).

Karlin – Wright 2004
Karlin, Fred – Wright, Rayburn. *On the Track: A Guide to Contemporary Film Scoring*, New York, Routledge, [2]2004.

Lack 2002
Lack, Russell. *Twenty Four Frames Under: A Buried History of Film Music*, London, Quartet Books, 2002.

Pope 2017
Pope, Conrad. Unpublished interview with the author, August 2017.

Sapiro 2016
Sapiro, Ian. *Scoring the Score: The Role of the Orchestrator in the Contemporary Film Industry*, New York, Routledge, 2016.

Thomas 1991
Thomas, Tony. *The Score: The Art & Craft of Movie Music*, Burbank, Riverwood Press, 1991.

TrailerAddict 2013
'Interview with John Williams (Composer) for The Book Thief', (2013), in: *TrailerAddict*, <https://www.traileraddict.com/the-book-thief/interview-john-williams>, accessed March 2018.

Yoho 2017
Yoho, Scott. 'May the Fourth Spotlight on JoAnn Kane Music', (2017), in: *Finale Blog*, <https://www.finalemusic.com/blog/may-the-fourth-spotlight-on-joann-kane-music>, accessed March 2018.

Orchestration Transformation: Examining Differences in the Instrumental and Thematic Colour Palettes of the *Star Wars* Trilogies

Nicholas Kmet
(New York University, NY)

Stylistically, John Williams has remained remarkably consistent since *Star Wars*[1] (George Lucas, 1977), his orchestral idiom and sonic palette immediately recognizable whether listening to the scores for *Raiders of the Lost Ark* (Steven Spielberg, 1981) or *Lincoln* (Steven Spielberg, 2012). While a number of his scores — such as *Memoirs of a Geisha* (Rob Marshall, 2005) and *Catch Me if You Can* (Steven Spielberg, 2002) — have deviated in sound and style, Williams has primarily remained true to the neoromantic, Classical-Hollywood style of music found in *A New Hope*.

However, like most composers, Williams's style has developed over the last 40 years, as he has increasingly relied on more contemporary styles and techniques, such as atonal, minimalist, and electronic idioms[2]. One aspect of Williams's film music that has seen interesting changes in the intervening decades is his approach to orchestration: Williams has gravitated towards different instrumentation and adjusted how he utilizes those instruments in his treatment of thematic material. Evaluating these changes at an empirical level can be difficult though, because while Williams has an identifiable style, each score remains an independent entity that is functionally disconnected from the others. It would be difficult, for example, to compare *Memoirs of a Geisha* and *Close Encounters of the Third Kind* (Steven Spielberg, 1977) and expect to draw many useful conclusions about his use of instrumentation.

The *Star Wars* franchise, then, provides a unique opportunity to evaluate Williams's music over the length of his career, as it has produced seven films scored by Williams over

[1]. For the rest of this chapter, I will refer to the 1977 film by the designation director George Lucas added for subsequent releases of the film — *A New Hope* — to differentiate from discussions about the *Star Wars* franchise as a whole.

[2]. Audissino 2014, p. 84.

nearly 40 years — with at least two more scheduled to be scored by Williams at the time of this writing. That the three trilogies are so spread out — 16 years between the original trilogy (1977-1983) and the prequel trilogy (1999-2005), and another 10 years before the sequel trilogy (2015-2019) — makes them especially useful for evaluating Williams's evolving style, as each represents a different portion of his career since the release of *A New* Hope in 1977. Each score is recognizable as belonging to the *Star Wars* canon, and yet a discernibly disparate sound exists across the spectrum of the three trilogies — they are as different as they are similar[3].

Preliminary Remarks: The Role of the Orchestrator and Music Editor

Before examining the scores themselves, it would be negligent to not cover the role of orchestrators and music editors in Williams's scoring process. Schedules for scoring films are usually tight — *A New Hope* required 90 minutes of music to be completed in six weeks[4]. As a result, Williams often relies on orchestrators to help complete his scores, something that most Hollywood composers do today. Williams collaborated extensively with Herbert Spencer as his primary orchestrator for over 20 years before his death in 1992; since then he has worked with a number of different orchestrators on the *Star Wars* franchise, including Conrad Pope, John Neufeld, Edward Karam, Paul S. Henning, and William Ross. Considering the notable changes to Williams's style over the course of his career, it does not seem difficult to conclude that the different personnel have had some kind of impact on his music. However, Williams is notable for providing his orchestrators with extremely detailed sketches and short scores, leaving little to interpretation[5]. It is thus unlikely that the orchestrators themselves would have had an outsized influence on the final scores[6].

In the late 1980s, filmmakers began using technology that allowed them to edit without the inordinate financial and labour costs associated with cutting film prints; George Lucas pioneered this technology following the release of *Return of the Jedi* (Richard Marquand, 1983): «In the early 1980s, following the triumphal releases of his *Star Wars* trilogy, director George Lucas and his engineers began development on what became known as the EditDroid. It featured a Unix computer controlling an array of video laserdiscs using a controller called the "Touchpad". While only 17 EditDroids were ever built,

[3]. The majority of this chapter will focus on the original and prequel trilogies, as Williams's scores for those are complete. At the time of this writing, only *The Force Awakens* (J. J. Abrams, 2015) from the sequel trilogy has been released; I will briefly discuss that score at the end of the chapter.

[4]. Anderson 2009, p. 467.

[5]. Darby – Du Bois 1990, p. 523.

[6]. On Williams and orchestrators, see also Ian Sapiro's chapter in this same volume.

they offered a tantalizing glimpse into the future of non-linear editing»[7]. The first truly digital system came in 1989 from Editing Machine Corporation, with Avid following suit later that year. Within a decade, non-linear, non-destructive editing software[8] became the standard method for editing motion pictures[9]. This would have a profound effect on how films were assembled, as directors could continuously edit their films long after traditional deadlines would have passed. While it was not uncommon for films to be edited after the music had been recorded prior to the use of digital editing systems — in his handbook on music editing from 1980, Milton Lustig plainly states that «there are always changes»[10] — the cost associated with the physical limitations of film would have made editing to the degree possible with digital technologies prohibitive. For a music editor, the destructive nature of cutting magnetic tape required making a copy from the master first, a process that could take up to a day and cost more than $100,000 per copy[11] — an exorbitant cost. Making even simple changes to the music — such as extending a sustained note — often involved multiple labour-intensive and time-consuming steps[12], a process now reduced to a few quick inputs on a personal computer. As a result, the role of music editors has grown significantly in post-production throughout the industry.

Non-linear digital editing featured heavily in Lucas's process for completing all three of the prequel films. The editing process for *The Phantom Menace* (George Lucas, 1999), for example, «extended from the time shooting started in England to just weeks before the film's release», a nearly two-year process that lasted months beyond the recording of the film's score[13]. As a result, thousands of edits were made to Williams's completed music. Rick Kline, the re-recording mixer for *Attack of the Clones* (George Lucas, 2002), has said in interviews that the Pro Tools sessions for each reel's[14] music averaged between 12,000 and 14,000 fades, with the smallest number of fades for a reel being 7,000[15]. While most of these edits likely involved very small changes to the music, or micro-edits, interviews with Williams and music editor Ken Wannberg indicate that there were several dramatic adjustments to the prequel scores that involved significant editing by Wannberg[16]. During

---

7. Arundale 2014, p. 12.

8. Non-destructive editing allows for the editing of sound and audio without permanently modifying the original material. Non-linear editing means that the video/audio can be manipulated in any sequence.

9. Arundale 2014, p. 14.

10. Lustig 1980, p. 144.

11. Kasow 2015.

12. Lustig 1980, pp. 160-163.

13. Bouzereau – Duncan 1999, p. 135.

14. A reel of positive film typically contains approximately 20 minutes of footage.

15. Blake 2002.

16. Wannberg, who also accrued more than 20 credits as a composer during his career, first worked with Williams on *Valley of the Dolls* (Mark Robson, 1967), consistently serving as Williams's primary music editor until his retirement in 2005. In that role, Wannberg would have been responsible for helping facilitate communication between Williams and directors, spotting films and calculating timings for the music,

the recording sessions for *The Phantom Menace*, Lucas screened a cut of the film for Steven Spielberg, whose suggestions resulted in significant editing to the final battle sequence of the film:

> Williams had completed his score to an earlier cut of the film. After consultation with Spielberg, though, Lucas had recently re-edited the sixth and final reel, the last 20 minutes of the film, which present simultaneous actions converging on the climax. Williams tries to be philosophical about the pickle this has dropped him into. «If I hit the ground running», he says, «I can write two minutes of music a day. If I were to have started all over again on the last reel, I would be ready to record in July — with the picture already in the theatres! So I've been making the music fit as we go along. That's why I'm constantly telling the players to drop measures 7 to 14[17].

However, significant edits continued to be made, and the original cue for the final battle sequence was scrapped altogether. In its place went a heavily edited version of "Duel of the Fates", which was originally meant to only accompany the end credits of the film[18]. Wannberg has described "Duel of the Fates" as a «utility track», noting that he often used it to replace music in other parts of the film after edits made the original music unusable[19]. The heavy editing of the score during this final battle sequence is readily apparent upon careful listening, as unrelated fragments of "Duel of the Fates" are mashed together to match the onscreen action.

This can be confirmed via a waveform analysis of the music as it appears in the film, made possible because two version of the soundtrack were released to the public — the original album released with the film in 1999[20], and a two-disc "Ultimate Edition" released in 2000[21]. The original album featured concert arrangements of the score, edited and approved by Williams — a typical 'soundtrack album' release. While the tracks on the original album do not reflect all the music that was recorded for *The Phantom Menace*, nor necessarily the original context in which it was written — some cues were likely combined or condensed — it is an accurate representation of how Williams wished his score to be heard by the general public[22]. The ultimate edition, however, presents the score entirely

overseeing the technical aspects of recording sessions, making necessary post-recording edits to the music, and representing Williams and the music during the final mix.

[17]. DYER 1999, pp. 18-19.

[18]. THAXTON 1999, p. 8.

[19]. *Ibidem*.

[20]. WILLIAMS, John. *Star Wars: Episode I – The Phantom Menace. Original Motion Picture Soundtrack*, Sony Classical SK61816, 1999. Henceforth (†).

[21]. ID. *Star Wars: Episode I – The Phantom Menace. The Ultimate Edition*, Sony Classical SK89460, 2000. Henceforth (§).

[22]. Williams is credited as the album producer, which would typically mean he had final say over the album's contents.

differently; according to its own packaging, it includes «every note of the original music that John Williams composed»[23]. This, however, is not entirely accurate; the ultimate edition soundtrack for *The Phantom Menace* is comprised of the music nearly exactly as it appears in the film — the vast majority of Wannberg's edits included — and excludes any music that was recorded but not used in the film. By comparing the waveforms of the music from the ultimate edition soundtrack to the music that appears on the album release produced by Williams, it becomes clear just how much Wannberg had to edit the recorded cues to fit the finished scene (see Fig. 1, p. 214).

In this two-and-one-half minute segment of the final battle sequence, Wannberg draws music from three separate tracks on the soundtrack album: "Qui-Gon's Noble End", "Duel of the Fates", and "Panaka; The Queen's Protectors". Combined, Wannberg's edited cues comprise three tracks on the ultimate edition soundtrack[24], each featuring the numerous micro-edits and repetitions he employs to conform the music to the scene. While the cues from the album release are to a degree idealized beyond their filmic context — edited to provide a more flawless representation — their musical coherence stands in stark contrast to the ultimate edition cues. Isolated from the film, the final score seemingly jumps at random through the musical material with little concern for structure or continuity, designed as it was to maximally match the onscreen action.

Because much of the music in the prequel trilogy is so heavily edited, and because complete releases do not exist for any of the prequel soundtracks, evaluating Williams's music in these cases is more difficult than evaluating the original trilogy. Are the shifts in orchestration that we hear in the scores for *The Phantom Menace*, *Attack of the Clones*, and *Revenge of the Sith* (George Lucas, 2005) the result of Wannberg's extensive music editing, or are they Williams's original intent? It is difficult to be entirely certain all the time. While I don't think this makes an analysis impossible, it certainly makes one more challenging, as a preponderance of musical evidence is necessary to draw any convincing conclusions. Carefully choosing which cues to analyse, however, can mitigate many of these problems fairly successfully.

Analysing the Instrumentation

Much like Darby and Du Bois do in *American Film Music*, it is paradoxically common for scholars and commentators to promote the notion of Williams as a traditionalist in style and instrumentation, as if his career began in 1977 with *A New Hope*: «Williams eschews many of the styles that arose during the 1950s and 1960s — jazz, limited ensembles, the song score — instead choosing to emphasize large and conventional sounds. He also

---

23. Bond 2000, p. 49.

24. Listen to "The Duel Begins" (§), "Anakin Takes Off in Spaceship" (§), and "The Duel Continues" (§).

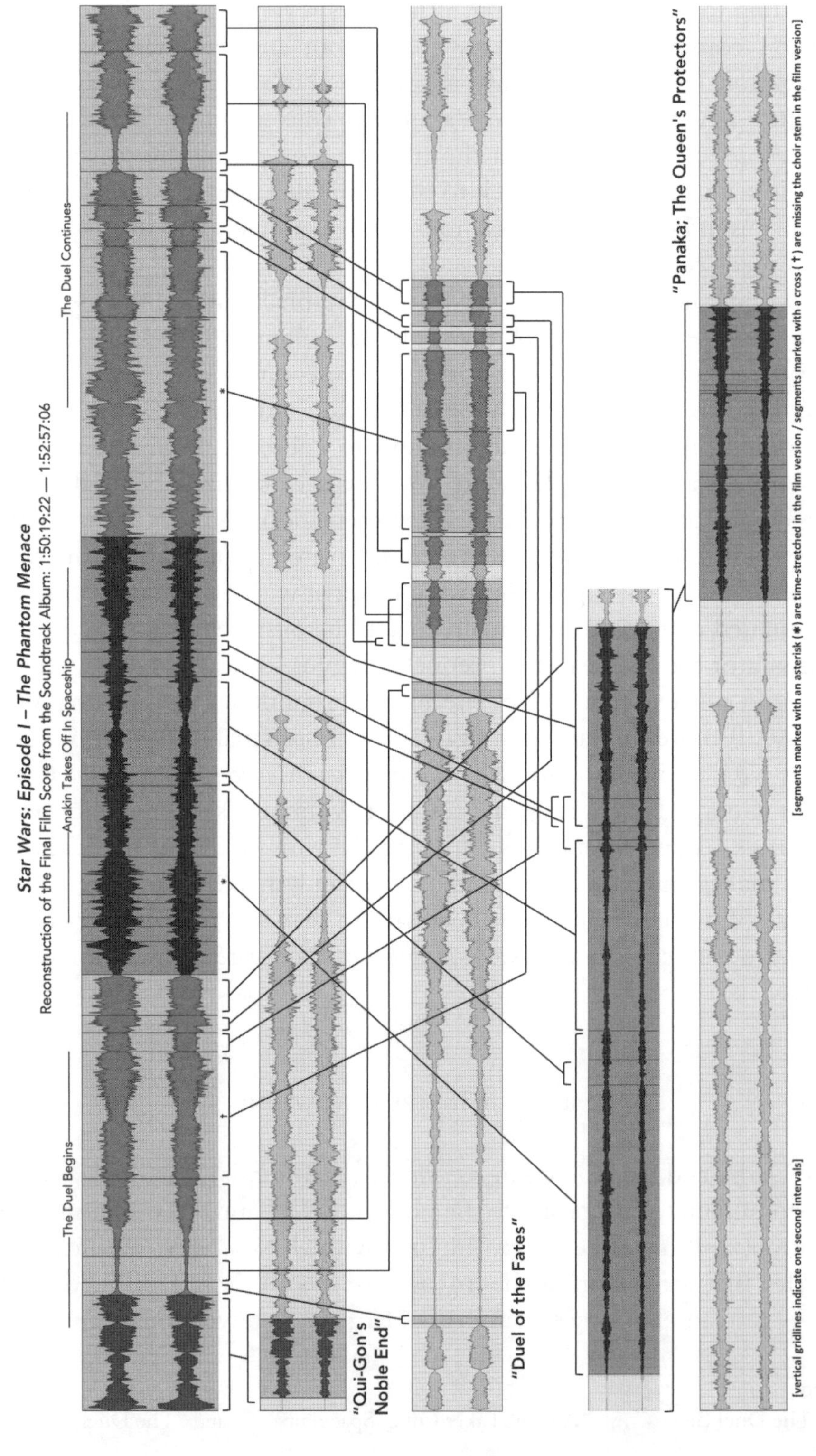

FIG. 1: waveform analysis/reconstruction of film score from *The Phantom Menace*. Graphic created by Nicholas Kmet. Used by permission.

downplays the combining of odd instruments, doesn't strive to create tunes that will spin off as independent entities and avoids the more modern sounds one associates with music videos and jazz»[25]. While *A New Hope* may have cemented the «conventional» neoromantic instrumentation and harmonic language as Williams's trademark style, it's important to remember that prior to *Jaws* (Steven Spielberg, 1975), Williams's music was far more in line with his contemporaries and with the prevailing industry trends. His score for Robert Altman's *Images* (1972), a collaboration with Japanese percussionist Stomu Yamashta, utilized percussive sculptures created by the Baschet brothers, other non-orchestral percussion, and numerous extended techniques in the string orchestra[26], reminiscent of Jerry Goldsmith's landmark score for *Planet of the Apes* (Franklin J. Schaffner, 1968). His score for *The Eiger Sanction* (Clint Eastwood, 1975), released the same year as *Jaws*, heavily features synthesizer and a jazz orchestra — including electric guitar and bass. Considering his background as a jazz pianist, it's hardly surprising that Williams would have utilized more contemporary instruments and styles.

However, *A New Hope* did represent a shift towards a conventional, neoromantic, Hollywood neoclassical style, at least temporarily. Many of Williams's scores in the immediate aftermath of *Star Wars* utilize such instrumentation — including *Close Encounters of the Third Kind*, *Superman* (Richard Donner, 1978), *Dracula* (John Badham, 1979), *Raiders of the Lost Ark*, and *E. T.: The Extra-Terrestrial* (Steven Spielberg, 1982) — and though there are exceptions, Williams's most successful scores (and films) utilize the neoromantic aesthetic[27] and instrumentation. And yet in the decades since, Williams has steadily moved to expand his sonic palette to include instrumentation outside of the traditional neoromantic aesthetic, much as he did prior to *A New Hope*. Williams readily embraced and prominently featured synthesized sounds throughout the 1990s, in P*resumed Innocent* (Alan J. Pakula, 1990), *Home Alone* (Chris Columbus, 1990), *JFK* (Oliver Stone, 1991), *Jurassic Park* (Steven Spielberg, 1993), and *Nixon* (Oliver Stone, 1995). Synthesized sounds continue to be an important part of his instrumental palette even in more overtly orchestral scores; the celeste used in Williams's three *Harry Potter* scores was a synthetic instrument developed by Randy Kerber[28]. Williams has expanded his palette in other ways as well, whether through a more overt embracing of his jazz background in the scores for films like *Catch Me if You Can*, *The Terminal* (Steven Spielberg, 2004), and *The Adventures of Tintin* (Steven Spielberg, 2011), or through the prominent use of ethnic instruments, such as in

---

25. Darby – Du Bois 1990, p. 521.

26. Bazelon 1975, pp. 202-206.

27. I refer to Williams's commitment to a number of practices consistent with romanticism and neoromanticism, such as the use of a large orchestra (winds in three, an expanded brass section, etc.), complex harmonic progressions, and a commitment to melody-centric, emotionally expressive scores. This stands in contrast with many of Williams's contemporaries, such as Hans Zimmer or Alexandre Desplat, who utilize different aesthetic approaches in their film scores.

28. *Cinesamples* 2013.

Memoirs of a Geisha and *Munich* (Steven Spielberg, 2005), further drifting from a purely neo-romantic aesthetic.

As I noted in my introduction to this chapter, Williams's scores for the *Star Wars* franchise are remarkably consistent in that each is easily identifiable as a *Star Wars* score; this consistency would seem to preclude dramatic changes in instrumentation. However, Williams greatly increased his use of exotic percussion, chorus/voice, and synthetically generated sounds in the prequel scores, mirroring the trend of diversification present in his scores outside of the franchise.

In the original trilogy, percussion is primarily limited to traditional orchestral instruments — timpani, snare drum, bass drum, cymbals, keyboard percussion — with the only exceptions coming from the music for the Sand People in *A New Hope*[29], and the Ewoks in *Return of the Jedi*[30]. These sequences utilize exotic sounding percussion — notably a wider array of pitched drums and wood instruments — to symbolize the 'primitive' nature of the characters they are associated with. The orchestral percussion is limited in its application as it is practically never foregrounded, and instead functions to accent figures in the orchestra. Even in many action sequences, such as the TIE fighter attack in *A New Hope*[31], the asteroid field in *The Empire Strikes Back* (Irvin Kershner, 1980)[32], and the sail barge assault and battle for Endor in *Return of the Jedi*[33], the percussion plays a supporting role, the rhythmic foundation and accentuating figures often primarily provided by other instrument groups — typically the low brass and strings — with sparse accompaniment from the percussion.

In the prequel trilogy, Williams is far more liberal with his use of percussion — including non-orchestral instruments. In *The Phantom Menace*, non-orchestral drums can be heard in several of the scenes on Tatooine[34], as the Gungans prepare for the final battle[35], briefly during the senate session[36], and in sequences featuring Darth Maul — including throughout the uses of "Duel of the Fates" during the final battle sequence[37]. Orchestral

29. Listen to "Landspeeder Search / Attack of the Sand People" from Williams, John. *Star Wars: Episode IV – A New Hope. Original Motion Picture Soundtrack*, Sony Classical S2K92950, 2004. Henceforth (Ω).

30. Listen to "The Levitation / Threepio's Bedtime Story", "Victory Celebration / End Title", and "Source Music: Ewok Feast / Part of The Tribe" from Id. *Star Wars: Episode VI – Return of the Jedi. Original Motion Picture Soundtrack*, Sony Classical S2K92952, 2004. Henceforth (£).

31. Listen to "Ben Kenobi's Death / Tie Fighter Attack" (Ω).

32. Listen to "The Asteroid Field" from Id. *Star Wars: Episode V: The Empire Strikes Back. Original Motion Picture Soundtrack*, Sony Classical SK92951, 2004. Henceforth (Δ).

33. Listen to "The Pit of Carkoon / Sail Barge Assault" (£) and "The Battle of Endor I" (£).

34. Listen to "The Arrival at Tatooine" (§), "Street Band of Mos Espa" (§), and "Desert Winds" (§).

35. Listen to "The Gungans March" (§).

36. Listen to "The Senate" (§).

37. Listen to "Darth Maul and The Sith Spacecraft" (§), "The Duel Begins" (§), "The Duel Continues" (§), "Qui-Gon Obi-Wan & Darth Maul Continue Battle" (§), and "The Death of Qui-Gon & The Surrender of The Gungans" (§).

percussion is also prominent, as the thematic material Williams employs to accompany the battle droids is primarily comprised of militaristic marches that rely heavily on snare, field, and bass drums[38], much like "The Imperial March" from *The Empire Strikes Back*. However, the percussion in these cues is considerably more foregrounded than anything found in the original trilogies. This increased use and prominence of percussion is further expanded upon in both *Attack of the Clones* and *Revenge of the Sith*. As Anakin and Obi-Wan chase Zam the Assassin through Coruscant at the beginning of *Attack of the Clones*, a cacophony of sounds accompanies the onscreen action, including a myriad of non-orchestral percussion that in the original trilogy could only have been heard accompanying the Sand People[39]. The opening sequence for *Revenge of the Sith* makes heavy use of orchestral percussion to provide a near-constant rhythmic underpinning for the action on screen[40], while an expanded percussion section accompanies Obi-Wan's search for General Grievous on Utapau[41], perhaps emphasizing the exotic nature of the locale[42].

Prior to *The Phantom Menace*, chorus of any kind was only heard in *Return of the Jedi*, for the Emperor's theme and the celebration music at the end of the film. The prequel trilogy, however, is marked by its use of chorus, a defining characteristic of much of its new thematic material. Chorus features heavily in *The Phantom Menace* — the emperor's theme from *Return of the Jedi* returns to accompany Darth Sidious[43] and chant-like passages in Sanskrit accompany the terrifying appearances of Darth Maul[44]; haunting, wordless passages are heard throughout the underwater sequences[45]; a fatalistic chorus accompanies the duel between the Sith and Jedi[46]; a mournful chorus presides over Qui-Gon's funeral[47]. *Attack of the Clones* utilizes chorus to a much more limited degree as it appears in only three places: during Obi-Wan's consultation with Yoda at the Jedi Temple[48], during Anakin's

---

[38]. Listen to "The Droid Invasion" (§) and "Activate the Droids" (§).

[39]. Listen to "Zam The Assassin and The Chase Through Coruscant" from Williams, John. *Star Wars: Episode ii – Attack of the Clones. Original Motion Picture Soundtrack*, Sony Classical SK89932-B1, 2002. Henceforth (Ø).

[40]. Listen to "Star Wars and Revenge of The Sith" from Id. *Star Wars: Episode iii – Revenge of the Sith. Original Motion Picture Soundtrack*, Sony Classical SK94220, 2005. Henceforth (€).

[41]. Listen to "General Grievous" (€).

[42]. In addition to offering rhythmic support for the on-screen action.

[43]. Listen to "Death Warrant for Qui-Gon and Obi-Wan" (§), "Darth Sidious" (§), "Enter Darth Maul" (§), "Darth Sidious and Darth Maul" (§), and "Nute & Rune Confer with Darth Sidious" (§).

[44]. Listen to "Darth Maul and the Sith Spacecraft" (§), "Qui-Gon & Darth Maul Meet" (§), and "The Death of Qui-Gon & The Surrender of The Gungans" (§).

[45]. Listen to "Swimming to Otoh Gunga" (§), "Inside the Bubble City" (§), "Attack of the Giant Fish" (§), and "Darth Sidious" (§).

[46]. Listen to "The Duel Begins" (§), "The Duel Continues" (§), and "Qui-Gon Obi-Wan & Darth Maul Continue Battle" (§).

[47]. Listen to "The Funeral of Qui-Gon" (§).

[48]. Listen to "Yoda and the Younglings" (Ø).

visit to the Sand People camp on Tatooine[49], and briefly during the duel between Yoda and Count Dooku[50]. Chorus plays a much larger role in *Revenge of the Sith*. First heard during General Grievous's conversation with Darth Sidious upon arriving at Utapau[51], it can also be heard as Anakin murders the remaining Jedi at the temple[52] and as Padmé is buried on Naboo[53]. It is an important component of the music that plays during the film's climax as the action cuts between two duels — Anakin versus Obi-Wan, and Palpatine versus Yoda[54]. Additionally, throat singing dominates the score during the opera house sequence[55], and a wailing female vocalist accompanies Padmé's ruminations over Anakin's fall to the dark side[56].

Synthesized sounds, mostly absent in the original trilogy[57], are heard throughout the prequel scores. Though limited in use and primarily for atmospheric effect, they nonetheless are added to the palette of sounds at Williams's disposal. According to Wannberg, the celebration parade sequence at the end of *The Phantom Menace*, was crafted almost entirely with synthesizers[58]. In *Revenge of the Sith*, synthesizer appears prominently during the "Anakin's Dream" and "Padmé's Ruminations" sequences. And while it does not appear in the film, the soundtrack version of the Coruscant chase music from *Attack of the Clones* includes a dramatic guitar solo[59].

ORCHESTRAL COLOUR: TREATMENT OF THEMATIC CONTENT[60]

Perhaps the most interesting changes in Williams's music can be found in his use of orchestral colour, specifically in his treatment of thematic content. As Doug Adams notes, Williams seems to adopt a more cellularized approach to much of his underscore, passing

49. Listen to "The Tusken Camp and the Homestead" (Ø).

50. Much of the music that plays during this sequence is not included on the soundtrack release for *Attack of the Clones*, however a portion of it can be heard at the beginning of "Confrontation with Count Dooku and Finale" (Ø).

51. Listen to "Grievous Speaks to Lord Sidious" (€).

52. Listen to "Anakin's Dark Deeds" (€).

53. Listen to "The Birth of the Twins and Padmé's Destiny" (€).

54. Listen to "Battle of the Heroes" (€) and "Anakin vs. Obi-Wan" (€) for the music that accompanies the duel between Anakin and Obi-Wan. The music that accompanies the Yoda / Palpatine duel is a re-recorded version of "Duel of the Fates" from *The Phantom Menace* that was not included on the soundtrack.

55. Listen to "Palpatine's Teachings" (€).

56. Listen to "Padmé's Ruminations" (€).

57. There are a few exceptions, notably "The Magic Tree" (Δ).

58. THAXTON 1999, p. 9.

59. It seems likely that the guitar solo was removed to avoid clashing with the sound effect for Zam's airspeeder, as it occupies much of the same frequency range as the sound effect.

60. See HUVET 2017. In the past, I have referred to this phenomenon in Williams's orchestration as 'arrangement'. This more descriptive title is an adaptation from a Ph.D. thesis by Chloé Huvet.

melodic statements throughout the orchestra as opposed to leaving them in one voice for extended passages:

> Williams's orchestration in the originals was like A Young Person's Guide to Film Scoring, where instrumental soloists stepped into the spotlight. In the [...] prequels, however, Williams concentrated more on doubled lines and denser orchestrations, ideas generally passing among instruments in each single statement. Had *Phantom's* dinner conversation in Anakin's hovel occurred in *A New Hope*, it's likely that the figure floating between French horn, flute and oboe would have stayed with one instrument for the duration[61].

Let's begin by examining the specific passage Adams refers to: the underscore for the dinner conversation in *The Phantom Menace*[62].

The cue opens with an eight-bar phrase that introduces much of the thematic material used throughout the rest of the cue. While the violins retain the melody for the duration of the phrase, the supporting orchestration evolves, as the lower strings are added one after another. The orchestration expands significantly from this point, as the cue is primarily divided into musical cells of two-to-three measures for its remainder. In measures 8-18 (Ex. 1, p. 220), the melody is alternately passed between flute and oboe, full strings, French horn, oboe, and violins — with none holding it for more than two measures. The accompaniment is similarly varied; the French horns carry the accompaniment from measures 8-10, though a shift in register occurs in the middle of measure 9. The strings accompany from measures 12-15, first with sustained chords for two measures, before transitioning to a more rhythmically varied figure. In measures 16-18, the cello accompanies with a rising figure that competes with the main melody for dominance.

The remainder of the cue is similarly varied; the melody at times passes through English horn, strings, oboe, glockenspiel, flute, clarinet, French horn, and synthesizer, with no group of instruments holding the melody for more than five measures — and most for less than three. No instrument gets a complete statement of any melody; instead, the melodies are fragmented as they are passed throughout the orchestra. The accompaniment is similarly fragmented, as no single texture is utilized for more than three bars at a time. The result is a highly cellularized cue, constantly evolving as it weaves around the dialogue heavy sequence.

As another example, consider this cue from *Attack of the Clones*, heard as Anakin and Padmé declare their love for each other before their intended execution in the Geonosis arena[63]. Much like "Talk of Podracing", this cue is built on a cellular construction; but this time each cell is four-measure long, rather than two. After a brief four-measure

---

61. Adams 2005, p. 34.

62. Listen to "Talk of Podracing" (§).

63. Listen to "Love Pledge and the Arena" (Ø).

Ex. 1: transcription of John Williams, "Talk of Podracing", from *Star Wars: Episode I – The Phantom Menace* (©1999 BMI), published by Bantha Music, administered by Warner-Tamerlane Publishing Corp., ear transcription from the film's soundtrack. Used in compliance with the U.S. Copyright Act, Section 107.

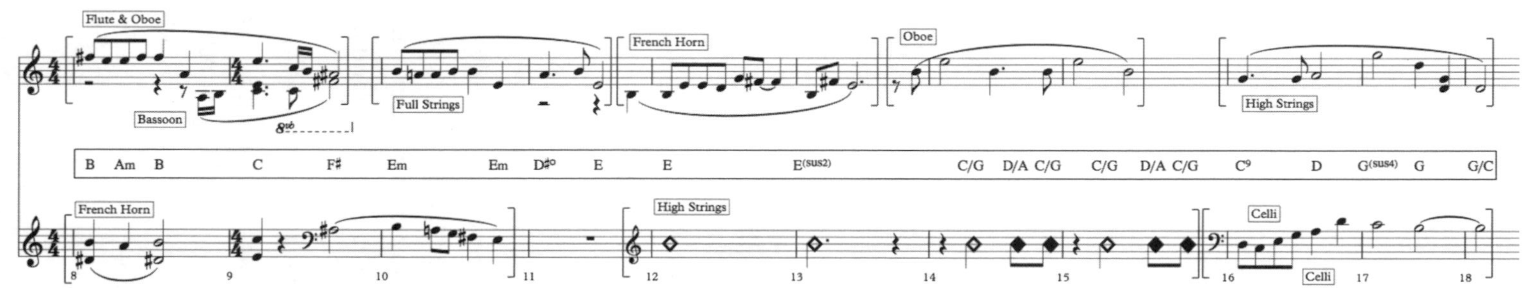

Ex. 2: transcription of John Williams, "Love Pledge and the Arena", from *Star Wars: Episode II – Attack of the Clones* (©2002 BMI), published by Bantha Music, administered by Warner-Tamerlane Publishing Corp., ear transcription from the film's soundtrack. Used in compliance with the U.S. Copyright Act, Section 107.

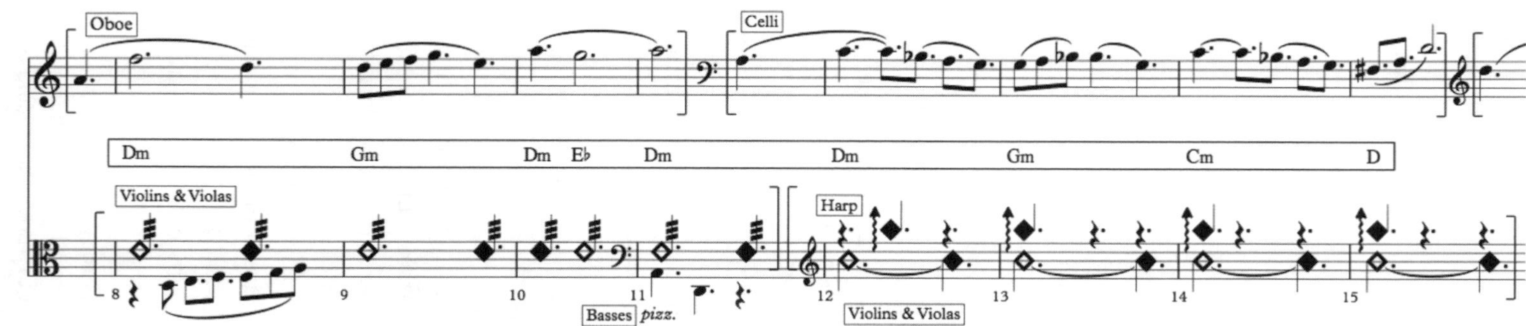

introduction, the cue opens with a rising melody in the violins, accompanied by a steadily moving figure in the lower strings. At measure eight, the melody is passed to the oboe for four measures (Ex. 2, p. 220).

The accompaniment shifts, as violins and violas play tremolo on chords that follow the harmonic rhythm of the melody. In measure twelve, the melody is passed to the cello section, while the violins and violas continue with the accompaniment. However, they shift up into a higher register, cease the tremolo articulation, and hold their chords across the entirety of each measure. They are also joined by short, ascending, harp glissandi.

In measure sixteen, the melody is handed back to the violins, accompanied by sustained chords in the lower strings and measure-length arpeggiations in the harp (Ex. 3, p. 222). After four measures, the melody shifts again, to flute and harpsichord, accompanied by sustained chords in the French horns and tremolo figures in the violins.

As the cue continues to unfold, the melody is passed to the violins, and eventually doubled in the cellos, while the accompanying figures become more fragmented in the French horns and low strings. As with "Talk of Podracing", no single instrument carries the melody beyond the four-bar cell it occupies, and none achieve a complete statement of the theme or its constituent periods. The accompaniment is similarly diverse, as subtle changes in texture, register, and harmonic rhythm occur for each four-bar cell.

Both of these cues are emblematic of Williams's writing in the prequel scores, as the orchestration is designed to shift rapidly while the melody proceeds through compact cells. In comparison, the scores from the original trilogy are much more static, relying on longer phrase structures with limited shifts in orchestration. Here, for example, are the opening bars of the cue that plays under a romantic moment between Han Solo and Princess Leia while the Millennium Falcon is trapped inside the giant space slug in *The Empire Strikes Back*[64] (Ex. 4, p. 222).

After a brief introduction of syncopated, descending figures in the woodwinds, and extended statement of the Han Solo / Princess Leia love theme is presented in solo French horn, accompanied by simple string chords and arpeggiating figures in harp and cello. The entire first phrase of the theme is stated before the orchestration changes; the melody is taken over by flute and oboe / English horn, while the accompaniment stays roughly the same, with the addition of a counter-melody of sorts in the celli and basses. As the melody moves to repeat the first phrase, it even remains in the flute and oboe / English horn, with only minor changes occurring in the accompaniment.

A similar approach is taken late in *Return of the Jedi* as Luke visits a dying Yoda[65]. This is a lengthy sequence, and Williams seamlessly weaves between thematic material as the dialogue during the sequence dictates. I have transcribed a segment of the of the cue that plays as Yoda foretells his death (Ex. 5, p. 223).

[64]. Listen to "Han Solo and the Princess" (Δ).

[65]. Listen to "The Emperor Arrives / The Death of Yoda / Obi-Wan's Revelation" (£).

Ex. 3: transcription of John Williams, "Love Pledge and the Arena", from *Star Wars: Episode II – Attack of the Clones* (©2002 BMI), published by Bantha Music, administered by Warner-Tamerlane Publishing Corp., ear transcription from the film's soundtrack. Used in compliance with the U.S. Copyright Act, Section 107.

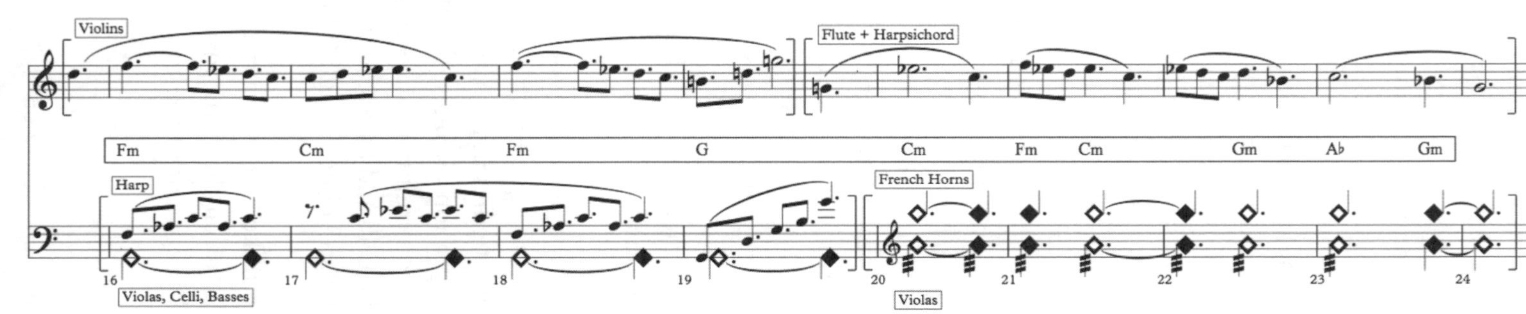

Ex. 4: transcription of John Williams, «Han Solo and the Princess», from *Star Wars: Episode V – The Empire Strikes Back* (©1980 BMI), published by Bantha Music, administered by Warner-Tamerlane Publishing Corp., ear transcription from the film's soundtrack. Used in compliance with the U.S. Copyright Act, Section 107.

Ex. 5: transcription of John Williams, "The Emperor Arrives / The Death of Yoda / Obi-Wan's Revelation", from *Star Wars: Episode VI – Return of the Jedi* (©1983 BMI), published by Bantha Music, administered by Warner-Tamerlane Publishing Corp, ear transcription from the film's soundtrack. Used in compliance with the U.S. Copyright Act, Section 107.

Ex. 6: transcription of John Williams, "The Scavenger", from *Star Wars: Episode VII – The Force Awakens* film score (©2015 BMI), published by Utapau Music, administered by Disney Music Publishing, ear transcription from the film's soundtrack. Used in compliance with the U.S. Copyright Act, Section 107.

This segment opens with a statement of "The Force Theme" in French horn, accompanied by simple chords in the strings. As the melody switches to "Yoda's Theme", it moves to the flute and oboe. The accompaniment also changes; the strings move to tremolo chords while the harp lays arpeggios and the basses hold a pedal. As the theme begins its second phrase, the accompaniment shifts again as the celli adopt a figure that mirrors the melody. The remainder of the cue follows a very similar structure; each time the melody changes, it moves to either a new instrument or to a different register, differentiating the melodies from each other. The accompaniment remains simple throughout, shifting its orchestration alongside the melody.

These significantly contrasting approaches are a key component of what makes the scores for each trilogy stand out as different from each other. Each of these scenes — from both trilogies — are similar in that they are both dialogue-heavy and expository. And yet, Williams's orchestration is considerably less dense for both of the original trilogy cues. Rather than weaving in and out of the dialogue with rapid changes in texture, register, instrumentation, and harmonic rhythm, a single instrument carries the melody for extended periods of time, coupled with a simple accompaniment designed to stay in the background. As a result, the melodies are less fragmented than their prequel trilogy counterparts, while the supporting orchestration draws considerably less attention to itself.

Conclusions

To what, then, do we attribute these changes in Williams's style? As subtle as they may seem on the surface, they do constitute a significant shift in his approach to orchestration. Audissino argues that Williams adopted a less melodic approach following *The Phantom Menace* after realizing that a modular approach would be more compatible with Lucas's new digital-editing approach, while different instrumentation would help to penetrate the aural wall of sound effects Lucas favoured[66]. While it is almost certain that Lucas's predilections had some effect on Williams's stylistic decisions and approach to the prequel scores, I'm not certain that these changes can be entirely explained as a reaction to Lucas's post-production process. Audissino primarily points to differences in Williams's approach to action sequences as evidence for his argument; however, as I illustrated with examples earlier in this chapter, Williams's cellularized approach can also be found in dialogue heavy, expository scenes as well. It is an approach in totality, rather than one strategically applied to problematic action sequences.

I would argue that this approach is not unique to *Star Wars*; as early as *Jurassic Park*, Williams seems to abandon melody as a driving force in action cues. His score to *Nixon* sounds prototypical in relation to *The Phantom Menace*. Even in a more traditional score like

[66]. Audissino 2017, pp. 228-229.

Saving Private Ryan (Steven Spielberg, 1998), melodic cellularization and fragmentation is endemic throughout. And these stylistic elements can certainly be found in scores written after *Revenge of the Sith*, such as in *Indiana Jones and the Kingdom of the Crystal Skull* (Steven Spielberg, 2008). Considering these shifts in approach can be found outside of the *Star Wars* prequel trilogy, I tend to think that these changes can be characterized as part of a more general transformation in Williams's approach to orchestration overall from the early 1990s through the late 2000s.

Thus far I have exclusively discussed differences between the original and prequel trilogies of the *Star Wars* franchise; this is primarily due to the fact that at the time of this writing, only the first film from the sequel trilogy — *The Force Awakens* (J. J. Abrams, 2015) — has been released. Drawing conclusions about Williams's orchestrations as they relate to the other trilogies in the franchise is thus an impossible exercise to conduct convincingly until the remaining two films — and their accompanying scores — have been released. And considering that Williams's overall film score output dropped precipitously after 2005[67] — the year that *Revenge of the Sith* was completed — the evaluation of his career since is somewhat challenging. The following discussion of the score to *The Force Awakens* should be considered tentative, and any broader conclusions should be tempered by the forthcoming scores.

Generally speaking, it would seem as though Williams has made a conscious effort to return to a style much more consistent with the original trilogy[68]. The outcome, I think, is perhaps a synthesis of two disparate sounds; much of the score for *The Force Awakens* seems to bridge the divide between the original and prequel trilogies. The clearest example comes in the instrumentation that Williams employs. Much like the original trilogy, the use of percussion is highly limited; exotic instruments are practically absent from the score, and Williams mostly limits himself to staples of the orchestra — timpani, snare drum, bass drum, cymbals, and keyboard percussion. He doesn't merely reduce the array of percussion; Williams limits its usage as well. Percussion no longer drives action sequences or occupies the foreground of cues. Instead, it accentuates figures already present elsewhere in the orchestra; it is the brass and strings that provide the rhythmic propulsion heard throughout the score[69].

67. Between the end of the prequel trilogy in 2005 and the beginning of the sequel trilogy in 2015 with the release of *The Force Awakens*, Williams only scored five feature length films. By comparison, between 1983 and 1999 — the end of the original trilogy and beginning of the prequel trilogy — Williams scored 27 feature films.

68. Note that while a complete version of the film score has not been released to the public, Disney also released a second version of the soundtrack online and to Academy members as part of their Academy Award campaign for the film. Many of the tracks on this version of this score contain music not heard on the album release. No physical version was released to the public. The album version [Williams, John. *Star Wars: The Force Awakens. Original Motion Picture Soundtrack*, Walt Disney Records D002177202, 2015] will henceforth be indicated by (ß), and the promo version [Id. *Star Wars: The Force Awakens. For Your Consideration – Best Original Score*, Lucasfilm Ltd., 2015] will henceforth be indicated by (‡).

69. Listen to "Scherzo for X-Wings" (ß) and "The Bombing Run" (‡).

Similarly, the use of chorus has been extremely diminished from its expansive role in the prequel trilogy; its only notable appearance is for Snoke's theme, a cue that utilizes throat singing eerily similar to the music that is heard during the opera house sequence in *Revenge of the Sith*[70]. Correspondingly, the role of synthesized sounds has been primarily focused on providing atmospheric effects; they never appear in the foreground[71].

In terms of how Williams treats thematic content throughout the score, it seems as though he uses a hybrid approach. There are a significant number of moments where Williams lets the thematic material linger in a single instrument, far beyond anything in the prequel trilogy. A prime example of this is when Rey sits down to eat her lunch; a solitary flute carries her theme for the entire length of the cue (Ex. 6, p. 223), an approach much more in line with the original trilogy[72].

There are other moments, though, where Williams shifts the orchestration at a breakneck pace, such as at the end of the film while Rey prepares to search for Luke[73]. As another example, Williams even reuses a portion of "Talk of Podracing" when Finn confesses to Rey at Maz's cantina[74]. The end result, I think, is a score that in many ways sounds closely related to both the original trilogy and prequel trilogy, providing a more cohesive sound to the entire *Star Wars* franchise.

Does this change from the prequel trilogy, however, represent an overall shift in Williams's approach to orchestration since the release of *Revenge of the Sith*? One of the difficulties in answering this question is that for the first time Williams was not working with George Lucas, who was notoriously hands off in providing direction for the score; Lucas typically heard Williams's scores for the first time as they were being recorded. It is unclear whether J. J. Abrams — director of *The Force Awakens* — took a similarly hands-off approach, or if the apparent return to a more classic *Star Wars* sound was a more directed approach. While Williams has produced few film scores in the intervening decade since the prequel trilogy ended, we can glean some supporting evidence from the scores he did complete. The score for *Lincoln*, for example, seems to exemplify many of the characteristics I've discussed that are inherent to the original trilogy – simplified instrumentation and a propensity for long melodic passages and limited shifts in orchestration. The same can be said for *War Horse* (Steven Spielberg, 2011) *The Book Thief* (Brian Percival, 2013). With an ear towards the forthcoming *Star Wars* scores, I think it is safe to say that Williams has once more reinvented his style and approach to orchestration. Once again, *Star Wars* sounds the same, and yet completely different.

70. Listen to "Snoke" (ß).

71. listen to "Lunchtime" (‡), "The Abduction" (‡), and "The Scavenger" (ß).

72. Listen to "The Scavenger" (ß).

73. Listen to "Farewell and the Trip" (ß).

74. Listen to "Finn's Confession" (ß).

Bibliography

Adams 2005

Adams, Doug. 'Revenge of the Sixth', in *Film Score Monthly*, x/3 (August 2005), pp. 33-35.

Anderson 2009

Anderson, Dana. 'The Film Music of John Williams', in: *Sound and Music in Film and Visual Media*, edited by Graeme Harper *et al.*, New York (NY), The Continuum International Publishing Group Inc., 2009, pp. 463-471.

Arundale 2014

Arundale, Scott – Trieu, Tashi. *Modern Post: Workflows and Techniques for Digital Filmmakers*, Hoboken, Taylor and Francis, 2014.

Audissino 2014

Audissino, Emilio. *John Williams's Film Music: «Jaws», «Star Wars», «Raiders of the Lost Ark», and the Return of the Classical Hollywood Music Style*, Madison (WI), University of Wisconsin Press, 2014 (Wisconsin Film Studies).

Audissino 2017

Id. 'John Williams and Contemporary Film Music', in: *Contemporary Film Music: Investigating Cinema Narratives and Composition*, edited by Lindsay Coleman and Joakim Tillman, London, Palgrave Macmillan, 2017, pp. 221-236.

Bazelon 1975

Bazelon, Irwin. *Knowing the Score: Notes on Film Music*, New York (NY), Van Nostrand Reinhold Company, 1975.

Blake 2002

Blake, Larry. '*Star Wars Episode ii: Attack of the Clones*', from <mixonline.com>, 1 June 2002, accessed February 2018.

Bond 2000

Bond, Jeff. 'Phantom Menace Ultimate CD Review', in: *Film Score Monthly*, v/9-10 (November-December 2000), pp. 49-50.

Bouzereau – Duncan 1999

Bouzereau, Laurent – Duncan, Jody. *«Star Wars»: The Making of «Episode i – The Phantom Menace»*, New York (NY), The Ballantine Publishing Group, 1999.

Cinesamples 2013

'Cinesamples Releases Randy's Celeste', from <randykerbermusic.com>, 8 February 2013, accessed February 2018.

Darby – Du Bois 1990

Darby, William – Du Bois, Jack. *American Film Music: Major Composers, Techniques, Trends, 1915-1990*, Jefferson (NC), McFarland & Company, 1990.

Dyer 1999
Dyer, Richard. 'Making *Star Wars* Sing Again', in: *Film Score Monthly*, iv/3 (June 1999), pp. 18-21.

Huvet 2017
Huvet, Chloé. *D'«Un nouvel espoir» (1977) à «La Revanche des Sith» (2005): écriture musicale et traitement de la partition au sein du complexe audio-visuel dans la saga «Star Wars»*, Ph.D. Diss., Rennes, Université Rennes 2; Montréal (QC), Université de Montréal, 2017.

Kasow 2015
Kasow, Todd. Unpublished interview by the author at New York University, 26 April 2015.

Lustig 1980
Lustig, Milton. *Music Editing for Motion Pictures*, New York (NY), Hastings House, 1980 (Communication Art Books).

Thaxton 1999
Thaxton, Ford A. '*Star Wars Episode One: The Phantom Menace*', in: *Soundtrack Magazine*, xviii (Summer 1999), pp. 8-9.

Discography

(†)
• Williams, John. *Star Wars: Episode i – The Phantom Menace. Original Motion Picture Soundtrack*, Sony Classical SK61816, 1999.
(§)
• Id. *Star Wars: Episode i – The Phantom Menace. The Ultimate Edition*, Sony Classical SK89460, 2000.
(Ø)
Id. *Star Wars: Episode ii – Attack of the Clones. Original Motion Picture Soundtrack*, Sony Classical SK89932-B1, 2002.
(Ω)
• Id. *Star Wars: Episode iv – A New Hope. Original Motion Picture Soundtrack*, Sony Classical S2K92950, 2004.
(Δ)
Id. *Star Wars: Episode v: The Empire Strikes Back. Original Motion Picture Soundtrack*, Sony Classical SK92951, 2004.
(£)
• Id. *Star Wars: Episode vi – Return of the Jedi. Original Motion Picture Soundtrack*, Sony Classical S2K92952, 2004.
(€)
• Id. *Star Wars: Episode iii – Revenge of the Sith. Original Motion Picture Soundtrack*, Sony Classical SK94220, 2005.
(‡)
• Id. *Star Wars: The Force Awakens. For Your Consideration – Best Original Score*, Lucasfilm Ltd., 2015.
(ß)
• Id. *Star Wars: The Force Awakens. Original Motion Picture Soundtrack*, Walt Disney Records D002177202, 2015.

The Villain's March Topic in John Williams's Film Music

Joakim Tillman
(Stockholm University)

John Williams is well-known for his striking and memorable themes for heroes like Luke Skywalker, Superman and Indiana Jones. With the exception of the "Imperial March" from the *Star Wars* series, though, his themes for the villains are less familiar. One of the theme types most frequently used to depict evil antagonists in Williams's film music is the villain's march, a style topic with a long history in Hollywood film music. One early example is Franz Waxman's theme for Dr. Pretorius (Ex. 1) in *The Bride of Frankenstein* (James Whale, 1935).

Ex. 1: Franz Waxman's "Dr. Pretorius's Theme" from *The Bride of Frankenstein* (© 1935 ASCAP), published by USI A Music Publishing, ear transcription from the film's soundtrack. Used in compliance with the U.S. Copyright Act, Section 107.

This villain's march displays the characteristic features exploited by Williams: a minor key march with a chromatic twist, often involving the tritone (the 'diabolus in musica')[1], which in this theme appears in the succession of two triads, C minor and F-sharp minor, whose roots are an augmented fourth apart. This chapter explores how Williams has been able to vary this seemingly simple formula depending on the kind of villains at hand, and the nature and degree of their evil. Besides characterizing the villains, the villain's march has many other narrative functions that will be analysed. For instance, it is used to underline the threat from the villains when they have the upper hand in the struggle between good

[1]. Latin for 'the devil in music', a supposedly late medieval nickname for the tritone (an augmented fourth or a diminished fifth), which was considered a dissonant and unstable interval. See Drabkin 2008 for a concise exposition of the tritone and its history. In nineteenth century Romantic opera, as Drabkin points out, «the tritone regularly portrays that which is ominous or evil».

and evil. Thus, the villain's march often functions like a negative counterpart to the hero's theme, which is used to lean on the thrill button (to use Steven Spielberg's expression[2]) when something heroic occurs. However, sometimes the villain's march also suggests the workings of evil even when the villains themselves are not explicitly present.

Williams's villain marches and their narrative functions are examined in six films: *Family Plot* (Alfred Hitchcock, 1976), *Superman* (Richard Donner, 1978), *Star Wars: Episode V – The Empire Strikes Back* (Irvin Kershner, 1980), *Indiana Jones and the Last Crusade* (Steven Spielberg, 1989), *Home Alone* (Chris Columbus, 1990), and *Harry Potter and the Sorcerer's Stone* (Chris Columbus, 2001). The disposition does not follow the films in chronological order, though, but starts with the most evil villains and ends with the comic burglars in *Home Alone*.

THE "IMPERIAL MARCH"

As the "Imperial March" is Williams's most well-known villain's theme, and also one of the most analysed[3], it is a good starting point for a discussion of this topic in his film music. The theme (Ex. 2a) is structured as a sentence[4], and starts with a two-measure basic idea which is followed by its varied repetition (mm. 3-4). The continuation (mm. 5-8) introduces more overt chromaticism, and the tritone appears in the harmonic progression between G minor and C-sharp minor.

Ex. 2a: John Williams's the "Imperial March", from *The Empire Strikes Back* (© 1980 BMI), published by Bantha Music/Warner-Tamerlane, ear transcription from the film's soundtrack. Used in compliance with the U.S. Copyright Act, Section 107.

However, only eight of the almost forty statements of the theme in *The Empire Strikes Back* feature the continuation. Because of the dominance of the basic idea and its varied repetition, the most salient feature of the theme is the progression between two minor triads whose roots are a major third apart. Matthew Bribitzer-Stull names this the "Tarnhelm" progression after the Tarnhelm motif in Richard Wagner's *Der Ring des Nibelungen*, the first example he has found that thematicizes the progression instead of just

[2]. SPIELBERG 1989.

[3]. For instance by BRIBITZER-STULL 2015, p. 149, BUHLER 2000, pp. 44-49, KALINAK 1992, pp. 194-198, and RICHARDS 2015B.

[4]. See ZACHAROPOULOS 2017, p. 258, and pp. 239-240 for a general presentation of this theme type in Williams's film music, using the *Superman* march as an example.

using it as an isolated foreground event. He points out that it «came to exhibit a remarkable commonality of connotation throughout the later nineteenth century, frequently evoking the sinister, the eerie, and the eldritch»[5]. He also calls attention to the importance of the "Tarnhelm" progression in film music for such genres as science fiction, fantasy and horror after 1975[6], and mentions the "Imperial March" as one of the most familiar examples[7].

On soundtrack recordings and in the published orchestral suite, the concert arrangement of the theme, "The Imperial March", has the subheading "Darth Vader's Theme" added in brackets. This indicates that the theme has a double association. According to Michael Matessino the theme is a «dark, but fun musical depiction of the might of the Empire which serves as a malevolent 'Hail to the Chief' for its principal figure, Darth Vader»[8], and in his liner notes for the special edition of the soundtrack, Matessino interchangeably uses the expressions the Imperial theme and Darth Vader's theme.

The opening of the Imperial theme (mm. 1-4) is introduced at the very beginning of *The Empire Strikes Back* as the camera pans down to reveal an imperial Star Destroyer. Played by the piccolo and not yet harmonized with the "Tarnhelm" progression, this statement of the theme is a far less imposing representation of evil than most versions heard later in the film. In this way it is a reminder that the Empire for now is a potential threat rather than an imminent danger. However, even though the association with the Empire is suggested, the theme's associations are not clearly defined until the imperial fleet and Darth Vader are first presented about twenty minutes later. In the previous scene, the rebels realized that the transmission from the imperial probe probably means that the Empire has discovered their secret base. Therefore, now the imperial fleet has become a real and imposing threat, and this gives rise to the first grand statement of the theme. As Matessino points out, the original music composed for this sequence was replaced with the opening of the concert arrangement, "The Imperial March", in the film[9]. The concert version opens with four measures of a martial rhythm pattern (Ex. 2b) which then accompanies the presentation of the complete Imperial theme (with two statements of the continuation).

Ex. 2b: John Williams's the "Imperial March", from *The Empire Strikes Back* (© 1980 BMI), published by Bantha Music/Warner-Tamerlane, ear transcription from the film's soundtrack. Used in compliance with the U.S. Copyright Act, Section 107.

5. Bribitzer-Stull 2015, p. 140.

6. *Ibidem*, pp. 133-134.

7. *Ibidem*, p. 149.

8. Matessino 1997, p. 6.

9. *Ibidem*, p. 12.

The cut from exterior shots of the imperial fleet to Vader on the bridge of his Star Destroyer occurs around the fourth beat in the first measure of the continuation (in its second statement). Introducing Vader in conjunction with the tritone progression of the theme is apt, but the theme's double association is more obvious in the music Williams originally composed for the scene[10]. The original music also begins with the martial rhythm, in a slightly different and shorter version, which then continues as the trombones play the first four measures of the Imperial theme. On the cut to Vader a second statement of the theme's opening four measures follow (with doublings in high woodwinds added for mm. 3-4), and it is this second presentation that introduces the full "Tarnhelm" harmonization.

When Captain Piett calls out to get Admiral Ozzel's attention, the tracked music from "The Imperial March" ends, and the cue continues as originally composed by Williams[11]. The exchange of views between the two officers is underscored with the continuation (mm. 5-8), which without the tracking of the concert version would have been the first appearance of this part of the Imperial theme in the film. Vader leaves the bridge and joins his officers. As he asks, «You have found something?» the "Tarnhelm" progression, without the theme, is heard in low trombones to indicate that the imperial threat to the rebels is about to become a reality. Vader looks at the computer screen and his immediate understanding that they have found the rebel's secret base is followed by the introductory martial rhythm. However the Imperial theme does not follow because Admiral Ozzel tries to raise objections to the conclusion of his superior commander. Vader interrupts him and orders the Admiral to set course for the Hoth system and then instructs General Veers to prepare his men. The martial rhythm starts again and the scene is brought to an end with a *fortissimo* statement of the Imperial theme's first two measures in the French horns. This scene, then, clearly establishes two of the Imperial theme's major associations, the Empire and Darth Vader, and also demonstrates several of its narrative functions: underscoring the imposing threat of the imperial fleet, characterizing Vader as dangerous and evil, and emphasizing his sinister intentions and actions.

According to Richards, the associations for Vader's theme are more narrowly defined that those for the Force theme. He states that the Force theme «does not have a single, consistent association, but instead can signify four interrelated concepts»[12]:

---

[10]. The original music for the scene can be heard on the Special Edition 2-CD set (BMG Classics 09026-68747-2, 1997), CD1, track 4 "The Imperial Probe/Aboard the Executor", 2:44-end of track. This source also reveals that the music originally started during the preceding scene in the rebel base, and a *piano* statement of the first two measures of the Imperial theme (in muted horns) was probably intended to follow C-3PO's line, «It could be an imperial code».

[11]. As the concert version, "The Imperial March", and the unused part of the cue are in the same key, G minor, and end with a return of the introductory martial rhythm, the transition between the tracked music and the original cue is smooth and completely seamless.

[12]. Richards 2015a.

- Character – Obi-Wan/the Jedi
- The Force – or Becoming a Jedi
- Struggle – of the Jedi/Good Guys
- Victory – of the Jedi/Good Guys

However, a similar scheme can be made for the Imperial theme:

- Character – Darth Vader/the Empire
- The Dark Side of the Force – or Turning to the Dark side of the Force
- Evil Action – of the Empire/Bad Guys
- Victory – of the Empire/Bad Guys

As Richards points out, most of the establishing shots of the imperial fleet in in *The Empire Strikes Back* are accompanied by the Imperial theme[13], and that also applies to other exterior shots of the fleet. In all, this accounts for almost a fourth of the theme's appearances in the film. In order to emphasize the imposing power and the magnitude of the threat represented by the Star Destroyers, the majority of these presentations are *fortissimo* statements with the theme played in octaves by four trumpets and four trombones. Maybe there was a feeling that this deployment of the theme risked being overused, and in two later occurrences it was replaced with just the introductory martial rhythm, while in another one it was not used at all[14]. Powerful statements in the brass are also used to underscore the success of the Empire and Vader. For instance, when imperial troops make their way into the rebel base on Hoth, the theme starts as Vader is revealed, and it returns moments later when he enters the rebel's abandoned command centre.

Kathryn Kalinak notes that the Imperial theme appears throughout *The Empire Strikes Back* when Vader's «presence literally or figuratively looms over the narrative»[15]. Sometimes it just emphasizes Vader as a figure of imposing evil, but more often it is used to express what Richards aptly designates «evil in action»[16], or what in a similar manner could be called evil intentions. For instance the theme is heard when Vader kills Admiral Ozzel, when he enters the prison cell in Cloud City to torture Han Solo, when the prisoners are taken to the carbon-freezing chamber, and when the platform lowers Han into the carbon-freezing equipment. Throughout the film, the theme is also deployed when Vader gives orders to his subordinate officers, usually planning some sort of action against the rebels, and also when these officers perform their orders (as when General

13. Richards 2015b.

14. The statement opening R6P3 was not used, while the appearances ending R6P5-R7P1 and R7P3 were replaced. The original versions can be heard on the special edition of the soundtrack album (see note 11).

15. Kalinak 1992, p. 197.

16. Richards 2015b.

Veers issues commands to his crew in the imperial snow walker, and later when the walker approaches its target and destroys the rebels' main power generators, disabling their energy shield defence). In these usages the dynamics vary between *mezzo forte* and *fortissimo* depending on the dramaturgic weight of the situation, or on practicalities like whether the theme is underscoring dialogue or not, and the theme is most often played by unison French horns supported by other brass instruments. According to Williams: «In the case of Darth Vader, brass suggests itself because of his military bearing and his authority and his ominous look. That would translate into a strong melody that's military, that grabs you right away, that is, probably simplistically, in a minor mode because he's threatening»[17]. In a couple of instances, though, the theme is orchestrated in different ways. When Lando Calrissian learns that his agreement with the Empire has been changed, he objects to the new conditions. After Vader's reply, «Perhaps you think you're being treated unfairly?» a *piano* rendition of the Imperial theme in low woodwinds ominously suggest the tenor of this veiled threat before Vader spells it out, «Good. It would be unfortunate if I had to leave a garrison here». And later when Calrissian protests against further alterations of the deal, a sinister statement in clarinets and oboes underscore Vader's response, «Pray I don't alter it any further». Thus, in contrast to the explicit evil displayed in Vader's actions against the rebels, and failing officers, the implied threats of evil consequences are accompanied by more subdued versions of the Imperial theme.

As indicated above, another association of the Imperial theme is the dark side of the Force. This association is suggested when Vader uses the Force to kill Admiral Ozzel. However, it is made explicit when the shimmering materialization of Ben warns Luke that he «will be tempted by the dark side of the Force», and the theme starts on the last words. As this is not yet an actual reality but a dark prophesy, a variation of the theme is played softly by bass clarinet and bassoons. The "Tarnhelm" progression, though, emphasizes the potential danger if Luke rushes off to help his friends instead of completing his training with Yoda. During this training, earlier in the film, Yoda teaches Luke that, «If once you start down the dark path forever will it dominate your destiny. Consume you it will as it did Obi-Wan's apprentice». In the unused cue that Williams composed for this training montage, these words are underscored with the first two measures of the Imperial theme, and as Luke replies «Vader», measures 3-4 follow[18]. Luke then wonders if the dark side is stronger. Yoda denies this, but explains that it is quicker, easier, and more seductive. During the last part of the film the Imperial theme is used to underscore Vader's seductive attempts to turn Luke to the dark side. The opening four measures of the theme follow the revelation that Vader is Luke's father, and the continuation accompany Vader's words that the emperor has foreseen that Luke

17. Byrd 1997, p. 20.

18. CD 1, track 11 "The Training of a Jedi Knight/The Magic Tree", 0:36-0:55 on the special edition of the soundtrack album (see note 11).

will destroy him, «It is your destiny. Join me, and together we can rule the galaxy as father and son». While the first four bars are rendered *forte* by all the six French horns to emphasize Luke's reaction, measures 5-8 are played by the English horn and two clarinets. The English horn is an instrument frequently associated with the Force theme, and together with Vader's words, the alluring, unspoken message is that the dark side is not fundamentally different and that Luke could use it for good purposes. Later, back on the bridge of his Star Destroyer, Vader uses the Force to reach out to Luke, who now is on the Millennium Falcon after having been rescued by Leia and Calrissian. To underline the distance between the characters and the telepathic nature of the communication, the Imperial theme is played softly by flutes and E♭ clarinet in high register. Here the theme is not harmonized with the "Tarnhelm" progression, but with a minor triad with the seventh in the bass, a convention that Williams describes as «an old signal of some evil, militaristic doer»[19]. Another transformation of the Imperial theme gives expression to Vader's resignation after the Millennium Falcon escapes into hyperspace. As Vader leaves the bridge of his Star Destroyer a statement of measure 3-4 begins. Admiral Piett looks to Vader with terror, but Vader just passes him without taking notice, and instead of ending resolutely in the usual way, the theme continues with the broken C-minor triad slowly descending towards the bass (Ex. 2c).

Ex. 2c: John Williams's the "Imperial March", from *The Empire Strikes Back* (© 1980 BMI), published by Bantha Music/Warner-Tamerlane, ear transcription from the film's soundtrack. Used in compliance with the U.S. Copyright Act, Section 107.

Nazi Villains

The march of the Nazis in *Indiana Jones and the Last Crusade* is a succinct and resolute motif that is never developed into a complete theme (Ex. 3). To emphasize the evilness of the Nazis, the motif ends on the raised fourth scale degree, and this tritone is emphasized by a *sforzando* and an unresolved dissonant chord (a French sixth) that contains two tritones.

[19]. Quoted in Audissino 2014, p. 153. In *Star Wars: Episode iv – A New Hope* (George Lucas, 1977), Williams brings together the convention of two minor triads whose roots are a major third apart and the minor chord with the seventh in the bass. When Darth Vader makes his first entrance there is a chord progression between B-flat minor and D minor over the C♯ in the bass.

Ex. 3: John Williams's Nazi march, from *Indiana Jones and the Last Crusade* (© 1989 BMI), published by Bantha Music, ear transcription from the film's soundtrack. Used in compliance with the U.S. Copyright Act, Section 107.

In contrast to Darth Vader the Nazis are real-life villains, and their motif does not exploit a cultural musical code like the "Tarnhelm" progression, which is associated with science fiction and fantasy. Apart from the chromatic tail ending with the augmented fourth, the Nazi motif is diatonic and could be an ominous version in minor of a real German march. Actually, the book burning rally in the film is accompanied by one of the most famous German military marches, "Der Königrätzer". Composed in 1866 by Johann Gottfried Piepfke (1817-1884), this march can be heard Leni Riefenstahl's Nazi propaganda film *Triumph of the Will* (1935). In *Indiana Jones and the Last Crusade* it is used as diegetic music to underline the frenzy of the crowd from the perspective of the Nazis. Williams's sinister Nazi motif, though, functions as commentary from the non-diegetic orchestral narration, and underscores the evilness of the Nazis. Such a use of diegetic and non-diegetic music to represent Nazi and anti-Nazi points of view has a precedent in *Casablanca* (Michael Curtiz, 1942). In one scene the German soldiers sing "Die Wacht am Rhein" [Watch on the Rhine], a nineteenth century patriotic song, to give expression to their nationalist feelings (before they are drowned out by "La Marseillaise"), but throughout his score Max Steiner represents the Nazi Germans, particularly Major Strasser, with sinister versions in minor keys of the "Deutschlandlied".

The Nazi motif is not deployed as frequently as the Imperial theme in *The Empire Strikes Back*. An obvious reason for this is that the Nazi motif is introduced rather late in *The Last Crusade*. It is first heard, almost halfway through the film, when Vogel, the Nazi colonel, enters the large hall in the Castle of Brunwald with the captive Indy and his father being ushered in behind him. A couple of minutes later, when Marcus Brody's hiding-place turns out to be the back of a Nazi truck, the motif returns as the swastika is seen on the rear door that is slammed behind Brody[20]. Thus, the association of the motif with the Nazis is confirmed, but at the same time the motif also indicates that the capture of Marcus will put Indy and his father in mortal danger. This is made explicit in the next scene where Indy and his father are sitting tied back-to-back in a pair of chairs. Vogel wishes to kill

[20]. Apart from this ending of the cue, the music composed by Williams was not used in the film. As can be heard on *Indiana Jones: The Soundtrack Collection* (disc 5, track 7, "Marcus is Captured/To Berlin"), the cue also starts with a statement of the Nazi motif which, given that the scene was not re-edited, should have started after Sallah's line that there is no museum in Iskenderun when one of the two men in black suits and hats asks for his papers. Thus, the music should have confirmed what the classical Hollywood dress code for villains had already suggested at the first appearance of these sinister men.

them immediately, but Elsa states that if they fail to recover from Brody the missing diary pages about the location of the Grail, they will need the Joneses alive.

When Donovan is leaving the castle, he gets a message telling that the Germans have Brody and the map, and another message from Berlin follows, stating that by personal command of the Führer the American conspirators should be eliminated. This sequence is underscored with a threefold statement of the Nazi motif. The first accompanies Vogel as he opens the car door for Donovan to let him get in, the second starts when Donovan gets and reads the first message, and the third follows on the last word, «map», and continues as the second message is delivered. Even though Donovan's concluding words to Vogel, «Germany has declared war on the Jones boys», is not accompanied by the Nazi motif, these words seem to encapsulate the narrative significance of the motif. The Nazi motif is heard every time the Wehrmacht has the upper hand in their war against Indy and his father (significantly, the motif is not introduced when Indy first discovers the presence of Nazis in the Brunwald castle). For instance, during the motorbike escape from the castle, the motif is heard when four Nazis on motorcycles appear behind Indy and Henry, chasing down the road after them. And later in the film, during the crossing of the desert towards the site of the Grail, the motif emphasizes the threat of the panzer tank when it appears behind Vogel, and a second statement accompanies the following long shot of Donovan's imposing exploration party. The motif returns when Henry is captured by the Nazis after trying to rescue Brody in the tank. And when Indy leaps onto the tank to save his father, the Nazi motif is heard as a close-up shows Vogel hate-staring at Indy in the turret. This is the final appearance of the motif in the film, making it clear that it is not associated with Donovan. Despite being the main villain of the film, he has very little screen time, and is not provided with a leitmotif. The association of the motif is with the Nazis, or more specifically, with Nazi military.

In comparison with the Imperial theme in *The Empire Strikes Back*, the Nazi motif in *The Last Crusade* is much less varied. The dynamics are loud and the orchestration is dominated by the brass, most often with trumpets playing the theme, and percussion in military style. The only exception is the presentation in muted French horns doubled by oboes and clarinets when Donovan reads the message about Brody's capture, but this more subdued version is probably caused by the need for the dialogue to be heard. The narrative functions of the Nazi motif are also more limited than those of the Imperial theme. One exception is the statement accompanying the shots of the huge Zeppelin as Indy and Henry leave the terminal building in Berlin. After boarding the airship, they sit down and with relief Indy states, «Well we made it». But the previous statement of the Nazi motif undermines his words, and we understand that they are still in peril. Of course, the swastika briefly seen at the Zeppelin's rudder also indicate that the «first available flight out of Germany» probably is not the safest one. The Zeppelin, though, is a civilian means of transportation and this presentation of the motif, with the melody in the French horns, does not feature percussion. After Indy realizes that the Zeppelin is turning around to take them back to Germany, the military character returns when the Nazi motif underscores the exterior shot of the U-turning airship. It is noteworthy that the motif is not used before the take off as Indy looks out the window and sees Vogel making his way to the Zeppelin. From the very start, the music sets a comedic tone for this scene, preparing for the «No ticket» gag, instead of hinting at potential danger.

The Evil Wizard

In *Harry Potter and the Sorcerer's Stone* there are no less than three themes for the main antagonist, the evil wizard Voldemort, but as the first theme is not a villain's march, I will not consider it in this essay[21]. Jamie Lynn Webster notes that they are related to each other: «All three themes are in duple meter, are performed at moderate tempi, have overtly chromatic melodies, and are relatively short (two to four measures long). As well, all three include dotted rhythms [...]»[22]. Another common feature is the prominent role played by the raised fourth scale degree, but Bribitzer-Stull points out that tritones and chromatic double neighbour notes around the fifth scale degree are common to a number of themes in Williams's scores for the first three *Harry Potter* films[23], not just the Voldemort themes. At first glance it may appear odd that the music for the protagonist and the antagonist share the same features. However, there is a narrative logic to this. When Voldemort tried to kill the baby Harry, he transferred some of his abilities to him, creating a connection between them. Also, as Michael L. Klein writes, «Within a universe of codes there is an economy of the musical sign that allows it to participate in more than one topic»[24]. According to Webster the martial rhythms, pervasive chromaticism and emphasis on brass and dark strings are characteristics that set the third Voldemort theme apart from the themes signifying benevolent magic or emotions, «which tend to use triple meter, lilting rhythms, and moderate chromaticism»[25].

Even though the themes in Exs. 4a and 4b both are associated with Voldemort, they address two different aspects of the character. As Webster notes, the first «tends to

---

[21]. For an insightful analysis of this theme, see Webster 2009, pp. 423-425.

[22]. *Ibidem*, p. 422.

[23]. Bribitzer-Stull 2015, p. 60. Chromatic neighbour notes, though, is a feature that Williams's also explores in themes for other films. For instance, it appears in the villain's march in *Home Alone* (see Ex. 7), like the first two instalments in the *Harry Potter* series a film directed by Chris Columbus, and in the Unicorn theme in *The Adventures of Tintin* (Steven Spielberg, 2011).

[24]. Klein 2005, p. 56.

[25]. Webster 2009, p. 428 and 422. However, I believe Webster's claim about pervasive versus moderate chromaticism is somewhat overstated. For instance, both Voldemort 2 and the most frequent version of Hedwig B feature two instances of the raised fourth scale degree.

align with indirect references to and the imminent presence of the adversary Voldemort», while the second «aligns with direct visual or dialogue references to Voldemort»[26]. The Voldemort 1 theme is first heard when Ollivander tells Harry that it is curious that he should be destined for the wand whose brother gave him his scar.

Ex. 4a: John Williams's "Voldemort 1", from *Harry Potter and the Sorcerer's Stone* (© 2001 BMI), published by Warner-Barham Music, ear transcription from the film's soundtrack. Used in compliance with the U.S. Copyright Act, Section 107.

Just moments later the theme is repeated a half-step up, heightening the dramatic tension, when Ollivander states that He-Who-Must-Not-Be-Named did great things even though his actions were terrible[27]. Back at the Leaky Cauldron Harry requests Hagrid to confirm his suspicion that he who killed his parents was the one who gave him the scar. After some hesitation, Hagrid tells Harry that not all wizards are good. In the unused music Williams composed for this conversation, Voldemort 1 accompanies Hagrid's reply[28]. In the film the music starts after the name of Voldemort has been uttered for the first time. As Hagrid starts to tell Harry about Voldemort, the Voldemort 2 theme is introduced, in G minor, as the evil wizard is seen, in a flashback, approaching the house of Harry's parents.

Ex. 4b: John Williams's "Voldemort 2", from *Harry Potter and the Sorcerer's Stone* (© 2001 BMI), published by Warner-Barham Music, ear transcription from the film's soundtrack. Used in compliance with the U.S. Copyright Act, Section 107.

When Voldemort kills Harry's mother the theme is stated again, in A minor providing another use of expressive tonality to increase tension. After Hagrid's flashback, Harry wonders what happened to the evil wizard, but he refrains from spelling out the name, and rephrases his question, «To You-Know-Who?». Voldemort 1 returns and underscores Hagrid's opinion that those who say that Voldemort died are mistaken, «Nope, I reckon he's out there still too tired to carry on».

---

[26]. *Ibidem*, pp. 425-426.

[27]. As Bribitzer-Stull 2015, p. 282, points out when discussing this scene, the repetition of a passage transposed up by semitone (or tone), rising the intensification, is a Wagnerian technique and he uses Wagner scholar Robert Bailey's concept of 'expressive tonality' for this phenomenon.

[28]. There is no official soundtrack release of this cue, 3M1 "Hagrid's Flashback" (*Harry Potter and the Sorcerer's Stone* (2001) – Complete Cue List, <http://www.jwfan.com/?p=3600>, accessed February 2018), but it can be heard on YouTube (<https://www.youtube.com/watch?v=VDS3czom13k>, accessed accessed February 2018).

In all the three statements of Voldemort 1, as well as in the unused version, the theme is played by muted French horns and low woodwinds (bass clarinet and bassoons) supported by low dyads in muted trombone and tuba (muted brass are regularly associated with evil in Williams's film music). The character is sinister, and the narrative function is to support Hagrid's belief that evil is still lurking in the shadows. The next time Voldemort 1 returns, much later in the film, is in the Forbidden Forest when Harry encounters some creature drinking the blood of a unicorn. The theme starts when the hooded figure gets on its feet and starts to approach Harry. Harry is feeling his scar burning, and the music gives expression to the suspicion that the monstrous creature may be Voldemort. To emphasize that evil is now emerging from the shadows, the theme is played *fortissimo* by French horns, trombones (both muted and open) and tuba, giving it a much more menacing character than before. Harry falls and as the hooded figure continues to approach, Voldemort 2 follows in trumpet and woodwinds, confirming that it indeed is the evil wizard. As this theme starts the camera angle changes to an over the shoulder shot from Voldemort's perspective, and it underlines that his intention is to kill Harry.

The two Voldemort themes are used in the same way when Harry finds Professor Quirrell in the chamber where the philosopher's stone is hidden. A statement of Voldemort 1 starts as a hissing disembodied voice is heard, requesting to speak to Harry, and when Quirrel unwraps his turban another statement follows. Both these statements are subdued, but when Voldemort's face is seen in the mirror, a more forceful version is played by flute, alto flutes, bassoons, French horns, and a muted trombone to emphasize the return of the evil wizard. Voldemort greets Harry, and as Harry utters his name the music continues *mezzo piano* with Voldemort 2 in low French horns, bassoons and bass clarinet. The French horns now play without mutes, but otherwise these are the same instruments and register most often used for the Voldemort 1 theme. The reasons for this choice of timbre are suggested by Voldemort's complaint that he does not have a body of his own, but must live off another as a mere parasite. A similar dark statement of Voldemort 2 is heard in the Forbidden Forest. After Firenze, the centaur, has told Harry about the terrible price you have to pay for killing a unicorn, Harry's suspicions are confirmed and he asks, «Do you mean to say that that thing that killed the unicorn, that was drinking its blood, that was Voldemort?». At the words «that thing», Voldemort 2 begins in bass clarinet, French horns and trombones.

The most forceful presentations of the second Voldemort theme, with trumpets and/or shrieking woodwinds, are reserved for those moments when Voldemort tries to kill Harry, as in Hagrid's flashback, in the Forbidden Forest, and during the Quidditch game. In the latter scene Hermione assumes that it is Snape who is jinxing with Harry's broom. As Webster points out, the music suggests that Snape is the servant of Voldemort, but, retrospectively, the music also corresponds with the yet unknown information that Quirrel is the one who cast the jinx and is the actual servant of the evil wizard[29]. Other statements

29. Webster 2009, p. 427.

by piercing woodwinds, but with somewhat lower dynamics, accompany Voldemort when he asks Harry to join him and promises to revive his parents if he gives him the stone. The music reveals Voldemort's unspoken motives, that is, with the Elixir of life he will be able to regain a body of his own, and carry on with his evil plans. However, Harry has already figured this out. In a previous scene after he understood that the hooded figure in the Forbidden was Voldemort, the centaur asks Harry if he knows what is hidden in the school. «The Philosopher's stone», answers Harry, and a *piano* statement of Voldemort 2 in flute, clarinet, celesta and harp, externalize his realization that Voldemort is after the Stone, and also why he wants it.

The two last statements of Voldemort 1 and 2 in *The Sorcerer's Stone* appear after Quirrell's demise. When Harry looks at the ashes that is all what remains of Quirrell, Voldemort 1 is played by low woodwinds, tuba and double basses. The low instruments and register makes this the darkest version of the theme in the film, and it suggests that even though Harry has vanquished Voldemort for now, the evil wizard has not disappeared for good. And indeed, Voldemort's spirit rises from the ashes and passes through Harry on its way out, a moment underscored with a *forte* statement of Voldemort 2 led by the trumpets, which emphasize that Voldemort will return with the intention of killing Harry.

THE MYSTERY VILLAINS

Family Plot, Alfred Hitchcock's last film, follows two couples, first separately but eventually the two plot lines are intertwined. Blanche Tyler is a fake medium who engage her boyfriend George Lumley, a cab driver, in the search for the lost heir of a rich elderly woman. Forty years earlier she had the son of her unmarried sister adopted, and if Blanche finds the boy, Edward Shoebridge, she will get a big reward. The other pair, the jeweller Arthur Adamson and his accomplice Fran, is a couple of hardened and sophisticated criminals who kidnap important people and demand precious diamonds as ransom.

The film begins with establishing the Blanche and George part of the intrigue. After a quarter of an hour, a mysterious woman, later identified as Fran, is seen crossing the street by George and Blanche in a point-of-view shot through the windshield of George's cab. In the following exterior shot the cab drives away and the camera pans and zooms in on Fran. This clever transition from the first plot line to the second provides a subtle hint that there eventually will be a connection between them. When the half-shot of Fran reveals that she is walking towards a sentry booth, an ominous ostinato (Ex. 5a) is introduced in the ARP synthesizer and the villain's theme (Ex. 5b) follows in the harpsichord and the strings.

Ex. 5a: John Williams's "Villain's Ostinato", from *Family Plot* (© 1976 BMI), published by USI B Music Publishing, ear transcription from the film's soundtrack. Used in compliance with the U.S. Copyright Act, Section 107.

Ex. 5b: John Williams's "Villain's Theme", from *Family Plot* (© 1976 BMI), published by USI B Music Publishing, ear transcription from the film's soundtrack. Used in compliance with the U.S. Copyright Act, Section 107.

Besides the sound of the harpsichord, the villain's theme is characterized by other traits reminiscent of eighteenth century music as the Alberti bass and certain melodic-rhythmic patterns (especially in mm. 3-4). However, these traits also appear in the theme for Blanche and George's sleuthing activities and are not unique for the villain's theme[30].

The villain's theme opens with a broken minor triad with a major seventh. Because of its importance in Bernard Herrmann's music for Hitchcock films, especially *Vertigo* (1958) and *Psycho* (1960), Royal S. Brown refers to this chord as the «Hitchcock cord»[31]. Herrmann was a close friend of Williams's, and even though the working relationship between Herrmann and Hitchcock had ended on a sour note a decade earlier, Williams looked for Herrmann's permission when asked to score *Family Plot*. A phone call to Herrmann cleared the matter when the older composer told Williams to «go ahead and do it»[32]. Therefore, Williams's reference to the «Hitchcock chord» is quite probably a conscious homage to an esteemed colleague. Like the other villain's themes considered in this chapter, the one in *Family Plot* features the tritone. When the basic idea is repeated in measure 5-6[33], the D♯ is harmonized with an A-minor chord, that is, it forms an augmented fourth with the root of the chord, and the interval also appears in measure 7 between G and C♯ in the melody.

30. For *Sleuth* (Joseph L. Mankiewicz, 1972), a film about a writer of detective novels, John Addison composed quasi-baroque music played by harpsichord, and in the 1960s Ron Goodwin used the harpsichord in his music for several films based on Agatha Christie's Miss Marple novels.

31. Brown 1994, p. 189.

32. Sullivan 2006, p. 310.

33. The theme is structured as a period. See Zacharopoulos 2017, p. 260 (who uses the designation Shoebridge theme), and pp. 241-243 for a general presentation of this theme type in Williams's film music.

The villain's theme appears five times in the scene where it is introduced. The first statement ends when the mysterious woman reaches a police sergeant in the sentry booth. After a phone call, the sergeant tells the woman to follow him, and the theme starts again, a half-step up to increase the tension. Upon entering the building the woman is revealed to have a gun in her hand, and as she slowly approaches the desk, a third, rhythmically augmented statement is played by low woodwinds. It is now revealed that the mysterious woman is a criminal who has arrived to collect the ransom, an enormous diamond, for a kidnapping victim. The police ask for assurance that the victim is still alive. The woman does not answer, but hands over a written note. When the police read the note a fourth statement of the theme, in A minor, is played by the harpsichord alone. The fifth statement, a half-step up in B-flat minor, starts as the party leaves the building and moves to the police helicopter that will transport the mysterious woman to a place of her choice.

After the helicopter has landed, the first two measures of the villain's theme return in the ARP synthesizer when the mysterious woman disappears into the dark wood, and it sets the mood for the introduction of Arthur Adamson who will turn out to be the criminal mastermind behind the kidnappings, and is the main villain of the film. Back at Adamson's house, the villain's ostinato starts as Fran states, «I don't know what's come over me tonight. I'm tingling all». The villain's theme then accompanies Adamson's answer, «I told you about danger didn't I? First it makes you sick. Then when you get through it, it makes you very, very loving». Thus, at this point in the film the association of the theme with the villains and their criminal activities has been clearly established.

The plot then returns to Blanche and George as the latter follows clues he hopes will lead him to the Shoebridge family and the adopted boy. The next statement of the villains' theme starts when George discovers the Shoebridge graves, and continues during the point of view shots of the two headstones. The theme is played again by the ARP synthesizer, doubled by the harps, in the bass while the high strings play dissonant chords connected by quarter-tone glissandos. The conventions are those of horror film music, but the music does more than provide a ghostly mood. First, the return of the villains' theme suggests that there is a connection between the villains and George's discovery. This will indeed be confirmed later, with the revelation that Edward Shoebridge faked his own death, disappeared and changed his name to Arthur Adamson. Second, as the theme has also been used to underscore the villain's criminal activity, it provides an anticipation of the yet unknown fact that Adamson was responsible for the murder of his adoptive parents. As the caretaker approaches, a variation of the theme is used as a red herring. Two further statements of the theme accompany George's realization that it is strange that there are two graves if the Shoebridge family died at the same time (alto flute and bassoon), and that the parents' headstone is old while the one on Edward's grave is new (bass clarinet, harps and ARP synthesizer). The caretaker can't or won't answer George's questions, but his continued investigations lead him to a Joseph P. Maloney who applied for Edward

Shoebridge's death certificate. When George visits Maloney's gas station, Maloney evades his questions, but as George drives away Maloney writes down his license number. The first two measures of the villain's theme, again played by the ARP synthesizer, do confirm that Maloney did have something to do with Edward Shoebridge's 'death', and in retrospect we also understand that the theme reveals his thought that he has to visit Adamson and tell him about George's visit.

In the immediately following cut to Adamson at the jewellery, the theme starts anew and reminds us of its original association, and further strengthens the suspicion that there is a connection between the two parallel plot lines of the film. This suspicion is confirmed when Maloney turns up in the shop. The following conversation reveals that Adamson was Eddie Shoebridge, and that he was responsible for the death of his adoptive parents, even though it was Maloney who lit the fire. There is no music during this conversation and the next cue start with a stinger when Maloney states that he will track down George and draws a knife. A subdued statement of the villain's theme in harp and electric piano follows as Adamson tells Maloney to go back home, and that he will look into the matter in his own quiet way. In the next part of the film the theme underscores the villains when they check Blanche's address, when they plot to get rid of Blanche and George in a faked accident, and when Adamson gets the news of Maloney's death and states that he will have to kill George and Blanche himself.

At Maloney's funeral his widow informs George that Eddie Shoebridge's new name is Adamson. This revelation is emphasized by the villain's theme (in the ARP). George passes this information on to Blanche, and from this point on the villain's theme is used to indicate that Blanche's search for Adamson is going to put her in a mortal danger, first when she visits the jewellery shop, and then when she arrives at Adamson's house. The theme also accompanies George when he breaks into Adamson's house, without knowing that Blanche was anesthetized and locked into the secret room where the villains hide the victims of their kidnappings. The last statement of the villain's theme appears when Adamson checks that Blanche is still asleep, and leaves the secret room to stage her faked suicide.

At the end of *Family Plot* it is obvious that the villain's theme is principally associated with Arthur Adamson, the main villain of the film. Adamson is a very different kind of villain than Darth Vader, the Nazis and Voldemort. He is not a military leader and he does not have supernatural powers. On the surface, Adamson is an ordinary man who leads a respectable life and has a calm and civilized demeanour. Therefore, his theme is never played by the brass. However, below the surface he is a psychopath who commits crimes for pleasure and not only for profit. An instrument which often plays the villain's theme (and the villain's ostinato) in *Family Plot* is the ARP synthesizer[34]. As Mervyn Cooke

34. Williams's most well-known use of this instrument is in *Close Encounters of the Third Kind* (Steven Spielberg, 1977), where it is heard diegetically in the musical communication with the aliens.

points out, an indelible association between electronics and the irrational was established in the 1940s and still persists today. Cooke mentions Miklós Rózsa's use of the theremin in Hitchcock's *Spellbound* (1945) as one early example where the electronic timbre is related to mental instability[35]. Thus, besides alluding to Herrmann's irrational 'Hitchcock chord', the sound of the ARP synthesizer is Williams's way of suggesting the villain's underlying mental disorder. The villain's theme is also played by other instruments. However, its presentations in strings or high woodwinds appear in scenes where Adamson's accomplice Fran runs his errands, or later when Blanche is looking for him.

The Comic Villains

In *Superman* (Richard Donner, 1978) the concert arrangement of the theme for Lex Luthor and Otis is explicitly labelled "The March of the Villains" (Ex. 6).

Ex. 6: John Williams's "The March of the Villains", from *Superman* (© 1978 BMI), published by Warner-Barham Music, ear transcription from the film's soundtrack. Used in compliance with the U.S. Copyright Act, Section 107.

The theme opens pompously with the tonic on the downbeat followed by a dotted rhythm on the dominant leading back to the tonic. However, the start of the theme is often undermined by a kind of hiccup in the form of a grace note preceding the first tonic on the downbeat. And then in the second measure the theme goes awry with a chromatically altered descending scale which ends in a syncopated rhythm having the effect of a stumble. Thus, the pompous and pretentious façade of the theme is subverted by features that make the music sound comical[36].

Like the Nazi motif in *Indiana Jones and the Last Crusade*, the villains' theme in *Superman* is introduced rather late, when we first see Otis almost one hour into the film, and of all the villain's themes considered in this chapter, the one in *Superman* is the most sparsely used. In its first presentation the theme is played by the bassoons, an instrument often referred to as the clown of the orchestra. When discussing «traditional connotative

[35]. Cooke 2008, pp. 113-114.

[36]. Unlike the other villain marches discussed in this chapter, this theme is not unequivocally in a minor key, but hovers between major and minor modes in an indeterminate way.

associations evoked by instrumental colours», Claudia Gorbman refers to Eric Sarnett's observation that «chubby-faced bassoons» are heard «when a fat man is seen coming along»[37].

The theme returns, after the dialogue between two cops tailing Otis, when he approaches a newspaper stand. Here the orchestration of the theme closely follows the action. A muted trumpet plays the first measure, but as Otis causally addresses the blind keeper of the stand, «Hey, Matt», the theme innocently continues in the flute. Otis pays for the newspaper, but steals a pretzel, and the third measure in the bassoon provides a humorous touch to this petty crime. He then tries to slip away accompanied by the fourth measure in the sneaky sound of the bass clarinet. However, the blind man's dog barks and catches Otis red-handed. «Okay. All right. See, I'm paying him. I got a pretzel too», says Otis, feigning an air of offended innocence. This is underlined by the villains' march in high woodwinds, in a new key to stress the surprise of being caught and the disappointment for a misdemeanour gone awry, but at the word pretzel the bassoons return to play the concluding measures of the theme in the original key.

When Otis enters the secret door leading to Luthor's lair the music starts again, and as he eats his peanuts the villains' march is played by the tuba. Like the bassoon, this is also an instrument often used in association with fat characters (as parodied in the *Family Guy* episode where Stewie follows overweight people playing the tuba[38]), or generally big, lumbering creatures. A notable example in John Williams's output is the tuba theme for Jabba the Hutt in *Star Wars: Episode VI – The Return of the Jedi* (Richard Marquand, 1983). In an unused portion of the «Introducing Otis» cue, the villain's march on the tuba (doubled by flutes four octaves higher) was to have accompanied an earlier cut to Otis eating a candy bar while walking through the train station.

The villain's march returns in the scene where Luthor stages a fake car accident in order to halt the truck convoy. Played by the tuba, the theme starts at the cut to Otis, who is using a tree branch like camouflage before sneaking aboard the missile transport. After a cross-cut to the military diverted by Miss Teshmacher lying seemingly unconscious on the road, a second statement in pizzicato strings accompanies Otis reprogramming the missiles. The use of pizzicato strings for sneaking and stealth has a long history in film music, and in *Superman* Williams also exploited this convention in the unused part of the cue «Introducing Otis», when Otis jumps down on the track and sneaks into the train tunnel leading to Luthor's lair. Finally, the villain's theme is heard a third time, in the tuba, as Otis returns to Luther and Miss Teschmacher in the ambulance.

---

37. Gorbman 1987, p. 86.

38. Season 5, Episode 16 (2007). This association has been established in the U.S. because of the song "Tubby the Tuba" (1945) and the cartoon based on the song (George Pal, 1947). A couple of years before *Superman*, a feature-length animated adaption of *Tubby the Tuba* (Alexander Schure, 1975) was released. The use of the tuba for big, lumbering creatures, though, has an earlier precedent in the music for Fafner as dragon in Richard Wagner's *Siegfried* (1856-1871).

The uses of the villains' march discussed so far makes it possible to question the plural «villains», as it only appears in conjunction with *one* villain, Otis. However, after Luthor has neutralized Superman with the Kryptonite necklace and pushed him into his pool, the theme also accompanies his scornful words to Superman before he leaves him to die. The theme comes to an end before Miss Teschmacher's line, «Lex, my mother lives in Hackensack», the place to which the second missile is directed due to Otis's mistake in reprogramming its directional vectors. Luthor looks at his watch, indifferently shakes his head, and as he exits the room the first notes of the villain's theme are heard. In this scene the theme is played by a muted trombone. Muted brass are regularly associated with (serious) villains in Williams's film music, and the use of the muted trombone here completely transforms the character of the theme, making it sinister instead of comic, underlining the cruelty and evilness of Luthor's actions and words.

Even though the villains' theme itself is not used in direct connection with Luthor earlier in the film, muted brass are heard elsewhere with the same narrative functions they have in this scene[39]. When Otis is introduced, sinister muted trombones are used on the first cut to the tailing cops. The significance of this is made clear when the second officer states that they should not arrest Otis, because he may lead them to the big man himself. A menacing accent in muted trombones precedes the first officer's answer, «Lex Luthor». Later in this sequence, the music starts again with low muted trombones when the officer who has been following Otis into the tunnel realizes that the wall indentation that Otis stepped back into as the train was passing is a hidden door leading to Luthor's lair. After the shot with Otis eating peanuts, there is, for the first time in the film, a cut to Luthor, yet unseen. As he sees the police officer on his CCTV monitor and speaks disparagingly about Otis's incompetence, we hear a descending semitone in stopped French horns. The policeman inspects the indentation where Otis disappeared. Menacing chords in muted trombones underscore the realization that he has found the secret way to Luthor, but also that this discovery has put him in grave danger. Luthor presses a button and the indentation in the wall moves forward, finally pushing the screaming policeman to his death on the tracks in front of the train rushing past.

Christian Clemmensen claims that in *Home Alone* (Chris Columbus, 1990) Williams's motif for the two villains is the most subtle and effective in the film:

> Instead of providing an ominous theme with one of the more powerful elements of the orchestra, the villains are accompanied only by woodwinds, an unexpected, but strangely appropriate choice for the idiots that these characters are. The dual performances of a bass [double] bassoon with a clarinet or oboe keep the theme low and mysterious while allowing the flexibility to toy with

39. This is also applies to the other films analysed in this chapter. For instance, when Vogel demonstrates how one says goodbye in Germany by punching Indy in the jaw in *Indiana Jones and the Last Crusade*, he is accompanied by low-pitched minor chords in muted trombones, and not the Nazi motif.

> their quirky personalities. That way, they are never quite that scary to kids in the audience, and Williams can sustain a light atmosphere for even the film's darkest moments[40].

The villains' march (Ex. 7) in *Home Alone* opens resolutely with a dominant anacrusis to the tonic on the downbeat.

Ex. 7: John Williams's "Villain's March", from *Home Alone* (© 1990 BMI), published by Fox Film Music Corporation, ear transcription from the film's soundtrack. Used in compliance with the U.S. Copyright Act, Section 107.

But then the long tonic note gives the impression that the music hesitates, making a small detour (double neighbour notes) returning to the tonic, before it continues upwards to the dominant. This is followed by a chromatic slide-slip to the raised fourth scale degree (the tritone), before the theme sinks back to the supertonic. The next phrase (mm. 5-8) begins with a precautious ascending semitone that returns to its starting point. A plunge down an octave leads to a new rising gesture, which is followed by a chromatic descent to F♯, before the second phrase ends on a low F. The consequent of the theme begins as the antecedent, but then the ascending gestures reach higher notes while the descending return to the deep register, thus increasing the contrast between the upward and downward movements. The short-breathed gestures with their constant changes between ascending and descending figures, as well as the low register and the *piano* dynamic, go back to conventions from silent film music. For instance, both the cues titled "Mysterious – Burglar Music" in J. S. Zamecnic's *Sam Fox Moving Picture Music volume 1* (1913), clearly display these features.

The burglar's theme is introduced early in the film after Kevin is startled by the policeman's twinkling gold tooth. Only the first four measures are used, but they immediately reveal that the seemingly solicitous cop, so concerned with the safety of the neighbourhood, is not who he pretends to be. And indeed, we will soon learn that he is Harry, a burglar that, together with his accomplice Marv, is planning to break into empty houses during the Christmas holidays. About fifteen minutes later in the film, after Harry's confident demonstration that he has figured out how all the automatic timers work in the houses where no one is home, the complete theme accompanies the discussion of the expected loot. The theme then follows the activities of Harry and Marv. In their first attempt to break into the McAllister house (where the little Kevin has been inadvertently

40. Clemmensen 1996/2016.

left behind by his vacationing family) the theme starts when Kevin sees their shadows through the window. The theme returns during the break into the neighbour house when Marv hears Kevin's father on the answering machine, thus figuring out that the MacAllister family has indeed gone away for Christmas. The theme is heard again when he starts flooding that house. As the burglars scout around the next day, Kevin recognizes Harry as the (fake) policeman who visited his house. Harry tells Marv that he didn't like the way the kid looked at him, and a menacing statement of the villains' theme emphasize his words. Later the theme underlines Harry's decision that they should break into the MacAllister house at nine o'clock that evening, as the only one home is the kid they saw the other day. During the break in, the burglar's theme is stated every time they, alone or together, regroup after having been caught in one of Kevin's traps. The character of the theme changes depending on the situation. For instance, when Harry and Marv try to climb along the line drawn between the attic and Kevin's tree house, the arrangement presents a tuba bass that makes the piece sound like circus music.

Conclusions

This chapter has explored how John Williams has been able to vary the seemingly simple formula of the villain's march topic — a minor key march with a chromatic twist, often involving the tritone — depending on the kind of villains at hand, and the nature and degree of their evil. The military villains, Darth Vader and the Nazis in *Indiana Jones and the Last Crusade*, are associated with resolute themes that are played by brass, accompanied by martial rhythms and mostly heard with loud dynamics. In contrast to Vader, though, the Nazis are real-life villains and their motif does not exploit minor chords whose roots are a major third apart, the most salient feature of Vader's theme (or the Imperial theme), a progression important in science fiction and fantasy films. Apart from the chromatic tail ending with the augmented fourth scale degree, the Nazi motif is diatonic and sounds like an ominous version in minor of a real German march. The march theme for the comic burglars in *Home Alone* is almost exclusively played by woodwinds, and the short-breathed gestures with constant changes between ascending and descending figures, the low register and the *piano* dynamic, go back to conventions for burglar music in silent-film music. In the villains' march in *Superman*, the pompous and pretentious façade of the theme is constantly undermined by features that make the music sound comical. The theme mostly appears in connection with Lex Luthor's sidekick, Otis, and is frequently played by the bassoon or the tuba, instruments associated with comic and fat characters. When used to underscore the evil and cruelty of Luthor, though, the theme is played by a muted trombone, and this completely transforms the character of the theme, making it sinister instead of comic. Muted brass are regularly associated with villains in Williams's film music, and one of Voldemort's themes in Harry *Harry Potter and the Sorcerer's Stone* is scored for muted French horns and low woodwinds accompanied by muted trombones and tuba. Tritones and chromatic double neighbour notes around the fifth scale degree are generally used to depict magic in Williams's Harry Potter music, but in Voldemort's three themes they are combined with other features to convey the evil of Voldemort. The main villain in Hitchcock's *Family Plot* is a seemingly ordinary jeweller, but behind the surface he is a psychopath who commits crimes for pleasure. To suggest the mental disorder below the surface, the villain's theme alludes to Bernard Hermann's "Hitchcock chord" and is often played by the ARP synthesizer — the use of electronics as a signifier of mental instability is a convention that was established in the 1940s in Hollywood film music.

Bibliography

Audissino 2014

Audissino, Emilio. *John Williams's Film Music: «Jaws», «Star Wars», «Raiders of the Lost Ark», and the Return of the Classical Hollywood Music Style*, Madison (WI), University of Wisconsin Press, 2014 (Wisconsin Film Studies).

Bribitzer-Stull 2015

Bribitzer-Stull, Matthew. *Understanding the Leitmotif: From Wagner to Hollywood Film Music*, Cambridge, Cambridge University Press, 2015.

Brown 1994

Brown, Royal S. *Overtones and Undertones: Reading Film Music*, Berkeley (CA), University of California Press, 1994 (Music).

Buhler 2000

Buhler, James. '*Star Wars*, Music, and Myth', in: *Music and Cinema*, edited by James Buhler, Caryl Flinn and David Neumeyer, Hanover (NH), Wesleyan University Press, 2000 (Music/Culture), pp. 33-57.

Byrd 1997

Byrd, Craig L. 'The *Star Wars* Interview: A New Talk', in: *Film Score Monthly*, ii/1 (January/February 1997), pp. 18-21.

Clemmensen 1996/2016

Clemmensen, Christian. 'Home Alone', in: *Filmtracks.com*, editorial review first published 1996, revised 2016, <http://filmtracks.com/titles/home_alone.html>, accessed February 2018.

Cooke 2008

Cooke, Mervyn. *A History of Film Music*, Cambridge, Cambridge University Press, 2008.

Drabkin 2008

Drabkin, William. 'Tritone', 2008, in: *Grove Music Online*, <http://www.oxfordmusiconline.com>, accessed February 2018.

Gorbman 1987

Gorbman, Claudia. *Unheard Melodies: Narrative Film Music*, Bloomington, Indiana University Press, 1987.

Kalinak 1992

Kalinak, Kathryn. *Settling the Score: Music and the Classical Hollywood Film*, Madison (WI), University of Wisconsin Press, 1992 (Wisconsin Studies in Film).

Klein 2005

Klein, Michael L. *Intertextuality in Western Art Music*, Bloomington, Indiana University Press, 2005 (Music Meaning and Interpretation).

Matessino 1997

Matessino, Michael. Liner notes for *The Empire Strikes Back*, Special Edition 2-CD set, BMG Classics (09026-68747-2), 1997.

Richards 2015a

Richards, Mark. 'Celebrating *Star Wars* Themes, Part 1 of 6: Uses of the Force Theme', 2015, <http://www.filmmusicnotes.com/celebrating-star-wars-part-1-of-6-uses-of-the-force-theme/>, accessed February 2018.

Richards 2015b

Id. 'Celebrating *Star Wars* Films, Part 2 of 6: Uses of Darth Vader's Theme', 2015, <http://www.filmmusicnotes.com/celebrating-star-wars-films-part-2-of-6-uses-of-darth-vaders-theme/>, accessed February 2018.

Spielberg 1989

Spielberg, Steven. Liner notes to *Indiana Jones and the Last Crusade, Original Motion Picture Soundtrack*, Warner Bros. 7599-25883-2, 1989.

Sullivan 2006

Sullivan, Jack. *Hitchcock's Music*, New Haven, Yale University Press, 2006.

Webster 2009

Webster, Jamie Lynn. 'The Music of *Harry Potter*: Continuity and Change in the First Five Films', Ph.D. Diss., Eugene (OR), University of Oregon, 2009.

Zacharopoulos 2017

Zacharopoulos, Konstantinos. 'Musical Syntax in John Williams's Film Music Themes', in: *Contemporary Film Music: Investigating Cinema Narratives and Composition*, edited by Lindsay Coleman and Joakim Tillman, Basingstoke, Palgrave Macmillan, 2017, pp. 237-262.

Musical Dramaturgy and Stylistic Changes in John Williams's *Harry Potter* Trilogy

Jamie Lynn Webster
(Pacific University, Forest Grove, OR)

Music in films expands the physical space of drama beyond the boundaries of what is seen, and likewise, is crucial in expanding the dimensions of the magical fantasy universe of the *Harry Potter* film versions, developing its own dramatic discourse and establishing its own temporal and spatial dimensions[1]. The *Harry Potter* film saga offers a notable perspective as one of few epic film series to subsequently employ four different directors and composers (for a total of five different collaborative combinations) over the course of the eight-film series, contributing to remarkably different perspectives on Harry's magical world[2]. As the first composer to work on the *Harry Potter* series, and also as the only composer on the series to work with two subsequent directors, John Williams established a template for how music would relate with the landscape of the story as well as initiating a model for how the musical landscape could flexibly change over the course of the narrative. In the process, we find a unique opportunity to examine Williams's own capacity for imagination, adaptation, and relevance for contemporary film scoring, providing an alternative reading to the common perception that Williams's formidably crafted, pervasive, Classic-Hollywood-style underscore is also somewhat dated

1. Smart 2004, Gorbman 1987, Chion 1994, Petrobelli 1994.

2. Other epic adventures (e.g. the *Indiana Jones* films and *The Lord of the Rings* trilogy) have maintained the same director and composer throughout. Similarly, while the *Star Wars* episodes employed different directors (for *The Empire Strikes Back* and *The Return of the Jedi*), John Williams composed scores for the first two trilogies, re-using leitmotifs and maintaining a consistent style throughout. Other series (e.g. *Superman*), have hired new orchestrators and arrangers yet required them to work with previously composed themes, thus contributing to a perception of musical continuity. A few director/composer teams have worked on various *Batman* films over the course of many decades, yet these films are episodic rather than serial, and therefore do not carry the same expectations for continuity. The *Star Trek* films, similarly, have used different director and composer collaborations, but are largely episodic rather than serial. Indeed, the production strategy of changing director/composer teams for high-profile film series may be an emerging trend, as observed again more recently in the *Twilight Saga*.

and predictable. In fact, an exploration of three audio-visual spheres relating to landscape — 1) music for the geographic and conceptual spaces that wizards and muggles (non-magical characters) inhabit, 2) Harry's annual journey to the Hogwarts School of Witchcraft and Wizardry, and 3) the temporal change of seasons during each year of schooling — provide a window on the significantly different perspectives on Harry Potter's world that Williams adopted when he wrote for the first director, Chris Columbus (for the first and second films), *vis-à-vis* the second director, Alfonso Cuarón (third film).

With the first director Chris Columbus, John Williams's music co-created a classic children's fantasy and his "Hedwig's Theme" became the identifying musical marker for the landscape of the wizarding world and the series as a whole. While Columbus brought expertise from his work on high-impact family-friendly Hollywood films, he also made choices aligning with what Troost calls the «heritage approach», faithfully preserving the storyline and characterizations, and visually emphasizing the objects and landscapes described in the novels[3]. Narrative spaces inhabited by Muggles and Magicals were respectively delineated with Dickensian murk and bright colours — that is, drab, shadowy colours for the Dursley house versus contrasting pigments and clear lighting for Hogwarts — establishing an immediate appeal for the magical world. Williams reported that music for *The Sorcerer's Stone* would naturally be «theatrical, magical and to capture a child's sense of wonder in the world»[4]. Thus, scenes depicting Harry's unhappy life with the Dursleys were left unaccompanied while those depicting his introduction to the magical world were saturated with underscore. By transferring (rather than transforming) the book's narrative to film, Columbus and Williams recognized the important relationship between fidelity and fan expectation, and viewers experienced a continuity and familiarity with the published books[5]. Critic Richard Corliss commented: «How to make a film out of such a cinematic experience that 100 million readers have seen in their minds' eyes? Either by transferring it like a lavishly illustrated volume of Dickens, or transforming it with a new vision. Columbus, along with screenwriter Steve Kloves and the Potter production team, chose Column A and made a handsomely faithful version, with actors smartly cast to type»[6]. While positive reception noted literary fidelity, criticism noted a pedestrian approach, and Williams's score, hailed as «magical» by some, was derided as a «a great clanging, banging music box that simply will not shut up» by others[7].

[3]. Troost 2007, pp. 75-89. Troost argues that the Hollywood-style approach generally favours successful marketability over literary fidelity. Alternatively, Troost describes the heritage approach as one that adheres to plots and characterizations, and emphasizes the authenticity of objects and geographies.

[4]. Williams quoted in Webster 2009, p. 90.

[5]. Ian Q. Hunter argues that literary fidelity is of greater importance in fantasy film because readers bring enormous expectations. Hunter 2007, pp. 154-166.

[6]. Corliss 2001.

[7]. Honeycutt 2001.

In collaboration with Columbus, Williams's scores for *The Sorcerer's Stone* and *The Chamber of Secrets* function like omniscient eyes that illustrate, define, and clarify the main ideas of the story in a tidy fashion[8]. Underscore performed by a large symphonic orchestra is almost always present, and Williams uses melodic leitmotifs for nearly every role of film music, expressing referential and connotative meanings with dance-like triple meters, plenty of chromaticism, unexpected harmonic progressions, and time-tested instrumental signifiers for magic such as harp and celeste[9]. Musical metaphors (symbolic theatrical conventions) call our attention to movements (their direction and speed), interpret the tenor of narrative elements with timbre and texture (e.g., delicate strings, bold brass, and so on), comment on character archetypes (e.g., French horns for heroes and bassoons for bad guys and oddballs), and elicit the emotional responses of viewers[10]. Williams's omniscient scores were said to «capture the soul of the Harry Potter world»[11].

These first two finely tuned film scores exemplify the style of Hollywood's Golden Age music, catching every action, and align with Williams's signature style which moviegoers have become accustomed to from other blockbuster epic adventures such as the *Star Wars* and *Indiana Jones* series[12]. Curiously, diegetic music, which can be employed as a potent tool for establishing time and place, is rarely used. Alternatively, every musical aspect of Williams's leitmotifs tends to resonate symbolically with visuals, and Williams's organization of the leitmotifs in relation to the visuals and to the other leitmotifs is the most complex of all the *Potter* soundtracks in *Sorcerer's Stone* and *Chamber of Secrets*. And yet, this approach also tends to represent narrative ideas in simpler, more straightforward terms, often telling viewers how to respond rather than engaging viewers in the experience of the story: sometimes the music telegraphs the outcome before the visual narrative plays out.

---

8. *Harry Potter and the Sorcerer's Stone* (Chris Columbus, 2001), *Harry Potter and the Chamber of Secrets* (Chris Columbus, 2002).

9. While Williams may use triple meter to convey Britishness (as it is largely used in British folk music), it is also consistent with Williams's approach to use triple meter to convey both magic and the magical realm as well as either feminine or childlike spheres. For instance, while all of his heroic anthems for the *Star Wars* films are in duple meter, scores for films such as *The Witches of Eastwick* emphasize triple meter. Likewise, an association between both chromaticism and unexpected harmonies and the supernatural world is a historic convention of the neo-romantic musical language that Williams employs. I cover the changing dramatic relationships between music and magic in the *Harry Potter* films in greater detail in WEBSTER 2012.

10. GORBMAN 1987, p. 84. My analysis of musical metaphors is greatly informed by the theoretical work of the late Steve Larson whose theories explore how metaphors of gravity, magnetism, and inertia can help explain movement (itself a metaphor) in melody, harmony, and rhythm. By using metaphors of motion to describe how film composers connect visual elements with metaphorical musical equivalents, one can help explain how music affects the listener emotionally. JOHNSON – LARSON 2003; LARSON – VAN HANDEL 2005; LARSON 2012.

11. From the CD liner notes, *Harry Potter and the Sorcerer's Stone: Original Motion Picture Soundtrack*.

12. Emilio Audissino's book-length study explores how Williams resurrected Hollywood's classical music style, launching a neoclassical trend. AUDISSINO 2014.

For instance, at the first Quidditch game of the season in *The Sorcerer's Stone*, phrases from two leitmotifs, a more general "Quidditch fanfare" (*Sorcerer's Stone* DVD: 1:16:11) and the victorious anthem "Hogwarts Forever!" (*Sorcerer's Stone* DVD: 1:16:21), alternate in time with the action while the Gryffindor and Slytherin team players fly onto the air field and the Quidditch game commences[13]. Whilst at first, the "Hogwarts Forever!" theme accompanies visuals of general school pride, including fans and players of both teams, the final statement before the game begins accompanies Harry as he takes his starting position, marking Harry as the designated champion, the pride of Hogwarts, and foreshadowing that his team will win the match (*Sorcerer's Stone* DVD: 1:16:55). In other words, Williams's music not only follows the form of the action, it also anticipates the form of what will occur later on.

Table 1: The Alternation of Leitmotifs for the Quidditch Match Scene in *The Sorcerer's Stone* as an Example of Music Following the Film's Form

Leitmotif Name	Starting Pitch	Visuals
Quidditch fanfare	E	Gryffindor team members enter field
Quidditch fanfare	F♯	Slytherin team members enter field
Hogwarts Forever!	A	Emcee announces the teams
Hogwarts Forever!	C	Hogwarts students cheer from the bleachers
10-beat extension		" " " " "
Quidditch fanfare	F♯	Teams fly toward starting positions
10-beat extension		" " " "
Hogwarts Forever!	E♭	Harry takes his starting position
Fade		Referee addresses teams

From left to right this chart shows how phrases of leitmotifs align with specific film gestures. From top to bottom, this chart shows how leitmotifs are alternated in order to attach interpretative meaning to the visuals. As a whole, one can see that music follows the form of the scene with alternating leitmotifs.

Director Alfonso Cuarón, best known for his more personal work on edgy, independent art-films, came on board as a singularly contrasting choice when Columbus left due to scheduling constraints. In contrast to Columbus's faithful approach, producers described Cuarón's contributions as «weird, wild, and wonderful», while Cuarón himself

[13]. These titles are congruent with those used in published materials. The Quidditch scene received high praise from viewers and critics for its ability to convey the airspace of the Wizarding world, and its success played an important role in the perceived success of the film's special effects.

cited faithfulness to the spirit of the narrative rather than to all details[14]. Cuarón made several changes to the magical universe as Columbus had envisioned it. Outdoor scenes moved from Gloucestershire and Northumberland, England, to Glencoe, Scotland, resulting in a wilder, more rugged landscape with a more subdued colour palette. Instead of saturated colours, verdant lawns, and a story-book forest, the new landscape included rocky, lichen coloured hillsides, an overgrown pumpkin patch filled with cawing ravens, old-growth forests with chirping birds, and sun-drenched mountainous vistas. Cuarón also re-configured the architectural structures at Hogwarts, contributing to a greater awareness of the landscape and layout[15]. Cuarón explained, «I'm trying to establish a universe around Harry that actually exists [rather than] just a backdrop for his adventures»[16].

In collaboration with Cuarón, Williams's new, less theatrical score for *The Prisoner of Azkaban* functions like a beating heart (instead of omniscient eyes), expanding and amplifying our emotional experience of Harry's world at a participatory level (rather than telling us the story at an informational level as the first scores tend to do)[17]. And it's the music itself, rather than the system of leitmotifs, which becomes more complex in almost all ways. The instrumental palette extends beyond the late-nineteenth-century orchestra to include Renaissance and Jazz instrumentation. The score presents fewer leitmotifs, described as «enchanting» and «hauntingly beautiful» (rather than whimsical and magical)[18], many of them new, in longer phrases to match Cuarón's longer-duration shooting style (in contrast to Columbus's faster edited, shorter-shot approach) with more varied harmonies and changing meters. Additionally, the relationship between music, visuals, and narrative ideas becomes richer, fluidly integrating source sounds in several provocatively complex examples of source music (for instance, in the scene involving Aunt Marge's visit, to be discussed later in detail), source scoring, sound effect, and what Michel Chion calls the «Elements of Auditory Setting» (E.A.S.) that engage the viewer in a freer experience of the narrative rather than merely interpreting the story for the viewer[19]. The varied levels of diegesis infuse Harry's experiences with feeling,

[14]. Jenson 2005.

[15]. For instance, Cuarón changed the location of Hagrid's hut, making it visible from Hogwarts Castle, and added a walking bridge and sundial to the Hogwarts grounds.

[16]. Dickey n.d.

[17]. *Harry Potter and the Prisoner of Azkaban* (Alfonso Cuarón, 2004).

[18]. Descriptions such as these are found among reviewer notes, fan sites, and online discussion boards on sites such as <http://www.musicfromthemovies.com>, <MuggleNet.com>, and <http://www.the-leaky-cauldron.org >, accessed February 2018.

[19]. Naturally, fluidity and richness may be perceived and valued to different degrees by different filmgoers. While some may value the complexity of the third film as a marker of artistry, others may find that the so-called artistry gets in the way of the story.

blur viewer perceptions of time and reality, and amplify the extent of Harry's emotional world[20]. Illustrating this point, a diegetic welcome song sung by Hogwarts choir, "Double Trouble", becomes the most prominent, most often-heard musical theme in the third film (usurping the role that "Hedwig's Theme" had in the previous films)[21]. Moreover, the relationship of music to itself develops over the course of the film, creating dramatic subtexts that enrich the viewer's experience and perception, upturning expectations, sometimes complete with humorous jabs at Williams's previous work[22]. In contrast to the clarifying role of music in the first two Potter films, this multi-layered approach reflects Cuarón's vision of representing a looser, less literal transformation (rather than transference) of the story with film, and Cuarón praised Williams's music for «breathing life into what has become a much better film»[23]. While some viewers found the discontinuities with the audio-visual design of the previous films «frustrating», positive consensus noted «intrigue around every turn»[24], due to the minute details of visuals and sound allowing the film to «breathe independently of the source material»[25] and enabling the viewer «to feel this wizarding world as an actual place with dense characters inhabiting real space»[26].

As such, Williams's approach changed so that some longer action scenes in *The Prisoner of Azkaban* receive unique themes with a unique treatment (eschewing the leitmotivic technique), effectively emphasizing the here-and-now (rather than relating to past and future leitmotifs). For instance, a single new theme scores the sequence of the third-year Quidditch game, during which powerful Dementors pull Harry off his broom (*Prisoner of Azkaban* DVD: 54:00)[27]. (A transcription of the main motif of the theme is given in Ex. 1 with brief analysis of its fugue-like properties.)

---

20. Webster 2012 offers a detailed examination of how reality and fantasy are depicted and delineated in each film.

21. This theme is melodically and harmonically related to the third section of the original version of Hedwig's Theme used in the first two films, though this theme is sometimes separated out in published materials under the title "Nimbus 2000".

22. For instance, audio-visuals poke fun at birds following the phenomenal success of Williams's "Hedwig's Theme" in the first film, so named for Harry's pet owl. For the second film, Williams mimicked the regal sound of Hedwig's theme though with an abrupt finish in parallel with the uncoordinated flight of Errol the owl. For the third film, Williams wrote a cheerful flute cadenza to accompany the flight of a songbird who meets a sudden end in the Whomping Willow's branches.

23. From the CD liner notes, Williams, John. *Harry Potter and the Prisoner of Azkaban: Original Motion Picture Soundtrack*, Warner Bros. 2004.

24. *Filmtracks* 2004.

25. Novikov 2008.

26. Pigeon 2007.

27. Composer Nicholas Hooper also borrowed this theme for the Quidditch game in the sixth film, *The Half-Blood Prince* (David Yates, 2009).

Ex. 1: the main motif for the Quidditch match, from *Harry Potter and the Prisoner of Azkaban* (© 2004 BMI), published by Warner-Barham Music LLC, ear transcription from the film's soundtrack. Used in compliance with the U.S. Copyright Act, Section 107.

Unlike the two alternating themes in Harry's first Quidditch match that referentially allude to the festive event with swashbuckler-like fanfares and adventure music, the tolling bell-like minor melody and the strong, agitated rhythm in this single fugato-style motif reflect the tension of the potentially violent wizard sport continuing in spite of a dark, rainy, thunderstorm, imparting a gravitas on the sequence that was absent in the previous examples. In order to fit the length and changing camera angles of the scene, the motif is repeated with changing instrumentation, played in ascending melodic sequence, extended through static repetition of accompanying harmonies, and varied at its beginning and end to accommodate following and preceding sections of music. The theme changes only briefly (to an alternating note ostinato played on harp) when Harry perceives the ominous shape of a black dog in the clouds ahead of him[28]. Diegetic sounds such as wind, thunder, breathing, and so on, continue to be audible alongside the music. Although agitated music foreshadows that danger looms, no specific musical gesture telegraphs the outcome. In other words, Williams simplifies the musical relationship (i.e., one theme, not tied to other narrative moments) while deepening the relationship with visuals.

Furthermore, in contrast to the truthful clarity of the first two film scores, music in the third film sometimes serves to deceive. For instance, the ominous ostinato accompanying the shape of the black dog in the clouds during the Quidditch match accurately reflects the characters' fear, while inaccurately reflecting the threat: the actual dog eventually turns out to be Harry's most loving advocate, his godfather Sirius Black. Similarly, in a different scene, a double-reed melody supporting the geo-cultural landscape depicted in the Weasley family's Egyptian vacation photos seems to be a piece of non-diegetic underscore at first, but turns out to be source music, coming from a child musician charming a snake-like rope in the background of the next, wider angle shot. That is, the musical cue is used effectively to confuse the viewers' perceptions about what is really going on. Instead of 'telling' the viewers that wizard life is unpredictable, the new approach provides an experience of unpredictability itself.

[28]. The ominous black dog is a recurring visual motif in the film, and only indirectly relates to the Quidditch game and its outcome.

Geographic and Temporal Dimensions

We gain a richer understanding of the contrasting strategies Williams used to create the narrative landscapes of the first three *Potter* films when we consider how music traverses spatial and temporal dimensions, bridging the inherent gaps of visual narration. For instance, music typically accompanies both Harry's annual journey to Hogwarts School of Witchcraft and Wizardry at the start of each school term, and the change of season throughout his school year there. An examination of music used at these transitions not only reveals Williams's varied aesthetic approaches, it also displays some of the ways in which humour is expressed between Williams's collaborations with Columbus and Cuaròn.

Spatial Discontinuity

In *The Sorcerer's Stone* and *The Chamber of Secrets*, Williams uses leitmotifs as agents of continuity when dealing with spatial discontinuity. When Harry boards the Hogwarts train in his first year, "Hedwig's Theme" accompanies the visuals of a birds-eye view of the train as it traverses the countryside (seemingly headed West by travelling from right to left, *Sorcerer's Stone* DVD: 34:03). Indeed, "Hedwig's Theme" occurs roughly 50 times throughout the first two films as a marker of many ideas and transitions. The volume of the music recedes to allow for the dialogue among the students. When the visuals show the train pulling up at the Hogsmeade station (now travelling left to right), "Hedwig's Theme" begins again (*Sorcerer's Stone* DVD: 37:50). Each shot/segment presents only one idea (e.g. either the train travelling, events on the train, or the train arriving), but the music facilitates a clear continuity between otherwise disjunct tableaux[29].

In his second year (*The Chamber of Secrets*) Harry doesn't ride the train to Hogwarts because he and his friend Ron miss their boarding time; instead, they drive a bewitched, flying Ford Anglia to school. The deviation from visual form in the narrative offers opportunity for musical change in the underscore. The accompanying set-piece (called "The Flying Car" on the CD) follows the contours of their path with an original melody, plenty of extensile music and a collection of leitmotifs from the first film, lending familiarity to the unfamiliar mode of travel. Likewise, while music makes way for dialogue and narrative developments when Harry rides the Hogwarts train in the first film, music in this case accompanies the entire action-packed journey in the Ford Anglia (*Chamber of Secrets* DVD: 23:37)[30]. Then, the music makes a transition to "Hedwig's Theme" when Harry and

[29]. The use of "Hedwig's Theme" for Harry's introduction into the magical sphere contributes to the continuity and form of the film as a whole. "Hedwig's Theme" is used for the introduction of magic during the opening scenes when owls like Hedwig delivered magic letters.

[30]. The flying car passes the Hogwarts train without musical comment, thus reinforcing the experience of the journey and a landscape, rather than signifying the train itself.

Ron arrive at Hogwarts (*Chamber of Secrets* DVD: 26:06). This example provides evidence that Williams used a variety of approaches even whilst working in the same collaboration.

In the third film, Williams and Cuarón use layered segues and sutures (consisting of both music and visuals) to create subtle, elegant transitions that are packed with narrative information. The new transition style favours subtlety over straightforwardness, and complexity over clarity. When Harry boards the Hogwarts train in his third year at Hogwarts, unaccompanied dialogue introduces the transition (*Prisoner of Azkaban* DVD: 19:05). At the end of the train ride, however, "Double Trouble" (a new theme that is melodically and harmonically related to the third section of "Hedwig's Theme") enters while visuals focus on Harry's reflection on the compartment window against a dark, rainy sky[31]. An instrumental prelude to the theme (*Prisoner of Azkaban* DVD: 23:55) begins just before the shadowy reflection of Harry's face segues into the shadowy reflection of moonlight across a puddle of water as carriages transport students from the train to Hogwarts Castle (*Prisoner of Azkaban* DVD: 23:57). Once inside the Great Hall, the focus is on a school choir and instrumentalists performing "Double Trouble" as a full choral piece (*Prisoner of Azkaban* DVD: 24:12). The lyrics of "Double Trouble" are taken from the dialogue of the three witches in Shakespeare's *MacBeth* (Act 4, Scene 1), except for the fourth line, «Something wicked this way comes», which is borrowed from the title of the 1962 Ray Bradbury novel:

Refrain
Double, double, toil and trouble
Fire burn and cauldron bubble
Double, double, toil and trouble
Something wicked this way comes!
Eye of newt and toe of frog
Wool of bat and tongue of dog
Adder's fork and blind-worm's sting
Lizard's leg and owlet's wing.

Refrain [...]
In the cauldron boil and bake
Fillet of a fenny snake
Scale of dragon, tooth of wolf
Witches mummy, maw and gulf.

Refrain [...]

31. In fact, a brief musical pre-cursor of "Double Trouble" occurs when the visuals leave the friends' conversation for a moment in order to present a wide-angle shot of the train curving around a loch (from left to right in this film, *Prisoner of Azkaban* DVD 19:37). The melody for the opening phrase of "Double Trouble" shares the same structural pitches and harmonies as the third section of "Hedwig's Theme" from the first two films. This third section was largely discarded in the subsequent films, except for its reframing as "Double Trouble".

In other words, a few subtle transitions weave together to convey a more important transition. The image of Harry's face makes a transition from Harry to his reflection, and then to the reflection of light in the puddle. The music makes a transition from apparent non-diegesis to a diegetic performance in the foreground. These elements integrate with Harry's ultimate geographic transition by train and then by carriage to the Hogwarts castle. Additionally, the manner of transition serves a broader narrative theme in the film: how interpretations change as perspectives shift.

Furthermore, the double meanings and hidden truths embedded in the transitions further reflect how circumstances are not as they initially seem. For example Shakespeare's amusingly macabre text could suggest serious threat, or simply mischief. Additionally, the provenance of the text blurs meta-contextual boundaries: poetic fiction uttered by Shakespeare's witches from the muggle literary sphere inform the understanding of muggle viewers of the magical world from a wizarding perspective. Finally, the implied formality of opening events at Hogwarts is juxtaposed with peculiar instrumentation highlighting bass clarinets, bassoons, recorders, harpsichord, and triangle (itself a historic dramatic symbol for the mysterious), and mixed gender choir augmented with the croaking of enormous toads[32].

Table 2: Musical Cues Bridging Spatial Discontinuity during Harry's Annual Journey to Hogwarts

	Film Title	Mode of travel	Leitmotifs	Music Makes Way for Dialogue
1.	*The Sorcerer's Stone*	Hogwarts Train	"Hedwig's Theme"	Yes
	The Chamber of Secrets	Flying Ford Anglia	Set-piece incorporating leitmotifs/"Hedwig's Theme"	No
2.	*The Prisoner of Azkaban*	Hogwarts Train	Set-piece, "Double Trouble"	Yes

This chart reveals the progression from a singular leitmotif accompanying Harry's journey, to an original set-piece quoting familiar leitmotifs, and finally, a journey accompanied only by an original theme.

Temporal Discontinuity, Timing… and Humour

An examination of temporal transitions similarly displays Williams's straightforward approach in his collaboration with Columbus versus the complexity of his approach with

32. These are the diegetic performing forces; the song was actually performed by an all-boy choir, with added sound effects. Furthermore, the act of singing is parodied later on in the film (via the circus adage «it isn't over until the fat lady sings») when the woman in the Gryffindor painting, known as 'the fat lady' tries to sing, but can only shriek (DVD 27:03). She tries to break a wine glass with her high note, but can not achieve it, so she smashes the glass instead, exclaiming, «Ah — Amazing! Just by the sound of my voice!» Thus, this set-piece may be part of an evolving commentary on singing.

Cuarón — though notably with an added layer of humour more prominently displayed than in the case of the geographic transitions. Humour, much like magic, consists of violations of the order of the normal world, and is amongst the main narrative elements that appeal to readers of the *Harry Potter* novels and viewers of the *Harry Potter* films. As depicted in Rowling's novels, the organization of the magical world seems to parody the real world through «humorous, exaggerated imitation», and sometimes additionally serves as a parody of traditional folklore and mythology by distorting the expected organization of the fantasy world[33]. Additionally, some of the musical cues poke fun at magical characters and at the magical world itself (that is, subverting what Veatch calls «the subjective moral» order of the magical world rather than just mocking the muggle world[34]). The act of normalizing the abnormal can result in a humorous effect. Likewise, musical incongruities with already humorous visuals may add a layer of comedy not present with the visuals alone[35]. The musical themes signifying magic in the films, such as "Hedwig's Theme", may be perceived as odd and funny by some because they exhibit characteristics against the tonal norm (e.g., strong chromaticism and unexpected harmonic progressions) that disrupt the listener's expectation without being too harsh on the ear. Like parody in literature, some musical themes for the magic world combine a nod toward established musical forms or styles with a wink of tongue-in-cheek imitation and exaggeration.

A temporal change to winter is presented simply and pleasurably in *The Sorcerer's Stone* when a folk-like melody with diatonic harmony and sleigh bells evokes Christmas during a cut-away scene of Hagrid dragging a large pine tree through the snow before the visuals change to the inside of Hogwarts on Christmas morning (*Sorcerer's Stone* DVD: 1:25:05). The same tune occurs again as the musical accompaniment for a wintertime cut-away in the *The Chamber of Secrets* when a brief moving tableau of horse-drawn carriages travelling through a snowy landscape precedes images of Christmas day inside Hogwarts (*Chamber of Secrets* DVD: 1:17:17), thus playing a role in the continuity between the first and second films. This straightforward depiction of the passing of time and change of season aligns with Columbus's intent to represent Harry's magical world with clarity.

---

33. Cross 2008, pp. 66-67.

34. Veatch 1998, pp. 164, 170-171, 212. Psychologist of humour Thomas C. Veatch explains, «humour occurs when it seems that things are normal while at the same time something seems wrong». That is to say, humour is an emotional response when the «subjective moral order» has been violated — when the moral order is «defined as the set of principles which an individual both has an affective commitment to and believes ought to hold». To the end that people have different levels of commitment to a moral order (culturally, and as individuals), that which is funny to one person may be perceived as either unremarkable or offensive to another.

35. Yet, Chion 1994 (p. 5) argues that the music always creates meaning out of visuals (rather than reflects it), and thus even so-called parallel music gestures create new meaning (rather than clarify one that already exists). However, Chion recognizes (as does Gorbman and others) that music that seems to contrast film visuals creates a different kind of new meaning.

In contrast, temporal changes in the third film are far more elaborate. Director Alfonso Cuarón uses the visual motifs of trees and birds as harbingers of the change of season; each presentation of these images serves as a unique vignette, and the collection of narrative motifs exhibits a coherent form that is both visual and musical. In the first seasonal change, a fast-paced flute melody in the foreground with background tolling clock bells accompanies a bluebird flying happily through a warm fall day (*Prisoner of Azkaban* DVD: 28:47), but then the bluebird bursts into a puff of feathers after being smashed by the magical Whomping Willow tree (*Prisoner of Azkaban* DVD: 29:04). In parallel with the role of mischief in the narrative, the filmmakers created an effect of audio-visual mischief through 'asynchronism' of the lighthearted music and the macabre visual punch line. In the second change of season vignette, "Hedwig's Theme" accompanies as Hedwig the owl takes flight in dry, fall weather (*Prisoner of Azkaban* DVD: 58:23), then continues to fly across the Hogwarts landscape as the sky produces snowflakes, and the ground turns white with snow (*Prisoner of Azkaban* DVD: 58:46)[36]. In the third seasonal change, sombre music continues from a previous scene (of Harry in the snow) to a transitional scene of a butterfly alighting on a bulb flower, and then to the Whomping Willow covered with melting snow (*Prisoner of Azkaban* DVD: 1:07:03). The Willow shakes its branches, and snow splatters the camera lens (producing a humorous violation of the camera's invisibility, *Prisoner of Azkaban* DVD: 1:07:12). The sombre music continues until the next scene when Harry meets with Professor Lupin after the Christmas holidays. The fourth and final seasonal change recalls the dark humour of the first presentation, when "Hedwig's Theme" accompanies again, this time following the lighthearted flight of a songbird who is subsequently extinguished by the limbs of the Whomping Willow tree — which are now covered in spring leaves (*Prisoner of Azkaban* DVD: 20:05:50).

As seen in Table 3, the audio-visual presentation creates a form of the seasonal motifs that includes a recapitulation when the songbird is smashed in the fourth presentation as it was in the first. As well, both the first and fourth statements include a bird and the tree, while the second and third statements include a bird and then a tree, respectively (producing a delay of expectation). The musical form is regulated with "Hedwig's Theme" for both the second and the fourth presentations of the change-of-season visual motif. The use of smaller forms such as this one within the larger form of the film helps to establish unity.

[36]. Notably, both the visuals and the music segue into the following scene. The flight of Hedwig leads the camera to the clock tower where Harry stands, and the final note of "Hedwig's Theme" becomes the first note of the theme associated with Harry's inner world.

Table 3: Four Temporal Transitions Using Bird and Tree Motifs with Musical Accompaniment in *The Prisoner of Azkaban*

Temporal Transition	Music	Visual
1. Fall	fast-paced flute	A bluebird is extinguished by the Whomping Willow
2. Fall to falling snow	Hedwig's Theme	Hedwig flies from fall to winter
3. Melting snow	somber-sounding	The Whomping Willow shakes snow off its branches
4. Spring	Hedwig's Theme	A bluebird is extinguished by the Whomping Willow

This table summarizes the audio-visual components of four seasonal changes in the third Potter film. The progression of musical themes follows an ABCB form. The form of the visuals (i.e., bird and tree motifs) includes an exposition, two variations, and a recapitulation. This provides evidence of the greater audio-visual complexity utilized by Williams in collaboration with Cuarón.

In fact, the different ways that the collaborators chose to frame "Hedwig's Theme" reveal further differences in approaches to humour. In spite of the major role "Hedwig's Theme" plays in representing the franchise and signifying the fantasy realm, it also often provides 'relief music' akin to 'relief laughter' in scenes depicting the resolution of minor conflicts. For instance, in *The Sorcerer's Stone*, "Hedwig's Theme" is used when Hagrid punishes Dudley Dursley for stealing and eating Harry's birthday cake by giving him a curly pig tail, punctuating the cartoonish visual and affirming the pleasure of a socially sanctioned transgression: sweet revenge[37]. In *The Chamber of Secrets*, Williams lampoons "Hedwig's Theme" with a new cue for the Weasley's infinitely clumsy owl Errol that subverts the symbolic glorification of the magical world that the real "Hedwig's Theme" had established by using abrupt stops in the musical phrase: a violation of propriety (see Ex. 2).

Ex. 2: two statements of "Errol the Owl", from *Harry Potter and the Chamber of Secrets* (© 2002 BMI), published by Warner-Barham Music LLC, ear transcription from the film's soundtrack. Used in compliance with the U.S. Copyright Act, Section 107.

In both examples, the melodic and rhythmic familiarity of Errol's lovely background music suggests that Errol has the same majestic qualities of Hedwig (and by extension,

37. Cross 2008, pp. 61-62. According to Cross, slapstick revenge is a socially sanctioned form of transgression that satisfies a subconscious need for subversive amusement and an «intuitive sense of justice».

the grandeur of the magic world as a whole). However, when Errol makes clumsy, disruptive landings — first smashing into a window and immediately dropping to the ground (*Chamber of Secrets* DVD: 13:31), and later crashing into bowls of cereal and other breakfast foods (*Chamber of Secrets* DVD: 33:45) — the propriety of elegant flight is violated by the untimely crashes much as the propriety of the beautiful music is violated by the untimely cessation of the musical phrase[38]. Thus over the course of the first three films, we see how "Hedwig's Theme" not only crosses boundaries of space and time, but also plays with the transgression of boundaries, punctuating slapstick humour and socially sanctioned transgressions in the pig tale scene, parodying itself with violations of propriety in the Errol the Owl scenes, and finally, subversively violating the sanctity of life in the bluebird and Whomping Willow seasonal transitions.

Segues, Parallels, and Spectacle

The elegant complexity of the musical cues in *The Prisoner of Azkaban* goes beyond the geographic and temporal transitions addressed above and warrants further discussion of what Gorbman calls «segues» and «sutures»[39]. When the musical soundtrack crosses boundaries between diegetic and nondiegetic space, it can aid rhythmic continuity by 'suturing' scenes in order to soften the edges of changing film angles, editing cuts, modifications in the perception of time, and evolving emotional dimensions. Williams's music for the third film seeps like a gel or a flow of water from one scene, physical space, and idea into the next, collaborating with Cuarón's visuals in a way that allows the story to unroll seamlessly before the viewer.

Visually, Cuarón sutures scenes together with the regular use of long travelling camera shots through the physical spaces of Hogwarts castle (for example, memorably panning up through the clock tower and down into the courtyard below), some of which also indicate temporal space (such as when the camera follows Hedwig as she circles the Hogwarts grounds from fall to winter). Musically, scenes are connected through motifs that continue from one shot to another, and sometimes by using a sound bridge leading to the next shot.

Case Study: Aunt Marge's Waltz, the Tango on the Television, and the Photo of Harry's Parents

The third film includes a number of musical set pieces that are rhythmically timed with the images to enhance visual pleasure, clarify humour, and streamline the delivery

---

[38]. In this second occurrence, the crash and abrupt musical stop happen later on in the theme to heighten the humour (by further subverting the expectation set by the first occurrence).

[39]. Gorbman 1987, p. 5.

of comedic dialogue. These set-pieces fall into a category that Gorbman defines as «spectacle», which «evoke larger-than-life dimensions, which, rather than involving us in the narrative, places us in contemplation of it»[40]. A particularly exemplary and subtle sequence involving segues and parallels occurs after Harry accidentally blows up his Aunt Marge to the size of a giant balloon. The sequence uses the motif of dancing and dance music to show absurdity, then banality, and then great tenderness, providing information about identities and relationships in addition to carrying the viewer from one shot to the next. In the process of exploring the physical dimensions of the magical world (and indeed, the magical erupting in the muggle world), Williams and Cuarón expand the conceptual dimensions as well.

When Aunt Marge insults Harry's deceased parents, Harry's unchecked magical energies blow her up like a balloon in retaliation and she floats away into the sky (*Prisoner of Azkaban* DVD: 4:18). A humorous theme called "Aunt Marge's Waltz" accompanies her physical inflation with a neo-classic combination of conventional orchestral instrumentation and form, and absurd-sounding harmonies in the style of Prokofiev's neo-classicism. The rollicking accompaniment pairs discordantly with the emotionally charged dialogue that precedes the event, and the violent images of the event itself, such that viewers may not register any violence at all[41]. The music tells us that Aunt Marge deserves her fate and that we should take pleasure in the dramatic justice at work. Moreover, initial close-ups focus on specific areas of Marge's inflation, facilitating the pleasure at her comeuppance while the music provides a melody-based laugh-track[42]. Indeed, this perspective is affirmed later when Harry defiantly tells his Uncle Dursley that «She deserved what she got!» (*Prisoner of Azkaban* DVD: 6:37).

The audio-visual combinations abound with metaphorical resonances. The contour of the piece follows the style of Rossini's famous comic-opera overtures, colouring the scene with operatic silliness. The oom-pah of low brass matches the bloated image of Marge and her disproportionate sense of self-righteousness (*Prisoner of Azkaban* DVD: 4:38). Likewise, the lunacy of the magical inflation is supported by the cuckoo clock's chime (*Prisoner of Azkaban* DVD: 4:40 and 5:12, and continuing in audio). The 'cuckoo' call of the bird (probably a sound effect not in the score), and the misalignment of the bird's call with musical phrases amplifies the craziness and the cacophony of the rapidly alternating, chaotic visual elements. Swiftly contrasting melodic changes from one musical

[40]. *Ibidem*, p. 68.

[41]. While readers of the novel know that Aunt Marge is ultimately rescued and deflated, I characterize the scene as violent because it includes abusive verbal interactions (a form of violent communication), which in turn motivates Harry's rage (a form of violent expression), and leads to the violation of Aunt Marge's physical body.

[42]. Music provides a melodic imitation of various patterns of laughter. Indeed, if each instrumental note were replaced by the vocalization 'ha' or 'he' the rhythm and melodic contour of most measures would sound like laughter.

measure to the next emphasize the preposterousness of the situation, and also reflect how characters (much like the viewer) have no idea of what will happen next. Such a contrast is evident between measure nine and measures ten through eleven (as assigned in the published piano reduction, and shown in Ex. 3).

Ex. 3: an example of an abrupt contrast between stability and instability in "Aunt Marge's Waltz", from *Harry Potter and the Prisoner of Azkaban* (© 2004 BMI), published by Warner-Barham Music LLC, transcribed from the piano reduction printed by Alfred Music. Used in compliance with the U.S. Copyright Act, Section 107.

Measure nine consists of only one persistent melodic note supported by a tonic G major chord, then in measures nine and ten, the melody suddenly traverses through two octaves (supported by an unexpected harmonic progression through E♭7 and DM7), creating an abrupt contrast between stability and instability (*Prisoner of Azkaban* DVD: 4:28 – 4:32). And yet, the gradual thickening of the orchestra, and the prominent rising and falling of the trombones in parallel with crashing cymbals and trilling piccolo, and the frequent use of Rossini's trademark crescendo, clearly reflect Marge's growing body, her new buoyant form, and the general frenzy of her spectacular ascent[43].

Juxtaposed against the pervasive humorous misalignment, three examples of audio-visual alignment are increasingly gratifying as both Marge and then Dudley suffer well-earned indignities. First, Aunt Marge's swelling neck busts apart her amber necklace, showering beads all over the dining room as the descending orchestral gesture cascades down. Second, Marge pops one of her shirt buttons which catapults across the table and smacks Dudley on the forehead on the musical downbeat (*Prisoner of Azkaban* DVD: 5:06). Last, Marge pops another shirt button that also smacks Dudley on the forehead, though this time it happens on a weak downbeat (subverting expectation by delaying gratification, *Prisoner of Azkaban* DVD: 5:11). In contrast to the many other misalignments in the scene, these three examples maximize the narrative interpretation that circumstances have aligned for the Dursleys to experience just desserts they have long deserved.

The music itself includes a humorous incongruency in that it contains qualities of both formality and folly. Much as magic disrupts the formal structure of the Dursley's home, the formal, seemingly symmetrical structure of the four measure waltz phrase is repeatedly subverted by phrase extensions, while the regularity of harmonic cadence is

[43]. While allusions to Prokofiev's style pervade Williams's works, reflecting this profound influence at a personal level, this is not the case with Rossini, thus imbuing this overt reference in this particular scene with a strong dramaturgic relevance.

subverted by multiple transitions to new key areas. Disruptive musical contrasts create fun and support the erratic nature of Harry's adolescent skills as well as Marge's unexpected physical experience — see Ex. 4.

Ex. 4: an example of multiple transitions in "Aunt Marge's Waltz", from *Harry Potter and the Prisoner of Azkaban* (© 2004 BMI), published by Warner-Barham Music LLC, transcribed from the piano reduction printed by Alfred Music. Used in compliance with the U.S. Copyright Act, Section 107.

For instance, a semi-tuneful French horn phrase (resembling the French horn motif from Richard Strauss's *Till Eulenspiegel's Merry Pranks* — see Ex. 5) beginning with the pick-up to measure 25 in the published piano score, combines legato with staccato notes, diatonicism with chromaticism, and triplets with non-measure preserving hemiola within the frame of eight measures (*Prisoner of Azkaban* DVD: 4:37 - 4:46). Strauss's tone poem depicts the mischief and mishaps of the unflappable German folk hero Till Eulenspiegel. Strauss's theme for Till, also played by a French horn and melodically emphasizing a cyclical motif from the first to the sixth scale degrees, is provided for comparison in Ex. 5.

Ex. 5: Till's theme from Richard Strauss's *Till Eulenspiegel* (1894-1895), ear transcription.

The association with Strauss's motif reminds (musically educated) audiences of the prank-like quality of Harry's effect on his aunt. When Aunt Marge ascends fully inflated into the sky, one hears the last strains of "Aunt Marge's Waltz" as it has transformed into a duple meter, triumphant, cadential fanfare in G major in the style of a classical Rossini closure (*Prisoner of Azkaban* DVD: 5:32).

The transition away from "Aunt Marge's Waltz" includes clever references to dancing in ways that further emphasize the off-putting behaviours of the Dursleys. The camera withdraws inside the house, leaving Petunia and Vernon Dursley on the back lawn waving as Marge drifts away. Inside the house, Harry's unconcerned cousin Dudley aloofly watches a tongue-in-cheek tango performed by a dancing woman and her inflatable-doll partner to Gerardo Matos Rodríguez's famous tango tune "La Cumparsita" (played in G harmonic-minor) on a variety show on television. There is a visual parallel here between the inflated Aunt Marge and the inflated dance partner, and a musical parallel between the waltz-tempo G-major music accompanying Aunt Marge and the G-minor tango tune accompanying the dancers on the television. The sound of the tango continues as the camera follows Harry rushing upstairs (*Prisoner of Azkaban* DVD: 6:11), and fades away when Harry enters his bedroom. Once inside, he sits on the bed, pausing a moment to reflect on the magically moving colour photograph of his late parents on the nightstand (*Prisoner of Azkaban* DVD: 6:20). In the picture, his father takes his mother's arms in a dance-like position and turns them both as if dancing together while autumn leaves drift around them. As Harry watches them, a plaintive G (natural) minor melody in slow waltz time is heard[44]. There is another visual parallel between Dudley watching the dancers on the television screen and Harry watching his parents dancing in the photograph, and likewise, another musical parallel between the diegetic tango tune (in G harmonic minor) with the non-diegetic plaintive waltz (in G natural minor). Importantly, these parallels create a comparison for the viewer amongst the absurdity of Aunt Marge's punishment, the vapidity of Dudley's television obsession, and finally the tenderness that Harry feels for his parents.

The different applications of music through this transition signify different levels of reality and truth — for the viewer and for the characters. "Aunt Marge's Waltz" fulfils a typical underscore role of helping make real (for the viewer) the otherwise unbelievable visuals of Marge's expanding body. The verisimilitude of the television programme engaging Dudley's attention (more than watching his Aunt float to the sky) adds a commentary on the level to which characters themselves accept the events as real. This might also be interpreted as a reflexive layer of commentary on the use of music in cinema itself: that the same mesmerizing principles that keep viewers glued to the film also keep Dudley glued to the television within the film. Further, the dance motifs make an emotional appeal to perceptions of reality and truth: although the dancers on the TV programme use formal positions and figures, the partnership with an inflatable-doll partner lacks substance; in contrast, although Harry's parents merely improvise a ballroom style turn out of context, we can perceive that their 'dance' is more authentic. Likewise, the musical parallels between the bombastic spectacle piece "Aunt Marge's Waltz," the cliché tango tune "La Cumparsita" and the plaintive waltz accompanying Harry's parents contribute to an emotional appeal distinguishing a deeper understanding of what 'real' family looks like. Having just experienced the folly of the Dursleys's conduct (indirectly contributing to

[44]. I call this the 'Love/Reflection/Longing' theme in Webster 2009, though official published materials call it "A Window to the Past". The theme figuratively and mimetically reflects Harry's emotional inner world.

Aunt Marge's inflation), and the vapidity of Harry's life in their home (depicted through Dudley Dursley's hypnotic attention to the television), the viewer comes to understand that Harry's longing and love for his parents and the love they had for him is not only real, it is something that truly matters. Music helps strengthen all these meanings by highlighting the parallels of these events and situations.

Conclusion

The *Harry Potter* films encompass one of the most popular narratives of our time: the seven-novel series has influenced an entire generation of readers worldwide, the *Harry Potter* films have been seen by millions of viewers, the franchise continues to operate in various media (including video games, newly illustrated editions of the novels, websites, theme parks, and so on), and the commercially successful *Harry Potter* film scores have developed award-winning reputations alongside and separate from the *Harry Potter* films (for instance, performed in concert and on the radio). Likewise, the role of fan and critical reception in the phenomenon is significant, and may have influenced producers to hire different collaborators in order to capitalize on this once in a lifetime literary/film phenomenon. As such, the different director-composer collaborations on the *Harry Potter* saga not only harboured different aesthetic visions, their output created decidedly different film experiences.

Williams's scores for the first two *Harry Potter* films meet the expectation for Classical Hollywood style of film music (through use of leitmotifs, mickey-mousing, and the use of rich and varied orchestral colours) while also hitting the typical markers of Williams's particular brand: namely, a prominent main theme ("Hedwig's Theme") and well-crafted leitmotifs that align meticulously with the visuals. Each score for the first two films prioritizes an organized clarity in storytelling, music faithfully accompanies the visuals and the narrative developments, and contributes to the lighthearted slapstick visual humour. For the third *Harry Potter* film, Cuarón's more experimental approach allowed Williams to incorporate alternative strategies, thus renegotiating the musical landscape set forth in the first films. The results were not only musically outstanding, they were compelling examples of creativity. The resulting score included a second hit main theme ("Double Trouble"), and well-crafted, longer leitmotifs that align with emotional resonances with the film's more complex narrative core. The audio-visual relationship prioritizes complex layers of meaning, multiple perspectives on truth and reality, and makes way for darker, sometimes macabre humour.

Importantly, the films feel different from one another because of the different strategies employed. While Williams's underscore for the first two films with director Chris Columbus established a relationship between music and visuals that carefully guided viewers in a re-telling of the novels, Williams's underscore for the third film with director Alfonso Cuarón took on the task of re-negotiating what he had originally set forth. It was Williams's distinction as the first composer to work on the saga and the only to work with two subsequent directors to set a course of musical change that ultimately echoed throughout the remaining three collaborations that rounded out the series. The success of the multi-collaboration experiment was made possible by Williams's successful endeavours to establish both continuity and change, a formula copied by more recent film sagas such as the *Twilight* series. Further, the examination of Williams's endeavours in the *Harry Potter* films attests to the capacity of his film scores to function adaptively and creatively by keeping up with the times. Indeed, the formidable music box that underscored the first Harry Potter films was also able to change its tune because of Williams's musical versatility and his adaptability to the needs of different directors, different tones, and different stories.

Bibliography

Audissino 2014

Audissino, Emilio. *John Williams's Film Music: «Jaws», «Star Wars», «Raiders of the Lost Ark», and the Return of the Classical Hollywood Music Style*, Madison (WI), University of Wisconsin Press, 2014 (Wisconsin Film Studies).

Chion 1994

Chion, Michel. *Audio-Vision: Sound on Screen*, edited and translated by Claudia Gorbman with a foreword by Walter Murch, New York, Columbia University, 1994.

Corliss 2001

Corliss, Richard. 'Wizardry without Magic', in: *Time*, 19 November 2001, <http://content.time.com/time/magazine/article/0,9171,184011,00.html>, accessed February 2018.

Cross 2008

Cross, Julie. 'Frightening and Funny: Humour in Children's Gothic Fiction', in: *The Gothic in Children's Literature: Haunting the Borders*, edited by Anna Jackson, Karen Coats and Roderick McGillis, New York, Routledge, 2008, pp. 57-76.

Dickey n.d.

Dickey, Lucinda. 'The Creators of *Harry Potter* Break Out of Character to Discuss *The Prisoner of Azkaban*', in: *Science Fiction Weekly*, <http://web.archive.org/web/20070819163554/http://www.scifi.com/sfw/issue372/interview.html>, accessed February 2018.

Filmtracks 2004

Filmtracks. '*Harry Potter and the Prisoner of Azkaban*', in: *Filmtracks.com*, 24 May 2004, <http://www.filmtracks.com/titles/prisoner_azkaban.html>, accessed February 2018.

Gorbman 1987

Gorbman, Claudia. *Unheard Melodies: Narrative Film Music*, Bloomington, Indiana University Press, 1987.

Honeycutt 2001

Honeycutt, Kirk. '*Harry Potter and the Sorcerer's Stone*', in: *The Hollywood Reporter*, 9 November 2001, <https://www.hollywoodreporter.com/review/harry-potter-sorcerers-stone-2001-review-946999>, accessed February 2018.

Hunter 2007

Hunter, Ian Q. 'Post-Classical Fantasy Cinema: *The Lord of the Rings*', in: *The Cambridge Companion to Literature on Screen*, edited by Deborah Cartmell and Imelda Whelehan, Cambridge, Cambridge University Press, 2007 (Cambridge Companions to Literature), pp. 154-166.

Jenson 2005

Jenson, Jeff. 'A Look Back: Producer David Heyman Recounts the Highs and Lows of Making the First Three "Potter" Movies, from Finding Harry to Losing Richard Harris', in: *Entertainment Weekly*, 4 November 2005, <http://ew.com/article/2005/11/04/potter-movie-producer-reflects-franchise>, accessed February 2018.

Johnson – Larson 2003

Johnson, Mark L. – Larson, Steve. 'Something in the Way She Moves – Metaphors of Musical Motion', in: *Metaphor and Symbol*, xviii/2 (2003), pp. 63-84.

Larson 2012

Larson, Steve. *Musical Forces: Motion, Metaphor, and Meaning in Music*, Bloomington, Indiana University Press, 2012 (Musical Meaning and Interpretation).

Larson – Van Handel 2005

Id. – Van Handel, Leigh. 'Measuring Musical Forces', in: *Music Perception*, xxiii/2 (2005), pp. 119-136.

Novikov 2008

Novikov, Eugene. 'From Page to Screen: *Harry Potter and the Prisoner of Azkaban*', in: *Cinematical.com*, 11 June 2008, <https://www.moviefone.com/2008/06/11/from-page-to-screen-harry-potter-and-the-prisoner-of-azkaban>, accessed February 2018.

Petrobelli 1994

Petrobelli, Pierluigi. *Music in the Theater: Essays on Verdi and Other Composers*, English translation by Roger Parker, Princeton, Princeton University Press, 1994 (Princeton Studies in Opera).

Pigeon 2007

Pigeon, Ted. 'Great Movies Can Come from Anywhere' in: *The Ted Pigeon Blogspot*, 23 July 2007, <http://tedpigeon.blogspot.com/2007/07/not-every-movie-can-be-great-but-great.html>, accessed February 2018.

Smart 2004

Smart, Mary Ann. *Mimomania: Music and Gesture in Nineteenth-Century Opera*, Berkeley (CA), University of California Press, 2004 (California Studies in 19th-Century Music, 13).

Troost 2007

Troost, Linda V. 'The Nineteenth-Century Novel on Film: Jane Austen', in: *The Cambridge Companion to Literature on Screen*, edited by Deborah Cartmell and Imelda Whelehan, Cambridge, Cambridge University Press, 2007 (Cambridge Companions to Literature), pp. 75-89.

Veatch 1998

Veatch, Thomas. 'A Theory of Humor', in: *Humor, the International Journal of Humor Research*, xi/2 (1998), pp. 161-215.

Webster 2009

Webster, Jamie Lynn. 'The Music of *Harry Potter*: Continuity and Change in the First Five Films', Ph.D. Diss., Eugene (OR), University of Oregon, 2009.

Webster 2012

Ead. 'Creating Magic with Music: The Changing Dramatic Relationship between Music and Magic in *Harry Potter* Films', in: *The Music of Fantasy Cinema*, edited by Janet K. Halfyard, Sheffield (UK), Equinox, 2012 (Genre, Music and Sound).

Case Studies

Sounding an Irish Childhood: John Williams's Score for *Angela's Ashes*

Laura Anderson
(Maynooth University, Ireland)

Frank McCourt's memoir of a childhood, *Angela's Ashes*, was a publishing sensation in 1996, winning the 1997 Pulitzer Prize for biography, the best nonfiction book award of 1996 by *Time Magazine*, the editors' choice for best book by *The New York Times* book review, the National Book Critics' Circle Award and *The Los Angeles Times* Award. It was even credited with contributing to the establishment of the 'misery lit' genre in the late 1990s due to themes of unrelenting poverty, frequent illness, and death woven through the book. Set during the Depression era in the newly-formed Free State Ireland, the story begins with the journey of the McCourt family from their home in Brooklyn back to Limerick where conditions are even harsher than those in New York. The memoir is presented from the perspective of Frank who describes his childhood and adolescent years in Limerick during which he always aspires to return to the United States. The key relationships in the story are with his long-suffering mother, Angela, his alcoholic father, Malachy, and his younger brothers. The author's formative experiences at school, playing with other children in the lanes, and his encounters with teachers and the Catholic Church are all vividly, and often amusingly, recounted. The McCourt family are trapped in a cycle of poverty due to Malachy's alcoholism and resulting inability to hold on to employment. Although Frank is a bright student he is forced to take on work as a teenager to support his family, assisting his neighbour Mr. Hannon to deliver coal and later working as a telegram boy at the post office. Through this work for the postal service, he meets his first love, Theresa Carmody, a young woman with tuberculosis and subsequently experiences his first heartbreak when she dies. He also meets the money lender Mrs Finucane who employs him as an assistant and it is through this job that he manages to save enough money to pay for his passage to America, ending the memoir on a note of hope.

Many readers interpreted the book with its themes of poverty, religion, and emigration as representing a particularly Irish childhood — as McCourt himself put it in the opening paragraphs: «When I look back on my childhood I wonder how I survived at all. It was, of course, a miserable childhood: the happy childhood is hardly worth your while. Worse than the ordinary miserable childhood is the miserable Irish childhood, and worse yet is the miserable Irish Catholic childhood». Yet, Frank's experiences evidently spoke to audiences far beyond Irish shores and, given the popularity of the book, it is unsurprising that when director Alan Parker first considered adapting it for the screen, he found that the rights had already been secured by David Brown who was going to produce the film for Paramount with Scott Rudin[1]. When the project returned to him a year later, a script had already been prepared by writer Laura Jones and Parker then began working on his own draft screenplay[2]. Parker filmed for seventy-five days at various locations around Ireland, including Dublin, Cork, and Limerick and at Ardmore Studios in Bray, with the shooting concluding on 22 December 1998[3].

Although the score for the film was composed after the shooting was complete, discussions among the producers about a suitable composer for the project were ongoing as early as April 1998. Correspondence held in the Alan Parker Archive at the British Film Institute reveals that John Williams expressed an interest in the project at this early stage[4]. In interview, Williams recalled, «I loved the book *Angela's Ashes* and I felt privileged to compose the score for the film»[5]. Securing Williams was a coup for Parker, as he recalled: «John Williams is *the* great maestro, I mean, I can't tell you how wonderful it was working with him»[6]. Williams's score was nominated for an International Film Music Critics Award in 1999 and for an Academy Award and a Golden Globe in 2000. This chapter proposes that the score played a crucial role in the successful adaptation of the memoir for the screen but, in contrast to many other contemporary films made about Ireland, it does not draw on clichéd Irish musical codes. Rather, through an emotional approach to the orchestral score, which features some subtle consistencies with Irish traditional music, the score supports the transformation of one boy's childhood into a universal story about humanity, suffering and survival. Following a discussion of how the score was conceptualized by Parker and Williams, I highlight some of the key characteristics of Williams's score for piano and orchestra, considering how the composer sounded out an Irish childhood and made the soul of the story accessible to a worldwide audience.

---

1. Parker 1999.
2. Parker 2003.
3. Parker 1999.
4. Gorfaine 1998.
5. Williams 2000.
6. Parker 2003.

Williams's Route to *Angela's Ashes*

Williams's career in the late 1990s was defined by several large-scale historical dramas, including *Saving Private Ryan* (Steven Spielberg, 1998) and *Amistad* (Steven Spielberg, 1997); the first instalment in the *Star Wars* prequel trilogy, *Star Wars Episode 1: The Phantom Menace* (George Lucas, 1999); and the adventure films, *Jurassic Park: The Lost World* (Steven Spielberg, 1997) and *Seven Years in Tibet* (Jean-Jacques Annaud, 1997). Narratively and stylistically, *Angela's Ashes* is an outlier of this period, but it was not the first film with an Irish theme that Williams had scored. He had already engaged with a story about the emigration of Irish people to America in his score for *Far and Away* (1992), directed and produced by Ron Howard. Set in 1892, the film tells the story of Joseph Donnelly, a young man from the West of Ireland who runs away to America with his landlord's wilful daughter, Shannon Christie. The pair are intent on securing land in the New World but are challenged by the harsh conditions they encounter on arrival. Their tale is set against the backdrop of the social unease in late nineteenth-century Ireland and the struggle of tenant farmers against the Anglo-Irish ascendency. Williams was influenced by his affection for the John Ford film *The Quiet Man* (John Ford, 1952), which like *Far and Away*, portrays a somewhat romanticized view of Irish culture. The film liberally quotes from Irish folk song and mixes traditional Irish instruments with orchestra. Williams recalled: «One of the films I admired the most when I was a very young person was a John Ford picture, *The Quiet Man*... I always felt I would love to write the score, and this opportunity came along through Ron Howard»[7].

Williams's score for *Far and Away* is obviously Irish in its stylistic codes, most clearly in its employment of The Chieftains whose music is in the main based on the folk-dance repertoire that can be heard in traditional music sessions. This was not the first time that The Chieftains were engaged with a film project: Ceoltóirí Chualann, the band from which they were formed, were employed by Seán Ó'Riada for the music in the seminal Irish film, *Mise Éire* (George Morrison, 1959)[8]. The Chieftains had also been employed by Stanley Kubrick for *Barry Lyndon* (1975), bringing their music to international film audiences.

Ron Howard had attended a concert given by The Chieftains in Pasadena, California during February 1984 and invited founder-member Paddy Moloney to compose the score for his next intended film, *The Rainbow Warrior*, but this project never came to fruition. Yet, the concert provided inspiration for *Far and Away* almost ten years later[9]. Howard recalled: «There was one song they played about an emigrant going off to America that was bittersweet, romantic and very Irish. [...] Then I started making a few notes and plot

7. Williams quoted in Audissino 2014, p. 225.

8. For discussion of the music in *Mise Éire*, see Cooper 2006.

9. Glatt 1997, p. 200.

ideas. That concert was point of origin for the movie, so it seemed fairly logical when John Williams was doing the music that we should bring The Chieftains in to play the main themes»[10]. Given the integral role played by The Chieftains in the conception of *Far and Away*, it is unsurprising that Williams's score was heavily influenced by their music.

The traditional timbres of The Chieftains (the group comprises two fiddles, flute, tin whistle, Uilleann pipes, harp and bodhrán) were married with the orchestra. The Chieftains received the orchestrations of Williams's score three days before the recording session with the full symphony orchestra at Sony Studios[11]. The group enjoyed a good working relationship with Williams who welcomed Moloney's amendments to the score to make it more «Chieftains-friendly»[12]. Williams described, «We needed Irish music played by Irish artistes [...]. These men are the best in the world — they're uniquely great. There's no side to them. They just turn up, play their instruments and get on with it»[13].

Some cues for *Far and Away* are played by The Chieftains without the orchestra, notably to accompany Joseph's fighting scenes, which lends the scenes a lighter character. For example, the first part of "The Fighting Donnellys" is a single jig in 6/8 time, with the typical crotchet-quaver lilting pattern that imbues the brothers' fight with a comical atmosphere. The audience knows that they are not seriously intent on harming each other. Williams's main titles for the film provide a good example of his fusion of traditional features with the symphony orchestra. He draws on instruments widely used in the Irish tradition: the Uilleann pipes, tin whistle, and the harp[14], combining these timbres with large string sections, infusing the melodies with ornamental figures in an Irish style, associated in particular with the sean nós performance style of slow airs. This includes the addition of grace notes, filling in large intervals, and the replacement of long sustained notes with shorter repeated notes. The melody, which has a clear modal quality, is presented on tin whistle, which would be idiomatic of melodic presentation in an Irish traditional music group. Williams also uses pan pipes, which although not typical of Irish traditional music are congruent with the overall Irish soundscape. Overall, it is abundantly clear to the audience that this soundscape functions to underline the fact that this is an Irish story (indeed, one of the reported working titles was *The Irish Story*[15]). While the original score with its exuberant folk-dance-like numbers and the contributions by The Chieftains works well for a film whose central theme is lively, romantic, and often light-hearted, its style would be incongruent with the much graver themes at stake in *Angela's Ashes*.

10. Quoted in *ibidem*, p. 252.
11. *ibidem*, p. 252.
12. *Ibidem*.
13. Quoted in *ibidem*.
14. The harp is the official symbol of the Irish state and often used in the performance of traditional airs.
15. *Far and Away* B.F.I. n.d.

DEVELOPMENT OF THE SOUNDSCAPE FOR *ANGELA'S ASHES*

The first distancing step from the *Far and Away* antecedent involved timbres: Williams dispensed with the sounds of Uilleann pipes and tin whistle for *Angela's Ashes*; the harp is the only instrument to nod to the Irish subject matter. He prepared a score that reflected his view of the book as a chamber piece with five principal characters: «I felt that a chamber music approach with musical protagonists that would more or less match the acting ones might work. I wrote a score that featured the piano, harp, oboe, and cello set in front of a string orchestra»[16]. The score required thirty-two violins, fourteen violas, twelve cellos, eight double basses, three flutes, three oboes (third oboe doubling cor anglais), four clarinets, three bassoons (third bassoon doubling contrabassoon), five horns, three tenor trombones and one bass trombone, one tuba, piano, harp, guitar, synthesizer, timpani, and percussion[17]. Williams composed a detailed condensed score consisting of forty-nine cues (including some alternative versions), which were then fully orchestrated by John Neufeld for the recording sessions at Sony Los Angeles between 28 June and 2 July 1999, with the cues requiring the largest orchestral forces recorded on the first date[18]. The most common instrumental combinations in the film are piano, harp, and strings with oboe often used for particularly poignant or nostalgic cues (2m5 "A Pint on the Day of the Funeral" when Frank is appalled to see his father resting his pint on his brother's coffin; 3m14 "Rejection at the Priest's House" when Frank is rejected as an altar boy; and 4m8 "The Holy Trinity is my Dad", which accompanies the description of Malachy's change of character when he drinks).

The alternation of solos with the renditions of the theme on strings characterizes the score[19]. The choice of oboe rather than flute solo and cello rather than violin arguably situates the soundscape in darker sonic territory than *Far and Away*. Solo piano initiates the theme in many of the cues and its intimate tone is well suited to the direct nature of the memoir — piano alone is used for cue 7m3 "Lying with Theresa", arguably the most personal moment of the film when Frank lies next to his girlfriend. The piano's timbre also blends well with the church bells that frequently share the film's soundscape. Although high strings are used in some cues, such as when Frank's father departs, when Frank leaves the house of his mother's abusive cousin, and when the family gather to watch the eclipse, most of the cues are grounded with large lower string sections. This emphasis on lower strings in the orchestration communicates the melancholic atmosphere very effectively. The cello is particularly prominent at times of grief such as in cue 2m4 "Lord, Why

16. Williams quoted in AUDISSINO 2014, p. 226.

17. RECORDING SESSION CUE LIST 1999.

18. *Ibidem*.

19. The instrumental soloists were John Ellis (oboe), Steve Erdody (cello), Jo Ann Turovsky (harp), and Randy Kerber (piano).

Do You Want the Wee Children?", when Malachy prays in despair; while cue 6m5 "Grandma's Funeral" is a simple combination of solo oboe and solo cello. Through the absence of sections of the orchestra for much of the film, the score suggests that Frank's life will only be complete when he escapes Ireland and emigrates to America. The full orchestra is reserved for the end of the film, with the addition of complete woodwind, brass, and percussion sections underlining the resolution and hope of Frank's successful arrival in New York harbour.

Williams's musical style in *Angela's Ashes* was shaped by Parker's wishes for the score and the director had clear ideas about both the original score and the pre-existing music featured in the film, even penning a song himself, "Kaiser Bill", for Malachy to perform in a scene of the family moving to a new house following their eviction from Roden Lane[20]. Parker had read the book closely and identified it as very cinematic and a story whose humanity would touch viewers internationally[21]. The director met with Williams in Boston during late May/early June 1999 to discuss the music for the project, and the details of the temp track discussed reveal the kind of soundscape that they hoped to achieve — as described by Ron Sadoff, «the temp track, in most cases, is a veritable blueprint of a film's soundtrack — a musical topography of score, songs, culture and codes»[22]. Yet, in an unusual move, the temp track for *Angela's Ashes* was not chosen by a Music Editor (as is the case in most film projects) but by Parker himself. On consideration of other projects by the director, this is not uncharacteristic, as described by Damon Wise: «Given that Parker is hands-on with every aspect of production — so Kubrickian, almost, that even he admits that, "It's a pain in the arse" — the process is even more complex. Parker oversees everything from script to score, grading the final print and making sure the video transfer corresponds to his original vision»[23]. Indeed, on earlier projects collaborating with Trevor Jones, Parker relished the opportunity to work with music «toolkits», collections of musical sounds that can be layered and built up by the director to create a range of atmospheric soundscapes[24]. In his work with Jones, Parker would handle pre-prepared musical stems, deciding on soundscapes for specific scenes. He recalled this earlier use of toolkits, which undoubtedly bolstered his confidence in preparing the temp track for *Angela's Ashes*:

> During the editing process I usually experiment with a 'tool kit' of music. On this film it was a particular pleasure as John Williams had agreed to do the finished score. I consequently laid up a miscellany of John's music, culled from his previous scores, to help me judge the ebb and flow of scenes

20. Parker initially wanted to use Al Jolson's song "Swanee", but this was too expensive so he composed his own song instead. PARKER 2003.

21. *Ibidem.*

22. SADOFF 2006, p. 166.

23. WISE 2000, p. 67.

24. SAPIRO 2014.

> but principally to aid the 'spotting' of just where we were going to need music. I showed John an early cut of the film in June and, after finishing his latest *Star Wars* opus, he began work on our score[25].

Parker's temp track for *Angela's Ashes* drew most frequently on *Seven Years in Tibet* (1997) (tracks twelve and nine[26]) for twenty-two cues; *Presumed Innocent* (Alan J. Pakula, 1990) (tracks two and ten) for six cues; one cue from *Nixon* (Oliver Stone, 1995); and *Sleepers* (Barry Levinson, 1996) for four cues related to the Church (track four "Saying the Rosary" is a choral piece that works perfectly in this context). Music by Zbigniew Preisner, most famous for his Romantic-style scores for Kryzystof Kieślowski, was used (although it is unclear which piece), and Parker chose track eight from Thomas Newman's *Oscar and Lucinda* (Gillian Armstrong, 1997) to accompany one scene. The most heavily used track, track twelve "Quiet Moments", from *Seven Years in Tibet*, shares obvious similarities with the score for *Angela's Ashes*, including the prominence accorded to cello and piano and the role of string orchestra. *Presumed Innocent* shares the use of the harp and the repetition of brief figures on piano accompanied by strings. *Nixon* also makes use of the harp and string orchestra and Williams described this score as «thematic but in a more motivic way [...] not a melody that you follow along [...] in a focussed direction, it's full of contrasts and difficulties»[27]. As will be discussed, this description of motivic thematicism holds true also for *Angela's Ashes*. These temp choices all share a reflective tone, a sense of intimacy in the use of solo instruments, and a prominent role for the string section of the orchestra. Parker and Williams annotated the list of temp tracks with some further amendments that would impact on the film editing, and Parker then distributed these changes to Gerry Hambling (Film Editor), Eddy Joseph (Supervising Sound Editor), David Wimbury (Line Producer), and Carolyne Chauncey (First Assistant Editor)[28].

The list of temp tracks included some pre-existing pieces that were retained in the final film, most frequently jazz standards, including recordings of Billie Holliday ("I Can't Give You Anything but Love", "Pennies from Heaven", "Your Mother's Son-in-Law"); Al Bowlly ("Bei Mir Bist du Schoen", "You Couldn't Be Cuter"); and Nat Gonella and His Georgians ("The Dipsy Doodle"). The use of music featured in the book can be contextualized within Parker's overall ambition to be loyal to the text. McCourt recalled that he did not like Irish traditional music while growing up, instead tuning the radio to the armed forces network and songs performed by Billie Holliday and Louis Armstrong[29]. Holliday's impact was such that McCourt described how he felt she was singing directly

---

25. PARKER 1999.

26. Based on analysis of the chosen tracks, it is assumed that the track numbers refer to the order of tracks on the official soundtrack.

27. WILLIAMS 1995.

28. TEMP MUSIC CUES 1999.

29. ROSE 1997.

to him[30]. Parker placed the jazz selections at light hearted moments in the story or scenes where Frank is happy, such as playing truant with his friends or at the cinema. "The Dipsy Doodle" is used when Frank's father gets a job, when Frank earns his first shilling as assistant to Mr. Hannon, and when he is preparing for work as a telegram boy in his new suit. In addition to alluding to Frank's love of American culture, Parker saw his choice of jazz as balancing with Williams's original score:

> I used a lot of sort of humorous music, really jazzy music, to balance what John Williams was doing with his score and also I wanted to avoid the cliché Irish music, I mean, which you hear in *every* single Irish film. And it was relevant to this story too because Frank had started out in Brooklyn and actually the music of the United States became very relevant to him thinking about getting back there. So I tried to use American music wherever possible to counterbalance the lyricism of John Williams's score[31].

Thus, through his discussions with Parker about the temp track, Williams was aware of the intended choice and placement of pre-existing songs as well as the emotional and lyrical atmosphere Parker had in mind for the original score before he started work.

Perhaps most striking about the temp track choices is that there is no attempt to draw on any typically Irish-sounding cues. The only Irish traditional music we encounter in the film is diegetic, Frank's father singing rebel songs ("Kevin Barry", "Roddy McCorley", "The Boys of Wexford"); his mother singing nostalgic Irish ballads; or the instrumental jigs and reels at dancing classes. Arguably, the universality of the film's themes encouraged avoidance of obvious Irish traditional musical tropes in the original score. In his study of Irishness and music, John O'Flynn points out that rejection of stereotypical Irishness in music usually involves a rejection of «kitsch», «twee», «stage-Irish» or «tourist-oriented performance»[32]. Parker recalls that he and Williams agreed to such a rejection early in the project:

> We were very keen not to go into the clichés of the kind of scores that are always associated with Irish films. We made a pact, John and I, very early on that there would be, from an instrumental point of view, there would be no bodhrán drums and Uilleann pipes and all the kind of things you normally associate with scores you see with Irish film, I mean, the *Riverdance* mentality, we were trying to avoid quite frankly[33].

Riverdance was an extraordinarily popular work of Irish music and dance, the creation of composer Bill Whelan and producer Moya Doherty, with choreography

30. McCourt 2004, p. 320.
31. Parker 2003.
32. O'Flynn 2009, p. 185.
33. Parker 2003.

by Jean Butler and Michael Flatley. It was premiered as the interval show at the 1994 Eurovision song contest hosted in Dublin. Musically, Whelan combined elements of Irish traditional music with orchestral and choral resources in a modern and confident representation of Irishness. As O'Flynn puts it, «this could glibly be described as a kind of Irishness-in-your-face»[34]. *Riverdance*'s popularity led to a range of spin off dance shows, notably Michael Flatley's *Lord of the Dance*, and the original show continues to tour nationally and internationally[35]. Although the combination of traditional instruments with orchestra might have been a viable compositional approach, the supercharged Irishness of *Riverdance* associated with modern affluent Ireland would not be compatible with the gritty tale of *Angela's Ashes* and might even undermine the sense of the memoir's authenticity. This is partially supported by the distinction between «Irish» and «Irishry» outlined by O'Flynn. He describes how within the association of Irish traditional music with Irishness, «a qualitative distinction is made between, on one side, music that sounds and feels Irish ('Irishy'), and, on the other side, music that sounds but does not feel Irish ('Irishry')»[36]. Yet, Parker and Williams were not interested in authenticity in the sense of Irish traditional music either. Rather, they aimed to achieve an *emotional* authenticity that should sound universal, in a score which would be true to the soul of the story and the characters' feelings about their daily struggles in dire poverty. Discussing his approach, Williams stated, «I thought that using a sort of Irish vernacular music might narrow the piece down [...]. Another way of going was to take a more universal approach, a more emotional approach, if you like, with the orchestra expressing the broad, human aspect of the experience. There was no need, I felt, for the music to emphasize the specifically Irish or Catholic aspect of the story»[37]. In the following section, I will discuss how this is borne out musically in a score that speaks to an international audience while suggesting some understated resonances of Irishness.

Hearing an Alternative Irishness in *Angela's Ashes*?

Investigating national identity in music presents many pitfalls, most obviously the threat of a reductive or simplistic analysis. As highlighted by John O'Flynn and Mark Fitzgerald, although the analytic construct of identity could be considered overused in existing scholarship, it retains currency because it continues to be used by people to categorize themselves and others[38]. While it would be impossible to argue that music

[34]. O'Flynn 2009, p. 39.

[35]. At the time of writing, *Riverdance* is midway through a summer run in Dublin's Gaiety Theatre.

[36]. O'Flynn 2009, p. 94.

[37]. Dyer 2000.

[38]. O'Flynn – Fitzgerald 2014, pp. 3-4.

itself is nationalistic in identity, certain musical traits come to be understood as nationalist thanks to cultural and political discourse around music's composition and reception[39]. This is apparent in the case of identifying music as Irish although, as O'Flynn argues, there is no one clear-cut conception of Irishness and the associations with music can be understood perceptually instead of «a definable set of essential meanings»[40]. Although an essential set of definitions for Irishness in music is impossible, there are some codes that listeners repeatedly identify as Irish. O'Flynn reveals a broad tendency to characterize Irish music as either «lively» (heavily associated with traditional dance music) or «haunting»[41]. He notes that this is reflected onscreen:

> The expressive characterization of Irish music as either 'lively' or 'haunting' is reflected in many representations of Irishness, notably, in TV and film. Here, I refer not only to Irish-produced film scores but also to major Hollywood and British productions that involve Irish themes and/or Irish(y) music, some examples being the films *Far and Away* (1992) and *Titanic* (1997) and the BBC drama series *Ballykissangel* (1996). Typically, music written in Irish reel or jig style is used to depict some brawl, chase or other 'humorous' event, while a solo female voice is often used to evoke feelings of passion, loneliness and suffering[42].

This description holds true for numerous contemporary films such as *Michael Collins* (Neil Jordan, 1996) and *The Wind That Shakes the Barley* (Ken Loach, 2006). Both films feature haunting renditions of folk songs by Irish singers as part of their soundtracks, including some sung in Gaelic in the latter film, and both films draw on ethnic instruments to underline the sense of place. By contrast, *Dancing at Lughnasa* (Pat O'Connor, 1998) features music by Bill Whelan written in Irish reel or jig style, falling into the «lively» category and strongly suggestive of *Riverdance*. Although *Angela's Ashes*' score can be described as haunting rather than lively, it is not explicitly Irish and does not borrow Irish folk song in this way. Instead, the main theme's contemplative character paired with the story told through the eyes of a child ensures that the audience is haunted by the poignancy of the combination.

I would suggest that Williams's engagement with McCourt's book is key to understanding his score and his identification of an Irish lilt in the text is illuminating: «What I love is the Irish lilt that lifts the story away from bleakest tragedy — that line near the end, for example, when he says, "There are three things an Irishman is allowed to love: God, children, and a horse that wins". Colour and humour like that help define a land in which the two great institutions are the church and the pub, both of them

39. WOOD 2012, p. 197.
40. O'FLYNN 2009, p. 18.
41. *Ibidem*, p. 150.
42. *Ibidem*, p. 150.

offering solace but not solutions»[43]. Arguably Williams reflected this identification in his score, which adopts the universal language of Hollywood — use of large orchestra with dominant strings, the primacy accorded the melody line, a thematic approach to motives underpinning the structure, and use of tonal harmony — but with a slight lilt that is suggestive of Irish traditional music.

The main theme encompasses several short motives that recur across the film. I wish to highlight three to consider some consistencies with typical features of Irish traditional music. The first motive (Ex. 1), which underpins the entire score, is first heard on piano and consists of two elements. It begins with a four bar-phrase that comprises two repeated bars introducing a plaintive melody, which continues over the repeated quaver patterns. This melody becomes bound up with the characterization of Frank due to its initial solo presentation as he begins his tale and recurrence at the close of the end credits, solidifying the connection with the end of his journey. The motive is suggestive of G minor with some borrowed chords at the opening. This minor-mode quality in conjunction with the slow pace, and association with the lead character, ensures that the melody is highly emotive. The opening leap followed by a step down a tone (highlighted in bar four) recalls the typical opening leaps of many Irish airs, most famously Thomas Moore's melodies[44], such as "The Last Rose of Summer", and thus subtly inflects the melody with a hint of Irishness[45].

Ex. 1: transcription of John Williams, "Theme from Angela's Ashes" (mm. 1-6), from *Angela's Ashes* (© 1999 BMI), published by Sony/ATV Melody and Universal Songs of Polygram International, Inc. Used in compliance with the U.S. Copyright Act, Section 107.

[43]. Dyer 2000.

[44]. Moore wrote the lyrics to airs in the main collected by Edward Bunting in his three volumes of *The Ancient Music of Ireland*.

[45]. Motherway 2013, p. 21.

The second motive (Ex. 2) functions as a countersubject to the first motive, consisting of just two bars and concluding with a half-close cadence, which means that it often appears as a self-contained motive or dovetailed with others.

Ex. 2: transcription of John Williams, "Theme from Angela's Ashes" (mm. 26-27), from *Angela's Ashes* (© 1999 BMI), published by Sony/ATV Melody and Universal Songs of Polygram International, Inc. Used in compliance with the U.S. Copyright Act, Section 107.

The third reflective motive (Ex. 3) consists of four chords and is evocative of the Dorian mode, although it cannot be classified as such and instead can be understood as continuing to circle around a d minor tonality established in the preceding bars but with some borrowed chords from g minor. Harmonically, it could be heard as a gentle allusion to Irish airs, which are typically minor modal. The passage feels detached, lonely, and separate from the rest of the score. This motive is used for contemplative moments, notably when Frank's Dad kisses him for the first time in his life at the hospital and the motive dovetails seamlessly into the first motive's melody on strings. Such transitioning from one brief motive to another, rather than expansive development of any one melody, is a key feature of the score for *Angela's Ashes*.

Ex. 3: transcription of John Williams, "Theme from Angela's Ashes" (m. 37), from *Angela's Ashes* (© 1999 BMI), published by Sony/ATV Melody and Universal Songs of Polygram International, Inc. Used in compliance with the U.S. Copyright Act, Section 107.

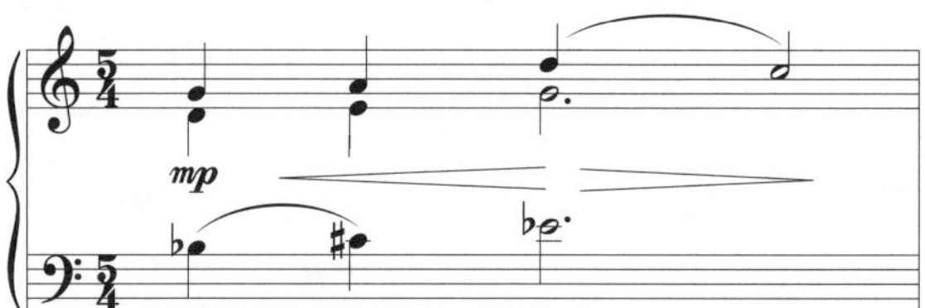

These motives are articulated in simple textures throughout the film with piano solo or supported by strings, usually monophonic or homophonic in texture. This is typical of textures of one Irish traditional music performance tradition — solo or groups of instruments playing the same melodic line without harmonic or polyphonic layers.

Rhythmically, the flowing quavers in compound time with use of semiquaver ornamentation of the first motive provide continuity across the film. They can also be seen to be consistent with the groupings of three in compound metres of Irish traditional dance music, particularly in the regular return of the opening four bar figures. The repetitive structures of traditional dance music were identified as Irish by listeners in O'Flynn's studies[46]:

> The idea of repetition came up with some frequency in interviews that were recorded at classical music events and at traditional music events. Significantly, ten interviewees at the informal pub sessions made reference to the repetitive structures of traditional dance music. Mostly, this involved positive terms such as «musical continuity», «alternations and repetitions», «the repeated structures», and «the way the dances go round and back to each other»[47].

Although the time signature changes in the opening bars (6/8 - 7/8 - 6/8 - 9/8 - 12/8 - 6/8 - 12/8), this can be interpreted as written out *rubato* in 6/8 which does not disrupt the flow of the music or prevent the audience hearing it as continuous until the change to 4/4 for the arrival of the second motive.

These melodic, rhythmic, and textural traits identified as consistent with features of Irishness in music are very understated and completely different to the surface level musical codes used in *Far and Away*. Indeed, reviews of the soundtrack noted that the film was remarkable in its avoidance of obvious Irishness: «The temptation to use Irish clichés may have been great but has been completely resisted, which has resulted in one of the best scores from one of the best composers»[48]; «For the most part eschewing the Oirish clichés that streamed through his score for *Far and Away*, John Williams' score for Alan Parker's cinematic recreation of Frank McCourt's childhood is much more low key than you would expect from the blockbuster merchant»[49].

CONCLUSION

McCourt never intended for his memoir to be a book about a specific place, considering it to be simply a book about poverty[50]. This ambition was recognized by Parker and Williams and for most listeners, the film's score will probably be heard as more evocative of the composer's earlier work than of any explicit sense of Irishness. Yet, when listening to the score in the context of viewing the film, whose images are full of visual codes of Irishness, it is much more likely that the audience are expecting to hear some

[46]. O'FLYNN 2009, p. 164.

[47]. *Ibidem*.

[48]. KEECH 2000, p. 27.

[49]. FREER 2000, pp. 130-131.

[50]. PARKER 1999.

Irish musical codes and are more likely to identify some of the subtle marks of Irishness discussed in this chapter. These suggestions of Irishness can be compared to the lilt that imbues McCourt's book — never the prime focus of our attention but identifiable in the background. Williams's musical language, employment of the symphony orchestra, and the presentation of the musical motives in both solo and orchestral renditions conform to the conventions of Hollywood scoring and to Williams's neo-Romantic style, famous from his many big budget projects. The music's lyricism complements Parker's choice of including more care-free pre-existing jazz, deepening the emotional impact of the story. International audiences can comfortably interpret the score according to the conventional codes of Hollywood scoring and, in this way, Williams supports the emotional connection the audience feels to the character of Frank. The score presents his perspective, reflective of the first-person mode of narration in the memoir, and it enables the transformation of the text for the screen, drawing out the key themes of poverty, struggle, and hope and making the story accessible to and relatable for audiences around the globe.

Bibliography

Primary Sources

McCourt 2004

McCourt, Frank. *Angela's Ashes: A Memoir of a Childhood*, London, Harper Perennial, 1996, rpt. 2004.

Parker 1999

Parker, Alan. '*Angela's Ashes*: The Making of the Film', 1999, at <http://alanparker.com/film/angelas-ashes/making/>, accessed March 2018.

Parker 2003

Id. 'Director's Commentary', in: *Angela's Ashes*, Paramount Pictures and Universal Pictures International, 2003 (DVD).

Rose 1997

Rose, Charlie. 'Interview with Frank McCourt', 1997, <https://www.youtube.com/watch?v=SskmdYBkNs4>, accessed March 2018.

Williams 1995

Williams, John. 'John Williams discusses his score for *Nixon*', 1995, <https://www.youtube.com/watch?v=jD9WCTioDME>, accessed March 2018.

Williams 2000

Id. Voiceover to broadcast of *Angela's Ashes* Suite, *Evening at the Pops*, 2000, <https://www.youtube.com/watch?v=JPw2pcm1krc>, accessed March 2018.

Alan Parker Archive, British Film Institute

GORFAINE 1998
Letter dated 13 April 1998 from Michael Gorfaine of The Gorfaine/Schwartz Agency to Scott Rudin. File Reference: PKR-1-21-5, Alan Parker Archive, British Film Institute.

RECORDING SESSION CUE LIST 1999
Angela's Ashes, Recording Session Cue List, dated 28 June – 2 July 1999. File Reference: PKR-1-21-5, Alan Parker Archive, British Film Institute.

TEMP MUSIC CUES 1999
Temp Music Cues, typed document dated 14 June 1999. File Reference: PKR-1-21-5, Alan Parker Archive, British Film Institute.

SECONDARY SOURCES

AUDISSINO 2014
AUDISSINO, Emilio. *John Williams's Film Music: «Jaws», «Star Wars», «Raiders of the Lost Ark» and the Return of the Classic Hollywood Music Style*, Madison (WI), University of Wisconsin Press, 2014 (Wisconsin Film Studies).

COOPER 2006
COOPER, David. 'Seán Ó'Riada and Irish Post-Colonial Film Music: George Morrison's *Mise Éire*', in: *European Film Music*, edited by Miguel Mera and David Burnand, Aldershot, Ashgate, 2006 (Ashgate Popular and Folk Music Series), pp. 100-115.

DYER 2000
DYER, Richard. 'John Williams reflects on *Angela's Ashes*: Maestro Chooses a 'Universal Approach' To an Irish Story', in: *The Boston Globe*, 3rd edn., 28 January 2000.

FAR AND AWAY B.F.I. N.D.
Far and Away, British Film Institute, <http://www.bfi.org.uk/films-tv-people/4ce2b7b4c76c3>, accessed January 2018.

FREER 2000
FREER, Ian. 'Review of *Angela's Ashes* Soundtrack', in: *Empire*, (2000), pp. 130-131.

GLATT 1997
GLATT, John. *The Chieftains: The Authorized Biography*, London, Century, 1997.

KEECH 2000
KEECH, Andrew. 'Review of *Angela's Ashes* Soundtrack', in: *Music for the Movies*, XXVI (2000), p. 27.

MOTHERWAY 2013
MOTHERWAY, Susan H. *The Globalization of Irish Traditional Song Performance*, Aldershot, Ashgate, 2013 (Ashgate Popular and Folk Music Series).

O'Flynn 2009
O'Flynn, John. *The Irishness of Irish Music*, Farnham, Surrey, Ashgate, 2009 (Ashgate Popular and Folk Music Series).

O'Flynn – Fitzgerald 2014
Id. – Fitzgerald, Mark. 'Introduction', in: *Music and Identity in Ireland and Beyond*, Farnham, Ashgate, 2014.

Sadoff 2006
Sadoff, Ronald H. 'The Role of the Music Editor and the "Temp Track" as Blueprint for the Score, Source Music, and Scource Music of Films', in: *Popular Music*, xxv/2 (2006), pp. 165-183.

Sapiro 2014
Sapiro, Ian. '"Simple, Medium and Shebang": Trevor Jones and the Development of the Toolkit', in: paper presented at *Music and the Moving Image ix*, New York, NYU Steinhardt School of Culture and Human Development, May 30 – June 1, 2014.

Wise 2000
Wise, Damon. 'In Person with Alan Parker', in: *Empire* (2000), <www.empireonline.com>.

Wood 2012
Wood, Nichola. 'Playing with "Scottishness": Musical Performance, Non-Representational Thinking and the Doings of National Identity', in: *Cultural Geographies*, ix/2 (2012), pp. 192-215.

John Williams and Sound Design: Shaping the Audiovisual World of *E. T.: The Extra-Terrestrial*

Chloé Huvet
(Université Rennes 2 / Univervisté de Montréal, QC)

E. T.: *The Extra-Terrestrial* (1982) is one of the magnum opuses of the Steven Spielberg-John Williams collaboration, which won its composer a fourth Oscar and set new box office records. Despite the film's importance, however, scholarship on the score and sound design of *E. T.* is quite scarce. Very little attention has been given to the soundtrack in cinema studies where commentaries on the score are sporadic if not absent[1]. Duncan Sinclair's article is the only journalistic paper entirely devoted to the music, but it merely consists of a list of the main themes without giving any consideration to the visual aspects of the film and, moreover, it is not entirely accurate[2]. Interesting musicological comments can be found in Peter Moormann's book on the scores composed by Williams for Spielberg's films[3], as well as in Jérôme Rossi's article devoted to Williams's harmonic language[4], but again their remarks are limited to only a few pages. In addition to the paragraphs he dedicated to *E. T.* in his book on Williams's style[5], Emilio Audissino has recently published an engaging comparative analysis of the scores of *Close Encounters of the Third Kind* and *E. T.*, aiming to show «how music operates on the emotive, perceptive, and cognitive levels»[6]. Furthermore, no study has, so far, explored the interactions between Williams's music and the other elements of the soundtrack which is surprising since the composer himself claims to be very sensitive to the other elements of the soundtrack — a specificity which distinctly manifests itself in *E. T.*

1. See Morris 2007, pp. 84-94; Gordon 2008, pp. 75-92; Kendrick 2014, pp. 23-68.
2. Sinclair 1989.
3. Moormann 2010.
4. Rossi 2011a.
5. See Audissino 2014, pp. 210-211.
6. Audissino 2017, p. 192.

This overall lack of in-depth musicological studies is all the more surprising since *E. T.* also has a special status in film history. Following *Star Wars* (George Lucas, 1977) and *Close Encounters of the Third Kind* (Steven Spielberg, 1977), it played an important part in reshaping the face of science-fiction cinema[7] by featuring a benevolent alien explorer accidentally left on Earth, a complete departure from the science-fiction films of the previous decades haunted by fears of the atomic bomb, totalitarianism and aggressive invasion[8]. In *E. T.*, the alien is the one being hunted down by faceless men. He ends up in the suburbs and encounters a broken family. First terrified by the children, he then bonds with Elliott, Gertie and Michael, who help him contact his fellows and leave Earth.

Williams's score for *E. T.* contributes significantly to this unusual approach and redefinition within the subgenre of alien invasion films[9]. The scope of this chapter is double: I aim to show how Williams carefully crafts his music of *E. T.* taking the visuals and the sound effects into account and, more specifically, to establish in what ways this personal approach to the image and sound design participate in the subtle mixture of science-fiction, melodrama and fairy tale. Drawing on a musicological analysis of the relation between the soundtrack, the image, and the manuscript of Melissa Mathison's screenplay kept in the archives of the Bibliothèque nationale de France, I first demonstrate how the thematic and orchestral treatment of the "Friendship Theme" focuses attention on the bond between Elliott and the extra-terrestrial, adding layers to the story and to the visual approach. I also show how the interactions between music and sound effects are carefully crafted so as to convey a sense of magic and wonder, re-enchanting the lonely children's daily life. The supernatural is, however, not devoid of terror and sadness in Spielberg's film; I argue that the soundtrack strongly supports the reading of *E. T.* as a bittersweet fairy tale, far from the unilateral and soppy story often depicted in the literature.

Re-enchanting the Lonely Children's Daily Life

While *E. T.* clearly falls within the science-fiction genre, one of the film's distinctive features is the focus on the relationship between a lonely boy and an extra-terrestrial, thus offering «a kind of intimate, very emotional suburb drama»[10], according to Audissino. But it also shares many characteristics with fairy tales, such as E. T.'s magical powers used

[7]. Gressard 1988, p. 104.

[8]. Representative examples of this trend are *The Man from Planet x*, (Edgar G. Ulmer, 1951), *The Thing from Another World* (Christian Nyby, 1951), *The War of the Worlds* (Byron Haskin, 1953), *Invasion of the Body Snatchers* (Don Siegel, 1956), *The Blob* (Irwin S. Yeaworth Jr., 1958), *Invasion of the Body Snatchers* (Philip Kaufman, 1978) and *The Thing* (John Carpenter, 1982).

[9]. See Heine 2016, pp. 52-59.

[10]. Audissino 2017, p. 206.

for benevolent purposes, the child hero, and his psychological maturation sparked off by his contact with the supernatural. The film also displays a «reversal of expected values», transforming «not only the strange into the familiar, but also the familiar [i.e. the suburban everyday life and the behaviour of adult human beings] into the strange»[11]. These fairy tale characteristics should not come as a surprise given Spielberg's admiration for Walt Disney[12] and his explicit references to *Peter Pan* (1953), *Pinocchio* (1940) or *Fantasia* (1940) in *Close Encounters for the Third Kind*, *E. T.*, *Hook* (1991), and *A. I. Artificial Intelligence* (2001).

The music and sound design of *E. T.* play a fundamental role in creating magic and wonder. They significantly contribute to the displacement of the primary genre of science-fiction by giving it a fairy-tale tone, an otherworldly and out-of-time dimension, first by depicting the exceptional relationship between E. T. and Elliott. These two central characters share a unique emotional and telepathic connection, summarized by the famous dialogue in which a scientist tells Elliott's big brother Michael, «Elliott thinks its thoughts», to which Michael replies, «No. Elliott feels his feelings».

John Williams has composed two themes for this special relationship, one of which has been described as a «Love theme» by the composer himself[13]. Since this theme — typically referred to as the "Flying Theme" — has already been the object of other studies[14], I will instead analyse the other theme — which I call the "Friendship Theme" — in its relation to the evolution of their friendship, which is varied and developed throughout the whole film — a typical Williams gesture that Audissino has labelled the «'gradual disclosure of the main theme' technique»[15].

The Treatment of the "Friendship Theme"

The "Friendship Theme", which is associated to the evolution of the relationship between the boy and the extraterrestrial, appears for the first time when Elliott lures E. T. into his room and is surprised to see that the alien imitates all his actions. Slow, gentle, and graceful, the theme (see Ex. 1) is played in the Aeolian mode on F♯ (but with an ambiguity with the Dorian mode on B, which contributes a delicate quality to the sound) and opened by a leap of perfect fifth, «an idiomatic trait of Williams's [writing]»[16] used in several other themes of *E. T.* but also in *Star Wars* or *Superman* (Richard Donner, 1978).

---

11. Gordon 1999, p. 114.
12. See Thoret 2006, p. 45.
13. Zailian 1982.
14. See Huvet 2011, pp. 112-119; and Audissino 2017, pp. 207-2011.
15. Audissino 2014, p. 126.
16. *Ibidem*, p. 75.

Ex. 1: John Williams, "Friendship Theme" from *E. T.: The Extra-Terrestrial* (© 1982 BMI), published by USI B Music Publishing, ear transcription from the film's soundtrack (*E. T.: The Extra-Terrestrial*, DVD no. 3, Universal Pictures, 905 226-9, 2002, 00:22:06). Used in compliance with the U.S. Copyright Act, Section 107.

A solo harp performs the theme in an improvisational manner; the timbre of the instrument, the fluctuating temporality[17], the mellifluous melodic line, and the delicate quavers endow it with a dreamlike, tender quality. Thus, the music here plays an essential role in highlighting Elliott's wonder and reinforcing the magic suggested by the decor of the child's room which, according to production designer Jim Bissell, was crafted to «show [the room] as [a] plac[e] to get away from harsh, cold realities»[18]. Several descending glissandi appear when Elliott yawns, closes his eyes and falls back on the chair like a sleepwalker. Beyond their quasi mickey-mousing accompaniment, the glissandi also create a hypnotic effect in line with the atmosphere of the scene. The final D-major chord closes the scene on a very bright and luminous tone, underlining the importance of the relationship between the two characters and its extraordinary nature, bound by a true symbiosis based on shared feelings. Through this subtle and graceful scoring, the composer accentuates the symbolic dimension of the scene and, from the very beginning, turns the friendship into a magic tale between the «shy, lonely boy in desperate need of a friend», and the one he finds in the creature «fallen out of the sky»[19].

This theme is then developed throughout its different iterations in the film. I focus here on one particularly important and representative scene. In the sequence where Mary reads *Peter Pan* to Gertie, the fairy-like musical accompaniment brings out the narrative

---

[17]. This is the translation I propose of Pierre Boulez's notion of «temps lisse» which he developed in Boulez 1963, pp. 107-108.

[18]. Quoted in Lowell 1983, p. 51.

[19]. Corliss 2003.

core of James M. Barrie's story, and the connection between childhood and the belief in magic. The alien's interest for the tender moment shared by the mother and her little girl, and his special bond to Elliott, are emphasized several times with chiming sounds, both notated in the score and created by the sound designer. First, when E. T. partially opens the closet's shutter, his gesture is brought out by quick ascending motives on the celeste, and the close-up on his tender expression is accompanied by a triangle and a vibraphone chord. When E. T.'s fingertip lights up as the alien realizes that Elliott has cut himself, this moment is underlined by a synthesized ringing sound in the high register reminiscent of a small bell, and in the orchestra by the triangle, an ascending glissando of the celeste, and quavers in the strings. The same process can be observed when the alien heals Elliott by touching his finger. The soundtrack also displays an interesting mixing choice: the voice of Mary reading the book totally disappears, and is not heard again until E. T.'s supernatural action is complete.

The careful combination of this handling of the soundtrack, the appearance of the theme, Williams's choices of orchestration, and the design of the sound effects all participate in reinforcing the magic and wonder, conveying a sense of enchantment. Elliott's healing, just like Tinkerbell's resuscitation, is closely linked to the belief in magic, to the ability to see and sense what is beyond the ordinary, everyday experience. This faith in the supernatural runs throughout Spielberg's whole filmography which, as Pierre Berthomieu argues, expresses «the return to an infancy of the eye and the avowal of a need for awed astonishment»[20].

Intertwining Music and Sound Design: Conveying Magic and Wonder

The scene just discussed also invites us to reconsider the widespread idea that «the symphonic sounds of Williams do not connect with sound design»[21] and vice versa. Here, the sound effects are, on the contrary, quite close to the sparkling tone of the music, and therefore the orchestra and sound design harmonize very well. In this regard, it is important to stress the fact that numerous discussions took place very early between the sound creators, the composer and the director[22], allowing them to exchange ideas about the different sound materials and the general sonic approach. Incidentally, these efforts were rewarded by two Academy Awards, besides Williams's own for Best Original Score: one for Best Sound Mixing to Robert Knudson, Robert Glass, Don Digirolamo and Gene Cantamessa and one for Best Sound Editing to Ben Burtt and Charles L. Campbell.

---

[20]. Berthomieu 2011, p. 546: «le retour de l'enfance du regard et l'aveu d'un besoin de sidération». All the English translations are mine.

[21]. Costantini s.d.

[22]. Digirolamo 2012.

The opening scene is particularly interesting in this regard. As in many fairy tales, the night is the primary place of the appearance of the supernatural, but, in *E. T.*, it is represented by Spielberg as comforting and soothing from the very opening of the film, thus establishing a fantasy atmosphere similar to the arrival of Mother Night in *Fantasia*. The director explains:

> Remember in Fantasia, Mother Night flying over with her cape, covering a daylight sky? [...] The Disney Mother Night was a beautiful woman with flowing, blue-black hair, and arms extended outward, twenty miles in either direction. And behind her was a very inviting cloak. She came from the horizon in an arc and swept over you until everything was a blue-black dome. And then there was an explosion, and the stars were suddenly made in this kind of animated sky. I wanted the opening of *E. T.* to be that kind of Mother Night[23].

The woodland environment is also essential in creating this fairy tale setting, and was suggested by screenwriter Melissa Mathison. Jim Bissell also explains the particular method of shooting and lighting the opening scene: «We did a week of location work near Crescent City, where we shot the redwood forest stuff. [...] We used a lot of stratified light there. That sequence had much of *Bambi* and some of *Peter Pan* in it»[24]. Several stars were also specifically superimposed to the night sky in post-production at Spielberg's request[25].

The carefully chosen layers of sound effects and music enhance this visually mysterious and bewitching opening. In sync with the pan shot of the starry sky, which gives the illusion of plunging us into deep space, the piccolo solo plays a motif associated with otherworldliness in the Lydian mode on A in the upper register (Ex. 2):

Ex. 2: John Williams, "Otherworldliness Motif" from *E. T.: The Extra-Terrestrial* (© 1982 BMI), published by USI B Music Publishing., ear transcription from the film's soundtrack (*E. T.: The Extra-Terrestrial* [1982], DVD no. 3, Universal Pictures, 905 226-9, 2002, 00:01:22). Used in compliance with the U.S. Copyright Act, Section 107.

The ethereal timbre, the delicate melody, the pared-down music material, the long note-values, and the swaying sextuplet quavers that generate a very smooth temporality, all cast onto the scene an oneiric and out-of-time quality. The last note, B, seems to stretch on

23. Sragow 2000, p 113.

24. Quoted in Lowell 1983, p. 51.

25. See Bouzereau 2002.

indefinitely and progressively reverts to silence in a long decrescendo. The music situates the action in an otherworldly enchanted place.

The melody appears in identical form a second time, but with a modified accompaniment: the rest on D♯ is correlated with a sort of orchestral awakening and a widening of the orchestral palette's range, with the statement of the melody by the horns adding a majestic aspect to the overall feeling of enchantment. Glistening effects are produced by the harp glissandi, the triangle, the violins playing in harmonics in the high register, and the superposition of an A major chord with a sustained C♮ played by the cellos and double basses. Interestingly, this shimmering awakening of the orchestra coincides with the coming to life of the nocturnal aural universe as a whole, creating an immersive sound environment. Several sound layers formed by the rattling of insects, the chirping of birds, and the rustling of leaves mingle with the music as the camera pans to finally reveal the place of action: huge redwood trees stand silhouetted against the starry background. Spielberg sought out this progressive unveiling in order to create a surprising and magical effect: «[Y]ou come down over the trees, you see the stars, and suddenly you think you're in space — wow, you're not, you're in a forest somewhere»[26].

Another representative example where the subtle interactions between sound design and music suggest magic occurs in the scene where Elliott does the washing up after a fight with his family. The close-up on his face framed from outside the window suggests his loneliness: nobody believes his story about the extra-terrestrial visitor. As he gazes towards the sky, the piccolo plays the motif associated with otherworldliness, accompanied by hazy harp glissandi which seem to translate into music the cloud of steam enveloping the child. The sound of water running and the harp accompaniment reinforce the mysterious and dream-like nature of the theme. We also notice the careful placement of music and sound effects within the acoustic spectrum: the sounds of water occupy the medium-low register, while the piccolo motif is concentrated in the upper-high register. Frequencies are distributed in such a way that the different sound materials cohabit in harmony without covering over one another. This is indeed one of Williams's main preoccupations, as he affirms: «I'm very sensitive to the sound effects and the dialogue — all the competition to my music […]. You do get film-wise after a while, and you learn to relate the colouration to the overall aural set-up: you know you've got horses' hooves to deal with, therefore X is better than Y, etc. […] It's part of the art of it»[27].

Interestingly, as the piccolo motif returns a second time, the sound of water is gradually replaced by nocturnal sounds like the stridulation of crickets, as the camera pulls away from Elliott. The soundtrack in its entirety signals how the little boy's mind falls into reverie and fantasy. The next shot establishes a symbolic setting where magic could take place: the backyard and the isolated small shed, delicately lit from the inside,

---

[26]. Quoted in Sragow 2000, p 113.

[27]. Quoted in Elley 1978, p. 24.

are presented as enchanted places, illuminated by moonlight and immersed in a blue-black luminous obscurity.

A significant part of *E. T.*'s soundtrack is thus devoted to creating a sense of wonder: Williams's writing and the sound design together bring out the magical aspect of the exterior settings, while the handling of the friendship theme heightens the special bond uniting E. T. and Elliott, emphasizing the way the alien comes to re-enchant the bleak life of the lonely boy.

A Tale Filled with Loneliness and Darkness

But this faith in magic and the supernatural, characteristic of Spielberg's cinema, is far from being unequivocal and «does not sweep away the threat of dark forces»[28]. Film scholars Pierre Berthomieu and James Kendrick have recently offered a major reconsideration of the approach of Spielberg's films, criticizing most of published studies for being blind to «one of the most compelling and central qualities of the majority of Spielberg's most well-regarded and popular films: the darkness»[29]. Like *Close Encounters*, *Hook*, or *A. I.*, *E. T.* has suffered from an ideological reading that portrays the film as a bland, conservative, and even mind-numbing fantasy, «sentimental and trite»[30] — a discourse that often stems from a criticism of blockbusters and their targeting of a large, mainstream audience and which has largely eclipsed an essential part of Spielberg's aesthetics[31]. Far from the «politics of bliss» depicted by Ilsa J. Black as a «sunny, peculiarly Reagan-era attitude of happiness bought with ignorance [and] magical wish-fullfilment»[32], the film is haunted by imagery of loneliness and terror.

The Threat of the Faceless Men

In the film, adults are either absent, remote from the children's preoccupations, or threatening. The men searching for the extra-terrestrial are shot as faceless and ruthless hunters. The menacing sounds assigned to them greatly contrast with the ones associated with E. T. and his benevolent magic as well as with the woodland and nocturnal settings. The sounds they make are aggressive, rough, metallic, and their dynamics are very unstable, swiftly shifting from one extreme to the other, thus causing a very unsettling and disturbing effect. For example, in her manuscript of the screenplay, Melissa Mathison describes the

[28]. Berthomieu 2011, pp. 545-546: «[Cette résurrection] ne balaie en rien la menace des ténèbres».

[29]. Kendrick 2014, p. 4.

[30]. Baxter 1996, p. 245.

[31]. See Kendrick 2014, pp. 2-5; and Audissino 2017, pp. 2-3.

[32]. Black 1992, p. 25.

first entrance of the character of Keys as follows: «Seen only from the waist down are: dark pants, heavy boots and a huge ring of keys hanging from his belt. The keys make a tremendous racket, displacing all other sounds of the night»[33].

The men are marked as antagonists not only by the sound effects, but also by the music. Williams has composed a motif which refers to Keys but also, more generally, to the hunt (Ex. 3):

Ex. 3: John Williams, "The Keys/Hunt Motif" from *E. T.: The Extra-Terrestrial* (© 1982 BMI), published by USI B Music Publishing, ear transcription from the film's soundtrack (*E. T.: The Extra-Terrestrial* [1982], DVD no. 3, Universal Pictures, 905 226-9, 2002, 00:05:07). Used in compliance with the U.S. Copyright Act, Section 107.

It connotes villainy by using signifiers of evil such as woodwinds and brass in the low register (bassoons, contrabassoon and bass clarinets, or horns predominantly play the motif), repeated notes, harmonic and rhythmic instability, and the plunging arpeggio shaping the melody. Whereas the theme is not much modified melodically during the movie, it circulates between different instrumental sections throughout the film, suggesting the presence of an ever-present and shape-shifting threat moving closer to Elliott's house with each new musical statement. In concert with Spielberg's direction, Williams's motif thus misguides the audience into thinking that the scientists are malevolent characters. After Michael and Gertie meet E. T. in the closet, the horns play the hunt theme in sync with the abrupt cut to the city seen from above, a complete rupture with the previous shot. Without any transition, the intimate atmosphere of the scene showing the children and E. T. in Elliott's room is suddenly broken by an exterior shot, and the subdued and magical lighting of the closet shots is brutally replaced by a strong and stark daylight. No character can be seen in this very long shot depicting the suburbs as a group of identical and impersonal houses. However, through the return of the theme, the music suggests the presence of the faceless men even before they appear on screen. The shot itself is quite revealing: the distortion brought by the dolly plus zoom generates a sense of uneasiness and dizziness that is accentuated by the high camera angle[34]. The horns play the opening call of the theme in the low register above a string pedal, punctuated by timpani and semitones on the celeste, reinforcing the threatening

[33]. Mathison 1981, p. 5. See also Friedman 2006, p. 29.

[34]. This shot (a combination of dolly in and zoom out) was popularized by *Vertigo* (Alfred Hitchcock, 1958) and famously used in *Jaws* (Steven Spielberg, 1975) as Brody witnesses with horror the second shark attack on the little boy Alex Kintner.

aspect of the image and of the cry of a bird of prey. It is interesting to remark that the opening notes resonate one last time on a nocturnal exterior shot of Elliott's house, thus hinting that the threat is much more focused than previously, and that both Elliott's secret and the peace of his family are endangered.

In accordance with this approach, the scene where the scientists enter Elliott's house is treated as a true invasion. Here, the phantasmagoria is transformed into a nightmare, with the visual and sound design borrowing techniques from the horror genre to create a frightening and bloodcurdling effect. As Mary decides to leave the house to protect her children from E. T., the otherworldliness motif occurs, but with a completely different character, as if corrupted: loud dissonances played by muted trumpets are overlaid upon the delicate timbre of the flute, like a dark sardonic parody of the original motif. The reaction shot on Michael is underlined by shrill repeated clusters, timpani rolls and bass drum accents like chilling thunderclaps which persist on the disturbing reverse shot showing a man in a white spacesuit. The cold, almost mechanical sound of the man's breathing, recorded from a very close perspective, amplified and reverberated, like Darth Vader's in the *Star Wars* saga[35], adds a very menacing hue to the hint he makes of a capture gesture. The protagonists are soon surrounded by other 'astronauts' blocking any possible exit at the sound of the hunt motif, while the toy train switches itself on, accentuating the nightmarish effect — a direct reference to little Barry's abduction in *Close Encounters of the Third Kind*. The several whistle blows of the train clearly signify danger for, as Barbara Flueckiger reminds us, alarm signals often «warn of concrete danger», indicating «threat or aggression. In [...] showdowns they are an indispensable means of raising the emotional stakes»[36] of the sequence. The wan light originating from outside also contributes to the overall feeling of peril for the lead characters by casting a ghostly halo over the room. In this regard, Jim Bissell insists that «it was uppermost in my mind that we had to make the home a lovely little nest so it would become more of an icy, cold nightmare when the scientists move in»[37]. This scene is all the more terrifying in that most of Spielberg's films are marked by the «endangerment of childhood figures»[38], whether John Hammond's grandchildren Lex and Tim in *Jurassic Park* (1993), the devoured Alex Kintner in *Jaws* (1975), the abducted Barry in *Close Encounters of the Third Kind* and John Anderton's son in *Minority Report* (2002), the murdered symbolic little girl with the red coat in *Schindler's List* (1993), or the abandoned and drowned child-robot David in *A. I. Artificial Intelligence*.

[35]. See Huvet 2017, pp. 477-479.

[36]. Flueckiger 2009, p. 159.

[37]. Quoted in Lowell 1983, p. 51.

[38]. Berthomieu 2003, p. 100 : «[Spielberg s'autorise] la mise en danger des figures enfantines». See also Cohen 2007, pp. 23-25.

A Melancholic Ending

If the scientists are eventually revealed as peaceful and willing to help save E. T., and if Keys may appear as a new father — and husband — figure, the film's ending does not sweep away the sadness, loneliness and bitterness that preceded that moment, as the very last close-up on Elliott's solemn face suggests. As Kendrick rightly remarks, Spielberg's films are «deeply conflicted, their surface pleasures often cracking open to reveal fissures of darkness, despair, loneliness, and regret that their conclusions, no matter how upbeat on the surface, couldn't fully resolve»[39]. In this regard, the clear-cut reading of *E. T.*'s last scene appears problematic and reductive. The final sequence has been widely criticized for its length — Charles Champlin deems it «vainly long and diluted»[40] — and its sentimentality — Andrew Sarris mockingly wonders whether, with all these adults and children around him, «E.T. was leaving for space or for a summer camp»[41]. The music itself is not spared this criticism: Vincent Canby rued the fact that Williams's score «sank into melodramatic excess»[42], and Bill Krohn judged the orchestration «too heavy»[43].

However, within the scene Williams makes room for intimate and delicate sections that are fundamental to note. One of these is the return of the motif associated with otherworldliness, played by the piccolo in the Lydian mode on C accompanied by harp glissandi, swift ascending arpeggios in G major on the celeste and divided dissonant tremolos on the violins. These polytonal layers and the instrumental timbres bestow a sad, ethereal, and hazy dimension upon the theme, like a distant call as the spaceship door gradually closes. Framed by triumphant music which was conceived as a «full-blown sort of operatic aria [and] musical denouement»[44], this thematic statement creates a sudden rupture of dynamics and orchestral texture, making viewers listen carefully. The return of the theme has also a particular meaning: the call of space and home prevails for the extra-terrestrial but at a cost — a bittersweet breaking up. Through these inflexions in the motif, the music draws attention on the painful emotional implications of this parting and clothes the shot in a subtle melancholic veil which clouds the perception of a happy ending[45].

As Jérôme Rossi has noted in *Jaws*[46], as Stefan Swanson demonstrates in *A. I.* in his chapter in the present volume, and as I myself have shown in articles on *Jurassic Park* and

[39]. Kendrick 2014, p. x.

[40]. Quoted in Krohn 1982, p. 19.

[41]. Quoted in *ibidem*.

[42]. Quoted in *ibidem*.

[43]. *Ibidem*, p. 23.

[44]. Quoted in Larson 1985, p. 303.

[45]. Jérôme Rossi had presented a similar interpretation in his paper «Les harmonies polytonales au cinéma» (Rossi 2011b).

[46]. *Ibidem*.

War of the Worlds[47], this melancholic approach is a constant in the music that Williams composes for the ending scenes of Spielberg films, though it is often overlooked. In *Jurassic Park* for example, as the characters are about to get onto the rescue helicopter, the shots are not accompanied by the triumphant "Adventure Theme" — the fanfare played at their arrival at Isla Nublar —, but by a segment from the "Remembering Petticoat Lane" cue. In a previous scene where this segment appeared, John Hammond expressed an unshakeable faith in the park, believing that technical enhancements could be made. The return of this very segment thus bears a melancholy dimension: it suggests that, if the survivors fortunately manage to leave the island, John's dream and vision are, however, broken. Similarly, for the final reunion of the family in *War of the Worlds*, after the ordeal the three main characters went through, Williams chooses a restrained approach: when Rachel runs into her mother's arms, a very sober piano theme is played in the Dorian mode on C. The soft and almost elegiac dimension of the music distances the scene from an effusive happy ending. Likewise, in *E. T.*, the composer's approach adds a rich and subtle subtext that challenges the reading of the film as a naive and overly sentimental fairy tale.

Conclusion

This study of the rich and complex relationship between sound effects, dialogue, music and moving images is in line with recent trends in film musicology. Scholars are willing to address new ways of understanding how these elements relate to each other, through the use of a cross-disciplinary approach and analysis that exceeds the traditional divisions between categories of sounds[48]. More specifically, through this chapter I aim to contribute to a more nuanced and appropriate understanding of John Williams's orchestral writing. The composer is always careful about writing his music having in mind not only the needs of the film, the narration, the visuals, but also the dialogue and sound effects. In this respect, I hope to have shown the multiple nuances of *E. T.*'s score and sound design, and the duality they embody between magic and darkness, contributing to the film's mixture of the genres of science-fiction, melodrama and fairy tale. Far from being authoritarian and from imposing one single reading of the narration and staging[49], throughout the film Williams's music weaves several, and sometimes deceptive, threads. It prevents a stable and passive audience positioning through the subtle interactions between the score, the on-screen action, and viewers' expectations[50].

47. See Huvet 2014 and Huvet 2018.
48. See Cathé 2007, Greene – Kulezic-Wilson 2016.
49. See in particular Lerner 2004.
50. For a detailed analysis of the film's explicit and implicit meanings, see Audissino 2017.

Furthermore, this chapter positions itself in the wake of recent research led by James Kendrick, Jérôme Rossi, Stefan Swanson, and Pierre Berthomieu that questions an overly simplistic and skewed interpretation of Spielberg's films as «emotionally manipulative and thematically hollow»[51]. *E. T.* is not so much about the extra-terrestrial and the supernatural itself but, as the music and sound design also suggest, about a lonely child's inner transformation through his contact with this fantastical creature, and his handling of everyday life, friendship, love, and loss. As Lester D. Friedman notes, «by finding memorable ways to express this need for something beyond the transient, something that partakes of the ethereal, Spielberg positions himself within the company of artists who sought to see radiance within the ordinary»[52].

Bibliography

Audissino 2014

Audissino, Emilio. *John Williams's Film Music: «Jaws», «Star Wars», «Raiders of the Lost Ark», and the Return of the Classical Hollywood Music Style*, Madison (WI), University of Wisconsin Press, 2014 (Wisconsin Film Studies).

Audissino 2017

Id. '*Close Encounters of the Third Kind* and *E. T. The Extra-Terrestrial*: The Bonding Power of Music', in: Id. *Film/Music Analysis. A Film Studies Approach*, Basingstoke, Palgrave Macmillan, 2017 (Palgrave Studies in Audio-Visual Culture), pp. 191-222 (chapter 8).

Baxter 1996

Baxter, John. *Steven Spielberg: The Unauthorised Biography*, London, Harper Collins, 1996.

Berthomieu 2003

Berthomieu, Pierre. *Le Cinéma hollywoodien: le temps du renouveau*, Paris, Nathan, 2003.

Berthomieu 2011

Id. *Hollywood moderne: le temps des voyants*, Pertuis, Rouge Profond, 2011 (Raccords).

Black 1992

Black, Ilsa J. 'The Look Back in *E. T.*', in: *Cinema Journal*, xxxi/4 (1992), p. 25.

Boulez 1963

Boulez, Pierre. *Penser la musique aujourd'hui*, Geneva, Gonthier, 1963 (Bibliothèque mediations, 13).

Bouzereau 2002

Bouzereau, Laurent. *The Music of «E. T.»: A Discussion with John Williams*, Los Angeles, Universal Studio Home Video, 2002.

---

51. This quotation in Friedman 2006, p. 118.

52. Friedman 2006, p. 118.

Cathé 2007

Cathé, Philippe. 'Bruit et musique dans la course des *Podracers* de *Star Wars, Episode 1, The Fantom Menace* (*La Menace fantôme*), 1999', in: *Musurgia*, xiv/2 (2007), pp. 53-69.

Cohen 2007

Cohen, Clélia. *Steven Spielberg*, Paris, Cahiers du cinéma/Le Monde, 2007 (Collection grands cinéastes, 2).

Corliss 2003

Corliss, Richard. 'That Old Feeling: *E. T.* Goes Home', in: *Time*, 30 March 2003, <http://www.time.com/time/arts/article/0,8599,221084,00.html>, accessed February 2018.

Costantini s.d.

Costantini, Gustavo. 'Leitmotif Revisited', in: *Filmsound*, <http://www.filmsound.org/gustavo/leitmotif-revisted.htm>, accessed February 2018.

Digirolamo 2012

Digirolamo, Son. 'Creating the Sights and Sounds of *E. T. The Extra-Terrestrial*', in: *Academy's Prime Tech Screening*, September 2012, <https://www.oscars.org/vef/load/7a257624f1427669a69910383660df8d?width=640&height=365&iframe=true>, accessed February 2018.

Elley 1978

Elley, Derek. 'The Film Composer: John Williams', in: *Films and Filming*, xxiv/10 (July 1978), pp. 20-24.

Flueckiger 2009

Flueckiger, Barbara. 'Strategies for Sound Effects in Film', in: *Sound and Music in Film and Visual Media: An Overview*, edited by Graeme Harper, London, Continuum, 2009, pp. 151-179.

Friedman 2006

Friedman, Lester D. *Citizen Spielberg*, Urbana, University of Illinois Press, 2006.

Gordon 1999

Gordon, Andrew M. '*E. T.* As Fairy Tale', in: *Nursery Realms: Children in the Worlds of Science Fiction, Fantasy, and Horror*, edited by Gary Westfahl and George Edgar Slusser, Athens, University of Georgia Press, 1999, pp. 111-127.

Gordon 2008

Id. *Empire of Dreams: The Science Fiction and Fantasy Films of Steven Spielberg*, Lanham, Rowman & Littlefield Publishers, 2008.

Gressard 1988

Gressard, Gilles. *Le Film de science-fiction*, Paris, J'ai lu, 1988 (J'ai lu cinéma, 10).

Greene – Kulezic-Wilson 2016

The Palgrave Handbook of Sound Design and Music in Screen Media: Integrated Soundtracks, edited by Liz Greene and Danijela Kulezic-Wilson, London, Palgrave Macmillan, 2016.

Heine 2016
Heine, Erik. *James Newton Howard's «Signs»: A Film Score Guide*, Lanham, Rowman & Littlefield, 2016 (Film Score Guides, 17).

Huvet 2011
Huvet, Chloé. *John Williams, héritier du symphonisme de l'âge d'or hollywoodien? Étude comparative d'«E. T. the Extra-Terrestrial» et de «Jurassic Park» de Steven Spielberg (1982-1993)*, Master's Diss., Lyon, École Normale Supérieure de Lyon, 2011.

Huvet 2014
Ead. 'La Dissociation musique/images dans *Jurassic Park*: un élargissement des pratiques compositionnelles de l'âge d'or hollywoodien dans la partition de John Williams', in: *Cahiers de la Société Québécoise de Recherche en Musique*, xv/2 (Fall 2014), pp. 23-39.

Huvet 2017
Ead. *D'«Un nouvel espoir» (1977) à «La Revanche des Sith» (2005): écriture musicale et traitement de la partition au sein du complexe audio-visuel dans la saga «Star Wars»*, Ph.D. Diss., Rennes, Université Rennes 2; Montréal (QC), Université de Montréal, 2017.

Huvet 2018
Ead. 'Le Son de l'apocalypse spielbergienne: musique et *sound design* dans *La Guerre des mondes* (2005)', in: *Formes d(e l')Apocalypse*, edited by Hélène Machinal, Monica Michlin and Arnaud Regnauld, forthcoming in 2018.

Kendrick 2014
Kendrick, James. *Darkness in the Bliss-Out: A Reconsideration of the Films of Steven Spielberg*, London/New York, Bloomsbury, 2014.

Krohn 1982
Krohn, Bill. 'L'Été de E. T.', in: *Cahiers du cinéma*, no. 342 (December 1982), pp. 17-24.

Larson 1985
Larson, Randall D. '*Déjà Vu*, The Music of John Williams', in: *Musique Fantastique: A Survey of Film Music in the Fantastic Cinema*, Metuchen (NJ) - London, Scarecrow Press, 1985, pp. 393-306 (chapter 14).

Lerner 2004
Lerner, Neil. 'Nostalgia, Masculinist Discourse, and Authoritarianism in John Williams' Scores for *Star Wars* and *Close Encounters of the Third Kind*', in: *Off the Planet: Music, Sound and Science Fiction Cinema*, edited by Philip Hayward, London, John Libbey Publishing, 2004, pp. 96-108.

Lowell 1983
Lowell, Allen D. 'Production Design for *E. T.*', in: *American Cinematographer*, lxiv/1 (January 1983), pp. 50-53.

Mathison 1981
Mathison, Melissa. *E .T. The Extraterrestrial: Scenario*, dact., 1981, Bibliothèque nationale de France, Département des Arts du spectacle, cote 4-MY-1540.

Moormann 2010
Moormann, Peter. *Spielberg-Variationen. Die Filmmusik von John Williams*, Baden-Baden, Nomos, 2010 (Schriftenreihe Filmstudien, 57).

Morris 2007
Morris, Nigel. *The Cinema of Steven Spielberg: Empire of Light*, London, Wallflower, 2007 (Directors' Cut).

Rossi 2011a
Rossi, Jérôme. 'Le dynamisme harmonique dans l'écriture filmique de John Williams: harmonie fonctionnelle versus harmonie non fonctionnelle', in: *John Williams: un alchimiste musical à Hollywood*, edited by Alexandre Tylski, Paris, L'Harmattan, 2011 (Univers Musical), pp. 113-140.

Rossi 2011b
Id. *Les Harmonies polytonales au cinéma: étude des ressources expressives de la polytonalité dans la musique de films de John Williams*, paper presented during a one-day workshop on polytonality, Paris-Sorbonne, 9 February 2011.

Sinclair 1989
Sinclair, Duncan. '*E. T. the Extra-Terrestrial*: a Brief Guide to Its Musical Themes and Some Suggestions as to Their Origins', in: *Soundtrack!*, viii/32 (December 1989), pp. 6-7.

Sragow 2000
Sragow, Michael. 'A Conversation with Steven Spielberg', in: *Steven Spielberg: Interviews*, edited by Lester D. Friedman and Brent Notbohm, Jackson, Mississipi University Press, 2000 (Conversations with Filmmakers Series), pp. 107-119.

Thoret 2006
Thoret, Jean-Baptiste. *Le Cinéma américain des années 70*, Paris, Cahiers du cinéma, 2006.

Zailian 1982
Zailian, Marian. 'John Williams: Master of Movie Scores', in: *San Francisco Examiner-Chronicle*, 18 July 1982.

«Today I'm Hearing with New Ears»: John Williams's Use of Audiovisual Incongruence to Convey Character Perspective in *Munich* and Spielberg's Historical Films

David Ireland
(University of Leeds)

Steven Spielberg's «suspense thriller» *Munich* (2005) is «[i]nspired by real events» according to the opening intertitle[1]. The film portrays a mission, covertly sanctioned by the Israeli government, to assassinate those believed to have ultimately been responsible for an attack that resulted in the massacre of eleven Israeli athletes at the 1972 Munich Olympic games. Given the narrative's origins in historical events *Munich* has been described as sharing qualities with nonfiction films «that dramatize actual events in the lives of real people»[2], and docudrama[3], a term that broadly refers to a hybrid of «'documentary' material with 'drama'»[4]. Spielberg claims that *Munich* is «not made to be a documentary. It's a story based on something that actually happened in history and it's not an effort [...] to be a crisp portrayal of exactly what happened»[5]. However, the film's composer, Spielberg's long-time collaborator John Williams, has also stated that he and Spielberg felt *Munich* was «closer [...] to a documentary film than to an action film», which influenced his approach to its music[6]. These comments reflect the tension between dramatic concerns and matters of authenticity when representing real people and events in films that take their inspiration from historical events: this tension results in a «dialogic relationship with history and fiction» in *Munich*[7]. For these reasons, and given its challenging subject, the film has proven controversial. However, little scholarly attention has been given to its

1. The opening description is quoted from the cover of the DreamWorks LLC and Universal Pictures 2007 DVD release of *Munich*. DSL1526.
2. Richter 2007, p. 140.
3. Morris 2007
4. Lipkin 1999, p. 370.
5. Spielberg 2007, [02.02].
6. Williams 2006, [05.50].
7. Morris 2007, p. 368.

music. The score provides interesting perspective on Williams's work as in several ways it challenges stereotypical views of the composer's approach that focus on the neoclassical style on which he «consolidated his reputation»[8]. Yet, whilst representing a sparser and darker output, parallels can be drawn between Williams's music for *Munich* and his scores for other Spielberg films that have their foundations in historical events. Therefore, analysis of *Munich*'s music aids consideration of aspects of Williams's approach to scoring films that are based on real people and events, particularly those that deal with violence and mass loss of life. Subsequently, such analysis also supports consideration of Williams and Spielberg's attitudes towards matters of representation and authenticity in such films.

To further explore these issues this chapter will primarily focus on Williams's score for three sequences from *Munich*. These sequences feature prominent emotive music and each depict moments from the 1972 attack, being the main times that these violent events are presented in the film. The idea of 'audiovisual incongruence' will be used to explore elements of Williams's music for these sequences. This term refers to a perceived lack of shared properties in the relationship between a film's images, narrative, and music, and psychological research has suggested that incongruent film music can result in the separate encoding of auditory and visual information[9]. This can create perceptual space that enables a perceiver to consider and question the nature and content of an audiovisual pairing, which is perhaps particularly important in films that address controversial real-life events and topics. As such, discussing potential audiovisual incongruities in Williams's music for these sequences from *Munich* provides a helpful lens through which to consider ideas of representation in nonfiction film. Given his similar placement of equally emotive cues in various other Spielberg nonfiction films (which will also be discussed), such analysis provides insight into an approach that Williams often uses when scoring history and tragedy, offering some suggestions as to why this might be an effective compositional strategy that is seemingly favoured by the composer in such contexts. However, before addressing these issues by analysing the sequences that portray the Munich massacre, it is important to contextualize these by first considering Williams's score for the film more broadly.

THE MUSIC OF *MUNICH*

Williams is arguably best known for writing scores that accompany a significant proportion of a film[10] and that use: orchestral resources; a neo-classical scoring style;

---

8. AUDISSINO 2017, p. 226.

9. E.g. BOLTZ 2004; LIPSCOMB – KENDALL 1994.

10. E.g. KALINAK 1992, p. 192 reports that Williams initially anticipated using 117 minutes of music for the 127 minute *Star Wars Episode V: The Empire Strikes Back* (Irvin Kershner, 1980).

and a thematic approach towards organizing material[11]. However, he is also a versatile practitioner who is adept at incorporating different musical idioms to suit the film at hand[12]. In *Munich* Williams complements the orchestra with wordless vocals and instruments like the oud, «a Middle Eastern lute»[13], and cimbalom, «a Hungarian zither»[14], to convey what he describes as an «atmosphere of the Middle East»[15]. Electronic sounds, including what Williams describes as a synthesized «heartbeat, drum-like» sound, also feature prominently in a series of cues that accompany the Israeli team's assassination attempts[16].

Perhaps more in line with stereotypes of Williams's thematic writing are a number of cues that use material from a theme associated with the team's leader, Avner (Eric Bana). This theme consists of a steady minor-key melody with a prominent repeated falling fourth interval in the second phrase. It is first heard at 00.27.24 as Avner and his team share a meal and is played on acoustic guitar with string accompaniment. Material from this theme occurs prominently: over *Munich*'s closing credits; following the deaths of two members of Avner's team; and in the final sequence where a guilt-ridden and exiled Avner, questioning the validity of his mission, refuses to return to Israel. Given this placement, it is perhaps easier to link this material with the team in general rather than just Avner, and to their identity and the sense of homeland that motivates them to undertake the mission. This interpretation resonates with Williams's claims of creating «a lyrical composition associated with Avner [...] and the home he leaves behind in Israel»[17].

Despite these cues there is a scarcity of thematic scoring in *Munich*. Indeed, very little of the film is scored, also challenging the aforementioned stereotypical perspectives on Williams's output. The composer suggests that *Munich* contains less music than most Spielberg films, describing his approach as one of «restraint» because realism and a stark character was «perhaps even more important and more desirable» given the film's content[18]. Holly Rogers highlights that traditional attitudes towards documentary film champion «minimum creative intervention in order to produce the illusion of a naturalistic chain of events»[19]. She writes that according to this view «the inclusion of a voice from beyond the filmed world can call into question what is being shown» and that «[i]t is feared that music may contradict the apparent spontaneity and naturalism of the documentary aesthetic»[20]. The lack of score throughout *Munich* resonates with these ideas. In the 150

11. Audissino 2014.
12. Audissino 2017.
13. Williams in Audissino 2014, p. 206.
14. *Ibidem*, p. 207.
15. Williams 2006, [06.24].
16. *Ibidem*, [06.50].
17. Cited in Audissino 2014, p. 206.
18. Williams 2006, [05.45].
19. Rogers 2015, p. 1.
20. *Ibidem*, pp. 1, 2.

minutes between the film's opening and the start of its closing credits there is just less than an hour of music, only 38 minutes circa of which are Williams's non-diegetic cues[21]. A significant proportion of this music occurs in the opening and closing half-hours. Just over 30% of the first half-hour features non-diegetic score, with almost six of these nine minutes occurring in the film's first 11 minutes. Contrastingly, only around 15% of *Munich*'s second 30 minutes has non-diegetic score. Non-diegetic music becomes more prominent towards the end of *Munich* and almost 45% of the final half-hour is non-diegetically scored. Therefore, aside from some instances of source music, large central sections remain unscored. However, the opening sequence and three episodes that present the Munich massacre are *entirely* scored, suggesting a different approach towards the presentation of this material: an approach that counters an unaccompanied, realist aesthetic of restraint. Just over 12 minutes in duration, the cues that accompany these sequences form almost a third of *Munich*'s non-diegetic score, reiterating questions of perspective and subjectivity surrounding the representation of these events.

The *Munich* Flashbacks

Munich's opening shows an armed group force entry into the Israeli athletes' residence. Williams's non-diegetic music accompanies the sequence and features prominent repeating chromatic ostinati that undulate around F (notably a recurring F–G♯–F–F♯ figure), primarily in the piano's lower register and cimbalom. Prior to this a pulsing rhythm is heard as the attackers initially gain entry into the Olympic village. The next sequence shows media coverage of the resulting siege and the eventual news that the hostages have been killed. Recreated and actual footage from the time shows the perspectives of those in the media and interested parties watching this news, rather than the attackers and their hostages — except for one moment that shows them watching unfolding events on a television inside the Olympic village. This entire sequence is unscored until the news breaks that the hostages have been killed.

Aside from these opening moments the only depictions of the Munich attack are presented as flashbacks. These are explicitly framed as Avner's perspective, which is a

[21]. In order to transparently emphasize the minimal amount of non-diegetic score in *Munich*, this total has been calculated including the full duration of two cues that integrate sections of source music that is challenging to disentangle from the non-diegetic orchestration. The first, beginning at 00.08.27, features material from 'Hatikvah' that appears to be emanating from a diegetic television and is then absorbed by the non-diegetic orchestra. The second, beginning at 00.33.47, accompanies the team's first assassination and is a fragmentary cue, which integrates music making from a nearby diegetic location. Discounting instances of what is likely pure source music within these cues results in a less absolutely accurate calculation but provides a revised total that is closer to 36.5 minutes circa.

central characteristic of the different approach taken within these sequences[22]. As a set the flashbacks are often highly stylized with selective use of slow-motion imagery, some muting of diegetic sound, and Williams's prominent non-diegetic music. The first flashback is framed by Avner staring out of a plane window as he flies to begin his mission and continues where the opening sequence finished, showing the violence inside the Olympic village as the athletes initially try to escape. The second, at 01.49.51, shows the hostages being transported by minibus as part of their captors' escape plan. This is framed by shots of Avner lying on a bed and then abruptly waking, implying the sequence was his nightmare. The final and longest flashback occurs slightly over 30 minutes later and just eight minutes before *Munich*'s closing credits. This depicts the massacre of the athletes and is intercut with images of a troubled Avner making love with his wife.

Generally, there is little motion in Williams's music for these flashbacks as the score largely features a reasonably slow rate of harmonic change. An exception is the first flashback, which features undulating figures in the bass that centre harmonically around a perfect fifth interval: these enter towards the end of the sequence creating greater movement. Otherwise, the accompaniment is often static and melodic figures are given relative prominence. In the first flashback the initial melodic material features sustained string pitches that evolve into more extended chromatic lines: identical material enters towards the end of the second flashback, which is arguably the least stylized of the three, and musically is initially characterized by at times barely-audible sustained and dissonant low register pitches and less prominent melodic identity. The final flashback repeats and extends melodic material from the opening titles, which feature Lisbeth Scott's «micro-tonal vocalises»[23]. Similar material is also heard on a wind instrument when the bass pattern enters towards the end of the first flashback. Much of this material is characterized by chromaticism (including: prominent shapes comprising a rising semitone followed by a rising augmented second interval; undulating phrases with prominent semitone intervals; and frequent use of major and minor second and third intervals), all of which could be interpreted as contributing towards the Middle-Eastern feel Williams claimed to be striving for.

This prominent music and stylized cinematography is counter to a sparse, objective, and realist aesthetic. Media theorist Nigel Morris contends that «[a]fter the prologue the status of the Munich reconstructions becomes ambiguous. Are they subjective flashbacks, as the editing suggests — except Avner was not there — or 'objective' drama-documentary to reinforce metonymically the modality of the fiction?»[24]. If these are Avner's subjective flashbacks then their temporal placement in the film's narrative is significant. David Richter identifies three main threads progressing throughout *Munich*[25]: the team's assassination

[22]. Richter 2007, p. 154.

[23]. Audissino 2017, p. 227.

[24]. Morris 2007, p. 364.

[25]. Richter 2007, p. 149.

attempts becoming increasingly complex; the team becoming targets as the mission progresses; and their growing qualms about the morality and validity of the mission. By the second flashback several innocents have been killed following the team's actions and suspected-CIA involvement has thwarted an attack on their primary target. By the final flashback, after the mission, and following the deaths of three of his team, Avner is concerned for the safety of his exiled family. By these points his realization of the personal and ethical implications of the mission is becoming readily apparent, as indicated by his increasing paranoia. Framing these flashbacks as Avner's subjectivity, and emphasizing this through a different use of music and cinematography compared to that employed elsewhere in the film, highlights character and narrative development. Thus, rather than just negating a realistic documentary aesthetic, Williams's prominent music here is central in emphasizing these sequences as something contrasting: Avner's personal perspectives on the Munich attack. This reading seems logical if *Munich* is to be interpreted as his story, which is likely given that the screenplay was developed from George Jonas's book *Vengeance*, a text that claims to cite testimony from the real Avner.

Spielberg describes approaching *Munich*'s subject matter via «empathy [...] because you can't understand the human motivation without empathy»[26]. Framing the violence that instigates the film's central plot from Avner's perspective is arguably one way that the director explores such notions of empathy. Carl Plantinga identifies a range of filmic elements that can influence empathic response. These include: prolonged shots of a character's face; narrative context; and affective congruence «between narrative context, character engagement, various uses of film style and technique, and the psychological impressions and responses they generate»[27]. Given camerawork that increasingly focuses on Avner's face and sustained string pitches in Williams's music to bridge the transition into the flashbacks, each of these sequences could be interpreted as sharing qualities with Plantinga's scene of empathy «in which the pace of the narrative momentarily slows and the interior emotional experience of a favored character becomes the locus of attention»[28]. Plantinga also suggests that the «conventional scene of empathy uses music for affective congruence and to encourage emotional contagion»[29]. However, given the different musical strategy that Williams adopts in these stylized flashbacks in contrast to the rest of

[26]. Spielberg 2007, [02.55].

[27]. Plantinga 1999, p. 253.

[28]. *Ibidem*, p. 239.

[29]. *Ibidem*, p. 254. For Plantinga, such scenes also promote empathy by eliciting emotional response. He notes that various factors influence emotional response and that facial cues that might influence empathic reactions can be complex, change over time, and not necessarily reflective of an character's interior state. Subsequently, empathic engagement involves congruent emotional response rather than emotions that directly match those experienced by a character. This position resonates with the flashbacks in *Munich* given Avner's vacant facial expressions, which may invite a range of interpretations about his exact internal emotions at these moments.

Munich, considering this music as *in*congruent is also beneficial when assessing how the score might contribute to the overall effect of these sequences.

Incongruence generally refers to «a lack of shared properties» in the film-music relationship and keeping this definition broad by not specifying on which levels of the audiovisual pairing this lack of shared properties may be present (e.g. semantic or structural levels), is theoretically advantageous[30]. This expanded definition reflects that incongruent film music is not necessarily judged as inappropriate for the images or narrative, nor necessarily consciously noticed given that attentional resources may instead be focused on the visual content[31]. Incongruence here becomes like the audiovisual difference that Nicholas Cook argues characterizes multimedia[32]. For Cook, audiovisual difference (information from separate audio and visual modalities) actively contributes to meaning in multimedia through complementary or contesting relationships, which may relate more directly to judgements of whether the pairing is holistically appropriate or not.

Empirical research suggests that in incongruent relationships auditory and visual information tends to be processed independently, in contrast to congruent relationships where such information is jointly encoded[33]. This separate encoding can influence attention and create perceptual space to consider the filmic and musical information, and the nature of their relationship. Conceiving Williams's foregrounded, emotive music during the *Munich* flashbacks as incongruent highlights that these complex, stylized sequences can be interpreted in various ways, supporting reflection on a range of potential responses and the perceptual strategies that belie these: arguably such matters are particularly important to consider in films with the subject matter of *Munich*, which relate to challenging contemporary political issues such as terrorist and counterterrorist activity and the Israel-Palestine conflict. Such theoretical context therefore invites debate about: which facets of Williams's music for the flashbacks might be interpreted as congruent or incongruent; what impact his music might have upon audience members; and how this music might reflect empathy-inducing strategies and/or realist aesthetics adopted by Williams and Spielberg in *Munich* and their other collaborations that represent real events and/or people and use similar audiovisual constructions.

Audiovisual (In)congruence in the *Munich* Flashbacks

Most immediately, given that the flashbacks reflect a different musical approach to much of the rest of *Munich*, they could be interpreted as creating intradomain

30. Ireland 2015.
31. Ireland 2017.
32. Cook 1998.
33. Boltz 2004; Lipscomb – Kendall 1994.

incongruence — incongruence within the soundtrack itself. Williams's prominent music in these episodes may call greater attention to itself due to the decision to largely eschew sustained foregrounded non-diegetic scoring elsewhere in the film. This may heighten the impact of the music in the flashbacks, regardless of any other properties that it may share with the visuals and narrative. The emotive qualities of Williams's music may promote greater empathic response towards Avner and/or other characters precisely because of this relative prominence, which occurs in some of *Munich*'s most emotionally charged moments. Arguably, this is particularly the case for the climactic third and most violent flashback: this flashback most consistently mutes diegetic sound in the initial parts of the sequence, which perhaps also draws greater attention to the music.

In this final flashback space in the musical texture gives emphasis to Scott's vocals, distinguishing this cue from the previous flashbacks. The prominent vocals, and thus the chromatic inflections encapsulated within these and much of Williams's melodic material across the three sequences, have been described as a «keening lament in an Arabic modality»[34]. Such qualities may lead to the music being judged as congruent with the sense of place, home and identity that is so central to *Munich*, particularly if these flashbacks are interpreted as Avner's perspective and thus associated with factors that initially motivated him to undertake the mission. Williams reuses melodic material between the first and second flashbacks, and between the opening titles and the final flashback: as such, this musical content may also be perceived as fitting due to its potential familiarity to the audience as a result of being used in similar sequences earlier in the film. Elements of the broader moods implied by Williams's music may too be deemed congruent in certain ways. Critics have described Scott's vocals as «mournful» and this character and the slow tempo that dominates the cues could be seen as emphasizing the human tragedy and loss of life depicted in these sequences[35]. However, the music could also be interpreted as incongruent given its previously discussed relatively static character in contrast to the violent, action-laden nature of many of the images, notably in the first and final flashbacks which depict violent struggles and gun battles.

On a broader level, such music could be judged as congruent given the frequent use of similar audiovisual tropes in contemporary multimedia. Common techniques like the association of slow, tranquil music with images of devastation and destruction can act like a schematic framework that aids audience interpretation given their likely familiarity with other similar filmic moments[36]. Recognition of this type of pairing might influence response and allow intertextual links to be made with other films that feature similar devices, such as the other Williams-Spielberg nonfiction films to be discussed in this chapter or the often-discussed use of Samuel Barber's "Adagio for Strings" alongside battle

[34]. Richter 2007, p. 155.

[35]. Goldwasser 2005.

[36]. Ireland 2017.

scenes in *Platoon* (Oliver Stone, 1986)[37]. Mervyn Cooke identifies «[a] common device» in film[38], where diegetic sound is suppressed and «slow-motion photography of brutal fighting [combines] with incongruously expressive music»[39]. Cooke's description clearly overlaps with aspects of the *Munich* flashbacks. His use of the adjective «incongruously» is perceptive and perhaps suggests that from his perspective the expressive character of such musical accompaniment does not capture something of the brutality and violence of such scenes, and maybe instead focuses on the human cost of these actions. This interpretation emphasizes the narrative complexity of sequences that present aggressive violence *and* great tragedy through the resultant loss of life. Describing such moments Cooke cites Chion's idea of anempathy, which refers to sound that seems conspicuously indifferent and does not match the mood of the filmic action[40]. Ideas of anempathy initially seem somewhat counter to the suggestion that Williams and Spielberg may be seeking to explore empathic response via the *Munich* flashbacks. However, such tensions can be addressed by considering anempathy within the present conceptualization of incongruence, which accounts for the apparent broader indifference of the music *and* the ways in which it might respond to or reflect the images. The final *Munich* flashback provides a good illustration of such tensions and how these might complement Williams and Spielberg's intentions for such sequences. Despite the consistently steady tempo and tonal register of Williams's music as this sequence climaxes and one of the attackers opens fire on the defenceless hostages, the strings swell and become increasingly dissonant, Scott's vocals become more agitated, and the editing becomes more rapid. Gunshots also become prominent following the almost total muting of diegetic sound prior to this point. Despite the broader apparent anempathy of the static, mournful music which seems to continue indifferently against the action-laden images, localized elements within the music, sound design, and narrative action (both that occurring in Munich and the intercut images of Avner and his wife making love) also share a closer relationship and climax together to reflect the dramatic trajectory of the sequence. Thus, whilst Williams and Spielberg may seek to promote empathy with Avner by reflecting his perspective and using emotive music to emphasize this, incongruities in the cinematic construction also enable the music to retain some anempathetic independent qualities, which as Chion notes may, perhaps paradoxically, intensify emotion[41].

---

37. For further detail see for example Howard 2007 who refers to the «juxtaposition of relentlessly violent images and the sustained serenity of the music» (p. 58) in *Platoon*.

38. Cooke 2008, p. 498.

39. *Ibidem*, p. 178.

40. Chion 1994, p. 221.

41. *Ibidem*, p. 8.

Williams's Approaches to Scoring Tragedy and History

As this analysis illustrates, there are many levels on which Williams's music for the *Munich* flashbacks might be considered congruent or incongruent. Recognizing such incongruities is valuable in offering perceptual explanations to explore *how* the flashbacks might influence audience response, including empathic identification with the characters, and thus *how* these stylized sequences and their music might complement Spielberg and Williams's intentions when presenting the film's broader subject matter. One of the main criticisms levelled against *Munich* is its perceived equation of terrorist and counter-terrorist actions but Morris argues that the film «strives to maintain detachment, challenging the spectator to reach a conclusion» about such issues[42]. In many ways the constructed nature of the flashbacks in a film that elsewhere eschews non-diegetic music to convey a realist tone challenges this aesthetic. Indeed, it could be argued that framing these sequences as Avner's perspective, and thus potentially inviting the audience to empathize with him, especially counters detached documentary qualities.

However, similar musical devices can be found in Williams's scores for various other Spielberg films that are based on historical situations, notably those dealing with mass loss of life, suggesting this is a recognized strategy for the pair when considering how music might support the presentation of such matters. For example, in the opening of *Amistad* (1997) shots depicting a mutiny on a ship as a group of enslaved Africans violently overpower their captors remain unscored. However, a later pivotal sequence in this film, which depicts the nineteenth century legal battle resulting from the group's actions and surrounding their rights, is presented as a flashback. The nearly 10 minute long flashback bridges two scenes in which Cinqué (the group's spokesman played by Djimon Hounsou) recounts his history to Baldwin (his legal representative played by Matthew McConaughey) and later as he relays this as testimony in court. The flashback shows Cinqué's abduction, the mistreatment and floggings he and others were subjected to, and the purposeful drowning of several chained captives. Before the flashback, non-diegetic music enters as Cinqué begins describing his past in response to Baldwin's questions, which aim to persuade Cinqué of his bravery and status as the group's leader so that he will testify on their behalf. The flashback concludes with shots from *Amistad*'s opening, this time with musical accompaniment similar to that heard throughout the flashback. Like the *Munich* flashbacks, moments in Williams's score combine haunting vocalises, this time choral rather than solo, with string accompaniment. African drumming patterns also feature and Morris contends that this instrumental and stylistic combination «assert[s] integration, a shared emotional and moral response, on the level of the music – a contemporary comment on past events»[43]. Lars Eckstein also suggests that the music and cinematography «work together to overwhelm the viewer with

[42]. Morris 2007, p. 372.

[43]. *Ibidem*, p. 267.

a cathartic overdose»[44]. Regardless of how one might interpret the historical authenticity or treatment of issues such as slavery and representations of race in the flashback, both of these readings recognize the emotive qualities of Williams's music: like the *Munich* flashbacks, the sequence may help the audience to empathize with a central character, partly by using prominent music featuring instrumentation that seeks to reflect something of the character's national identity and that is placed in such a way as to reflect aspects of character development (in *Amistad* as Cinqué evolves as the group's leader, and in *Munich* as Avner becomes increasingly troubled by the consequences of his mission).

Saving Private Ryan (1998) also provides an interesting example for consideration. Much of this film is technically a flashback, bookended by two sequences showing an initially unidentified veteran and his family visiting the war graves in Normandy. Audissino notes a «sobriety» in the score[45], and Spielberg has described «restraint», the same word Williams used to describe his approach to scoring *Munich*, as the composer's «primary objective. He did not want to sentimentalize or create emotion from what already existed in raw form»[46]. As such, the pair decided not to score the battle sequences and the 162 minute film features just 40 minutes of non-diegetic music[47]. The opening sequences reflect this aesthetic well. A sustained, high-pitched dissonant string pedal, and increasingly prominent sounds of waves, accompany a 24 second shot that gradually zooms in on the former soldier's face, providing the transition into the flashback. The following recreation of the Omaha Beach landing is just over 20 minutes long and features no music. The horror and chaos of battle is conveyed by seemingly diegetic sound, including moments of point-of-audition sound design reflecting the disoriented perspective of Captain Miller (Tom Hanks)[48]. Music returns at battle's end as shots showing soldiers' corpses strewn across the beach are presented following a close-up shot of Miller's face as he acknowledges to a fellow soldier that the sight is «quite a view». Williams again creates an intradomain incongruence with the preceding sustained blend of sound design and chaotic action through his introduction of a «slow diatonic chorale»[49], which Decker describes as «elegiac»[50]: again this musical entry is connected with the perspective of a central character[51].

---

[44]. Eckstein 2008, p. 77.

[45]. Audissino 2014, p. 217.

[46]. Cited *ibidem*.

[47]. Decker 2017, p. 231.

[48]. Grajeda 2016.

[49]. Lehman 2015, p. 417.

[50]. Decker 2017, pp. 231-233.

[51]. For Lehman 2015, Williams here demonstrates his Americana style, which draws upon Aaron Copland's influences, including «sparking orchestration and constant melodiousness — with allowances for the occasional non-disruptive dissonance» (p. 417).

Similar musical devices can also be found in other Spielberg-Williams films when the relevant sequences are not framed as flashbacks[52]. In *Lincoln* (2012) Williams's score is again «restrained», only accompanying around a third of the film[53]. However, a scene around 15 minutes before *Lincoln*'s ending presents the horrors of the Civil War from the titular president's (Daniel Day-Lewis) perspective as he rides through a battlefield strewn with corpses. The music features solo piano, and later, subtle string accompaniment. It progresses at a steady pace and features largely consonant harmony centred around G minor, and includes greater chromatic motion in the bass at a moment where the camera focuses on the bodies on the ground. The cue is described as «delicate» and «somber» by Burgoyne and Trafton, who suggest that «Lincoln is a stand-in for the spectator, revisiting the violence of war»[54].

Considering point-of-view representations of violence in Spielberg films, Burgoyne and Trafton also identify moments from *Schindler's List* (1993) where the extent of the atrocities being committed against the Jews is framed by Schindler's (Liam Neeson) perspective. As with *Munich*, discussing the approach he and Spielberg decided to take given *Schindler's List*'s subject, Williams talks about using music «sparingly», complementing the approach taken in the cinematography (including the decision to present the film in black and white)[55]. One scene that does feature prominent music addresses the incineration of Jews at the concentration camps and is framed by Schindler's reactions to these events: firstly his noticing ash from the camp chimney's falling onto his car; and then his noticing the body of the girl in the red coat from an earlier sequence on a passing cart piled with corpses. This is accompanied by Williams's orchestral and choral "Immolation" cue, which uses Hebrew liturgical text[56]. The moment echoes the earlier sequence where the Krakow ghetto is cleared and many of its residents executed, which is framed by shots of Schindler watching events from a nearby hill. The sequence is largely unscored but after nearly 10 minutes a non-diegetic children's choir's rendition of the traditional Yiddish song "Oyfn Pripetshik" enters and the shot returns to show Schindler watching on.

Finally, comparisons may be drawn with an early sequence from *Munich* itself where the news of the athletes' deaths breaks via television reports. After the initial announcement, the report listing the names of the victims is watched by Avner and his wife. "Hatikvah", the Israeli national anthem, accompanies the sequence, initially at a quiet volume, likely emanating from the television. This music is later performed by the non-diegetic orchestra

---

52. Arguably, most sequences in *Saving Private Ryan* do not feel like flashbacks given that most of the narrative is itself a flashback: consequently, episodes such as the Omaha Beach sequence arguably do not sustain the same sense of temporal disruption with their surrounding scenes as the much briefer *Munich* flashbacks.

53. Audissino 2014, p. 221.

54. Burgoyne – Trafton 2017, p. 379.

55. Cited in Dyer 1994.

56. *Ibidem*.

and the report intercut with images of Mossad agents listing the targets of their retaliatory mission. Again, the tragedy of the Munich massacre is filtered through Avner's eyes and accompanied by emotive music that infers nationalistic qualities.

Conclusions

Using flashbacks and/or point-of-view editing each of these sequences depicts horrific moments that replicate or are inspired by actual events. They present the perspectives of central characters and Williams often scores these sequences using emotive music that may further imply these perspectives by using stylistic and instrumental inflections that suggest something of the characters' identities or heritage. Williams also often makes prominent use of the voice in such sequences, which is interesting given recent empirical research that has linked the voice and instruments with qualities that sound like the human voice (e.g. string instruments, which also feature prominently in many of these examples), with negative emotions like sadness[57]. Any emotion induction or empathic response prompted by these sequences may help an audience to process the violent acts depicted. However, such compositional devices arguably undermine claims for neutral historical authenticity, not least given Williams and Spielberg's choice to avoid music at other prominent moments in these films. Moreover, such strategies, that might encourage an audience to empathize with the characters, raise various questions surrounding perspective and identification: indeed, encouraging the audience to empathize with characters like Avner perhaps raises particularly problematic questions in contrast with equivalent framing in films like *Schindler's List* given Schindler's efforts to save life and Avner's mission to take life. An alternative interpretation, which negates such questions to some extent, is that rather than encouraging identification with Avner or the characters identified above, perhaps any attempts to induce empathy via these musically-supported flashbacks derive from giving the audience another human, someone, anyone, to empathize with purely to help to process the gravity of the depicted events. Regardless, each of these sequences suggests Williams and Spielberg's awareness of the potential functions of music in films with weighty content and historical origins, not least in flashback and point-of-view sequences.

Rogers observes that it is a common device in documentary film to use «music to suggest a move back in time in the form of a re-enactment to illustrate the recollection of an interviewee»[58]. She quotes the director Errol Morris's suggestion that «re-enactment is not re-enacting anything, it's there to make you think about reality, about what we take to be reality, what we think is reality, what claims to be reality»[59]. The constructed,

57. E.g. Huron – Anderson – Shanahan 2014; Juslin – Harmat – Eerola 2014.

58. Rogers 2015, p. 12.

59. Cited *ibidem*, p. 13.

potentially empathy-inducing nature of sequences like the *Munich* flashbacks share qualities with Morris's re-enactments and therefore, perhaps paradoxically, might not simply challenge realism in such moments but also actually complement the ideals of these films to document or represent historical individuals and events. Whilst perhaps promoting empathic identification, these sequences and their associated music might simultaneously help to maintain some sense of detachment because of their overtly-constructed nature in contrast to other less overtly-stylized moments like the reconstructed news footage near the start of *Munich,* which may imply greater authenticity and objectivity. Morris describes the use of devices like the muting of diegetic sound, as happens in the *Munich* flashbacks, as «enhancing psychological realism and emphasising textuality»[60]: the transitions between the more overtly-stylized and scored, and the seemingly more realistic, documentary-like sequences may also promote such qualities. Morris suggests that by using such devices *Munich* promotes a «partly detached spectator»[61]. It is via such partial detachment that spectators can question the depicted events, the way in which history is represented, and their own responses to such content. Incongruities in the audiovisual relationship when music is used as Williams often does in such sequences can contribute to such processes due to the perceptual space created by the separate encoding of auditory and visual information, providing perceptual explanation for a potential plethora of responses. Therefore, even if the audience does empathize with the characters, other incongruities in the audiovisual relationship may still cause them to question the representation of the depicted events and consequently their responses to the character's plight. There are many levels on which a lack of shared properties might be identified in such film-music constructions. Williams and Spielberg are likely aware of these potential effects of the music, given their frequent use of such techniques. In such contexts, (as for many other directors and composers given the aforementioned common use of this filmic trope), an often used strategy for Williams and Spielberg is to present steady, incongruously expressive music against images of devastation and destruction, perhaps to emphasize tragedy and loss of life rather than the aggression and brutality of violence. Similarly, this analysis suggests that Williams and Spielberg recognize the emotive potential of the intradomain incongruities that result from contrasting this prominent scoring with other sequences that remain unscored to convey a more objective realist aesthetic[62].

---

[60]. Morris 2007, p. 369.

[61]. *Ibidem*, p. 366.

[62]. It is worth noting that this represents just one approach taken by Williams when scoring nonfiction and history films. An interesting point of comparison, (which given the different director and his different approach falls beyond the scope of this chapter), is Williams's scores for Oliver Stone's presidential trilogy *Born on the Fourth of July* (1989), *JFK* (1991), and *Nixon* (1995). Lehman's 2015 penetrating analysis discusses how Williams's abilities as a musical mythmaker complement Stone's countermythical films, which 'make no claim to the [...] neutral recounting of fact, and instead employ cinematic devices to rhetorical ends' (p. 415) supporting readings of Stone as a '*reinterpretive* historian' (p. 420).

Morris suggests that expectations of «authoritative documentary exposition» in *Munich* are «inappropriate»[63]. He writes: «[d]ebate about distortion and bias could continue endlessly, missing the point that no representation is neutral»[64]. Considering the debates that will influence her sanctioning of the retaliatory mission depicted in *Munich,* Israeli Prime Minister Golda Meir (Lynn Cohen) remarks: «Today I'm hearing with new ears». Williams's music for the events that prompted this mission echoes techniques he has used elsewhere to score violence, tragedy, and history, and allows the audience to do exactly that as they too engage with the content of Spielberg's provocative film and his other representations of historical events and individuals.

Bibliography

Audissino 2014

Audissino, Emilio. *John Williams's Film Music: «Jaws», «Star Wars», «Raiders of the Lost Ark», and the Return of the Classical Hollywood Music Style*, Madison (WI), University of Wisconsin Press, 2014 (Wisconsin Film Studies).

Audissino 2017

Id. 'John Williams and Contemporary Film Music', in: *Contemporary Film Music: Investigating Cinema Narratives and Composition*, edited by Lindsay Coleman and Joakim Tillman, London, Palgrave Macmillan, 2017, pp. 221-236.

Boltz 2004

Boltz, Marilyn G. 'The Cognitive Processing of Film and Musical Soundtracks', in: *Memory and Cognition*, xxxii/7 (2004), pp. 1194-1205.

Burgoyne – Trafton 2017

Burgoyne, Robert – Trafton, John. 'Violence and Memory in Spielberg's *Lincoln*', in: *A Companion to Steven Spielberg*, edited by Nigel Morris, Malden (MA), Wiley Blackwell, 2017 (Wiley Blackwell Companions to Film Directors, 16), pp. 374-386.

Chion 1994

Chion, Michel. *Audio-Vision: Sound on Screen*, English translation by Claudia Gorbman, New York, Columbia University Press, 1994.

Cook 1998

Cook, Nicholas. *Analysing Musical Multimedia*, Oxford, Oxford University Press, 1998.

Cooke 2008

Cooke, Mervyn. *A History of Film Music*, Cambridge, Cambridge University Press, 2008.

---

63. Morris 2007, p. 372.

64. *Ibidem*, p. 373.

Decker 2017
Decker, Todd R. *Hymns for the Fallen: Combat Movie Music and Sound after Vietnam*, Oakland (CA), University of California Press, 2017.

Dyer 1994
Dyer, Richard. 'John Williams: Making Movie-Music History: *Schindler* Composer Is up for Fifth Oscar', in: *Boston Globe*, 20 March 1994.

Eckstein 2008
Eckstein, Lars. 'The Pitfalls of Picturing Atlantic Slavery: Steven Spielberg's *Amistad* vs Guy Deslauriers's *The Middle Passage*', in: *Cultural Studies Review*, xiv/1 (2008), pp. 72-84.

Goldwasser 2005
Goldwasser, Dan. 'Review – *Munich*', in: *Soundtrack.Net*, (2005), <http://www.soundtrack.net/album/munich>, accessed February 2018.

Grajeda 2016
Grajeda, Tony. 'Listening to Violence: Point-of-audition Sound, Aural Interpellation, and the Rupture of Hearing', in: *The Palgrave Handbook of Sound Design and Music in Screen Media*, edited by Liz Green and Danijela Kulezic-Wilson, London, Palgrave Macmillan, 2016, pp. 169-182.

Howard 2007
Howard, Luke. 'The Popular Reception of Samuel Barber's *Adagio for Strings*', in: *American Music*, xxv/1 (2007), pp. 50-80.

Huron – Anderson – Shanahan 2014
Huron, David – Anderson, Neesha – Shanahan, Daniel. '"You Can't Play a Sad Song on the Banjo": Acoustic Factors in the Judgment of Instrument Capacity to Convey Sadness', in: *Empirical Musicology Review*, ix/1 (2014), pp. 29-41.

Ireland 2015
Ireland, David. 'Deconstructing Incongruence: A Psycho-Semiotic Approach toward Difference in the Film-Music Relationship', in: *Music and the Moving Image*, viii/2 (2015), pp. 48-57.

Ireland 2017
Id. 'Great Expectations? The Changing Role of Audiovisual Incongruence in Contemporary Multimedia', in: *Music and the Moving Image*, x/3 (2017), pp. 21-35.

Juslin – Harmat – Eerola 2014
Juslin, Patrik N. – Harmat, Lászlő – Eerola, Tuomas. 'What Makes Music Emotionally Significant? Exploring the Underlying Mechanisms', in: *Psychology of Music*, xlii/4 (2014), pp. 599-623.

Kalinak 1992
Kalinak, Kathryn. *Settling the Score: Music and the Classical Hollywood Film*, Madison (WI), University of Wisconsin Press, 1992 (Wisconsin Studies in Film).

Lehman 2015

Lehman, Frank. 'Scoring the President: Myth and Politics in John Williams's *JFK* and *Nixon*', in: *Journal of the Society for American Music*, ix/4 (2015), pp. 409-444.

Lipkin 1999

Lipkin, Steve. 'Defining Docudrama: *In the Name of the Father*, *Schindler's List*, and *JFK*', in: *Why Docudrama? Fact-Fiction on film and TV*, edited by Alan Rosenthal, Carbondale, Southern Illinois University Press, 1999, pp. 370-383.

Lipscomb – Kendall 1994

Lipscomb, Scott D. – Kendall, Roger A. 'Perceptual Judgement of the Relationship between Musical and Visual Components in Film', in: *Psychomusicology*, xiii/1 (1994), pp. 60-98.

Morris 2007

Morris, Nigel. *The Cinema of Steven Spielberg: Empire of Light*, London, Wallflower Press, 2007 (Directors' Cut).

Plantinga 1999

Plantinga, Carl. 'The Scene of Empathy and the Human Face on Film', in: *Passionate Views: Film, Cognition, and Emotion*, edited by Carl Plantinga and Greg M. Smith, Baltimore (MD), The John Hopkins University Press, 1999, pp. 239-255.

Richter 2007

Richter, David H. 'Keeping Company in Hollywood: Ethical Issues in Nonfiction Film', in: *Narrative*, xv/2 (2007), pp. 140-166.

Rogers 2015

Rogers, Holly. 'Introduction: Music, Sound and the Nonfiction Aesthetic', in: *Music and Sound in Documentary Film*, edited by Holly Rogers, New York, Routledge, 2015 (Routledge Music and Screen Media Series), pp. 1-19.

Spielberg 2007

Spielberg, Steven. 'Introduction', in: *Munich* DVD, DreamWorks LLC and Universal Pictures, 2007. DSL1526.

Williams 2006

Williams, John. 'And the Nominees Are…: Academy Nominees 2006', 2011, <https://www.youtube.com/watch?v=b8zh8gy1xYw>, accessed February 2018.

John Williams and the Musical Avant-garde: The Score for *War of the Worlds*

Irena Paulus
(Franjo Lučić Art School, Velika Gorica)

When thinking of John Williams, one thinks of the memorable themes and hummable melodies composed for the *Star Wars* saga created by George Lucas (1977-ongoing), *Superman* (Richard Donner, 1978), *E. T.* (Steven Spielberg, 1982), the *Indiana Jones* saga (Steven Spielberg, 1981-ongoing) — to name just the most celebrated scores. Being both supportive of the picture and enjoyable to listen to, Williams's music became a signpost not only of Hollywood film scoring, but of film music in general. Yet, in the early 2000s, particularly in Steven Spielberg's new millennial science-fiction trilogy, John Williams wrote more modernistic scores than usual.

The score for *Artificial Intelligence* (Steven Spielberg, 2001), based on a Stanley Kubrick project that Spielberg had inherited, features partly «atonal dialect and a sort of futuristic minimalism — with colouring touches of synthesizers and electric guitars»[1]. In *Minority Report* (Steven Spielberg, 2002), inspired by a Philip K. Dick short story, even more non-functional harmonic writing was present, blended with elements of old film noir music, with a special nod to Bernard Herrmann[2]. The third instalment of Spielberg's science fiction trilogy, *War of the Worlds* (2005) was an adaptation of the famous novel by Herbert George Wells. The score offered very few tonally stable cues and was dominated by non-functional harmonies.

Steven Spielberg noticed that:

> For *War of the Worlds* John reached for something not of this earth and composed a score that you feel on your skin, even before you become aware that you are actually hearing it. He has laid down a musical foundation of atmospherics and textural events, achieving a rhythmic propulsion that is so utterly primal it crawls up inside of you and makes you wonder how one composer could make such a radical departure in style from such masterworks

1. Audissino 2014, p. 217.
2. *Ibidem*, p. 218; Rossi 2011a, p. 137.

of melodic phrasing as the "Flying Theme" from *E.T.* to the enduring themes of *Star Wars* series and come up with a new sound that gives *War of the Worlds* much of its ultra-realism[3].

Change in Williams's Musical Language?

The score for *War of the Worlds* emerged from the composer's long career, where scores written with advanced modern techniques (such as the music for Robert Altman's 1972 film, *Images*) or composed to dodge tonality through a kind of semi-atonality (as for Spielberg's *Close Encounters of the Third Kind*, 1977) share room with memorable scores characterized by tonality and based on broad themes, attractive harmonic progressions and ever-interesting instrumentation. In a 1975 interview with Irwin Bazelon[4] Williams pointed out the composers he loved and had come to be influenced by. Beside the film composers of the classical Hollywood period, such as Alfred Newman, Max Steiner, Franz Waxman, and Bernard Herrmann, interestingly he mentioned the names of two composers who, although from different countries, both ended up in California: Igor Stravinsky and Arnold Schoenberg. However, they weren't nearly as appreciated by him as Sir Peter Maxwell Davies, the prolific English composer who could write in a variety of styles, some of them being highly experimental and violent in character, such as his theatre piece *Eight Songs for a Mad King* (1969), and some more accessible, such as his eclectic orchestral piece *St. Thomas Wake* (1969).

Despite the appreciation stated in that interview, Williams's work has never been as radical as Davies's. Yet, it does seem that the tone of Williams's film scores slightly changed at the beginning of new millennium, with *Artificial Intelligence*, *Minority Report* and *War of the Worlds* becoming darker in instrumentation and harmonization, more intellectually oriented and more grasping beyond the boundaries of tonality. And during this period Williams also scored Alfonso Cuarón's *Harry Potter and the Prisoner of Azkaban* (2004) which was ominous in tone, and not at all childish, as one would expect and anticipate from the two previous *Harry Potter* films[5].

Out with Commercialism, in with Contemporary Art-Music?

Williams has always accompanied his film career with a regular output for the concert stage, believing that this domain presented him with opportunities that he «wouldn't have

3. Spielberg 2005, n.p.
4. Bazelon 1975, pp. 193-206.
5. See Jamie Lynn Webster's chapter on *Harry Potter* in this volume.

in the restricted areas of composing film music»[6]. Concert oeuvres offer another look at the composer's work; in these pieces he has applied his mastery to the area of art-music that most contemporary film composers avoid, because they mostly come from the world of popular music.

On the other hand, in the same interview in which he pointed out Maxwell Davies as his first-choice composer, Williams expressed some firm, even 'blasphemous' views on the usage of popular music in films. Prompted by Bazelon, who asked him about the tendency of pop forms to infiltrate films, he stated that «it is natural for pop to end up in the film»[7], that «the idea of music earning money [...] is a healthy thing»[8] and that he didn't like to term the popular music dialect «lower art», because he believed in democracy in arts[9]. Commercialism of film music is not a discovery — Jerry Goldsmith, another composer Williams admired, also noticed that most film composers came from pop backgrounds, and that music can sometimes be «a completely commercial device»[10]. Did Williams write these different, darker film scores in the early 2000s, after thirty years of successful artistic achievements characterize by more melodic/thematic scores, to eventually move his style closer to that art-music figures he had professed his admiration for? Could this stylistic change, culminated in the music for *War of the Worlds*, be a sign of his willingness to embrace a more art-music-oriented language and depart from the commercialism of mainstream film scoring?

The score presented possibly the heaviest deviations from the composer's musical language as typically used in other films. Indeed, Williams's die-hard fans seemingly had some difficulty accepting the change. One commented that the music was an extremely difficult listen and that «only those with a true fanboy masochistic streak will be able to withstand such a continuous and ominous barrage of sci-fi dissonance»[11]. Others felt that the music was «unglamorous» (unlike other Williams's scores) and «merely an average background listening experience»[12]; one claimed that there was a surprisingly small quantity of music in the film[13].

Instead, those who did not perceive dissonances as a negative listening experience — mostly music professionals — described *War of the Worlds* as the «ultimate case [where] harmonic dynamism continues to function, but, without themes, the moments of

6. Mangan 2005.

7. *Ibidem*, p. 194.

8. *Ibidem*, p. 195.

9. *Ibidem*, p. 196.

10. Bazelon 1975, p. 190.

11. Monger 2005, online.

12. Clemmensen 2005-2011.

13. «The score is striking partly as a result of how sparingly it is used. For long stretches of the movie, you hear no music at all» (Scott 2005). In reality, *War of the Worlds* is another extensively scored movie, as are all the Spielberg-Williams collaborations.

functional harmonies are opposed without a big contrast to the moments of non-functional harmonies»[14]. Scholars also emphasized the presence of «piercing dissonance, disorienting atonality, stalking rhythms, and frenetic percussions»[15] and concluded that the music tends to «oscillate between tonality, polytonality and atonality»[16].

The film itself gained some exceptionally negative reactions, notably from renowned film critic Roger Ebert[17]. Ebert felt that *War of the Worlds* was «curiously rudimentary in its action»; he thought it was full of clichés, found the story unconvincing, and said the human characters were «disappointingly one-dimensional»; the alien fighting machines, the Tripods, were «designed for heavy lifting» and obviously needed «to modernize [their] equipment and techniques»; the film lacked «the zest and joyous energy we expect from Steven Spielberg [...] the sense of wonder [of *Close Encounters of the Third Kind*] [...], the dazzling imagination of *Minority Report*».

General reviews of *War of the Worlds* were not as negative as Ebert's. In fact, the film was basically a commercial success, although it did has not become as 'timeless' as Spielberg's earlier science-fiction films, like *Close Encounters of the Third Kind* or *E. T.* Unfortunately, the same has happened with its score, which soon fell into semi-obscurity.

FROM H. G. WELLS TO SPIELBERG

Written in 1898, Herbert George Wells's novel *The War of the Worlds* became one of the most influential texts in science-fiction history. It inspired Orson Welles to broadcast his notorious 1938 radio show; it was adapted as a major film in 1953, directed by Byron Haskin; it originated two seasons of the *War of the Worlds* television series (1988-1990) and several direct-to-DVD films[18]; it was the basis for the animated science-fiction film *War of the Worlds: Goliath* (Joe Pearson, 2012), the Canadian/UK semi-documentary *The Great Martian War 1913-1917* (Mike Slee, 2013), and numerous comic books[19] and video games[20]. It even inspired two conceptual albums conceived by American composer Jeff Wayne: *Jeff*

[14]. ROSSI 2011A, p. 138.

[15]. AUDISSINO 2014, p. 220.

[16]. ROSSI 2011A, p. 138.

[17]. EBERT 2005.

[18]. Some of these were variants of the same material shown in *H. G. Wells' The War of the Worlds* directed by Timothy Hines in 2005.

[19]. Comic books were published by Classics Illustrated, Now-Age Illustrated, Eternity Comics, Marvel Comics, Caliber Comics, Dark Horse Comics, etc.

[20]. For example, *War of the Worlds*, monochrome vector arcade game created in 1982; *Jeff Wayne's The War of the Worlds,* a real-time strategy video game released for Windows-based PCs in 1998; *The War of the Worlds*, a human survival online game launched in 2005 by Paramount; *The War of the Worlds*, a 2011 single-player side-scrolling 2D action-adventure video game, etc.

Wayne's Musical Version of the War of the Worlds (1978) and *Jeff Wayne's Musical Version of The War of the Worlds – The New Generation* (2012), which, in turn, became the basis of a stage show, a combination of live musical performances, theatre and multimedia inserts[21].

The everlasting success of Wells's novel, classified at the end of nineteenth century as a 'scientific romance', was due to its merging of fantasy and realism. With the theme of the invasion from Mars[22] open to be interpreted as *any* invasion[23], it provided an opportunity to explore human behaviour in extreme, war-like situations.

In Steven Spielberg's version of *War of the Worlds*, the story is told from the perspective of a longshoreman, Ray Ferrier. He works at the docks of Brooklyn, and lives in Bayonne, New Jersey. He is divorced and he is temporarily in care of his two children, teenage son Robbie and ten-year old daughter Rachel, while his ex-wife is off visiting her parents in Boston. Ray is estranged from his children, but this attitude gradually changes as they all learn that Earth is being attacked by ruthless alien invaders, and they have to bond in order to survive.

In his version of the story, Spielberg decided not to mention the provenance of the aliens, despite the prominence Wells had given to Martians in the science-fiction genre. Otherwise, the director tried to stay as close to the novel as possible in the context of the new political situation of the early twenty-first century, and the new locale[24].

John Williams approached the scoring of the film with these peculiarities in mind. He probably also kept in mind Leith Stevens's score for the 1953 film, which was stylistically advanced for its time[25]. So, contrary to his more famous compositional approach and in line with the trend of contemporary film music, Williams abandoned the thematic treatment inherited from Wagnerian drama and decided to treat each scene separately, depending on its narrative content. While doing so, he maintained cohesion in his usage of intervallic and harmonic material, and developed a specific style that sounds at the verge of tonality.

---

21. For more about Jeff Wayne's project, see Beck 2016, pp. 275-288.

22. Wells chose Mars, because it was scientifically reliable. By his time, people had been observing Mars through telescopes for three centuries. Also, by appearing in Wells's novel, Martians became a universal trope for aliens in the science fiction genre.

23. In Wells's case, invasion put Victorian England in jeopardy. In the cases of later adaptations of the novel, there were direct references to World War I and pre-World War II world crises (in Orson Welles's radio drama); to Cold War, notably the 1950-1953 Korean War and the Soviet Union's first hydrogen bomb test in August 1953 (in the 1953 film version); to 9/11/2001 terrorist attack, and the 2003-2011 Iraq War (in Spielberg's 2005 version).

24. Orson Welles's version moved Wells's story from Woking, London and the nineteenth century English countryside to Grover's Mill, New Jersey; the 1953 film version moved it to Linda Rosa and Los Angeles in California; Spielberg moved it to New York, New Jersey and Boston.

25. Stevens's score was based on the harmony of fourths on two tonics, taken from Joseph Schillinger's music system. For more about this score, see Rosar 2006.

Consider the scene where Ray, shaken by events that he assumes are cause by an abnormal storm, walks out onto the street. A neighbour points out the sudden disruption of all electric devices, including every single car. Because of this event, Ray notices that his son Robbie has borrowed Ray's car without permission. Robbie is at the same time shaken by the unfolding odd events and feels guilty for having taken the car. Ray is firstly relieved to see that Robbie is safe but then warns him: the next time Robbie does something like that, Ray will call the Police.

The scene is accompanied by a motif, repeated in different variations — see Ex. 1. It contains a minor second and a minor third as the main intervals and varies them, anticipating many similar motifs, chords, and even clusters with the same or similar intervallic content that will appear later in the score.

Ex. 1: transcription of John Williams, "An Abnormal Storm" (tentative title) from the *War of the Worlds* film score (© 2005 BMI), published by Songs of SKG, ear transcription from the film's soundtrack. Used in compliance with the U.S. Copyright Act, Section 107.

The music seems to literally communicate the twitch in Ray's stomach as he passes his neighbour and talks to Robbie. Another element to notice is that Williams's music is closely synchronized to the events, although the scene presents a rather simple action, an introductory situation seemingly not too important in the context of the developing events[26].

Apart from creating tension and a feeling of nervous anticipation, the motivic movement gives space to dialogue as well. Firstly, by going up in a pitch and changing slightly its melodic content (with a persistent usage of the same intervals) during the comments of Ray's neighbour; secondly, by blending with the timbre of Robbie's teenage voice (music is played by violins and vibraphone), and then complementing Ray's tenor voice by diving in deeper register (music is played by violas).

An Athematic Score?

Considered within the Williams canon, the most frequent objection to the *War of the Worlds* score is that it doesn't have melodies; it doesn't even have a title theme. Indeed, what we hear over the appearance of the film's title could hardly be called a theme: two harsh timpani strokes with the sticks left to bounce freely to add more sound body.

[26]. Gorbman uses the term «narrative cueing» (Gorbman 1987, pp. 73, 82-89); Audissino uses the notion of «tailoring music to the picture» (see Audissino 2014).

Yet the general statement that the *War of the Worlds* score lacks thematic material is not completely true. A closer listen reveals, if not full-fledged melodies, plenty of themes. There is the beautiful trumpet trio playing when Ray finds the wreckage of a Boeing 747 that crashed in front of his ex-wife's house[27]; the violas playing two long contrapuntal lines that express the refugees' desperation; the piano melody that accompanies the final family reunion in Boston; even the gradually accumulating string lines in a high-pitched register that accompany the horrified Rachel as she realizes that there are more and more dead bodies floating in the river.

Themes, in terms of linear writing, do exist in *War of the Worlds*. The thing is that they are effectively embedded in the sound mix of the film and remain unnoticed in the background. Due to their intervallic and harmonic construction, these themes are not melodically 'pleasant' to the ear of the common listener and, contrary to Williams's trademark leitmotivic technique, they are not repeated across the film.

The harsh sound of the themes reflects the film's narrative: the characters are experiencing mortally dangerous and emotionally taxing situations, which make them re-examine their attitudes towards each other. The needs of this narrative must have led Williams to use a melodic construction unfamiliar to the wider audiences: themes appear over pedal tones, which often result in bitonality (as in the aeroplane wreckage scene and during the family reunion in Boston); or they produce dissonant counterpoint, often in the course of largely expanded tonality (as in the scene where Rachel sees dead bodies floating in the river, or in the scene where clothes fall from the sky). Nevertheless, themes also appear in the more familiar context of (mostly) minor-mode writing (for example, in the scene where Robbie drives after a stressful quarrel with his father, and the family sees lots of sorrowful refugees), and even acquire a memorable march-like quality at the end of the film (as in the scene of the final return to Boston, where Ray notices that the alien red weeds are dead and that the Tripod acts oddly and seemingly sickly[28]).

---

[27]. As stated in Bouzereau 2005, the trumpet trio was previously written for the "Epilogue" cue, and was moved by Spielberg to the aeroplane wreckage scene. It also plays over the film's end credits. This melody stands out not because it openly uses thirds (above the pedal tone, which is also a minor third), but because it comes after several tense action cues ("Intersection Scene", "Escape from the City"). Broadly looking, it sounds like a military trumpet honouring the victims of the (terrorist, Second World-, alien...) war. Namely, apart from being an obvious reference to the 9/11 terrorist attacks, the scene also refers to Orson Welles's radio show where fighter planes succeed in taking down a Martian tripod through a kamikaze attack (Ingvarsson 2013, p. 275).

[28]. The march-like quality in the victorious part of the "Return to Boston" sequence doesn't lead anywhere, though. Williams composed it to signify a victory with some reservations. By doing this, he grouped the cue with other musical cues at the end of a film which point to the 'fake happy ending' as also seen in the original Wells novel (the cue "Reunion in Boston", similarly composed 'with reservation', is analysed in Rossi 2011b, pp. 186-188).

Contrary to the general, superficial opinion, the score of *War of the Worlds* is rich in themes. What it lacks is not themes, but repetitions of melodies representing the film's characters, i.e. leitmotifs. This lack of leitmotifs could have been an anomaly in the film scores of the 1930s, 1940s, and even the late 1970s and 1980s, when Williams revived the classical Hollywood music style «almost single-handedly»[29]. Yet in 2005, when the simplification of film music due to the development of digital technology had already started, this was not the case[30].

Ominous Timbres of the Alien Invasion

Orchestral colours are of utmost importance to Williams. In the score to *War of the Worlds* the timbre of different instrumental combinations comes to the fore, surpassing the importance of themes and motifs. Williams uses a standard symphony orchestra, but enhanced for the purposes of the science-fiction genre. In the prologue and epilogue, where the world of the microscopic beings is shown to be as important as the whole universe, we can specifically hear a luminous, ethereal sound produced by synthesizers. In "The Intersection Scene", where the alien machine emerges from the ground and starts attacking humans, synthesizers are paired with women's voices. Together, they create the eerie effect of the human bodies being vaporized (the voices slide from cluster to cluster, mostly using their breath, producing a sound somewhere between the vowels 'a' and 'e').

Aliens are accompanied by a whole array of sounds, some of them produced by the sound effects department[31]. Most of the other sounds were instead created by carefully planned instrumental pairings, but also with specific chords and clusters to evoke an otherworldly, aggressive, and outlandish atmosphere. For example, in "The Ferry scene", where Tripods attack the crowd which desperately tries to get on board, Williams uses male voices, in an extremely low register, sounding threatening, but at the same time almost like the 'ohm' as sung by Tibetan monks[32].

---

29. Audissino 2014, p. 4.

30. On film music in the time of digital film-making, see Vernallis 2013. For more about Williams's music in the digital era see Audissino 2017.

31. The cry of the Tripods, first heard in "The Intersection Scene", although containing recognizable tones (which include minor third, an interval Williams often exploits), is a sound effect, not composed music. Nevertheless, Williams organizes orchestra around the "Tripod Sound", preparing carefully its first, and other sinister appearances (like in "The Ferry Sequence"), mostly by silencing the orchestra before a "Tripod Sound", and unleashing the music afterwards. As said before, Tripods are associated with an array of sounds: except for the sounds of their movement being mimicked by the orchestra, there are mechanical sounds (especially prominent in the scene set in the deserted countryside and heard from Ogilvy's basement, and in "The Basket Scene"). It seems that these sounds were inspired by the novel itself, since Wells described Tripods as perpetually crying an alternation of two notes, «ulla, ulla, ulla» (Wells 2011, pp. 266-270).

32. Williams in Bouzereau 2005.

The voices in the score (especially male ones) are infrequent and mostly have a mere colouring function. More important are the brass instruments — horns and trombones specifically, which (sometimes reinforced by trumpets) produce the trebling, threatening, pulsating, violently accentuated flutter noise that is often prominent in the action scenes with the alien Tripods. Woodwinds, particularly those with a bright timbre like flutes and oboes, are much less usedy[33]. On the other hand, bass clarinet has an important role as the 'sound' of the alien probe and of other sinister situations in Harlan Ogilvy's basement in the second part of the film[34].

The overall sound of the film is dark, ominous and somewhat pessimistic; the string section is led by violas, not by violins, to materialize a darker sound more appropriate to this apparently hopeless story. Williams relies more on combinations of instruments rather than individual voices. He often divides the melodic line among different instrument groupings of similar colour, as happens in the aforementioned scene of Ray and Robbie's conversation in the street. Another example is a quotation of the "Dies Irae" motif in the "Return to Boston" cue, where the medieval "Day of Wrath" motif is passed around — alternatively — among horns, cellos and contrabasses[35].

Percussion instruments have a central role, but Williams provides rhythm patterns and driving pulse through the whole orchestra as well. Percussion, generally timpani and bass drum, provide the basis which is coloured by orchestral instruments, including strings and winds, synthesizer and piano. Its most prominent use is in the scene where Ogilvy is killed, with Rachel singing "Hushabye Mountain" over wildly aggressive orchestral punches created by various — pitched and non-pitched — instruments. The sounding metal reverberation that can be heard after the killing is over comes from the piano. It is important to note that the whole scene, with the camera staying on Rachel's face as close as possible while the killing takes place offscreen, wouldn't have worked this effectively if the music had not so tangibly and vividly illustrated the events we are not allowed to see.

33. Piccolo flutes and other bright-coloured instruments stand out in the high-pitch chord that intensifies Rachel's screaming when she is spotted by the Tripod at the small hill overgrown with the alien red weed.

34. The strange character of Harlan Ogilvy, masterfully played by Tim Robbins, was created as a combination of three different characters from Wells's original story. These were the astronomer Ogilvy who dies at the very beginning of the novel; the artilleryman who boasted many pieces of advice about how to defeat Martians but was too passive to act; and the curate who was specifically disliked by the narrator, reflecting Wells's own attitude towards religion.

35. There is another musical quotation in *War of the Worlds*. In the scene where the flabby three-fingered hand of the alien falls out from the open Tripod, Williams cites Max Steiner's *King Kong* motif from the 1933 movie, played by horns. There is a parallel in the downfall of the monster(s) in both stories; also, this was the occasion for Williams to give a nod of admiration to one of his predecessors from the classical Hollywood era.

Reaching Out of Tonality

At the very beginning of *War of the Worlds*, Spielberg uses, twice, a device that can be very effective in sound films: the complete absence of sound. It first occurs after the abnormal storm that terrified everyone (Ray and Rachel hid under the table). Its second occurrence is after the Tripod has emerged from under the ground: people (including Ray) gather to look at the alien machine with curiosity, as the machine is looking at them in turn. Then, the machine releases a strange sound (the cry of the Tripod) and it starts to move in order to attack. We hear mechanically rhythmic sounds, pulsating and persistent, and we might think that they come from the Tripod. But they come from the musical score — see Ex. 2 and Ex. 3. Set in triple meter, and coloured with the dark tones of the trombones and other wind instruments doubled by the piano, the sound for the Tripod's walk brings to the fore interesting chord combinations. It is an alternation of D-F♯/B♭-E♭-G♭ and E♭-G/A-D, before it changes position to G-B/E♭-G♭-B♭ alternating with A-C♯/D-F.

Ex. 2: transcription of John Williams, "The Tripod's Walking Motif" (tentative title) from the *War of the Worlds* film score (© 2005 BMI), published by Songs of SKG, ear transcription of the film's soundtrack. Used in compliance with the U.S. Copyright Act, Section 107.

Ex. 3: transcription of John Williams, "The Tripod's Walking Motif, second version" (tentative title) from the *War of the Worlds* film score (© 2005 BMI), published by Songs of SKG, ear transcription of the film's soundtrack. Used in compliance with the U.S. Copyright Act, Section 107.

The first structure suggests bitonal combination of D major/E♭ minor and E♭ major/D minor; but it could be also read as two variants of the same chord, the first being a (minor) ninth chord, and the second a (major incomplete) eleventh chord, both rooted on the note E♭. Another position of the chords suggests G major/E♭ minor and A major/D minor combinations, but both could be read differently, mainly as 'normal' chords. The first is a kind of 'tonal cluster' containing simultaneously two minor thirds (E♭-G♭ and G-B♭) and two major thirds (E♭-G and G-B) in a vertical structure, E♭-G♭-G-B♭-B, indicating all types of triad, again rooted on the note E♭. The second one is a minor seventh chord rooted on D (D-F-A-C♯).

This kind of bitonal writing, put in a context that conveys a rhythmically strong impetus with an emphasis on tone colour — with the idea of creating a kind of orchestral 'noise' — recalls Igor Stravinsky's writing in the *Rite of Spring* (1913). Consider Stravinsky's 'Les Augures' chord, transcribed in Ex. 4.

Ex. 4: transcription of Igor Stravinsky, 'Les Augures' chord from the *Rite of the Spring* score (1967) printed by Dover Publications, 1989. Used in compliance with the U.S. Copyright Act, Section 107.

This chord oscillates between the first inversion of dominant seventh chord in the (possible) tonality of A-flat and a F♭-major triad, bringing together tones of two chords, one rooted on the note E♭ and the other one rooted on the E in the bass, so close that they almost resemble a twelve-tone row (the bitonal combination in "Les augures printaniers" can be also seen as a thirteenth chord rooted on the fundamental tone E♭, an interpretation which is also possible in the case of Williams's chords). Daniel Chua stated that Stravinsky «fine-tuned» the chord to achieve «tonal noise» that is rhythmically oriented and, through many repetitions and different accentuation, impulse-driven[36].

The same could be said about Williams's chords: they are sometimes evidently set in a bitonal context that clashes to our ears, especially when organized in certain (often changing, often asymmetric) meters and enriched with accents that fall on and off the beat. Apart from the scene where the Tripods show their destructive power for the first time, this type of writing can be detected in other action cues. Some examples: the scene where Ray escapes with Robbie and Rachel in the back seat of a stolen car; the scene where the Tripods attack the ferry overloaded with people; the silent fight between Ray and Ogilvy while the aliens search Ogilvy's basement; and the scene where Rachel and Ray are captured with other people in a Tripod's gigantic basket.

Chords are on the verge of becoming clusters, and some clusters used here emerge directly from chords. They are mostly small in scale: some of them contain third(s); some of them are built from the tones of a diatonic tetrachord, or from the motifs already applied horizontally. Therefore, clusters in Williams's writing are put in a tonal (mostly

36. Chua 2007, p. 77.

minor) context[37] and they tend to sound tonal even when they produce sinister sounds, pounding rhythms or eerie effects. Williams sometimes uses chords which come in bitonal combinations, while at other times he uses quartal harmonies (often inserting tritone among perfect fourths), which makes the diversity of his chord-building techniques exceptionally wide.

Although the *War of the Worlds* score is often described as «mostly atonal» and «tough to listen to», when closely analysed it reveals that true atonality is used only rarely. Williams rather writes in some kind of 'semi-tonality': the strong points of tonality are weakened by a pandiatonic approach, by the use of altered chords, unsolved dissonances, chromaticism and clusters. The free floating of the musical discourse from one tonal centre to another enables modulation to become a natural and constant event.

As the story progresses and the alien invasion seems to leave no hope to the human kind, Williams's writing becomes denser and denser. But atonal writing proper, in the sense of the adoption of twelve-tone rows or serial technique, remains extremely rare. Twelve-tone rows are hard to detect by ear[38], but it seems that they are employed in the scene in Ogilvy's basement, where Harlan Ogilvy, citing Wells, compares the war between aliens and men with the war between men and maggots. One can also discern a rigid control of dynamics borrowed from serialism in the scene where Rachel, spotted by a Tripod, screams. There is a strong accent on the appearance of the quartal chord that emphasizes her scream, followed by sudden *piano*. There are also examples of *Klangfarbenmelodie*, since Williams at times gradually changes the instrumental colour of the cluster in use (for example, in the scene where Ray searches for Rachel in Ogilvy's house in panic, assuming she has been abducted or killed by aliens): clusters for high-register strings rapidly change colour with the addition of low-register strings and then brass.

Conclusion

The music for *War of the Worlds* can't be compared to Maxwell Davies's, but it could be to Igor Stravinsky's and — to some extent — Arnold Schoenberg's. However, by 2005, their techniques — including the usage of bitonality, twelve tone rows, *Klangfarbenmelodie*, serialism and even quarter-tone music (all used sporadically in *War of the Worlds*, with the latter technique mentioned above used possibly for the gliding female voices in the scene of the Tripods evaporating human bodies) — were almost a hundred years old. The compositional techniques used in *War of the Worlds* were not at all new or modern; they were just not commonly used in films. Their more frequent usage in Williams's works in the early 2000s, with the peak reached in *War of the Worlds*, may reflect the composer's

[37]. The only chord that clearly sounds like a major chord appears at the end of the movie.

[38]. Since the orchestral score of *War of the Worlds* is not available, all analyses have been done by ear.

maturity and his willingness to expand the musical vocabulary. Yet, these 'modernistic' musical devices applied to the *War of the Worlds* score were all prompted by the film's story. Williams used twelve-tone rows because of Ogilvy's mental state; his usage of serial technique and *Klangfarbenmelodie* were triggered by Rachel's horror and Ray's panic about the idea that he might have lost his daughter forever. Since there is lots of music in the film, with many different compositional techniques, much of it escapes memorization because of its lack of melodic traits. In Williams's musical language all decisions follow the film's story: themes and leitmotifs, orchestration and dynamics, the usage of rhythm and meter, the shaping of chords and clusters, one compositional technique over another, the specific musical form of a cue... And these elements combine and support each other in a savvy musical composition put in the service of the events shown on the screen. The old principle of film music's inaudibility is brought to perfection — the viewer is not aware of synch points or mickey-mousing effects used in a sophisticated manner throughout the film[39]. At first, the score to *War of the Worlds* might sound unusually radical and experimental within the Williams canon. But a closer listen of the score *within* the film, brings only one conclusion to the fore: Williams did not really depart from his style just for the sake of experimentation, in order to pursue a more contemporary art-music sound. He employed more modernistic devices in *War of the Worlds* because the film required them. *War of the Worlds* was just *one* among other film assignments he worked on in 2005. In the same year, he composed the scores to Steven Spielberg's *Munich* and Rob Marshall's *Memoirs of Geisha* — receiving his 44th and 45th Academy Award nominations — and he also scored the sixth instalment of George Lucas's *Star Wars* Saga, *Episode III*: *Revenge of the Sith*. Those four film 2005 scores couldn't be more different, and aptly reflect the variety of idioms of the twenty-first century classical and non-classical music, all of which are part of Williams's compositional toolkit. And the scores composed after 2005, like *Indiana Jones and the Kingdom of the Crystal Scull* (Steven Spielberg, 2008), *The Adventures of Tintin* (Steven Spielberg, 2011), *War Horse* (Steven Spielberg, 2011) or *The Book Thief* (Brian Percival, 2013) do not show a radical re-orientation in Williams's writing. He has continued to put all his energy, skills, experience and invention to write the type of film music that serves the story of the film at hand. Thus, far from being an anomaly or a sign of discontent for the film-scoring craft, the *War of the Worlds* score is the affirmation of the composer's absolute dedication to film and scoring. With its combination of carefully chosen art-music techniques and their thoughtful application to the context of the film's narrative, *War of the Worlds* is one of John Williams's finest works, an example of both his musical versatility and his dramaturgical acumen.

---

[39]. The most prominent example of the usage of the mickey-mousing technique is the scene where alien probe searches for humans in Ogilvy's basement. Music is formed out of symmetrically built phrases, but the viewer is not aware of the symmetry — he feels only tension.

Bibliography

Audissino 2014

Audissino, Emilio. *John Williams's Film Music: «Jaws», «Star Wars», «Raiders of the Lost Ark», and the Return of the Classical Hollywood Music Style*, Madison (WI), University of Wisconsin Press, 2014 (Wisconsin Film Studies).

Audissino 2017

Id. 'John Williams and Contemporary Film Music', in: *Contemporary Film Music: Investigating Cinema Narratives and Composition*, edited by Lindsay Coleman and Joakim Tillman, London, Palgrave Macmillan, 2017, pp. 221-236.

Bazelon 1975

Bazelon, Irwin. *Knowing the Score: Notes on Film Music*, New York, Arco Publishing Inc., 1975.

Beck 2016

Beck, Peter J. *The War of the Worlds: from H. G. Wells to Orson Welles, Jeff Wayne, Steven Spielberg & Beyond*, London, Bloomsbury, 2016.

Bouzereau 2005

Bouzereau, Laurent. *War of the Worlds*, documentary, DreamWorks Home Entertainment, 2005.

Chua 2007

Chua, Daniel K. L. 'Rioting with Stravinsky: A Particular Analysis of the *Rite of the Spring*', in: *Music Analysis*, xxvi/1-2 (2007), pp. 59-109.

Clemmensen 2005-2011

Clemmensen, Christian. '*War of the Worlds*', in: *filmtracks.com*, (2005-2011), <http://filmtracks.com/titles/war_worlds.html>, accessed February 2018.

Ebert 2005

Ebert, Roger. '*War of the Worlds*', in: *RogertEbert.com*, 2005, <http://www.rogerebert.com/reviews/war-of-the-worlds-2005>, accessed February 2018.

Gorbman 1987

Gorbman, Claudia. *Unheard Melodies: Narrative Film Music*, London, Indiana University Press, 1987.

Ingvarsson 2013

Ingvarsson, Jonas. 'Literature through Radio: Distance and Silence in *The War of the Worlds*, 1938/1898', in: *Adaptation Studies: New Challenges, New Directions*, edited by Jørgen Bruhn, Anne Gejlsvik and Eirik Frisvold Hanssen, London, Bloomsbury, 2013, pp. 269-286.

Mangan 2005

Mangan, Timothy. 'John Williams interview: "It's not hard work that makes success; it's sustained hard work that makes success"', in: *Gramophone*, (2005), <https://www.gramophone.co.uk/feature/john-williams-interview-its-not-hard-work-that-makes-success-its-sustained-hard-work-that>, accessed February 2018.

Monger 2005
Monger, James Christopher. '*War of the Worlds*', in: *AllMusic*, 2005, <http://www.allmusic.com/album/mw0000702519>, accessed February 2018.

Paulus 2014
Paulus, Irena. 'Williams Versus Wagner or an Attempt at Linking Musical Epics', in: *Film in Concert: Film Scores and Their Relation to Classical Concert Music*, edited by Sebastian Stoppe, Glückstadt, Verlag Werner Hülsbusch, 2014, pp. 63-107.

Rosar 2006
Rosar, William H. 'Music for Martians: Schillineger's Two Tonics and Harmony of Fourths in Lieth Stevens' Score for *War of the Worlds* (1953)', in: *The Journal of Film Music*, 1/4 (2006), pp. 395-438.

Rossi 2011a
Rossi, Jérôme. 'Le Dynamisme harmonique dans l'écriture filmique de John Williams: Harmonie fonctionnelle *versus* harmonie non fonctionnelle', in: *John Williams: un alchimiste musical à Hollywood*, edited by Alexandre Tylski, Paris, L'Harmattan, 2011 (Univers musical), pp. 113-140.

Rossi 2011b
Id. 'Les Harmonies polytonales dans la musique de films de John Williams: étude des ressources expressives de la polytonalité', in: *Polytonalités*, edited by Philippe Malhaire, Paris, L'Harmattan, 2011 (L'univers esthétique), pp. 179-200.

Scott 2005
Scott, Anthony Oliver. 'Another Terror Attack, but Not by Humans', in: *New York Times*, 29 June 2005, online, http://www.nytimes.com/2005/06/29/movies/another-terror-attack-but-not-by-humans.html. Accessed 1 July 2017.

Spielberg 2005
Spielberg, Steven. Liner notes for the *War of the Worlds*, CD, Decca Records, 2005.

Vernallis 2013
Vernallis, Carol. *Unruly Media: Youtube, Music Video, and the New Digital Cinema*, Oxford, Oxford University Press, 2013.

Wells 2011
Wells, Herbert George. *War of the Worlds*, Planet Publishing PDF, 2011, <http://www.planetpublish.com/wp-content/uploads/2011/11/The_War_of_the_Worlds_NT.pdf.>, accessed February 2018.

Out of Darkness: John Williams's Violin Concerto

Tom Schneller
(Ithaca College, Ithaca, NY)

This is the Hour of Lead —
Remembered, if outlived,
As Freezing persons, recollect the Snow —
First — Chill — then Stupor — then the letting go —
Emily Dickinson[1]

Instead of leading to paralysis, in some composers the experience of personal tragedy seems to produce a surge of urgent creative energy. Beethoven's deafness was the «painful chrysalis within which his 'heroic' style came to maturity»[2]. Verdi suffered the devastating loss of his wife less than two years before his career breakthrough, the triumphant premiere of *Nabucco* in 1842, which inaugurated a decade of feverish activity that saw the creation of 16 operas in 11 years. Schoenberg unlocked the gates of atonality in 1908 during a traumatic marital crisis. For John Williams, the sudden death of his wife Barbara Ruick Williams in March of 1974 preceded a period of remarkable creative efflorescence which resulted, within a few years, in the musical landmarks of *Jaws* (Steven Spielberg, 1975), *Star Wars* (George Lucas, 1977), *Close Encounters of the Third Kind* (Steven Spielberg, 1977), and *Superman* (Richard Donner, 1978) — works that permanently transformed the terrain of film scoring through their brilliance and dramatic power. If, as Donald MacLeod suggests, the «fantastical and soaring melodies [of Williams's] iconic scores [...] were, for the composer, solace at a time of deep personal loss»[3], the heroic optimism of much of Williams's film music of this period assumes a different aspect: thrown into relief, as it were, against a dark background of bereavement.

---

1. Dickinson 1998, vol. 1, p. 170.
2. Solomon 1998, p. 162.
3. Williams 2012.

Background

Although Williams's career soared in the years following Barbara Ruick's passing (he won his second Academy Award for *Jaws* in 1975, and quickly became one of the most sought-after composers in Hollywood), the mid-1970s were a difficult time for the composer. He recalls being «in a state of shock that year and the year after, so when all of these accolades were going on, I was barely aware of it»[4]. According to a friend of the Williams family, «he became almost reclusive after [Ruick] passed away»[5]. At a recent panel discussion, Williams movingly described the transformative impact his wife's death had on his own subsequent development:

> When I was about 40 years old, I lost somebody very, very, very close to me unexpectedly, and before that point in my life, I didn't [know] what I was doing. But after that point in my writing, in my approach to music, and everything that I was doing, I felt clear about what it is I was trying to do [...] It was a huge emotional turning point in my life [...] but one that resonates with me still, and taught me about who I was and what I was doing and what it meant. This is a deeply emotional thing, and in a way, that was the greatest gift ever given to me — if I can put it that way — by anyone. And certainly, a pivotal moment in my thinking, in my living of my life, and approaching the blank page *absolutely*. I immediately knew where to go with this emotionally[6].

In response to Barbara Ruick's death, Williams composed what is arguably his most intensely personal work: the *Concerto for Violin and Orchestra* (1974-1976), which is dedicated to the memory of his wife. Forged in a crucible of grief, the work marked a point of stylistic introspection. Shortly after its completion, Williams described it as «the closest I've been able to come to a genuine, idiosyncratic expression. [...] For the first time in my life, at a relatively late age, I began to feel some kind of real crystallization of personal idiom». Not until the violin concerto did the synthesis of modernism and neoromantic expression which characterizes most of his mature concert works emerge. «As I was working on [the concerto]», Williams recalls, «I was just beginning to feel my wings — much more than in the *Symphony* or the wind works. I had more difficulty with style and idiom in those; with the violin concerto I was beginning to find a style which [...] was still Romantic, but the kind of Romantic Atonality, in an American way, which I was seeking»[7].

During the period Williams was writing the concerto, his film music moved away from the more experimental and often jazz-tinged scores of the early 1970s toward the grand symphonism of the late 1970s. Its composition bridges the first part of his career,

---

4. Burlingame 2002.
5. Jones 2006.
6. Williams 2014.
7. Elley 1978, p. 33.

during which he consolidated his formidable musicodramatic craftsmanship, and the second, which saw him ascend to the zenith of success in his collaborations with Steven Spielberg and George Lucas. In both musical and biographical terms, then, the violin concerto represents a pivotal work in Williams's canon.

A Musical Romance

The connection between John Williams and Barbara Ruick was, from the start, not only personal, but also musical. In 1948, the Williams family moved from New York to Los Angeles. Williams, aged 16, enrolled at North Hollywood High School (NHHS), where he soon «found himself attracted to a fellow student named Barbara Ruick»[8]. Like many students at NHHS, the vivacious and precociously talented girl was a scion of a show business family, and she was already an accomplished vocalist when they met: «I did very little acting in school [...] but the music bug bit me early and at 14 I started singing with a school band at dances and benefits»[9]. One of the bands she sang with was headed by John 'Curley' Williams, who in 1949 had formed a jazz quintet comprised of fellow NHHS students (all of whom were, like Williams, sons of well-known West Coast musicians). Dubbed the «hottest band in Hollywood» by Time Magazine[10], Curley Williams and His Boys performed weekly at the Dri-Nite Club in Van Nuys, the «hottest spot in town for Van Nuys teenagers»[11]. Their shows drew sizable crowds: on 26 September 1949, for example, «one hundred sixty-nine teenagers danced [...] to the music of Curley Williams and his band»[12]. Joining the quintet that night was Barbara Ruick, who was by then a regular guest vocalist with the group. «Those schooldays were wonderful», she would later recall fondly, «Five fellows and I started a radio show in a San Fernando station [KGIL]. It was called "Teen Time". We broadcast each Saturday night from a place called "The Dry Night Club". It was strictly for teenagers; and only soft drinks were served»[13]. After enrolling at UCLA, Williams continued to work with Ruick as a piano accompanist[14], but their paths diverged in the early 1950s. During Williams's enlistment in the Air Force (1951-55), which he spent mostly in Texas, Arizona, and Newfoundland, and his subsequent studies with Rosina Lhévinne at the Juilliard School in New York City, Barbara Ruick established herself as a rising starlet at MGM. Her first prominent role was in the 1953 campus farce

[8]. KOLODIN 1968.
[9]. SCOTT 1952.
[10]. *TIME* 1949.
[11]. *THE VAN NUYS NEWS* 1949A.
[12]. *THE VAN NUYS NEWS* 1949B.
[13]. HOPPER 1953.
[14]. GALLOWAY 1954.

The Affairs of Dobie Gillies (Don Weis). The same year, she married fellow MGM actor Robert Horton. Her marriage to Horton turned out to be turbulent and unhappy; on 10 August 1955, Ruick filed for divorce, charging cruelty, although the couple temporarily reconciled before splitting up for good in 1956[15].

After shooting the Rodgers and Hammerstein musical *Carousel* (Henry King) in the summer and fall of 1955, Ruick relocated to New York City in December to record an album for Columbia Records and take part in the spring 1956 City Center revival of *Kiss Me, Kate*. She shared an apartment with her *Carousel* co-star and best friend, Shirley Jones, and it was during this time that she reconnected with Williams, who was making a name for himself in New York as a jazz pianist and arranger. Shirley Jones recalls the intensity of Williams's feelings for Ruick: «When we were living together in New York in this lovely apartment, she said "Oh, I met this young man who's a wonderful musician". [...] Well, in walked John Williams, into this little apartment we had, and he was wild about Barbara. I mean, he just — the way he looked at her, and the way — you could tell, he was just head over heels. And finally, she said [...] "I'm going to marry this wonderful man"»[16]. Although her divorce from Robert Horton was not finalized until the summer of 1956, Williams and Ruick eloped to Mexico in April to begin a marriage that would last 18 years[17].

The year 1956 thus represents a key juncture in the lives of both Williams and Ruick, not only personally but professionally as well. Williams moved back to the West Coast and began his career in Hollywood as a studio pianist at Columbia and 20th-Century Fox. Following the premiere of *Carousel* in February 1956, Ruick was poised on the cusp of breakthrough as an actress, having garnered glowing reviews for her performance as Carrie Pipperidge (a trade paper cites her, along with Shirley MacLaine and Anita Ekberg, as a «brilliant newcomer» with «definite potentialities for stardom»[18]). However, her marriage marked a decisive turn away from the screen, the stage, and the recording studio. Jennifer, the first of their three children, was born in January 1957, and from then until her untimely death, Ruick remained focused primarily on her family — although she continued to make occasional appearances on stage and TV (most notably, as one of the wicked stepsisters in the Rodgers and Hammerstein TV musical *Cinderella* [Charles S. Dubin, 1965]). «I quit when Jennifer was born», she confided to reporter Cecil Smith in 1959, «I grew up with it, you know — being a show business child. Mother and father away on the road, on location. My kids weren't going to have it»[19].

15. *Los Angeles Times* 1955.
16. Jones 2006.
17. Parsons 1956.
18. Sidney 1956.
19. Smith 1959.

3 March 1974

In early February 1974, John Williams celebrated his forty-second birthday. He had come a long way since his days as a studio pianist: having established himself as one of the most versatile and technically accomplished composers in Hollywood, he had won two Emmys and an Oscar, and collaborated with top-notch directors such as William Wyler and Robert Altman. At the same time, he had been able to maintain a double life as a composer of concert works (including his *Symphony No. 1*, premiered by André Previn with the Houston Symphony in 1966). He had plans to write a violin concerto for Isaac Stern, with whom he had collaborated on *Fiddler on the Roof* in 1971, but had not gotten around to it yet[20].

Barbara Ruick, too, was balancing two different worlds. Now that their children were older (17, 15, and 13), she accepted her first — and, as it turned out, final — role in a feature film since *Carousel*: a small part as a wisecracking barmaid in Robert Altman's gambling drama *California Split*. On Thursday, 28 February, Ruick was filming on location in Reno, Nevada at the Mapes Hotel. That weekend, «she had planned to drive to Tahoe with her children [...] if her husband didn't come up, in which case they planned to spend the weekend together»[21]. It was not to be. On the night of Saturday, March 2, she complained of headache and nausea, and retired early to her hotel room. At 12:30 PM the next day, a maid discovered her lifeless body and called the police. The coroner identified the cause of death as an intracerebral hemorrhage brought on by a berry aneurysm[22]. On 9 March, Williams's colleague, the composer Lyn Murray, noted in his diary: «Dear, sweet, joyous Barbara Ruick, married to Johnny Williams, is dead»[23].

Aftermath

It is a poignant coincidence that Barbara Ruick passed away in the same month that saw the premiere of *The Sugarland Express*[24] — the film which inaugurated Williams's celebrated partnership with Steven Spielberg. In the years ahead, his work with Spielberg and other directors would provide Williams with the distraction and solace of creative collaboration. Along with his responsibilities as a parent, it was his dedication to music that sustained him in the aftermath of Barbara Ruick's death:

---

20. Palmer 1972.
21. Church 1974.
22. *Reno Gazette-Journal* 1974.
23. Murray 1987, p. 308.
24. In New York on 31 March 1974.

> When my wife passed away, [my children] were teenagers, and the question of going on was just a basic, simple necessity. One needed to keep working, keep going, keep supporting and helping the children, and offering the kind of strength and support that they needed at that time. And secondly — the solace that's found in music, in solitude or in public: [...] when Barbara passed. [...] I found great comfort in my work, certain in the knowledge that she wanted me to continue. [...] Her father was a violinist, and she was always egging me on to write a violin concerto, and I thought well, now I have the time [...] to try and write one[25].

The composition of the concerto would occupy Williams for the next two and a half years (he completed the orchestration on 19 October 1976[26]). During this time, he also composed the scores for *Earthquake* (Mark Robson, 1974), *The Towering Inferno* (John Guillermin, 1974), *The Eiger Sanction* (Clint Eastwood, 1975), *Jaws*, *Family Plot* (Alfred Hitchcock, 1976), *The Missouri Breaks* (Arthur Penn, 1976), *Midway* (Jack Smight, 1976), and *Black Sunday* (John Frankenheimer, 1977), in addition to his only stage musical, *Thomas and the King*, which premiered in London in October 1975 — a staggering workload that caused his progress on the concerto to be constantly interrupted. «It was on my piano», Williams recalls, «I kept leaving it [for other projects] and coming back to it. I'm kind of a stonemason in that I have to keep chipping away at it, refining it, writing and rewriting»[27]. Given this sporadic compositional process, the formal and stylistic cohesion of the concerto is a testament to the composer's prodigious technique and powers of concentration.

The Concerto Takes Wing

Although Williams stressed in a 1978 interview that «writing the *Violin Concerto* was enough in itself» and that he was «beyond the point of having to hear it»[28], it was not long before the work would be presented to the public. Having completed his first season as conductor of the Boston Pops, he was busy «polishing» the concerto in November of 1980 for its world premiere, which took place on 29 January 1981 in St. Louis. Leonard Slatkin conducted the St. Louis Symphony with the young Russian émigré virtuoso Mark Peskanov as soloist. On 2 February Slatkin and Peskanov took the concerto to New York City's Carnegie Hall; in December, they reunited in London to record it with the London Symphony.

25. Williams 2012.
26. Williams 1983.
27. Pasles 1997.
28. Elley 1978.

The first reviews were uniformly hostile. Williams was taken to task for having written an «academic»[29] and «imitative»[30] concerto. Undeterred by the initial reception, Williams conducted the piece with Alexander Treger and the Los Angeles Philharmonic in November of 1983; a month later, he led the Toronto Symphony with Mark Peskanov as soloist. Again, the critical consensus was overwhelmingly negative. «[T]he piece, despite solid craftsmanship, lacked an overall design or purpose. It merely pushes buttons for alternating currents (lean, drifting lyricism versus vehement agitation) — a.k.a. movie-scoring technique», Donna Perlmutter sneered in *Ovation*[31]. «This incessantly busy music, it must be said, does avoid the simplistic black and white of film composition», sniffed Martin Bernheimer of the *Los Angeles Times*, «Unfortunately, it adheres instead to a murky gray»[32]. And *Strad's* Henry Roth sniggered: «[M]uch ado about nothing. And, of course, it does not contain a single memorable theme»[33].

The venom directed against Williams by Bernheimer *et al.* reveals less about the concerto than it does about the tin ears and ideological blinders of his critics, who evidently had no inkling of just how sophisticated the music was they were busily tearing to shreds. What these early reviews of the concerto reflect above all is the bias of the critical establishment against composers marked by the 'scarlet letter' of Hollywood. This, of course, was nothing new — Erich Wolfgang Korngold, Miklós Rózsa, Leonard Rosenman and others had to contend with the same ingrained and mindless prejudice.

But by the late 1980s, the musical climate was changing. When Williams performed the concerto with the Houston Symphony in April 1987 and with the San Francisco Symphony in 1993, reviews were markedly warmer[34]. More importantly, the artistic value of the work was being recognized by other musicians. The concerto found a brilliant young champion in Gil Shaham, who first performed it with Williams and the Boston Symphony at Tanglewood in 1998 (and three years later recorded it for Deutsche Grammophon). Since then, the concerto has been taken up by violinists Emmanuelle Boisvert and James Ehnes, as well as by prominent conductors including Esa-Pekka Salonen and Stéphane Denéve. It has been performed by the National Symphony, the Detroit Symphony, the Philadelphia Orchestra, and other top ensembles. Even the music critics have mostly changed their tune: «romanticism of the first order»[35], «the work deserves a higher profile»[36], «bracing, energetic, and adventurous [...]. The concerto belongs in the standard repertory»[37].

---

29. Peters 1981.
30. Rothstein 1981.
31. Perlmutter 1984.
32. Bernheimer 1983.
33. Roth 1984.
34. Ward 1987 and Tucker 1993.
35. Johnson 2010.
36. Stryker 2010.
37. Dyer 2002.

As the towering contribution by John Williams to American musical life is finally being recognized in academia, it is time to devote serious analytical attention not only to his film music, but his concert works as well. The violin concerto, in particular, holds a central place in Williams's oeuvre, but beyond that, I would argue that it ranks as one of the masterpieces of late 20th-century concert music. On a variety of levels, in fact, the Williams violin concerto can be heard as an American counterpart to Alban Berg's violin concerto (dedicated to the memory of Alma Mahler's daughter Manon Gropius, who died unexpectedly of polio in 1935). Both concerti are musical epitaphs; both inhabit a bittersweet harmonic twilight zone between tonality and atonality; both display a tension between structural rigor and deep emotional expression, in which a subcurrent of grief runs beneath a polished surface of impeccable technical craftsmanship. But whereas Berg's concerto marked the end of an artistic career (it was the last piece he completed before his death), Williams's concerto, as we have seen, stands at the beginning of his compositional maturity.

The concerto has gone through at least three revisions since it was written. The following analysis is based on its most recent version, as recorded in 2011 by Emmanuelle Boisvert, Leonard Slatkin, and the Detroit Symphony[38]. Since the score is not available commercially as of this writing, I will use timestamps ([minutes:seconds]) based on the 2011 Slatkin/Boisvert recording to refer to specific passages in the music. The focus of my analysis will be on the thematic structure of the concerto, which features not only an intricate network of interrelationships between the melodic material of all three movements, but a dynamic, organic process of motivic evolution that culminates in the apotheotic transformation of the concerto's opening motif in the last movement. The way Williams leads up to this moment of arrival provides an object lesson in his use of teleological genesis: the gradual emergence of an extended melodic idea that develops out of motivic seeds planted early in the piece. This technique is a characteristic of many Williams scores, both for film and the concert hall (it is extensively applied, for example, in the scores for *Close Encounters*, *E. T.*, and *A. I.*)[39]. Williams's sophisticated use of teleological genesis situates the concerto within an organicist lineage that can be traced back, via Schoenberg, to the Romantic aesthetic of unity within diversity. At the same time, it provides the structural framework for an emotional trajectory that transmutes raw grief into acceptance and release. The concerto thereby encapsulates, in musical terms, the process that allowed the composer to emerge from personal catastrophe into a period of extraordinary creative fecundity.

---

[38]. John Williams, *Concerto for Violin and Orchestra* (Leonard Slatkin, Detroit Symphony Orchestra; Emanuelle Boisvert, violin), Naxos Music Library (2011).

[39]. Schneller 2014.

First Movement («Moderato»)

The first movement is based on three distinct but interrelated subjects, arranged in a palindromic pattern that recalls sonata-rondo form. These are contrapuntally combined in a brief development section at the centre of the movement. The first and third subjects are lyrical in character, in contrast to the jaunty second subject which appears intermittently, like a fleeting will-o-the-whisp, amid an otherwise sombre musical environment (FIG. 1).

FIG. 1: first movement, form. Timings refer to the 2011 recording (Slatkin, Boisvert)[40].

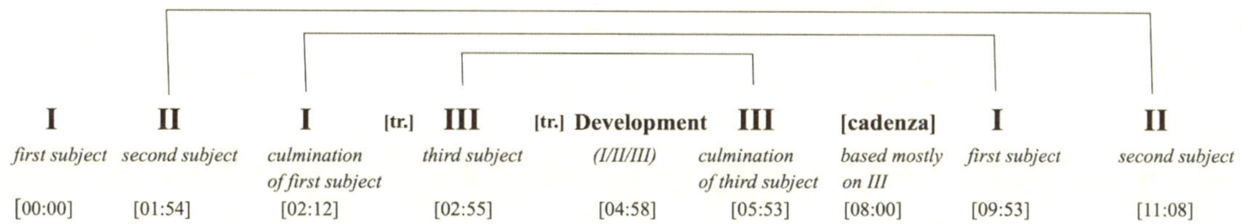

First Subject

The movement begins in solitude and sorrow, with an unaccompanied statement of the first subject by the solo violin (EX. 1). Cast in the AA'B structure of a Schoenbergian sentence, the subject evolves organically out of its first four notes, which consist of two pairs of ascending minor sixths (motif X1). In the first two phrases, this motif undergoes a series of transformations which can be summarized as X1 (m6↑/m6↑) - X2 (M6↓/M6↑) - X3 (m3↓/m3↑). Note the trajectory of intervallic compression within four-note groups: the sixths of phrase A1 are inverted into thirds in phrase A2. In phrase B, the prevalent melodic motion is tightened yet further, to the stepwise octatonic tetrachords labelled motif o. From these motivic prototypes, a plethora of derived shapes will be generated in the course of the concerto.

Like the intervallic span, the rhythmic structure of the first subject undergoes a process of compression, from quarter notes via eighth notes to the triplet figure in m.9. The melodic apex in ms. 6-7 temporarily suspends the gathering momentum; the chromatic changing tone pattern C♯-C-D-C♯, highlighted by lengthened note values, will become another important motivic building block (motif n).

40. To assure that timings line up correctly, use a professional or semi-professional audio playback or editing program with a reliable time display (like GarageBand or Audacity) for playback of the mp3 file, rather than Quicktime or iTunes, which can be off by several seconds.

Ex. 1: first movement, first subject. Arches indicate phrase structure; brackets indicate motivic components. John Williams, *Concerto for Violin and Orchestra* (© 1976/2007 BMI), published by Marjer Music/Warner-Tamerlane, transcription from the Naxos recording with Emmanuelle Boisvert, violin, and the Detroit Symphony Orchestra, conducted by Leonard Slatkin, 2011, digital download. Used in compliance with the U.S. Copyright Act, Section 107.

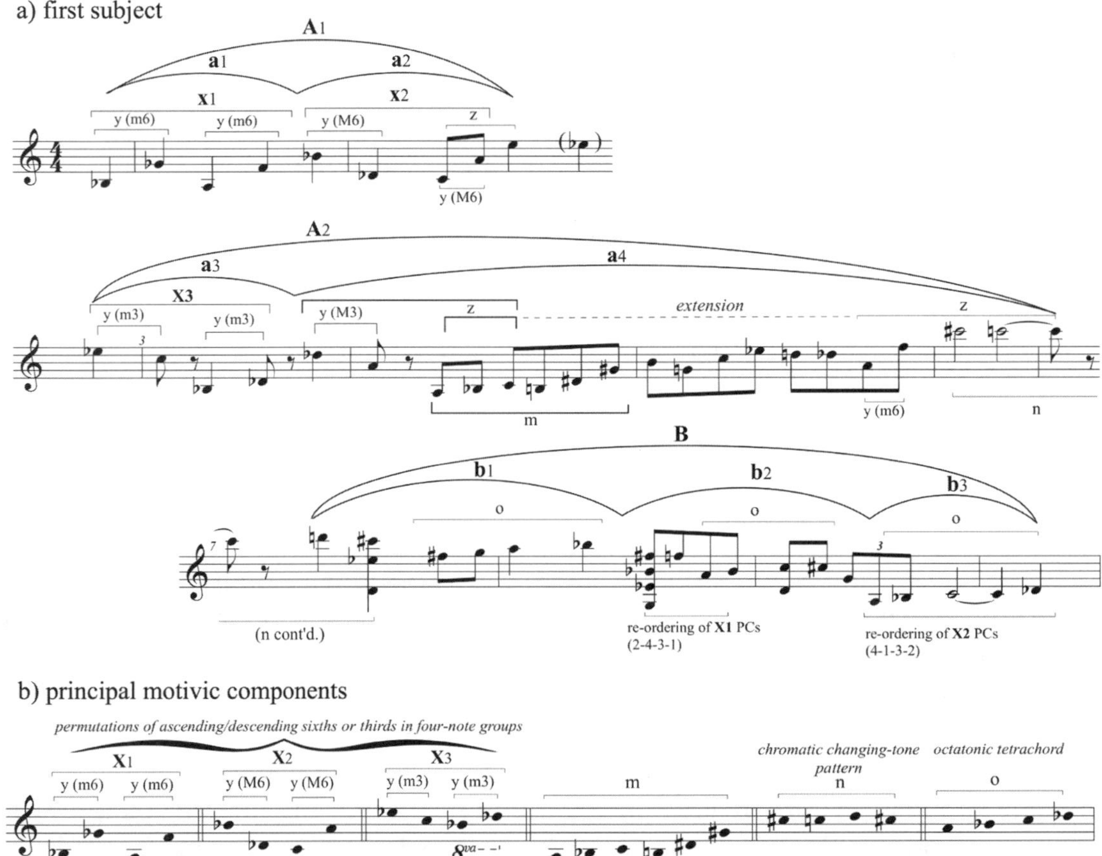

Just as the first subject is developed from its opening four notes, the theme itself provides the 'seed' from which the entire concerto grows (see Appendix 2 for a comprehensive chart of motivic interrelationships). The sixths and thirds of the X motifs, in particular, function as key generative intervals. The consistency with which Williams derives subsequent material from this motivic fountainhead evokes Schoenberg's vision of total organicism: «[w]hatever happens in a piece of music is nothing but the endless reshaping of a basic shape […] or in other words, there is nothing in music but what comes from the theme, springs from it and can be traced back to it»[41].

41. Schoenberg 1975, pp. 289-294.

While it gives rise to a multitude of derived shapes, the first subject itself undergoes only minimal variation (mostly through rhythmic modification, truncation, and transposition). Like an agonizing question posed over and over again — ten times in all — it haunts the movement without coming to a resolution. The opening of the concerto, in fact, resembles a passacaglia in its emphasis on thematic reiteration: after two statements of the first subject by the unaccompanied soloist, the flute takes up the theme, then passes it on to the strings, while the soloist is engaged in virtuosic passagework.

Second Subject

Once the tension generated by thematic repetition and increasing contrapuntal and orchestrational density reaches a breaking point, however, the first subject releases its grip as the soloist launches into the propulsive rhythmic energy of the second subject, which recalls the demonic scherzi of Prokofiev (Ex. 2, [01:54-02:11]). This modular theme consists of four motivic cells that can be rotated in various combinations — a structural feature that will be exploited in the development section.

Ex. 2: first movement, second subject. John Williams, *Concerto for Violin and Orchestra* (© 1976/2007 BMI), published by Marjer Music/Warner-Tamerlane, transcription from the Naxos recording with Emmanuelle Boisvert, violin, and the Detroit Symphony Orchestra, conducted by Leonard Slatkin, 2011, digital download. Used in compliance with the U.S. Copyright Act, Section 107.

The second subject provides only a temporary escape from the oppressive shadows of the opening. After a mere ten measures, the first subject, now in the brass, breaks through once more in a dark orchestral wave that sweeps away the soloist and culminates in the first climax of the movement [02:12-02:46]. Like an obsessive, tormenting thought, the first subject cannot be eluded for long. In fact, its presence permeates even the apparently contrasting second subject: module a is derived from the major sixths of motif X2, module b from motif m (Ex. 3).

Ex. 3: first movement, derivation of second subject from first subject. John Williams, *Concerto for Violin and Orchestra* (© 1976/2007 BMI), published by Marjer Music/Warner-Tamerlane, transcription from the Naxos recording with Emmanuelle Boisvert, violin, and the Detroit Symphony Orchestra, conducted by Leonard Slatkin, 2011, digital download. Used in compliance with the U.S. Copyright Act, Section 107.

Third Subject

Following the climactic restatement of the first subject, the music subsides into a quiet transition [02:47-02:54] that leads to the third principal subject, which is comprised of two distinct melodic ideas spun out into an A1-A2-B1-B2-B3 form (Ex. 4, [02:55-04:16]). Sung by the solo violin in its high register, the theme is based on the nonatonic scale, which can also be found in the music of Alexander Tcherepnin and Olivier Messiaen (who referred to it as his «third mode of limited transposition»). It conveys a haunting, bittersweet sense of longing; a remembrance, perhaps, of things past and forever out of reach. We have arrived not only at the structural but also at the emotional core of the movement[42].

Ex. 4: first movement, third subject. John Williams, *Concerto for Violin and Orchestra* (© 1976/2007 BMI), published by Marjer Music/Warner-Tamerlane, transcription from the Naxos recording with Emmanuelle Boisvert, violin, and the Detroit Symphony Orchestra, conducted by Leonard Slatkin, 2011, digital download. Used in compliance with the U.S. Copyright Act, Section 107.

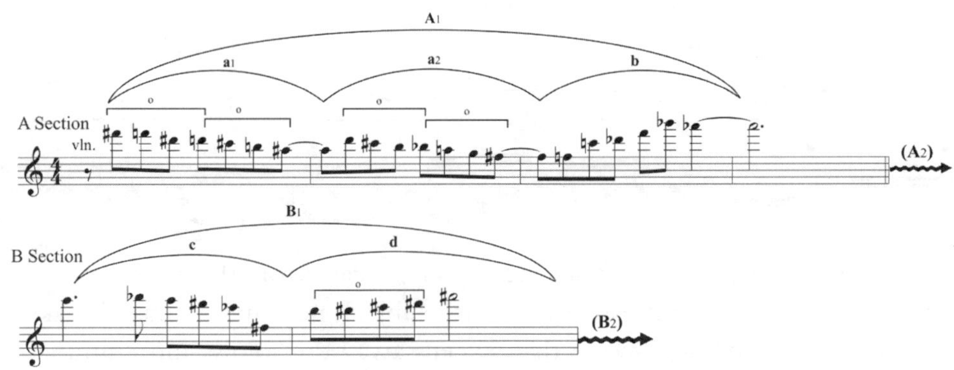

[42]. There is some evidence that Williams associated the expressive descending scalar pattern of the third subject with grief: in his score for Brian de Palma's *The Fury* (1978), an almost identical motif accompanies the unexpected, bloody death of Hester, the lover of Peter Sandza ("Gillian's Escape", [0:03:24]). This apparent reference to the violin concerto is a rare intertextual link between Williams's film and concert music.

Again, a number of subtle links to the first subject can be observed. As its point of departure, the theme takes the first minor sixth of motif X1 (B♭-G♭), inverts it, and fills in the gap with two conjunct octatonic tetrachords related — again by inversion — to motif o. Recall that the first subject proceeds from minor sixths to octatonic tetrachords, an intervallic trajectory that is now compressed into a single melodic gesture. While the A section of the third subject uses the minor sixth as a melodic framework filled in by step, in the B section it emerges into the melodic foreground (Ex. 5).

Ex. 5: derivation of third subject from first subject. John Williams, *Concerto for Violin and Orchestra* (© 1976/2007 BMI), published by Marjer Music/Warner-Tamerlane, transcription from the Naxos recording with Emmanuelle Boisvert, violin, and the Detroit Symphony Orchestra, conducted by Leonard Slatkin, 2011, digital download. Used in compliance with the U.S. Copyright Act, Section 107.

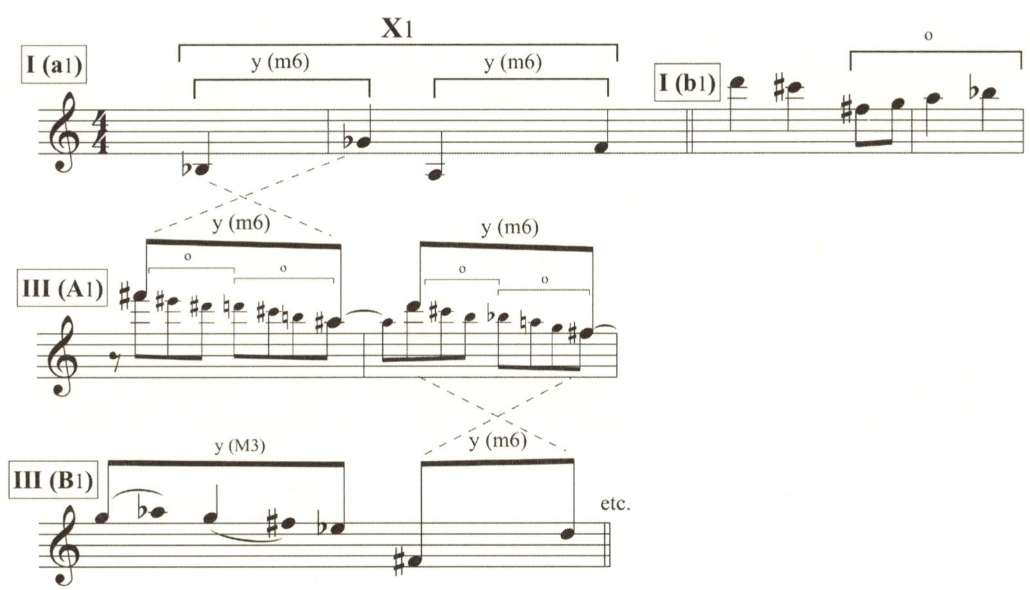

Development, Recapitulation of Third Subject, Cadenza, and Conclusion

Now that all themes have been introduced, they are subjected to a brief but vigorous developmental 'working-out' that focuses on the contrapuntal combination of the first and second subjects [04:58-05:52]. In lilting triple meter, the first subject is stated by celli and violas, then by flute and clarinet. At the same time, the solo violin recombines the four modules of the second subject in a kaleidoscopic array of rotational transformation (Ex. 6).

Ex. 6: contrapuntal combination of first and second subjects in the development. John Williams, *Concerto for Violin and Orchestra* (© 1976/2007 BMI), published by Marjer Music/Warner-Tamerlane, transcription from the Naxos recording with Emmanuelle Boisvert, violin, and the Detroit Symphony Orchestra, conducted by Leonard Slatkin, 2011, digital download. Used in compliance with the U.S. Copyright Act, Section 107.

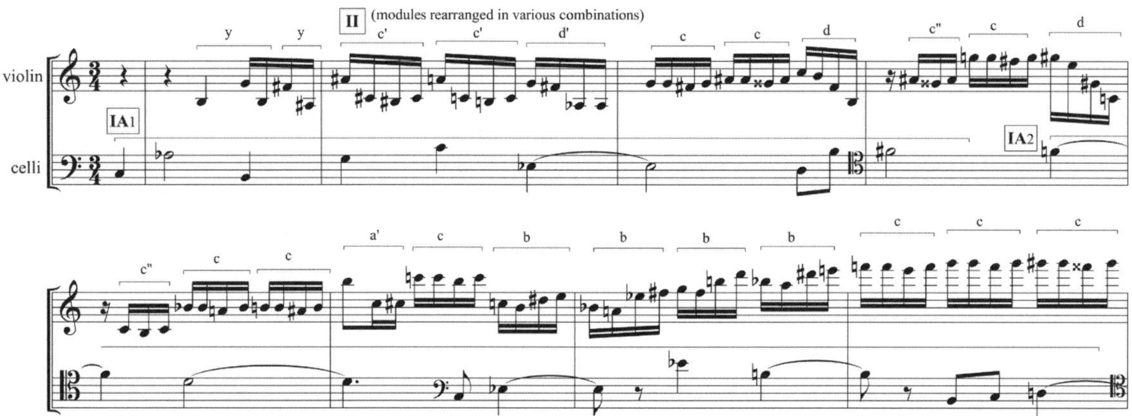

Near the end of the development section, the opening phrase of the third subject appears in the flute and oboe, setting the stage for a rhapsodic recapitulation of the complete theme by the orchestra in alternation with the violin [05:53-07:44]. But this apotheosis of reminiscence proves to be ephemeral: after the violin has soared to its highest register, the orchestra fades into silence, leaving the soloist, once more, in solitude. From this still point emerges the cadenza [08:00-09:52], an anguished meditation on the third subject during which its A phrase is ingeniously folded in on itself through the contrapuntal combination of the a and b segments; later, the B phrase is embroidered through arpeggios and figuration.

A hushed recapitulation of the first subject follows the cadenza [09:53-11:07]. The clarinet poses the same question with which the movement began, answered only by a canonic echo in the bassoon. As the theme migrates to ghostly strings for its final statement, the soloist reenters with ruminative figurations (Ex. 7, [10:25]). Embedded within this figuration is a motivic seed that will come to fruition in the next movement: X4 (m3↓/m3↓), which is a permutation of the first subject's X3 (m3↓/m3↑) and thus represents another evolution of the concerto's protean opening motif.

As the first act of this musical drama draws to a quiet, unresolved close, the puckish second subject in the solo violin flits across the stage one last time before the curtain descends with a hollow pizzicato [11:08].

Ex. 7: first movement, motif X4. John Williams, *Concerto for Violin and Orchestra* (© 1976/2007 BMI), published by Marjer Music/Warner-Tamerlane, transcription from the Naxos recording with Emmanuelle Boisvert, violin, and the Detroit Symphony Orchestra, conducted by Leonard Slatkin, 2011, digital download. Used in compliance with the U.S. Copyright Act, Section 107.

Second Movement («Slowly»)

If the first movement blends elements of rondo and sonata form, the second movement merges slow movement and scherzo into a compound ternary design (Fig. 2). Note, again, the prevalence of structural palindromes: the lyrical A section is a ternary form built from two contrasting themes, while the B section features a short trio embedded within the scherzo.

Fig. 2: second movement, form.

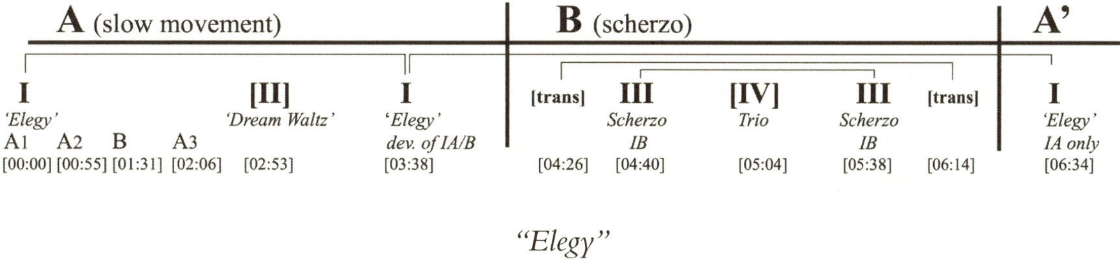

"Elegy"

The movement begins with an ethereal cantilena for the solo violin that unfolds over a sighing accompanimental pattern in the strings (Ex. 8). This theme, which I call "Elegy", consists of two contrasting melodic modules (A and B) arranged in an A1 A2 B A3 pattern.

The surface calm of the music balances on an edge of pain, evoking, as Wordsworth puts it, «thoughts that [...] lie too deep for tears». In the opening phrase (A), the bittersweet harmony migrates from D Minor to D Major by way of a tormented progression of chromatic dissonances; the resolution that awaits the listener at the end of the phrase is approached through a thicket of thorns.

Ex. 8: "Elegy", phrase A1 [00:00-00:54]. John Williams, *Concerto for Violin and Orchestra* (© 1976/2007 BMI), published by Marjer Music/Warner-Tamerlane, transcription from the Naxos recording with Emmanuelle Boisvert, violin, and the Detroit Symphony Orchestra, conducted by Leonard Slatkin, 2011, digital download. Used in compliance with the U.S. Copyright Act, Section 107.

The harmonic trajectory from minor to major, from dissonance to resolution, assumes a deeper significance when we consider that the theme begins with a subtle allusion to the Bach chorale quoted near the end of Alban Berg's violin concerto (Ex. 9). The chorale is a plea for deliverance («It is enough! Lord, if it please you, unyoke me now at last!»). In Berg's concerto, which is dedicated «To the Memory of an Angel» (Manon Gropius), the chorale symbolizes an acceptance of death as release from suffering. Williams's nod to Bach as filtered through Berg establishes another point of resonance between the two concerti, and links the memory of one «angel» to that of another.

Ex. 9: "Elegy", allusion to Alban Berg's violin concerto.

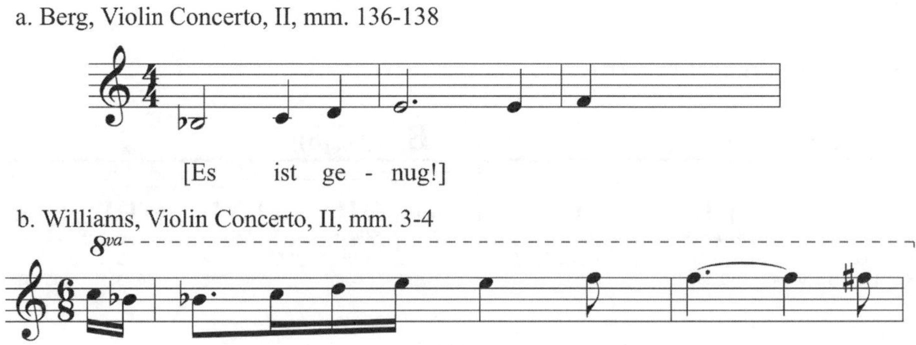

But the first phrase also presents a new transformation of motif X: as in the third subject of the first movement, the initial sixth (B♭-G♭) of X1 provides an intervallic framework filled in by stepwise motion (in this case, an ascending lydian scale). The lineage of the theme can thus be traced back, via the third subject, to the very opening of the concerto (Ex. 10).

Ex. 10: derivation of "Elegy" phrase A1 from motif X. John Williams, *Concerto for Violin and Orchestra* (© 1976/2007 BMI), published by Marjer Music/Warner-Tamerlane, transcription from the Naxos recording with Emmanuelle Boisvert, violin, and the Detroit Symphony Orchestra, conducted by Leonard Slatkin, 2011, digital download. Used in compliance with the U.S. Copyright Act, Section 107.

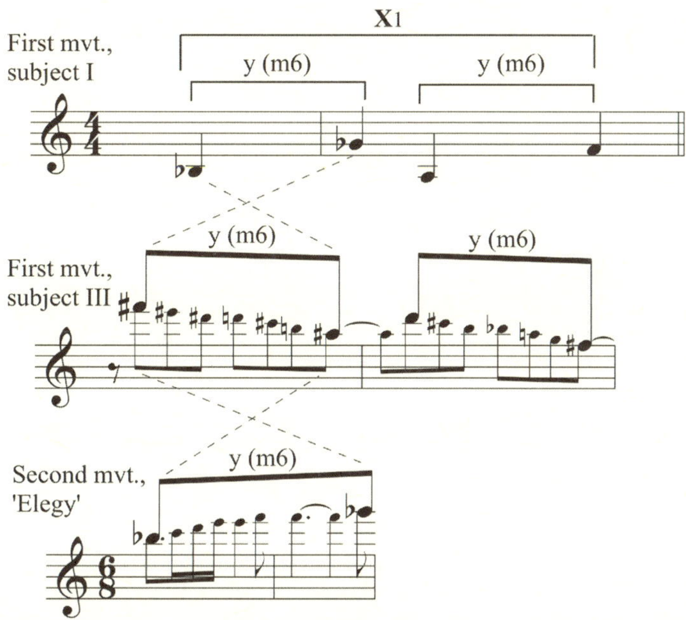

If the A sections of the theme suggest an attempt to find peace through acquiescence, in the B section the orchestra wells up from the depths to rage against the dying of the light [01:31-02:05]. In an agitated series of sequential phrases, the B section introduces X5 (m3↑/m3↓) — yet another permutation of motif X1, which appears in conjunction with variants of motif m (Ex. 11). As the waves of sorrow subside, the first statement of "Elegy" concludes with a tranquil statement of A3 in the solo horn and clarinet [02:06-02:52]. The A and B sections of the theme seem to encapsulate a struggle between acceptance and defiance — a struggle that will not be resolved until the end of the movement.

Ex. 11: "Elegy", B section. John Williams, *Concerto for Violin and Orchestra* (© 1976/2007 BMI), published by Marjer Music/Warner-Tamerlane, transcription from the Naxos recording with Emmanuelle Boisvert, violin, and the Detroit Symphony Orchestra, conducted by Leonard Slatkin, 2011, digital download. Used in compliance with the U.S. Copyright Act, Section 107.

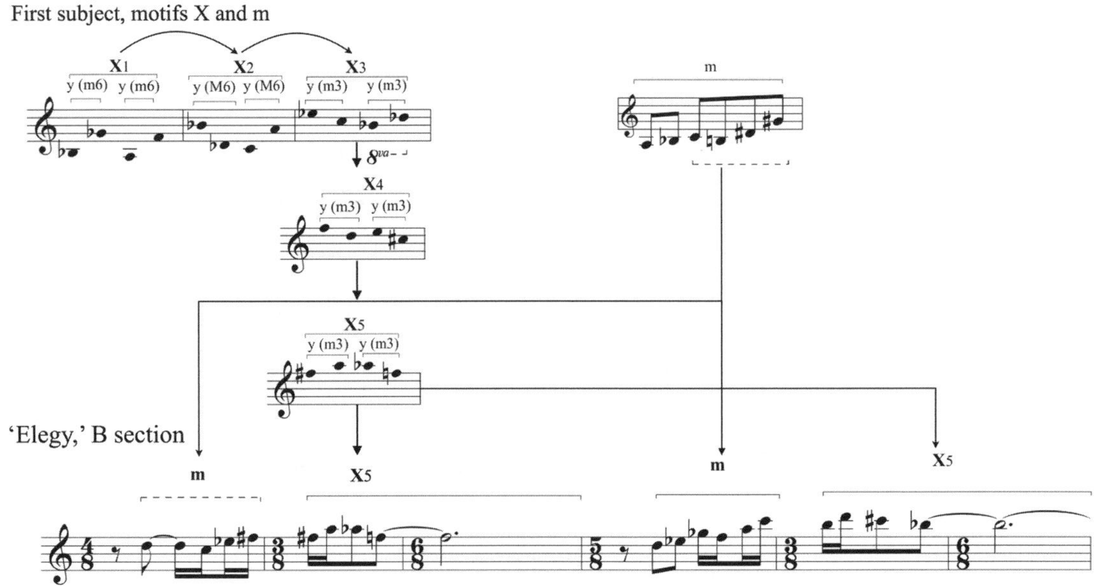

"Dream Waltz" and development of "Elegy"

The second theme (which I call "Dream Waltz") is introduced by the solo violin, then taken up by the flute [02:53-03:37]. Surreal and fantastical in mood, "Dream Waltz" unspools reams of 16th-notes that conjure up a ghostly dance. As illustrated in Ex. 12, the melodic line is constructed largely from the retrograde of motif n — the chromatic changing tone pattern which marks the registral apex of the first subject in the previous movement.

Ex. 12: "Dream Waltz". John Williams, *Concerto for Violin and Orchestra* (© 1976/2007 BMI), published by Marjer Music/Warner-Tamerlane, transcription from the Naxos recording with Emmanuelle Boisvert, violin, and the Detroit Symphony Orchestra, conducted by Leonard Slatkin, 2011, digital download. Used in compliance with the U.S. Copyright Act, Section 107.

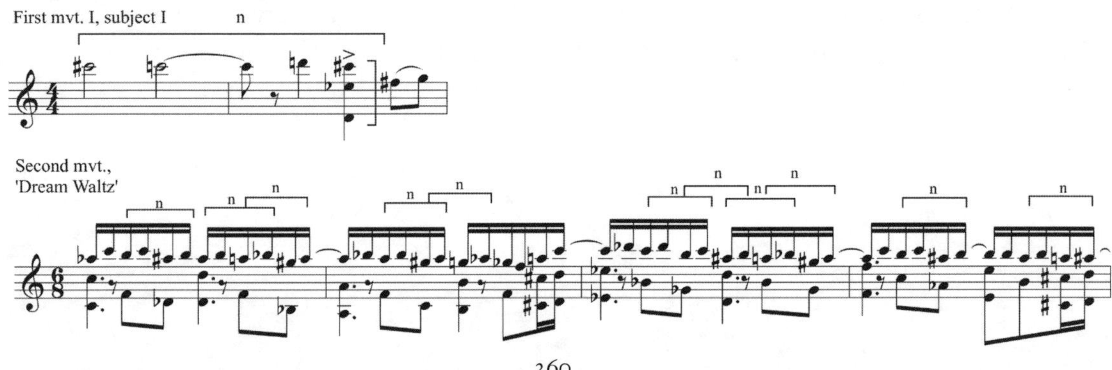

But like a wistful memory, "Dream Waltz" provides only a fleeting diversion from the sorrow of the opening: after two statements of the theme, it whirls away, never to be heard again, while the orchestra launches into a stormy development of "Elegy" at [03:38] in which fragments of the A and B sections intertwine in an anguished embrace that builds to the movement's central climax. In a magnification of the tormented cadence that concludes the first phrase of the theme, a series of dissonant chords converge on a luminous A Major triad.

Scherzo/Trio

Out of this triad emerges the solo violin with a transition to the scherzo section (Ex. 13a, [04:26-04:39]). The transition alternates between scalar passages and the interlocking thirds of motif X4 (which was introduced at the very end of the first movement); both motivic components will figure prominently in the scherzo, which Williams describes as «a brisk middle section based on rushing 'tetrachordal' figures that are tossed back and forth between soloist and orchestra. The mood of the opening is always present, however, as the rushing and playing about continue to be accompanied by hints of a return to the movement's more introspective opening»[43]. These «hints of return» consist of fragments drawn from the B section of "Elegy", in particular motif X5, which whirls throughout the atomized, pointillistic texture (Ex. 13b, [04:40-05:03]). Shorn of its previous pathos, "Elegy" now appears fractured and distorted, as though the movement had been invaded by a horde of goblins who make a mockery of the solemn proceedings. As Gil Shaham notes, the whiff of brimstone exuded by the scherzo evokes a tradition of «devil-in-the-violin»[44] writing that can be traced from Stravinsky's *L'Histoire du soldat* via Saint-Saëns's *Danse macabre* to Paganini, the 'Devil's violinist' (Williams himself made a memorable contribution to this trope in his 1987 score for *The Witches of Eastwick* [George Miller]).

The brittle repartee between soloist and winds briefly gives way to the warm, flowing legato phrases of the trio (Ex. 13c, [05:04-05:37]). The strings arch upward yearningly, then descend in a long stepwise line highlighted by the flute. But soon the goblins are back to reprise the scherzo, before they are ushered out at [06:14] by the rushing scales and flurries of the transition (which now leads to the closing section of the movement).

[43]. Williams 1983.

[44]. Shaham 2013.

Ex. 13: transition, scherzo and trio — motivic components. John Williams, *Concerto for Violin and Orchestra* (© 1976/2007 BMI), published by Marjer Music/Warner-Tamerlane, transcription from the Naxos recording with Emmanuelle Boisvert, violin, and the Detroit Symphony Orchestra, conducted by Leonard Slatkin, 2011, digital download. Used in compliance with the U.S. Copyright Act, Section 107.

Reprise of "Elegy"

In the telescoped reprise of "Elegy", only the melancholy, tranquil A section of the theme remains — the agitated B section has evaporated, as though it had been driven out with the scherzo in a kind of motivic exorcism [06:34-09:56]. The A section is intoned in four successive variants, first by the solo flute over the sighing accompaniment of the opening, then thrice by the violin. The movement concludes with a radiant C major chord approached by dissonant cadence: a gesture that both echoes previous cadential points and sums up the emotional trajectory of the movement.

Third Movement («Broadly, Quickly»)

In the final movement, Williams expertly pulls together the principal motivic threads of the concerto and builds toward an apotheosis of motif X1 that is the culmination of the work as a whole. The movement is a 7-part rondo, A B A C A B A, expanded by two interpolations (Fig. 3). As we will see, the bustling rondo and the timeless, mystical interpolations establish two opposing soundworlds that, in the apotheotic second interpolation, are brought into alignment with each other.

Fig. 3: third movement, form.

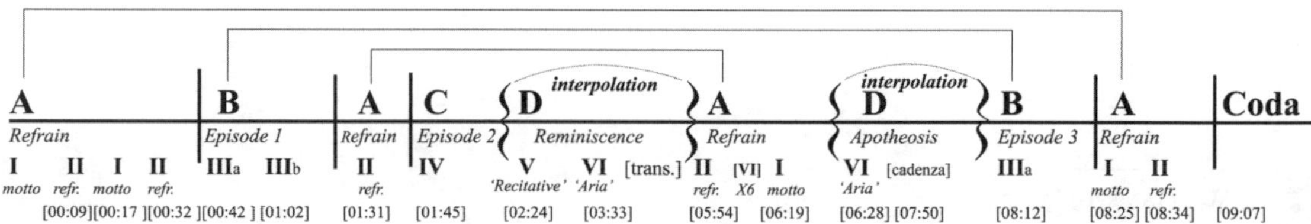

Motto and Refrain

The movement begins with six dissonant 'chiming' chords in the orchestra, the top line of which traces motif X5 in the piccolo and first violins (Ex. 14, [00:00-00:08]). In a motto-like fashion, variants of this opening gesture recur throughout the movement at important structural points. Each of the four statements of the motto pivots around a repeating pitch that is sounded, inexorably, throughout the progression (G in the first two statements; B and E in the others). In its harsh dissonance and massive scoring, the motto suggests a menacing colossus bestriding a narrow world, like the «terrible and fatal statue»[45] conjured up by the opening theme in Messiaen's *Turangalîla Symphony*.

Ex. 14: motto, first statement. John Williams, *Concerto for Violin and Orchestra* (© 1976/2007 BMI), published by Marjer Music/Warner-Tamerlane, transcription from the Naxos recording with Emmanuelle Boisvert, violin, and the Detroit Symphony Orchestra, conducted by Leonard Slatkin, 2011, digital download. Used in compliance with the U.S. Copyright Act, Section 107.

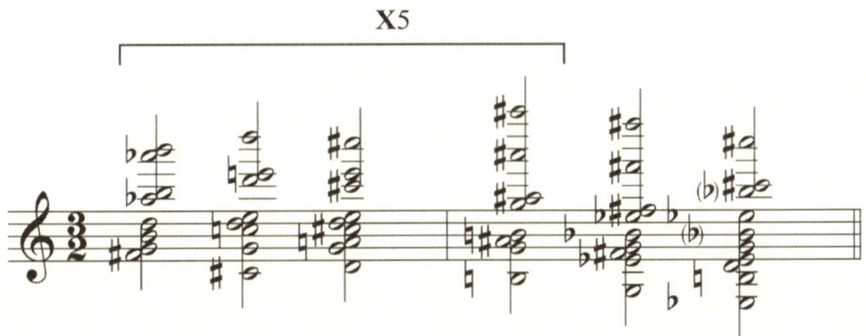

Scurrying between the towering orchestral sound masses of the motto's first two statements is the rondo refrain in the violin: a kinetic moto perpetuo theme which fuses the sixths of motif X1, the ascending lydian pentachord of "Elegy", and the chromatic changing-tone figure of motif n into a unified framework (Ex. 15, [00:09-00:16]). Note the melodic pattern G-B/A-C♯ in the second measure, woven seamlessly into the fabric of the theme. In the course of the movement, these ascending thirds will emerge as a distinct, independent motivic entity: X6, the final transformation of motif X1.

[45]. Sherlaw-Johnson 2009, p. 83.

Ex. 15: synthesis of motivic elements in refrain. John Williams, *Concerto for Violin and Orchestra* (© 1976/2007 BMI), published by Marjer Music/Warner-Tamerlane, transcription from the Naxos recording with Emmanuelle Boisvert, violin, and the Detroit Symphony Orchestra, conducted by Leonard Slatkin, 2011, digital download. Used in compliance with the U.S. Copyright Act, Section 107.

Episode 1 - Refrain - Episode 2

The first episode (B) divides into two sections ([00:42-00:54] and [01:02-01:30]), separated by a transition featuring triple stops in the violin ([00:55-01:01]). Both sections centre on a figure of oscillating sixths in the winds that is related to motif X1 (Ex. 16).

Ex. 16: episode 1 — oscillating sixth motif. John Williams, *Concerto for Violin and Orchestra* (© 1976/2007 BMI), published by Marjer Music/Warner-Tamerlane, transcription from the Naxos recording with Emmanuelle Boisvert, violin, and the Detroit Symphony Orchestra, conducted by Leonard Slatkin, 2011, digital download. Used in compliance with the U.S. Copyright Act, Section 107.

Before long, the second refrain whirls by ([01:31-01:44]). Embedded within the tail end of the theme is the first independent statement of motif X6 (the ascending third pattern E-G/F♯-A), which has now detached itself from the first phrase of the refrain and assumed an independent — if still embryonic — identity (Ex. 17). This process of expansion will continue in the third refrain, where motif X6 vies for dominance with the moto perpetuo theme itself.

Ex. 17: refrain 2 — emergence of X6 as independent motif. John Williams, *Concerto for Violin and Orchestra* (© 1976/2007 BMI), published by Marjer Music/Warner-Tamerlane, transcription from the Naxos recording with Emmanuelle Boisvert, violin, and the Detroit Symphony Orchestra, conducted by Leonard Slatkin, 2011, digital download. Used in compliance with the U.S. Copyright Act, Section 107.

Until now, the violin has been playing almost continuously, but in the second episode (C), it yields to the orchestra, which launches into a sweeping, improvisatory reconfiguration of motivic components drawn from the first subject of the opening movement (Ex. 18, [01:45-02:23]). Note the saturation of the melodic line with thirds and sixths — Williams is preparing the ear for the resurrection of the transformed first subject, fragments of which have been lurking beneath the motivic surface throughout, but which is now starting to emerge more insistently into the foreground.

Ex. 18: episode 2 — connection to first subject. John Williams, *Concerto for Violin and Orchestra* (© 1976/2007 BMI), published by Marjer Music/Warner-Tamerlane, transcription from the Naxos recording with Emmanuelle Boisvert, violin, and the Detroit Symphony Orchestra, conducted by Leonard Slatkin, 2011, digital download. Used in compliance with the U.S. Copyright Act, Section 107.

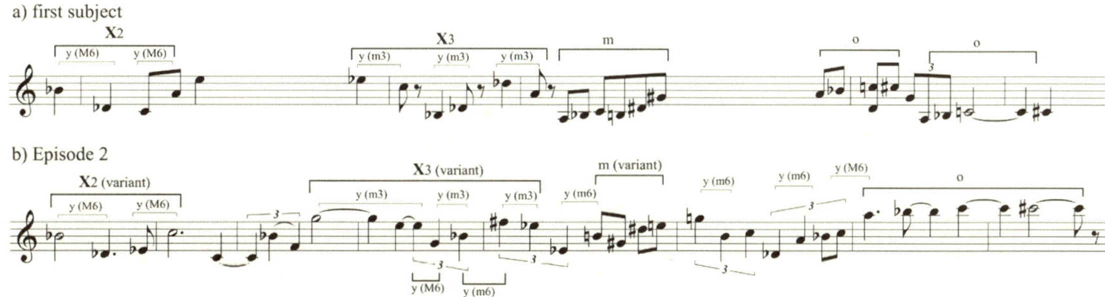

Interpolation 1: Reminiscence and Transformation

Having crested in the tutti of the second episode, the frenetic momentum of the rondo suddenly dissipates at [02:10] into a sustained chord aquiver with swirling arpeggios, as though the orchestral fabric had dissolved to reveal a vast firmament beyond. This breach into a mystical musical space marks the beginning of the first interpolation (D). A caesura in both the structural and emotional sense, it serves at once a recapitulatory and a transformative function. The melodic sixths that had, in the preceding episode, appeared as horizontal intervals are now verticalized into crystalline parallel sixths in the vibraphone and winds. The mood is enigmatic and reverential; we are witnessing a moment of transfiguration, in which familiar musical objects will emerge in a new, otherworldly light. The violin intones the minor sixth G – E♭, then wistfully recalls the first phrase of "Elegy" ([02:35-03:00]). While its signature lydian pentachord is preserved, the outline and rhythmic profile of the theme appears in a dreamlike distortion, as though examined through a prism (Ex. 19).

Ex. 19: interpolation 1 — reminiscence of "Elegy" in the instrumental recitative. John Williams, *Concerto for Violin and Orchestra* (© 1976/2007 BMI), published by Marjer Music/Warner-Tamerlane, transcription from the Naxos recording with Emmanuelle Boisvert, violin, and the Detroit Symphony Orchestra, conducted by Leonard Slatkin, 2011, digital download. Used in compliance with the U.S. Copyright Act, Section 107.

In its declamatory, free-flowing rhythm and phrase structure, the first part of the interpolation resembles an instrumental recitative ([02:24-03:32]). In the second part, this 'recitative' coalesces into a lyrical 'aria' in which, as Williams puts it, «insistent intervals, borrowed from the first movement, [are] 'sung' by the solo violin»[46] (Example 20, [03:33-05:53]). The minor sixths of motif X1 have permutated into the minor thirds of X6, which provides the basic motivic cell that is spun out, through repetition and sequential transposition, into the extended melodic line of the aria.

46. Williams 1983.

Ex. 20: interpolation 1 — 'Aria'. John Williams, *Concerto for Violin and Orchestra* (© 1976/2007 BMI), published by Marjer Music/Warner-Tamerlane, transcription from the Naxos recording with Emmanuelle Boisvert, violin, and the Detroit Symphony Orchestra, conducted by Leonard Slatkin, 2011, digital download. Used in compliance with the U.S. Copyright Act, Section 107.

Here at last, it seems, is the answer to the question posed in the first movement — the tormented opening of the concerto has been distilled into a simple, pure cantabile constructed almost entirely from rising thirds. As the violin ascends into the stratosphere, the music suggests a seraphic vision akin, perhaps, to the dream described three centuries earlier by John Milton, another bereaved husband mourning the recent death of his wife:

> Her face was veiled; yet to my fancied sight,
> Love, sweetness, goodness, in her person shined
> So clear, as in no face with more delight.
> But oh! as to embrace me she inclined
> I waked, she fled, and day brought back my night[47].

As in Milton's poem, the vision does not last — after the violin has attained its highest note (D♯), it descends in a mournful sequence based on X3 that marks the first overt recapitulation of first subject material since the opening movement. The thematic telos is thus followed by its point of departure, making explicit both the motivic origin of the aria and the inescapability of the solitude to which the soloist returns, again and again, in the concerto.

47. Milton 1993, p. 65.

Refrain/Motto and Interpolation 2 (Apotheosis)

However, the moment of contemplative melancholy is almost immediately interrupted by the orchestra, which energetically rushes in with the third statement of the refrain ([05:54-06:18]). As we have seen, motif X6 has grown with each rotation of the refrain; this time, the motif takes centre stage in a transition between the moto perpetuo theme and the third statement of the motto, to which it builds up in heroic, canonically staggered triplets (Ex. 21, [06:11-06:18]). The wall separating the world of the rondo from that of the interpolations has become translucent and permeable. It is about to be breached altogether by the herculean chords of the motto ([06:19-06:27]).

Ex. 21: refrain 3 — transition to motto chords based on motif X6. John Williams, *Concerto for Violin and Orchestra* (© 1976/2007 BMI), published by Marjer Music/Warner-Tamerlane, transcription from the Naxos recording with Emmanuelle Boisvert, violin, and the Detroit Symphony Orchestra, conducted by Leonard Slatkin, 2011, digital download. Used in compliance with the U.S. Copyright Act, Section 107.

After nine tutti strokes, the wall crumbles, and the motto strides onward into the climactic apotheosis of the "aria" (Ex. 22, [06:28-07:27]). But in crossing the threshold between sections, the motto is magically transformed: while it continues inexorably advancing in half notes, its violent, clashing sound masses have been burnished into a tender, hushed pandiatonic chorale. The colossus has been tamed, iron transmuted into stained glass. Over these luminously reharmonized chords, the aria in the violin soars like a phoenix arisen from the ashes of the first subject. In a moment of hallucinatory intensity, the world of the rondo and the world of the interpolations, the physical and the metaphysical, the temporal and the timeless, love and loss, joy and pain, fuse into one ecstatic hymn.

At the end of the apotheosis, the violin climbs to the same stratospheric D# that marked the apex of the first interpolation, and once again, motif X3 returns — but now it, too, has been transfigured. In place of the mournful descending sequence that concluded the first interpolation, the rising and falling thirds of motif X3 range freely across registers, and are embellished with playful trills and warbles, as though the motif was testing its new wings ([07:28-07:49]). The second interpolation concludes with a brief cadenza based on the rising thirds of motif X6 ([07:50-08:11]).

Ex. 22: motto chords (end of refrain 3) and apotheosis (interpolation 2). John Williams, *Concerto for Violin and Orchestra* (© 1976/2007 BMI), published by Marjer Music/Warner-Tamerlane, transcription from the Naxos recording with Emmanuelle Boisvert, violin, and the Detroit Symphony Orchestra, conducted by Leonard Slatkin, 2011, digital download. Used in compliance with the U.S. Copyright Act, Section 107.

Episode 3 - Motto/Refrain - Coda

In the remainder of the movement, Williams resumes and concludes the interrupted rondo. The third episode ([08:12-08:24]) reprises the oscillating sixths of the first episode. The final refrain begins with the fourth and last statement of the dissonant motto chords, which are now joined by wild arpeggiations, across three octaves, in the violin ([08:25-08:33]). A brisk, galloping coda over a pounding timpani pulse builds to a brilliant bravura conclusion at [9:07].

Conclusions

Maynard Solomon writes in reference to Beethoven that «heroism defines itself in conflict with mortality, and mortality is in turn superseded by renewed and transfigured life»[48]. This, in a nutshell, captures the emotional trajectory of John Williams's violin concerto as well. Its energetic, exuberant conclusion is a hard-won triumph, a consequence of its confrontation with the tragedy that galvanized its creation. The organic web of interrelated material, in which all themes and motives are derived from the opening, thus assumes not only a structural but a symbolic significance as well — try as it might, the violin cannot escape the constraints of the first four notes of the concerto, but through inverting and permutating and thus quite literally turning them on their head, it can come to terms with *what they mean*. The negative 'absence' that drives the concerto from tormented questioning to nostalgic recollection to agonized defiance leads, finally, to a positive 'presence' in the apotheosis of the aria: a deepened understanding, perhaps, of

48. Solomon 1998, p. 253.

the fragility of existence, an urgent sense that time's winged chariot is hurrying near, and that what remains of life must be dedicated with renewed vigour to creative work. «The pursuit of excellence is what life ought to be about», Williams observed in 1989. «I am defined by my work, by the details of the process of making music. My work is what I am»[49]. In describing his emotional turning point after Barbara Ruick's death as «the greatest gift ever given to me», perhaps the composer was alluding, in part, to this single-minded sublimation of self into art — a sublimation that found its most profound and personal expression in the violin concerto.

Appendix 1
Performances of the Violin Concerto[50]

DATE	ORCHESTRA	CONDUCTOR	SOLOIST	LOCATION
29/31 Jan. 1981	St. Louis Symphony	Leonard Slatkin	Mark Peskanov	St. Louis, MO (Powell Symphony Hall)
6 Feb. 1982	St. Louis Symphony	Leonard Slatkin	Mark Peskanov	New York, NY (Carnegie Hall)
10 Nov. 1983	L.A. Philharmonic	John Williams	Alexander Treger	Los Angeles, CA (Dorothy Chandler Pavillion)
1 Dec. 1983	Toronto Symphony	John Williams	Mark Peskanov	Toronto, Canada (Roy Thomson Hall)
4 April 1987	Houston Symphony	John Williams	Alexander Treger	Houston, TX (Jones Hall)
28 Nov. 1993	San Francisco Symphony	John Williams	Alexander Treger	San Francisco, CA (Davies Symphony Hall)
19 Dec. 1997	L.A. Philharmonic	John Williams	Alexander Treger	Orange County, CA (Orange County Perfroming Arts Center)
18, 20-21 Dec. 1997	L.A. Philharmonic	Esa-Pekka Salonen	Alexander Treger	Los Angeles, CA (Dorothy Chandler Pavillion)
July 1998	Boston Symphony	John Williams	Gil Shaham	Tanglewood, MA (Koussevitsky Shed)
11 Aug. 2001	Grant Park Symphony Orchestra	Carlos Kalmar	Gil Shaham	Chicago, IL (Petrillo Music Shell)
21 July 2002	Brevard Music Center Orchestra	Arthur Fagan	Gil Shaham	Asheville, NC (Brevard Music Center)
18 July 2004	Aspen Festival Orchestra	John Williams	Gil Shaham	Apen, CO (Benedict Music Tent)
4/28-30, 2005	National Symphony Orchestra	John Williams	Gil Shaham	Washington, D.C (Kennedy Center)
23 June 2007	Music Academy of the West Festival Orchestra	John Williams	Gil Shaham	Santa Barbara, CA (Santa Barbara Bowl)
14-17 Jan. 2010	Detroit Symphony	Leonard Slatkin	Emmanuelle Boisvert	Detroit, MI (Orchestra Hall)
8-9 Nov. 2013	Chicago Symphony	John Williams	Gil Shaham	Chicago, IL (Symphony Center)
17-19 March 2016	Boston Symphony Orchestra	Stéphane Denève	Gil Shaham	Boston, MA (Symphony Hall)
5-7 May 2016	Philadelphia Orchestra	Stéphane Denève	James Ehnes	Philadelphia, PA (Kimmel Center)
25 July 2017	Los Angeles Philharmonic	Stéphane Denève	Gil Shaham	Los Angeles, CA (Hollywood Bowl)

49. Christy 1989.
50. This list may not be comprehensive.

Appendix 2: Principal Motivic Interrelationships

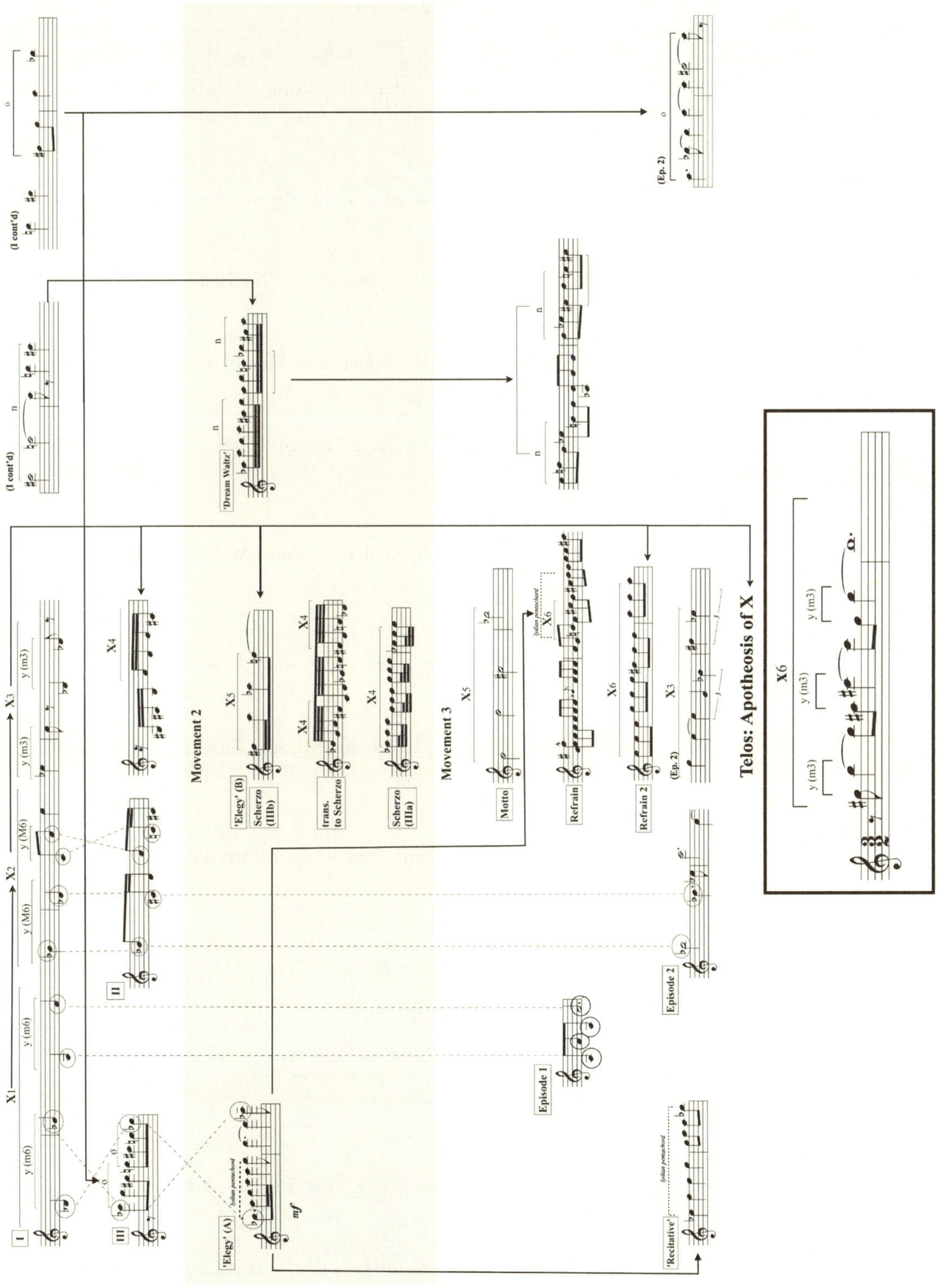

Movement 1

I X1 X2 X3

y (m6) y (m6) y (M6) y (M6) y (m3) y (m3)

(I cont'd) n

(I cont'd) o

III o o

II

X4

Movement 2

'Elegy' (A) lydian pentachord

mf

'Elegy' (B) Scherzo (IIIb) X5

trans. to Scherzo X4 X4

Scherzo (IIIa) X4

'Dream Waltz' n n

n n

Movement 3

Motto X5

Episode 1

Refrain lydian pentachord X6

Refrain 2 X6

'Recitative' lydian pentachord

Episode 2

(Ep. 2) X3

(Ep. 2) o

Telos: Apotheosis of X

X6

y (m3) y (m3) y (m3)

Bibliography

Bernheimer 1983
Bernheimer, Martin, 'Pop! John Williams on Philharmonic podium', in: *Los Angeles Times*, 12 November 1983.

Burlingame 2002
Burlingame, Jon. 'A Career of Epic Proportions', in: *Los Angeles Times*, 3 February 2002.

Christy 1989
Christy, Marian. 'John Williams' Pursuit of Excellence', in: *The Boston Globe*, 4 July 1989.

Church 1974
Church, Foster. 'Center Stage', in: *Reno Gazette-Journal*, 8 March 1974.

Dickinson 1998
Dickinson, Emily. *The Poems of Emily Dickinson*, edited by R. W. Franklin, 3 vols., Cambridge, Harvard University Press, 1998.

Dyer 2002
Dyer, Richard. 'Boston Symphony with Gil Shaham, violin, Williams', in: *The Boston Globe*, 17 January 2002.

Elley 1978
Elley, Derek. 'John Williams, Part Two', in: *Films and Filming*, xxiv/11 (August 1978), pp. 30-33.

Galloway 1954
Galloway, Paul. 'Airman Composes Way to Movie Musical Career', in: *The Beacon*, 27 August 1954.

Hopper 1953
Hopper, Hedda. 'On Hollywood: Acting Came Easy, Opportunity Hard', in: *The Baltimore Sun*, 16 August 1953.

Johnson 2010
Johnson, Lawrence B. 'With Firm Grip, Slatkin Retakes Reins of DSO', in: *Detroit News*, 15 January 2010.

Jones 2006
Jones, Shirley. DVD Audio Commentary, *Carousel: 50th Anniversary Edition*, dir. Henry King, Beverly Hills (CA), 20th Century Fox, 2006.

Kolodin 1968
Kolodin, Irving. 'Parents Can Be a Help', in: *Battle Creek Enquirer*, 4 February 1968.

Los Angeles Times 1955
'Actress Barbara Ruick Files Suit for Divorce', in: *Los Angeles Times*, 11 August 1955.

Milton 1993
Milton, John. *Selected Poems*, edited by Stanley Appelbaum, Toronto, Dover Thrift Editions, 1993.

Murray 1987
Murray, Lyn. *Musician: A Hollywood Journal of Wives, Women, Writers, Lawyers, Directors, Producers and Music*, Secaucus (NJ), Lyl Stuart, 1987.

Palmer 1972
Palmer, Christopher. 'The Changing World of Film Music: Composer John Williams', in: *Crescendo International*, x (April 1972), p. 8.

Parsons 1956
Parsons, Louella. 'Hollywood', in: *Corsicana Daily Sun*, 24 September 1956.

Pasles 1997
Pasles, Chris. 'Experimental Craft', in: *Los Angeles Times*, 19 December 1997.

Perlmutter 1984
Perlmutter, Donna. 'Giulini's Valedictory Season', in: *Ovation*, iv (February 1984), p. 27.

Peters 1981
Peters, Frank. 'Mahler Work Impressive at Powell Hall', in: *St. Louis Post-Dispatch*, 30 January 1981.

Reno Gazette-Journal 1974
'Actress' Death Ruled Natural', in: *Reno Gazette-Journal*, 5 March 1974.

Roth 1984
Roth, Henry, 'Los Angeles Philharmonic/Williams/Treger (violin)', in: *The Strad*, xciv (January 1984), p. 596.

Rothstein 1981
Rothstein, Edward. 'Symphony at Carnegie Hall: Energetic, Youthful Sound', in: *St. Louis Post-Dispatch*, 9 February 1981.

Schneller 2014
Schneller, Tom. 'Sweet Fulfillment: Allusion and Teleological Genesis in John Williams's *Close Encounters of the Third Kind*', in: *The Musical Quarterly*, xcvii/1 (March 2014), pp. 98-131.

Schoenberg 1975
Schoenberg, Arnold. *Style and Idea*, Berkeley-Los Angeles, University of California Press, 1975.

Scott 1952
Scott, John. 'Barbara Ruick "Real Gone" among the Bop Set', in: *Los Angeles Times*, 6 July 1952, p. D3.

Shaham 2013
Shaham, Gil. 'Gil Shaham Talks «Star Wars», the Violin and the New York Knicks', posted online on 8 November 2013 by Noel Morris, <https://noelmorris.net/2013/11/08/gil-shaham-talks-star-wars-the-violin-and-the-new-york-knicks/>, accessed February 2018.

Sherlaw-Johnson 2009
Sherlaw-Johnson, Robert. *Messiaen*, London, Omnibus Press, [3]2009.

Sidney 1956
Sidney, George. 'The Cry for New Faces', in: *The Independent Film Journal*, 30 June 1956.

Smith 1959
Smith, Cecil. "'Boy Friend' Bounces Back", in: *Los Angeles Times*, 15 February 1959.

Solomon 1998
Solomon, Maynard. *Beethoven*, New York, Schirmer, 1998.

Stryker 2010
Stryker, Mark. 'Slatkin Returns to Podium in Fine Form', in: *Detroit Free Press*, 16 January 2010.

Time 1949
'Phuff?', in: *Time Magazine*, 31 October 1949.

The Van Nuys News 1949a
'Optimist Dri-Nite Club Bringing "Surprise Package" to Teen-Agers', in: *The Van Nuys News*, 4 August 1949.

The Van Nuys News 1949b
'Teen-Agers Pack Dri-Nite Club for Dancing, Program', in: *The Van Nuys News*, 26 September 1949.

Tucker 1993
Tucker, Marilyn. 'Symphony Goes to the Movies – *E. T.*, *Star Wars* Composer Conducts', in: *San Francisco Chronicle*, 30 November 1993.

Ward 1987
Ward, Charles, 'Williams Lifts Baton, Leads Own Works', in: *Houston Chronicle*, 5 April 1987.

Williams 1983
Williams, John. 'The Violin Concerto', liner notes to *John Williams: Violin Concerto – Flute Concerto*, Mark Peskanov, Leonard Slatkin, Varese Sarabande VSD-5345, 1983.

Williams 2012
Id. Interview by Donald MacLeod, *Composer of the Week*, BBC3, 18 January 2012, online, <http://www.bbc.co.uk/programmes/b01px3j8>, accessed February 2018.

Williams 2014
Id. 'John Williams: A Pivotal Moment in His Life and Work', from the Academy event 'Behind the Score: The Art of the Film Composer' at LACMA's Bing Theatre, 21 July 2014, <https://www.youtube.com/watch?v=bE9IWvLz6Dk>, accessed February 2018.

Happily Never After: Williams's Musical Exploration of the 'Controversial' Ending to *A. I.: Artificial Intelligence*

Stefan Swanson
(New York University, NY)

Steven Spielberg's 2001 film *A. I.: Artificial Intelligence* is a futuristic reworking of the Pinocchio story that substitutes a robot boy (David) for the wooden puppet as the protagonist. David is given advanced artificial intelligence that enables him to love, but this causes him endless conflict in a human world. The film addresses complex themes about humanity, love, and creation, and the conflicts these themes create between *orga* (humans) and *mecha* (lifelike, human-created robots). One of the most important factors in this exploration is the score composed by John Williams. This chapter shows how the music explores the dichotomy of 'human'-related subjects (referred to as *orga* in this chapter) and 'artificial'-related subjects (referred to as *mecha* in this chapter) present in the story.

A. I.: Artificial Intelligence received mixed reviews upon its release in 2001, and the most criticized element was certainly the third act, the «disappointing, needlessly cathartic ending [Spielberg] thrusts upon us»[1]. Roger Ebert's review of *A. I.* was largely positive but even he called the ending «too facile and sentimental, given what has gone before»[2]. Brian Aldiss, who wrote the original short story *A. I.* was loosely inspired by, said the ending «is one of the 'ifs' of film history — at least the ending indicates Spielberg adding some sugar to Kubrick's wine. The actual ending is overly sympathetic and moreover rather overtly engineered by a plot device that does not really bear credence»[3].

As demonstrated by the Aldiss quote, Spielberg himself is often blamed for the sentimentality of the third act. Thomas Morrissey says, «it is so very clear where Kubrick's dark vision gives way to Spielberg's attempt at a rosy ending», continuing that «[David's]

---

1. Reid 2001, p. D7.
2. Ebert 2001.
3. Aldiss 2001.

schmaltzy perfect day with Mommy sugar coats the bitter core of the film»[4]. Throughout his career, Spielberg has been criticized for the insertion of 'overly sentimental' moments in his films, from Oscar Schindler's emotional breakdown at the end of *Schindler's List* (1993) to Captain Miller's «Earn this» in *Saving Private Ryan* (1998) to the 'happy ending' in the otherwise bleak *Minority Report* (2002). Royal Brown says, «Spielberg films are a sucker punch: the director sets you up with all sorts of things that you just *have* to love — childhood, motherhood, cuddly aliens, patriotism, even paranoid adults and great white sharks (not much difference there, eh?) — and then, not unlike Sally Field at the Academy Awards ceremonies a few years back, just stands there and begs you to love him»[5].

In the final act in *A. I.*, David is allowed one more day with his mother Monica, whom he has been searching for throughout the entire film. Throughout this act, Williams's music, dominated by "Monica's Theme", mixes orga and mecha elements in ways that suggest the ending is perhaps darker than it appears, just an illusion created for David's comfort[6]. While blaming *A. I.*'s conclusion on Spielberg's penchant for sentimentality is reasonable, according to Spielberg, this is a misunderstanding:

> People assume that Stanley ended *A. I.* with David and Teddy underwater trapped by the Ferris wheel and then end credits roll, and they're going to be down there until their batteries run out. That's where they assume Stanley ended it, and I of course get criticized for carrying the film 2000 years into an advanced future where the robots that were created have replaced us and super-mechas rule the world. They become a silicon-based society, no longer a carbon based society, and they certainly assume that's how I wrecked Stanley's movie, when in fact Stanley's treatment, along with Ian Watson, went right into the 2000 year future. And this was where Stanley was going to take the movie had he lived to direct it, and this is where I was obligated to take the picture[7].

This is further supported by Kubrick's own notes from 1993[8]. If the ending comes from Kubrick, whose finales include nuclear doomsday in *Dr. Strangelove* (1964), the 'curing' of Alex in *A Clockwork Orange* (1971), and the mercy kill in *Full Metal Jacket* (1987), perhaps the interpretation that *A. I.*'s ending is 'happy' is not entirely accurate.

Tim Kreider's 2002 *Film Quarterly* review argues that Spielberg is ultimately manipulating the audience throughout the film and the seemingly saccharine final act is actually a grim conclusion to David's story. A musical analysis of the final act, emphasizing "Monica's Theme", demonstrates specifically how the music helps manipulate the audience,

---

4. Morrissey 2004, p. 257.
5. Brown 2001, p. 330.
6. Kreider 2002, p. 39.
7. Spielberg 2006.
8. Struthers 2009, p. 23.

supporting Kreider's review. On the surface the film's conclusion appears to be a 'happy' reunion, but the music ultimately reveals a darker, more complicated truth. It concludes that Williams is musically setting up the ending as a tragic continuation of David's prior conflicts with humans and emotions.

Methodology

The link between the music and the content of *A. I.* is paramount, therefore my analyses and reductions are based on the soundtrack found on the 2002 Dreamworks Video DVD release. For his soundtrack albums, Williams typically records separate cues specifically written for the album and «tries to arrange the tracks in a more interesting way than just in the order they are heard in the film»[9]. Because of this rearranging, soundtrack albums often differ from the material found in the final cut of the film. Even the cues written for the film are sometimes edited and rearranged after recording so the written score does not coincide with the music as heard in the finished film[10]. Any discrepancies between the music as presented in this chapter and the music found on the original soundtrack album or the final versions of the scores as prepared by Conrad Pope and John Neufield will be due to changes made during the post-recording editing process. Because film music is a collaborative effort between the filmmaker and the composer, it is important to analyse the music in its final form, that is the music track in the film's sound mix.

Furthermore a Catalogue of Cues is found at the conclusion of this chapter for reference, detailing each musical cue specifically as heard in the film, including both non-diegetic and diegetic music. Specific information about timings for each cue such as start and end times, along with overall cue length is included. Musical descriptions detailing instrumentation, textures, themes, etc., and other notes relating to dramatic/filmic features are also included. Throughout the chapter, parenthetical references such as <29 Escape from Rouge City / Manhattan> and <4 Introduction to David> guide the reader to the specific cues in the Catalogue for more information. The purpose of this Catalogue is to provide a comprehensive overview of all music in the film and contextualize the music specifically discussed in the chapter.

Because the score explores the dichotomy of orga and mecha elements in the film, this paper uses a semiotic methodology that differentiates between musical representations of orga and mecha. Table 1 shows the main signifiers and their counterparts that will be explored. Each is explained in detail after the chart.

---

9. Wannberg 1999.

10. «Steven Spielberg advised George Lucas to change the edits of the combats at the end of the movie. John just said "Oh. I think I will let Kenny handle that". So it was up to Ken Wannberg to cut up everything». Conrad Pope, John Williams's orchestrator for *A. I.* in Huvet 2017.

Table 1: Signifier Dichotomy

Orga Signifiers *Late-Romantic style*	Mecha Signifiers *Avoidance of Romanticism*
Lyrical melody with long, sustained phrases	Overt use of repetition, including Minimalism
Acoustic instrumentation	Electronic instrumentation

Orga Signifiers: Late-Romantic Style

The late-Romantic style associated with Richard Wagner and Richard Strauss has been a primary influence on film music composers since Golden Age Hollywood, despite the style's being «several decades out of date in the concert hall»[11]. Several reasons for this association have been offered including the immigration of European composers at that time[12], the studios' assumption that «the public would refuse to tolerate any music more modern-sounding than Liszt symphonic poem»[13], and film scoring's connection to opera. Roy Prendergast writes, «When confronted with the kind of dramatic problems films presented to them, Steiner, Korngold, and Newman merely looked [...] to those composers who had, for the most part solved almost identical problems in their operas»[14]. Christopher Palmer presents the connection as a product of musical escapism, with the marriage of such anachronistic music to modern story-telling stemming from Hollywood functioning as a 'dream factory' and Romanticism being the music of fantasy, dream, and illusion[15].

Caryl Flinn suggests the tradition of using Romantic styles in film music has to do with a «utopian function», or «an impression of perfection and integrity in an otherwise imperfect, unintegrated world», and that «has been assigned to [...] film music of the 1930s and 1940s in particular»[16]. This music supplies something missing as «a result of a fundamental ontological deficiency of the cinema»[17], or as Bernard Herrmann suggests, «a piece of film, by its nature, lacks a certain ability to convey emotional overtones»[18]. Susan McClary critiques this relationship, stating, «Romanticism also offered spectators a means of escape into a mythologized and culturally elite past»[19].

11. Cooke 2008, p. 78.
12. *Ibidem*.
13. Palmer 1990, p. 25.
14. Prendergast 1992, p. 39.
15. Palmer 1990, p. 23.
16. Flinn 1992, p. 9.
17. *Ibidem*, p. 44.
18. Manvel – Huntley 1957, p. 244.
19. Mcclary 2007, p. 50.

Williams's connection to this Romantic style is deeply rooted in his own work. His main model for the music to *Star Wars* was the prominent Golden Age composer Erich Wolfgang Korngold[20]. Using Palmer's, Flinn's, and McClary's critiques of this association, I examine the usage of Romantic gestures in this score as critical signifiers of 'human' concepts. These range from pure emotions, to failures and shortcomings, to the 'utopian' function of David's need to be loved.

The usage of leitmotif in film comes from the same late-Romantic operatic tradition of Wagner and Strauss that Prendergast discussed before. T. W. Adorno critiques the early usage of leitmotif in film music when he says the sole function «is to announce heroes and situations so as to help the audience to orient itself more easily»[21]. James Buhler counters Adorno's notion saying John Williams's use of leitmotifs in the original *Star Wars* trilogy «comes as close as any film music to the tone of Wagner»[22], whose primary purpose «is the production of myth not signification»[23]. This is important when looking at the usage of themes as leitmotifs in *A. I.* because themes are sometimes brought back in situations in which the obvious signification makes little sense.

Lyrical Melody with Long, Sustained Phrases

Williams's music in this film often uses lyrical melodies with long, sustained phrases to signify orga, an approach to melody often associated with Romantic music[24]. As demonstrated by Gino Stefani, melody is a difficult term to define, but he proposes «'melody' is a notion belonging essentially to everyday culture, to popular culture»[25]. In other words, its recognition stems from a gathered human experience. Stefani often uses the word 'singable' in his exploration for a definition of melody. According to Lewis Rowell, Wagner viewed melody as being able to «articulate expressions of inarticulate human feeling»[26]. These are in direct contrast with the other elements such as Minimalism and repetitive phrasing that feature so prominently in the score. Furthermore the melodies are mostly associated with situations in the film relating to Monica, an orga subject.

Acoustic Instrumentation

Because Williams uses acoustic instrumentation in the music that represents both the orga and mecha, (e.g. minimalist styles), this is a less categorically defined signifier that

20. AUDISSINO 2014, p. 72.
21. ADORNO 2005, p. 36.
22. BUHLER 2000, p. 44.
23. *Ibidem*, p. 43.
24. SZABOLCSI 1970, p. 278.
25. STEFANI 1987, p. 21.
26. ROWELL 2004, p. 28.

relates more to its usage in conjunction with other signifiers. When it is used with other orga signifiers, it represents orga alone — see the string sections of <4 Introduction to David>. When used with other signifiers of the 'artificial', acoustic instrumentation either serves to enhance the artificial quality — see <29 Escape from Rouge City / Manhattan> — or mix in some measure of orga — see <13 Abandoned in the Woods>.

MECHA SIGNIFIERS: AVOIDANCE OF LATE-ROMANTIC STYLE

If late-Romantic associations signify orga elements, then the conspicuous use of styles and techniques not related to those found in late-Romantic music signifies mecha elements.

Overt Use of Repetition, Including Minimalism

Rebecca Eaton notes that the use of minimalism to signify the mechanical is common, and this association can be traced back to early reviews of minimalist works in the 1970s[27]. She lists dozens of examples of multimedia works that all use minimalism in conjunction with machines or technology, including Philip Glass's score to *Koyaanisqatsi* (Godfrey Reggio,1982), one Audi commercial whose music was stylistically so close to Glass that a lawsuit ensued (1996), and Williams's score to *A. I.* Her reasoning for this connection is that minimalism «features a regular, steady pulse. It is not melodically based, but repetition-based. It typically displays limited dynamic contrast. All of these musical attributes are also characteristics of the working of machines, be they are manifested in sound, visually observed motion, or internal process»[28]. This is in direct contrast with the Romantic idiom signifying human emotion. For instance, in cues dominated by minimalism, the emotion from the scene is controlled by Romantic procedures such as varying the dynamic range, expanding the range of the instruments, and frequent harmonic shifts — see <13 Abandoned in the Woods>. In line with Eaton's analysis, I conclude that the usage of minimalism is customarily a signifier of the mecha.

I further this notion to include conspicuous repetition on larger structural levels. For instance, while minimalism generally features a repeated pattern of just a few notes or measures, *A. I.* features examples of phrase and structural repetitions that are sometimes separated by several dozen measures. Arved Ashby discusses how the mechanical repetition in the context of recorded music changes the way we form musical memories since the listener is able to hear an exact replica of a given piece of music countless times[29]. While

27. EATON 2014, p. 5.
28. *Ibidem*, p. 6.
29. ASHBY 2010, p. 62.

not as immediately obvious as repetitions of specific phrases/gestures (e.g. a four-note chordal arpeggio repeated twenty times in a row), these higher-level repetitions are still easily recognizable, and in the case of *A. I.* usually come in conflict with orga music such as lyrical melodies.

Electronic Instrumentation

One obvious way music can evoke artificiality is through the use of electronics or synthesizers. Williams is mainly known for his orchestral scores, however, he has used synthesizers on several notable occasions, including a pivotal moment in *The Empire Strikes Back* (Irvin Kershner, 1980) when Luke Skywalker ventures off to the Magic Tree to face his greatest fears, along with films depicting such inhuman acts as murder and rape, such as *Presumed Innocent* (Alan J. Pakula, 1990), *Sleepers* (Barry Levinson, 1996), and *Munich* (Steven Spielberg, 2005). Interestingly, the example that best matches his usage of electronics in *A. I.* actually comes from the lesser-known film *Heartbeeps* (Allan Arkush, 1981) in which Williams uses a plethora of electronic sounds, in combination with the usual orchestra, to underscore the love story between two robots.

Because these signifiers are not always black and white in the score and often blend into each other, making a definitive statement is sometimes difficult. For instance, in <29 Escape from Rouge City / Manhattan>, a pervasive minimalist style runs throughout, however it is scored with a large, Romantic-style orchestra with little to no electronics. I will explore these issues and how their very existence augments Williams's musical exploration of the 'orga versus the mecha' narrative theme.

Analysis of "Monica's Theme"

The relationship between David and his programmed mother Monica is the driving force of the drama in *A. I.* She receives him as a gift from her husband because she is having difficulty accepting that their sick, cryogenically frozen son will most likely never wake up. Although Monica is initially repulsed by the artificiality of David, she begins to warm up to him. She ultimately programs David to 'love' her, but after realizing her mistake, she abandons him in the woods. David then begins an obsessive search to find the woman he 'loves'.

In the composer's words, "Monica's Theme" is a «cantilena», with associations to lullabies, that «although both simple and direct, has its complexities»[30]. The first statement of this theme, albeit just a fragment in solo piano, actually occurs at a very pivotal moment

[30]. Williams in Bouzereau 2002.

in the first of act of the film when David calls Monica «Mommy» after she completes the imprinting process. The usage of the theme is telling as it implies David's love for Monica is immediate and programmed. The solo piano foreshadows the treatment of "Monica's Theme" when it dominates David's 'ultimate day' at the end of the film. Up to this point, Monica's interactions with David have been largely negative: 1) She yells at her husband for bringing him home. 2) She is so upset when he asks to be dressed for bed (he of course does not need to sleep), that she has to urgently leave the room. 3) Their game of hide and seek, while appearing for a moment to be the turning point where Monica starts to accept him, ends awkwardly when David finds her on the toilet. 4) During dinner, David laughs to an inappropriately exaggerated degree. 5) When Monica finally does dress David for bed, she still flashes back to her frozen son Martin. Williams's use of her theme after the imprinting process tells us that David now loves Monica, but these interactions offer no evidence that she loves him back, or that he even has reason to love her. His immediate love is simply programmed. Neither party has earned it.

Outside of an additional small statement of the theme when Monica reads *Pinocchio* to Martin, "Monica's Theme" does not come back until the third act, when the advanced mechas awaken David from his 2000-year 'slumber' (<34 Stored Memories>). The theme starts out in solo piano with a mechanical, repetitive alternation between B and D eighth notes (see Ex. 1), implying a robotic quality to David's searching. This implication is further supported by the fact that the eighth note rhythm in the left hand does not cease until he hears the woman's voice later in the scene.

Ex. 1: repetitive alternation. John Williams, "Stored Memories" from *A. I.: Artificial Intelligence* (© 2001 BMI), published by Songs of SKG/Warner Barham Music, LLC, ear transcription from the film's soundtrack. Used in compliance with the U.S. Copyright Act, Section 107.

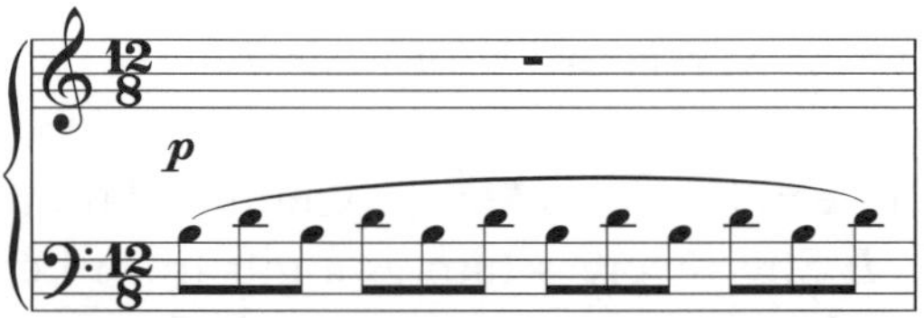

After two measures of this pattern, the melody finally closes and establishes G major as the tonic. The construction of the melody itself, when taken on its own, also supports the drama unfolding on screen as David is searching throughout the house calling for his mother. The first two notes heard are an ascending, octave leap from the lower dominant to the upper dominant. This is followed by another ascending leap up to the tonic.

The first six measures alone serve as a representation of the David character to this point in the film (see Ex. 2). The first two measures, with their empty harmonic content and unwavering repetition (section a. in Ex. 2), signify David's cold, robotic beginnings, constantly watching and calculating his surrounding environment, but never quite fitting into the orga world. Measures three and four, with the wide leaps and early melodic peak on tonic (section b. in Ex. 2), mirror the tragedy of Monica imprinting David before she is truly ready, changing him from a simple machine to a more complex being trapped in-between the worlds of orga and mecha. He is cursed with an unattainable goal of getting his orga mother to love his mecha self. Measures five and six are seemingly heading for 'home', but with a break in the ascending pattern (F♯ moving down to E instead of up to G), the final arrival on tonic being displaced by an octave (section c. in Ex. 2), and the settling on the relative minor harmony instead of the tonic fit with the current scene as David believes he is home («Teddy, we're home!») but is soon to find out that is false.

Ex. 2: "Monica's Theme" as David's character. John Williams, "Stored Memories" from *A. I.: Artificial Intelligence* (© 2001 BMI), published by Songs of SKG/Warner Barham Music, LLC, ear transcription from the film's soundtrack. Used in compliance with the U.S. Copyright Act, Section 107.

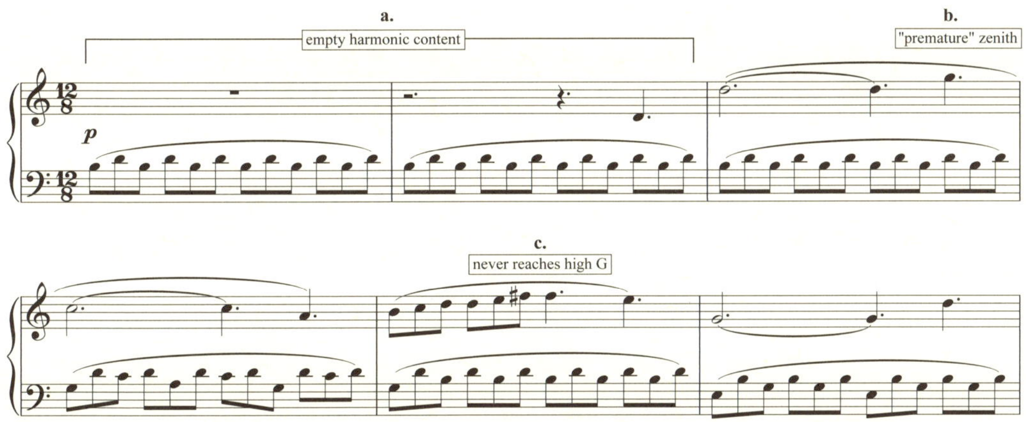

A dominant pickup in the melody begins a descending stepwise pattern (simple inversion of the ascending pattern from before) down to E, followed by slow alternations between A and E. Unlike the ascending steps before, the 'goal' of the melody here is not clear. The accompanying harmony (implied A minor with a pedal G) remains static for two bars, which along with the lack of direction in the melody create a sense of musical 'stalling out'. Listeners may expect that the A minor harmony is serving as a 'typical' pre-dominant leading to a final perfect authentic cadence. The result is less climactic (as shown in Ex. 3).

Ex. 3: avoiding the perfect authentic cadence. John Williams, "Stored Memories" from *A. I.: Artificial Intelligence* (© 2001 BMI), published by Warner Barham Music, LLC, ear transcription from the film's soundtrack. Used in compliance with the U.S. Copyright Act, Section 107.

What follows is a resting point that feels forced or artificial, almost as a formality. The melody drops down a fifth to the dominant D while a full, rich tonic triad is played underneath. Very little has paved the way for this resolution. The key of G major has been present from the beginning, leading listeners to the idea that the resolution should eventually come back there. Simply moving from Am/G to G, especially when considering how dramatic the false resolution on E minor sounded a few measures earlier, feels hollow. A Schenker graph (see Ex. 4) of the first melodic phrase shows that the melody is clearly descending stepwise from the dominant to the tonic, however the tonic arrival never comes. When looking at the tenor line, another descending stepwise line from dominant to tonic is forming, but just as with the melody, it never arrives on the tonic[31].

Ex. 4: Schenker graph of "Monica's Theme".

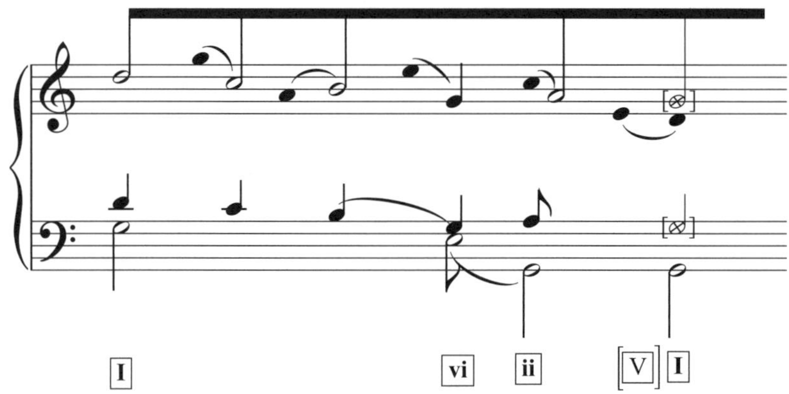

This also reinforces the previous thought regarding this melody as a representation of the David character throughout the film. The film ends with David falling asleep with his mother one final time after she tells him she loves him. Although the conclusion works in a thematic sense — David's journey is over and now he gets the happy ending he worked so hard for — something about it rings forced. It is ambiguous whether this is his real mother or just a vision of David's desire implanted by the advanced mechas. Even the narrating voice over this final scene is not explicit as to whether this is real or not: «And as the day wore on, David thought it was the happiest day of his life. All the problems seem to have disappeared from his Mommy's mind. There was no Henry. There was no Martin. There was no grief. It was only David». The inclusion of the words 'thought' and 'seem' focus the narration on David's point-of-view, or at least what he believes whether this is 'objectively' true. Also, the wording of this passage heavily implies Monica's grief was caused by Henry and Martin, her husband and son, an interpretation that can only be true in David's mind. In reality they were the cause of David's grief.

[31]. These 'expected' but never fulfilled musical events are included in the graph and bracketed.

Eventually David's ultimate wish comes true when Monica says to him, «I love you. I always loved you». While this might be, as the voice over states, «the everlasting moment [David] had been waiting for», the audience is left unfulfilled. From an orga perspective, David has not earned his mother's love. As mentioned before, most of their interactions surrounding the imprinting process were unsettling for Monica[32]. Their last contact was Monica abandoning him in the woods and instead of David feeling any resentment or anger towards her, or Monica showing any regret towards him, they both offer a blissful, blind (perhaps 'robotic') acceptance, as if nothing had happened. As a dramatic conclusion to a story this can be suitable, however the lack of genuine, 'human' emotions and interactions leaves the audience unfulfilled. It merely mimics orga behaviour, but never authentically acquires it.

In the film, as David searches for his mother in this illusory house, an unexpected sonic moment occurs, blurring the line between diegesis and underscore. A woman's voice calls out to David [02:03:13], singing his name on E and C♯, in perfect consonance with the underlying harmony of the non-diegetic underscore (see Ex. 5). The voicing of the A major arpeggio here is the fullest and richest voicing of a triad thus far in the cue. Seldom does a root-position fully-voiced triad occur. The look on David's face and the warmth of this chord suggests he feels this could be his mother calling to him. The piano eventually settles on a lone D as David is fixated on this voice and moves towards it. Harmonically speaking this could set up the next iteration of "Monica's Theme" in the original, tonic key. Instead the music moves to a completely different direction in both timbre and key.

Ex. 5: woman's voice. John Williams, "Stored Memories" from *A. I.: Artificial Intelligence* (© 2001 BMI), published by Songs of SKG/Warner Barham Music, LLC, ear transcription from the film's soundtrack. Used in compliance with the U.S. Copyright Act, Section 107.

As David starts to enter the room where the voice is coming from [02:03:21], "Monica's Theme" disappears and instead a slow moving, homophonic, almost hymnal set of chords are stated in quiet, but full strings (shown in Ex. 6). This creates a religious-like atmosphere as the source of the voice is slowly revealed to be the Blue Fairy, the figure

32. These interactions include David spilling her favourite perfume, his creeping her out with his phone trick, his damaging himself eating the spinach, his not being phased while receiving 'surgery', his attempt at cutting her hair while she's sleeping and scratching her eye, and his almost drowning her son.

David was last seen praying to in seeming perpetuity. Once again the woman's voice sings David's name on E and C♯ [02:03:31], but the strings resolve to an F♯-minor chord on the latter note, reflecting the disappointment as David realizes this is not Monica.

Ex. 6: slow moving, homophonic chords. John Williams, "Stored Memories" from *A. I.: Artificial Intelligence* (© 2001 BMI), published by Songs of SKG/Warner Barham Music, LLC, ear transcription from the film's soundtrack. Used in compliance with the U.S. Copyright Act, Section 107.

The hymnal chords in the strings continue over the next several minutes of David's conversation with the Blue Fairy, constantly wavering between related major and minor chords. This, along with the addition of added notes just a second away from chord tones and a soft, women's chorus, creates a still atmosphere, somewhere between major and minor (see Ex. 7). The lack of musical change and material throughout this section is noteworthy because while David attentively listens to the Blue Fairy, he never fully understands the implications of what she is telling him. He is blindly focused on Monica's reincarnation, even though that means she will have to die all over again.

Ex. 7: between major and minor. John Williams, "Stored Memories" from *A. I.: Artificial Intelligence* (© 2001 BMI), published by Songs of SKG/Warner Barham Music, LLC, ear transcription from the film's soundtrack). Used in compliance with the U.S. Copyright Act, Section 107.

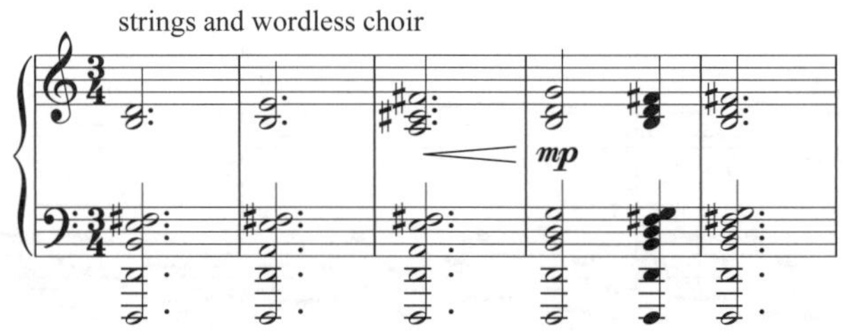

Seemingly unfazed by the Blue Fairy's warnings, David wonders how he will be able to bring Monica back. A stubborn eighth note pattern in the lower electronics (shown in Ex. 8) concludes this scene as David looks at the Blue Fairy and coldly declares, «Now you can bring her back» [02:06:41]. This is followed by the entrance of the hymnal chords in the strings while the lower electronic ostinato continues undeterred. After ten literal repetitions of the ostinato, the music slows to a quiet close. David's mecha mind has been made up and he will not accept anything less than one more day with Monica, emphasized by the incessantly repeated ostinato and the use of the electronics.

Ex. 8: synth ostinato. John Williams, "Stored Memories" from *A. I.: Artificial Intelligence* (© 2001 BMI), published by Songs of SKG/Warner Barham Music, LLC, ear transcription from the film's soundtrack. Used in compliance with the U.S. Copyright Act, Section 107.

The aforementioned concluding scene, when David and Monica finally have their moment <36 David's Day with Monica>, initially follows a near identical iteration of "Monica's Theme" for solo piano [02:11:50]. The first major change in the music comes after the E♭ major, G major, A major, D major progression. In <34 Stored Memories> David thinks the female voice calling to him is his mother, but ultimately discovers otherwise. Her voice calls to him over the A major triad in the score. In this final cue, when the same A major triad sounds, David says to what he thinks is his real mother, «I found you», recalling his unfulfilled moment from before.

What follows is the first statement of the refrain to "Monica's Theme". While it begins with new material, a simple held supertonic resolving to tonic (see Ex. 9a), it quickly settles back to material nearly identical to the second phrase of the initial verse of "Monica's Theme" (see Ex. 9b). The refrain finishes with varied sequences of this material and even ends with a similar E♭, G, A, D progression (this time the G triad is minor). What started out as a promising change from the theme that has been heard several times already, ultimately falls back to the same patterns found before. This suggests that while appearing to be the conclusion David has been waiting for (along with the audience), nothing has really changed. David has merely completed the mission he was programmed to do.

Ex. 9a: "Monica's Theme" refrain. John Williams, "Monica's Theme" from *A. I.: Artificial Intelligence* (© 2001 BMI), published by Songs of SKG/Warner Barham Music, LLC, ear transcription from the film's soundtrack. Used in compliance with the U.S. Copyright Act, Section 107.

Ex. 9b: material related to verse. John Williams, "Monica's Theme" from *A. I.: Artificial Intelligence* (© 2001 BMI), published by Songs of SKG/Warner Barham Music, LLC, ear transcription from the film's soundtrack. Used in compliance with the U.S. Copyright Act, Section 107.

Further support for the idea that this is merely a 'programmed' conclusion for David can be found in how Williams repeats "Monica's Theme" four times in its full iteration with little change in the accompanying figures during this finale. While the key does change from G major to A-flat major to A major, the harmonic progressions in relation to the melody remain mostly the same, and the eighth-note arpeggio rhythms continue in near perpetuity. There is one noticeable interruption of this theme when the "Bonding Theme" takes over as David is showing Monica his paintings [02:14:55], here tossed between oboe and synth with 16th note chords wavering back and forth in strings. This theme was originally featured prominently in <6 Hide and Seek> where Monica is beginning to explore motherly feelings for David. It is warm and mostly tonal, but with a brief hint of bitonality to show Monica's bonding is never quite perfect. Ultimately, though, the music settles back to "Monica's Theme" for good when he guides her to her room [02:16:07]. Here the refrain is stated in woodwinds and strings in the key of A-flat major and settles down for Monica to say «I love you, David».

What follows is a very jarring modulation from A-flat major to A major. Because the new key has little to no relation to the preceding key, nor was it set up, the entrance of "Monica's Theme" here (in the same piano arrangement that has been heard three times in this cue alone) sounds more like a programmed formality, musically speaking. Monica says, «I love you, David», so the only proper solution is to score it with this theme, again. Even for Williams this is a very literal usage of themes[33].

All throughout both of these cues, the use of electronics in "Monica's Theme" is minimal. Almost every statement of the theme involves piano, sometimes accompanied by strings, harp, or woodwinds. While electronics are present behind these statements, creating a soft, hazy background ambiance, they are never brought to the forefront like they are in <6 Hide and Seek> and <7 Programming David / Perfume>. This, along with the usage of long, lyrical melodies suggest the music is playing to the orga qualities. It may be David has learned to become orga and this is a 'happy' ending after all.

Perhaps though it is difficult for an audience «conditioned by decades of pandering and manipulation»[34] in Spielberg films to see anything but saccharine 'fluff' in the ending to *A. I.* It could be just another happy ending in a long line of Spielbergian happy endings. But the uncertainty presented in the narration along with the hazy visuals suggests this is all an illusion. Williams's score, "Monica's Theme" in particular, supports this reading with the amount of repetition on both the large and small scale and the unfulfilled melodic and harmonic promises the music sets up. It indicates a more complicated look

[33]. Note the famous moment in Williams's score to *Star Wars* (George Lucas, 1977) when Luke looks at the binary sunset and the "Force Theme" plays in sweeping strings. There is no mention of the Force to this point, but the aesthetic match of the visual to and the music takes primary importance.

[34]. Kreider 2002, p. 32.

at the ending as forced and unfulfilled, superficially 'real' but ultimately 'artificial', at least from our human perspective. As Kreider says, «David has been given a comforting illusion, like the one Spielberg's narrator offers us in this ending, if, like children, we choose to believe it»[35].

Bibliography

Adorno 2005

Adorno, Theodor Ludwig Wiesengrund. *Versuch über Wagner*, Berlin, Suhrkamp Verlag, 1952, English translation by Rodney Livingstone, *In Search of Wagner*, London, Verso, 2005 (Verso Modern Classics Series).

Aldiss 2001

Aldiss, Brian. 'The Mind Behind A. I.', in: *BBC News*, 2001, <http://news.bbc.co.uk/2/hi/in_depth/sci_tech/2001/artificial_intelligence/1542794.stm>, accessed February 2018.

Ashby 2010

Ashby, Arved. *Absolute Music, Mechanical Reproduction*, Berkeley (CA), University of California Press, 2010.

Audissino 2014

Audissino, Emilio. *John Williams's Film Music: «Jaws», «Star Wars», «Raiders of the Lost Ark», and the Return of the Classical Hollywood Music Style*, Madison (WI), University of Wisconsin Press, 2014 (Wisconsin Film Studies).

Bouzereau 2002

Bouzereau, Laurent. 'The Music of *A. I.*' in: *A. I.: Artificial Intelligence – Disc 2, Special Features*, DVD, Dreamworks LLC and Warner Bros., 2002.

Brown 2001

Brown, Royal S. 'Soundtracks: Williams – *A. I. Artificial Intelligence* Original Film Score', in: *Fanfare – The Magazine for Serious Collectors*, (November-December 2001), p. 330.

Buhler 2000

Buhler, James. 'Star Wars, Music, and Myth', in: *Music and Cinema*, edited by James Buhler, Caryl Flinn and David Neumeyer, Hanover (OR), Weslyan University Press, 2000 (Music/Culture), pp. 33-57.

Cooke 2008

Cooke, Mervyn. *A History of Film Music*, Cambridge, Cambridge University Press, 2008.

Eaton 2014

Eaton, Rebecca M. Doran. 'Marking Minimalism: Minimal Music as a Sign of Machines and Mathematics in Multimedia', in: *Music and the Moving Image*, vii/1 (2014), pp. 3-23.

35. *Ibidem*, p. 39.

Ebert 2001

Ebert, Roger. '*A. I.: Artificial Intelligence*', in: *Roger Ebert.com*, 2001, <http://www.rogerebert.com/reviews/ai-artificial-intelligence-2001>, accessed February 2018.

Flinn 1992

Flinn, Caryl. *Strains of Utopia: Gender, Nostalgia, and Hollywood Film Music*, Princeton, Princeton University Press, 1992.

Gengaro 2013

Gengaro, Christine Lee. *Listening to Stanley Kubrick: The Music in His Films*, Lanham (MD), Scarecrow Press, 2013.

Huvet 2017

Huvet, Chloé. *D'«Un nouvel espoir» (1977) à «La Revanche des Sith» (2005): transformations de l'écriture musicale de John Williams et du traitement de la partition au sein du complexe audio visuel de la saga «Star Wars»*, Ph.D. Diss., Rennes, Université Rennes 2; Montréal (QC), Université de Montréal, 2017.

Kreider 2002

Kreider, Tim. '*A. I.: Artificial Intelligence*', in: *Film Quarterly*, lvi/2 (2002), pp. 32-39.

Manvel – Huntley 1957

Manvel, Roger – Huntley, John. *The Technique of Film Music*, New York, Hasting House, 1957 (Communication Arts Books).

Mcclary 2007

Mcclary, Susan. 'Minima Romantica', in: *Beyond the Soundtrack: Representing Music in Cinema*, edited by Daniel Goldmark, Lawrence Kramer, and Richard Leppert, Berkeley (CA), University of California Press, 2007, pp. 48-65.

Morrissey 2004

Morrissey, Thomas. 'Growing Nowhere: Pinocchio Subverted in Spielberg's *A. I. Artificial Intelligence*', in: *Extrapolation*, xlv/3 (Fall 2004), pp. 249-262.

Palmer 1990

Palmer, Christopher. *The Composer in Hollywood*, New York, Marion Boyars, 1990.

Prendergast 1992

Prendergast, Roy. *Film Music: A Neglected Art: A Critical Study of Music in Film*, New York, W. W. Norton, 1992.

Reid 2001

Reid, Michael. 'Boy, Robot: Spielberg's Take on Artificial Intelligence an Homage to Kubrick', in: *Times Colonist*, Victoria (BC), 11 December 2001.

Rowell 2004

Rowell, Lewis. 'Time in the Romantic Philosophies of Music' in: *Indiana Theory Review*, xxv (Spring/Fall 2004), pp. 139-175.

Spielberg 2006
Spielberg, Steven. Interview by Richard Schickel, 'Age & Innocence', in: *DGA.org*, 2006, <https://www.dga.org/Craft/DGAQ/All-Articles/0604-Winter2006-07/DGA-Interview-Steven-Spielberg.aspx>, accessed February 2018.

Stefani 1987
Stefani, Gino. 'Melody: A Popular Perspective', in: *Popular Music*, vi/1 (January 1987), pp. 21-35.

Struthers 2009
Struthers, Jane M. 'The Birth of *A. I.*', in: *A. I.: Artificial Intelligence: From Stanley Kubrick to Steven Spielberg: The Vision Behind the Film*, edited by Jan Harlan and Jane M. Struthers, London, Thames and Hudson, 2009, pp. 10-25.

Szabolcsi 1970
Szabolcsi, Bence. 'The Decline of Romanticism: End of the Century, Turn of the Century – Introductory Sketch of an Essay', in: *Studia Musicologica Academiae Scientiarum Hungaricae*, xii/1-4 (1970), pp. 263-289.

Wannberg 1999
Wannberg, Kenneth. Interview by Ford A. Thaxton, 'Music Editor Ken Wannberg', in: *Soundrack*, 1999, <http://web.archive.org/web/20010129044o/http://www.soundtrackmag.com/kwannberg.html>, accessed February 2018.

Appendix

Catalogue of Cues

This Catalogue of Cues was created using the Dreamworks Video 2002 DVD release of *A. I.: Artificial Intelligence*. It includes all music in the film including both diegetic (grey background) and non-diegetic (white background). The organization and designation of the cues was derived solely from the music as heard in the DVD version of the film and therefore is not related to the official soundtrack album or the written score.

cue	scene	time	length	musical description	themes	spotting notes	musical perspective
1	Cryogenics	6:50 - 8:02	1:12	- single mid/high celli line playing Cryogenics Theme *** Khachaturian - Gayaneh's "Adagio" (same key/instruments) - violins come in when parents enter Cryogenics (7:35) - Dm chord on shot of Robin Hood book	Cryogenics	- begins after "But in the beginning, didn't God create Adam to love him?" - ends when Monica takes speaker out of purse	Monica
2	Son Cryo-ed	8:10 - 8:55	:45	- "Garland Waltz" from Sleeping Beauty		- begins when Monica turns on player - ends right after "I can still hear you."	
3	Henry/Doctor Discuss Monica	8:55 - 10:14	1:19	- related celli line from cue 1 - violin chords accompany - changes to single line at "Martin is merely 'pending'" (9:13) - violin counterline comes in "all her grief goes undigested" (9:21) - back to chords over celli line at cut to Hobby's office (9:38) - Dm chord on shot of dad's picture	Cryogenics	- begins right after "I can still hear you." - washes over from previous Tchaikovsky - ends when Henry comes home	Monica
4	Introduction to David	10:35 - 14:16	3:41	- high electronic pads - brings in violin note when he touches floor (10:52) - synth celesta with Nostalgia Theme when he turns around (11:07) - mid string sustains, w/ harp when Monica is arguing (11:21) * almost warm, Romantic - English horn when she starts to rethink (11:47) - after he says, "A mecha child," Curiosity Theme in electronics (12:22) - piano version of the Nostalgia Theme when David looks at pictures (12:33) - colder strings when Henry explains to Monica (13:05) - synth celesta after Monica says, "Of course I'm not sure." (14:07)	Nostalgia Curiosity	- begins on alien-like shot/reveal of David - ends on shot of mobile in David's room	Monica
5	David Changes	14:58 - 15:34	:36	- low electronic pad followed by higher pads - piano/harp atonal arpeggio		- begins when Monica shuts door - ends at coffee the next morning	Monica
6	Hide and Seek	15:34 - 18:28	2:54	- repetitive harp figure - Curiosity Theme in electronics when Monica takes coffee (15:41) - repetitive, meandering piano Theme when David studies coffee (15:49) - Curiosity Theme in electronics when Monica notices David (16:09) - piano theme again when David studies her cup (16:16) - Curiosity Theme in electronics when he startles her making bed (16:29) - horn/celli when he's smiling at her (16:34) * Curiosity Theme continues over top - repetitive harp figure when she walks away (16:48) - music pauses when she's startled by him (16:54) - filled out version of harp figure, mixing strings, harp, electronics (16:57) - horn theme from before now in woodwinds, glockenspiel when she continues her business (17:03) * canonic treatment, like it's chasing itself - repetitive harp figure (17:19) - Curiosity Theme in electronics when she remembers David in closet (17:34) - horn theme from before now in piano/flute when gets him from closet (17:38) - string filigree when he finds her in bathroom (18:10) * one quiet statement of horn theme in piano	Curiosity Bonding	- begins on "double" shot of David's eyes - ends when he shuts door to bathroom (Monica on toilet)	Monica (David?)
7	Programming David/Perfume	20:35 - 28:40	8:05	- harp playing Nostalgia Theme when she's tucking David in * although warm, synth celesta sound creates unsettled feeling when Monica is staring at him - electronic pads on shot of Monica picturing frozen Martin (21:17) - pads continue when Monica sets David up to be imprinted * repeated piano/harp notes added - strings take over when Monica starts explaining to David (22:16) * very quiet harp octaves on Searching Theme - a touch of the Blue Fairy Theme when she touches his neck to start the imprinting (22:35) - electronic pads back in when she starts the imprinting (22:48) * another quiet statement of Searching Theme in piano - synth celesta when David's face changes (23:29) - Monica's Theme in piano when David calls her "Mommy" (23:53) * scene curiously ends with synth celesta after "touching moment" - synth celesta continues into scene with Henry and Monica getting ready for party (24:22) - solo ENGLISH HORN when David appears (24:50) - two statements of Curiosity Theme in electronics when David notices perfume (25:08) - solo oboe right before David appears again (25:25) - Curiosity Theme again on shot of spilled perfume (25:49) - warm strings and harp after David asks if Monica will die (26:05) * gradually becomes more unsettled as he puts his head in her lap - Nostalgia in solo piano when David whispers "I love you, Mommy. I hope you never die." (26:41) *** reliance on "the motive" connects this to Abandonment Theme - playful oboe with Teddy's Theme on appearance of Teddy (27:30) - sustained violins when Monica leaves (28:18)	Nostalgia Searching Monica Blue Fairy Curiosity Abandonment Teddy	- begins on Monica preparing David for bed (after the awkward dinner) - ends on shot of David and Teddy in doorway when Monica and Henry leave	Monica then David
8	Martin Comes Home	29:33 - 30:22	:49	- starts with soft piano when Monica realizes Martin's awake (29:32) - Abandonment Theme in oboe (29:39) for Martin's arrival - soft, dissonant brass chords with atonal piano when David looks at Martin (30:05)	Abandonment	- begins when Monica listens on phone - ends after shot of David starring at Martin in wheelchair	Monica (foreshadowing) then David
9	David Draws the "Bird"	32:54 - 33:59	1:05	- high strings * horn enters when says his first memory is a bird - oboe solo when he draws the bird (33:30) * snippet of Bonding Theme? - electronics on close-up of drawing (33:38)	Bonding?	- begins after Martin asks when his "build day" was - ends on shot of spinning pills	David
10	Reading Pinocchio	34:24 - 35:53	1:29	- starts with repetitive variation of Cryogenics Theme in violins - solo piano plays Monica's Theme when she starts reading about the Blue Fairy (35:17)	Cryogenics Monica	- begins when Martin asks Monica to read Pinocchio - ends on first shot of table	Monica then David
11	Eating Spinach/Scissors	36:36 - 41:44	4:43	- nearly inaudible violin or viola entrance - slowly grows to unsettled chords - brass/electronics punctuate the drooping face - barely perceptible electronic high pitch for surgery (37:21) - piano comes in on shot of Martin looking at Monica holding David's hand (38:27) - dark strings when Martin attempts to deceive David (38:34) * soft music box notes, oboe notes sporadically - mix of short string washes, sustained brass, and dark electronic pads when David appears with scissors (40:07) * Bonding Theme? - two sustained oboe notes when he leans in to cut (40:52) - back to string washes when he snips (41:07)	Bonding?	- begins on close-up of David eating spinach - ends on them setting up for birthday party	Monica then David
12	Near Drowning	44:02 - 45:31	1:29	- low rumble on look of fear - mix of soft, atonal string tremolo chords and brass - more pronounced electronics on shot of David in pool (44:50) - no musical release when Martin is revived * more string chords and horn - harp/piano arpeggio and synth voices on overhead shot of David (45:16)		- begins right when David is poked - ends on David coloring in his room	David

cue	scene	time	length	musical description	themes	spotting notes	musical perspective
13	Abandoned in the Woods	45:32 - 52:29	6:57	- soft, repetitive piano figure - Nostalgia Theme in piano when Monica looks at David's paintings (46:12) - back to piano figure when she looks back to him (46:53) - warm strings when she sits next to him (47:11) - oboe and synth celesta play Abandonment Theme when David asks "and Teddy?" (47:25) - beginning of piano and string arpeggios on cut to car ride (47:52) * very Glass-like - more urgent version of the repetitive piano figure when David asks her questions in the car (48:06) - Abandonment Theme in oboe and synth celesta when Monica sees Cybertronics sign (48:38) - long "vamp" in strings and piano while Monica stops and decides to turn car (48:47) - music dies down to a few sporadic, repetitive rumbles when David exits car (49:14) - dissonant string figures when Monica approaches David (49:34) - piano playing Abandonment Theme when David asks if he'll be alone (50:25) * each phrase punctuated by Glass-like piano arpeggio - music escalates when David pleads (51:04) - back to fuller, Glass-like arpeggios in strings when she runs to car (51:11) - Abandonment Theme in horns when she explains to him where not to go (51:19) - music increases in urgency after Monica pushes David down (51:55) - full, dramatic statement of Abandonment Theme in strings over Glass-like arpeggio (52:02) - dissonant piano crashes on shot of David as car drives away (52:13)	Nostalgia Abandonment	- begins on shot of David coloring in his room - ends on black	Monica then both?
14	Joe Convincing Client	53:59 - 54:59	1:00	- "I Only Have Eyes for You" sung by Dick Powell - starts out as tinny, radio music - broadens (both arrangement and stereo space) when he puts her down		- begins when Joe snaps his head - ends on Joe outside walking down street	
15	Street Music	54:49 - 56:13	1:24	- diegetic music playing from street		- begins when Joe's outside walking down street - ends when he turns on his hand mirror	
16	Stairs to Client	55:57 - 56:32	:35	- ambient, soundscape		- begins when he holds up room key - ends just before he snaps on "Guys and Dolls"	N/A
17	Joe's Second Client	56:33 - 57:20	:47	- "Guys and Dolls" sung by Stubby Kaye and Johnny Silver		- begins when Joe snaps his head - when Joe answers the guy's question	
18	Joe Cuts Off Barcode	57:44 - 58:25	:41	- ambient, soundscape		- begins when Joe steps out onto street - ends when David and Teddy are walking in woods at night	N/A
19	Scrounging for Parts/Rounding Up	59:15 - 1:05:50	6:35	- low, dark strings, piano, brass, perc when the parts are dumped - electronic music for chase		- begins on shot of pile of mecha parts - ends on shot of Teddy watching moon fly away	David
20	Nanny's Lullaby	1:05:06 - 1:05:50	:44	- "Dodo, l'enfant do" (traditional French lullaby) - mixes with score		- begins when the mechas are being hauled away - ends on shot of Teddy watching moon fly away	
21	Flesh Fair	1:05:50 - 1:14:40	8:50*	- "What About Us" by Ministry - heavy metal		- begins at Flesh Fair - ends when Johnson-Johnson drags David out into open - *it comes as goes throughout scene	
22	Hobby's Pictures of David	1:17:35 - 1:19:43	2:08	- small section of strong comforting horns/strings when Joe and David are set free - solo piano playing Nostalgia Theme over sustained strings on shot of pictures (1:17:50) - strings swell on shot of Hobby (1:18:15) - solo clarinet with Nostalgia Theme when employees tell Hobby the found David (1:18:29) * solo taken up by solo flute - repetitive harp (electronics?) figure on cut to David and Joe in woods (1:18:59) - figure intensifies on shot of moon (1:19:10) - strings play ominous chords when David decides to go the other way (1:19:28)	Nostalgia	- begins when David and Joe escape the Flesh Fair - ends with Joe asking David if he's in bad trouble	Hobby then David
23	Joe Knows Women	1:20:21 - 1:20:51	:30	- "Cheek to Cheek" sung by Fred Estaire		- begins when Joe snaps his head - ends when he snaps head again	
24	Road to Rouge City	1:20:59 - 1:23:46	2:47	- harp/strings/oboe music of excitement - minimalist marimba/strings start when Joe and David start walking (1:21:23) * playful, also excitement * sustained notes over repetitive marimba figure - minimalist gestures continue, brass more prevalent on cut to car (1:22:28) *** Strauss - Der Rosenkavalier quotation (1:23:15) * minimalist gestures still continue underneath		- begins when Joe points to moon - ends when they're on escalator	David
25	Rouge City Streets	1:23:43 - 1:25:40	1:57	- diegetic music playing from street		- begins when they're on escalator - ends when they're in Dr. Know's place	
26	Joe's Radio Music	1:25:13 - 1:25:17	:04	- "I Only Have Eyes for You" sung by Dick Powell		- begins when Joe snaps his head - ends when he snaps head again	
27	Dr. Know	1:25:37 - 1:30:10	4:33	- blurs the line at times between diegetic and non-diegetic		- begins when they're in Dr. Know's place - ends after David asks how the Blue Fairy can make a robot into a real boy	
28	Joe's Warning About Humans	1:31:03 - 1:33:56	2:53	- barely perceptible pad - no change when David starts back at Joe - more electronics added when Joe responds (1:32:00) - harp comes in when Joe says, "She cannot love you." (1:32:18) * snippet of Bonding? - dark string/brass chords when Joe explains why humans hate them (1:32:22) - brass/percussive piano when they exit to the street (1:33:07)	Bonding?	- begins when David leaves Dr. Know - ends when David starts the amphibicopter	David
29	Escape from Rouge City/Manhattan	1:33:58 - 1:39:05	5:07	- electronic beats (similar to "rounding up" music) when David starts amphibicopter - strings/horns start more rising, majestic figure when Joe comes to amphibicopter (01:34:28) - minimalist marimba/string/brass music, similar to "road to Rouge City," when they start flying (01:34:52) * Searching Theme in strings - more urgent trumpet repeated notes when Manhattan border is reached (01:35:49) * Gershwin-esque? * another Searching Theme statement in strings - texture thickens with strings and more brass when they see the weeping lions (01:36:45) * what seems to be the Searching Theme becomes that "motive" - more dramatic with flute/pic arpeggios on close up of lion's face - synth pads playing Searching??? Theme when they enter the building (01:37:59) - harp while Joe reads door (01:38:10) - solo horn as Joe guides David to enter room (01:38:18) * Bonding Theme??? - synth celesta and strings when David enters room (01:38:36) - repeated harp note when David approaches chair (01:38:51)	Searching	- begins when David moves amphibicopter - ends after Hobby sits David down	David
30	Meeting David/Hobby	1:39:06 - 1:41:54	2:48	- dark, electronic rumblings, dissonant strings/brass when other David appears - eerie synth pad, string sustains when David talks to David (01:39:16) - string sustains as Hobby approaches David (01:40:33) - bowed cymbal, tam-tam as David starts to threaten David (01:40:03) - harsh, violent string, piccolo, brass gestures when David starts swinging the lamp (01:40:12) - oboe with Bonding Theme when David asks about Blue Fairy (01:41:57) * unsettled harmony underneath	Bonding	- begins when David meets David in chair - ends after Hobby sits David down	David

cue	scene	time	length	musical description	themes	spotting notes	musical perspective
31	**Other Davids/Suicide**	1:43:51 - 1:49:20	5:29	- voiceless choir note sustains when David starts to get out of chair (01:43:51) * other voices, string harmonics, electronics layer * strange, electronic flourish when camera pans past Hobby's son's picture (01:44:11) - layers thicken, darken on shot of hanging David robots (01:44:24) - everything cuts out except two choral lines at shot David through the eye holes (01:45:19) * low synth, string, brass, and upper woodwinds swell when he looks through the eyes - Searching Theme in celli/horns when Cryogenics statue is revealed (01:45:45) - dramatic, cluster of orchestral and choral sounds builds with zoom in on David's empty face (01:46:32) *** Ligeti - Lux Aeterna, "Kyrie" from Requiem, and Atmosphères - texture thins out to choral and string sustains as David sits on ledge (01:46:51) * Searching Theme in oboe or English horn and synth celesta (01:46:55) - string sustains, bubbling harp/piano figure as David is underwater (01:47:34) * Cryogenics Theme in violas? (01:48:08) * pronounced Cryogenics Theme statement in violins (01:48:27) - solo oboe when David starts to see something (01:48:59)	Searching Cryogenics	- begins when David starts to get out of chair - ends when David is pulled away underwater	David
32	**Finding the Blue Fairy**	1:50:12 - 1:55:38	5:26	- dark brass and string chords as the amphibicopter enters the water * Searching Theme? - synth celesta playing murky figure over wavering strings on shot of Pinocchio (1:51:20) * oom-pah figure in synth calliope - repeated piano note as amphibicopter climbs stairs (1:51:54) - Blue Fairy Theme in voice and synth celesta on shot of Blue Fairy (1:52:30) * several repetitions (similar to David's repeated pleas to her?) * ends on Dm chord	Searching Blue Fairy	- begins when David's amphibicopter goes underwater - ends when it cuts to the ice	David
33	**Into the Ice**	1:55:37 - 2:01:33	5:56	- voiceless chorus with a contrapuntal variation of the Cryogenics Theme - atonal piano arpeggios over synth pads, strings, choir, and perc when David is activated (1:58:02) - sustained violins on shot of Blue Fairy (1:59:10) * previous eerie music continues underneath - Searching Theme in oboe when Blue Fairy crumbles? (2:00:01)	Cryogenics Searching	- begins on cut to ice - ends when David "wakes up"	Mechas then David
34	**Stored Memories/Blue Fairy**	2:01:33 - 2:07:07	5:34	- synth pads and quiet violin flourishes as David wakes up - repetitive piano accompaniment figure when David gets up (2:02:00) - Monica's Theme in solo piano when David thinks he's home (2:02:08) * quiet synth pads underneath * not actually his home * modulates to match woman's voice singing "David" (02:03:11) - religious-like, warm string chords as David talks to the Blue Fairy (02:03:21) * women's voices join - solo piano and harp join when Teddy approaches David (2:06:00) - Monica's Theme in synth celesta when Teddy pulls out lock of hair (2:06:17) - repetitive harp figure as David implores the Blue Fairy (2:06:38)	Monica	- begins when Davd "wakes up" - ends after Blue Fairy says, "your wish is my command."	David (Mechas?)
35	**Explaining to David**	2:07:08 - 2:11:03	3:55	- silence, then excited strings when David hears door knock - excited strings flourishes when David goes to answer door (02:07:41) - synth pads when advanced mecha comes in room (02:07:59) * solo oboe when they hold hands (02:08:12) - harp plays Blue Fairy Theme when advanced mecha starts explaining (02:08:20) * F#m chord when advanced mecha say resurrectees die * solo cello when advanced mecha explains David is the living memory of humans (02:10:24) * F#m chord when advanced mecha agrees to bring Monica back (02:10:57)	Blue Fairy	- begins on shot of mobile - ends when day breaks	David (Mechas?)
36	**David's Day with Monica**	2:11:03 - 2:18:47	7:44	- "awakening" music in strings and clarinets - repetitive lead in to Monica's Theme in piano as David opens her bedroom door (2:11:50) - Monica's Theme in solo piano when he enters her room (2:11:56) * full version, even to the refrain * repeated several times * often accompanied by light strings, English horn counter line - whimsical strings and harp when David shows paintings (2:14:53) * Bonding Theme in oboe - refrain of Monica's Theme in strings and horn when David walks her to her bed (2:16:05) - repetitive piano lead in when Monica says "I do love you" (2:16:57) - Monica's Theme in solo piano when voice over comes in (2:17:04)	Monica Bonding	- begins when day breaks - ends at end	David (Mechas?)

The Performer's Viewpoint

John Williams Seen from the Podium: An Interview with Maestro Keith Lockhart

Emilio Audissino – Frank Lehman
(University of Southampton – Tufts University, Medford, MA)

In January 1980 John Williams was appointed new Principal Conductor and Music Director of America's Orchestra, the Boston Pops, succeeding to the outstanding fifty-year-long tenure of Arthur Fiedler. Part of the Boston Symphony Orchestra, the Boston Pops has specialized, since 1885, in concert programmes of light symphonic music: popular favourites excerpted from the classical repertoire, American marches and songs, highlights from the opera, operetta and Broadway repertoires, symphonic jazz, and pop pieces in orchestral arrangements. Williams led this prominent ensemble until 1993, when he resigned to focus on composition, and assumed the title of Boston Pops Laureate Conductor, maintaining a steady relationship through his regular appearances on the orchestra's podium. The first Hollywood composer to be assigned a role of such prestige and visibility with a top American symphonic institution, Williams expanded the Pops' offerings with the best of the past and present output of the film-music repertoire[1]. He also pioneered the now-popular format of 'film concerts' — film screenings in which the music is played live by an orchestra[2].

In 1995 Keith Lockhart succeeded to Williams as the 20th Music Director and Principal Conductor of the Boston Pops. A graduate in Piano from Furman University with a Master's in Orchestral Conducting from the Carnegie Mellon University, he has served as Music Director of the Utah Symphony Orchestra (1998-2009) and is currently also Principal Conductor of the BBC Concert Orchestra, Artistic Advisor and Principal Conductor of the Brevard Music Center Summer Institute and Festival, and has appeared as a guest conductor in a number of major orchestras all over the world. At the Boston Pops, Keith Lockhart has built upon Williams's legacy, maintaining film music as a staple of the Pops concerts. An accomplished conductor with a thorough knowledge of both

[1]. On Williams's tenure at the Boston Pops and his innovations, see Audissino 2013 and Audissino 2014a, pp. 183-196.

[2]. On 'Film concerts' — or 'multimedia films' — see Audissino 2014b and Audissino 2014c.

the classical and the popular repertoire — and a deep connoisseur of Williams's music — Maestro Lockhart is the best person to provide insights into Williams's music from a conductor's viewpoint[3].

Can you talk about your relationship with John Williams and your arrival in Boston as his successor?

I have a friendly relationship with John Williams. I don't know if I'd characterize this as close because we don't see each other all that often. But of course our common link is the Boston Pops, and he is always available whenever I've looked to him for any guidance or to answer any questions, or most notably to offer up any of his music, to make it available for concert use. When I came into the orchestra in 1995, a lot of John's repertoire was already 'repertoire standards' for them, and the Boston Pops is probably the only standing orchestra which that is true for[4]. Before coming to Boston I had done the usual *Star Wars* "Main Title", "The Imperial March", some music from *Jaws* — the things that were out for rental at that point, much before the Hal Leonard Signature Editions were published and made largely available. Much of John's music that was played in Boston then was unavailable to other orchestras. A lot of the scores I still conduct from are the manuscript scores which he brought to Boston; these were originally derived from unedited movie cues and were only slowly converted over into the Hal Leonard editions that have since come out. This of course has allowed John to edit further and look over things during his Boston Pops years. When I arrived I learnt a lot of this repertoire kind of on the fly, with pieces that the orchestra already knew but that I myself had never conducted. So, rather than teaching these pieces to the orchestra I kind of learned them *from* the orchestra. Since then a lot of things have come in that we have learned together, or that John does with the orchestra, because we try to let him have the first crack of some of these pieces — after all, he wrote them — and then I pick them up and they become a standard part of the orchestra's repertoire.

What is that makes Williams's film music particularly attractive to performers and listeners?

John's music is very demanding, and it's demanding in a good way. There are film composers whose music is difficult to play especially in live-concert situations because, honestly, they are less skilled composers. There are difficulties because of the inadequacy of the material. Occasionally you see things with other composers that are simply unplayable.

3. We met with Keith Lockhart at Boston's Symphony Hall on 24 May 2017. He also kindly invited us to sit through the rehearsals of the film concert of *Jaws* (Steven Spielberg, 1975) whose world premiere was given by Maestro Lockhart and the Boston Pops on 25 May 2017.

4. The Boston Pops has a section of their library called "John Williams Music Library" which holds the Williams pieces from the film-music and the concert repertoire that were premiered during his conductorship.

I mean, it might be assemblable in a studio environment where you can patch soundtrack cues together from many takes into one. Or they're demanding just because they are exhaustively repetitive, or something like that.

On the other hand, there is a kind of musical difficulty that arises because the composer knows the orchestra well enough to write to the full extent of performers' abilities. And John's music is demanding in this last sense. When you look at the symphonic repertoire, at, for example, Gustav Mahler — which was a particular favourite of mine in the more 'legitimate' side of my career — you see things that were written absolutely to the limits of the players' individual technique. But nobody would ever argue that Mahler symphonies were 'unplayable', because the composer has a mastery and knowledge of the instruments they are writing for. And John of course employs orchestrators when scoring a film, but his work, just like everything he does, is so meticulous and detailed that what you're getting even in his orchestrational sketches is his own highly detailed intentions[5]. The basic thing is that, as opposed to a lot of other film music, John's music is extremely involved and highly difficult, and actually requires the same amount of rehearsal time one might give to a piece in the more core classical repertoire. But on the other hand it also bears a fruit, artistically, that's worth the difficulty.

One of the other things that makes his music particularly different is its integrity. It's possible to do film-music concerts of almost anybody's music. I've worked with the Hollywood in Vienna people. They honour a different composer each year, and it's possible to excerpt a lot of people's material — especially if you're using video montages or film clips. But rarely is there somebody whose music is able to sustain enough interest if you take the film away, that is compelling enough to perform it on its own for a live audience. That to me is what distinguishes Williams's music: it is both perfectly fit to the film it is going with and it has enough core integrity that it is never just mere 'accompaniment'.

Do you think, knowing Williams's working process, that he writes his film music so that it will stand up once detached from the film, as a kind of pure music?

I think he's a Hollywood creature at the end of the day. I'm not sure it would be in the service of the film to be thinking «Well, this will stand fine by itself». I think he just writes this music and then he turns around and goes, «Well, that would work». But

[5]. The use of orchestrators is a common practice in the Hollywood music industry aimed at saving time, and using an orchestrator does not necessarily mean that a composer is incapable of writing for full orchestra and doing her/his own orchestrations. Williams produces very detailed eight/twelve-staff condensed scores (in a sort of musical shorthand) which are then passed on to an orchestrator that expands them into twenty-and-more-staff full scores and makes them more clearly readable. In this case, to use Lawrence Morton's definition, the orchestrator acts like an «intelligent copyist» (Morton 2012, p. 134) and the orchestral effects and textures in Williams's music come all from him. On the use of orchestrators in Williams's film music, see Ian Sapiro's chapter in this volume.

even then it requires some kind of assembling. Think of "Star Gazers", essentially a harp concerto he extracted out of *E. T.* Not one measure of "Star Gazers" exists in literal form in *E. T.* There are bits and pieces of that music there, but there's nothing as effective that he could have excerpted because in the film it's eight bars and then it goes to something else. It wasn't intended to be a concert piece, it was intended to fulfil the action of the screen.

What piece/pieces do you find particularly compelling?

The temptation is to say all the fun action/adventure sort of stuff, *Star Wars*, *Raiders of the Lost Ark*, which is in particular a really really good score. But the things I have most respect for, maybe the most awe for, are the things that, honestly, sound the least like John Williams. I mean, there is a John Williams sound; there are people who say, «This must be John Williams!», and for things like *Star Wars* that's particularly true. But if you look at scores like *Schindler's List* — not just the famous violin excerpts that everybody plays but the whole thing — it is written with a kind of extremely advanced chromatic harmony, an early twentieth-century German sort of sound, with a little Klezmer thrown in because of the Polish-Jewish element of the film. That is one score that for me just leaps off the page as being extraordinary, because it doesn't sound like John Williams. Another one would be *Memoirs of a Geisha*, in which he uses Western instruments, particularly the cello, to create sounds that are very un-Western. I have conducted the whole *Geisha* suite with Johannes Moser, and I've done the *Schindler's List* excerpts, including some things that are not published, like the "Immolation Scene".

In 2017 — in celebration of Williams's eighty-fifth birthday — you and the Boston Pops released the album *Lights, Camera… Music! Six Decades of John Williams*, an anthology spanning from lesser known 1960s scores like *Heidi* to the latest *Star Wars* instalment *The Force Awakens*. Could you talk a little about it?

This album allowed me to study pieces that even I didn't know John had written the score for — let alone our audience — like *Heidi*, which I remember seeing as an eight-year old and which is exactly what it should be; it's big, you can see merry horns twirling on the hilltops in Switzerland, it's a very *Sound of Music* sort of sound. And *Sleepers*, a really chilling and strong use of the score. And *Munich*… I guess I kind of like the deep-cuts, but that's possibly also because I know the other ones, like *Star Wars*, well enough already. One of my favourite little excerpts to do is the "Devil's Dance" from *The Witches of Eastwick* because I think it is an orchestrational masterpiece. And it is something that John put together himself. We asked him, «Gee, where did you come up with these sounds?», and we learned those were *his* orchestrations. He didn't go to an orchestrator and ask them, «Make this sound scary». It is all Williams's own orchestration — low brass, the Harmon mutes, all the nasty snarling things, the vibraslap, the thunder sheets…

Does Williams tinker with his works? There are multiple versions of his concert pieces, both from the film-music repertoire ("Main Title" from *Star Wars*, "Excerpts from *Close Encounters of the Third Kind*", "Scherzo for Motorcycle and Orchestra" from *Indiana Jones and the Last Crusade*...) and the concert-hall repertoire (for example, the *Violin Concerto*, the *Cello Concerto*, *Song for World Peace*, the perennially under-revision *Symphony*...).

It's an interesting combination. When you write film music, it's a little more along the lines of *Gebrauchsmusik*. You finish one assignment and you're onto the next project. You don't say: «These are my nine symphonies for posterity». So, especially when we approach Williams about this stuff, for some things it was obvious that he honestly just didn't remember writing. YouTube is a great resource; all these people have put up soundtracks that had been out of print for forty years. And with a lot of these things, he's really like, «Oh, I guess I did write that!». That's understandable, you don't get to remember everything you wrote for the last sixty years! So, for some things it's like, «Sure, if you like that we'll see if we can find the sketches», and people dug around for them. I think earlier in his career he was probably less aware of the legacy, he was a bit more of a working-stiff composer, wrote things and threw them into a desk somewhere.

For the CD we managed to unearth *Heidi*, for instance, and *Goodbye Mr. Chips*, both from the late 1960s. Some of them had to be recreated from short scores, but his short scores are very detailed. Especially with this Hal Leonard Signature series that has come out, I think projects like these are giving him an opportunity to revisit his works. And what has happened when he's revisited them has shown him to be a bit of a tinkerer because — I'm sure to the somewhat occasional frustration of Hal Leonard — things were ready to go to print and then he goes, «Oh, wait. You know, I've never really liked how this transition goes», and then he redraws it. We had two or three versions of *The BFG* before it came out with that one John will be doing next week [*31 may/01 June 2017*]. We have two versions of *The Patriot*: we played the shorter Hal Leonard version in the past but for the CD we went to the one John originally played with us because we liked it better, actually. And also there are commercial interests at hand when you publish for everybody. I wouldn't say 'dumbed down', but there are some arrangements that are probably not as hard as they were in the original, because not every ensemble is the most skilled Hollywood orchestra, or the Boston Pops for that matter. There are articulations, for instance, that are changed even in things as basic as *Star Wars*, that are different from the way we do them, because we do them in the way John originally wanted us to do them, even if that is much more technically demanding. I suspect that it is a judicious change to allow for good performances at every level of decent orchestra. So, it's not like Beethoven — I don't think Williams is somebody who has twenty-five versions of everything he ever wrote — but I do think for him it is not one of those «one and done, I wrote it, it's done, it's gone» situations. He does go back, he does listen to the result, and he does make adjustments.

Do you think he is concerned with the legacy that you mentioned?

I think more and more he is. Who wouldn't be? I hate to speak for someone else, he could probably answer that question better, but I think it would be impossible to be unaware of how important his body of work has become to the whole art of film scoring. And I think when you do that you, you want the record to reflect accurately what you wanted to do. And fortunately this project with Hal Leonard, which has become huge, has allowed for this stuff to be out in the public marketplace, to an extent no other film composer has even come close to. They are real scores, with a fairly high level of editorial work. This stuff has been treated — I say this with tongue-in-cheek — as real music.

What is the status of film music in concert now?

I think because of John Williams there has been an explosion in the way that orchestras all over the country and the world have embraced film music. A glaring example is the more and more frequent live concert phenomenon, the 'film concerts', which not long ago were such a rarity[6]. I have done a lot of them now but I didn't do them until very recently. For one thing, the technology had to catch up to a point where you can actually dodge the orchestra out of film sound tracks[7]. That's still pretty spotty when you're dealing with older films where music, dialogue, and sound-effects are not on separate tracks, or that are not digital. It's a lot harder to remove them out, to remove the orchestra for the old scores. With a multitrack film it would be easier, but it isn't when you do the older films. For example, I have done *The Wizard of Oz* and *Singin' in the Rain*... With *The Wizard of Oz* you could hear the ghost of the other orchestra all the time because for performance, we keep the original vocal tracks, which were recorded on separate tracks; but it's really hard even in the digital era to pull everything out. So, in a way the film-in-concert performance has become a phenomenon because we can do it.

But, beyond that, I think it is a recognition by the orchestral world that the world of film scores is the popular interface with the world of orchestras. It's kind of like opera was at the beginning of the seventeenth century, or like ballet scores during the nineteenth century. Here were classical composers composing something that was seen as more user-friendly than a symphony. So in a way, if the light classical music of the nineteenth century

[6]. The phenomenon of 'film concerts' has blossomed in the last five years. See BURLINGAME 2015.

[7]. Sound films come with a soundtrack that is the combination of three audio tracks: the music track; the dialogue track; the effect track. In 'film concerts' the original dialogue and effect tracks are kept and played with the visual track, while the music track is performed live by the orchestra. This entails a preparatory technical manipulation of the original film in which the music track is removed from the final sound mix. For recent films, the separate tracks are available and the selective muting of the music track is thus easy. This is not the case with old films, particularly the ones with low-res monaural soundtracks: what survives is mostly only the final sound mix in which the three tracks are fused together. Until the recent progress in digital audio processing, it was impossible to remove the music track without touching the other two tracks too. The preparation of 'film concerts' is explained in MUHLFRIEDEL 2016 and LICHTENSTEIN 2017.

was Von Suppé overtures, Rossini and Delibes, that sort of thing, the light classical music of this century, from 1930-something on, is film music. And I've been kind of amazed at how popular this has become, and not only here in Boston. New York, all the major orchestras, and a lot of the minor orchestras too, are doing the same kind of projects we're doing here. With things like *West Side Story* — that level of iconicity — because it was composed by Bernstein specifically they're even doing them on their classical subscription as an alternative to the stage version, which does show a great degree of legitimization. It's wonderful to have the live presence of the orchestra there with the films, you can hear a lot of things you may have not noticed before. It's not so much the case with John's scores because the recording technology is more modern, but in the tracks on the old movies the orchestra is so muddy and it is so hard to hear it. When you look at the score of *The Wizard of Oz*, for instance, the orchestration is ingenious, but you could never tell that from listening to the low-res sound of the old soundtrack.

Speaking about the 'film concert' phenomenon, could you tell us a bit about the process of synchronization of the live orchestral performance with the film? What synch aids do you use? Click-track? Streamers and punches[8]?

There are a number of ways to keep the orchestra in synch with the film, some that are traditional and date back to the earliest days of sound-stage scoring, and others more modern approaches. There are basically visual aids and aural aids. The aural aids include click-track, primarily, or simply following the film's sound. When I do *Singin' in the Rain* or something like that, I just accompany the singer, as though I were conducting an opera. I wouldn't want to look at visual aids for that, I just want to slow down when, you know…

[8]. The click-track is an aural aid to keep an orchestra in synchronization with a film: the conductor and players wear headphones in which they hear a metronome-like pulse (click, click, click…) that, if strictly followed, makes the musical performance adhere to the visual flow. The relentless and rigid pulse has the tendency of straight-jacketing the music into a mechanical performance. Streamers and punches are visual aids and provide a less constrictive guidance. Punches are holes that used to be made in the film strip at regular intervals, resulting in a series of white flashes that communicated the pulse to follow in order to keep the synchronization — a visual version of the click-track. Streamers are even less intruding: a diagonal line was traced across the filmstrip leading to the frame with a synch-point to be hit musically — for example, a stab to be mirrored by a blast of the brass. The synch-point frame was punched with a hole. The visual effect for the conductor is a white line that crosses the screen from left to right, usually taking two seconds, at the end of whose journey a white dot flashes. The appearance of the line on the left side alerts the conductor that a synch-point is approaching, which is to be hit exactly when the line touches the right side, on the appearance of the white flash. These visual aids are paired with matching markings on the score: a horizontal line above the measures quantifies the length covered by the streamer's journey, and the line terminates with an X mark, which indicates the synch-point and coincides with the white flash. Nowadays both the streamers and punches are superimposed digitally with time-processor software like The Auricle (<http://auricle.com/site/>, accessed February 2018). In the recording studio these visual aids are visible on the big screen above the orchestra; in concerts they are only displayed on the conductor's LCD monitor.

[*sings*] «You are my lucky star...». It's just like there is an opera; it's an opera where the singer is not paying any attention to you the conductor, there's not that give and take... Which is the core difficulty to doing these things. I think that what people don't realize is that this is not the way it was ever intended to be done. This is reverse engineering. When you make a film you have the musical idea, you cut the film then, to some extent, you either conduct the music in short chunks that can be lined up or you edit the film to make it go two more seconds before it. There's a famous story about the bicycle chase in *E.T.* that John tried to score against an already filmed thing and he couldn't make it up. So Spielberg recut the movie because he loved the music and he didn't want to change any of it, which is a rare collaboration, I'm sure.

Then there is click-track. Click-track is effective when you're keeping a rock band together, when you're keeping an orchestra together with a rock band. I find it pretty much useless when it is used with something like John's music. And not only useless, but detrimental to flow, because basically click-tracks are an averaged beat, which just flattens everything down — no room for nuance, no freedom from strict phrasing. And it's really impossible to conduct against them. You get [*imitates the relentless beat of the click-track*] «click, click, click, click...», and you can't say, «Oh, let's take some time here and make it up in the next bar». There's no *rubato*. What they are good for is something like a generic action score where you have five minutes of [*mimics*] «tu-thump, tu-thump, tu-thump, tu-thump». And then you give click-tracks [*through headphones*] to the players too, because they understand what it is that you are pushing against, and when they hear it they come with you.

In the old days they also used, of course, the big analogue clock, the time-code clock. The first film score I did was *Alexander Nevsky* and in that it was an actual clock, the clock with the mechanical attachment to the time-code that would reset at fifteen seconds until start and then when it hit zero you would start, and then what you have all through was, «I need to be at the downbeat at bar four at second twelve and a half», and you would time it out just against that. Then they started taking the modern version of that, like for *An American in Paris* for instance, a split screen for the conductor with the action on one screen and the clock next to it, but the clock is now a picture of a clock — those clocks were probably all built in the thirties and have probably all died by now!

The more modern thing that most people use is the streamers and punches, which takes a bit to get used to, but I'm very comfortable with it now. You get to the point where you really can just sense as the thing sweeps across, you know exactly where the next downbeat is. It's kind of like watching a violinist's bow. If I'm doing a concerto, I can tell when they're going to change in the same way I can tell when this is going to come across. It's one of the most exhausting concentration things I've ever done as a conductor, including Mahler's Eighth, because you can't stop looking and thinking about that or — in a long cue like in the *Indiana Jones* fight scenes — you'll end up hopelessly lost, because there's so much going on and it just keeps changing tempos. If you don't keep track of where you are in the music, you'll end up lost. I use the streamers but I also use the bar count because most of these have «15: 1, 2, 3, 4; 16: 1, 2, 3, 4...» going on top of the conductor's monitor and the score has clearly printed the measure numbers in it[9]. It is a kind of a visual version of click. And a lot of times the bar count allows you to supplement the streamers with a visual «click, click, click...» for every other downbeat. In something like *Jaws* which has so many variants of «da-dah, da-dah, da-dah...» at different speeds, to do that really allows you to keep it locked in to a quarter of beat.

What skills does the live accompaniment of films require from the conductor and orchestra compared to traditional performances?

I have an interesting anecdote about this. I made my debut last year with the Academia di Santa Cecilia, the big orchestra in Rome, a wonderful orchestra. We had a great time, we did *Fantasia*, which is really hard because the music is so dense and so classical, and because the older part, the part from the Stokowski one, is badly edited, there are missing bits. And with Stokowski you just need to catch up, because Stokowski's tempos are from a different age, they're really pushed to their extremes[10]. The tempo of the *Sourcerer's Apprentice* is like... [*sings the theme at breakneck speed*], which is faster that humanly possible. So, basically you're just beating the orchestra, driving them. And then Stokowski does his own transcription of *Clair de Lune* and it is so slow that I swear babies are born between the first and the second half! It is so hard to just pace yourself and to mirror something done at that tempo. But this action on screen is very precise, all those little fairies, and Pegasus, and the things in Beethoven's 'Pastoral' like the storm scene, the thunderbolts... The orchestra of the Academia di Santa Cecilia had never ever done something like this before. They don't do Pops concerts. This is like crossing the gap. The material is all classical, of course, and they really enjoyed it because it is something they don't do every day. A guy came up to me and he said, «Maestro, I so like this week. It's like a videogame for conductor and orchestra». And he was exactly right! Because conducting is normally a two-way street.

---

9. During the rehearsals of *Jaws* we had the opportunity to see Maestro Lockhart at work on a 'film concert'. He uses an LCD monitor next to his music stand, on which a copy of the film is played with visual synchronization aids that are not shown on the big screen above the orchestra. A yellow streamer alerts that a musical cues is about to start; this is followed by a green streamer, which leads to the actual start of the musical piece (during the two-second green streamer the conductor gets the orchestra ready to start). White streamers keep crossing the screen during the whole segment, each taking two measures to travel from the left to the right side. On the top left corner of the monitor the time-code of the film runs (hours:minutes:seconds:frames) which allows for a precise identification of every synch-point. On the top right corner there is an indicator of the number of the current bar followed by the number of the current beat, which shows what part of the music should be playing over that part of the film.

10. Since *Fantasia* was animated and edited to Stokowski's rendition, to hit the synch-points in a live accompaniment the orchestra must replicate the exact tempo that Stokowski chose.

You normally set the tempo, you give an idea physically of what you want somebody to do. If they take more time than you would have at the end of their solo, you don't just go, «Oh! I can't follow that!». You listen to them and you adjust your beat, and you say, «Well, I think he needs a little bit more of that…». It's a communication, and a good conductor both sets an overall interpretational context and also allows people and their own artistry within that context. But with these live-accompanied film concerts there is neither that or this. It is, «I don't care what they're doing! I want them to do what I want them to do!». So for the conductor, it's like managing to stay with this but also *show* what is necessary to stay *precisely* with this, which is not exactly the same thing. For instance, the orchestra would have a tendency to play a certain kind of rhythmic figure and slow down. You can't do that, you need to know where it is that you can goose it forward of pull it back without making the music start to sound like jumpy. For the orchestra it's this opportunity to say, «Well, assuming this conductor has a good technique, can we follow *exactly* what he wants us to do?». Most conductors are saved by *not* having an orchestra do exactly what they want them to do! So, it's a fun challenge and I think people here in America perceive it as a challenge in that way too. One of the things that seems funny is that there are a lot of films these days that I'm *not* sure have the musical merit to really deserve the film-concert treatment. For example, *Love Actually* has just came out as a live concert with film. I love the movie but I can't say I'm thinking, «Oh, wow! I've always wanted to hear that score performed!».

How do you prepare and practice to conduct these 'film concert' performances?

One marks the score differently for these concerts. You mark signposts in your score when you're marking a symphony — larger structures, four-bar subsets, things that allow you to remember that all of a sudden the composer puts an extra extension in the phrase, that sort of thing. Here, that's true as well, but what you're also marking is a signpost you can very easily see peripherally that keeps track of where the streamers are — for example, that the guy who sets the streamers sets them three bars apart there and two bars apart there. When you see the streamer you automatically start to try fill the amount of space to get to the next streamer. As for practising, these days they kindly provide digital guide-tracks — practice videos that have the sound on them and the streamers to follow as well. What I do is this: I go through, I look at each cue and learn the music, which means I usually listen to the music once before I turn it off and mark it as if I were doing a concert piece. And then I go back and turn the sound off — you can turn the sound off to follow that take in the streamers. And I keep doing it until I can hear all those changes, whether I'm singing it to myself or just thinking through the music. Because conducting is all about anticipation, about being able to change your gesture in advance of the thing happening. You don't want a conductor to go like, «Oh, no! It's faster now!».

When you conduct 'film concerts' are you responding dynamically to dialogue levels or things that in a film proper would be mixed during post-processing?

The balance is mostly done when a film is prepared for a 'film concert' screening. They put dynamics in that were not probably in the original dubbing, in which they usually just dipped the orchestra down under the dialogue. It's still a problem in live performance. I mean, you don't want to get rid of this music as it's great, but people onscreen are yelling over the dub and there's only so much dynamic adjustment of volume one can ask for before the gain is totally unnatural in the voices and sound-effects. But most of that balancing is already done when these films are prepared for live accompaniment, and mostly is a matter of reminding yourself that you have to pay careful attention to those other sound elements. You get playing this stuff, it's a really great cue, and you don't want to all of a sudden to go like this [*mimics silencing the orchestra*]... because somebody onscreen says something.

Going back to the big picture for the conclusion, what do you think has been the contribution of Williams's tenure at the Boston Pops in terms of legitimization of film music as a valid repertoire for concert programmes?

One of the first things that changed the viewpoint of the way film music was perceived in the broader world of orchestral music was John's appointment here in Boston. That's not his music specifically; it's taking a Hollywood composer seriously enough to give him a position in the world of orchestral music, which is the starchiest and most rigid of all performing arts. I wasn't around here in 1980 but I'm sure that there were people going, «Well, I wonder what he is just playing... Just *that* stuff?». And without question the answer was to some extent «not just that stuff», but that's the stuff John knows, not just his own music but Korngold, Waxman, Rózsa... All that stuff entered the repertoire, stuff that Fiedler had probably never touched. What Fiedler knew, in terms of the body of work, was Von Suppé overtures and Rossini, and movements from major symphonic works. For John this job must have been a huge challenge and a huge responsibility, because parts of this job that I don't have to think about are the symphonic warhorses. When we have violinists coming and they're doing Mendelssohn's *Violin Concerto*, or pianists coming and they're doing the last movement of the "Rach 2", this is my bread and butter, this is the stuff I have been studying since I was twenty-one. By the time I came here I had fifteen years of that sort of work under my belt. The reason I can concentrate on all the new things, the commissions and things like that, is because I already know all that standard repertoire. But imagine if that stuff had been new to learn, which was the case with John! All John had conducted was his own work in the studio, basically. Like a lot of the studio composers, he conducted his own recording sessions. But it's a different thing when you have to start interpreting everybody else's work too. So, my hat's off to him. I'm sure we was a very busy boy! And at the same time composing film scores, at that point probably four or five a year!…

With many thanks to Amanda Severin for her assistance

Bibliography

Audissino 2013

Audissino, Emilio. 'Archival Research and the Study of the Concert Presentations of Film Music. The Case of John Williams and the Boston Pops Orchestra', in: *The Journal of Film Music*, vi/2 (2013), pp. 147-173.

Audissino 2014a

Id. *John Williams's Film Music: «Jaws», «Star Wars», «Raiders of the Lost Ark», and the Return of the Classical Hollywood Music Style*, Madison (WI), University of Wisconsin Press, 2014 (Wisconsin Film Studies).

Audissino 2014b

Id. 'Film Music and Multimedia: An Immersive Experience and a Throwback to the Past', in: *Jahrbuch Immersiver Medien 2014*, (October 2014), pp. 46-56.

Audissino 2014c

Id. 'Overruling a Romantic Prejudice. Forms and Formats of Film Music in Concert Programs', in: *Film in Concert, Film Scores and their Relation to Classical Concert Music*, edited by Sebastian Stoppe, Glücksstadt, Verlag Werner Hülsbusch Verlag, 2014, pp. 25-43.

Burlingame 2015

Burlingame, Jon. 'Live Movie Concerts A Cash Cow for Orchestras', in: *Variety*, 29 April 2015, online, <http://variety.com/2015/music/features/live-movie-concerts-a-cash-cow-for-orchestras-1201483456/>, accessed February 2018.

Lichtenstein 2017

Lichtenstein, Grace. 'Film Concerts Go Mainstream', in: *Bachtrack.com*, 2 May 2017, online, <https://bachtrack.com/screenings-with-live-orchestra-film-game-music-month-may-2017>, accessed February 2018.

Morton 2012

Morton, Lawrence. 'Film Music of the Quarter', (1951), in: *The Routledge Film Music Sourcebook*, edited by James Wierzbicki, Nathan Platte and Colin Roust, New York, Routledge, 2012, pp. 131-136.

Muhlfriedel 2016

Muhlfriedel, Marina. 'Live Movie Concerts: Experiencing Classic Films with Composer and Conductor David Newman', in: *Harman.com*, 22 August 2016, <http://pro.harman.com/insights/harman-pro/live-movie-concerts-experiencing-classic-films-with-composer-and-conductor-david-newman>, accessed February 2018.

John Williams Seen from the Piano: An Interview with Maestro Simone Pedroni

Maurizio Caschetto
(Colonnesonore.net, Italy)

Internationally acclaimed Italian pianist Simone Pedroni is only one of the latest of a recent generation of musicians — including Gustavo Dudamel and Stéphane Denève — that has been nurtured by the music of John Williams since a very young age and is now performing it regularly on the concert stage. He graduated from Milano's 'Giuseppe Verdi' Conservatory in 1990 and in 1995 he took his Master's Degree at the Accademia Pianistica in Imola, Italy, where he studied with Lazar Berman, Franco Scala and Piero Rattalino. In 1993, he was awarded the Gold Medal at the Ninth Van Cliburn International Piano Competition. Since then, Pedroni has played with the Royal Philharmonic Orchestra, the Moscow Virtuosi, the Orchestra of Maggio Musicale — Florence, the RAI Orchestra — Turin, the Oslo Philharmonic, the National Polish Radio Symphony Orchestra in Katowice, the Prague Chamber Orchestra, the Santa Cecilia Orchestra of Rome, to name a few, and under the such conductors as Sir Yehudi Menuhin, Vladimir Ashkenazy, Zubin Mehta, Eliahu Inbal, Pinchas Steinberg, Roberto Abbado, Leonard Slatkin, Riccardo Chailly, Gianandrea Noseda, Louis Langrée, Lü Jia, Xian Zhang. He is Artist-in-Residence at the Orchestra Sinfonica di Milano 'Giuseppe Verdi' (aka 'La Verdi'). Besides works by Brahms, Tchaikovsky, Schumann and the full cycle of Beethoven's piano concerti, with La Verdi he also premiered a Piano Concerto composed for him by Luis Enriquez Bacalov. As a recording artist, Pedroni has released albums featuring works by Mussorgsky, Rachmaninoff, Liszt and Hindemith, and Bach's *Goldberg* Variations, among others[1].

Pedroni has cultivated a special relationship with the music of John Williams for a long time, regularly performing his own piano transcriptions of Williams's film music in several piano recitals. In 2015, he made his debut as a conductor with the Orchestra Sinfonica di Milano 'Giuseppe Verdi' and Chorus in a series of sold-out and critically-

[1]. Simone Pedroni's full bibliographical information and the catalogue of his performances and recordings are available on his official website, <http://www.simonepedroni.com/bio-eng-1>, accessed January 2018.

acclaimed concerts presenting an entire programme devoted to Williams's music from the *Star Wars* films, featuring the complete series of concert arrangements prepared by the composer himself. In 2017, he released for Varèse Sarabande *John Williams: Themes and Transcriptions for Piano*, an album of Williams music for solo piano featuring both the composer's original piano arrangements of *Lincoln* and *The Book Thief* and Pedroni's own transcriptions from scores like *Harry Potter, Presumed Innocent* and the *Star Wars* saga. Pedroni's penchant for Williams's music is another example of this composer's ability to reach out to a broad, cross-generational audience that includes both simple fans and master musicians all around the world. Pedroni is indeed convinced that one of the secrets of Williams's success lies in the way the composer has always been able to keep alive an inner childlike spirit which is reflected in his art. As the Los Angeles Times' music critic Mark Swed wrote in 2014, «Williams' most lasting legacy is likely to be his influence on children. [...] No composer in history has so infused young people with symphonic joy»[2].

Could you tell us your first encounter with John Williams's music? How and when your interest for his music, as pianist and interpreter, was born?

My interest in the music of John Williams started in my teenage years, more precisely in 1983, the year when I saw *Return of the Jedi* at the movie theatre. My schoolmates told me about *The Empire Strikes Back*, but I missed that one at the cinema. I remember seeing *Star Wars* a few years before in a small movie theatre in my hometown, but for some reason the lightning struck when I saw *Jedi* for the first time. I still vividly remember being very impressed by the film, but even more than that, I was blown away by the music I was hearing in the background — a huge symphony orchestra playing incredibly complex music almost from the beginning to the end of the film. I noticed that it was indeed the music that gave gravitas and deeper meaning to what I was seeing on screen — Luke Skywalker's inner conflict with his father Darth Vader, the unusual love story between Han Solo and Princess Leia, the playful and epic battle of the Ewoks against the Empire and the evil presence of the Emperor. The music was telling me what the images couldn't say, what neither the acting nor the editing could express. Also, the music had the power of making you believe what you were seeing with an almost Wagnerian flair. It's not a coincidence that the *Star Wars* saga is also categorized as a 'space opera'. After this almost 'mystical' experience, I was immediately interested in playing Williams's music on my instrument, the piano, but I soon discovered that nothing was officially available to perform. I remember that I transcribed a version for solo piano of the "Luke and Leia" theme by ear from the original soundtrack album. I started to search for other available records, which in those years were mostly stuff for collectors. Every new soundtrack was a revelation for me, as I became more and more aware of Williams's uncanny ability to

[2]. Swed 2014.

come up with the right sound and the right music for any film. Everything in his composing style was fascinating for me, especially becoming aware that he had a very personal style and unmistakable language. I still remember my wonder in listening to *Empire of the Sun* and *The Witches of Eastwick* — these were written and released in the same year (1987), but they couldn't have been more different in style and character. Williams's music fuelled my imagination through the way it sounded in my ears, filling my heart with its deep and true sincerity. All of this happened just a few years after I completely fell in love with Beethoven's symphonies and also Tchaikovsky's. Therefore I never saw Williams's music as something stylistically inferior only because it was written for film. I was interested in the music itself.

Williams is also trained as a classical pianist. When he was young he wanted to become a concert pianist and he studied at the renowned Juilliard School of Music in New York with the esteemed Rosina Lhévinne, the same teacher of Van Cliburn and one of the most famous teachers of that era. Do you think Williams's music contains specific elements that we can trace back to his formation as a pianist?

I think the piano studies he made at the Juilliard School were only a segment of a larger musical education that touched upon a wide variety of genres and quite diverse experiences. Williams undertook his musical training in a very singular and clever way. Of course the classical piano studies with Rosina Lhévinne were crucial to his formation as a composer, but I would also add his experience as an arranger for the US Air Force Band, his years as a jazz performer, the influence of his own father (who was a talented percussionist) and his composition studies with Mario Castelnuovo-Tedesco. All these training grounds were all equally important. If we consider all these experiences together, we get an idea of the incredible and very diverse range of influences that might have gone into his own compositional voice.

The piano has a central role in several film scores composed by Williams. There are extended piano parts in scores like *The Accidental Tourist* (Lawrence Kasdan, 1988), *Angela's Ashes* (Alan Parker, 1999), but also more recently in *Lincoln* (Steven Spielberg, 2012) and *The Book Thief* (Brian Percival, 2013), just to name a few. We can also find a few important piano solos in earlier scores such as *Jane Eyre* (Delbert Mann, 1970) and *Images* (Robert Altman, 1972). Would you be able to define what Williams's piano style is?

Yes, the piano solo is often present in many of his film scores, especially in intimate dramas like *Angela's Ashes*, *War Horse*, *Schindler's List* and *Presumed Innocent*, but as you said also in earlier films like *Images* or the sparkling *How to Steal a Million*. I would say that Williams often uses the piano solo for the scenes that are the emotional pinnacle of those films, for example the final sequences of *War Horse* and *Schindler's List*, as if it's the soul of the main character that comes out through the sound of the piano. Williams's piano style is very peculiar — I'd say it's rigorous. There aren't passages in octaves which might help to enrich the writing and therefore sound more 'orchestral' in character, but instead he usually opts for a very quartet-like style of writing. We can hear this in *Lincoln*, *The Book Thief*, *Angela's Ashes* and *Sabrina*. But we could say the same of several of his recordings from the 1960s where he performs his own piano arrangements from Gershwin and others.

Williams is known for his great command of the symphony orchestra and its many colours, especially the ability to give the orchestra a major role in the musical accompaniment of a motion picture. You are a pianist and you started to work on transcriptions and performances of Williams's music specifically for solo piano, almost stripping off these compositions of their trade-mark big symphonic character. What have you discovered during this process of study and re-interpretation?

I was especially happy to discover that Williams himself prepared for the first time a piano reduction for his scores to *Lincoln* and *The Book Thief*. The biggest surprise was to discover that several pieces contained music not found both in the film or on the original soundtrack album. We had his own piano arrangements for *Sabrina* and *Schindler's List*, but both involved the main theme only. For *Lincoln* and *The Book Thief* we have full piano suites authored for the first time by the composer. Working and studying these two suites, I realized that what makes Williams's music so special and full of significance is indeed the music itself and his own personal language. The orchestral suites are richer in sound of course, but I think the piano solo versions are just as special. It's not a mere reduction of its orchestral counterpart, but a sort of 'first pass' in which we can find all the things that make his music so unique. Stylistically, it's quite similar to Prokofiev's piano transcriptions, as in his own piano version of *Romeo and Juliet*. It's an essential, almost austere writing, like a pencil drawing that however reveals the essential truth on which the orchestral version is based.

Despite having written a large number of concertos for almost every single instrument of the orchestra and several chamber music pieces, Williams composed only two pieces specifically for piano: a *Scherzo for Piano and Orchestra*[3] and the piano suite *Conversations*[4]. The former work is a virtuosic excursus

3. *Scherzo for Piano and Orchestra* was composed in 2014 for the "Music in the Summer Air" festival in Beijing, China, and premiered on 1 July by the China Philharmonic Orchestra conducted by Long Yu with pianist Lang Lang.

4. *Conversations*, a suite in four movements for piano solo, was written for pianist Gloria Cheng. The first two movements premiered at Tanglewood, Massachusetts, on 10 August 2012. The third and fourth movements premiered at the "Piano Spheres" series in Los Angeles, California, on 12 November 2013.

around the many sonic possibilities of the instrument (and sounds almost like a first movement of a larger work), while the latter instead is a collection of sombre, wistful pieces in which Williams seems to look back on his past as a young jazz musician. What are your reflections about these two compositions?

What strikes me the most, aside from some typical gestures of Williams's piano writing (like the fast passages in unison with the hands distanced by two, three or even four octaves), is the sublimation of his language. Stylistically it's much different from his orchestral music written for films, but at the same time it deepens some of its specific traits. I think it is a wrong approach that of comparing the orchestral writing to the writing for a solo instrument. I mean, *Conversations* would be pretty impossible to transcribe for full orchestra because it is intrinsically pianistic but that does not mean it is 'poorer' than the *Piano Concerto*, which is for piano *and orchestra*. On the contrary, to me this is the proof that when Williams writes something — and, by the way, he always writes at the piano, as he said many times — the piece is already perfect and fully formed in its expressive traits. The orchestra is *one* option. The piano is *another* option, not a choice that necessarily means a reduction. In terms of pianism, I'd like to elaborate a little more on *Conversations*, the only extended concert piece for piano solo written by Williams so far. I think it's important to start by recalling what the composer himself has said about it:

> I began to think of what a conversation might be like between the great jazz pianist Phineas Newborn, Jr. and Elizabeth Freeman, known as Mumbett [...]. Two strong personalities, one pianistic and the other most surely vocal and hymnal... meet for a chat. I imagined them having their conversation near the Sedgwick Pie in Stockbridge, Massachusetts [...]. Next came Claude and Monk. Not the Claude you might think I mean, but Claude Thornhill... a seminal figure in jazz history, principally remembered for his mentoring of Gil Evans. Thornhill, who loved Debussy, and who I knew during my childhood, understood the sea change in piano sonorities discovered by Debussy, and those equally radical ones invented by Thelonious Monk. It's delicious to imagine an exchange between these two giants. Chet Baker and Miles Davis possessed markedly opposing personalities, however they did have much in common. They both eschewed bravura and needless display, and always revealed their art with the barest minimum of fuss. They could be brief and often quiet, but their message was invariably brought forth with great force and power. Finally, "Strays" (Billy Strayhorn), Duke (that one, of course...) and Blind Tom, another former slave and somewhat forgotten 19th-Century figure in American pianistic history... here gather to unravel the secrets surrounding the birth of 'stride'. And dear listener/reader, if you're still with us... don't listen too intently to identify the voices named within. Theirs will remain inimitable and incomparable. However, that we might be permitted to overhear these

The recording is available on the album *Montage: Great Fim Composers and the Piano*, released in 2015 on the Harmonia Mundi label (Gloria Cheng, piano).

> luminaries chatting in some undiscovered time zone… unrestrained by such things as clefs and bar lines… is a notion that is indeed enticing, and I hope that these minor musings might, in some small way, be worthy of the memory of these notable antecedents of ours[5].

In addition to his well-known humility, what strikes me is both the originality of the approach and the fact that the piano writing is here looking at the jazz style, even though abstractly, but at the same time also at the innovations brought in by contemporary art composers like Ligeti — for example some passages in the *Études for Piano*. The whole suite is permeated by a very dream-like character. The use of legato, especially in some figures that cover long melodic lines with wide intervals, is instead very expressionistic. Looking at the movements, I think that this sense of evocation is very strong and present. It's almost the opposite of film music, which is the description or the illustration of something that is already existent. Williams once said, with his typical charming restraint, that writing 'pure' music is much more difficult for him than writing for film. It may be true, but in this piece the sense of evocation flows powerfully like a great river, as if he were putting down on paper what lies in the deepest corners of his memory and his personal life.

"Phineas and Mumbett" has a writing influenced by both Anton Webern's *Variationen* and Debussy's piano style, even though the syntax is different. It's rich in dissonance, but it also has a very personal and peculiar harmonic language. It's almost a transcribed improvisation, and this impression is confirmed when one looks at the score — the piece is written as a single bar with free rhythm. Nonetheless, we can find a clear structure consisting of an introduction, rondo and coda. The language is atonal, but there is a constant reference to the key of D Major, even though 'tarnished' with some jazz-like chords. Very significant are also the expressive markings on the score: «Mist», «Plaintly», «Hymn-Like», «Jazzy», «A full old-time Be-Bop 'flare'», «Lion's roar», «Blues».

"Claude and Monk" is a *perpetuum mobile* in quadruplets, with a structure of A-B-A. Williams's tempo indication on the score is «Magico». He indeed creates a magical, suspended atmosphere that becomes more anxious with the use of counter-rhythms and *sforzando* passages, but always plunged in a kind of sonic 'fog' generated by the uninterrupted flow of the quadruplets. While the composer advises not to identify too much the musicians who inspired the pieces, if we look at the B section of this movement («Broadly») there seems to be a clear depiction of the enigmatic Thelonious Monk and his stylistic innovations for jazz piano. That being said, Williams remains truthful to himself. He doesn't quote or refer a specific style, but tries to imagine — from his composer's perspective — a hypothetical musical conversation between these two geniuses. Claude Thornhill is a great catalyst for Williams and his language — the piece *Heartwood*, for cello and orchestra, was also inspired by him. Thornhill brought Debussy's atmospheres in jazz music.

[5]. Williams 2013.

"Chet and Miles" is also inspired by Debussy, but only as an external factor, I would say. The language has nothing to do with Debussy. The piece is two pages long and is written on three staves. It starts with the indication «Cool and calm». Both the sparse texture and the sudden bursts of energy truly recall the attitude and the laconic language of both Miles Davis and Chet Baker. What Williams explores (and partly takes from Debussy's piano style) is the possibility of an illusory effect, as if two pianos were playing together or two performers were superimposed one over another, giving the listener the impression of a sound coming from different directions. I think it's important to remember that Debussy worked out his own peculiar, magical piano style after hearing the Javanese gamelan orchestras during the Paris Expo in 1889. He was so impressed by that sound that he tried to reproduce something similar on the piano.

In "Strays, Duke… and Blind Tom" Williams pays homage to the 'stride' piano style in a very striking way. The harmonic progression is elusive and almost creates a sense of estrangement, but it also gives the listener a feeling of growing excitement, something that is important when it comes to a live performance. This is certainly the most virtuosic movement of the whole suite. After a first slow section, with an improvisatory character marked «Freely, Take time» (frequently used in the other movements as well), the rhythm of the stride starts to appear, first with a hesitant character, then more and more energetic («Full Stride tempo»), then even faster («High Stride») and finally reaching a furious climax («Thunderously») before closing out with a cluster in the lowest part of the keyboard.

When he's not writing for a film, Williams remains faithful to one of his ethical standards, which is to write music as a moment of personal growth and experimentation. Therefore, I believe *Conversations* is a very important addition to the piano repertoire in general and also a significant step forward for Williams's own style. It adds a new and unexpected piece to the overall mosaic of his own catalogue of compositions.

Let's go back to Williams's film music. In your album *John Williams: Themes and Transcriptions for Piano* there are numerous selections aside from the suites from *Lincoln* and *The Book Thief*. How did you choose the pieces that ended up on the album?

When I found out about the piano suites from *Lincoln* and *The Book Thief*, I started to think about the idea of doing a full recording project around them. I thought that I could also include some of the transcriptions I had prepared over the years for my own piano recitals. I picked pieces that could be very effective on solo piano without losing anything in comparison to the original orchestral versions. I wanted to have pieces that could reveal the spark of the original inspiration and that had already been written by Williams himself with the solo piano in mind, so I chose pieces from *Sabrina*, *Presumed Innocent* and *Schindler's List*. Then I wanted to feature something from *Star Wars* — I thought the main theme wasn't the ideal pick for a solo piano piece as it would lose too much of its character. I opted instead for "The Asteroid Field" (which is a Toccata-like piece) and the Nocturne-like "Luke and Leia". Finally, I chose some selections from the *Harry Potter* films, which I thought could be rendered very well in a Prokofiev-like transcription. Other pianists have done their own transcriptions of the music of John Williams, but I think my own project is substantially different from all the others. Without sounding too pretentious, I didn't want just to play popular themes and pieces. My goal was to perform Williams's music with the same respect and attitude I apply to classical composers such as Brahms and Rachmaninoff and give the music a character that would enhance its own piano qualities. For me, it was a very personal journey back to the origin of my love for music and it fulfilled a dream I have had for almost 30 years.

In 2015, you debuted as a conductor with a sold-out concert in Milano, Italy, entirely devoted to the music from the *Star Wars* films, featuring the concert suites from all the six movies. In 2016, you performed this programme again, also featuring the Italian premiere of music from the seventh episode, *The Force Awakens*[6]. You once said that the core idea was to present a classical concert that would be like 'an opera without singing'. Can you elaborate further on what brought you to this specific idea?

In 1999, sixteen years after the original trilogy films, Williams returned to the world of *Star Wars* to compose music for the prequel trilogy. For these films, he wrote scores of impeccable craftsmanship and incredible substance. As the years went by, he has been able to develop the musical language he created for the original three films. It was a work of deep diving that was probably inconscious for the most part, but I think it hugely helped strengthen the integrity of these works and the success of the films themselves. It was spontaneous for me to imagine and prepare a concert that would tell the story of the fall and redemption of Anakin Skywalker/Darth Vader through Williams's music only, without any film clips or narration added and using only the official concert versions prepared by the composer himself. I was confident that these could be successful concerts, so I insisted for a few years with the orchestra's management to put it into their regular concert season and finally they agreed. The sold-out concerts in 2015 were surprising to many people. I think we were among the first orchestras in the world to present a concert featuring all of the available concert versions in a chronological order, from *Episode I* to *Episode VI*. Then, the following year, I added the suite from *The Force Awakens*. When experienced in such a format, these works truly become like an opera without singing (even though there is a choir in some pieces). The variety and diversity of the pieces, coupled with their strong emotional power, created an electrifying experience for both the orchestra

6. "Star Wars: A Musical Journey", performed by Orchestra Sinfonica & Coro Sinfonico di Milano 'Giuseppe Verdi' on September 3 and 6, 2015 and July 14, 15 and 17, 2016 at the Auditorium di Milano, Italy.

and the audience, much like we would have when experiencing a great symphonic piece in a concert hall or a fully staged opera at the theatre. I was also confident that such a programme would gather a very diverse audience, including people that probably had never experienced a live classical concert before. I think this is one of John Williams's greatest achievements — he brought the sound of the symphony orchestra to millions of people. During his years as Principal Conductor of the Boston Pops Orchestra, Williams did an immense work in terms of legitimization of the film-music repertoire and made the audience aware of its importance in our contemporary music culture. And the music of the *Star Wars* films, specifically the concert suites he has prepared over the years, are really a masterwork of orchestration. It's almost a paradox, but when experienced in a live concert setting, I think the music tells the story even better than the films themselves do. Also, the profound impact of hearing it in a live performance makes the audience concentrate more on the musical language than just on remembering the images the music is associated with. That's why I called it 'opera without singing'. It's truly a new form of musical representation that lies in-between ballet, opera and incidental music.

Over the last few years, the music of John Williams became a regular presence in the programmes of many symphony orchestras around the globe. In January 2017, the classical music website Bachtrack.com placed John Williams at Number 2 in a Top Ten ranking of the most-performed contemporary composers in concert halls all over the world[7]. Williams's music is becoming more and more a part of traditional concert repertoire despite its origin as film music, or applied music. The last remnants of prejudice, which a lot of music critics and academics nurtured for many years toward this composer and the film music repertoire at large, seem to be finally disappearing. What are the main reasons for this small 'revolution', according to you?

One essential factor for Williams's success is that his music is not only much enjoyed by the listeners but it is also very satisfying to play for the performers. It's very demanding and virtuosic music, it engages the performers in full stride. After one of the *Star Wars* concerts we did in Milan, the first clarinet of 'La Verdi' Orchestra (Fausto Ghiazza) told me that despite he didn't have any solo part, he really played almost non-stop for the whole concert, much more than with the usual repertoire. This was a very interesting observation that confirmed how much orchestration and the richness of orchestral colours are something very dear to Williams. This aspect — how he uses the orchestra, but also how Williams he is able to evoke different images through the art of orchestration — is surely one of the key components of its success. As a performer, I'm also very aware of the importance of Williams's music as a means of social gathering and communal experience.

7. "Classical music statistics 2016 – more top tens", in <Bachtrack.com>, 11 January 2017, <https://bachtrack.com/statistics-more-top-tens-january-2017>, accessed January 2018.

That is one of the reasons why I started a summer music festival in northern Italy called *Da Bach a Williams* ('From Bach to Williams')[8], where we perform music from both the classical and the film repertoire, and the audience response is enthusiastic and trans-generational — elderly, adult, young and even children come to enjoy the music. I believe Williams elevated film music to something closer to classical repertoire, so in his case it's actually useless to stick a label on it. And then, let me say this: time is the greatest dispenser of justice. For many years, Williams had a huge popular success among the audience, but at the same time suffered a backlash from music critics. The same thing happened to Puccini and Rachmaninov during their lifetime. In the end, it's not difficult to understand why — the success of anyone makes a lot of people envious and blind towards the real artistic merits. This happens in every artistic field all the time. But now that Williams is 86 years old and has accomplished so many goals, it's easier to look at him and at his music with a clearer critical perspective. Commercial success might be something fleeting and ephemeral, but the real interest in Williams's artistic production showed by a generation of composers and musicians (including myself) is something you can't ignore or bypass. Many musicians all over the world just open up one of Williams's scores and look with admiration at his ability to produce music of great beauty. I and many other musicians like me were already conscious of this from the first moment we encountered his music, so I'm very happy to live a moment where a lot of people are finding treasures that were only waiting to be discovered. My piano teacher at the Conservatory of Milano, Piero Rattalino, is also a historian of musical interpretation and performance. He has always been a very insightful observer of the great changes happening throughout the history of music. When he talked about the 'critical problem' represented by Rachmaninov, he used to say that when a composer reaches success and recognition for more than two generations, then he rightfully becomes part of the history of music even if the critics lambasted him.

Finally, I think it's important to bring up another element. I believe Williams's music goes deep into the soul of the listener and the performer not only because the 'right' notes comes from his pencil after a long and hard work of finishing touches, but also because his music truly reflects his own personality and character. I had the honour of meeting him in person in Boston to present him with a copy of my CD of his piano music — he was aware of this project and had given his approval to the album. Well, I can confirm what many others have said about him. He welcomed me with kindness and gratitude and when we talked, Williams kept looking in my eyes and listened to what I had to say. When I told him how much his music helped my personal growth as a musician and as a human being, he graciously replied that he didn't deserve all that appreciation. I think his humility and

---

8. Simone Pedroni is the founder and artistic curator of the Alagna Summer Music Festival *Da Bach a Williams*, held every year since 2014 in Alagna Valsesia, Vercelli, a location situated near Italian Alps in northern Italy. During the festival, both pieces from classical and film repertoire are regularly performed within the same programmes with no distinction whatsoever.

his genuine sincerity are probably his greatest qualities. He has been able to keep alive a spiritual inner childhood. That's why his music will last for generations and will continue to fascinate performers and listeners for many years to come.

Bibliography

Swed 2014

Swed, Mark. 'John Williams' Mastery on Display at L. A. Philharmonic Season Opener', in *Los Angeles Times*, 1 October 2014, <http://www.latimes.com/entertainment/arts/la-et-cm-la-phil-gala-review-20141002-column.html>, accessed January 2018.

Williams 2013

Williams, John. 'Programme notes to *Conversations*', 2013, <http://www.jwfan.com/?p=6331>, accessed January 2018.

Abstracts and Biographies

Emilio Audissino, *Introduction: John Williams, Composer*

The opening chapter provides the context and historical outlines of John Williams's career and biography, traces an overview of the scholarly literature on John Williams, introduces the rationale for the book, and gives a brief presentation of each of the following chapters.

A film scholar and a film musicologist, Emilio Audissino (University of Southampton) holds one Ph.D. in History of Visual and Performing Arts from the University of Pisa, and one Ph.D. in Film Studies from the University of Southampton. He specializes in Hollywood and Italian cinema, and his interests are film analysis, film style and technique, comedy, horror, and film sound and music. His book *Film/Music Analysis: A Film Studies Approach* (2017) concerns a method to analyse music in films that blends Neoformalism, Gestalt Psychology, and Leonard Meyer's musicology. A John Williams specialist, he is the author of *John Williams's Film Music: «Jaws», «Star Wars», «Raiders of the Lost Ark» and the Return of the Classical Hollywood Music Style* (2014), the first book in English on the composer.

John Williams and the Musical Landscapes: Film, Television, Jazz, and Concert Halls

Mervyn Cooke, *A New Symphonism for a New Hollywood: The Musical Language of John Williams's Film Scores*

What are the musical ingredients which make up Williams's much-loved style of orchestral film scoring, and how does his music transcend its many homages to earlier composers and achieve a coherent and original compositional voice? This chapter explores the oft-noted influence of Korngold and other Hollywood composers on Williams's blockbuster scores, alongside other seminal influences from the classical arena, including Russian, German, American and British music of the late nineteenth and twentieth centuries. While classical exemplars in temp tracks notoriously led to some rather close imitations – most obviously in the Holst and Stravinsky templates which helped shape some of the cues in the *Star Wars* series – Williams's idiom is shown to be as fresh, vibrant, and narratively compelling as the finest composing of his Golden Age Hollywood forebears, while at the same time speaking to a new generation of filmgoers by updating the romanticism at the music's heart with more modern elements such as jazz, expressionism, and minimalism.

Mervyn Cooke is Professor of Music at the University of Nottingham. The author of *A History of Film Music* (2008) and editor of *The Hollywood Film Music Reader* (2010), he has also published widely in the fields of Britten studies and jazz: his other books include *Britten and the Far East* (1998), several volumes of Britten's correspondence, and monographs on the same composer's *Billy Budd* (1993) and *War Requiem* (1996). He has edited Cambridge Companions devoted to film music, jazz, twentieth-century opera, and Britten, and has published two illustrated histories of jazz for Thames & Hudson. His most recent book is an analytical study of the ECM recordings of guitarist and composer Pat Metheny (2017).

Paula Musegades, *John Williams: Television Composer*

With over 100 Oscar, Emmy, and Grammy nominations to his name, John Williams is arguably the most recognized film composer in Hollywood's history. Before Williams's success in the world of film, however, he first wrote music for television. Composing catchy themes and successful scores for dozens of television shows, including *M-Squad* (1957-1960), *Kraft Suspense Theater* (1963-1965), and *Lost in Space* (1965-1968), Williams was already developing his familiar compositional style by the 1960s. This chapter investigates two formative assignments during Williams's television career, the detective series, *Checkmate* (1961-1963) and the anthology show, *Alcoa Premiere* (1961-1963). Building upon Emilio Audissino's position on Williams as a neoclassic film composer, I suggest that even during his early career, Williams practised this neoclassic style; his blending of the classic Hollywood sound with modern twentieth century music helps mark these early television scores as distinctly 'Williams'.

Paula Musegades is an Assistant Professor in the Music Department and American Studies Program at Brandeis University where she teaches a range of courses on American music. Specializing in Hollywood film scores from the first half of the twentieth century, her forthcoming book, *Aaron Copland's Hollywood Film Music*, investigates Copland's five Hollywood film scores composed between 1939-1949.

Ryan Patrick Jones, *"Catch as Catch Can": Jazz, John Williams, & Popular Music Allusion*

Little of John Williams's cinematic output bespeaks his formative work in popular music settings. The lush, late-nineteenth-century European style typifying his most well known film scores inherently eschews commercial music sources. In those rarer instances where his writing does reference popular strains, Williams often refashions their presentation akin to the process by which he effected the familiar, yet suitably alien, 'swing' of his *Star Wars* cantina band. Before his 2002 score for *Catch Me if You Can*, virtually none of Williams's efforts assumed a pop aesthetic so directly. Exploring his early flirtation with jazz alongside reflections from collaborators with the Boston Pops who participated in live concert presentations of *Catch Me* under his baton as laureate conductor, this chapter frames analysis of Williams's approach to invoking jazz sound and style against his customary compositional direction. While certain elements appropriated from jazz (such as instrumentation and rhythmic interest) clearly inform his score, this study further examines those ways in which this hybrid work is also indebted to the classical concert music tradition – most notably in its preference for notated improvisatory gesture over outright improvisation.

Ryan Patrick Jones is Professor of Music History in the Department of Music and Theatre Arts at the University of Wisconsin-Eau Claire. Dr. Jones's research in jazz has traced the educational arc of Julian "Cannonball" Adderley's early training and career in music (*Current Musicology*, 2006), and examined the challenges of Stan Kenton's early Artistry in Rhythm Orchestra as its leader eschewed dance music from the receding swing era to embrace concert presentations of jazz (*Jazz Research Journal*, 2008). A contributor to the second edition of the *Grove Dictionary of American Music* (Oxford University Press), Dr. Jones also authored the *Instructor's Manual* accompanying both *Jazz: Essential Listening* (W. W. Norton, 2011) and the second edition of its parent text, *Jazz*, by Scott DeVeaux and Gary Giddins.

Emile Wennekes, *No Sharks, No Stars, Just Idiomatic Scoring and Sounding Engagement: John Williams as a 'Classical' Composer*

This contribution addresses 'the other' John Williams: 'the classical composer'. His classical oeuvre consists most notably of concerti, chamber music and occasional works in various instrumentations. These pieces will be contextualized, whereas conclusions will be drawn on how this musical sub-segment sh/could be understood within his overall compositional oeuvre. Williams's own ideas will be evaluated in correlation to the reception of these specific 'absolute' works in which motivic structures and references differ from his film scores. No sharks, no stars here, albeit that extra-musical references have still been cast in relevant roles. Zooming in on the solo concerti for string instruments (violin and cello), these pieces will be juxtaposed to Williams's film scores. Mutual relationships between scores and underscores will be discussed, whereas the western art music canon as a source of inspiration for Williams's soundtracks will be addressed and analyzed.

EMILE WENNEKES is Chair Professor of Musicology: Music and Media in the School, Media and Culture Studies at Utrecht University, in the Netherlands. He has published on diverse subjects including Amsterdam's Crystal Palace, Bernard Haitink, Bach, Liszt, Mahler and Mozart reception, conductor films, Vitaphone shorts, and contemporary music in the Netherlands; some books are available in translation (six European languages and Chinese). Wennekes previously worked as a journalist for the Dutch dailies *NRC Handelsblad* and *de Volkskrant*, and was artistic advisor and orchestral programmer before intensifying his academic career. He chairs the Study Group Music and Media (MaM) under the auspices of the International Musicological Society.

SEBASTIAN STOPPE, *John Williams's Film Music in the Concert Halls*

John Williams is well known for regularly preparing suites or excerpts from his film scores for performances in the concert hall. This chapter examines his contribution on how film music is regarded as serious concert repertoire today. The study focusses on the post-Williams era at the Boston Pops Orchestra and the development of the New York Philharmonic's film-music concerts, with an analysis of their past film-music concerts and programme booklets. In addition, it examines the film-music concerts of the Gewandhaus Orchestra Leipzig, which took place in the 2000s under the direction of John Mauceri and in which Williams's music was prominently featured.

SEBASTIAN STOPPE is a Research Associate at Leipzig University Library, Germany. His primary research field – among others – is film and television studies and especially music for film and television. In 2014, he edited a volume about film music in the concert halls (*Film in Concert, Film Scores and their Relation to Classical Concert Music*, Verlag Werner Hülsbusch, Glückstadt, Germany). He wrote his Ph.D. thesis on the television franchise *Star Trek* as a political utopia, which was also published in 2014 under the title *Unterwegs zu neuen Welten* (*On the Way to New Worlds*, Büchner-Verlag, Darmstadt, Germany). Sebastian has studied Communication and Media Studies, Political Sciences and History at Leipzig University, Germany.

THE WILLIAMS TOUCH: STYLE AND MUSICAL DRAMATURGY

MARK RICHARDS, *The Use of Variation in John Williams's Film Music Themes*

This chapter explores relationships between the structure and narrative association of Williams's film themes that are based on variation, which occur with a greater frequency in his scores than in those of his contemporaries. A detailed methodology establishes conceptual categories for the analysis of thematic structures before demonstrating how a theme's opening idea may be varied and how this variation affects the theme's expressive import. Types of variation-based themes are then identified and, in those which Williams most prefers, musical expressions of their narrative associations are analysed. Finally, after Williams's film scores are divided into style periods, the associations of variation-based themes are more deeply investigated in the period where they appear with the highest concentration: the mid 1970s through the early 1990s, or what is labelled his 'second period'.

Abstracts and Biographies

Mark Richards is an Assistant Professor of Music Theory at Florida State University. His research interests include associations of thematic structures in film music, tonality and harmony in popular music, and form and style change in Beethoven. His work has appeared in such journals as *Music Theory Spectrum*, *Music Theory Online*, and *Music Analysis*, and he has presented his work at the annual meetings of the Society for Music Theory, the Music Theory Society of New York State, and the European Music Analysis Conference.

Frank Lehman, *The Themes of «Star Wars»: Catalogue and Commentary*

With nine thematically interlinked films and counting, the *Star Wars* saga stands as the widest leitmotivically-driven canvas in the history of cinema. Accordingly, thematic materials have received intense and consistent attention in both technical and critical discourses surrounding the series. Despite the sheer familiarity of these musical materials, however, many aspects of thematic structure and usage that could benefit from systematic analysis have been left unexamined in favour of more superficial or informal approaches. This essay provides a thorough and authoritative catalogue of recurrent thematic materials in the *Star Wars* musical universe, compiled in a systematic manner and with an eye for the complexities – and inconsistencies – of (leit)motivic scoring. In addition to the catalogue itself, which includes both true leitmotifs and more ad hoc 'incidental motifs,' a substantial portion of this essay is dedicated to exploring issues that inevitably arise when identifying recurrent musical thoughts in an evolving, decade-spanning musical text like *Star Wars*. Questions of thematic categorization, semantic flexibility, and patterns of usage are not matters of secondary importance, but central concerns for any scholarly approach to theme-rich film music, and are accordingly explored in depth in relation to Williams's neo-Wagnerian approach to this influential franchise.

Frank Lehman is an Assistant Professor of Music at Tufts University. He received his Ph.D. in Music Theory in 2012 from Harvard University. His research explores issues of structure, meaning, and interpretation for contemporary cinema and nineteenth century art music, with a special emphasis on neo-Riemannian and formal methodologies. His publications have appeared in *Music Theory Spectrum*, *Music Analysis*, *Music Theory Online*, *The Journal of Film Music*, and *The Journal of the Society for American Music*. Recent projects include analyses of ambient and electroacoustic repertoires and a series of detailed investigations into the style and cultural impact of composer John Williams. His book on chromaticism and wonderment in American cinema, *Hollywood Harmony*, appears in Oxford University Press's Music/Media series.

Ian Sapiro, *Star Scores: Orchestration and the Sound of John Williams's Film Music*

Despite acknowledgement of the importance of the symphony orchestra to much of John Williams's filmic output, his use of instrumental resources through the orchestration of his music has received little attention relative to discussions of musical style and his use of melodies and leitmotifs. While Williams's filmography shows that a number of orchestrators (some of whom have not been credited) have worked on his scores, closer inspection highlights that he maintained long working relationships with just four principal orchestrators – Herbert Spencer (1977-1990), John Neufeld (1989-2004), Conrad Pope (1993-2011) and Eddie Karam (2001-2011) – prior to a change in his underlying processes in 2012. This chapter investigates the role that orchestration plays in Williams's compositional and creative process, and analyses the use of instrumental resources across his career to date, exploring consistencies and developments in the construction of the 'John Williams sound'.

Ian Sapiro is a Lecturer in Music at the University of Leeds specializing in film music, musical theatre, orchestration, production processes, and the overlaps between them. He is author of *Scoring the Score: The Role of the Orchestrator in the Contemporary Film Industry* (Routledge, 2016), *Ilan Eshkeri's «Stardust»: A Film*

Score Guide (Scarecrow, 2013) and book chapters on film-score orchestration, the British musical and the pop industry, and the film adaptation of *Les Misérables*. Forthcoming publications include a co-authored book on film composer Trevor Jones, and a book chapter on adaptations of *Annie* for the big and small screens.

NICHOLAS KMET, *Orchestration Transformation: Examining Differences in the Instrumental and Thematic Colour Palettes of the «Star Wars» Trilogies*

Since his revival of the lush, neoromantic orchestra that once dominated Hollywood with his score to *Star Wars* (1977), John Williams has practically occupied his own genre of film music. However, Williams's style has seen changes across his career, especially in his approach and choices related to orchestration. Perhaps no better example of these changes can be found than in the seven *Star Wars* scores Williams has scored to date. Each score is immediately recognizable as his, and yet a greatly disparate sound exists across the spectrum of films. Much of these differences can be attributed to the transformation and maturation of Williams's style of orchestration over the last four decades. This chapter examines the evolution of John Williams's orchestrations throughout his scores for the *Star Wars* franchise, reflecting the broader transformations of his orchestrational style and contextualizing the approach of one Hollywood's greatest film composers.

NICHOLAS KMET is a Ph.D. candidate at New York University, studying film music composition. He has worked professionally as a composer, music editor, and sound designer. He holds a M.M. in Scoring for Film and Multimedia from New York University and a B.A. in Music from Whitworth University. His research focuses on the music of John Williams, the collaborative nature of film music, and how digital technology affects the scoring process, particularly in its relation to music editing.

JOAKIM TILLMAN, *The Villain's March Topic in John Williams's Film Music*

John Williams is well-known for his striking and memorable themes for heroes like Luke Skywalker, Superman and Indiana Jones. With the exception of the "Imperial March" from the *Star Wars* series, though, his themes for the villains are less familiar. One of the theme types frequently used to depict evil antagonists in William's film music is the villain's march, a style topic with a long history in Hollywood film music. One early example, Franz Waxman's theme for Dr. Pretorius in *The Bride of Frankenstein* (James Whale, 1935), displays the characteristic features exploited by Williams: a minor key march with a chromatic twist, often involving the tritone (the diabolus in musica). The chapter explores how Williams has been able to vary this seemingly simple formula depending on the kind of villains at hand and the degree their evil. Besides characterizing the villains, the villain's march has many other narrative functions. For instance, it is used to underline the threat from the villains when they have the upper hand in the struggle between Good and Evil. Thus, the villain's march functions like a negative counterpart to the hero's theme, which is used to lean on the thrill button when something heroic occurs. However, sometimes the villain's march also suggests the workings of evil forces even when the villains themselves are not explicitly present. Williams's villain marches are examined in six films: *Family Plot* (Alfred Hitchcock, 1976), *Superman* (Richard Donner, 1978), *Star Wars: Episode V – The Empire Strikes Back* (Irvin Kershner, 1980), *Indiana Jones and the Last Crusade* (Steven Spielberg, 1989), *Home Alone* (Chris Columbus, 1990), and *Harry Potter and the Philosopher's Stone* (Chris Columbus, 2001).

JOAKIM TILLMAN is an Assistant Professor of Musicology at Stockholm University, where he teaches courses in music analysis, 19th- and 20th-century music history, film and game music, and opera. He has published in numerous scholarly journals and edited volumes, including the article '*Topoi* and Intertextuality: Narrative Function in Hans Zimmer's and Lisa Gerrard's Music to *Gladiator*', in: *Music in Epic Film: Listening to Spectacle*, edited by Stephen C. Meyer (New York, Routledge, 2017), and he is co-editor of the book *Contemporary film music: Investigating cinema narratives and composition* (Basingstoke, Palgrave Macmillan, 2017). His current research focuses on the film music of Elliot Goldenthal, James Horner, and Hans Zimmer.

Jamie Lynn Webster, *Musical Dramaturgy and Stylistic Changes in John Williams's «Harry Potter» Trilogy*

The Harry Potter films provided a rare opportunity to observe how audio-visual relationships evolved over the course of a film series using different composers and directors. It was Williams's distinction as both the first composer, and the only to work with two subsequent directors to both establish a template and set a course for musical change that ultimately echoed throughout the remaining collaborations. With first director Chris Columbus, Williams's music co-created a classic children's fantasy and his "Hedwig's Theme" became the identifying musical marker for the series as a whole. With director Alfonso Cuarón, his less theatrical underscore included new music applied differently, integrated source music, expanded musical forces beyond Williams's signature style, and humorous examples poking fun at his previous scores. The differences between these scores highlight Williams's relevance for contemporary film scoring through his musical versatility and his adaptability to the needs of different directors, different tones, and different stories.

Jamie Lynn Webster, Ph.D. (Musicology and Ethnomusicology, University of Oregon) is a performer, choral conductor, and researcher specializing in music for drama and dance, ritual, and expressive folklore on stage, screen, and in cultural contexts. Her work on *Harry Potter* film scores interrogates matters of dramaturgy, folklore, and gender. Other publications and interests explore singing traditions in practice and performance among America's hyphenated ethnic groups (Polish-American, Welsh-American, and Anglo-Saxon) and affinity groups (American women singing Balkan songs), and the interrelationships between music and dance in both classical and folkloric story telling. She teaches music history and world music courses at Pacific University.

Case Studies

Laura Anderson, *Sounding an Irish Childhood: John Williams's Score for «Angela's Ashes»*

Alan Parker's film *Angela's Ashes* adapted Frank McCourt's Pulitzer prize-winning autobiography for the screen, securing John Williams to compose the score. While many audience members interpreted the book as representing a particularly Irish childhood, Parker noted that McCourt intended his book to be about the broader theme of poverty rather than its particular geographical location. Considering issues of Irish identity in film, this chapter explores how Williams created a score that, in contrast to many other contemporary films made about Ireland, does not draw on surface-level Irish musical markers and codes, yet creates a musical language for piano and orchestra that transforms the written text for the screen and makes it accessible to a worldwide audience.

Laura Anderson is an Irish Research Council Post-Doctoral Fellow at Maynooth University. Her interdisciplinary project, 'Disruptive Soundscapes: Music and Sound Design in French Post-War Cinema' offers a new view of avant garde post-war French film sound design by examining its relationship with wider cultural developments. Her main research interests are in the areas of film music, film sound design, and French music. Between 2013 and 2016 Laura was part of the research team on the AHRC-funded project, 'The Professional Career and Output of Trevor Jones' at the University of Leeds.

Abstracts and Biographies

Chloé Huvet, *John Williams and Sound Design: Shaping the Audiovisual World of «E. T.: The Extra-Terrestrial»*

Despite the importance of *E. T.: The Extra-Terrestrial* (1982) within the Spielberg/Williams collaboration, scholarship on the score and sound design is quite scarce. This lack of in-depth studies is all the more surprising since *E. T.* also has a special status in film history. The scope of this chapter is double: I aim to show how Williams carefully crafts his music of *E. T.* taking the visuals and the sound effects into account and, more specifically, to establish in what ways this personal approach to the image and sound design participate in the subtle mixture of science-fiction, melodrama and fairy tale. I show that the soundtrack strongly supports the reading of *E. T.* as a bittersweet fairy tale, far from the naïve and mushy story often depicted in the literature.

Chloé Huvet obtained her Ph.D. from the Université Rennes 2 (France) and Université de Montréal (Canada). Her research focuses on the evolving relationship between music, sound effects and technology in the *Star Wars* saga, under the supervision of Professors Gilles Mouëllic and Michel Duchesneau. A former student of Lyon's École Normale Supérieure, she was valedictorian of *agrégation externe de musique*, France's highest competitive examination for posts in National Education. Her publications include articles about the music of *Star Wars*, *Eyes Wide Shut*, *Jurassic Park*, *The Pianist*, *The Tudors* as well as composers Georges Delerue, Bruno Coulais and Wojciech Kilar. She teaches film analysis at Université Rennes 2, film music history and analysis at the Université de Montréal.

David Ireland, *«Today I'm Hearing with New Ears»: John Williams's Use of Audiovisual Incongruence to Convey Character Perspective in «Munich» and Spielberg's Historical Films*

Williams's score for Spielberg's 2005 quasi-historical suspense thriller *Munich* presents some departures from the more overtly Romanticised neoclassical style often most readily associated with the composer. Rather than wall-to-wall orchestral accompaniment sharing a close relationship with the images, much of *Munich* remains unscored. Williams's music is arguably most prominent in moments presented as the protagonist's flashback-like memories of the massacre of several Israeli Olympic athletes. This chapter will conceptualize these moments as incongruent: that is where film music displays some lack of shared properties with the concurrent images. Exploring these complementary and contesting audiovisual relationships, this chapter will consider how these scoring strategies in *Munich* and other Spielberg-Williams films that are based on real-life individuals and events, contribute to the emotive properties of these sequences and relate to the presentation of character perspective that challenges the docudrama qualities attributed to *Munich* (Morris, 2007).

David Ireland is a Lecturer in music psychology at the School of Music at the University of Leeds. His research particularly addresses the role of music in the perception of meaning in, and emotional response to, film. His thesis, supervised by Dr Luke Windsor and Prof. David Cooper and funded by a University Research Scholarship, incorporated approaches from music psychology and film music studies to theorize incongruent film music. David has published on the incongruent soundtrack in *The Soundtrack* and *Music and the Moving Image* journals, and is currently writing a monograph on the topic for Palgrave Macmillan.

Irena Paulus, *John Williams and the Musical Avant-garde: The Score for «War of the Worlds»*

The style of John Williams, known for its basically tonal and yet inventive compositional techniques, started to change at the beginning of 2000s. While not becoming unrecognizable, it featured more frequent usage of atonality, dissonances and some rhythmic and instrumentational peculiarities. The culmination of this 'deviation' from the typical Williams tonality-led melodic style which had marked his film music of the 1980s was Steven Spielberg's *War of the Worlds* (2005). Due to its brutal rhythms, complex chords and lack of typical leitmotivic treatment, this score has been typically neglected amongst Williams's analysts and fans. But it interestingly shows 'some other' Williams.

IRENA PAULUS graduated in Musicology at the Music Academy of the University of Zagreb, Croatia; specialized in Film Music at the European Film College, Denmark; and earned her M.A. and Ph.D. degrees from the Faculty of Humanities and Social Sciences of the University of Zagreb. Paulus is a tenured teacher at the Franjo Lučić Art School in Velika Gorica, Croatia. She also teaches film music courses at the Academy of Dramatic Art and the Faculty of Humanities and Social Sciences in Zagreb. She is a long-time collaborator of the Croatian National Radio. Paulus has written four books: *Music from the Screen: Croatian Film Music Between 1942 and 1990*, *Brainstorming: Notes on Film Music*, *Kubrick's Musical Odyssey*, and *Theory of Film Music through Theory of Film Sound*.

TOM SCHNELLER, *Out of Darkness: John Williams's Violin Concerto*

In March 1974, John Williams's marriage to Barbara Ruick was abruptly cut short by her unexpected death. In response to this tragic event, Williams composed what is arguably his most intense and personal concert work: the *Concerto for Violin and Orchestra* (1974–1976). In this chapter, I examine the genesis as well as the performance and reception history of the concerto before providing a structural analysis that focuses on the intricate motivic relationships between its three movements. These motivic links coalesce in the last movement, in which Williams presents an ecstatic transfiguration of the concerto's elegiac opening theme that serves as a culmination of the work as a whole.

TOM SCHNELLER is a Lecturer in music history and theory at Ithaca College. His research focusses on Hollywood music, in particular the work of Bernard Herrmann and John Williams. He has published articles and book reviews on film music in *The Musical Quarterly*, *The Journal of Film Music*, and *Popular Music History*, and recently contributed a chapter on music for Doppelganger films to *The Routledge Companion to Screen Music and Sound*. Tom holds a D.M.A. from Cornell University, where he studied with Steven Stucky, Roberto Sierra, and David Rosen. He lives in Ithaca, New York, with his wife and two children.

STEFAN SWANSON, *Happily Never After: Williams's Musical Exploration of the 'Controversial' Ending to «A. I.: Artificial Intelligence»*

This chapter looks at how John Williams's score for the 2001 film *A. I.: Artificial Intelligence* supports Tim Kreider's reading of the ending that director Steven Spielberg is ultimately manipulating the audience throughout the film and the seemingly saccharine final act is actually a grim conclusion to David's story. I analyze the controversial finale demonstrating specifically how the juxtaposition and mixing of styles and techniques helps manipulate the audience into seeing what on the surface appears to be a 'happy' reunion, but ultimately reveals the darker truth. Drawing from Caryl Flinn's *Strains of Utopia* and Rebecca Eaton's article 'Marking Minimalism: Minimal Music as a Sign of Machines and Mathematics in Multimedia', I conclude that Williams uses minimalist and neo-romantic styles to represent 'artificial' and 'human' subjects respectively, thus musically setting up the ending as a tragic continuation of David's prior conflicts with humans and emotions.

STEFAN SWANSON is a film/concert composer with a Ph.D. from Rutgers University who currently teaches composition and film scoring at California State University, Northridge and New York University.

He has written over sixty compositions for the concert hall, including commissions from the Harmonium Choral Society and Lakeland College. He has scored nearly fifty films including *Gun Hill Road*, and his music has been heard on HBO, Cinemax, NBC, and BET, as well the Sundance, Tribeca, and Cannes film festivals. He is a recipient of the Susan and Ford Schumann Award, the Film Music Museum Award, and the Singing City Prize.

The Performer's Viewpoint

Emilio Audissino – Frank Lehman, *John Williams Seen from the Podium: An Interview with Maestro Keith Lockhart*

In this exclusive interview, Keith Lockhart, the Music Director and Principal Conductor of the Boston Pops Orchestra, who succeeded to Williams in 1995, talks about his predecessor's music, the challenges that conducting this repertoire demands from the orchestra and the conductor, and the technicalities and difficulties of conducting live to films.

Maurizio Caschetto, *John Williams Seen from the Piano. An Interview with Maestro Simone Pedroni*

In this exclusive interview, world-renowned pianist and conductor Simone Pedroni, a long-time performer of piano transcriptions from the Williams repertoire who has released a CD of Williams piano music for Varése Sarabande, talks about his encounter with this composer's music. In particular focussing on *Conversations* and his experiences conducting Williams's *Star Wars* music with the Giuseppe Verdi Symphony Orchestra of Milan, Italy, Pedroni provides insights into why Williams's music is so appealing.

Maurizio Caschetto is a writer/producer for a global entertainment media company and also a long-time 'student' of John Williams's music and film music at large. He's one of the founders and editors of *ColonneSonore.net*, the only resource about film and media music in the Italian language available online. For the *ColonneSonore* website he wrote several articles and conducted interviews with such composers as Howard Shore, Elliot Goldenthal, Alexandre Desplat, Dario Marianelli and conductors Keith Lockhart and Richard Kaufman. A series of writings and reviews dedicated to John Williams and his music are available at <www.colonnesonore.net>. He lives and works in Milan, Italy.

Index of Names

C